A VEBLEN TREASURY

From Leisure Class to War, Peace, and Capitalism

STUDIES IN INSTITUTIONAL ECONOMICS

GARDINER C. MEANS
INSTITUTIONALIST AND POST KEYNESIAN
Warren J. Samuels and Steven G. Medema

THE HETERODOX ECONOMICS OF GARDINER C. MEANS
A COLLECTION
Frederic S. Lee and Warren J. Samuels, editors

UNDERGROUND ECONOMICS
A DECADE OF INSTITUTIONALIST DISSENT
William M. Dugger

THE STRATIFIED STATE
RADICAL INSTITUTIONALIST THEORIES OF
PARTICIPATION AND DUALITY
William M. Dugger and William T. Waller, Jr., editors

A VEBLEN TREASURY
FROM LEISURE CLASS TO WAR,
PEACE, AND CAPITALISM
Rick Tilman, editor

A VEBLEN TREASURY

From Leisure Class to War, Peace, and Capitalism

Rick Tilman
Editor

M.E. Sharpe
Armonk, New York
London, England

80 Business Park Drive, Armonk, New York 10504

Library of Congress Cataloging-in-Publication Data

Veblen, Thorstein, 1857–1929.
A Veblen treasury: from leisure class to war, peace, and capitalism / edited by Rick Tilman.
p. cm
Includes bibliographical references and index.
ISBN 1-56324-261-3 — ISBN 1-56324-262-1 (pbk.)
1. Economics. 2. Sociology. 3. Social sciences
4. Veblen, Thorstein, 1857–1929.
I. Title.
HB171.V42 1993
330′.092—dc20
93-26762
CIP

Printed in the United States of America.

The paper used in this publication meets the minimum requirements of American National Standard for Information Sciences—Permanence of Paper for Printed Library Materials, ANSI Z 39.48-1084.

BM (c) 10 9 8 7 6 5 4 3 2 1
BM (p) 10 9 8 7 6 5 4 3 2 1

Contents

THE CASE OF THE UNITED STATES

CULTURE, RELIGION, AND EDUCATION

ON WAR, PEACE, AND CAPITALISM

Acknowledgments

The editor gratefully acknowledges the aid of Donna Evans, Diana Sjoberg, Grace Skelly, and Ruth Porter-Tilman in preparing this manuscript for publication. In addition, the editor thanks the Sabbatical Leave Committee and the Research Committee (College of Business and Economics) of the University of Nevada, Las Vegas. Thanks are also due to the following for permission to quote from unpublished correspondence and manuscripts: University of Chicago Library, Presidents' Papers 1889–1925; the State Historical Society of Wisconsin, Thorstein Veblen Collection; the University of Missouri, Western Historical Manuscript Collection, Jacob Warshaw Papers, 1910–1944; and the Minnesota Historical Society, Andrew A. Veblen Papers.

Editor's Introduction

Veblen the Man

The neglect of the ideas of Thorstein Veblen (1857–1929) is a major academic scandal. Veblen undoubtedly ranks with John Dewey and C.S. Peirce as the most seminal mind of his generation of American thinkers, yet to many professional social scientists and laypersons alike his name conjures up little more than vague recollections of "conspicuous consumption," if that. One reason for this is that he was a caustic critic of American business culture in a society in which business has a hegemonic hold on the mind of much of the underlying population. Then too, Veblen wrote in a manner that is difficult to decipher, for his prose is studded with latinates that require a large vocabulary to comprehend. During his thirty-year academic career he attacked every major institution and practice in American life that had been or were regarded as sacrosanct; these included emulatory consumption and waste, institutional religion, absentee ownership, sports and games, the subjugation of women, and aspects of academic life, including the entrepreneurial role of administrators. Little of this criticism endeared him to the powers that be, in or out of the economics profession, and he was thus often consigned to the underworld of economic heretics.

However, Veblen's reputation as a seminal thinker in economics and sociology is well established among institutional economists, intellectual historians, and radical American sociologists, thanks in part to the massive study of him by Joseph Dorfman. Dorfman gives an able analysis of his economics and sociology, even if he occasionally fails to offer a clear or consistent portrayal of him as a human being. Veblen scholars owe Dorfman a serious debt, and the lacunae left by him with regard to Veblen's personal traits and life can be filled in part by using materials not available to him between 1926 and 1934, when he wrote *Thorstein Veblen and His America.*[1] Future biographers of Veblen may want to revise Dorfman's conclusions regarding Veblen's late acquisition of English, the cultural and social isolation of the Veblen family, and its material circumstances when he was young. In any case, interested readers are referred to Dorfman's writings even though he is not always a reliable source on Veblen's childhood and adolescence. Dorfman exaggerated the cultural isolation of the Norwegian-Lutheran settlements in which the Veblen family lived by downplaying the fact that many of their neighbors and acquaintances were of Yankee origin and still others were Catholics. It is also interesting to note that many of the Veblen siblings, including Thorstein, married individuals of British origin. It appears, then, that his idiosyncratic personality and ideas had sources other than the social marginality induced by living in an ethnic Norwegian environment.[2]

Both of Veblen's marriages were to women who were, or became, mentally or emotionally ill. Of course, much has been made of Veblen's "womanizing," but insufficient attention has been paid to the mental state of his wives as a plausible explanation of this. Andrew Veblen, Thorstein's older brother, wrote of his first wife that:

> She was interested in a theosophical establishment, the headquarters of which I understood was situated at Halcyon. This was a branch of the cult of theosophy which consisted of followers of Madame Blavatsky. . . . She was much absorbed in spiritual-religious matters and problems.[3]

Veblen divorced Ellen Rolfe Veblen in 1911, but they apparently corresponded for many years thereafter. Only one letter, written in 1920, has survived, but it is quite revealing of her state of mind:

> Think of all that has happened in our lifetime! The Bahai Movement, Spiritualism, Theosophy, Christian Science, Darwin, Blavatsky, Healers of all sorts, the upheaval of the nation, Bolshevism, Karl Marx, the world war in progress [unintelligible], radio, art, and as I hear, a new ray which renders metal permanently hot. Then, also, the oscilloscope.[4]

History does not record Veblen's reaction to this bizarre juxtaposition of ideas, thinkers, religious movements, and inventions, but the excerpt provides insight into his first wife's mind-set and emotional state. It is also interesting to note that Veblen's second wife, Ann Bradley, a former student whom he married in 1914, was committed to Maclean Hospital, a mental asylum, in 1919.

That university administrators used Veblen's dalliances with women as a reason for firing him is beyond doubt. Evidence of this is provided in a sanctimonious message written by the president of Stanford University to the president of the University of Chicago. In a letter marked "confidential," David Starr Jordan told Harry Pratt Judson that:

> I have been able, with the help of Mrs. Veblen, to find out the truth in detail as to Professor Veblen's relations. He seems unable to resist the "femme mecomprise". It is fair to say, that in my final talk with him, he [indecipher-

> able] behaved in manly fashion, with no attempt at denial or evasion. He has tendered his resignation to later effect at my discretion. This will probably mean with July of next year. For the University cannot condone these matters, much as its officials may feel compassion for the individual.[5]

Clearly, Veblen's philandering was offensive to academic administrators. Yet the truth about his several dismissals from academic posts is more complex, for his ideological leanings also influenced administrators against him. Interestingly, however, President Jordan's later correspondence with Veblen indicates that he still read and admired Veblen's work and bore him no personal ill will.[6]

Perhaps the most focused analysis of Veblen the man came from Jacob Warshaw, professor of romance languages at the University of Missouri, who came to know him well during his seven-year stay in Columbia. Warshaw read Dorfman's *Thorstein Veblen and His America* when it was published in 1934. He believed that while it mostly did justice to Veblen's sociology and economics, it failed to adequately capture some of his basic personality traits. The following reflections are based on Warshaw's acquaintance with Veblen when the latter was in his mid-to-late fifties.

> Though I always felt sorry for Veblen as a misunderstood man and a man of sorrows—if he had known of my compassion he would have withered me with a look—I never thought of him as, in his heart, the suave, imperturbable, sphinx-like character who stands out in Dorfman. He struck me rather as a man of spontaneous passions who had found it not the easiest task in the world to keep smiling and to say nothing.[7]

The only major scholarly portrait of Veblen based on primary sources available to us is the Dorfman book. Most other commentaries on his personality made by other Veblen scholars are from this source and are thus derivative. Obviously, Warshaw knew Veblen far better than Dorfman did, so his commentaries on the man and on Dorfman's study of him are an invaluable source of information. Up to now, the thirteen-page Warshaw sketch has rarely been used, but it is likely that some future revisionist biographer of Veblen will systematically exploit it. However, the significant point is that at least one of Veblen's contemporaries saw him differently from the way Dorfman did.

> The general impression that I get from Dorfman is that Veblen was a quiet, suave, passionless person who broke loose only once or twice in his life and never laughed. Had I not known Veblen pretty well that would have been my picture of him out of Dorfman. My recollections, however, are different. Veblen could get as irritated as the next man and gave signs of his irritation. . . . He once gave me a dirty look when I declined one of his Russian cigarettes on the ground that my stomach was out of whack and that I thought I was losing weight through smoking too much. . . . If you didn't appreciate a joke of his, a frown would form on his face or his eyes would take on a somber look.[8]

For those who remain convinced of the value of psychobiography in explaining the relationship between personality and theory, Warshaw's analysis of Dorfman's work is more penetrating than David Riesman's study *Thorstein Veblen: A Critical Interpretation*, although the latter relied heavily on Dorfman for information regarding Veblen. In what is perhaps Warshaw's most discerning comments he writes:

> [U]nder the surface, Veblen was highly emotional. His philandering with women was one indication. His constant, bitter irony and sarcasm—which are good exhaust valves when you are inhibited from doing bodily damage—may be regarded as another. To realize this emotional quality in Veblen is, it seems to me, to get another light on his ideas and projects, to forgive him most of his cynicism, and to find him a more sympathetic and human individual than he is usually credited with being. He was never a cold-blooded, calculating radical—at least, so it appears to me.[9]

Veblen's sense of humor, and the emotional structure of which it provides evidence, were not adequately expressed in his sardonic scholarly posture. The bitter cynicism and sarcasm noted by Dorfman, which found outlet in his theories, was only one part of Veblen's temperament. Warshaw points to another aspect of it:

> As for his ability to smile and laugh, I can say that I never found him markedly lacking in it. . . . Where he was to a certain extent in the public gaze, his smile was somewhat pinched and guarded, but in our rambles over the golf links it was frequent, natural, and infectious. In fact, his smile is one of the features that I best remember him by. It was a kindly, amused, rather Olympian smile, and thoroughly genuine. I have also heard him laugh—not once, but a number of times.[10]

Dorfman treated Veblen essentially as a social scientist and satirist whose main interests were the social order, the government, and the economy. But Warshaw, a scholar of romance languages and literature, discerningly portrays the humanist in him.

> Few of the readers of Dorfman will realize . . . that they have been reviewing the life of one of the most learned and most curious of latter-day humanists. By "humanist" I mean in this case "a lover of learning" and not merely "a lover of polite learning or the humanities," as was true during the Renaissance. . . . It is this insatiable curiosity and this accumulation of all kinds of knowledge that I should call Veblen's humanism. There was probably a limit to the stock of knowledge that he could hold and manipulate, but I never saw it reached. He would have been in his glory among the Renaissance humanists or the eighteenth-century encyclopedists.[11]

Since Warshaw was an accomplished linguist, his comments on Veblen in this regard are significant and provide still another link with the latter's humanism.

> As a linguist alone, Veblen was unusual. Among students the legend ran that he knew twenty-six languages. The combination of languages that he could handle was somewhat uncommon. It included, along with the classics and the more widely known modern languages, Spanish, Dutch, and the Scandinavian tongues, including Icelandic. I do not doubt that Veblen had a working knowledge of other languages not usually studied and that he was capable, in an incredibly short time, of "getting up" in any language that he was interested in or had need of. His accomplishments in French, Spanish, and Italian I can vouch for. Whether or not he could speak them I can't be sure. But he surprised me frequently with his familiarity with minutiae of the Romance literatures and once or twice with his shrewd analyses of the history of Romance words. I did not know at the time that he had once had ambitions of becoming a philologist.[12]

Warshaw was also an observer of Veblen's personal idiosyncracies. These oddities shed light not only on his personal tastes but also on his capacity for absorbing and assimilating knowledge. Warshaw interpreted one this way:

> He preferred not to have anybody read his newspaper over his shoulder. That may have been due either to his abnormal personal sensitiveness or to his faculty, mentioned several times to me by one of his close friends, of being able to read two columns of print simultaneously—a circumstance that would keep him and the onlooker woefully out of step.[13]

That Veblen could read two columns of print simultaneously, if true, may shed light on how it was that he could master such an extraordinary amount of printed material.

Warshaw also knew the personal side of Veblen from the perspective of one who had enjoyed the hospitality of the Veblen home, an opportunity of which few could boast.

> He could be whole-heartedly congenial, as the few persons who visited him in his home can testify. Lounging about in his loose dressing-gown and looking not nearly as anemic and fragile as in his street clothes, he reminded one, with his drooping mustaches and Nordic features, of nothing so much as a hospitable Viking taking his ease at his own fireside. At such times, he was at his best, pouring out curious information, throwing off a little malicious gossip which, in view of his seclusiveness, he must have picked miraculously out of the air, mixing picturesque slang with brilliant phrases of his own coinage, solicitously watching out for his guests' comfort, and in general, behaving like a "regular guy." An evening with him—when you were fortunate enough to get one—was as good as a French salon or an eighteenth-century London coffee-house. When it was over you wished that you had had a Boswellian memory and eye.[14]

Warshaw concluded: "The fact is that Veblen the friendly companion was quite a different person from Veblen the ponderous, pontifical writer and dangerous iconoclast."[15]

An anecdote about a New York bookstore trying to sell a customer a copy of *The Theory of the Leisure Class* shortly after the end of World War I also provides insight: Madge Jenison, a bookseller, recalled:

> A man used to appear every six or eight weeks quite regularly, an ascetic, mysterious person with keys to unlock things, I took him to be, and with a gentle air. He wore his hair long and looked Scandinavian. I do not know just why or when I made him a Swedenborgian minister. . . . I used to try to interest him in economics. . . . I even once tried to get him to begin with *The Theory of the Leisure Class*. I explained to him what a brilliant port of entry it is to social consciousness. But it became clear that if he was ever to be interested in sociology and economics, he would not be interested in them by me. He listened attentively to all I said and melted like a snow drop through the door. One day he ordered a volume of Latin hymns. "I shall have to take your name because we will order this expressly for you," I told him. "We shall not have an audience for such a book as this again in a long time, I am afraid." "My name is Thorstein Veblen," he breathed rather than said.[16]

Why did Veblen not explain in his numerous visits to the bookstore who he was, particularly after being encouraged to buy a famous book he wrote? No doubt his droll sense of humor needed some outlet at times and, as he grew older, perhaps there were fewer opportunities to express it. Nevertheless, the account by Jenison reveals an unusual detachment from self or, perhaps, unusual qualities of self-deprecation.

Andrew Veblen, in a letter to economist Edward Bemis, who had once been Veblen's colleague at the University of Chicago, described his brother's death in 1929 in these words:

> My youngest daughter with her husband and two children, near, and at times with, whom he had lived in Chicago, made him a visit in July; and they, as well as Becky [his stepdaughter], were there with him when he was taken ill and died. It seemed he had been anticipating, lately, that the end might come though this only became evident afterward. He was taken with a fainting attack, and lived only an hour, or a little more, part of the time he was conscious, but did not seem to have much pain. This was the afternoon of August 3.[17]

Thus ended the life of the American iconoclast and satirist and, perhaps, unwitting founder of institutional economics.

Veblen Retrieved

With Veblen's personality and temperament as an adult described, it is time to retrieve other facets of him. Those familiar with the corpus of his writings will recall the importance of "idle curiosity," which apparently had roots in his early life. As a boy of eight or nine, living with his Norwegian immigrant parents and many siblings on a farm in rural Minnesota, he made snares of horsehair and trapped gophers and squirrels with them, not to destroy the rodents, but so he could study them. He carried them about inside his shirt while he observed them and then released them after satisfying his curiosity. His interest in botany manifested itself when the Veblen children went picking berries in the woods and fields, for he was likely to detect any plant that he had not seen before and carefully investigate it. Further evidence of his interest in natural phenomena is found in his failure to return one day to the farm after having been sent on an errand. When he did not return as expected, one of his brothers went looking for him. In the meantime, a powerful storm had arisen. When the brother found him, he was lying on his back beside the road, studying the storm with intense interest, the family dog curled up next to him. Such were the forms that "idle curiosity" took in Veblen, the boy, and it is not surprising that he later assigned it a key role in human motivation.[18]

Various stories about Veblen's sense of humor from youth to old age can be told, and they mostly give evidence of his social marginality and iconoclasm. As a boy he defended the rights of native Americans against the encroachment of white settlers in the Midwest; he wrote curses in Greek on the fence of a neighbor whom he disliked. As an undergraduate he defended drunkenness in a tongue-in-cheek campus presentation.

Joseph Dorfman stressed the influence of Veblen's parents. His mother was an able and altruistic woman who often served as an amateur doctor in the frontier settlements where they lived. His father was a skilled carpenter and builder who was also a competent and successful farmer. Veblen once described his father as having the finest mind he ever encountered. The latter placed a premium on higher education and, unlike other farmers in the neighborhood of Nerstrand, Minnesota, where they permanently settled in 1865, sent all of the dozen or so Veblen children, girls included, who survived to adulthood were sent to preparatory school or college. In fact, Thomas Anderson Veblen and his sons built a house in Northfield, Minnesota, near Carleton College for the siblings to live in while they attended college.

Veblen received three years of preparatory schooling at the academy attached to Carleton and three years at the college itself. His interests were primarily in economics, philology, philosophy, and biology. It may well be that this multidisciplinary background was the genesis of his focus on the study of cultures as a whole. To illustrate, as an undergraduate he worked under John Bates Clark, who later became an eminent neoclassical economist; later, in graduate school at Johns Hopkins University, he was the student of the noted economist Richard Ely and of Charles Sanders Peirce, who is recognized as one of the greatest American philosophers. Still later, at Yale University, where he earned a doctorate in philosophy, he studied Immanuel Kant with President Noah Porter and economics with the noted social Darwinist William Graham Sumner. During his years on the faculty of the University of Chicago his acquaintances included the philosophers John Dewey and George Herbert Mead and the eminent physiologist Jacques Loeb. Later, when he lived in New York, the anthropologist Franz Boas and the historian Charles A. Beard were included among his friends. His European acquaintances included the heterodox English economist John Hobson, the British sociologist Victor Branford, and the Scottish scientist, social philosopher, and urban planner Patrick Geddes. The point of all this academic name-dropping is to note the breadth and depth of Veblen's knowledge, the stature of his intellectual acquaintances, and some of the sources of the broad-gauged structure of his theory.

Before Veblen's career could get under way he had to obtain an academic post, a task that took him seven years. During this period he was plagued intermittently with illness. To make matters worse, because of his agnosticism he was unable to obtain employment at the denominational colleges where he sought posts. Apparently, during this period of recuperation and unemployment he spent most of his time reading. Finally, in 1891, he returned to graduate school at Cornell University; J. Laurence Laughlin, head of the economics department, was so impressed by him that he obtained a fellowship for him. The next year, when the University of Chicago opened, he took Veblen with him. Veblen, now thirty-five, began to publish in the fields of sociology and economics. Although he served as managing editor of the *Journal of Political Economy* and was rapidly becoming a noted publicist, his salary was small, promotions were slow, the availability of other academic posts was limited, and he was unable to get funds for research. Veblen's radicalism, his satirical writing, and his unconventional life-style did not endear him to university presidents or to philanthropic benefactors.

More to the point, however, was the fact that Veblen was a caustic critic of neoclassical economics and economists. Although neoinstitutional economists have done yeoman work in clarifying and further developing his ideas in order to reconstruct economics along the lines he suggested, critics have often been genuinely puzzled by the thrust of his attack on the received economic wisdom. If his primary aim was to destroy or at least radically change economic science, what did he intend to put in its place?

He did not want economics to remain a defense of an arbitrary and functionless absentee ownership. When he demanded an "evolutionary" economic science, what he wanted was one that would be a science of collective welfare; that is, a means of advancing the instrumental adaptive powers of the entire community to ceaseless change. He emphasized not the capitalization of intangible assets for personal gain but the industrial arts as a community possession. In his view, economics as a discipline should not be a form of apologetics for the diversion of the corporate income stream to the upper class and its satellites but a defense of the social dividend bequeathed to the community by the progress of science and technology. He thus attacked neoclassical economics for focusing far too narrowly on the study of the allocation of scarce resources through the price system and market mechanism with little heed for the use value of what was produced and consumed with regard to the health, vitality, and future of the community.

Veblen's Dualisms

Veblen's theory is powerfully dualistic, and in his interlocking dualisms his own values are vitally evident. One conflict in his work is the struggle between the animistic and the matter-of-fact, between superstition and science, between that which is magical and that which is empirically demonstrable. A second dualism manifest throughout his work is that which pits technology, that is, the machine process and the industrial arts, against stagnant, change-resistant institutions that impede technology's progress. A variation on this is the conflict between business and industry, that is, the cleavage between pecuniary and industrial employments, between those who make money and those who produce socially useful goods and services. A conflict thus exists between those who perform what Veblen sees as socially wasteful roles and those who have useful social functions. In the realm of consumption, the dualism translates into an emulatory status process rooted in conspicuous consumption and ostentatious display versus consumption aimed at the satisfaction of functional and biological needs which serve what Veblen calls the "generic ends of life."

Also, Veblen's social psychology led him to construct a dualism between predatory exploit and warlike animus on the one hand, and peaceable congeniality and workmanlike efficiency on the other; thus the emergence in his thought of a conflict between the predatory and the peaceful. Consequently, a dualism separates the pecuniary and sporting proclivities of the predatory type, which exhibit themselves in force and fraud, from the amiable pacifism of the opposite type, whose behavior is channeled into idle curiosity, the parental bent, and the propensity for workmanship.

World War I and Its Aftermath

Interpreters of Veblen often suggest that there were two Veblens. One was the detached intellectual who was reluctant to take sides; the other, the revolutionary Veblen, emerged more clearly during and after World War I. In this view critics note that, while there is little in Veblen's later work that he did not deal with earlier, his later writings take the form of concrete application and propaganda, moving away from the abstraction, aloofness, and greater objectivity of his earlier work.

In 1914 Veblen published *The Instinct of Workmanship*, which he believed was his most important book and which can profitably be read as a sequel to *The Theory of the Leisure Class*. In it Veblen modified the instinct psychology and racialism that influenced his early work. This he accomplished by defining "instinct" as purposive, learned behavior and by asserting that all Europeans were racial hybrids with little to separate them in terms of their natural endowment. Veblen's erudition was evident in his further development of the phases through which he believed humanity has evolved, including the savage, the barbarian, the handicraft, and the industrial stages. What separates these stages from each other, in addition to the level of economic development reached, is the degree to which the predatory instincts have contaminated the peaceful traits; in short, the extent to which the sporting and pecuniary instincts have impacted the instincts of idle curiosity, parenthood, and workmanship.

Veblen's main commentary on American universities was *The Higher Learning in America* (1918), which he subtitled "A Memorandum on the Conduct of Universities by Business Men." Originally at least part of this book was incorporated in *The Theory of Business Enterprise* (1904); and while it was still in manuscript form President William Rainey Harper, Veblen's administrative superior at the University of Chicago, read it. Veblen's unflattering portrayal of the "captains of erudition," which, at least by implication, included Harper, may have contributed to his dismissal in 1905. In any case, when the book was finally published in 1918, it contributed mightily to Veblen's indictment of American business culture, for it attributed the flaws in the university to "businesslike" management and to leisure-class values.

The outbreak of war in 1914 was a catalyst that altered the nature and direction of Veblen's work. Much of what he wrote before the war had a timeless, cosmological quality about it; what he wrote after the war was often polemical, prescriptive, and contemporary; his work during the war combined the qualities of both. When the United States entered the war in April 1917, Veblen offered his services to the federal government. He wanted to participate in the planning for peace, and he wrote several memoranda on a "League of Pacific Peoples" and on a plan for international control of foreign investments and for the economic penetration of underdeveloped areas. Although Veblen probably had little appreciable impact on President Wilson's policies, he was finally given a job with the federal Food Administration, and for several months he did statistical surveys and wrote reports for it.

Veblen made several proposals for aiding the war effort at home. The first was to end the persecution of the leaders of the Industrial Workers of the World, a union that represented agricultural workers in the Midwest, so they could successfully harvest the wheat crop. The second was to do away with merchants in country towns and to supply farmers via a mail-order system. The last was to levy a steep progressive tax on employers of domestic servants to free up wasted manpower. Evidence is lacking that the Food Administration or President Wilson paid attention to these proposals or that they had any effect on policy.

At the war's end in 1918 Veblen went to New York to be one of the editors of *The Dial*, a literary and political journal. The two major themes of the early postwar era were peace and the antiradical hysteria that was beginning to sweep the country. In his editorials Veblen referred to the first as an attempt to "make the world safe" for the "vested interests," and the second he called "dementia praecox" (precocious insanity). He ridiculed the establishment's fears of a revolutionary uprising. As he put it: "The Guardians have allowed the known facts of the case to unseat their common sense. Hence the pitiful spectacle of official hysteria and the bedlamite conspiracies in restraint of sobriety."[19]

At the same time as he wrote editorials for *The Dial* in 1918 and 1919, he also wrote two series of articles. One became *The Vested Interests and the State of the Industrial Arts* (1919), which was mostly a popularization of his thoughts on nationalism, business enterprise, technology, and natural rights. Written in a more polemical and argumentative style than his work before the war, it was a succinct summation of his basic ideas, but there was little new in it. The other series of articles became *The Engineers and the Price System* (1921). He knew that there was little revolutionary potential among American farmers or workers, so he now turned to the engineers and technicians for an examination of their transformative capacities. They were the creative technologists whose intelligence and skill determined the state of the industrial arts, and they conceivably could operate the existing industrial plant without the obstructiveness of its pecuniary institutional encumbrances. But Veblen doubted their revolutionary potential also. A decade later, during the Great Depression, Howard Scott, who claimed to be under Veblen's influence, achieved fleeting fame for his Technocracy movement, but Scott's proposals for economic reconstruction bore only vague resemblance to Veblen's analysis of the revolutionary potential of a "soviet of engineers."

When *The Dial* editorship came to an end Veblen was hired by the newly founded New School for Social Research. He probably was never an effective teacher for the common run of student, and that he was in ill health and in late middle age did not improve his effectiveness. Each semester his classes began with a large registration but soon dwindled away to only the committed. When the New School had to be reorganized, he became an expensive luxury the school could not afford. Even though he was at the peak of his influence as a publicist, his academic career was at an end.

Veblen's Social and Economic Theory

During the thirty years Veblen held academic posts at Chicago, Stanford, Missouri, and the New School for Social Research, he became the most influential and best-known dissenting economist in the United States. After the publication in 1899 of his most famous book, *The Theory of the Leisure Class*, in which he developed his theory of status emulation, his heterodoxy was widely known by professional economists and sociologists.

Veblen argued in his theory of status emulation that social classes competitively emulate the social strata next above them. This is done wittingly or not in order to increase their own social status and thus their sense of self-worth and esteem. But emulatory consumption itself is not a value-neutral type of behavior; rather, it is an often intense form of competitive rivalry aimed at status enhancement and, perhaps, also at power aggrandizement. In any case, Veblen believed that those classes most able to conspicuously consume, waste, and avoid useful labor are most likely to command social honor and deference from other classes. More recently scholars working in the Veblenian tradition have fleshed out and updated his analysis. Briefly, what they have done is to place consumption into three categories: (1) sybaritic, (2) status enhancing or emulatory, and (3) functional or instrumental.

Sybaritic consumption, named after an ancient people, the Sybarites, was renowned for its emphasis on sensual delights and luxury, but it is here noted for providing evidence of self-indulgence, not ability to conspicuously consume. Sybaritic consumption may be private or public, but it does not aim at status enhancement, and Veblen thus paid it little heed. The emulatory consumption to which he paid much attention aims at improving one's social position or at least the perception of it by others. American economist Harvey Leibenstein breaks it into three forms, which he calls (1) "Veblen effects," where price is the main consideration; the higher the price paid for a commodity the more status it gives, (2) "bandwagon effects," where exceeding one's peers in ability to purchase and display conspicuously is not the intent; instead the aim is to achieve rough equality with them, that is, join them on the "bandwagon," and (3) "snob effects," where emphasis is on the acquisition of culturally esoteric artifacts which only the cultural elite have the expertise or education to appreciate. To this third category Robert Steiner and Joseph Weiss have added a fourth; which they call "counter-snobbery" it signifies a reversion to more austere and simple tastes and lifestyles. This also aims at status enhancement, but employs a different method for achieving it.

Clearly, Veblen preferred consumption that was functional, that is, instrumental in enhancing the life process of the community. Such consumption aimed at the satisfaction of biological rather than status needs, at human serviceability, not self-indulgence or status display. Veblen was aware that most goods and services achieve some of both, but argued that it was often possible to differentiate the one purpose from the other as the primary function of the commodity. The achievement of the generic ends of life impersonally considered, or "fullness of life," as he sometimes put it, thus depended upon the community's ability to distinguish between functional and status-enhancing consumption.

In his satirical study of the leisure class and the underlying social strata that emulate it, he argued that conspicuous consumption, waste, and ostentatious avoidance of useful work were practices that enhanced social status. In short, Veblen contended that individual utility preferences could not be understood except in relation to the utility preferences of upper-class others. Individuals were emulating others to strengthen their own sense of self-worth by commanding more social esteem. The assumptions of atomistic individualism and consumer sovereignty, deemed valid by microeconomists, were thus shown to be specious on social-psychological grounds alone.

The Theory of the Leisure Class also contained many ideas on the nature of social value that were fundamentally different from the ideas of the utilitarian tradition that formed the basis of the neoclassical approach to value. Veblen was unconvinced by the conventional view of individuals as "globules of desire" who tried to maximize pleasure and minimize pain. He was also caustic in his repudiation of the moral agnosticism he found pervasive in the neoclassical view of value as subjective preference measurable only by price. The latter led to the claim that interpersonal comparisons of utility were impossible or irrelevant because consumer preferences were autonomously rooted in private, subjective states of mind and thus were not subject to public scrutiny.

Veblen's rejection of neoclassical value theory did not end in nihilism, however, for he outlined an alternative to both neoclassicism and classical Marxism. He wrote of the "generic ends" of life "impersonally considered" and of "fullness of life." In his evolutionary—that is, Darwinian—mode of analysis this implied the existence of some transcultural set of values. He found these values embedded in workmanship, parenthood, and idle curiosity, all of which flourish in a properly developing society. To Veblen, the "instincts" of craftsmanship, altruism, and critical intelligence were dominant values and processes if communities were to develop in a noninvidious manner. But in communities that were not so developing, these "instincts," propensities, or values/processes would be contaminated by the pecuniary and sporting traits, which were invidious and destructive.

Veblen's second book, *The Theory of Business Enterprise* (1904), contains his explanation of business cycles and an extended treatment of the cultural and social psychological incidence of the machine process. Contrary to conventional analysts of business cycles, Veblen saw no "natural" equilibrating tendencies in the American economy. He argued that instability was endemic in the American business system because of excessive capitalization and credit inflation. His analysis focused on the tendency of firms to borrow too much by overestimating their future earning power. At some point their creditors would recognize that loans made to these firms had been unwarranted because their earning power was less than anticipated. Their loans would then be called in, with the inevitable consequences of bankruptcy and liquidation. A protracted period of depression would follow, with large-scale unemployment and unused industrial capacity. Gradually, however, the earning power and credit rating of firms would move toward convergence with each other, and recovery would occur. A period of prosperity would then ensue, until overcapitalization and credit inflation recurred and the cycle began anew. Veblen anticipated that the growth of monopoly and wasteful government expenditures might check cyclical instability, but his disciples looked to the social control of industry and better government planning to offset the deficiencies of the system.

Much of Veblen's reputation as a dissenting economist was based on his critique of classical and neoclassical economics. Included in his analysis of the received economic theory and doctrines was rejection of (1) hedonism and utilitarianism, (2) the static bias of price theory, (3) the taxonomic method, and (4) the infection of economics with teleology. Veblen labeled these deficiencies "predarwinian," that is, rooted in a pre-evolutionary mind-set which had not yet come to terms with the scientific revolution for which Charles Darwin was the chief catalyst.

Veblen criticized the hedonistic and utilitarian theory for portraying humans as passive agents reacting to external forces only when impinged upon. His reading in cultural anthropology convinced him that humanity was active rather than quiescent and that, in any case, the Benthamite claim that pleasure and pain were "sovereign masters of us all" was merely tautological. When Veblen accused eminent neoclassicists, such as his former teacher John Bates Clark and Yale's Irving Fisher, of mere "taxonomy" he was, of course, charging them with mistaking classification, inventorying, and labeling for genuine scientific explanation, which in his view dealt primarily with the establishment of cumulative causal relationships. Indeed, Veblen's essentially negative view of neoclassicism rested on his belief that it failed to move beyond the taxonomic stage of inquiry.

Veblen attacked the static bias of neoclassicism for its inability to account for change; general and partial equilibrium theory failed to capture the flux of evolutionary processes, including changes in both the market mechanism and the underlying institutions that direct and channel exchange. Finally, Veblen criticized neoclassicism for its retention of the residues of teleology that so badly infected classical economics. His most often cited example was the neoclassical claim that equilibrium between supply and demand constitutes a "normal" state of affairs toward which markets inevitably and invariably tend.

However, the central feature of Veblen's work as a dissenting economist was not his critique of neoclassicism, his contribution to business cycle theory, or even his theory of status emulation, as important as these were. Instead, what most set him off from the conventional paradigm was his development and use of the dichotomy between business and industry, which his disciples later called the "ceremonial-technological dichotomy." They and Veblen employed it as an analytic device, as an approach to the larger problem of value in economics, and as part of a theory of social change. In his usage the dichotomy included salesmanship as opposed to workmanship, free income versus tangible performance, individual gain as opposed to community serviceability, invidious emulation versus technological efficiency, and competitive advertising versus the provision of valuable information and guidance.

To Veblen much of the activity in which the business community engaged was wasteful and futile, for the profitability of market exchange did not necessarily measure the value of commodities in achieving the generic ends of life. In spite of his lack of specificity about which pursuits are industrial, which are businesslike, and which have both traits, it is clear in retrospect that such judgments depend on the meaning assigned by Veblen to "fullness of life, impersonally considered," which was his way of indicating that the generic ends of life are transcultural in nature and often not served by profit-making. The dichotomy between business and industry can be understood, as Veblen intended, if it is recognized that those values and processes most conducive to fullness of life, such as idle curiosity, the parental bent, and proficiency of workmanship, cannot always be adequately measured by a price system or through market exchange. It follows that business enterprise will often dissipate resources rather than produce commodities that contribute to the generic ends of life. In the final analysis, what is business and what is industry in the Veblenian dichotomy can only be ascertained by reference to these ends.

Conventional income distribution theory, according to Veblen, is based on the untenable assumption that remuneration measures production. The modern captain of industry and the absentee owner are considered productive agents who receive in remuneration the exchange equivalence of their productivity. Thus, pecuniary activities are not treated as the controlling factor about which the modern economic process turns but are assumed to be productive operations effecting the distribution of goods from producer to consumer. At various times Veblen cast aspersions on all the prevailing theories and rationalizations of the existing distribution of income. He satirized, castigated, or considered irrelevant the abstinence, risk, and time (period of waiting) rationales for the receipt of rent, interest, and profit, and he indicated that marginal utility theory was tautological and thus without explanatory power. He believed that there was no objective way to ascertain the value of an individual's contribution without taking into consideration the social nature of production. Consequently, he criticized the Marxian theory because he thought it assigned to the individual worker the value of his labor and ignored the fact that technology itself was a collective legacy. Although he never specifically articulated a theory of income distribution, his evolutionary view of social change suggests an unending process of adjusting means to ends, and ends to means, with community serviceability (social usefulness) as the standard of value for economic activity. Income should thus be distributed so as to facilitate the instrumentally adaptive efforts of society to achieve the generic ends of life as well as successfully cope with unending change.

As an economic historian and theorist of growth, Veblen is best known for his "institutionalism," a term coined by Walton Hamilton during World War I. In one sense the term is misleading, because Veblen was critical of existing institutions due to their inhibitive impact on technological change. In his theory of cultural lag, he develops the idea that institutions are inhibitory and backward-looking, while science and technology are themselves dynamic and oriented toward change. The question at any point in time is whether institutions are sufficiently malleable to permit efficient exploitation of existing technological potential. As the "tool continuum" evolves, it may become more or less absorptive of culturally cross-fertilized processes that bring together more and different tools and make possible new technologies. Veblen explains the economic history of the West by linking cultural anthropology and social history with changes in the technoeconomic base; the main variables in his explanation are the degree of institutional rigidity and the force exerted on it by technology.

Veblen's theory of economic growth is closely linked with his ideas regarding economic waste. In his theory, the rate of economic growth cannot be maximized if all output is not serviceable and if efficiency is sacrificed to pecuniary interests. The rate of maximum growth is thus governed by technological advance, which controls the size of the nation's economic surplus, although this rate is also a matter of the disposition of the surplus between serviceable and disserviceable uses. In short, Veblen incorporates a theory of waste—that is, unproductive consumption, investment, and labor—within his theory of social change. This permits him to show the conditions under which economic growth will stagnate and, also, the conditions under which growth will not be synonymous with the economic welfare of the community. The concept of economic efficiency is thus clarified and linked with the processes of social change and noninvidious economic growth.

Veblen's last three books, *The Vested Interests and the State of the Industrial Arts* (1919), *The Engineers and the Price System* (1921), and *Absentee Ownership and Business Enterprise in Recent Times* (1923), focus on the predation and waste of the corporate capitalist order. Writing in a more polemical style than before, Veblen endorsed the displacement of absentee owners and business-minded executives from the American corporation. He also recommended, perhaps tongue-in-cheek, that engineers and technicians form an alliance with workers and run enterprises themselves. At this point in his career, Veblen interacted for a short time with politically progressive engineers and emphasized the role they might play in the establishment of an industrial republic. But the many allegations by his critics that Veblen was a technocratic elitist who wanted to establish an autocracy dominated by engineers and technicians exaggerate this element in his thought.[20]

It was inevitable in his role as a dissenting economist that Veblen would favor large-scale changes in the capitalist order, although it was unusual for him to make serious policy recommendations. What distinguished him from other radicals was his view of the means that were available to make these changes. Orthodox Marxists often put their faith in a proletariat whether it was revolutionary or not, but Veblen was skeptical of this "labor metaphysic," as C. Wright Mills was later to call it.[21] Nevertheless, he persisted in his search for a social change agent, a political technology, and a vehicle for structural change. Early in his career the American proletariat and Bellamyite socialism attracted his attention in these regards. After them, anarcho-syndicalism in the form of the Industrial Workers of the World aroused his sympathies, and, of course, he later endorsed, perhaps satirically, progressive engineers and technicians as the wave of the future. Ultimately, however, he retreated into pessimism toward the American scene, believing that "imbecile institutions" were dominant.

But his own analysis of the social psychology of classes makes uncertain the outcome of industrial civilization. The machine process had an emancipatory impact on the psyche of industrial workers which turned them against social convention and presumably in favor of socialism; on the other hand, status emulation infected the working class and served as a social bonding agent to offset both the class mentality and the conflict induced by the machine process. Status emulation was in turn reinforced by patriotism, which Veblen defined as "a sense of partisan solidarity in respect of prestige."[22] Would the machine process triumph and turn the working class against capitalism, as suggested in *The Theory of Business Enterprise*, or would emulatory consumption reinforced by patriotism triumph? In the final analysis, despite his pessimism, Veblen did not know—or at least he did not say.

Estimates of Veblen's creative contribution as a dissenting economist vary greatly, depending on the political and social philosophy of the critic. Most neoclassical economists who are politically conservative find little merit in his work because they see themselves correctly, both as economists and as consumers, as the objects of his satire. Political liberals react differently to Veblen, depending on how far left they are in the political spectrum. To illustrate, those still partly under the influence of classical liberalism find little of value in his work other than his humor, while collectivist liberals often respect both his satire and his social theory. However, it is on the radical left that Veblen's theory and doctrine meet with greatest approval, although Marxists like Paul Baran and Theodor Adorno were very critical of his work.[23]

The creation of the Association for Evolutionary Economics in 1966 and the *Journal of Economic Issues* have provided a forum for the study of Veblen and his ideas. More recently, the Association for Institutional Thought (1979), the European Association for Evolutionary Political Economy (1988), and the International Thorstein Veblen Association (1992) provide evidence of the continued growth of a dissenting tradition with Veblenian roots. Veblen's theoretical and doctrinal arsenal as a dissenter from conventional economics is thus more widely accessible to a new generation of economists in search of a viable alternative to the neoclassical paradigm.

Veblen's Social Criticism, Social Theory, and Critics

Veblen is sometimes criticized for not having developed a systematic theory. Those who make such criticisms apparently have theorists like Karl Marx, Max Weber, and Talcott Parsons in mind as models of systematic theorizing. In my opinion, such criticisms are often wide of their mark, for Veblen at his best was both a systematic thinker and theorist. Such misunderstandings might have been avoided had his critics been more cognizant of the prime influences on Veblen's theoretical system—that is, Charles Darwin and the Darwinian revolution in Western thought, and socialism broadly construed, particularly its American variants. It is Darwinism that is most important in grasping the essentials of Veblen's theory.

What Veblen took from Darwin's approach was not the conservative "social Darwinism," which glorified competition and economic predation; indeed, Veblen stood William Graham Sumner and Herbert Spencer on their heads by emphasizing a different set of values and processes. He favored not economic ruthlessness and exploit but peacableness, critical intelligence, altruism, and proficiency of workmanship. Veblen took from Darwin the essential scientific method, which studies humanity in its process of continuous adaptation to both its social and natural environment and which sees the conditions of human existence as subject to ceaseless change. Although he was not always consistent in his use of Darwinian principles, it is impossible to appreciate the systematic nature of his theory without grasping its Darwinian origins.

For many, Veblen is a prophet with an ethical and an aesthetic message. Others view him simply as an insightful social scientist. Although Veblen's significance is still widely disputed, the secondary literature dealing with his ideas indicates that he was an original thinker, responsible for introducing and popularizing a host of important concepts and insights. A partial catalogue would include the ideas of conspicuous consumption, display, and emulation, which are significant in explaining not only ruling-class hegemony but also consumer behavior, corporate predation, international politics, militarism, sports, and fashion changes. Veblen is also credited with demonstrating the linkage between ostentatious display and the oppression of women.

Political sociologists and students of modernization respond sympathetically to such Veblenian concepts as "the merits of borrowing" and "the penalty for taking the lead" in industrialization, the notion of "trained incapacity," and the idea of "conscious withdrawal of efficiency." Veblen is also recognized for his contributions to the theory of latent and manifest functions so popular in sociology. He is praised for his ideas regarding social stratification and the sociology of knowledge. Finally, radical political theorists often refer to his critique of social institutions and their linkage to corporate power centers.

Veblen's interpreters have focused on themes of contemporary significance in his work. In the 1920s their attention was riveted on what appeared to be the prime deficiencies of the American capitalist order, namely, its waste of resources on luxury items and its indulgence in emulatory consumption. Also, his satirical wit and irony were appreciated as part of an exposé of conformist leisure-class morals and foibles. In the 1930s, however, the focus shifted to Veblen's study of business cycles and the roots of economic instability, exploitation of the working class, and responsibility of corporations for the depression debacle.

Early in World War I, Veblen had written *Imperial Germany and the Industrial Revolution* and, a little later, articles on Imperial Japan. He argued that both imperial Germany and Japan were volatile mixtures of modern science and technology with archaic feudal institutions and suggested that only time would tell if they could successfully shed their obsolescent social structure and fully achieve modernity. By the late 1930s, with the rise of fascism, Veblen's predictions regarding a resurgence of authoritarianism in Germany and Japan attracted attention for their obvious relevance to understanding those two political systems. In the 1940s and 1950s, focus was on Veblen's work on the linkage among imperialism, colonialism, and war, as critics grappled with understanding first World War II and later the cold war. Those scholars writing in the area of international relations during this period often saw validity in Veblen's theories explaining American foreign policy and cold war politics. Still, only a few years later the New Left paid little attention to him, perhaps because of its fascination with Marxism and anarchism, although institutional economists continued to stress the explanatory power of his social theory and the appeal of his values.

Radicals often criticized Veblen for not offering plausible solutions to social ills and for having little to say on current political issues. They believed he was, unfortunately, silent regarding the role of unskilled workers and the general population in the new social order that seemed to be emerging. Also, Veblen's Darwinian evolutionary view of the future was perceived as vague, cynical, or pessimistic. Radicals sometimes claimed that he rejected not only business civilization but also the socialist alternative and that he had no viable third alternative. His espousal of the empirical study of institutions provided the inspiration and set the stage for the important school of institutionalism. Yet his avowed followers, the institutionalists, stood accused of having shed his radicalism and being bound to him only by their devotion to factual study and quantitative methods, thus giving his work an atheoretical bias which stripped it of much of its moral and political thrust.

However, in rebuttal of the above criticisms, five ideas are found in Veblen that are representative of his thinking and that are of enduring significance. The first is his emphasis on the emancipatory potential of the machine process, provided it can be harnessed to community serviceability. The second is the antithesis between business and industry, with its stress on the difference between making money and making socially useful goods. He rightly emphasized the antisocial tendency of business enterprise on account of its emphasis on profit instead of community serviceability. Third is Veblen's view of legal and political institutions as representing the vesting of economic interests or, in contemporary jargon, a "zero-sum game" in which the wealthy and powerful "win" and the underlying population "loses." Fourth is Veblen's emphasis on the compulsive force of idea patterns and the inability of the common man to overcome their hold on him, which is exemplified in his theory of emulatory consumption. Fifth is Veblen's belief in the "bankruptcy" of commercial values, and a business culture dominated by them, which is rooted in his conviction that they thwart realization of the generic ends of life: critical intelligence (idle curiosity), altruism (parental bent), and proficiency of craftsmanship (instinct of workmanship).

Characteristically, Veblen did not distinguish between economics and politics. For him, business interests dominated both industry and politics, and that domination resulted in economic stagnation and waste. Reformers often criticized Veblen for not realizing that social legislation and government control of business would serve to indefinitely stabilize the system. However, Veblen's view of an upper-class hegemony in modern society led him to discount the likelihood of social reform.

Veblen ignited controversy not only in economics, his primary interest, but also in sociology, history, and political science. The number and quality of the responses to his work provides evidence of the novelty and explanatory power of his ideas. This collection of his writings will enable the reader to sample the broad spectrum of his thought and to reach his or her own conclusions regarding its present relevance.

What I have attempted to do in organizing this anthology is to make enough selections to give a sense of Veblen's range of insights, so the reader is exposed to the flavor and power of his ideas; to do justice to his scholarly academic social and economic theory without neglecting his commentaries on social institutions and cultural practices; and to keep in mind both the academic specialist and the layperson with no prior knowledge of Veblen. I have used much of the format and many of the selections of Max Lerner's *The Portable Veblen*, now long out of print. *A Veblen Treasury: From Leisure Class to War, Peace, and Capitalism* differs in that it includes a new introduction based partly on sources that were not available to Lerner, several articles Lerner did not include for whatever reasons, and an updated bibliography. American spelling and punctuation has been used for this volume.

Notes

1. Joseph Dorfman, *Thorstein Veblen and His America* (New York: Viking Press, 1934).
2. This interpretation of Veblen's life is taken from chapter 1 of the editor's *Thorstein Veblen and His Critics, 1891–1963: Conservative, Liberal and Radical Critics* (Princeton: Princeton University Press, 1992).
3. Andrew Veblen to Edward Bemis, October 4, 1929, Andrew Veblen Papers, Minnesota Historical Society, St. Paul, Minnesota.
4. Ellen Rolfe Veblen to Thorstein Veblen, May 16, 1920, Thorstein Veblen Collection, Wisconsin Historical Society, Madison, Wisconsin. For a brief portrait of Ellen Rolfe Veblen, see Robert Duffus, *Innocents at Cedro* (New York: Macmillan, 1944), pp. 143–49.
5. David Starr Jordan to Harry Pratt Judson, October 6, 1909, University President's Papers, 1889–1925, Regenstein Library, University of Chicago.
6. See David Starr Jordan to Thorstein Veblen, August 22, 1917, Thorstein Veblen

7. Jacob Warshaw, "A Few Footnotes to Dorfman's Veblen," p. 2. University of Missouri Western Historical Manuscript Collection, Columbia, Missouri.

8. Ibid., p. 3.

9. Ibid.

10. Ibid., p. 4.

11. Ibid., p. 5.

12. Ibid., pp. 8, 12.

13. Ibid., p. 10.

14. Ibid., p. 5.

15. Ibid., p. 4.

16. Madge Jenison, *Sunwise Turn: A Human Comedy of Bookselling* (New York: E. P. Dutton, 1923), pp. 125–26.

17. Andrew Veblen to Edward Bemis, October 4, 1929, Andrew Veblen Papers.

18. Other incidents regarding him are related by Florence Veblen in "Thorstein Veblen: Reminiscences of His Brother Orson," *Social Forces*, 10 (December 1931): 187–95.

19. For other expressions of his state of mind during this period, see *Essays in Our Changing Order* (New York: Augustus M. Kelley, 1964), pp. 391–461.

20. See Rick Tilman, "Veblen's Ideal Political Economy and Its Critics," *American Journal of Economics and Sociology*, 31 (July 1972): 307–17.

21. C. Wright Mills, *The Marxists* (New York: Dell, 1972), p. 129.

22. Thorstein Veblen, *The Nature of Peace* (New York: Macmillan, 1917), p. 31.

23. See especially Theodor Adorno, "Veblen's Attack on Culture," *Studies in Philosophy and Social Science*, 9 (1941): 389–413.

The Theory of the Leisure Class

Preface

It is the purpose of this inquiry to discuss the place and value of the leisure class as an economic factor in modern life, but it has been found impracticable to confine the discussion strictly within the limits so marked out. Some attention is perforce given to the origin and the line of derivation of the institution, as well as to features of social life that are not commonly classed as economic.

At some points the discussion proceeds on grounds of economic theory or ethnological generalization that may be in some degree unfamiliar. The introductory chapter indicates the nature of these theoretical premises sufficiently, it is hoped, to avoid obscurity. A more explicit statement of the theoretical position involved is made in a series of papers published in Volume IV of the *American Journal of Sociology*, on "The Instinct of Workmanship and the Irksomeness of Labour," "The Beginnings of Ownership," and "The Barbarian Status of Women." But the argument does not rest on these—in part novel—generalizations in such a way that it would altogether lose its possible value as a detail of economic theory in case these novel generalizations should, in the reader's apprehension, fall away through being insufficiently backed by authority or data.

Partly for reasons of convenience, and partly because there is less chance of misapprehending the sense of phenomena that are familiar to all men, the data employed to illustrate or enforce the argument have by preference been drawn from everyday life, by direct observation or through common notoriety, rather than from more recondite sources at a farther remove. It is hoped that no one will find his sense of literary or scientific fitness offended by this recourse to homely facts, or by what may at times appear to be a callous freedom in handling vulgar phenomena or phenomena whose intimate place in men's life has sometimes shielded them from the impact of economic discussion.

Such premises and corroborative evidence as are drawn from remoter sources,

All readings in this Part are reprinted from *The Theory of the Leisure Class*. New York: The Macmillan Company, 1899.

as well as whatever articles of theory or inference are borrowed from ethnological science, are also of the more familiar and accessible kind and should be readily traceable to their source by fairly well read persons. The usage of citing sources and authorities has therefore not been observed. Likewise the few quotations that have been introduced, chiefly by way of illustration, are also such as will commonly be recognized with sufficient facility without the guidance of citation.

Introductory

The institution of a leisure class is found in its best development at the higher stages of the barbarian culture; as, for instance, in feudal Europe or feudal Japan. In such communities the distinction between classes is very rigorously observed; and the feature of most striking economic significance in these class differences is the distinction maintained between the employments proper to the several classes. The upper classes are by custom exempt or excluded from industrial occupations, and are reserved for certain employments to which a degree of honor attaches. Chief among the honorable employments in any feudal community is warfare; and priestly service is commonly second to warfare. If the barbarian community is not notably warlike, the priestly office may take the precedence, with that of the warrior second. But the rule holds with but slight exceptions that, whether warriors or priests, the upper classes are exempt from industrial employments, and this exemption is the economic expression of their superior rank. Brahmin India affords a fair illustration of the industrial exemption of both these classes. In the communities belonging to the higher barbarian culture there is a considerable differentiation of sub-classes within what may be comprehensively called the leisure class; and there is a corresponding differentiation of employments between these sub-classes. The leisure class as a whole comprises the noble and the priestly classes, together with much of their retinue. The occupations of the class are correspondingly diversified; but they have the common economic characteristic of being non-industrial. These non-industrial upper-class occupations may be roughly comprised under government, warfare, religious observances, and sports.

At an earlier, but not the earliest, stage of barbarism, the leisure class is found in a less differentiated form. Neither the class distinctions nor the distinctions between leisure-class occupations are so minute and intricate. The Polynesian islanders generally show this stage of the development in good form, with the exception that, owing to the absence of large game, hunting does not hold the usual place of honor in their scheme of life. The Icelandic community in the time of the Sagas also affords a fair instance. In such a community there is a rigorous distinction between classes and between the occupations peculiar to each class. Manual labor, industry, whatever has to do directly with the everyday work of getting a livelihood, is the exclusive occupation of the inferior class. This inferior class includes slaves and other dependents, and ordinarily also all the women. If there are several grades of aristocracy, the women of high rank are commonly exempt from industrial employment, or at least from the more vulgar kinds of manual labor. The men of the upper classes are not only exempt, but by prescriptive custom they are debarred, from all industrial occupations. The range of employments open to them is rigidly defined. As on the higher plane already spoken of, these employments are government, warfare, religious observances, and sports. These four lines of activity govern the scheme of life of the upper classes, and for the highest rank—the kings or chieftains—these are the only kinds of activity that custom or the common sense of the community will allow. Indeed, where the scheme is well developed even sports are accounted doubtfully legitimate for the members of the highest rank. To the lower grades of the leisure class certain other employments are open, but they are employments that are subsidiary to one or another of these typical leisure-class occupations. Such are, for instance, the manufacture and care of arms and accoutrements and of war canoes, the dressing and handling of horses, dogs, and hawks, the preparation of sacred apparatus, etc. The lower classes are excluded from these secondary honorable employments, except from such as are plainly of an industrial character and are only remotely related to the typical leisure-class occupations.

If we go a step back of this exemplary barbarian culture, into the lower stages of barbarism, we no longer find the leisure class in fully developed form. But this lower barbarism shows the usages, motives, and circumstances out of which the institution of a leisure class has arisen, and indicates the steps of its early growth. Nomadic hunting tribes in various parts of the world illustrate these more primitive phases of the differentiation. Any one of the North American hunting tribes may be taken as a convenient illustration. These tribes can scarcely be said to have a defined leisure class. There is a differentiation of function, and there is a distinction between classes on the basis of this difference of function, but the exemption of the superior class from work has not gone far enough to make the designation "leisure class" altogether applicable. The tribes belonging on this economic level have carried the economic differentiation to the point at which a marked distinction is made between the occupations of men and women, and this distinction is of an invidious character. In nearly all these tribes the women are, by prescriptive custom, held to those employments out of which the industrial occupations proper develop at the next advance. The men are exempt from these vulgar employments and are reserved for war, hunting, sports, and devout observances. A very nice discrimination is ordinarily shown in this matter.

This division of labor coincides with the distinction between the working and the leisure class as it appears in the higher barbarian culture. As the diversification and specialization of employments proceed, the line of demarcation so drawn comes to divide the industrial from the non-industrial employments. The man's occupation as it stands at the earlier barbarian stage is not the original out of which any appreciable portion of later industry has developed. In the later development it survives only in employments that are not classed as industrial—war, politics, sports, learning, and the priestly office. The only notable exceptions are a portion of the fishery industry and certain slight employments that are doubtfully to be classed as industry; such as the manufacture of arms, toys, and sporting goods. Virtually the whole range of industrial employments is an outgrowth of what is classed as woman's work in the primitive barbarian community.

The work of the men in the lower barbarian culture is no less indispensable to the life of the group than the work done by the women. It may even be that the men's work contributes as much to the food supply and the other necessary consumption of the group. Indeed, so obvious is this "productive" character of the men's work that in the conventional economic writings the hunter's work is taken as the type of primitive industry. But such is not the barbarian's sense of the matter. In his own eyes he is not a laborer, and he is not to be classed with the women in this respect; nor is his effort to be classed with the women's drudgery, as labor or industry, in such a sense as to admit of its being confounded with the latter. There is in all barbarian communities a profound sense of the disparity between man's and woman's work. His work may conduce to the maintenance of the group, but it is felt that it does so through an excellence and an efficacy of a kind that cannot without derogation be compared with the uneventful diligence of the women.

At a farther step backward in the cultural scale—among savage groups—the differentiation of employments is still less elaborate and the invidious distinction between classes and employments is less consistent and less rigorous. Unequivocal instances of a primitive savage culture are hard to find. Few of those groups or communities that are classed as "savage" show no traces of regression from a more advanced cultural stage. But there are groups—some of them apparently not the result of retrogression—which show the traits of primitive savagery with some fidelity. Their culture differs from that of the barbarian communities in the absence of a leisure class and the absence, in great measure, of the animus or spiritual attitude on which the institution of a leisure class rests. These communities of primitive savages in which there is no hierarchy of economic classes make up but a small and inconspicuous fraction of the human race. As good an instance of this phase of culture as may be had is afforded by the tribes of the Andamans, or by the Todas of the Nilgiri Hills. The scheme of life of these groups at the time of their earliest contact with Europeans seems to have been nearly typical, so far as regards the absence of a leisure class. As a further instance might be cited the Ainu of Yezo, and, more doubtfully, also some Bushman and Eskimo groups. Some Pueblo communities are less confidently to be included in the same class. Most, if not all, of the communities here cited may well be cases of degeneration from a higher barbarism, rather than bearers of a culture that has never risen above its present level. If so, they are for the present purpose to be taken with allowance, but they may serve none the less as evidence to the same effect as if they were really "primitive" populations.

These communities that are without a defined leisure class resemble one another also in certain other features of their social structure and manner of life. They are small groups and of a simple (archaic) structure; they are commonly peaceable and sedentary; they are poor; and individual ownership is not a dominant feature of their economic system. At the same time it does not follow that these are the smallest of existing communities, or that their social structure is in all respects the least differentiated; nor does the class necessarily include all primitive communities which have no defined system of individual ownership. But it is to be noted that the class seems to include the most peaceable—perhaps all the characteristically peaceable—primitive groups of men. Indeed, the most notable trait common to members of such communities is a certain amiable inefficiency when confronted with force or fraud.

The evidence afforded by the usages and cultural traits of communities at a low stage of development indicates that the institution of a leisure class has emerged gradually during the transition from primitive savagery to barbarism; or more precisely, during the transition from a peaceable to a consistently warlike habit of life. The conditions apparently necessary to its emergence in a consistent form are: (1) the community must be of a predatory habit of life (war or the hunting of large game or both); that is to say, the men, who constitute the inchoate leisure class in these cases, must be habituated to the infliction of injury by force and stratagem; (2) subsistence must be obtainable on sufficiently easy terms to admit of the exemption of a considerable portion of the community from steady application to a routine of labor. The institution of a leisure class is the outgrowth of an early discrimination between employments, according to which some employments are worthy and others unworthy. Under this ancient distinction the worthy employments are those which may be classed as exploit; unworthy are those necessary everyday employments into which no appreciable element of exploit enters.

This distinction has but little obvious significance in a modern industrial community, and it has therefore, received but slight attention at the hands of economic writers. When viewed in the light of that modern common sense which has guided economic discussion, it seems formal and insubstantial. But it persists with great tenacity as a commonplace preconception even in modern life, as is shown, for instance, by our habitual aversion to menial employments. It is a distinction of a personal kind—of superiority and inferiority. In the earlier stages of culture, when the personal force of the individual counted more immediately and obviously in shaping the course of events, the element of exploit counted for more in the everyday scheme of life. Interest centered about this fact to a greater degree. Consequently a distinction proceeding on this ground seemed more imperative and more definitive then than is the case today. As a fact in the sequence of development, therefore, the distinction is a substantial one and rests on sufficiently valid and cogent grounds.

The ground on which a discrimination between facts is habitually made changes as the interest from which the facts are habitually viewed changes. Those features of the facts at hand are salient and substantial upon which the dominant interest of the time throws its light. Any given ground of distinction will seem insubstantial to any one who habitually apprehends the facts in question from a different point of view and values them for a different purpose. The habit of distinguishing and classifying the various purposes and directions of activity prevails of necessity always and everywhere; for it is indispensable in reaching a working theory or scheme of life. The particular point of view, or the particular characteristic that is pitched upon as definitive in the classification of the facts of life depends upon the interest from which a discrimination of the facts is sought. The grounds of discrimination, and the norm of procedure in classifying the facts, therefore, progressively change as the growth of culture proceeds; for the end for which the facts of life are apprehended changes, and the point of view consequently changes also. So that what are recognized as the salient and decisive features of a class of activities or of a social class at one stage of culture will not retain the same relative importance for the purposes of classification at any subsequent stage.

But the change of standards and points of view is gradual only, and it seldom results in the subversion or entire suppression of a standpoint once accepted. A distinction is still habitually made between industrial and non-industrial occupations; and this modern distinction is a transmuted form of the barbarian distinction between exploit and drudgery. Such employments as warfare, politics, public worship, and public merrymaking, are felt, in the popular apprehension, to differ intrinsically from the labor that has to do with elaborating the material means of life. The precise line of demarcation is not the same as it was in the early barbarian scheme, but the broad distinction has not fallen into disuse.

The tacit, common-sense distinction today is, in effect, that any effort is to be accounted industrial only so far as its ultimate purpose is the utilization of non-human things. The coercive utilization of man by man is not felt to be an industrial function; but all effort directed to enhance human life by taking advantage of the non-human environment is classed together as industrial activity. By the economists who have best retained and adapted the classical tradition, man's "power over nature" is currently postulated as the characteristic fact of industrial productivity. This industrial power over nature is taken to include man's power over the life of the beasts and over all the elemental forces. A line is in this way drawn between mankind and brute creation.

In other times and among men imbued with a different body of preconceptions, this line is not drawn precisely as we draw it today. In the savage or the barbarian scheme of life it is drawn in a different place and in another way. In all communities under the barbarian culture there is an alert and pervading sense of antithesis between two comprehensive groups of phenomena, in one of which barbarian man includes himself, and in the other, his victual. There is a felt antithesis between economic and non-economic phenomena, but it is not conceived in the modern fashion; it lies not between man and brute creation, but between animate and inert things.

It may be an excess of caution at this day to explain that the barbarian notion which it is here intended to convey by the term "animate" is not the same as would be conveyed by the word "living." The term does not cover all living things, and it does cover a great many others. Such a striking natural phenomenon as a storm, a disease, a waterfall, are recognized as "animate"; while fruits and herbs, and even inconspicuous animals, such as house-flies, maggots, lemmings, sheep, are not ordinarily apprehended as "animate" except when taken collectively. As here used the term does not necessarily imply an indwelling soul or spirit. The concept includes such things as in the apprehension of the animistic savage or barbarian are formidable by virtue of a real or imputed habit of initiating action. This category comprises a large number and range of natural objects and phenomena. Such a distinction between the inert and the active is still present in the habits of thought of unreflecting persons, and it still profoundly affects the prevalent theory of human life and of natural processes; but it does not pervade our daily life to the extent or with the far-reaching practical consequences that are apparent at earlier stages of culture and belief.

To the mind of the barbarian, the elaboration and utilization of what is afforded by inert nature is activity on quite a different plane from his dealings with "animate" things and forces. The line of demarcation may be vague and shifting, but the broad distinction is sufficiently real and cogent to influence the barbarian scheme of life. To the class of things apprehended as animate, the barbarian fancy imputes an unfolding of activity directed to some end. It is this teleological unfolding of activity that constitutes any object or phenomenon an "animate" fact. Wherever the unsophisticated savage or barbarian meets with activity that is at all obtrusive, he construes it in the only terms that are ready to hand—the terms immediately given in his consciousness of his own actions. Activity is, therefore, assimilated to human action, and active objects are in so far assimilated to the human agent. Phenomena of this character—especially those whose behavior is notably formidable or baffling—have to be met in a different spirit and with proficiency of a different kind from what is required in dealing with inert things. To deal successfully with such phenomena is a work of exploit rather than of industry. It is an assertion of prowess, not of diligence.

Under the guidance of this naive discrimination between the inert and the animate, the activities of the primitive social group tend to fall into two classes, which would in modern phrase be called exploit and industry. Industry is effort that goes to create a new thing, with a new purpose given it by the fashioning hand of its maker out of passive ("brute") material; while exploit, so far as it results in an outcome useful to the agent, is the conversion to his own ends of energies previously directed to some other end by another agent. We still speak of "brute matter" with something of the barbarian's realization of a profound significance in the term.

The distinction between exploit and drudgery coincides with a difference between the sexes. The sexes differ, not only in stature and muscular force, but perhaps even more decisively in temperament, and this must early have given rise to a corresponding division of labor. The general range of activities that come under the head of exploit falls to the males as being the stouter, more massive, better capable of a sudden and violent strain, and more readily inclined to self-assertion, active emulation, and aggression. The difference in mass, in physiological character, and in temperament may be slight among the members of the primitive group; it appears, in fact, to be relatively slight and inconsequential in some of the more archaic communities with which we are acquainted—as for instance the tribes of the Andamans. But so soon as a differentiation of function has well begun on the lines marked out by this difference in physique and animus, the original difference between the sexes will itself widen. A cumulative process of selective adaptation to the new distribution of employments will set in, especially if the habitat or the fauna with which the group is in contact is such as to call for a considerable exercise of the sturdier virtues. The habitual pursuit of large game requires more of the manly qualities of massiveness, agility, and ferocity, and it can therefore scarcely fail to hasten and widen the differentiation of functions between the sexes. And so soon as the group comes into hostile contact with other groups, the divergence of function will take on the developed form of a distinction between exploit and industry.

In such a predatory group of hunters it comes to be the able-bodied men's office to fight and hunt. The women do what other work there is to do—other members who are unfit for man's work being for this purpose classed with the women. But the men's hunting and fighting are both of the same general character. Both are of a predatory nature; the warrior and the hunter alike reap where they have not strewn. Their aggressive assertion of force and sagacity differs obviously from the women's assiduous and uneventful shaping of materials; it is not to be accounted productive labor, but rather an acquisition of substance by seizure. Such being the barbarian man's work, in its best development and widest divergence from women's work, any effort that does not involve an assertion of prowess comes to be unworthy of the man. As the tradition gains consistency, the common sense of the community erects it into a canon of conduct; so that no employment and no acquisition is morally possible to the self-respecting man at this cultural stage, except such as proceeds on the basis of prowess—force or fraud. When the predatory habit of life has been settled upon the group by long habituation, it becomes the able-bodied man's accredited office in the social economy to kill, to destroy such competitors in the struggle for existence as attempt to resist or elude him, to overcome and reduce to subservience those alien forces that assert themselves refractorily in the environment. So tenaciously and with such nicety is this theoretical distinction between exploit and drudgery adhered to that in many hunting tribes the man must not bring home the game which he has killed, but must send his woman to perform that baser office.

As has already been indicated, the distinction between exploit and drudgery is an invidious distinction between employments. Those employments which are to be classed as exploit are worthy, honorable, noble; other employments, which do not contain this element of exploit, and especially those which imply subservience or submission, are unworthy, debasing, ignoble. The concept of dignity, worth, or honor, as applied either to persons or conduct, is of first-rate consequence in the development of classes and of class distinctions, and it is therefore necessary to say something of its derivation and meaning. Its psychological ground may be indicated in outline as follows.

As a matter of selective necessity, man is an agent. He is, in his own apprehension, a center of unfolding impulsive activity—"teleological" activity. He is an agent seeking in every act the accomplishment of some concrete, objective, impersonal end. By force of his being such an agent he is possessed of a taste for effective work, and a distaste for futile effort. He has a sense of the merit of serviceability or efficiency and of the demerit of futility, waste, or incapacity. This aptitude or propensity may be called the instinct of workmanship. Wherever the circumstances or traditions of life lead to an habitual comparison of one person with another in point of efficiency, the instinct of workmanship works out in an emulative or invidious comparison of persons. The extent to which this result follows depends in some considerable degree on the temperament of the population. In any community where such an invidious comparison of persons is habitually made, visible success becomes an end sought for its own utility as a basis of esteem. Esteem is gained and dispraise is avoided by putting one's efficiency in evidence. The result is that the instinct of workmanship works out in an emulative demonstration of force.

During that primitive phase of social development, when the community is still habitually peaceable, perhaps sedentary, and without a developed system of individual ownership, the efficiency of the individual can be shown chiefly and most consistently in some employment that goes to further the life of the group. What emulation of an economic kind there is between the members of such a group will be chiefly emulation in industrial serviceability. At the same time the incentive to emulation is not strong, nor is the scope for emulation large.

When the community passes from peaceable savagery to a predatory phase of life, the conditions of emulation change. The opportunity and the incentive to emulation increase greatly in scope and urgency. The activity of the men more and more takes on the character of exploit; and an invidious comparison of one hunter or warrior with another grows continually easier and more habitual. Tangible evidences of prowess—trophies—find a place in men's habits of thought as an essential feature of the paraphernalia of life. Booty, trophies of the chase or of the raid, come to be prized as evidence of pre-eminent force. Aggression becomes the accredited form of action, and booty serves as *prima facie* evidence of successful aggression. As accepted at this cultural stage, the accredited, worthy form of self-assertion is contest; and useful articles or services obtained by seizure or compulsion, serve as a conventional evidence of successful contest. Therefore, by contrast, the obtaining of goods by other methods than seizure comes to be accounted unworthy of man in his best estate. The performance of productive work, or employment in personal service, falls under the same odium for the same reason. An invidious distinction in this way arises between exploit and acquisition by seizure on the one hand and industrial employment on the other hand. Labor acquires a character of irksomeness by virtue of the indignity imputed to it.

With the primitive barbarian, before the simple content of the notion has been obscured by its own ramifications and by a secondary growth of cognate ideas, "honorable" seems to connote nothing else than assertion of superior force. "Honorable" is "formidable"; "worthy" is "prepotent." A honorific act is in the last analysis little if anything else than a recognized successful act of aggression; and where aggression means conflict with men and beasts, the activity which comes to be especially and primarily honorable is the assertion of the strong hand. The naive, archaic habit of construing all manifestations of force in terms of personality or "will power" greatly fortifies this conventional exaltation of the strong hand. Honorific epithets, in vogue among barbarian tribes as well as among peoples of a more advanced culture, commonly bear the stamp of this unsophisticated sense of honor. Epithets and titles used in addressing chieftains, and in the propitiation of kings and gods, very commonly impute a propensity for overbearing violence and an irresistible devastating force to the person who is to be propitiated. This holds true to an extent also in the more civilized communities of the present day. The predilection shown in heraldic devices for the more rapacious beasts and birds of prey goes to enforce the same view.

Under this common-sense barbarian appreciation of worth or honor, the taking of life—the killing of formidable competitors, whether brute or human—is honorable in the highest degree. And this high office of slaughter, as an expression of the slayer's prepotence, casts a glamour of worth over every act of slaughter and over all the tools and accessories of the act. Arms are honorable, and the use of them, even in seeking the life of the meanest creatures of the fields, becomes an honorific employment. At the same time, employment in industry becomes correspondingly odious, and, in the common-sense apprehension, the handling of the tools and implements of industry falls beneath the dignity of able-bodied men. Labor becomes irksome.

It is here assumed that in the sequence of cultural evolution primitive groups of men have passed from an initial peaceable stage to a subsequent stage at which fighting is the avowed and characteristic employment of the group. But it is not implied that there has been an abrupt transition from unbroken peace and goodwill to a later or higher phase of life in which the fact of combat occurs for the first time. Neither is it implied that all peaceful industry disappears on the transition to the predatory phase of culture. Some fighting, it is safe to say, would be met with at any early stage of social development. Fights would occur with more or less frequency through sexual competition. The known habits of primitive groups, as well as the habits of the anthropoid apes, argue to that effect, and the evidence from the well-known promptings of human nature enforces the same view.

It may therefore be objected that there can have been no such initial stage of peaceable life as is here assumed. There is no point in cultural evolution prior to which fighting does not occur. But the point in question is not as to the occurrence of combat, occasional or sporadic, or even more or less frequent and habitual; it is a question as to the occurrence of an habitual bellicose frame of mind—a prevalent habit of judging facts and events from the point of view of the fight. The predatory phase of culture is attained only when the predatory attitude has become the habitual and accredited spiritual attitude for the members of the group; when the fight has become the dominant note in the current theory of life; when the common-sense appreciation of men and things has come to be an appreciation with a view to combat.

The substantial difference between the peaceable and the predatory phase of culture, therefore, is a spiritual difference, not a mechanical one. The change in spiritual attitude is the outgrowth of a change in the material facts of the life of the group, and it comes on gradually as the material circumstances favorable to a predatory attitude supervene. The inferior limit of the predatory culture is an industrial limit. Predation cannot become the habitual, conventional resource of any group or any class until industrial methods have been developed to such a degree of efficiency as to leave a margin worth fighting for, above the subsistence of those engaged in getting a living. The transition from peace to predation therefore depends on the growth of technical knowledge and the use of tools. A predatory culture is similarly impracticable in early times, until weapons have been developed to such a point as to make man a formidable animal. The early development of tools and of weapons is of course the same fact seen from two different points of view.

The life of a given group would be characterized as peaceable so long as habitual recourse to combat has not brought the fight into the foreground in men's everyday thoughts, as a dominant feature of the life of man. A group may evidently attain such a predatory attitude with a greater or less degree of completeness, so that its scheme of life and canons of conduct may be controlled to a greater or less extent by the predatory animus. The predatory phase of culture is therefore conceived to come on gradually, through a cumulative growth of predatory aptitudes, habits, and traditions, this growth being due to a change in the circumstances of the group's life, of such a kind as to develop and conserve those traits of human nature and those traditions and norms of conduct that make for a predatory rather than a peaceable life.

The evidence for the hypothesis that there has been such a peaceable stage of primitive culture is in great part drawn from psychology rather than from ethnology, and cannot be detailed here. It will be recited in part in a later chapter, in discussing the survival of archaic traits of human nature under the modern culture.

Pecuniary Emulation

In the sequence of cultural evolution the emergence of a leisure class coincides with the beginning of ownership. This is necessarily the case, for these two institutions result from the same set of economic forces. In the inchoate phase of their development they are but different aspects of the same general facts of social structure.

It is as elements of social structure—conventional facts—that leisure and ownership are matters of interest for the purpose in hand. An habitual neglect of work does not constitute a leisure class; neither does the mechanical fact of use and consumption constitute ownership. The present inquiry, therefore, is not concerned with the beginning of indolence, nor with the beginning of the appropriation of useful articles to individual consumption. The point in question is the origin and nature of a conventional leisure class on the one hand and the beginnings of individual ownership as a conventional right or equitable claim on the other hand.

The early differentiation out of which the distinction between a leisure and a working class arises is a division maintained between men's and women's work in the lower stages of barbarism. Likewise the earliest form of ownership is an ownership of the women by the able-bodied men of the community. The facts may be expressed in more general terms, and truer to the import of the barbarian theory of life, by saying that it is an ownership of the woman by the man.

There was undoubtedly some appropriation of useful articles before the custom of appropriating women arose. The usages of existing archaic communities in which there is no ownership of women is warrant for such a view. In all communities the members, both male and female, habitually appropriate to their individual use a variety of useful things; but these useful things are not thought of as owned by the person who appropriates and consumes them. The habitual appropriation and consumption of certain slight personal effects goes on without raising the question of ownership; that is to say, the question of a conventional, equitable claim to extraneous things.

The ownership of women begins in the lower barbarian stages of culture, apparently with the seizure of female captives. The original reason for the seizure and appropriation of women seems to have been their usefulness as trophies. The practice of seizing women from the enemy as trophies gave rise to a form of ownership-marriage, resulting in a household with a male head. This was followed by an extension of slavery to other captives and inferiors, besides women, and by an extension of ownership-marriage to other women than those seized from the enemy. The outcome of emulation under the circumstances of a predatory life, therefore, has been on the one hand a form of marriage resting on coercion, and on the other hand the custom of ownership. The two institutions are not distinguishable in the initial phase of their development; both arise from the desire of the successful men to put their prowess in evidence by exhibiting some durable result of their exploits. Both also minister to that propensity for mastery which pervades all predatory communities. From the ownership of women the concept of ownership extends itself to include the products of their industry, and so there arises the ownership of things as well as of persons.

In this way a consistent system of property in goods is gradually installed. And although in the latest stages of the development, the serviceability of goods for consumption has come to be the most obtrusive element of their value, still, wealth has by no means yet lost its utility as a honorific evidence of the owner's prepotence.

Wherever the institution of private property is found, even in a slightly developed form, the economic process bears the character of a struggle between men for the possession of goods. It has been customary in economic theory, and especially among those economists who adhere with least faltering to the body of modernized classical doctrines, to construe this struggle for wealth as being substantially a struggle for subsistence. Such is, no doubt, its character in large part during the earlier and less efficient phases of industry. Such is also its character in all cases where the "niggardliness of nature" is so strict as to afford but a scanty livelihood to the community in return for strenuous and unremitting application to the business of getting the means of subsistence. But in all progressing communities an advance is presently made beyond this early stage of technological development. Industrial efficiency is presently carried to such a pitch as to afford something appreciably more than a bare livelihood to those engaged in the industrial process. It has not been unusual for economic theory to speak of the further struggle for wealth on this new industrial basis as a competition for an increase of the comforts of life—primarily for an increase of the physical comforts which the consumption of goods affords.

The end of acquisition and accumulation is conventionally held to be the consumption of the goods accumulated—whether it is consumption directly by the owner of the goods or by the household attached to him and for this purpose identified with him in theory. This is at least felt to be the economically legitimate end of acquisition, which alone it is incumbent on the theory to take account of. Such consumption may of course be conceived to serve the consumer's physical wants—his physical comfort—or his so-called higher wants—spiritual, aesthetic, intellectual, or what not; the latter class of wants being served indirectly by an expenditure of goods, after the fashion familiar to all economic readers.

But it is only when taken in a sense far removed from its naïve meaning that consumption of goods can be said to afford the incentive from which accumulation invariably proceeds. The motive that lies at the root of ownership is emulation; and the same motive of emulation continues active in the further development of the institution to which it has given rise and in the development of all those features of the social structure which this institution of ownership touches. The possession of wealth confers honor; it is an invidious distinction. Nothing equally cogent can be said for the consumption of goods, nor for any other conceivable incentive to acquisition, and especially not for any incentive to the accumulation of wealth.

It is of course not to be overlooked that in a community where nearly all goods are private property the necessity of earning a livelihood is a powerful and ever-present incentive for the poorer members of the community. The need of subsistence and of an increase of physical comfort may for a time be the dominant motive of acquisition for those classes who are habitually employed at manual labor, whose subsistence is on a precarious footing, who possess little and ordinarily accumulate little; but it will appear in the course of the discussion that even in the case of these impecunious classes the predominance of the motive of physical want is not so decided as has sometimes been assumed. On the other hand, so far as regards those members and classes of the community who are chiefly concerned in the accumulation of wealth, the incentive of subsistence or of physical comfort never plays a considerable part. Ownership began and grew into a human institution on grounds unrelated to the subsistence minimum. The dominant incentive was from the outset the invidious distinction attaching to wealth, and, save temporarily and by exception, no other motive has usurped the primacy at any later stage of the development.

Property set out with being booty held as trophies of the successful raid. So long as the group had departed but little from the primitive communal organization, and so long as it still stood in close contact with other hostile groups, the utility of things or persons owned lay chiefly in an invidious comparison between their possessor and the enemy from whom they were taken. The habit of distinguishing between the interests of the individual and those of the group to which he belongs is apparently a later growth. Invidious comparison between the possessor of the honorific booty and his less successful neighbors within the group was no doubt present early as an element of the utility of the things possessed, though this was not at the outset the chief element of their value. The man's prowess was still primarily the group's prowess, and the possessor of the booty felt himself to be primarily the keeper of the honor of his group. This appreciation of exploit from the communal point of view is met with also at later stages of social growth, especially as regards the laurels of war.

But so soon as the custom of individual ownership begins to gain consistency, the point of view taken in making the invidious comparison on which private property rests will begin to change. Indeed, the one change is but the reflex of the other. The initial phase of ownership, the phase of acquisition by naive seizure and conversion, begins to pass into the subsequent stage of an incipient organization of industry on the basis of private property (in slaves); the horde develops into a more or less self-sufficing industrial community; possessions then come to be valued not so much as evidence of successful foray, but rather as evidence of the prepotence of the possessor of these goods over other individuals within the community. The invidious comparison now becomes primarily a comparison of the owner with the other members of the group. Property is still of the nature of trophy, but, with the cultural advance, it becomes more and more a trophy of successes scored in the game of ownership carried on between the members of the group under the quasi-peaceable methods of nomadic life.

Gradually, as industrial activity further displaces predatory activity in the community's everyday life and in men's habits of thought, accumulated property more and more replaces trophies of predatory exploit as the conventional exponent of prepotence and success. With the growth of settled industry, therefore, the possession of wealth gains in relative importance and effectiveness as a customary basis of repute and esteem. Not that esteem ceases to be awarded on the basis of other, more direct evidence of prowess; not that successful predatory aggression or warlike exploit ceases to call out the approval and admiration of the crowd, or to stir the envy of the less successful competitors; but the opportunities for gaining distinction by means of this direct manifestation of superior force grow less available both in scope and frequency. At the same time opportunities for industrial aggression, and for the accumulation of property by the quasi-peaceable methods of nomadic industry, increase in scope and availability. And it is even more to the point that property now becomes the most easily recognized evidence of a reputable degree of success as distinguished from heroic or signal achievement. It therefore becomes the conventional basis of esteem. Its possession in some amount becomes necessary in order to any reputable standing in the community. It becomes indispensable to accumulate, to acquire property, in order to retain one's good name. When accumulated goods have in this way once become the accepted badge of efficiency, the possession of wealth presently assumes the character of an independent and definitive basis of esteem. The possession of goods, whether acquired aggressively by one's own exertion or passively by transmission through inheritance from others, becomes a conventional basis of reputability. The possession of wealth, which was at the outset valued simply as an evidence of efficiency, becomes, in popular apprehension, itself a meritorious act. Wealth is now itself intrinsically honorable and confers honor on its possessor. By a further refinement, wealth acquired passively by transmission from ancestors or other antecedents presently becomes even more honorific than wealth acquired by the possessor's own effort; but this distinction belongs at a later stage in the evolution of the pecuniary culture and will be spoken of in its place.

Prowess and exploit may still remain the basis of award of the highest popular esteem, although the possession of wealth has become the basis of commonplace reputability and of a blameless social standing. The predatory instinct and the consequent approbation of predatory efficiency are deeply ingrained in the habits of thought of those peoples who have passed under the discipline of a protracted predatory culture. According to popular award, the highest honors within human reach may, even yet, be those gained by an unfolding of extraordinary predatory efficiency in war, or by a quasi-predatory efficiency in statecraft; but for the purposes of a commonplace decent standing in the community these means of repute have been replaced by the acquisition and accumulation of goods. In order to stand well in the eyes of the community, it is necessary to come up to a certain, somewhat indefinite, conventional standard of wealth; just as in the earlier predatory stage it is necessary for the barbarian man to come up to the tribe's standard of physical endurance, cunning, and skill at arms. A certain standard of wealth in the one case, and of prowess in the other, is a necessary condition of reputability, and anything in excess of this normal amount is meritorious.

Those members of the community who fall short of this, somewhat indefinite, normal degree of prowess or of property suffer in the esteem of their fellow-men; and consequently they suffer also in their own esteem, since the usual basis of self-respect is the respect accorded by one's neighbors. Only individuals with an aberrant temperament can in the long run retain their self-esteem in the face of the disesteem of their fellows. Apparent exceptions to the rule are met with, especially among people with strong religious convictions. But these apparent exceptions are scarcely real exceptions, since such persons commonly fall back on the putative approbation of some supernatural witness of their deeds.

So soon as the possession of property becomes the basis of popular esteem, therefore, it becomes also a requisite to that complacency which we call self-respect. In any community where goods are held in severalty it is necessary, in order to his own peace of mind, that an individual should possess as large a portion of goods as others with whom he is accustomed to class himself; and it is extremely gratifying to possess something more than others. But as fast as a person makes new acquisitions, and becomes accustomed to the resulting new standard of wealth, the new standard forthwith ceases to afford appreciably greater satisfaction than the earlier standard did. The tendency in any case is constantly to make the present pecuniary standard the point of departure for a fresh increase of wealth; and this in turn gives rise to a new standard of sufficiency and a new pecuniary classification of one's self as compared with one's neighbors. So far as concerns the present question, the end sought by accumulation is to rank high in comparison with the rest of the community in point of pecuniary strength. So long as the comparison is distinctly unfavorable to himself, the normal, average individual will live in chronic dissatisfaction with his present lot; and when he has reached what may be called the normal pecuniary standard of the community, or of his class in the community, this chronic dissatisfaction will give place to a restless straining to place a wider and ever-widening pecuniary interval between himself and this average standard. The invidious comparison can never become so favorable to the individual making it that he would not gladly rate himself still higher relatively to his competitors in the struggle for pecuniary reputability.

In the nature of the case, the desire for wealth can scarcely be satiated in any individual instance, and evidently a satiation of the average or general desire for wealth is out of the question. However widely, or equally, or "fairly," it may be distributed, no general increase of the community's wealth can make any approach to satiating this need, the ground of which is the desire of every one to excel every one else in the accumulation of goods. If, as is sometimes assumed, the incentive to accumulation were the want of subsistence or of physical comfort, then the aggregate economic wants of a community might conceivably be satisfied at some point in the advance of industrial efficiency; but since the struggle is substantially a race for reputability on the basis of an invidious comparison, no approach to a definitive attainment is possible.

What has just been said must not be taken to mean that there are no other incentives to acquisition and accumulation than this desire to excel in pecuniary standing and so gain the esteem and envy of one's fellow-men. The desire for added comfort and security from want is present as a motive at every stage of the process of accumulation in a modern industrial community; although the standard of sufficiency in these respects is in turn greatly affected by the habit of pecuniary emulation. To a great extent this emulation shapes the methods and selects the objects of expenditure for personal comfort and decent livelihood.

Besides this, the power conferred by wealth also affords a motive to accumulation. That propensity for purposeful activity and that repugnance to all futility of effort which belong to man by virtue of his character as an agent do not desert him when he emerges from the naïve communal culture where the dominant note of life is the unanalyzed and undifferentiated solidarity of the individual with the group with which his life is bound up. When he enters upon the predatory stage, where self-seeking in the narrower sense becomes the dominant note, this propensity goes with him still, as the pervasive trait that shapes his scheme of life. The propensity for achievement and the repugnance to futility remain the underlying economic motive. The propensity changes only in the form of its expression and in the proximate objects to which it directs the man's activity. Under the regime of individual ownership the most available means of visibly achieving a purpose is that afforded by the acquisition and accumulation of goods; and as the self-regarding antithesis between man and man reaches fuller consciousness, the propensity for achievement—the instinct of workmanship—tends more and more to shape itself into a straining to excel others in pecuniary achievement. Relative success, tested by an invidious pecuniary comparison with other men, becomes the conventional end of action. The currently accepted legitimate end of effort becomes the achievement of a favorable comparison with other men; and therefore the repugnance to futility to a good extent coalesces with the incentive of emulation. It acts to accentuate the struggle for pecuniary reputability by visiting with a sharper disapproval all shortcoming and all evidence of shortcoming in point of pecuniary success. Purposeful effort comes to mean, primarily, effort directed to or resulting in a more creditable showing of accumulated wealth. Among the motives which lead men to accumulate wealth, the primacy, both in scope and intensity, therefore, continues to belong to this motive of pecuniary emulation.

In making use of the term "invidious," it may perhaps be unnecessary to remark, there is no intention to extol or depreciate, or to commend or deplore any of the phenomena which the word is used to characterize. The term is used in a technical sense as describing a comparison of persons with a view to rating and grading them in respect of relative worth or value—in an aesthetic or moral sense—and so awarding and defining the relative degrees of complacency with which they may legitimately be contemplated by themselves and by others. An invidious comparison is a process of valuation of persons in respect of worth.

Conspicuous Leisure

If its working were not disturbed by other economic forces or other features of the emulative process, the immediate effect of such a pecuniary struggle as has just been described in outline would be to make men industrious and frugal. This result actually follows, in some measure, so far as regards the lower classes, whose ordinary means of acquiring goods is productive labor. This is more especially true of the laboring classes in a sedentary community which is at an agricultural stage of industry, in which there is a considerable subdivision of property, and whose laws and customs secure to these classes a more or less definite share of the product of their industry. These lower classes can in any case not avoid labor, and the imputation of labor is therefore not greatly derogatory to them, at least not within their class. Rather, since labor is their recognized and accepted mode of life, they take some emulative pride in a reputation for efficiency in their work, this being often the only line of emulation that is open to them. For those for whom acquisition and emulation is possible only within the field of productive efficiency and thrift, the struggle for pecuniary reputability will in some measure work out in an increase of diligence and parsimony. But certain secondary features of the emulative process, yet to be spoken of, come in to very materially circumscribe and modify emulation in these directions among the pecuniarily inferior classes as well as among the superior class.

But it is otherwise with the superior pecuniary class, with which we are here immediately concerned. For this class also the incentive to diligence and thrift is not absent; but its action is so greatly qualified by the secondary demands of pecuniary emulation, that any inclination in this direction is practically overborne and any incentive to diligence tends to be of no effect. The most imperative of these secondary demands of emulation, as well as the one of widest scope, is the requirement of abstention from productive work. This is true in an especial degree for the barbarian stage of culture. During the predatory culture labor comes to be associated in men's habits of thought with weakness and subjection to a master. It is therefore a mark of inferiority, and therefore comes to be accounted unworthy of man in his best estate. By virtue of this tradition labor is felt to be debasing, and this tradition has never died out. On the contrary, with the advance of social differentiation it has acquired the axiomatic force due to ancient and unquestioned prescription.

In order to gain and to hold the esteem of men it is not sufficient merely to possess wealth or power. The wealth or power must be put in evidence, for esteem is awarded only on evidence. And not only does the evidence of wealth serve to impress one's importance on others and to keep their sense of one's importance alive and alert, but it is of scarcely less use in building up and preserving one's self-complacency. In all but the lowest stages of culture the normally constituted man is comforted and upheld in his self-respect by "decent surroundings" and by exemption from "menial offices." Enforced departure from his habitual standard of decency, either in the paraphernalia of life or in the kind and amount of his everyday activity, is felt to be a slight upon his human dignity, even apart from all conscious consideration of the approval or disapproval of his fellows.

The archaic theoretical distinction between the base and the honorable in the manner of a man's life retains very much of its ancient force even today. So much so that there are few of the better class who are not possessed of an instinctive repugnance for the vulgar forms of labor. We have a realizing sense of ceremonial uncleanness attaching in an especial degree to the occupations which are associated in our habits of thought with menial service. It is felt by all persons of refined taste that a spiritual contamination is inseparable from certain offices that are conventionally required of servants. Vulgar surroundings, mean (that is to say, inexpensive) habitations, and vulgarly productive occupations are unhesitatingly condemned and avoided. They are incompatible with life on a satisfactory spiritual plane—with "high thinking." From the days of the Greek philosophers to the present, a degree of leisure and of exemption from contact with such industrial processes as serve the immediate everyday purposes of human life has ever been recognized by thoughtful men as a prerequisite to a worthy or beautiful, or even a blameless, human life. In itself and in its consequences the life of leisure is beautiful and ennobling in all civilized men's eyes.

This direct, subjective value of leisure and of other evidences of wealth is no doubt in great part secondary and derivative. It is in part a reflex of the utility of leisure as a means of gaining the respect of others, and in part it is the result of a mental substitution. The performance of labor has been accepted as a conventional evidence of inferior force; therefore it comes itself, by a mental short-cut, to be regarded as intrinsically base.

During the predatory stage proper, and especially during the earlier stages of the quasi-peaceable development of industry that follows the predatory stage, a life of leisure is the readiest and most conclusive evidence of pecuniary strength, and therefore of superior force; provided always that the gentleman of leisure can live in manifest ease and comfort. At this stage wealth consists chiefly of slaves, and the benefits accruing from the possession of riches and power take the form chiefly of personal service and the immediate products of personal service. Conspicuous abstention from labor therefore becomes the conventional mark of superior pecuniary achievement and the conventional index of reputability; and conversely, since application to productive labor is a mark of poverty and subjection, it becomes inconsistent with a reputable standing in the community. Habits of industry and thrift, therefore, are not uniformly furthered by a prevailing pecuniary emulation. On the contrary, this kind of emulation indirectly discountenances participation in productive labor. Labor would unavoidably become dishonorable, as being an evidence of poverty, even if it were not already accounted indecorous under the ancient tradition handed down from an earlier cultural stage. The ancient tradition of the predatory culture is that productive effort is to be shunned as being unworthy of able-bodied men, and this tradition is reinforced rather than set aside in the passage from the predatory to the quasi-peaceable manner of life.

Even if the institution of a leisure class had not come in with the first emergence of individual ownership, by force of the dishonor attaching to productive employment, it would in any case have come in as one of the early consequences of ownership. And it is to be remarked that while the leisure class existed in theory from the beginning of predatory culture, the institution takes on a new and fuller meaning with the transition from the predatory to the next succeeding pecuniary stage of culture. It is from this time forth a "leisure class" in fact as well as in theory. From this point dates the institution of the leisure class in its consummate form.

During the predatory stage proper the distinction between the leisure and the laboring class is in some degree a ceremonial distinction only. The able-bodied men jealously stand aloof from whatever is, in their apprehension, menial drudgery; but their activity in fact contributes appreciably to the sustenance of the group. The subsequent stage of quasi-peaceable industry is usually characterized by an established chattel slavery, herds of cattle, and a servile class of herdsmen and shepherds; industry has advanced so far that the community is no longer dependent for its livelihood on the chase or on any other form of activity that can fairly be classed as exploit. From this point on, the characteristic feature of leisure-class life is a conspicuous exemption from all useful employment.

The normal and characteristic occupations of the class in this mature phase of its life history are in form very much the same as in its earlier days. These occupations are government, war, sports, and devout observances. Persons unduly given to difficult theoretical niceties may hold that these occupations are still incidentally and indirectly "productive"; but it is to be noted as decisive of the question in hand that the ordinary and ostensible motive of the leisure class in engaging in these occupations is assuredly not an increase of wealth by productive effort. At this as at any other cultural stage, government and war are, at least in part, carried on for the pecuniary gain of those who engage in them; but it is gain obtained by the honorable method of seizure and conversion. These occupations are of the nature of predatory, not of productive, employment. Something similar may be said of the chase, but with a difference. As the community passes out of the hunting stage proper, hunting gradually becomes differentiated into two distinct employments. On the one hand it is a trade, carried on chiefly for gain; and from this the element of exploit is virtually absent, or it is at any rate not present in a sufficient degree to clear the pursuit of the imputation of gainful industry. On the other hand, the chase is also a sport—an exercise of the predatory impulse simply. As such it does not afford any appreciable pecuniary incentive, but it contains a more or less obvious element of exploit. It is this latter development of the chase—purged of all imputation of handicraft—that alone is meritorious and fairly belongs in the scheme of life of the developed leisure class.

Abstention from labor is not only an honorific or meritorious act, but it presently comes to be a requisite of decency. The insistence on property as the basis of reputability is very naïve and very imperious during the early stages of the accumulation of wealth. Abstention from labor is the conventional evidence of wealth and is therefore the conventional mark of social standing; and this insistence on the meritoriousness of wealth leads to a more strenuous insistence on leisure. *Nota notæ est nota rei ipsius.* According to well-established laws of human nature, prescription presently seizes upon this conventional evidence of wealth and fixes it in men's habits of thought as something that is in itself substantially meritorious and ennobling; while productive labor at the same time and by a like process becomes in a double sense intrinsically unworthy. Prescription ends by making labor not only disreputable in the eyes of the community, but morally impossible to the noble, freeborn man, and incompatible with a worthy life.

This tabu on labor has a further consequence in the industrial differentiation of classes. As the population increases in density and the predatory group grows into a settled industrial community, the constituted authorities and the customs governing ownership gain in scope and consistency. It then presently becomes impracticable to accumulate wealth by simple seizure, and, in logical consistency, acquisition by industry is equally impossible for high-minded and impecunious men. The alternative open to them is beggary or privation. Wherever the canon of conspicuous leisure has a chance undisturbed to work out its tendency, there will therefore emerge a secondary, and in a sense spurious, leisure class—abjectly poor and living a precarious life of want and discomfort, but morally unable to stoop to gainful pursuits. The decayed gentleman and the lady who has seen better days are by no means unfamiliar phenomena even now. This pervading sense of the indignity of the slightest manual labor is familiar to all civilized peoples, as well as to peoples of a less advanced pecuniary culture. In persons of delicate sensibility, who have long been habituated to gentle manners, the sense of the shamefulness of manual labor may become so strong that, at a critical juncture, it will even set aside the instinct of self-preservation. So, for instance, we are told of certain Polynesian chiefs, who, under the stress of good form, preferred to starve rather than carry their food to their mouths with their own hands. It is true, this conduct may have been due, at least in part, to an excessive sanctity or tabu attaching to the chief's person. The tabu would have been communicated by the contact of his hands, and so would have made anything touched by him unfit for human food. But the tabu is itself a derivative of the unworthiness or moral incompatibility of labor; so that even when construed in this sense the conduct of the Polynesian chiefs is truer to the canon of honorific leisure than would at first appear. A better illustration, or at least a more unmistakable one, is afforded by a certain king of France, who is said to have lost his life through an excess of moral stamina in the observance of good form. In the absence of the functionary whose office it was to shift his master's seat, the king sat uncomplaining before the fire and suffered his royal person to be toasted beyond recovery. But in so doing he saved his Most Christian Majesty from menial contamination.

Summum crede nefas animam præferre pudori,
Et propter vitam vivendi perdere causas.

It has already been remarked that the term "leisure," as here used, does not connote indolence or quiescence. What it connotes is non-productive consumption of time. Time is consumed non-productively (1) from a sense of the unworthiness of productive work, and (2) as an evidence of pecuniary ability to afford a life of idleness. But the whole of the life of the gentleman of leisure is not spent before the eyes of the spectators who are to be impressed with that spectacle of honorific leisure which in the ideal scheme makes up his life. For some part of the time his life is perforce withdrawn from the public eye, and of this portion which is spent in private the gentleman of leisure should, for the sake of his good name, be able to give a convincing account. He should find some means of putting in evidence the leisure that is not spent in the sight of the spectators. This can be done only indirectly, through the exhibition of some tangible, lasting results of the leisure so spent—in a manner analogous to the familiar exhibition of tangible, lasting products of the labor performed for the gentleman of leisure by handicraftsmen and servants in his employ.

The lasting evidence of productive labor is its material product—commonly some article of consumption. In the case of exploit it is similarly possible and usual to procure some tangible result that may serve for exhibition in the way of trophy or booty. At a later phase of the development it is customary to assume some badge or insignia of honor that will serve as a conventionally accepted mark of exploit, and which at the same time indicates the quantity or degree of exploit of which it is the symbol. As the population increases in density, and as human relations grow more complex and numerous, all the details of life undergo a process of elaboration and selection; and in this process of elaboration the use of trophies develops into a system of rank, titles, degrees and insignia, typical examples of which are heraldic devices, medals, and honorary decorations.

As seen from the economic point of view, leisure, considered as an employment, is closely allied in kind with the life of exploit; and the achievements which characterize a life of leisure, and which remain as its decorous criteria, have much in common with the trophies of exploit. But leisure in the narrower sense, as distinct from exploit and from any ostensibly productive employment of effort on objects which are of no intrinsic use, does not commonly leave a material product. The criteria of a past performance of leisure therefore commonly take the form of "immaterial" goods. Such immaterial evidences of past leisure are quasi-scholarly or quasi-artistic accomplishments and a knowledge of processes and incidents which do not conduce directly to the furtherance of human life. So, for instance, in our time there is the knowledge of the dead languages and the occult sciences; of correct spelling; of syntax and prosody; of the various forms of domestic music and other household art; of the latest proprieties of dress, furniture, and equipage; of games, sports, and fancy-bred animals, such as dogs and race-horses. In all these branches of knowledge the initial motive from which their acquisition proceeded at the outset, and through which they first came into vogue, may have been something quite different from the wish to show that one's time had not been spent in industrial employment; but unless these accomplishments had approved themselves as serviceable evidence of an unproductive expenditure of time, they would not have survived and held their place as conventional accomplishments of the leisure class.

These accomplishments may, in some sense, be classed as branches of learning. Beside and beyond these there is a further range of social facts which shade off from the region of learning into that of physical habit and dexterity. Such are what is known as manners and breeding, polite usage, decorum, and formal and ceremonial observances generally. This class of facts are even more immediately and obtrusively presented to the observation, and they are therefore more widely and more imperatively insisted on as required evidences of a reputable degree of leisure. It is worth while to remark that all that class of ceremonial observances which are classed under the general head of manners hold a more important place in the esteem of men during the stage of culture at which conspicuous leisure has the greatest vogue as a mark of reputability, than at later stages of the cultural development. The barbarian of the quasi-peaceable stage of industry is notoriously a more high-bred gentleman, in all that concerns decorum, than any but the very exquisite among the men of a later age. Indeed, it is well known, or at least it is currently believed, that manners have progressively deteriorated as society has receded from the patriarchal stage. Many a gentleman of the old school has been provoked to remark regretfully upon the under-bred manners and bearing of even the better classes in the modern industrial communities; and the decay of the ceremonial code—or as it is otherwise called, the vulgarization of life—among the industrial classes proper has become one of the chief enormities of latter-day civilization in the eyes of all persons of delicate sensibilities. The decay which the code has suffered at the hands of a busy people testifies—all deprecation apart—to the fact that decorum is a product and an exponent of leisure-class life and thrives in full measure only under a régime of status.

The origin, or better the derivation, of manners is, no doubt, to be sought elsewhere than in a conscious effort on the part of the well-mannered to show that much time has been spent in acquiring them. The proximate end of innovation and elaboration has been the higher effectiveness of the new departure in point of beauty or of expressiveness. In great part the ceremonial code of decorous usages owes its beginning and its growth to the desire to conciliate or to show good-will, as anthropologists and sociologists are in the habit of assuming, and this initial motive is rarely if ever absent from the conduct of well-mannered persons at any stage of the later development. Manners, we are told, are in part an elaboration of gesture, and in part they are symbolical and conventionalized survivals representing former acts of dominance or of personal service or of personal contact. In large part they are an expression of the relation of status—a symbolic pantomime of mastery on the one hand and of subservience on the other. Wherever at the present time the predatory habit of mind, and the consequent attitude of mastery and of subservience, gives its character to the accredited scheme of life, there the importance of all punctilios of conduct is extreme, and the assiduity with which the ceremonial observance of rank and titles is attended to approaches closely to the ideal set by the barbarian of the quasi-peaceable nomadic culture. Some of the Continental countries afford good illustrations of this spiritual survival. In these communities the archaic ideal is similarly approached as regards the esteem accorded to manners as a fact of intrinsic worth.

Decorum set out with being symbol and pantomime and with having utility only as an exponent of the facts and qualities symbolized; but it presently suffered the transmutation which commonly passes over symbolical facts in human intercourse. Manners presently came, in popular apprehension, to be possessed of a substantial utility in themselves; they acquired a sacramental character, in great measure independent of the facts which they originally prefigured. Deviations from the code of decorum have become intrinsically odious to all men, and good breeding is, in everyday apprehension, not simply an adventitious mark of human excellence, but an integral feature of the worthy human soul. There are few things that so touch us with instinctive revulsion as a breach of decorum; and so far have we progressed in the direction of imputing intrinsic utility to the ceremonial observances of etiquette that few of us, if any, can dissociate an offense against etiquette from a sense of the substantial unworthiness of the offender. A breach of faith may be condoned, but a breach of decorum cannot. "Manners maketh man."

None the less, while manners have this intrinsic utility, in the apprehension of the performer and the beholder alike, this sense of the intrinsic rightness of decorum is only the proximate ground of the vogue of manners and breeding. Their ulterior, economic ground is to be sought in the honorific character of that leisure or non-productive employment of time and effort without which good manners are not acquired. The knowledge and habit of good form come only by long-continued use. Refined tastes, manners, and habits of life are a useful evidence of gentility, because good breeding requires time, application, and expense, and can therefore not be compassed by those whose time and energy are taken up with work. A knowledge of good form is *prima facie* evidence that that portion of the well-bred person's life which is not spent under the observation of the spectator has been worthily spent in acquiring accomplishments that are of no lucrative effect. In the last analysis the value of manners lies in the fact that they are the voucher of a life of leisure. Therefore, conversely, since leisure is the conventional means of pecuniary repute, the acquisition of some proficiency in decorum is incumbent on all who aspire to a modicum of pecuniary decency.

So much of the honorable life of leisure as is not spent in the sight of spectators can serve the purposes of reputability only in so far as it leaves a tangible, visible result that can be put in evidence and can be measured and compared with products of the same class exhibited by competing aspirants for repute. Some such effect, in the way of leisurely manners and carriage, etc., follows from simple persistent abstention from work, even where the subject does not take thought of the matter and studiously acquire an air of leisurely opulence and mastery. Especially does it seem to be true that a life of leisure in this way persisted in through several generations will leave a persistent, ascertainable effect in the conformation of the person, and still more in his habitual bearing and demeanor. But all the suggestions of a cumulative life of leisure, and all the proficiency in decorum that comes by the way of passive habituation, may be further improved upon by taking thought and assiduously acquiring the marks of honorable leisure, and then carrying the exhibition of these adventitious marks of exemption from employment out in a strenuous and systematic discipline. Plainly, this is a point at which a diligent application of effort and expenditure may materially further the attainment of a decent proficiency in the leisure-class proprieties. Conversely, the greater the degree of proficiency and the more patent the evidence of a high degree of habituation to observances which serve no lucrative or other directly useful purpose, the greater the consumption of time and substance impliedly involved in their acquisition, and the greater the resultant good repute. Hence, under the competitive struggle for proficiency in good manners, it comes about that much pain is taken with the cultivation of habits of decorum; and hence the details of decorum develop into a comprehensive discipline, conformity to which is required of all who would be held blameless in point of repute. And hence, on the other hand, this conspicuous leisure of which decorum is a ramification grows gradually into a laborious drill in deportment and an education in taste and discrimination as to what articles of consumption are decorous and what are the decorous methods of consuming them.

In this connection it is worthy of notice that the possibility of producing pathological and other idiosyncrasies of person and manner by shrewd mimicry and a systematic drill have been turned to account in the deliberate production of a cultured class—often with a very happy effect. In this way, by the process vulgarly known as snobbery, a syncopated evolution of gentle birth and breeding is achieved in the case of a goodly number of families and lines of descent. This syncopated gentle birth gives results which, in point of serviceability as a leisure-class factor in the population, are in no wise substantially inferior to others who may have had a longer but less arduous training in the pecuniary proprieties.

There are, moreover, measurable degrees of conformity to the latest accredited code of the punctilios as regards decorous means and methods of consumption. Differences between one person and another in the degree of conformity to the ideal in these respects can be compared, and persons may be graded and scheduled with some accuracy and effect according to a progressive scale of manners and breeding. The award of reputability in this regard is commonly made in good faith, on the ground of conformity to accepted canons of taste in the matters concerned, and without conscious regard to the pecuniary standing or the degree of leisure practiced by any given candidate for reputability; but the canons of taste according to which the award is made are constantly under the surveillance of the law of conspicuous leisure, and are indeed constantly undergoing change and revision to bring them into closer conformity with its requirements. So that while the proximate ground of discrimination may be of another kind, still the pervading principle and abiding test of good breeding is the requirement of a substantial and patent waste of time. There may be some considerable range of variation in detail within the scope of this principle, but they are variations of form and expression, not of substance.

Much of the courtesy of everyday intercourse is of course a direct expression of consideration and kindly good-will, and this element of conduct has for the most part no need of being traced back to any underlying ground of reputability to explain either its presence or the approval with which it is regarded; but the same is not true of the code of proprieties. These latter are expressions of status. It is of course sufficiently plain, to any one who cares to see, that our bearing towards menials and other pecuniarily dependent inferiors is the bearing of the superior member in a relation of status, though its manifestation is often greatly modified and softened from the original expression of crude dominance. Similarly, our bearing towards superiors, and in great measure towards equals, expresses a more or less conventionalized attitude of subservience. Witness the masterful presence of the high-minded gentleman or lady, which testifies to so much of dominance and independence of economic circumstances, and which at the same time appeals with such convincing force to our sense of what is right and gracious. It is among this highest leisure class, who have no superiors and few peers, that decorum finds its fullest and maturest expression; and it is this highest class also that gives decorum that definitive formulation which serves as a canon of conduct for the classes beneath. And here also the code is most obviously a code of status and shows most plainly its incompatibility with all vulgarly productive work. A divine assurance and an imperious complaisance, as of one habituated to require subservience and to take no thought for the morrow, is the birthright and the criterion of the gentleman at his best; and it is in popular apprehension even more than that, for this demeanor is accepted as an intrinsic attribute of superior worth, before which the base-born commoner delights to stoop and yield.

As has been indicated in an earlier chapter, there is reason to believe that the institution of ownership has begun with the ownership of persons, primarily women. The incentives to acquiring such property have apparently been: (1) a propensity for dominance and coercion; (2) the utility of these persons as evidence of the prowess of their owner; (3) the utility of their services.

Personal service holds a peculiar place in the economic development. During the stage of quasi-peaceable industry, and especially during the earlier development of industry within the limits of this general stage, the utility of their services seems commonly to be the dominant motive to the acquisition of property in persons. Servants are valued for their services. But the dominance of this motive is not due to a decline in the absolute importance of the other two utilities possessed by servants. It is rather that the altered circumstances of life accentuate the utility of servants for this last-named purpose. Women and other slaves are highly valued, both as an evidence of wealth and as a means of accumulating wealth. Together with cattle, if the tribe is a pastoral one, they are the usual form of investment for a profit. To such an extent may female slavery give its character to the economic life under the quasi-peaceable culture that the woman even comes to serve as a unit of value among peoples occupying this cultural stage—as for instance in Homeric times. Where this is the case there need be little question but that the basis of the industrial system is chattel slavery and that the women are commonly slaves. The great, pervading human relation in such a system is that of master and servant. The accepted evidence of wealth is the possession of many women, and presently also of other slaves engaged in attendance on their master's person and in producing goods for him.

A division of labor presently sets in, whereby personal service and attendance on the master becomes the special office of a portion of the servants, while those who are wholly employed in industrial occupations proper are removed more and more from all immediate relation to the person of their owner. At the same time those servants whose office is personal service, including domestic duties, come gradually to be exempted from productive industry carried on for gain.

This process of progressive exemption from the common run of industrial employment will commonly begin with the exemption of the wife, or the chief wife. After the community has advanced to settled habits of life, wife-capture from hostile tribes becomes impracticable as a customary source of supply. Where this cultural advance has been achieved, the chief wife is ordinarily of gentle blood, and the fact of her being so will hasten her exemption from vulgar employment. The manner in which the concept of gentle blood originates, as well as the place which it occupies in the development of marriage, cannot be discussed in this place. For the purpose in hand it will be sufficient to say that gentle blood is blood which has been ennobled by protracted contact with accumulated wealth or unbroken prerogative. The woman with these antecedents is preferred in marriage, both for the sake of a resulting alliance with her powerful relatives and because a superior worth is felt to inhere in blood which has been associated with many goods and great power. She will still be her husband's chattel, as she was her father's chattel before her purchase, but she is at the same time of her father's gentle blood; and hence there is a moral incongruity in her occupying herself with the debasing employments of her fellow-servants. However completely she may be subject to her master, and however inferior to the male members of the social stratum in which her birth has placed her, the principle that gentility is transmissible will act to place her above the common slave; and so soon as this principle has acquired a prescriptive authority it will act to invest her in some measure with that prerogative of leisure which is the chief mark of gentility. Furthered by this principle of transmissible gentility the wife's exemption gains in scope, if the wealth of her owner permits it, until it includes exemption from debasing menial service as well as from handicraft. As the industrial development goes on and property becomes massed in relatively fewer hands, the conventional standard of wealth of the upper class rises. The same tendency to exemption from handicraft, and in the course of time from menial domestic employments, will then assert itself as regards the other wives, if such there are, and also as regards other servants in immediate attendance upon the person of their master. The exemption comes more tardily the remoter the relation in which the servant stands to the person of the master.

If the pecuniary situation of the master permits it, the development of a special class of personal or body servants is also furthered by the very grave importance which comes to attach to this personal service. The master's person, being the embodiment of worth and honor, is of the most serious consequence. Both for his reputable standing in the community and for his self-respect, it is a matter of moment that he should have at his call efficient specialized servants, whose attendance upon his person is not diverted from their chief office by any by-occupation. These specialized servants are useful more for show than for service actually performed. In so far as they are not kept for exhibition simply, they afford gratification to their master chiefly in allowing scope to his propensity for dominance. It is true, the care of the continually increasing household apparatus may require added labor; but since the apparatus is commonly increased in order to serve as a means of good repute rather than as a means of comfort, this qualification is not of great weight. All these lines of utility are better served by a larger number of more highly specialized servants. There results, therefore, a constantly increasing differentiation and multiplication of domestic and body servants, along with a concomitant progressive exemption of such servants from productive labor. By virtue of their serving as evidence of ability to pay, the office of such domestics regularly tends to include continually fewer duties, and their service tends in the end to become nominal only. This is especially true of those servants who are in most immediate and obvious attendance upon their master. So that the utility of these comes to consist, in great part, in their conspicuous exemption from productive labor and in the evidence which this exemption affords of their master's wealth and power.

After some considerable advance has been made in the practice of employing a special corps of servants for the performance of a conspicuous leisure in this manner, men begin to be preferred above women for services that bring them obtrusively into view. Men, especially lusty, personable fellows, such as footmen and other menials should be, are obviously more powerful and more expensive than women. They are better fitted for this work, as showing a larger waste of time and of human energy. Hence it comes about that in the economy of the leisure class the busy housewife of the early patriarchal days, with her retinue of hard-working hand-maidens, presently gives place to the lady and the lackey.

In all grades and walks of life, and at any stage of the economic development, the leisure of the lady and of the lackey differs from the leisure of the gentleman in his own right in that it is an occupation of an ostensibly laborious kind. It takes the form, in large measure, of a painstaking attention to the service of the master, or to the maintenance and elaboration of the household paraphernalia; so that it is leisure only in the sense that little or no productive work is performed by this class, not in the sense that all appearance of labor is avoided by them. The duties performed by the lady, or by the household or domestic servants, are frequently arduous enough, and they are also frequently directed to ends which are considered extremely necessary to the comfort of the entire household. So far as these services conduce to the physical efficiency or comfort of the master or the rest of the household, they are to be accounted productive work. Only the residue of employment left after deduction of this effective work is to be classed as a performance of leisure.

But much of the services classed as household cares in modern everyday life, and many of the "utilities" required for a comfortable existence by civilized man, are of a ceremonial character. They are, therefore, properly to be classed as a performance of leisure in the sense in which the term is here used. They may be none the less imperatively necessary from the point of view of decent existence; they may be none the less requisite for personal comfort even, although they may be chiefly or wholly of a ceremonial character. But in so far as they partake of this character they are imperative and requisite because we have been taught to require them under pain of ceremonial uncleanness or unworthiness. We feel discomfort in their absence, but not because their absence results directly in physical discomfort; nor would a taste not trained to discriminate between the conventionally good and the conventionally bad take offense at their omission. In so far as this is true the labor spent in these services is to be classed as leisure; and when performed by others than the economically free and self-directing head of the establishment, they are to be classed as vicarious leisure.

The vicarious leisure performed by housewives and menials, under the head of household cares, may frequently develop into drudgery, especially where the competition for reputability is close and strenuous. This is frequently the case in modern life. Where this happens, the domestic service which comprises the duties of this servant class might aptly be designated as wasted effort, rather than as vicarious leisure. But the latter term has the advantage of indicating the line of derivation of these domestic offices, as well as of neatly suggesting the substantial economic ground of their utility; for these occupations are chiefly useful as a method of imputing pecuniary reputability to the master or to the household on the ground that a given amount of time and effort is conspicuously wasted in that behalf.

In this way, then, there arises a subsidiary or derivative leisure class, whose office is the performance of a vicarious leisure for the behoof of the reputability of the primary or legitimate leisure class. This vicarious leisure class is distinguished from the leisure class proper by a characteristic feature of its habitual mode of life. The leisure of the master class is, at least ostensibly, an indulgence of a proclivity for the avoidance of labor and is presumed to enhance the master's own well-being and fullness of life; but the leisure of the servant class exempt from productive labor is in some sort a performance exacted from them, and is not normally or primarily directed to their own comfort. The leisure of the servant is not his own leisure. So far as he is a servant in the full sense, and not at the same time a member of a lower order of the leisure class proper, his leisure normally passes under the guise of specialized service directed to the furtherance of his master's fullness of life. Evidence of this relation of subservience is obviously present in the servant's carriage and manner of life. The like is often true of the wife throughout the protracted economic stage during which she is still primarily a servant—that is to say, so long as the household with a male head remains in force. In order to satisfy the requirements of the leisure-class scheme of life, the servant should show not only an attitude of subservience, but also the effects of special training and practice in subservience. The servant or wife should not only perform certain offices and show a servile disposition, but it is quite as imperative that they should show an acquired facility in the tactics of subservience—a trained conformity to the canons of effectual and conspicuous subservience. Even today it is this aptitude and acquired skill in the formal manifestation of the servile relation that constitutes the chief element of utility in our highly paid servants, as well as one of the chief ornaments of the well-bred housewife.

The first requisite of a good servant is that he should conspicuously know his place. It is not enough that he knows how to effect certain desired mechanical results; he must, above all, know how to effect these results in due form. Domestic service might be said to be a spiritual rather than a mechanical function. Gradually there grows up an elaborate system of good form, specifically regulating the manner in which this vicarious leisure of the servant class is to be performed. Any departure from these canons of form is to be deprecated, not so much because it evinces a shortcoming in mechanical efficiency, or even that it shows an absence of the servile attitude and temperament, but because, in the last analysis, it shows the absence of special training. Special training in personal service costs time and effort, and where it is obviously present in a high degree, it argues that the servant who possesses it, neither is nor has been habitually engaged in any productive occupation. It is *prima facie* evidence of a vicarious leisure extending far back in the past. So that trained service has utility, not only as gratifying the master's instinctive liking for good and skillful workmanship and his propensity for conspicuous dominance over those whose lives are subservient to his own, but it has utility also as putting in evidence a much larger consumption of human service than would be shown by the mere present conspicuous leisure performed by an untrained person. It is a serious grievance if a gentleman's butler or footman performs his duties about his master's table or carriage in such unformed style as to suggest that his habitual occupation may be ploughing or sheepherding. Such bungling work would imply inability on the master's part to procure the service of specially trained servants; that is to say, it would imply inability to pay for the consumption of time, effort, and instruction required to fit a trained servant for special service under an exacting code of forms. If the performance of the servant argues lack of means on the part of his master, it defeats its chief substantial end; for the chief use of servants is the evidence they afford of the master's ability to pay.

What has just been said might be taken to imply that the offense of an under-trained servant lies in a direct suggestion of inexpensiveness or of usefulness. Such, of course, is not the case. The connection is much less immediate. What happens here is what happens generally. Whatever approves itself to us on any ground at the outset, presently comes to appeal to us as a gratifying thing in itself; it comes to rest in our habits of thought as substantially right. But in order that any specific canon of deportment shall maintain itself in favor, it must continue to have the support of, or at least not be incompatible with, the habit or aptitude which constitutes the norm of its development. The need of vicarious leisure, or conspicuous consumption of service, is a dominant incentive to the keeping of servants. So long as this remains true it may be set down without much discussion that any such departure from accepted usage as would suggest an abridged apprenticeship in service would presently be found insufferable. The requirement of an expensive vicarious leisure acts indirectly, selectively, by guiding the formation of our taste—of our sense of what is right in these matters—and so weeds out unconformable departures by withholding approval of them.

As the standard of wealth recognized by common consent advances, the possession and exploitation of servants as a means of showing superfluity undergoes a refinement. The possession and maintenance of slaves employed in the production of goods argues wealth and prowess, but the maintenance of servants who produce nothing argues still higher wealth and position. Under this principle there arises a class of servants, the more numerous the better, whose sole office is fatuously to wait upon the person of their owner, and so to put in evidence his ability unproductively to consume a large amount of service. There supervenes a division of labor among the servants or dependents whose life is spent in maintaining the honor of the gentleman of leisure. So that, while one group produces goods for him, another group, usually headed by the wife, or chief wife, consumes for him in conspicuous leisure; thereby putting in evidence his ability to sustain large pecuniary damage without impairing his superior opulence.

This somewhat idealized and diagrammatic outline of the development and nature of domestic service comes nearest being true for that cultural stage which has here been named the "quasi-peaceable" stage of industry. At this stage personal service first rises to the position of an economic institution, and it is at this stage that it occupies the largest place in the community's scheme of life. In the cultural sequence, the quasi-peaceable stage follows the predatory stage proper, the two being successive phases of barbarian life. Its characteristic feature is a formal observance of peace and order, at the same time that life at this stage still has too much of coercion and class antagonism to be called peaceable in the full sense of the word. For many purposes, and from another point of view than the economic one, it might as well be named the stage of status. The method of human relation during this stage, and the spiritual attitude of men at this level of culture, is well summed up under that term. But as a descriptive term to characterize the prevailing methods of industry, as well as to indicate the trend of industrial development at this point in economic evolution, the term "quasi-peaceable" seems preferable. So far as concerns the communities of the Western culture, this phase of economic development probably lies in the past; except for a numerically small though very conspicuous fraction of the community in whom the habits of thought peculiar to the barbarian culture have suffered but a relatively slight disintegration.

Personal service is still an element of great economic importance, especially as regards the distribution and consumption of goods; but its relative importance even in this direction is no doubt less than it once was. The best development of this vicarious leisure lies in the past rather than in the present; and its best expression in the present is to be found in the scheme of life of the upper leisure class. To this class the modern culture owes much in the way of the conservation of traditions, usages, and habits of thought which belong on a more archaic cultural plane, so far as regards their widest acceptance and their most effective development.

In the modern industrial communities the mechanical contrivances available for the comfort and convenience of everyday life are highly developed. So much so that body servants, or, indeed, domestic servants of any kind, would now scarcely be employed by anybody except on the ground of a canon of reputability carried over by tradition from earlier usage. The only exception would be servants employed to attend on the persons of the infirm and the feeble-minded. But such servants properly come under the head of trained nurses rather than under that of domestic servants, and they are, therefore, an apparent rather than a real exception to the rule.

The proximate reason for keeping domestic servants, for instance, in the moderately well-to-do household of today, is (ostensibly) that the members of the household are unable without discomfort to compass the work required by such a modern establishment. And the reason for their being unable to accomplish it is (1) that they have too many "social duties," and (2) that the work to be done is too severe and that there is too much of it. These two reasons may be restated as follows: (1) Under a mandatory code of decency, the time and effort of the members of such a household are required to be ostensibly all spent in a performance of conspicuous leisure, in the way of calls, drives, clubs, sewing-circles, sports, charity organizations, and other like social functions. Those persons whose time and energy are employed in these matters privately avow that all these observances, as well as the incidental attention to dress and other conspicuous consumption, are very irksome but altogether unavoidable. (2) Under the requirement of conspicuous consumption of goods, the apparatus of living has grown so elaborate and cumbrous, in the way of dwellings, furniture, bric-a-brac, wardrobe and meals, that the consumers of these things cannot make way with them in the required manner without help. Personal contact with the hired persons whose aid is called in to fulfill the routine of decency is commonly distasteful to the occupants of the house, but their presence is endured and paid for, in order to delegate to them a share in this onerous consumption of household goods. The presence of domestic servants, and of the special class of body servants in an eminent degree, is a concession of physical comfort to the moral need of pecuniary decency.

The largest manifestation of vicarious leisure in modern life is made up of what are called domestic duties. These duties are fast becoming a species of services performed, not so much for the individual behoof of the head of the household as for the reputability of the household taken as a corporate unit—a group of which the housewife is a member on a footing of ostensible equality. As fast as the household for which they are performed departs from its archaic basis of ownership-marriage, these household duties of course tend to fall out of the category of vicarious leisure in the original sense; except so far as they are performed by hired servants. That is to say, since vicarious leisure is possible only on a basis of status or of hired service, the disappearance of the relation of status from human intercourse at any point carries with it the disappearance of vicarious leisure so far as regards that much of life. But it is to be added, in qualification of this qualification, that so long as the household subsists, even with a divided head, this class of non-productive labor performed for the sake of household reputability must still be classed as vicarious leisure, although in a slightly altered sense. It is now leisure performed for the quasi-personal corporate household, instead of, as formerly, for the proprietary head of the household.

Conspicuous Consumption

In what has been said of the evolution of the vicarious leisure class and its differentiation from the general body of the working classes, reference has been made to a further division of labor—that between different servant classes. One portion of the servant class, chiefly those persons whose occupation is vicarious leisure, come to undertake a new, subsidiary range of duties—the vicarious consumption of goods. The most obvious form in which this consumption occurs is seen in the wearing of liveries and the occupation of spacious servants' quarters. Another, scarcely less obtrusive or less effective form of vicarious consumption, and a much more widely prevalent one, is the consumption of food, clothing, dwelling, and furniture by the lady and the rest of the domestic establishment.

But already at a point in economic evolution far antedating the emergence of the lady, specialized consumption of goods as an evidence of pecuniary strength had begun to work out in a more or less elaborate system. The beginning of a differentiation in consumption even antedates the appearance of anything that can fairly be called pecuniary strength. It is traceable back to the initial phase of predatory culture, and there is even a suggestion that an incipient differentiation in this respect lies back of the beginnings of the predatory life. This most primitive differentiation in the consumption of goods is like the later differentiation with which we are all so intimately familiar, in that it is largely of a ceremonial character, but unlike the latter it does not rest on a difference in accumulated wealth. The utility of consumption as an evidence of wealth is to be classed as a derivative growth. It is an adaptation to a new end, by a selective process, of a distinction previously existing and well established in men's habits of thought.

In the earlier phases of the predatory culture the only economic differentiation is a broad distinction between an honorable superior class made up of the able-bodied men on the one side, and a base inferior class of laboring women on the other. According to the ideal scheme of life in force at that time it is the office of the men to consume what the women produce. Such consumption as falls to the women is merely incidental to their work; it is a means to their continued labor, and not a consumption directed to their own comfort and fullness of life. Unproductive consumption of goods is honorable, primarily as a mark of prowess and a perquisite of human dignity; secondarily, it becomes substantially honorable in itself, especially the consumption of the more desirable things. The consumption of choice articles of food, and frequently also of rare articles of adornment, becomes tabu to the women and children; and if there is a base (servile) class of men, the tabu holds also for them. With a further advance in culture this tabu may change into simple custom of a more or less rigorous character; but whatever be the theoretical basis of the distinction which is maintained, whether it be a tabu or a larger conventionality, the features of the conventional scheme of consumption do not change easily. When the quasi-peaceable stage of industry is reached, with its fundamental institution of chattel slavery, the general principle, more or less rigorously applied, is that the base, industrious class should consume only what may be necessary to their subsistence. In the nature of things, luxuries and the comforts of life belong to the leisure class. Under the tabu, certain victuals, and more particularly certain beverages, are strictly reserved for the use of the superior class.

The ceremonial differentiation of the dietary is best seen in the use of intoxicating beverages and narcotics. If these articles of consumption are costly, they are felt to be noble and honorific. Therefore the base classes, primarily the women, practice an enforced continence with respect to these stimulants, except in countries where they are obtainable at a very low cost. From archaic times down through all the length of the patriarchal regime it has been the office of the women to prepare and administer these luxuries, and it has been the perquisite of the men of gentle birth and breeding to consume them. Drunkenness and the other pathological consequences of the free use of stimulants therefore tend in their turn to become honorific, as being a mark, at the second remove, of the superior status of those who are able to afford the indulgence. Infirmities induced by over-indulgence are among some peoples freely recognized as manly attributes. It has even happened that the name for certain diseased conditions of the body arising from such an origin has passed into everyday speech as a synonym for "noble" or "gentle." It is only at a relatively early stage of culture that the symptoms of expensive vice are conventionally accepted as marks of a superior status, and so tend to become virtues and command the deference of the community; but the reputability that attaches to certain expensive vices long retains so much of its force as to appreciably lessen the disapprobation visited upon the men of the wealthy or noble class for any excessive indulgence. The same invidious distinction adds force to the current disapproval of any indulgence of this kind on the part of women, minors, and inferiors. This invidious traditional distinction has not lost its force even among the more advanced peoples of today. Where the example set by the leisure class retains its imperative force in the regulation of the conventionalities, it is observable that the women still in great measure practice the same traditional continence with regard to stimulants.

This characterization of the greater continence in the use of stimulants practiced by the women of the reputable classes may seem an excessive refinement of logic at the expense of common sense. But facts within easy reach of any one who cares to know them go to say that the greater abstinence of women is in some part due to an imperative conventionality; and this conventionality is, in a general way, strongest where the patriarchal tradition—the tradition that the woman is a chattel—has retained its hold in greatest vigor. In a sense which has been greatly qualified in scope and rigor, but which has by no means lost its meaning even yet, this tradition says that the woman, being a chattel, should consume only what is necessary to her sustenance—except so far as her further consumption contributes to the comfort or the good repute of her master. The consumption of luxuries, in the true sense, is a consumption directed to the comfort of the consumer himself, and is, therefore, a mark of the master. Any such consumption by others can take place only on a basis of sufferance. In communities where the popular habits of thought have been profoundly shaped by the patriarchal tradition we may accordingly look for survivals of the tabu on luxuries at least to the extent of a conventional deprecation of their use by the unfree and dependent class. This is more particularly true as regards certain luxuries, the use of which by the dependent class would detract sensibly from the comfort or pleasure of their masters, or which are held to be of doubtful legitimacy on other grounds. In the apprehension of the great conservative middle class of Western civilization the use of these various stimulants is obnoxious to at least one, if not both, of these objections; and it is a fact too significant to be passed over that it is precisely among these middle classes of the Germanic culture, with their strong surviving sense of the patriarchal proprieties, that the women are to the greatest extent subject to a qualified tabu on narcotics and alcoholic beverages. With many qualifications—with more qualifications as the patriarchal tradition has gradually weakened—the general rule is felt to be right and binding that women should consume only for the benefit of their masters. The objection of course presents itself that expenditure on women's dress and household paraphernalia is an obvious exception to this rule; but it will appear in the sequel that this exception is much more obvious than substantial.

During the earlier stages of economic development, consumption of goods without stint, especially consumption of the better grades of goods—ideally all consumption in excess of the subsistence minimum—pertains normally to the leisure class. This restriction tends to disappear, at least formally, after the late peaceable stage has been reached, with private ownership of goods and an industrial system based on wage labor or on the petty household economy. But during the earlier quasi-peaceable stage, when so many of the traditions through which the institution of a leisure class has affected the economic life of later times were taking form and consistency, this principle has had the force of a conventional law. It has served as the norm to which consumption has tended to conform, and any appreciable departure from it is to be regarded as an aberrant form, sure to be eliminated sooner or later in the further course of development.

The quasi-peaceable gentleman of leisure, then, not only consumes of the staff of life beyond the minimum required for subsistence and physical efficiency, but his consumption also undergoes a specialization as regards the quality of the goods consumed. He consumes freely and of the best, in food, drink, narcotics, shelter, services, ornaments, apparel, weapons and accoutrements, amusements, amulets, and idols or divinities. In the process of gradual amelioration which takes place in the articles of his consumption, the motive principle and the proximate aim of innovation is no doubt the higher efficiency of the improved and more elaborate products for personal comfort and well-being. But that does not remain the sole purpose of their consumption. The canon of reputability is at hand and seizes upon such innovations as are, according to its standard, fit to survive. Since the consumption of these more excellent goods is an evidence of wealth, it becomes honorific; and conversely, the failure to consume in due quantity and quality becomes a mark of inferiority and demerit.

This growth of punctilious discrimination as to qualitative excellence in eating, drinking, etc., presently affects not only the manner of life, but also the training and intellectual activity of the gentlemen of leisure. He is no longer simply the successful, aggressive male—the man of strength, resource, and intrepidity. In order to avoid stultification he must also cultivate his tastes, for it now becomes incumbent on him to discriminate with some nicety between the noble and the ignoble in consumable goods. He becomes a connoisseur in creditable viands of various degrees of merit, in manly beverages and trinkets, in seemly apparel and architecture, in weapons, games, dancers, and the narcotics. This cultivation of the aesthetic faculty requires time and application, and the demands made upon the gentleman in this direction therefore tend to change his life of leisure into a more or less arduous application to the business of learning how to live a life of ostensible leisure in a becoming way. Closely related to the requirement that the gentleman must consume freely and of the right kind of goods, there is the requirement that he must know how to consume them in a seemly manner. His life of leisure must be conducted in due form. Hence arise good manners in the way pointed out in an earlier chapter. High-bred manners and ways of living are items of conformity to the norm of conspicuous leisure and conspicuous consumption.

Conspicuous consumption of valuable goods is a means of reputability to the gentleman of leisure. As wealth accumulates on his hands, his own unaided effort will not avail to sufficiently put his opulence in evidence by this method. The aid of friends and competitors is therefore brought in by resorting to the giving of valuable presents and expensive feasts and entertainments. Presents and feasts had probably another origin than that of naïve ostentation, but they acquired their utility for this purpose very early, and they have retained that character to the present; so that their utility in this respect has now long been the substantial ground on which these usages rest. Costly entertainments, such as the potlatch or the ball, are peculiarly adapted to serve this end. The competitor with whom the entertainer wishes to institute a comparison is, by this method, made to serve as a means to the end. He consumes vicariously for his host at the same time that he is a witness to the consumption of that excess of good things which his host is unable to dispose of single-handed, and he is also made to witness his hosts' facility in etiquette.

In the giving of costly entertainments other motives, of a more genial kind, are of course also present. The custom of festive gatherings probably originated in motives of conviviality and religion; these motives are also present in the later development, but they do not continue to be the sole motives. The latter-day leisure-class festivities and entertainments may continue in some slight degree to serve the religious need and in a higher degree the needs of recreation and conviviality, but they also serve an invidious purpose; and they serve it none the less effectively for having a colorable non-invidious ground in these more avowable motives. But the economic effect of these social amenities is not therefore lessened, either in the vicarious consumption of goods or in the exhibition of difficult and costly achievements in etiquette.

As wealth accumulates, the leisure class develops further in function and structure, and there arises a differentiation within the class. There is a more or less elaborate system of rank and grades. This differentiation is furthered by the inheritance of wealth and the consequent inheritance of gentility. With the inheritance of gentility goes the inheritance of obligatory leisure; and gentility of a sufficient potency to entail a life of leisure may be inherited without the complement of wealth required to maintain a dignified leisure. Gentle blood may be transmitted without goods enough to afford a reputably free consumption at one's ease. Hence results a class of impecunious gentlemen of leisure, incidentally referred to already. These half-caste gentlemen of leisure fall into a system of hierarchical gradations. Those who stand near the higher and the highest grades of the wealthy leisure class, in point of birth, or in point of wealth, or both, outrank the remoter-born and the pecuniarily weaker. These lower grades, especially the impecunious, or marginal, gentlemen of leisure, affiliate themselves by a system of dependence or fealty to the great ones; by so doing they gain an increment of repute, or of the means with which to lead a life of leisure, from their patron. They become his courtiers or retainers, servants; and being fed and countenanced by their patron they are indices of his rank and vicarious consumers of his superfluous wealth. Many of these affiliated gentlemen of leisure are at the same time lesser men of substance in their own right; so that some of them are scarcely at all, others only partially, to be rated as vicarious consumers. So many of them, however, as make up the retainers and hangers-on of the patron may be classed as vicarious consumers without qualification. Many of these again, and also many of the other aristocracy of less degree, have in turn attached to their persons a more or less comprehensive group of vicarious consumers in the persons of their wives and children, their servants, retainers, etc.

Throughout this graduated scheme of vicarious leisure and vicarious consumption the rule holds that these offices must be performed in some such manner, or under some such circumstance or insignia, as shall point plainly to the master to whom this leisure or consumption pertains, and to whom therefore the resulting increment of good repute of right inures. The consumption and leisure executed by these persons for their master or patron represents an investment on his part with a view to an increase of good fame. As regards feasts and largesses this is obvious enough, and the imputation of repute to the host or patron here takes place immediately, on the ground of common notoriety. Where leisure and consumption is performed vicariously by henchmen and retainers, imputation of the resulting repute to the patron is effected by their residing near his person so that it may be plain to all men from what source they draw. As the group whose good esteem is to be secured in this way grows larger, more patent means are required to indicate the imputation of merit for the leisure performed, and to this end uniforms, badges, and liveries come into vogue. The wearing of uniforms or liveries implies a considerable degree of dependence, and may even be said to be a mark of servitude, real or ostensible. The wearers of uniforms and liveries may be roughly divided into two classes—the free and the servile, or the noble and the ignoble. The services performed by them are likewise divisible into noble and ignoble. Of course the distinction is not observed with strict consistency in practice; the less debasing of the base services and the less honorific of the noble functions are not infrequently merged in the same person. But the general distinction is not on that account to be overlooked. What may add some perplexity is the fact that this fundamental distinction between noble and ignoble, which rests on the nature of the ostensible service performed, is traversed by a secondary distinction into honorific and humiliating, resting on the rank of the person for whom the service is performed or whose livery is worn. So, those offices which are by right the proper employment of the leisure class, are noble; such are government, fighting, hunting, the care of arms and accoutrements, and the like—in short, those which may be classed as ostensibly predatory employments. On the other hand, those employments which properly fall to the industrious class are ignoble; such as handicraft or other productive labor, menial services, and the like. But a base service performed for a person of very high degree may become a very honorific office; as for instance the office of a Maid of Honor or of a Lady in Waiting to the Queen, or the King's Master of the Horse or his Keeper of the Hounds. The two offices last named suggest a principle of some general bearing. Whenever, as in these cases, the menial service in question has to do directly with the primary leisure employments of fighting and hunting, it easily acquires a reflected honorific character. In this way great honor may come to attach to an employment which in its own nature belongs to the baser sort.

In the later development of peaceable industry, the usage of employing an idle corps of uniformed men-at-arms gradually lapses. Vicarious consumption by dependents bearing the insignia of their patron or master narrows down to a corps of liveried menials. In a heightened degree, therefore, the livery comes to be a badge of servitude, or rather of servility. Something of an honorific character always attaches to the livery of the armed retainer, but this honorific character disappears when the livery becomes the exclusive badge of the menial. The livery becomes obnoxious to nearly all who are required to wear it. We are yet so little removed from a state of effective slavery as still to be fully sensitive to the sting of any imputation of servility. This antipathy asserts itself even in the case of the liveries or uniforms which some corporations prescribe as the distinctive dress of their employees. In this country the aversion even goes the length of discrediting—in a mild and uncertain way—those government employments, military and civil, which require the wearing of a livery or uniform.

With the disappearance of servitude, the number of vicarious consumers attached to any one gentleman tends, on the whole, to decrease. The like is of course true, and perhaps in a still higher degree, of the number of dependents who perform vicarious leisure for him. In a general way, though not wholly nor consistently, these two groups coincide. The dependent who was first delegated for these duties was the wife, or the chief wife; and, as would be expected, in the later development of the institution, when the number of persons by whom these duties are customarily performed gradually narrows, the wife remains the last. In the higher grades of society a large volume of both these kinds of service is required; and here the wife is of course still assisted in the work by a more or less numerous corps of menials. But as we descend the social scale, the point is presently reached where the duties of vicarious leisure and consumption devolve upon the wife alone. In the communities of the Western culture, this point is at present found among the lower middle class.

And here occurs a curious inversion. It is a fact of common observation that in this lower middle class there is no pretense of leisure on the part of the head of the household. Through force of circumstances it has fallen into disuse. But the middle-class wife still carries on the business of vicarious leisure, for the good name of the household and its master. In descending the social scale in any modern industrial community, the primary fact—the conspicuous leisure of the master of the household—disappears at a relatively high point. The head of the middle-class household has been reduced by economic circumstances to turn his hand to gaining a livelihood by occupations which often partake largely of the character of industry, as in the case of the ordinary business man of today. But the derivative fact—the vicarious leisure and consumption rendered by the wife, and the auxiliary vicarious performance of leisure by menials—remains in vogue as a conventionality which the demands of reputability will not suffer to be slighted. It is by no means an uncommon spectacle to find a man applying himself to work with the utmost assiduity, in order that his wife may in due form render for him that degree of vicarious leisure which the common sense of the time demands.

The leisure rendered by the wife in such cases is, of course, not a simple manifestation of idleness or indolence. It almost invariably occurs disguised under some form of work or household duties or social amenities, which prove on analysis to serve little or no ulterior end beyond showing that she does not and need not occupy herself with anything that is gainful or that is of substantial use. As has already been noticed under the head of manners, the greater part of the customary round of domestic cares to which the middle-class housewife gives her time and effort is of this character. Not that the results of her attention to household matters, of a decorative and mundificatory character, are not pleasing to the sense of men trained in middle-class proprieties; but the taste to which these effects of household adornment and tidiness appeal is a taste which has been formed under the selective guidance of a canon of propriety that demands just these evidences of wasted effort. The effects are pleasing to us chiefly because we have been taught to find them pleasing. There goes into these domestic duties much solicitude for a proper combination of form and color, and for other ends that are to be classed as aesthetic in the proper sense of the term; and it is not denied that effects having some substantial aesthetic value are sometimes attained. Pretty much all that is here insisted on is that, as regards these amenities of life, the housewife's efforts are under the guidance of traditions that have been shaped by the law of conspicuously wasteful expenditure of time and substance. If beauty or comfort is achieved—and it is a more or less fortuitous circumstance if they are—they must be achieved by means and methods that commend themselves to the great economic law of wasted effort. The more reputable, "presentable" portion of middle-class household paraphernalia are, on the one hand, items of conspicuous consumption, and on the other hand, apparatus for putting in evidence the vicarious leisure rendered by the housewife.

The requirement of vicarious consumption at the hands of the wife continues in force even at a lower point in the pecuniary scale than the requirement of vicarious leisure. At a point below which little if any pretense of wasted effort, in ceremonial cleanness and the like, is observable, and where there is assuredly no conscious attempt at ostensible leisure, decency still requires the wife to consume some goods conspicuously for the reputability of the household and its head. So that, as the latter-day outcome of this evolution of an archaic institution, the wife, who was at the outset the drudge and chattel of the man, both in fact and in theory—the producer of goods for him to consume—has become the ceremonial consumer of goods which he produces. But she still quite unmistakably remains his chattel in theory; for the habitual rendering of vicarious leisure and consumption is the abiding mark of the unfree servant.

This vicarious consumption practiced by the household of the middle and lower classes can not be counted as a direct expression of the leisure-class scheme of life, since the household of this pecuniary grade does not belong within the leisure class. It is rather that the leisure-class scheme of life here comes to an expression at the second remove. The leisure class stands at the head of the social structure in point of reputability; and its manner of life and its standards of worth therefore afford the norm of reputability for the community. The observance of these standards, in some degree of approximation, becomes incumbent upon all classes lower in the scale. In modern civilized communities the lines of demarcation between social classes have grown vague and transient, and wherever this happens the norm of reputability imposed by the upper class extends its coercive influence with but slight hindrance down through the social structure to the lowest strata. The result is that the members of each stratum accept as their ideal of decency the scheme of life in vogue in the next higher stratum, and bend their energies to live up to that ideal. On pain of forfeiting their good name, and their self-respect in case of failure, they must conform to the accepted code, at least in appearance.

The basis on which good repute in any highly organized industrial community ultimately rests is pecuniary strength; and the means of showing pecuniary strength, and so of gaining or retaining a good name, are leisure and a conspicuous consumption of goods. Accordingly, both of these methods are in vogue as far down the scale as it remains possible; and in the lower strata in which the two methods are employed, both offices are in great part delegated to the wife and children of the household. Lower still, where any degree of leisure, even ostensible, has become impracticable for the wife, the conspicuous consumption of goods remains and is carried on by the wife and children. The man of the household also can do something in this direction, and, indeed, he commonly does; but with a still lower descent into the levels of indigence—along the margin of the slums—the man, and presently also the children, virtually cease to consume valuable goods for appearances, and the woman remains virtually the sole exponent of the household's pecuniary decency. No class of society, not even the most abjectly poor, foregoes all customary conspicuous consumption. The last items of this category of consumption are not given up except under stress of the direst necessity. Very much of squalor and discomfort will be endured before the last trinket or the last pretense of pecuniary decency is put away. There is no class and no country that has yielded so abjectly before the pressure of physical want as to deny themselves all gratification of this higher or spiritual need.

From the foregoing survey of the growth of conspicuous leisure and consumption, it appears that the utility of both alike for the purposes of reputability lies in the element of waste that is common to both. In the one case it is a waste of time and effort, in the other it is a waste of goods. Both are methods of demonstrating the possession of wealth, and the two are conventionally accepted as equivalents. The choice between them is a question of advertising expediency simply except so far as it may be affected by other standards of propriety, springing from a different source. On grounds of expediency the preference may be given to the one or the other at different stages of the economic development. The question is, which of the two methods will most effectively reach the persons whose convictions it is desired to affect. Usage has answered this question in different ways under different circumstances.

So long as the community or social group is small enough and compact enough to be effectually reached by common notoriety alone—that is to say, so long as the human environment to which the individual is required to adapt himself in respect of reputability is comprised within his sphere of personal acquaintance and neighborhood gossip—so long the one method is about as effective as the other. Each will therefore serve about equally well during the earlier stages of social growth. But when the differentiation has gone farther and it becomes necessary to reach a wider human environment, consumption begins to hold over leisure as an ordinary means of decency. This is especially true during the later, peaceable economic stage. The means of communication and the mobility of the population now expose the individual to the observation of many persons who have no other means of judging of his reputability than the display of goods (and perhaps of breeding) which he is able to make while he is under their direct observation.

The modern organization of industry works in the same direction also by another line. The exigencies of the modern industrial system frequently place individuals and households in juxtaposition between whom there is little contact in any other sense than that of juxtaposition. One's neighbors, mechanically speaking, often are socially not one's neighbors, or even acquaintances; and still their transient good opinion has a high degree of utility. The only practicable means of impressing one's pecuniary ability on these unsympathetic observers of one's everyday life is an unremitting demonstration of ability to pay. In the modern community there is also a more frequent attendance at large gatherings of people to whom one's everyday life is unknown; in such places as churches, theaters, ballrooms, hotels, parks, shops, and the like. In order to impress these transient observers, and to retain one's self-complacency under their observation, the signature of one's pecuniary strength should be written in characters which he who runs may read. It is evident, therefore, that the present trend of the development is in the direction of heightening the utility of conspicuous consumption as compared with leisure.

It is also noticeable that the serviceability of consumption as a means of repute, as well as the insistence on it as an element of decency, is at its best in those portions of the community where the human contact of the individual is widest and the mobility of the population is greatest. Conspicuous consumption claims a relatively larger portion of the income of the urban than of the rural population, and the claim is also more imperative. The result is that, in order to keep up a decent appearance, the former habitually live hand-to-mouth to a greater extent than the latter. So it comes, for instance, that the American farmer and his wife and daughters are notoriously less modish in their dress, as well as less urbane in their manners, than the city artisan's family with an equal income. It is not that the city population is by nature much more eager for the peculiar complacency that comes of a conspicuous consumption, nor has the rural population less regard for pecuniary decency. But the provocation to this line of evidence, as well as its transient effectiveness, are more decided in the city. This method is therefore more readily resorted to, and in the struggle to outdo one another the city population push their normal standard of conspicuous consumption to a higher point, with the result that a relatively greater expenditure in this direction is required to indicate a given degree of pecuniary decency in the city. The requirement of conformity to this higher conventional standard becomes mandatory. The standard of decency is higher, class for class, and this requirement of decent appearance must be lived up to on pain of losing caste.

Consumption becomes a larger element in the standard of living in the city than in the country. Among the country population its place is to some extent taken by savings and home comforts known through the medium of neighborhood gossip sufficiently to serve the like general purpose of pecuniary repute. These home comforts and the leisure indulged in—where the indulgence is found—are of course also in great part to be classed as items of conspicuous consumption; and much the same is to be said of the savings. The smaller amount of the savings laid by the artisan class is no doubt due, in some measure, to the fact that in the case of the artisan the savings are a less effective means of advertisement, relative to the environment in which he is placed, than are the savings of the people living on farms and in the small villages. Among the latter, everybody's affairs, especially everybody's pecuniary status, are known to everybody else. Considered by itself simply—taken in the first degree—this added provocation to which the artisan and the urban laboring classes are exposed may not very seriously decrease the amount of savings; but in its cumulative action, through raising the standard of decent expenditure, its deterrent effect on the tendency to save cannot but be very great.

A felicitous illustration of the manner in which this canon of reputability works out its results is seen in the practice of dram-drinking, "treating," and smoking in public places, which is customary among the laborers and handicraftsmen of the towns, and among the lower middle class of the urban population generally. Journeymen printers may be named as a class among whom this form of conspicuous consumption has a great vogue, and among whom it carries with it certain well-marked consequences that are often deprecated. The peculiar habits of the class in this respect are commonly set down to some kind of an ill-defined moral deficiency with which this class is credited, or to a morally deleterious influence which their occupation is supposed to exert, in some unascertainable way, upon the men employed in it. The state of the case for the men who work in the composition and press rooms of the common run of printing-houses may be summed up as follows. Skill acquired in any printing-house or any city is easily turned to account in almost any other house or city; that is to say, the inertia due to special training is slight. Also, this occupation requires more than the average of intelligence and general information, and the men employed in it are therefore ordinarily more ready than many others to take advantage of any slight variation in the demand for their labor from one place to another. The inertia due to the home feeling is consequently also slight. At the same time the wages in the trade are high enough to make movement from place to place relatively easy. The result is a great mobility of the labor employed in printing; perhaps greater than in any other equally well-defined and considerable body of workmen. These men are constantly thrown in contact with new groups of acquaintances, with whom the relations established are transient or ephemeral, but whose good opinion is valued none the less for the time being. The human proclivity to ostentation, reenforced by sentiments of goodfellowship, leads them to spend freely in those directions which will best serve these needs. Here as elsewhere prescription seizes upon the custom as soon as it gains a vogue, and incorporates it in the accredited standard of decency. The next step is to make this standard of decency the point of departure for a new move as advance in the same direction—for there is no merit in simple spiritless conformity to a standard of dissipation that is lived up to as a matter of course by every one in the trade.

The greater prevalence of dissipation among printers than among the average of workmen is accordingly attributable, at least in some measure, to the greater ease of movement and the more transient character of acquaintance and human contact in this trade. But the substantial ground of this high requirement in dissipation is in the last analysis no other than that same propensity for a manifestation of dominance and pecuniary decency which makes the French peasant-proprietor parsimonious and frugal, and induces the American millionaire to found colleges, hospitals and museums. If the canon of conspicuous consumption were not offset to a considerable extent by other features of human nature, alien to it, any saving should logically be impossible for a population situated as the artisan and laboring classes of the cities are at present, however high their wages or their income might be.

But there are other standards of repute and other, more or less imperative, canons of conduct, besides wealth and its manifestation, and some of these come in to accentuate or to qualify the broad, fundamental canon of conspicuous waste. Under the simple test of effectiveness for advertising, we should expect to find leisure and the conspicuous consumption of goods dividing the field of pecuniary emulation pretty evenly between them at the outset. Leisure might then be expected gradually to yield ground and tend to obsolescence as the economic development goes forward, and the community increases in size; while the conspicuous consumption of goods should gradually gain in importance, both absolutely and relatively, until it had absorbed all the available product, leaving nothing over beyond a bare livelihood. But the actual course of development has been somewhat different from this ideal scheme. Leisure held the first place at the start, and came to hold a rank very much above wasteful consumption of goods, both as a direct exponent of wealth and as an element in the standard of decency, during the quasi-peaceable culture. From that point onward, consumption has gained ground, until, at present, it unquestionably holds the primacy, though it is still far from absorbing the entire margin of production above the subsistence minimum.

The early ascendancy of leisure as a means of reputability is traceable to the archaic distinction between noble and ignoble employments. Leisure is honorable and becomes imperative partly because it shows exemption from ignoble labor. The archaic differentiation into noble and ignoble classes is based on an invidious distinction between employments as honorific or debasing; and this traditional distinction grows into an imperative canon of decency during the early quasi-peaceable stage. Its ascendancy is furthered by the fact that leisure is still fully as effective an evidence of wealth as consumption. Indeed, so effective is it in the relatively small and stable human environment to which the individual is exposed at that cultural stage, that, with the aid of the archaic tradition which deprecates all productive labor, it gives rise to a large impecunious leisure class, and it even tends to limit the production of the community's industry to the subsistence minimum. This extreme inhibition of industry is avoided because slave labor, working under a compulsion more rigorous than that of reputability, is forced to turn out a product in excess of the subsistence minimum of the working class. The subsequent relative decline in the use of conspicuous leisure as a basis of repute is due partly to an increasing relative effectiveness of consumption as an evidence of wealth; but in part it is traceable to another force, alien, and in some degree antagonistic, to the usage of conspicuous waste.

This alien factor is the instinct of workmanship. Other circumstances permitting, that instinct disposes men to look with favor upon productive efficiency and on whatever is of human use. It disposes them to deprecate waste of substance or effort. The instinct of workmanship is present in all men, and asserts itself even under very adverse circumstances. So that however wasteful a given expenditure may be in reality, it must at least have some colorable excuse in the way of an ostensible purpose. The manner in which, under special circumstances, the instinct eventuates in a taste for exploit and an invidious discrimination between noble and ignoble classes has been indicated in an earlier chapter. In so far as it comes into conflict with the law of conspicuous waste, the instinct of workmanship expresses itself not so much in insistence on substantial usefulness as in an abiding sense of the odiousness and aesthetic impossibility of what is obviously futile. Being of the nature of an instinctive affection, its guidance touches chiefly and immediately the obvious and apparent violations of its requirements. It is only less promptly and with less constraining force that it reaches such substantial violations of its requirements as are appreciated only upon reflection.

So long as all labor continues to be performed exclusively or usually by slaves, the baseness of all productive effort is too constantly and deterrently present in the mind of men to allow the instinct of workmanship seriously to take effect in the direction of industrial usefulness; but when the quasi-peaceable stage (with slavery and status) passes into the peaceable stage of industry (with wage labor and cash payment) the instinct comes more effectively into play. It then begins aggressively to shape men's views of what is meritorious, and asserts itself at least as an auxiliary canon of self-complacency. All extraneous considerations apart, those persons (adults) are but a vanishing minority today who harbor no inclination to the accomplishment of some end, or who are not impelled of their own motion to shape some object or fact or relation for human use. The propensity may in large measure be overborne by the more immediately constraining incentive to a reputable leisure and an avoidance of indecorous usefulness, and it may therefore work itself out in make-believe only; as for instance in "social duties," and in quasi-artistic or quasi-scholarly accomplishments, in the care and decoration of the house, in sewing-circle activity or dress reform, in proficiency at dress, cards, yachting, golf, and various sports. But the fact that it may under stress of circumstances eventuate in inanities no more disproves the presence of the instinct than the reality of the brooding instinct is disproved by inducing a hen to sit on a nestful of china eggs.

This latter-day uneasy reaching-out for some form of purposeful activity that shall at the same time not be indecorously productive of either individual or collective gain marks a difference of attitude between the modern leisure class and that of the quasi-peaceable stage. At the earlier stage, as was said above, the all-dominating institution of slavery and status acted resistlessly to discountenance exertion directed to other than naïvely predatory ends. It was still possible to find some habitual employment for the inclination to action in the way of forcible aggression or repression directed against hostile groups or against the subject classes within the group; and this served to relieve the pressure and draw off the energy of the leisure class without a resort to actually useful, or even ostensibly useful employments. The practice of hunting also served the same purpose in some degree. When the community developed into a peaceful industrial organization, and when fuller occupation of the land had reduced the opportunities for the hunt to an inconsiderable residue, the pressure of energy seeking purposeful employment was left to find an outlet in some other direction. The ignominy which attaches to useful effort also entered upon a less acute phase with the disappearance of compulsory labor; and the instinct of workmanship then came to assert itself with more persistence and consistency.

The line of least resistance has changed in some measure, and the energy which formerly found a vent in predatory activity, now in part takes the direction of some ostensibly useful end. Ostensibly purposeless leisure has come to be deprecated, especially among that large portion of the leisure class whose plebeian origin acts to set them at variance with the tradition of the *otium cum dignitate*. But that canon of reputability which discountenances all employment that is of the nature of productive effort is still at hand, and will permit nothing beyond the most transient vogue to any employment that is substantially useful or productive. The consequence is that a change has been wrought in the conspicuous leisure practiced by the leisure class; not so much in substance as in form. A reconciliation between the two conflicting requirements is effected by a resort to make-believe. Many and intricate polite observances and social duties of a ceremonial nature are developed; many organizations are founded, with some specious object of amelioration embodied in their official style and title; there is much coming and going, and a deal of talk, to the end that the talkers may not have occasion to reflect on what is the effectual economic value of their traffic. And along with the make-believe of purposeful employment, and woven inextricably into its texture, there is commonly, if not invariably, a more or less appreciable element of purposeful effort directed to some serious end.

In the narrower sphere of vicarious leisure a similar change has gone forward. Instead of simply passing her time in visible idleness, as in the best days of the patriarchal regime, the housewife of the advanced peaceable stage applies herself assiduously to household cares. The salient features of this development of domestic service have already been indicated.

Throughout the entire evolution of conspicuous expenditure, whether of goods or of services or human life, runs the obvious implication that in order to effectually mend the consumer's good fame it must be an expenditure of superfluities. In order to be reputable it must be wasteful. No merit would accrue from the consumption of the bare necessities of life, except by comparison with the abjectly poor who fall short even of the subsistence minimum; and no standard of expenditure could result from such a comparison, except the most prosaic and unattractive level of decency. A standard of life would still be possible which should admit of invidious comparison in other respects than that of opulence; as, for instance, a comparison in various directions in the manifestation of moral, physical, intellectual, or aesthetic force. Comparison in all these directions is in vogue today; and the comparison made in these respects is commonly so inextricably bound up with the pecuniary comparison as to be scarcely distinguishable from the latter. This is especially true as regards the current rating of expressions of intellectual and aesthetic force or proficiency; so that we frequently interpret as aesthetic or intellectual a difference which in substance is pecuniary only.

The use of the term "waste" is in one respect an unfortunate one. As used in the speech of everyday life the word carries an undertone of deprecation. It is here used for want of a better term that will adequately describe the same range of motives and of phenomena, and it is not to be taken in an odious sense, as implying an illegitimate expenditure of human products or of human life. In the view of economic theory the expenditure in question is no more and no less legitimate than any other expenditure. It is here called "waste" because this expenditure does not serve human life or human well-being on the whole, not because it is waste or misdirection of effort or expenditure as viewed from the standpoint of the individual consumer who chooses it. If he chooses it, that disposes of the question of its relative utility to him, as compared with other forms of consumption that would not be deprecated on account of their wastefulness. Whatever form of expenditure the consumer chooses, or whatever end he seeks in making his choice, has utility to him by virtue of his preference. As seen from the point of view of the individual consumer, the question of wastefulness does not arise within the scope of economic theory proper. The use of the word "waste" as a technical term, therefore, implies no deprecation of the motives or of the ends sought by the consumer under this canon of conspicuous waste.

But it is, on other grounds, worth noting that the term "waste" in the language of everyday life implies deprecation of what is characterized as wasteful. This common-sense implication is itself an outcropping of the instinct of workmanship. The popular reprobation of waste goes to say that in order to be at peace with himself the common man must be able to see in any and all human effort and human enjoyment an enhancement of life and well-being on the whole. In order to meet with unqualified approval, any economic fact must approve itself under the test of impersonal usefulness—usefulness as seen from the point of view of the generically human. Relative or competitive advantage of one individual in comparison with another does not satisfy the economic conscience, and therefore competitive expenditure has not the approval of this conscience.

In strict accuracy nothing should be included under the head of conspicuous waste but such expenditure as is incurred on the ground of an invidious pecuniary comparison. But in order to bring any given item or element in under this head it is not necessary that it should be recognized as waste in this sense by the person incurring the expenditure. It frequently happens that an element of the standard of living which set out with being primarily wasteful, ends with becoming, in the apprehension of the consumer, a necessary of life; and it may in this way become as indispensable as any other item of the consumer's habitual expenditure. As items which sometimes fall under this head, and are therefore available as illustrations of the manner in which this principle applies, may be cited carpets and tapestries, silver table service, waiter's services, silk hats, starched linen, many articles of jewelry and of dress. The indispensability of these things after the habit and the convention have been formed, however, has little to say in the classification of expenditures as waste or not waste in the technical meaning of the word. The test to which all expenditure must be brought in an attempt to decide that point is the question whether it serves directly to enhance human life on the whole—whether it furthers the life process taken impersonally. For this is the basis of award of the instinct of workmanship, and that instinct is the court of final appeal in any question of economic truth or adequacy. It is a question as to the award rendered by a dispassionate common sense. The question is, therefore, not whether, under the existing circumstances of individual habit and social custom, a given expenditure conduces to the particular consumer's gratification or peace of mind; but whether, aside from acquired tastes and from the canons of usage and conventional decency, its result is a net gain in comfort or in the fullness of life. Customary expenditure must be classed under the head of waste in so far as the custom on which it rests is traceable to the habit of making an invidious pecuniary comparison—in so far as it is conceived that it could not have become customary and prescriptive without the backing of this principle of pecuniary reputability or relative economic success.

It is obviously not necessary that a given object of expenditure should be exclusively wasteful in order to come in under the category of conspicuous waste. An article may be useful and wasteful both, and its utility to the consumer may be made up of use and waste in the most varying proportions. Consumable goods, and even productive goods, generally show the two elements in combination, as constituents of their utility; although, in a general way, the element of waste tends to predominate in articles of consumption, while the contrary is true of articles designed for productive use. Even in articles which appear at first glance to serve for pure ostentation only, it is always possible to detect the presence of some, at least ostensible, useful purpose; and on the other hand, even in special machinery and tools contrived for some particular industrial process, as well as in the rudest appliances of human industry, the traces of conspicuous waste, or at least of the habit of ostentation, usually become evident on a close scrutiny. It would be hazardous to assert that a useful purpose is ever absent from the utility of any article or of any service, however obviously its prime purpose and chief element is conspicuous waste; and it would be only less hazardous to assert of any primarily useful product that the element of waste is in no way concerned in its value, immediately or remotely.

The Pecuniary Standard of Living

For the great body of the people in any modern community, the proximate ground of expenditure in excess of what is required for physical comfort is not a conscious effort to excel in the expensiveness of their visible consumption, so much as it is a desire to live up to the conventional standard of decency in the amount and grade of goods consumed. This desire is not guided by a rigidly invariable standard, which must be lived up to, and beyond which there is no incentive to go. The standard is flexible; and especially it is indefinitely extensible, if only time is allowed for habituation to any increase in pecuniary ability and for acquiring facility in the new and larger scale of expenditure that follows such an increase. It is much more difficult to recede from a scale of expenditure once adopted than it is to extend the accustomed scale in response to an accession of wealth. Many items of customary expenditure prove on analysis to be almost purely wasteful, and they are therefore honorific only, but after they have once been incorporated into the scale of decent consumption, and so have become an integral part of one's scheme of life, it is quite as hard to give up these as it is to give up many items that conduce directly to one's physical comfort, or even that may be necessary to life and health. That is to say, the conspicuously wasteful honorific expenditure that confers spiritual well-being may become more indispensable than much of that expenditure which ministers to the "lower" wants of physical well-being or sustenance only. It is notoriously just as difficult to recede from a "high" standard of living as it is to lower a standard which is already relatively low; although in the former case the difficulty is a moral one, while in the latter it may involve a material deduction from the physical comforts of life.

But while retrogression is difficult, a fresh advance in conspicuous expenditure is relatively easy; indeed, it takes place almost as a matter of course. In the rare cases where it occurs, a failure to increase one's visible consumption when the means for an increase are at hand is felt in popular apprehension to call for explanation, and unworthy motives of miserliness are imputed to those who fall short in this respect. A prompt response to the stimulus, on the other hand, is accepted as the normal effect. This suggests that the standard of expenditure which commonly guides our efforts is not the average, ordinary expenditure already achieved; it is an ideal of consumption that lies just beyond our reach, or to reach which requires some strain. The motive is emulation—the stimulus of an invidious comparison which prompts us to outdo those with whom we are in the habit of classing ourselves. Substantially the same proposition is expressed in the commonplace remark that each class envies and emulates the class next above it in the social scale, while it rarely compares itself with those below or with those who are considerably in advance. That is to say, in other words, our standard of decency in expenditure, as in other ends of emulation, is set by the usage of those next above us in reputability; until, in this way, especially in any community where class distinctions are somewhat vague, all canons of reputability and decency, and all standards of consumption, are traced back by insensible gradations to the usages and habits of thought of the highest social and pecuniary class—the wealthy leisure class.

It is for this class to determine, in general outline, what scheme of life the community shall accept as decent or honorific; and it is their office by precept and example to set forth this scheme of social salvation in its highest, ideal form. But the higher leisure class can exercise this quasi-sacerdotal office only under certain material limitations. The class cannot at discretion effect a sudden revolution or reversal of the popular habits of thought with respect to any of these ceremonial requirements. It takes time for any change to permeate the mass and change the habitual attitude of the people; and especially it takes time to change the habits of those classes that are socially more remote from the radiant body. The process is slower where the mobility of the population is less or where the intervals between the several classes are wider and more abrupt. But if time be allowed, the scope of the discretion of the leisure class as regards questions of form and detail in the community's scheme of life is large; while as regards the substantial principles of reputability, the changes which it can effect lie within a narrow margin of tolerance. Its example and precept carries the force of prescription for all classes below it; but in working out the precepts which are handed down as governing the form and method of reputability—in shaping the usages and the spiritual attitude of the lower classes—this authoritative prescription constantly works under the selective guidance of the canon of conspicuous waste, tempered in varying degree by the instinct of workmanship. To these norms is to be added another broad principle of human nature—the predatory animus—which in point of generality and of psychological content lies between the two just named. The effect of the latter in shaping the accepted scheme of life is yet to be discussed.

The canon of reputability, then, must adapt itself to the economic circumstances, the traditions, and the degree of spiritual maturity of the particular class whose scheme of life it is to regulate. It is especially to be noted that however high its authority and however true to the fundamental requirements of reputability it may have been at its inception, a specific formal observance can under no circumstances maintain itself in force if with the lapse of time or on its transmission to a lower pecuniary class it is found to run counter to the ultimate ground of decency among civilized peoples, namely, serviceability for the purpose of an invidious comparison in pecuniary success.

It is evident that these canons of expenditure have much to say in determining the standard of living for any community and for any class. It is no less evident that the standard of living which prevails at any time or at any given social altitude will in its turn have much to say as to the forms which honorific expenditure will take, and as to the degree to which this "higher" need will dominate a people's consumption. In this respect the control exerted by the accepted standard of living is chiefly of a negative character; it acts almost solely to prevent recession from a scale of conspicuous expenditure that has once become habitual.

A standard of living is of the nature of habit. It is an habitual scale and method of responding to given stimuli. The difficulty in the way of receding from an accustomed standard is the difficulty of breaking a habit that has once been formed. The relative facility with which an advance in the standard is made means that the life process is a process of unfolding activity and that it will readily unfold in a new direction whenever and wherever the resistance to self-expression decreases. But when the habit of expression along such a given line of low resistance has once been formed, the discharge will seek the accustomed outlet even after a change has taken place in the environment whereby the external resistance has appreciably risen. That heightened facility of expression in a given direction which is called habit may offset a considerable increase in the resistance offered by external circumstances to the unfolding of life in the given direction. As between the various habits, or habitual modes and directions of expression, which go to make up an individual's standard of living, there is an appreciable difference in point of persistence under counteracting circumstances and in point of the degree of imperativeness with which the discharge seeks a given direction.

That is to say, in the language of current economic theory, while men are reluctant to retrench their expenditures in any direction, they are more reluctant to retrench in some directions than in others; so that while any accustomed consumption is reluctantly given up there are certain lines of consumption which are given up, with relatively extreme reluctance. The articles or forms of consumption to which the consumer clings with the greatest tenacity are commonly the so-called necessaries of life, or the subsistence minimum. The subsistence minimum is of course not a rigidly determined allowance of goods, definite and invariable in kind and quantity; but for the purpose in hand it may be taken to comprise a certain, more or less definite, aggregate of consumption required for the maintenance of life. This minimum, it may be assumed, is ordinarily given up last in case of a progressive retrenchment of expenditure. That is to say, in a general way, the most ancient and ingrained of the habits which govern the individual's life—those habits that touch his existence as an organism—are the most persistent and imperative. Beyond these come the higher wants—later-formed habits of the individual or the race—in a somewhat irregular and by no means invariable gradation. Some of these higher wants, as for instance the habitual use of certain stimulants, or the need of salvation (in the eschatological sense), or of good repute, may in some cases take precedence of the lower or more elementary wants. In general, the longer the habituation, the more unbroken the habit, and the more nearly it coincides with previous habitual forms of the life process, the more persistently will the given habit assert itself. The habit will be stronger if the particular traits of human nature which its action involves, or the particular aptitudes that find exercise in it, are traits or aptitudes that are already largely and profoundly concerned in the life process or that are intimately bound up with the life history of the particular racial stock.

The varying degrees of ease with which different habits are formed by different persons, as well as the varying degrees of reluctance with which different habits are given up, goes to say that the formation of specific habits is not a matter of length of habituation simply. Inherited aptitudes and traits of temperament count for quite as much as length of habituation in deciding what range of habits will come to dominate any individual's scheme of life. And the prevalent type of transmitted aptitudes, or in other words the type of temperament belonging to the dominant ethnic element in any community, will go far to decide what will be the scope and form of expression of the community's habitual life process. How greatly the transmitted idiosyncrasies of aptitude may count in the way of a rapid and definitive formation of habit in individuals is illustrated by the extreme facility with which an all-dominating habit of alcoholism is sometimes formed; or in the similar facility and the similarly inevitable formation of a habit of devout observances in the case of persons gifted with a special aptitude in that direction. Much the same meaning attaches to that peculiar facility of habituation to a specific human environment that is called romantic love.

Men differ in respect of transmitted aptitudes, or in respect of the relative facility with which they unfold their life activity in particular directions; and the habits which coincide with or proceed upon a relatively strong specific aptitude or a relatively great specific facility of expression become of great consequence to the man's well-being. The part played by this element of aptitude in determining the relative tenacity of the several habits which constitute the standard of living goes to explain the extreme reluctance with which men give up any habitual expenditure in the way of conspicuous consumption. The aptitudes or propensities to which a habit of this kind is to be referred as its ground are those aptitudes whose exercise is comprised in emulation; and the propensity for emulation—for invidious comparison—is of ancient growth and is a pervading trait of human nature. It is easily called into vigorous activity in any new form, and it asserts itself with great insistence under any form under which it has once found habitual expression. When the individual has once formed the habit of seeking expression in a given line of honorific expenditure—when a given set of stimuli have come to be habitually responded to in activity of a given kind and direction under the guidance of these alert and deep-reaching propensities of emulation—it is with extreme reluctance that such an habitual expenditure is given up. And on the other hand, whenever an accession of pecuniary strength puts the individual in a position to unfold his life process in larger scope and with additional reach, the ancient propensities of the race will assert themselves in determining the direction which the new unfolding of life is to take. And those propensities which are already actively in the field under some related form of expression, which are aided by the pointed suggestions afforded by a current accredited scheme of life, and for the exercise of which the material means and opportunities are readily available—these will especially have much to say in shaping the form and direction in which the new accession to the individual's aggregate force will assert itself. That is to say, in concrete terms, in any community where conspicuous consumption is an element of the scheme of life, an increase in an individual's ability to pay is likely to take the form of an expenditure for some accredited line of conspicuous consumption.

With the exception of the instinct of self-preservation, the propensity for emulation is probably the strongest and most alert and persistent of the economic motives proper. In an industrial community this propensity for emulation expresses itself in pecuniary emulation; and this, so far as regards the Western civilized communities of the present, is virtually equivalent to saying that it expresses itself in some form of conspicuous waste. The need of conspicuous waste, therefore, stands ready to absorb any increase in the community's industrial efficiency or output of goods, after the most elementary physical wants have been provided for. Where this result does not follow, under modern conditions, the reason for the discrepancy is commonly to be sought in a rate of increase in the individual's wealth too rapid for the habit of expenditure to keep abreast of it; or it may be that the individual in question defers the conspicuous consumption of the increment to a later date—ordinarily with a view to heightening the spectacular effect of the aggregate expenditure contemplated. As increased industrial efficiency makes it possible to procure the means of livelihood with less labor, the energies of the industrious members of the community are bent to the compassing of a higher result in conspicuous expenditure, rather than slackened to a more comfortable pace. The strain is not lightened as industrial efficiency increases and makes a lighter strain possible, but the increment of output is turned to use to meet this want, which is indefinitely expansible, after the manner commonly imputed in economic theory to higher or spiritual wants. It is owing chiefly to the presence of this element in the standard of living that J.S. Mill was able to say that "hitherto it is questionable if all the mechanical inventions yet made have lightened the day's toil of any human being."

The accepted standard of expenditure in the community or in the class to which a person belongs largely determines what his standard of living will be. It does this directly by commending itself to his common sense as right and good, through his habitually contemplating it and assimilating the scheme of life in which it belongs; but it does so also indirectly through popular insistence on conformity to the accepted scale of expenditure as a matter of propriety, under pain of disesteem and ostracism. To accept and practice the standard of living which is in vogue is both agreeable and expedient, commonly to the point of being indispensable to personal comfort and to success in life. The standard of living of any class, so far as concerns the element of conspicuous waste, is commonly as high as the earning capacity of the class will permit—with a constant tendency to go higher. The effect upon the serious activities of men is therefore to direct them with great singleness of purpose to the largest possible acquisition of wealth, and to discountenance work that brings no pecuniary gain. At the same time the effect on consumption is to concentrate it upon the lines which are most patent to the observers whose good opinion is sought; while the inclinations and aptitudes whose exercise does not involve an honorific expenditure of time or substance tend to fall into abeyance through disuse.

Through this discrimination in favor of visible consumption it has come about that the domestic life of most classes is relatively shabby, as compared with the éclat of that overt portion of their life that is carried on before the eyes of observers. As a secondary consequence of the same discrimination, people habitually screen their private life from observation. So far as concerns that portion of their consumption that may without blame be carried on in secret, they withdraw from all contact with their neighbors. Hence the exclusiveness of people, as regards their domestic life, in most of the industrially developed communities; and hence, by remoter derivation, the habit of privacy and reserve that is so large a feature in the code of proprieties of the better classes in all communities. The low birthrate of the classes upon whom the requirements of reputable expenditure fall with great urgency is likewise traceable to the exigencies of a standard of living based on conspicuous waste. The conspicuous consumption, and the consequent increased expense, required in the reputable maintenance of a child is very considerable and acts as a powerful deterrent. It is probably the most effectual of the Malthusian prudential checks.

The effect of this factor of the standard of living, both in the way of retrenchment in the obscurer elements of consumption that go to physical comfort and maintenance, and also in the paucity or absence of children, is perhaps seen at its best among the classes given to scholarly pursuits. Because of a presumed superiority and scarcity of the gifts and attainments that characterize their life, these classes are by convention subsumed under a higher social grade than their pecuniary grade should warrant. The scale of decent expenditure in their case is pitched correspondingly high, and it consequently leaves an exceptionally narrow margin disposable for the other ends of life. By force of circumstances, their own habitual sense of what is good and right in these matters, as well as the expectations of the community in the way of pecuniary decency among the learned, are excessively high—as measured by the prevalent degree of opulence and earning capacity of the class, relatively to the non-scholarly classes whose social equals they nominally are. In any modern community where there is no priestly monopoly of these occupations, the people of scholarly pursuits are unavoidably thrown into contact with classes that are pecuniarily their superiors. The high standard of pecuniary decency in force among these superior classes is transfused among the scholarly classes with but little mitigation of its rigor; and as a consequence there is no class of the community that spends a larger proportion of its substance in conspicuous waste than these.

Pecuniary Canons of Taste

The caution has already been repeated more than once, that while the regulating norm of consumption is in large part the requirement of conspicuous waste, it must not be understood that the motive on which the consumer acts in any given case is this principle in its bald, unsophisticated form. Ordinarily his motive is a wish to conform to established usage, to avoid unfavorable notice and comment, to live up to the accepted canons of decency in the kind, amount, and grade of goods consumed, as well as in the decorous employment of his time and effort. In the common run of cases this sense of prescriptive usage is present in the motives of the consumer and exerts a direct constraining force, especially as regards consumption carried on under the eyes of observers. But a considerable element of prescriptive expensiveness is observable also in consumption that does not in any appreciable degree become known to outsiders—as, for instance, articles of underclothing, some articles of food, kitchen utensils, and other household apparatus designed for service rather than for evidence. In all such useful articles a close scrutiny will discover certain features which add to the cost and enhance the commercial value of the goods in question, but do not proportionately increase the serviceability of these articles for the material purposes which alone they ostensibly are designed to serve.

Under the selective surveillance of the law of conspicuous waste there grows up a code of accredited canons of consumption, the effect of which is to hold the consumer up to a standard of expensiveness and wastefulness in his consumption of goods and in his employment of time and effort. This growth of prescriptive usage has an immediate effect upon economic life, but it has also an indirect and remoter effect upon conduct in other respects as well. Habits of thought with respect to the expression of life in any given direction unavoidably affect the habitual view of what is good and right in life in other directions also. In the organic complex of habits of thought which make up the substance of an individual's conscious life the economic interest does not lie isolated and distinct from all other interests. Something, for instance, has already been said of its relation to the canons of reputability.

The principle of conspicuous waste guides the formation of habits of thought as to what is honest and reputable in life and in commodities. In so doing, this principle will traverse other norms of conduct which do not primarily have to do with the code of pecuniary honor, but which have, directly or incidentally, an economic significance of some magnitude. So the canon of honorific waste may, immediately or remotely, influence the sense of duty, the sense of beauty, the sense of utility, the sense of devotional or ritualistic fitness, and the scientific sense of truth.

It is scarcely necessary to go into a discussion here of the particular points at which, or the particular manner in which, the canon of honorific expenditure habitually traverses the canons of moral conduct. The matter is one which has received large attention and illustration at the hands of those whose office it is to watch and admonish with respect to any departures from the accepted code of morals. In modern communities, where the dominant economic and legal feature of the community's life is the institution of private property, one of the salient features of the code of morals is the sacredness of property. There needs no insistence or illustration to gain assent to the proposition that the habit of holding private property inviolate is traversed by the other habit of seeking wealth for the sake of the good repute to be gained through its conspicuous consumption. Most offenses against property, especially offenses of an appreciable magnitude, come under this head. It is also a matter of common notoriety and byword that in offenses which result in a large accession of property to the offender he does not ordinarily incur the extreme penalty or the extreme obloquy with which his offense would be visited on the ground of the naïve moral code alone. The thief or swindler who has gained great wealth by his delinquency has a better chance than the small thief of escaping the rigorous penalty of the law; and some good repute accrues to him from his increased wealth and from his spending the irregularly acquired possessions in a seemly manner. A well-bred expenditure of his booty especially appeals with great effect to persons of a cultivated sense of the proprieties, and goes far to mitigate the sense of moral turpitude with which his dereliction is viewed by them. It may be noted also—and it is more immediately to the point—that we are all inclined to condone an offense against property in the case of a man whose motive is the worthy one of providing the means of a "decent" manner of life for his wife and children. If it is added that the wife has been "nurtured in the lap of luxury," that is accepted as an additional extenuating circumstance. That is to say, we are prone to condone such an offense where its aim is the honorific one of enabling the offender's wife to perform for him such an amount of vicarious consumption of time and substance as is demanded by the standard of pecuniary decency. In such a case the habit of approving the accustomed degree of conspicuous waste traverses the habit of deprecating violations of ownership, to the extent even of sometimes leaving the award of praise or blame uncertain. This is peculiarly true where the dereliction involves an appreciable predatory or piratical element.

This topic need scarcely be pursued farther here; but the remark may not be out of place that all that considerable body of morals that clusters about the concept of an inviolable ownership is itself a psychological precipitate of the traditional meritoriousness of wealth. And it should be added that this wealth which is held sacred is valued primarily for the sake of the good repute to be got through its conspicuous consumption.

The bearing of pecuniary decency upon the scientific spirit or the quest of knowledge will be taken up in some detail in a separate chapter. Also as regards the sense of devout or ritual merit and adequacy in this connection, little need be said in this place. That topic will also come up incidentally in a later chapter. Still, this usage of honorific expenditure has much to say in shaping popular tastes as to what is right and meritorious in sacred matters, and the bearing of the principle of conspicuous waste upon some of the commonplace devout observances and conceits may therefore be pointed out.

Obviously, the canon of conspicuous waste is accountable for a great portion of what may be called devout consumption; as, e.g., the consumption of sacred edifices, vestments, and other goods of the same class. Even in those modern cults to whose divinities is imputed a predilection for temples not built with hands, the sacred buildings and the other properties of the cult are constructed and decorated with some view to a reputable degree of wasteful expenditure. And it needs but little either of observation or introspection—and either will serve the turn—to assure us that the expensive splendor of the house of worship has an appreciable uplifting and mellowing effect upon the worshipper's frame of mind. It will serve to enforce the same fact if we reflect upon the sense of abject shamefulness with which any evidence of indigence or squalor about the sacred place affects all beholders. The accessories of any devout observance should be pecuniarily above reproach. This requirement is imperative, whatever latitude may be allowed with regard to these accessories in point of aesthetic or other serviceability.

It may also be in place to notice that in all communities, especially in neighborhoods where the standard of pecuniary decency for dwellings is not high, the local sanctuary is more ornate, more conspicuously wasteful in its architecture and decoration, than the dwelling-houses of the congregation. This is true of nearly all denominations and cults, whether Christian or Pagan, but it is true in a peculiar degree of the older and maturer cults. At the same time the sanctuary commonly contributes little if anything to the physical comfort of the members. Indeed, the sacred structure not only serves the physical well-being of the members to but a slight extent, as compared with their humbler dwelling-houses; but it is felt by all men that a right and enlightened sense of the true, the beautiful, and the good demands that in all expenditure on the sanctuary anything that might serve the comfort of the worshipper should be conspicuously absent. If any element of comfort is admitted in the fittings of the sanctuary, it should at least be scrupulously screened and masked under an ostensible austerity. In the most reputable latter-day houses of worship, where no expense is spared, the principle of austerity is carried to the length of making the fittings of the place a means of mortifying the flesh, especially in appearance. There are few persons of delicate tastes in the matter of devout consumption to whom this austerely wasteful discomfort does not appeal as intrinsically right and good. Devout consumption is of the nature of vicarious consumption. This canon of devout austerity is based on the pecuniary reputability of conspicuously wasteful consumption, backed by the principle that vicarious consumption should conspicuously not conduce to the comfort of the vicarious consumer.

The sanctuary and its fittings have something of this austerity in all the cults in which the saint or divinity to whom the sanctuary pertains is not conceived to be present and make personal use of the property for the gratification of luxurious tastes imputed to him. The character of the sacred paraphernalia is somewhat different in this respect in those cults where the habits of life imputed to the divinity more nearly approach those of an earthly patriarchal potentate—where he is conceived to make use of these consumable goods in person. In the latter case the sanctuary and its fittings take on more of the fashion given to goods destined for the conspicuous consumption of a temporal master or owner. On the other hand, where the sacred apparatus is simply employed in the divinity's service, that is to say, where it is consumed vicariously on his account by his servants, there the sacred properties take the character suited to goods that are destined for vicarious consumption only.

In the latter case the sanctuary and the sacred apparatus are so contrived as not to enhance the comfort or fullness of life of the vicarious consumer, or at any rate not to convey the impression that the end of their consumption is the consumer's comfort. For the end of vicarious consumption is to enhance, not the fullness of life of the consumer, but the pecuniary repute of the master for whose behoof the consumption takes place. Therefore priestly vestments are notoriously expensive, ornate, and inconvenient; and in the cults where the priestly servitor of the divinity is not conceived to serve him in the capacity of consort, they are of an austere, comfortless fashion. And such it is felt that they should be.

It is not only in establishing a devout standard of decent expensiveness that the principle of waste invades the domain of the canons of ritual serviceability. It touches the ways as well as the means, and draws on vicarious leisure as well as on vicarious consumption. Priestly demeanor at its best is aloof, leisurely, perfunctory, and uncontaminated with suggestions of sensuous pleasure. This holds true, in different degrees of course, for the different cults and denominations; but in the priestly life of all anthropomorphic cults the marks of a vicarious consumption of time are visible.

The same pervading canon of vicarious leisure is also visibly present in the exterior details of devout observances and need only be pointed out in order to become obvious to all beholders. All ritual has a notable tendency to reduce itself to a rehearsal of formulas. This development of formula is most noticeable in the maturer cults, which have at the same time a more austere, ornate, and severe priestly life and garb; but it is perceptible also in the forms and methods of worship of the newer and fresher sects, whose tastes in respect of priests, vestments, and sanctuaries are less exacting. The rehearsal of the service (the term "service" carries a suggestion significant for the point in question) grows more perfunctory as the cult gains in age and consistency, and this perfunctoriness of the rehearsal is very pleasing to the correct devout taste. And with a good reason, for the fact of its being perfunctory goes to say pointedly that the master for whom it is performed is exalted above the vulgar need of actually proficuous service on the part of his servants. They are unprofitable servants, and there is an honorific implication for their master in their remaining unprofitable. It is needless to point out the close analogy at this point between the priestly office and the office of the footman. It is pleasing to our sense of what is fitting in these matters, in either case, to recognize in the obvious perfunctoriness of the service that it is a *pro forma* execution only. There should be no show of agility or of dexterous manipulation in the execution of the priestly office, such as might suggest a capacity for turning off the work.

In all this there is of course an obvious implication as to the temperament, tastes, propensities, and habits of life imputed to the divinity by worshippers who live under the tradition of these pecuniary canons of reputability. Through its pervading men's habits of thought, the principle of conspicuous waste has colored the worshippers' notions of the divinity and of the relation in which the human subject stands to him. It is of course in the more naïve cults that this suffusion of pecuniary beauty is most patent, but it is visible throughout. All peoples, at whatever stage of culture or degree of enlightenment, are fain to eke out a sensibly scant degree of authentic information regarding the personality and habitual surroundings of their divinities. In so calling in the aid of fancy to enrich and fill in their picture of the divinity's presence and manner of life they habitually impute to him such traits as go to make up their ideal of a worthy man. And in seeking communion with the divinity the ways and means of approach are assimilated as nearly as may be to the divine ideal that is in men's minds at the time. It is felt that the divine presence is entered with the best grace, and with the best effect, according to certain accepted methods and with the accompaniment of certain accepted methods and with the accompaniment of certain material circumstances which in popular apprehension are peculiarly consonant with the divine nature. This popularly accepted ideal of the bearing and paraphernalia adequate to such occasions of communion is, of course, to a good extent shaped by the popular apprehension of what is intrinsically worthy and beautiful in human carriage and surroundings on all occasions of dignified intercourse. It would on this account be misleading to attempt an analysis of devout demeanor by referring all evidences of the presence of a pecuniary standard of reputability back directly and baldly to the underlying norm of pecuniary emulation. So it would also be misleading to ascribe to the divinity, as popularly conceived, a jealous regard for his pecuniary standing and a habit of avoiding and condemning squalid situations and surroundings simply because they are under grade in the pecuniary respect.

And still, after all allowance has been made, it appears that the canons of pecuniary reputability do, directly or indirectly, materially affect our notions of the attributes of divinity, as well as our notion of what are the fit and adequate manner and circumstances of divine communion. It is felt that the divinity must be of a peculiarly serene and leisurely habit of life. And whenever his local habitation is pictured in poetic imagery, for edification or in appeal to the devout fancy, the devout word-painter, as a matter of course, brings out before his auditors' imagination a throne with a profusion of the insignia of opulence and power, and surrounded by a great number of servitors. In the common run of such presentations of the celestial abodes, the office of this corps of servants is a vicarious leisure, their time and efforts being in great measure taken up with an industrially unproductive rehearsal of the meritorious characteristics and exploits of the divinity; while the background of the presentation is filled with the shimmer of the precious metals and of the more expensive varieties of precious stones. It is only in the crasser expressions of devout fancy that this intrusion of pecuniary canons into the devout ideals reaches such an extreme. An extreme case occurs in the devout imagery of the negro population of the South. Their word-painters are unable to descend to anything cheaper than gold; so that in this case the insistence on pecuniary beauty gives a startling effect in yellow—such as would be unbearable to a soberer taste. Still, there is probably no cult in which ideals of pecuniary merit have not been called in to supplement the ideals of ceremonial adequacy that guide men's conception of what is right in the matter of sacred apparatus.

Similarly it is felt—and the sentiment is acted upon—that the priestly servitors of the divinity should not engage in industrially productive work; that work of any kind—any employment which is of tangible human use—must not be carried on in the divine presence, or within the precincts of the sanctuary; that whoever comes into the presence should come cleansed of all profane industrial features in his apparel or person, and should come clad in garments of more than everyday expensiveness; that on holidays set apart in honor of or for communion with the divinity no work that is of human use should be performed by any one. Even the remoter, lay dependents should render a vicarious leisure to the extent of one day in seven.

In all these deliverances of men's uninstructed sense of what is fit and proper in devout observance and in the relations of the divinity, the effectual presence of the canons of pecuniary reputability is obvious enough, whether these canons have had their effect on the devout judgment in this respect immediately or at the second remove.

These canons of reputability have had a similar, but more far-reaching and more specifically determinable, effect upon the popular sense of beauty or serviceability in consumable goods. The requirements of pecuniary decency have, to a very appreciable extent, influenced the sense of beauty and of utility in articles of use or beauty. Articles are to an extent preferred for use on account of their being conspicuously wasteful; they are felt to be serviceable somewhat in proportion as they are wasteful and ill adapted to their ostensible use.

The utility of articles valued for their beauty depends closely upon the expensiveness of the articles. A homely illustration will bring out this dependence. A hand-wrought silver spoon, of a commercial value of some ten to twenty dollars, is not ordinarily more serviceable—in the first sense of the word—than a machine-made spoon of the same material. It may not even be more serviceable than a machine-made spoon of some "base" metal, such as aluminum, the value of which may be no more than some ten to twenty cents. The former of the two utensils is, in fact, commonly a less effective contrivance for its ostensible purpose than the latter. The objection is of course ready to hand that, in taking this view of the matter, one of the chief uses, if not the chief use, of the costlier spoon is ignored; the hand-wrought spoon gratifies our taste, our sense of the beautiful, while that made by machinery out of the base metal has no useful office beyond a brute efficiency. The facts are no doubt as the objection states them, but it will be evident on reflection that the objection is after all more plausible than conclusive. It appears (1) that while the different materials of which the two spoons are made each possesses beauty and serviceability for the purpose for which it is used, the material of the hand-wrought spoon is some one hundred times more valuable than the baser metal, without very greatly excelling the latter in intrinsic beauty of grain or color, and without being in any appreciable degree superior in point of mechanical serviceability; (2) if a close inspection should show that the supposed hand-wrought spoon were in reality only a very clever imitation of hand-wrought goods, but an imitation so cleverly wrought as to give the same impression of line and surface to any but a minute examination by a trained eye, the utility of the article, including the gratification which the user derives from its contemplation as an object of beauty, would immediately decline by some eighty or ninety per cent, or even more; (3) if the two spoons are, to a fairly close observer, so nearly identical in appearance that the lighter weight of the spurious article alone betrays it, this identity of form and color will scarcely add to the value of the machine-made spoon, nor appreciably enhance the gratification of the user's "sense of beauty" in contemplating it, so long as the cheaper spoon is not a novelty, and so long as it can be procured at a nominal cost.

The case of the spoons is typical. The superior gratification derived from the use and contemplation of costly and supposedly beautiful products is, commonly, in great measure a gratification of our sense of costliness masquerading under the name of beauty. Our higher appreciation of the superior article is an appreciation of its superior honorific character, much more frequently than it is an unsophisticated appreciation of its beauty. The requirement of conspicuous wastefulness is not commonly present, consciously, in our canons of taste, but it is none the less present as a constraining norm selectively shaping and sustaining our sense of what is beautiful, and guiding our discrimination with respect to what may legitimately be approved as beautiful and what may not.

It is at this point, where the beautiful and the honorific meet and blend, that a discrimination between serviceability and wastefulness is most difficult in any concrete case. It frequently happens that an article which serves the honorific purpose of conspicuous waste is at the same time a beautiful object; and the same application of labor to which it owes its utility for the former purpose may, and often does, go to give beauty of form and color to the article. The question is further complicated by the fact that many objects, as, for instance, the precious stones and metals and some other materials used for adornment and decoration, owe their utility as items of conspicuous waste to an antecedent utility as objects of beauty. Gold, for instance, has a high degree of sensuous beauty; very many if not most of the highly prized works of art are intrinsically beautiful, though often with material qualification; the like is true of some stuffs used for clothing, of some landscapes, and of many other things in less degree. Except for this intrinsic beauty which they possess, these objects would scarcely have been coveted as they are, or have become monopolized objects of pride to their possessors and users. But the utility of these things to the possessor is commonly due less to their intrinsic beauty than to the honor which their possession and consumption confers, or to the obloquy which it wards off.

Apart from their serviceability in other respects, these objects are beautiful and have a utility as such; they are valuable on this account if they can be appropriated or monopolized; they are, therefore, coveted as valuable possessions, and their exclusive enjoyment gratifies the possessor's sense of pecuniary superiority at the same time that their contemplation gratifies his sense of beauty. But their beauty, in the naïve sense of the word, is the occasion rather than the ground of their monopolization or of their commercial value. "Great as is the sensuous beauty of gems, their rarity and price adds an expression of distinction to them, which they would never have if they were cheap." There is, indeed, in the common run of cases under this head, relatively little incentive to the exclusive possession and use of these beautiful things, except on the ground of their honorific character as items of conspicuous waste. Most objects of this general class, with the partial exception of articles of personal adornment, would serve all other purposes than the honorific one equally well, whether owned by the person viewing them or not; and even as regards personal ornaments it is to be added that their chief purpose is to lend éclat to the person of their wearer (or owner) by comparison with other persons who are compelled to do without. The aesthetic serviceability of objects of beauty is not greatly nor universally heightened by possession.

The generalization for which the discussion so far affords ground is that any valuable object in order to appeal to our sense of beauty must conform to the requirements of beauty and of expensiveness both. But this is not all. Beyond this the canon of expensiveness also affects our tastes in such a way as to inextricably blend the marks of expensiveness, in our appreciation, with the beautiful features of the object, and to subsume the resultant effect under the head of an appreciation of beauty simply. The marks of expensiveness come to be accepted as beautiful features of the expensive articles. They are pleasing as being marks of honorific costliness, and the pleasure which they afford on this score blends with that afforded by the beautiful form and color of the object; so that we often declare that an article of apparel, for instance, is "perfectly lovely," when pretty much all that an analysis of the aesthetic value of the article would leave ground for is the declaration that it is pecuniarily honorific.

This blending and confusion of the elements of expensiveness and of beauty is, perhaps, best exemplified in articles of dress and of household furniture. The code of reputability in matters of dress decides what shapes, colors, materials, and general effects in human apparel are for the time to be accepted as suitable; and departures from the code are offensive to our taste, supposedly as being departures from aesthetic truth. The approval with which we look upon fashionable attire is by no means to be accounted pure make-believe. We readily, and for the most part with utter sincerity, find those things pleasing that are in vogue. Shaggy dress-stuffs and pronounced color effects, for instance, offend us at times when the vogue is goods of a high, glossy finish and neutral colors. A fancy bonnet of this year's model unquestionably appeals to our sensibilities today much more forcibly than an equally fancy bonnet of the model of last year; although when viewed in the perspective of a quarter of a century, it would, I apprehend, be a matter of the utmost difficulty to award the palm for intrinsic beauty to the one rather than to the other of these structures. So, again, it may be remarked that, considered simply in their physical juxtaposition with the human form, the high gloss of a gentleman's hat or of a patent-leather shoe has no more of intrinsic beauty than a similarly high gloss on a threadbare sleeve; and yet there is no question but that all well-bred people (in the Occidental civilized communities) instinctively and unaffectedly cleave to the one as a phenomenon of great beauty, and eschew the other as offensive to every sense to which it can appeal. It is extremely doubtful if any one could be induced to wear such a contrivance as the high hat of civilized society, except for some urgent reason based on other than aesthetic grounds.

By further habituation to an appreciative perception of the marks of expensiveness in goods, and by habitually identifying beauty with reputability, it comes about that a beautiful article which is not expensive is accounted not beautiful. In this way it has happened, for instance, that some beautiful flowers pass conventionally for offensive weeds; others that can be cultivated with relative ease are accepted and admired by the lower middle class, who can afford no more expensive luxuries of this kind; but these varieties are rejected as vulgar by those people who are better able to pay for expensive flowers and who are educated to a higher schedule of pecuniary beauty in the florist's products; while still other flowers, of no greater intrinsic beauty than these, are cultivated at great cost and call out much admiration from flower-lovers whose tastes have been matured under the critical guidance of a polite environment.

The same variation in matters of taste, from one class of society to another, is visible also as regards many other kinds of consumable goods, as, for example, is the case with furniture, houses, parks, and gardens. This diversity of views as to what is beautiful in these various classes of goods is not a diversity of the norm according to which the unsophisticated sense of the beautiful works. It is not a constitutional difference of endowments in the aesthetic respect, but rather a difference in the code of reputability which specifies what objects properly lie within the scope of honorific consumption for the class to which the critic belongs. It is a difference in the traditions of propriety with respect to the kinds of things which may, without derogation to the consumer, be consumed under the head of objects of taste and art. With a certain allowance for variations to be accounted for on other grounds, these traditions are determined, more or less rigidly, by the pecuniary plane of life of the class.

Everyday life affords many curious illustrations of the way in which the code of pecuniary beauty in articles of use varies from class to class, as well as of the way in which the conventional sense of beauty departs in its deliverances from the sense untutored by the requirements of pecuniary repute. Such a fact is the lawn, or the close-cropped yard or park, which appeals so unaffectedly to the taste of the Western peoples. It appears especially to appeal to the tastes of the well-to-do classes in those communities in which the dolicho-blond element predominates in an appreciable degree. The lawn unquestionably has an element of sensuous beauty, simply as an object of apperception, and as such no doubt it appeals pretty directly to the eye of nearly all races and all classes; but it is, perhaps, more unquestionably beautiful to the eye of the dolicho-blond than to most other varieties of men. This higher appreciation of a stretch of greensward in this ethnic element than in the other elements of the population, goes along with certain other features of the dolicho-blond temperament that indicate that this racial element had once been for a long time a pastoral people inhabiting a region with a humid climate. The close-cropped lawn is beautiful in the eyes of a people whose inherited bent it is to readily find pleasure in contemplating a well-preserved pasture or grazing land.

For the aesthetic purpose the lawn is a cow pasture; and in some cases today—where the expensiveness of the attendant circumstances bars out any imputation of thrift—the idyl of the dolicho-blond is rehabilitated in the introduction of a cow into a lawn or private ground. In such cases the cow made use of is commonly of an expensive breed. The vulgar suggestion of thrift, which is nearly inseparable from the cow, is a standing objection to the decorative use of this animal. So that in all cases, except where luxurious surroundings negate this suggestion, the use of the cow as an object of taste must be avoided. Where the predilection for some grazing animal to fill out the suggestion of the pasture is too strong to be suppressed, the cow's place is often given to some more or less inadequate substitute, such as deer, antelopes, or some such exotic beast. These substitutes, although less beautiful to the pastoral eye of Western man than the cow, are in such cases preferred because of their superior expensiveness or futility, and their consequent repute. They are not vulgarly lucrative either in fact or in suggestion.

Public parks of course fall in the same category with the lawn; they too, at their best, are imitations of the pasture. Such a park is of course best kept by grazing, and the cattle on the grass are themselves no mean addition to the beauty of the thing, as need scarcely be insisted on with any one who has once seen a well-kept pasture. But it is worth noting, as an expression of the pecuniary element in popular taste, that such a method of keeping public grounds is seldom resorted to. The best that is done by skilled workmen under the supervision of a trained keeper is a more or less close imitation of a pasture, but the result invariably falls somewhat short of the artistic effect of grazing. But to the average popular apprehension a herd of cattle so pointedly suggests thrift and usefulness that their presence in the public pleasure ground would be intolerably cheap. This method of keeping grounds is comparatively inexpensive, therefore it is indecorous.

Of the same general bearing is another feature of public grounds. There is a studious exhibition of expensiveness coupled with a make-believe of simplicity and crude serviceability. Private grounds also show the same physiognomy wherever they are in the management or ownership of persons whose tastes have been formed under middle-class habits of life or under the upper-class traditions of no later a date than the childhood of the generation that is now passing. Grounds which conform to the instructed tastes of the latter-day upper class do not show these features in so marked a degree. The reason for this difference in tastes between the past and the incoming generation of the well-bred lies in the changing economic situation. A similar difference is perceptible in other respects, as well as in the accepted ideals of pleasure grounds. In this country as in most others, until the last half century but a very small proportion of the population were possessed of such wealth as would exempt them from thrift. Owing to imperfect means of communication, this small fraction were scattered and out of effective touch with one another. There was therefore no basis for a growth of taste in disregard of expensiveness. The revolt of the well-bred taste against vulgar thrift was unchecked. Wherever the unsophisticated sense of beauty might show itself sporadically in an approval of inexpensive or thrifty surroundings, it would lack the "social confirmation" which nothing but a considerable body of like-minded people can give. There was, therefore, no effective upper-class opinion that would overlook evidences of possible inexpensiveness in the management of grounds; and there was consequently no appreciable divergence between the leisure-class and the lower middle-class ideal in the physiognomy of pleasure grounds. Both classes equally constructed their ideals with the fear of pecuniary disrepute before their eyes.

Today a divergence in ideals is beginning to be apparent. The portion of the leisure class that has been consistently exempt from work and from pecuniary cares for a generation or more is now large enough to form and sustain an opinion in matters of taste. Increased mobility of the members has also added to the facility with which a "social confirmation" can be attained within the class. Within this select class the exemption from thrift is a matter so commonplace as to have lost much of its utility as a basis of pecuniary decency. Therefore the latter-day upper-class canons of taste do not so consistently insist on an unremitting demonstration of expensiveness and a strict exclusion of the appearance of thrift. So, a predilection for the rustic and the "natural" in parks and grounds makes its appearance on these higher social and intellectual levels. This predilection is in large part an outcropping of the instinct of workmanship; and it works out its results with varying degrees of consistency. It is seldom altogether unaffected, and at times it shades off into something not widely different from that make-believe of rusticity which has been referred to above.

A weakness for crudely serviceable contrivances that pointedly suggest immediate and wasteless use is present even in the middle-class tastes; but it is there kept well in hand under the unbroken dominance of the canon of reputable futility. Consequently it works out in a variety of ways and means for shamming serviceability—in such contrivances as rustic fences, bridges, bowers, pavilions, and the like decorative features. An expression of this affectation of serviceability, at what is perhaps its widest divergence from the first promptings of the sense of economic beauty, is afforded by the cast-iron rustic fence and trellis or by a circuitous drive laid across level ground.

The select leisure class has outgrown the use of these pseudo-serviceable variants of pecuniary beauty at least at some points. But the taste of the more recent accessions to the leisure class proper and of the middle and lower classes still requires a pecuniary beauty to supplement the aesthetic beauty, even in those objects which are primarily admired for the beauty that belongs to them as natural growths.

The popular taste in these matters is to be seen in the prevalent high appreciation of topiary work and of the conventional flower-beds of public grounds. Perhaps as happy an illustration as may be had of this dominance of pecuniary beauty over aesthetic beauty in middle-class tastes is seen in the reconstruction of the grounds lately occupied by the Columbian Exposition. The evidence goes to show that the requirement of reputable expensiveness is still present in good vigor even where all ostensibly lavish display is avoided. The artistic effects actually wrought in this work of reconstruction diverge somewhat widely from the effect to which the same ground would have lent itself in hands not guided by pecuniary canons of taste. And even the better class of the city's population view the progress of the work with an unreserved approval which suggests that there is in this case little if any discrepancy between the tastes of the upper and the lower or middle classes of the city. The sense of beauty in the population of this representative city of the advanced pecuniary culture is very chary of any departure from its great cultural principle of conspicuous waste.

The love of nature, perhaps itself borrowed from a higher-class code of taste, sometimes expresses itself in unexpected ways under the guidance of this canon of pecuniary beauty, and leads to results that may seem incongruous to an unreflecting beholder. The well-accepted practice of planting trees in the treeless areas of this country, for instance, has been carried over as an item of honorific expenditure into the heavily wooded areas; so that it is by no means unusual for a village or a farmer in the wooded country to clear the land of its native trees and immediately replant saplings of certain introduced varieties about the farmyard or along the streets. In this way a forest growth of oak, elm, beech, butternut, hemlock, basswood, and birch is cleared off to give room for saplings of soft maple, cottonwood, and brittle willow. It is felt that the inexpensiveness of leaving the forest trees standing would derogate from the dignity that should invest an article which is intended to serve a decorative and honorific end.

The like pervading guidance of taste by pecuniary repute is traceable in the prevalent standards of beauty in animals. The part played by this canon of taste in assigning her place in the popular aesthetic scale to the cow has already been spoken of. Something to the same effect is true of the other domestic animals, so far as they are in an appreciable degree industrially useful to the community—as, for instance, barnyard fowl, hogs, cattle, sheep, goats, draught-horses. They are of the nature of productive goods, and serve a useful, often a lucrative end; therefore beauty is not readily imputed to them. The case is different with those domestic animals which ordinarily serve no industrial end; such as pigeons, parrots and other cage-birds, cats, dogs, and fast horses. These commonly are items of conspicuous consumption, and are therefore honorific in their nature and may legitimately be accounted beautiful. This class of animals are conventionally admired by the body of the upper classes, while the pecuniary lower classes—and that select minority of the leisure class among whom the rigorous canon that abjures thrift is in a measure obsolescent—find beauty in one class of animals as in another, without drawing a hard and fast line of pecuniary demarcation between the beautiful and the ugly.

In the case of those domestic animals which are honorific and are reputed beautiful, there is a subsidiary basis of merit that should be spoken of. Apart from the birds which belong in the honorific class of domestic animals, and which owe their place in this class to their non-lucrative character alone, the animals which merit particular attention are cats, dogs, and fast horses. The cat is less reputable than the other two just named, because she is less wasteful; she may even serve a useful end. At the same time the cat's temperament does not fit her for the honorific purpose. She lives with man on terms of equality, knows nothing of that relation of status which is the ancient basis of all distinctions of worth, honor, and repute, and she does not lend herself with facility to an invidious comparison between her owner and his neighbors. The exception to this last rule occurs in the case of such scarce and fanciful products as the Angora cat, which have some slight honorific value on the ground of expensiveness, and have, therefore, some special claim to beauty on pecuniary grounds.

The dog has advantages in the way of uselessness as well as in special gifts of temperament. He is often spoken of, in an eminent sense, as the friend of man, and his intelligence and fidelity are praised. The meaning of this is that the dog is man's servant and that he has the gift of an unquestioning subservience and a slave's quickness in guessing his master's mood. Coupled with these traits, which fit him well for the relation of status—and which must for the present purpose be set down as serviceable traits—the dog has some characteristics which are of a more equivocal aesthetic value. He is the filthiest of the domestic animals in his person and the nastiest in his habits. For this he makes up in a servile, fawning attitude towards his master, and a readiness to inflict damage and discomfort on all else. The dog, then, commends himself to our favor by affording play to our propensity for mastery, and as he is also an item of expense, and commonly serves no industrial purpose, he holds a well-assured place in men's regard as a thing of good repute. The dog is at the same time associated in our imagination with the chase—a meritorious employment and an expression of the honorable predatory impulse.

Standing on this vantage ground, whatever beauty of form and motion and whatever commendable mental traits he may possess are conventionally acknowledged and magnified. And even those varieties of the dog which have been bred into grotesque deformity by the dog-fancier are in good faith accounted beautiful by many. These varieties of dogs—and the like is true of other fancy-bred animals—are rated and graded in aesthetic value somewhat in proportion to the degree of grotesqueness and instability of the particular fashion which the deformity takes in the given case. For the purpose in hand, this differential utility on the ground of grotesqueness and instability of structure is reducible to terms of a greater scarcity and consequent expense.

The commercial value of canine monstrosities, such as the prevailing styles of pet dogs both for men's and women's use, rests on their high cost of production, and their value to their owners lies chiefly in their utility as items of conspicuous consumption. Indirectly, through reflection upon their honorific expensiveness, a social worth is imputed to them; and so, by an easy substitution of words and ideas, they come to be admired and reputed beautiful. Since any attention bestowed upon these animals is in no sense gainful or useful, it is also reputable; and since the habit of giving them attention is consequently not deprecated, it may grow into an habitual attachment of great tenacity and of a most benevolent character. So that in the affection bestowed on pet animals the canon of expensiveness is present more or less remotely as a norm which guides and shapes the sentiment and the selection of its object. The like is true, as will be noticed presently, with respect to affection for persons also; although the manner in which the norm acts in that case is somewhat different.

The case of the fast horse is much like that of the dog. He is on the whole expensive, or wasteful and useless—for the industrial purpose. What productive use he may possess, in the way of enhancing the well-being of the community or making the way of life easier for men, takes the form of exhibitions of force and facility of motion that gratify the popular aesthetic sense. This is of course a substantial serviceability. The horse is not endowed with the spiritual aptitude for servile dependence in the same measure as the dog; but he ministers effectually to his master's impulse to convert the "animate" forces of the environment to his own use and discretion and so express his own dominating individuality through them. The fast horse is at least potentially a racehorse, of high or low degree; and it is as such that he is peculiarly serviceable to his owner. The utility of the fast horse lies largely in his efficiency as a means of emulation; it gratifies the owner's sense of aggression and dominance to have his own horse outstrip his neighbor's. This use being not lucrative, but on the whole pretty consistently wasteful, and quite conspicuously so, it is honorific, and therefore gives the fast horse a strong presumptive position of reputability. Beyond this, the racehorse proper has also a similarly non-industrial but honorific use as a gambling instrument.

The fast horse, then, is aesthetically fortunate, in that the canon of pecuniary good repute legitimates a free appreciation of whatever beauty or serviceability he may possess. His pretensions have the countenance of the principle of conspicuous waste and the backing of the predatory aptitude for dominance and emulation. The horse is, moreover, a beautiful animal, although the racehorse is so in no peculiar degree to the uninstructed taste of those persons who belong neither in the class of racehorse fanciers nor in the class whose sense of beauty is held in abeyance by the moral constraint of the horse fancier's award. To this untutored taste the most beautiful horse seems to be a form which has suffered less radical alteration than the racehorse under the breeder's selective development of the animal. Still, when a writer or speaker—especially of those whose eloquence is most consistently commonplace—wants an illustration of animal grace and serviceability, for rhetorical use, he habitually turns to the horse; and he commonly makes it plain before he is done that what he has in mind is the racehorse.

It should be noted that in the graduated appreciation of varieties of horses and of dogs, such as one meets with among people of even moderately cultivated tastes in these matters, there is also discernible another and more direct line of influence of the leisure-class canons of reputability. In this country, for instance, leisure-class tastes are to some extent shaped on usages and habits which prevail, or which are apprehended to prevail, among the leisure class of Great Britain. In dogs this is true to a less extent than in horses. In horses, more particularly in saddle horses—which at their best serve the purpose of wasteful display simply—it will hold true in a general way that a horse is more beautiful in proportion as he is more English; the English leisure class being, for purposes of reputable usage, the upper leisure class of this country, and so the exemplar for the lower grades. This mimicry in the methods of the apperception of beauty and in the forming of judgments of taste need not result in a spurious, or at any rate not a hypocritical or affected, predilection. The predilection is as serious and as substantial an award of taste when it rests on this basis as when it rests on any other; the difference is that this taste is a taste for the reputably correct, not for the aesthetically true.

The mimicry, it should be said, extends further than to the sense of beauty in horseflesh simply. It includes trappings and horsemanship as well, so that the correct or reputably beautiful seat or posture is also decided by English usage, as well as the equestrian gait. To show how fortuitous may sometimes be the circumstances which decide what shall be becoming and what not under the pecuniary canon of beauty, it may be noted that this English seat, and the peculiarly distressing gait which has made an awkward seat necessary, are a survival from the time when the English roads were so bad with mire and mud as to be virtually impassable for a horse travelling at a more comfortable gait; so that a person of decorous tastes in horsemanship today rides a punch with docked tail, in an uncomfortable posture and at a distressing gait, because the English roads during a great part of the last century were impassable for a horse travelling at a more horse-like gait, or for an animal built for moving with ease over the firm and open country to which the horse is indigenous.

It is not only with respect to consumable goods—including domestic animals—that the canons of taste have been colored by the canons of pecuniary reputability. Something to the like effect is to be said for beauty in persons. In order to avoid whatever may be matter of controversy, no weight will be given in this connection to such popular predilection as there may be for the dignified (leisurely) bearing and portly presence that are by vulgar tradition associated with opulence in mature men. These traits are in some measure accepted as elements of personal beauty. But there are certain elements of feminine beauty, on the other hand, which come in under this head, and which are of so concrete and specific a character as to admit of itemized appreciation. It is more or less a rule that in communities which are at the stage of economic development at which women are valued by the upper class for their service, the ideal of female beauty is a robust, large-limbed woman. The ground of appreciation is the physique, while the conformation of the face is of secondary weight only. A well-known instance of this ideal of the early predatory culture is that of the maidens of the Homeric poems.

This ideal suffers a change in the succeeding development, when, in the conventional scheme, the office of the high-class wife comes to be a vicarious leisure simply. The ideal then includes the characteristics which are supposed to result from or to go with a life of leisure consistently enforced. The ideal accepted under these circumstances may be gathered from descriptions of beautiful women by poets and writers of the chivalric times. In the conventional scheme of those days ladies of high degree were conceived to be in perpetual tutelage, and to be scrupulously exempt from all useful work. The resulting chivalric or romantic ideal of beauty takes cognizance chiefly of the face, and dwells on its delicacy, and on the delicacy of the hands and feet, the slender figure, and especially the slender waist. In the pictured representations of the women of that time, and in modern romantic imitators of the chivalric thought and feeling, the waist is attenuated to a degree that implies extreme debility. The same ideal is still extant among a considerable portion of the population of modern industrial communities; but it is to be said that it has retained its hold most tenaciously in those modern communities which are least advanced in point of economic and civil development, and which show the most considerable survivals of status and of predatory institutions. That is to say, the chivalric ideal is best preserved in those existing communities which are substantially least modern. Survivals of this lackadaisical or romantic ideal occur freely in the tastes of the well-to-do classes of Continental countries.

In modern communities which have reached the higher levels of industrial development, the upper leisure class has accumulated so great a mass of wealth as to place its women above all imputation of vulgarly productive labor. Here the status of women as vicarious consumers is beginning to lose its place in the affections of the body of the people; and as a consequence the ideal of feminine beauty is beginning to change back again from the infirmly delicate, translucent, and hazardously slender, to a women of the archaic type that does not disown her hands and feet, nor, indeed, the other gross material facts of her person. In the course of economic development the ideal of beauty among the peoples of the Western culture has shifted from the woman of physical presence to the lady, and it is beginning to shift back again to the woman; and all in obedience to the changing conditions of pecuniary emulation. The exigencies of emulation at one time required lusty slaves; at another time they required a conspicuous performance of vicarious leisure and consequently an obvious disability; but the situation is now beginning to outgrow this last requirement, since, under the higher efficiency of modern industry, leisure in women is possible so far down the scale of reputability that it will no longer serve as a definitive mark of the highest pecuniary grade.

Apart from this general control exercised by the norm of conspicuous waste over the ideal of feminine beauty, there are one or two details which merit specific mention as showing how it may exercise an extreme constraint in detail over men's sense of beauty in women. It has already been noticed that at the stages of economic evolution at which conspicuous leisure is much regarded as a means of good repute, the ideal requires delicate and diminutive hands and feet and a slender waist. These features, together with the other, related faults of structure that commonly go with them, go to show that the person so affected is incapable of useful effort and must therefore be supported in idleness by her owner. She is useless and expensive, and she is consequently valuable as evidence of pecuniary strength. It results that at this cultural stage women take thought to alter their persons, so as to conform more nearly to the requirements of the instructed taste of the time; and under the guidance of the canon of pecuniary decency, the men find the resulting artificially induced pathological features attractive. So, for instance, the constricted waist which has had so wide and persistent a vogue in the communities of the Western culture, and so also the deformed foot of the Chinese. Both of these are mutilations of unquestioned repulsiveness to the untrained sense. It requires habituation to become reconciled to them. Yet there is no room to question their attractiveness to men into whose scheme of life they fit as honorific items sanctioned by the requirements of pecuniary reputability. They are items of pecuniary and cultural beauty which have come to do duty as elements of the ideal of womanliness.

The connection here indicated between the aesthetic value and the invidious pecuniary value of things is of course not present in the consciousness of the valuer. So far as a person, in forming a judgment of taste, takes thought and reflects that the object of beauty under consideration is wasteful and reputable, and therefore may legitimately be accounted beautiful; so far the judgment is not a *bona fide* judgment of taste and does not come up for consideration in this connection. The connection which is here insisted on between the reputability and the apprehended beauty of objects lies through the effect which the fact of reputability has upon the valuer's habits of thought. He is in the habit of forming judgments of value of various kinds—economic, moral, aesthetic, or reputable—concerning the objects with which he has to do, and his attitude of commendation towards a given object on any other ground will affect the degree of his appreciation of the object when he comes to value it for the aesthetic purpose. This is more particularly true as regards valuation on grounds so closely related to the aesthetic ground as that of reputability. The valuation for the aesthetic purpose and for the purpose of repute are not held apart as distinctly as might be. Confusion is especially apt to arise between these two kinds of valuation, because the value of objects for repute is not habitually distinguished in speech by the use of a special descriptive term. The result is that the terms in familiar use to designate categories or elements of beauty are applied to cover this unnamed element of pecuniary merit, and the corresponding confusion of ideas follows by easy consequence. The demands of reputability in this way coalesce in the popular apprehension with the demands of the sense of beauty, and beauty which is not accompanied by the accredited marks of good repute is not accepted. But the requirements of pecuniary reputability and those of beauty in the naïve sense do not in any appreciable degree coincide. The elimination from our surroundings of the pecuniarily unfit, therefore, results in a more or less thorough elimination of that considerable range of elements of beauty which do not happen to conform to the pecuniary requirement.

The underlying norms of taste are of very ancient growth, probably far antedating the advent of the pecuniary institutions that are here under discussion. Consequently, by force of the past selective adaptation of men's habits of thought, it happens that the requirements of beauty, simply, are for the most part best satisfied by inexpensive contrivances and structures which in a straightforward manner suggest both the office which they are to perform and the method of serving their end.

It may be in place to recall the modern psychological position. Beauty of form seems to be a question of facility of apperception. The proposition could perhaps safely be made broader than this. If abstraction is made from association, suggestion, and "expression," classed as elements of beauty, then beauty in any perceived object means that the mind readily unfolds its apperceptive activity in the directions which the object in question affords. But the directions in which activity readily unfolds or expresses itself are the directions to which long and close habituation has made the mind prone. So far as concerns the essential elements of beauty, this habituation is an habituation so close and long as to have induced not only a proclivity to the appreciative form in question, but an adaptation of physiological structure and function as well. So far as the economic interest enters into the constitution of beauty, it enters as a suggestion or expression of adequacy to a purpose, a manifest and readily inferable subservience to the life process. This expression of economic facility or economic serviceability in any object—what may be called the economic beauty of the object—is best served by neat and unambiguous suggestion of its office and its efficiency for the material ends of life.

On this ground, among objects of use the simple and unadorned article is aesthetically the best. But since the pecuniary canon of reputability rejects the inexpensive in articles appropriated to individual consumption, the satisfaction of our craving for beautiful things must be sought by way of compromise. The canons of beauty must be circumvented by some contrivance which will give evidence of a reputably wasteful expenditure, at the same time that it meets the demands of our critical sense of the useful and the beautiful, or at least meets the demand of some habit which has come to do duty in place of that sense. Such an auxiliary sense of taste is the sense of novelty; and this latter is helped out in its surrogateship by the curiosity with which men view ingenious and puzzling contrivances. Hence it comes that most objects alleged to be beautiful, and doing duty as such, show considerable ingenuity of design and are calculated to puzzle the beholder—to bewilder him with irrelevant suggestions and hints of the improbable—at the same time that they give evidence of an expenditure of labor in excess of what would give them their fullest efficiency for their ostensible economic end.

This may be shown by an illustration taken from outside the range of our everyday habits and everyday contact, and so outside the range of our bias. Such are the remarkable feather mantles of Hawaii, or the well-known carved handles of the ceremonial adzes of several Polynesian islands. These are undeniably beautiful, both in the sense that they offer a pleasing composition of form, lines, and color, and in the sense that they evince great skill and ingenuity in design and construction. At the same time the articles are manifestly ill fitted to serve any other economic purpose. But it is not always that the evolution of ingenious and puzzling contrivances under the guidance of the canon of wasted effort works out so happy a result. The result is quite as often a virtually complete suppression of all elements that would bear scrutiny as expressions of beauty or of serviceability, and the substitution of evidences of misspent ingenuity and labor, backed by a conspicuous ineptitude; until many of the objects with which we surround ourselves in everyday life, and even many articles of everyday dress and ornament, are such as would not be tolerated except under the stress of prescriptive tradition. Illustrations of this substitution of ingenuity and expense in place of beauty and serviceability are to be seen, for instance, in domestic architecture, in domestic art or fancy work, in various articles of apparel, especially of feminine and priestly apparel.

The canon of beauty requires expression of the generic. The "novelty" due to the demands of conspicuous waste traverses this canon of beauty, in that it results in making the physiognomy of our objects of taste a congeries of idiosyncrasies; and the idiosyncrasies are, moreover, under the selective surveillance of the canon of expensiveness.

This process of selective adaptation of designs to the end of conspicuous waste, and the substitution of pecuniary beauty for aesthetic beauty, has been especially effective in the development of architecture. It would be extremely difficult to find a modern civilized residence or public building which can claim anything better than relative inoffensiveness in the eyes of any one who will dissociate the elements of beauty from those of honorific waste. The endless variety of fronts presented by the better class of tenements and apartment houses in our cities is an endless variety of architectural distress and of suggestions of expensive discomfort. Considered as objects of beauty, the dead walls of the sides and back of these structures, left untouched by the hands of the artist, are commonly the best feature of the building.

What has been said of the influence of the law of conspicuous waste upon the canons of taste will hold true, with but a slight change of terms, of its influence upon our notions of the serviceability of goods for other ends than the aesthetic one. Goods are produced and consumed as a means to the fuller unfolding of human life; and their utility consists, in the first instance, in their efficiency as means to this end. The end is, in the first instance, the fullness of life of the individual, taken in absolute terms. But the human proclivity to emulation has seized upon the consumption of goods as a means to an invidious comparison, and has thereby invested consumable goods with a secondary utility as evidence of relative ability to pay. This indirect or secondary use of consumable goods lends an honorific character to consumption, and presently also to the goods which best serve this emulative end of consumption. The consumption of expensive goods is meritorious, and the goods which contain an appreciable element of cost in excess of what goes to give them serviceability for their ostensible mechanical purpose are honorific. The marks of superfluous costliness in the goods are therefore marks of worth—of high efficiency for the indirect, invidious end to be served by their consumption; and conversely, goods are humilific, and therefore unattractive, if they show too thrifty an adaptation to the mechanical end sought and do not include a margin of expensiveness on which to rest a complacent invidious comparison. This indirect utility gives much of their value to the "better" grades of goods. In order to appeal to the cultivated sense of utility, an article must contain a modicum of this indirect utility.

While men may have set out with disapproving an inexpensive manner of living because it indicated inability to spend much, and so indicated a lack of pecuniary success, they end by falling into the habit of disapproving cheap things as being intrinsically dishonorable or unworthy because they are cheap. As time has gone on, each succeeding generation has received this tradition of meritorious expenditure from the generation before it, and has in its turn further elaborated and fortified the traditional canon of pecuniary reputability in goods consumed; until we have finally reached such a degree of conviction as to the unworthiness of all inexpensive things, that we have no longer any misgivings in formulating the maxim, "Cheap and nasty." So thoroughly has this habit of approving the expensive and disapproving the inexpensive been ingrained into our thinking that we instinctively insist upon at least some measure of wasteful expensiveness in all our consumption, even in the case of goods which are consumed in strict privacy and without the slightest thought of display. We all feel, sincerely and without misgiving, that we are the more lifted up in spirit for having, even in the privacy of our own household, eaten our daily meal by the help of hand-wrought silver utensils, from hand-painted china (often of dubious artistic value) laid on high-priced table linen. Any retrogression from the standard of living which we are accustomed to regard as worthy in this respect is felt to be a grievous violation of our human dignity. So, also, for the last dozen years candles have been a more pleasing source of light at dinner than any other. Candle-light is now softer, less distressing to well-bred eyes, than oil, gas, or electric light. The same could not have been said thirty years ago, when candles were, or recently had been, the cheapest available light for domestic use. Nor are candles even now found to give an acceptable or effective light for any other than a ceremonial illumination.

A political sage still living has summed up the conclusion of this whole matter in the dictum: "A cheap coat makes a cheap man," and there is probably no one who does not feel the convincing force of the maxim.

The habit of looking for the marks of superfluous expensiveness in goods, and of requiring that all goods should afford some utility of the indirect or invidious sort, leads to a change in the standards by which the utility of goods is gauged. The honorific element and the element of brute efficiency are not held apart in the consumer's appreciation of commodities, and the two together go to make up the unanalyzed aggregate serviceability of the goods. Under the resulting standard of serviceability, no article will pass muster on the strength of material sufficiency alone. In order to completeness and full acceptability to the consumer it must also show the honorific element. It results that the producers of articles of consumption direct their efforts to the production of goods that shall meet this demand for the honorific element. They will do this with all the more alacrity and effect, since they are themselves under the dominance of the same standard of worth in goods, and would be sincerely grieved at the sight of goods which lack the proper honorific finish. Hence it has come about that there are today no goods supplied in any trade which do not contain the honorific element in greater or less degree. Any consumer who might, Diogenes-like, insist on the elimination of all honorific or wasteful elements from his consumption, would be unable to supply his most trivial wants in the modern market. Indeed, even if he resorted to supplying his wants directly by his own efforts, he would find it difficult if not impossible to divest himself of the current habits of thought on this head; so that he could scarcely compass a supply of necessaries of life for a day's consumption without instinctively and by oversight incorporating in his home-made product something of this honorific, quasi-decorative element of wasted labor.

It is notorious that in their selection of serviceable goods in the retail market, purchasers are guided more by the finish and workmanship of the goods than by any marks of substantial serviceability. Goods, in order to sell, must have some appreciable amount of labor spent in giving them the marks of decent expensiveness, in addition to what goes to give them efficiency for the material use which they are to serve. This habit of making obvious costliness a canon of serviceability of course acts to enhance the aggregate cost of articles of consumption. It puts us on our guard against cheapness by identifying merit in some degree with cost. There is ordinarily a consistent effort on the part of the consumer to obtain goods of the required serviceability at as advantageous a bargain as may be; but the conventional requirement of obvious costliness, as a voucher and a constituent of the serviceability of goods, leads him to reject as under grade such goods as do not contain a large element of conspicuous waste.

It is to be added that a large share of those features of consumable goods which figure in popular apprehension as marks of serviceability, and to which reference is here had as elements of conspicuous waste, commend themselves to the consumer also on other grounds than that of expensiveness alone. They usually give evidence of skill and effective workmanship, even if they do not contribute to the substantial serviceability of the goods; and it is no doubt largely on some such ground that any particular mark of honorific serviceability first comes into vogue and afterward maintains its footing as a normal constituent element of the worth of an article. A display of efficient workmanship is pleasing simply as such, even where its remoter, for the time unconsidered, outcome is futile. There is a gratification of the artistic sense in the contemplation of skillful work. But it is also to be added that no such evidence of skillful workmanship, or of ingenious and effective adaptation of means to end, will, in the long run, enjoy the approbation of the modern civilized consumer unless it has the sanction of the canon of conspicuous waste.

The position here taken is enforced in a felicitous manner by the place assigned in the economy of consumption to machine products. The point of material difference between machine-made goods and the hand-wrought goods which serve the same purposes is, ordinarily, that the former serve their primary purpose more adequately. They are a more perfect product—show a more perfect adaptation of means to end. This does not save them from disesteem and depreciation, for they fall short under the test of honorific waste. Hand labor is a more wasteful method of production; hence the goods turned out by this method are more serviceable for the purpose of pecuniary reputability; hence the marks of hand labor come to be honorific, and the goods which exhibit these marks take rank as of higher grade than the corresponding machine product. Commonly, if not invariably, the honorific marks of hand labor are certain imperfections and irregularities in the lines of the hand-wrought article, showing where the workman has fallen short in the execution of the design. The ground of the superiority of hand-wrought goods, therefore, is a certain margin of crudeness. This margin must never be so wide as to show bungling workmanship, since that would be evidence of low cost, nor so narrow as to suggest the ideal precision attained only by the machine, for that would be evidence of low cost.

The appreciation of those evidences of honorific crudeness to which hand-wrought goods owe their superior worth and charm in the eyes of well-bred people is a matter of nice discrimination. It requires training and the formation of right habits of thought with respect to what may be called the physiognomy of goods. Machine-made goods of daily use are often admired and preferred precisely on account of their excessive perfection by the vulgar and the underbred who have not given due thought to the punctilios of elegant consumption. The ceremonial inferiority of machine products goes to show that the perfection of skill and workmanship embodied in any costly innovations in the finish of goods is not sufficiency of itself to secure them acceptance and permanent favor. The innovation must have the support of the canon of conspicuous waste. Any feature in the physiognomy of goods, however pleasing in itself, and however well it may approve itself to the taste for effective work, will not be tolerated if it proves obnoxious to this norm of pecuniary reputability.

The ceremonial inferiority or uncleanness in consumable goods due to "commonness," or in other words to their slight cost of production, has been taken very seriously by many persons. The objection to machine products is often formulated as an objection to the commonness of such goods. What is common is within the (pecuniary) reach of many people. Its consumption is therefore not honorific, since it does not serve the purpose of a favorable invidious comparison with other consumers. Hence the consumption, or even the sight of such goods, is inseparable from an odious suggestion of the lower levels of human life, and one comes away from their contemplation with a pervading sense of meanness that is extremely distasteful and depressing to a person of sensibility. In persons whose tastes assert themselves imperiously, and who have not the gift, habit, or incentive to discriminate between the grounds of their various judgments of taste, the deliverance of the sense of the honorific coalesce with those of the sense of beauty and of the sense of serviceability—in the manner already spoken of; the resulting composite valuation serves as a judgment of the object's beauty or its serviceability, according as the valuer's bias or interest inclines him to apprehend the object in the one or the other of these aspects. It follows not infrequently that the marks of cheapness or commonness are accepted as definitive marks of artistic unfitness, and a code or schedule of aesthetic proprieties on the one hand, and of aesthetic abominations on the other, is constructed on this basis for guidance in questions of taste.

As has already been pointed out, the cheap, and therefore indecorous, articles of daily consumption in modern industrial communities are commonly machine products; and the generic feature of the physiognomy of machine-made goods as compared with the handwrought article is their greater perfection in workmanship and greater accuracy in the detail execution of the design. Hence it comes about that the visible imperfections of the hand-wrought goods, being honorific, are accounted marks of superiority in point of beauty, of serviceability, or both. Hence has arisen that exaltation of the defective, of which John Ruskin and William Morris were such eager spokesmen in their time; and on this ground their propaganda of crudity and wasted effort has been taken up and carried forward since their time. And hence also the propaganda for a return to handicraft and household industry. So much of the work and speculations of this group of men as fairly comes under the characterization here given would have been impossible at a time when the visibly more perfect goods were not the cheaper.

It is of course only as to the economic value of this school of aesthetic teaching that anything is intended to be said or can be said here. What is said is not to be taken in the sense of depreciation, but chiefly as a characterization of the tendency of this teaching in its effect on consumption and on the production of consumable goods.

The manner in which the bias of this growth of taste has worked itself out in production is perhaps most contently exemplified in the book manufacture with which Morris busied himself during the later years of his life; but what holds true of the work of the Kelmscott Press in an eminent degree, holds true with but slightly abated force when applied to latter-day artistic book-making generally—as to type, paper, illustration, binding materials, and binder's work. The claims to excellence put forward by the later products of the book-maker's industry rest in some measure on the degree of its approximation to the crudities of the time when the work of book-making was a doubtful struggle with refractory materials carried on by means of insufficient appliances. These products, since they require hand labor, are more expensive; they are also less convenient for use than the books turned out with a view to serviceability alone; they therefore argue ability on the part of the purchaser to consume freely, as well as ability to waste time and effort. It is on this basis that the printers of today are returning to "old-style," and other more or less obsolete styles of type which are less legible and give a cruder appearance to the page than the "modern." Even a scientific periodical, with ostensibly no purpose but the most effective presentation of matter with which its science is concerned, will concede so much to the demands of this pecuniary beauty as to publish its scientific discussions in old-style type, on laid paper, and with uncut edges. But books which are not ostensibly concerned with the effective presentation of their contents alone, of course go farther in this direction. Here we have a somewhat cruder type, printed on hand-laid, deckel-edged paper, with excessive margins and uncut leaves, with bindings of a painstaking crudeness and elaborate ineptitude. The Kelmscott Press reduced the matter to an absurdity—as seen from the point of view of brute serviceability alone—by issuing books for modern use, edited with the obsolete spelling, printed in black-letter, and bound in limp vellum fitted with thongs. As a further characteristic feature which fixes the economic place of artistic book-making, there is the fact that these more elegant books are, at their best, printed in limited editions. A limited edition is in effect a guarantee—somewhat crude, it is true—that this book is scarce and that it therefore is costly and lends pecuniary distinction to its consumer.

The special attractiveness of these book-products to the book-buyer of cultivated taste lies, of course, not in a conscious, naïve recognition of their costliness and superior clumsiness. Here, as in the parallel case of the superiority of hand-wrought articles over machine products, the conscious ground of preference is an intrinsic excellence imputed to the costlier and more awkward article. The superior excellence imputed to the book which imitates the products of antique and obsolete processes is conceived to be chiefly a superior utility in the aesthetic respect; but it is not unusual to find a well-bred book-lover insisting that the clumsier product is also more serviceable as a vehicle of printed speech. So far as regards the superior aesthetic value of the decadent book, the chances are that the book-lover's contention has some ground. The book is designed with an eye single to its beauty, and the result is commonly some measure of success on the part of the designer. What is insisted on here, however, is that the canon of taste under which the designer works is a canon formed under the surveillance of the law of conspicuous waste, and that this law acts selectively to eliminate any canon of taste that does not conform to its demands. That is to say, while the decadent book may be beautiful, the limits within which the designer may work are fixed by requirements of a non-aesthetic kind. The product, if it is beautiful, must also at the same time be costly and ill adapted to its ostensible use. This mandatory canon of taste in the case of the book-designer, however, is not shaped entirely by the law of waste in its first form; the canon is to some extent shaped in conformity to that secondary expression of the predatory temperament, veneration for the archaic or obsolete, which in one of its special developments is called classicism.

In aesthetic theory it might be extremely difficult, if not quite impracticable, to draw a line between the canon of classicism, or regard for the archaic, and the canon of beauty. For the aesthetic purpose such a distinction need scarcely be drawn, and indeed it need not exist. For a theory of taste the expression of an accepted ideal archaism, on whatever basis it may have been accepted, is perhaps best rated as an element of beauty; there need be no question of its legitimation. But for the present purpose—for the purpose of determining what economic grounds are present in the accepted canons of taste and what is their significance for the distribution and consumption of goods—the distinction is not similarly beside the point.

The position of machine products in the civilized scheme of consumption serves to point out the nature of the relation which subsists between the canon of conspicuous waste and the code of proprieties in consumption. Neither in matters of art and taste proper, nor as regards the current sense of the serviceability of goods, does this canon act as a principle of innovation or initiative. It does not go into the future as a creative principle which makes innovations and adds new items of consumption and new elements of cost. The principle in question is, in a certain sense, a negative rather than a positive law. It is a regulative rather than a creative principle. It very rarely initiates or originates any usage or custom directly. Its action is selective only. Conspicuous wastefulness does not directly afford ground for variation and growth, but conformity to its requirements is a condition to the survival of such innovations as may be made on other grounds. In whatever way usages and customs and methods of expenditure arise, they are all subject to the selective action of this norm of reputability; and the degree in which they conform to its requirements is a test of their fitness to survive in the competition with other similar usages and customs. Other things being equal, the more obviously wasteful usage or methods stands the better chance of survival under this law. The law of conspicuous waste does not account for the origin of variations, but only for the persistence of such forms as are fit to survive under its dominance. It acts to conserve the fit, not to originate the acceptable. Its office is to prove all things and to hold fast that which is good for its purpose.

Dress as an Expression of the Pecuniary Culture

It will be in place, by way of illustration, to show in some detail how the economic principles so far set forth apply to everyday facts in some one direction of the life process. For this purpose no line of consumption affords a more apt illustration than expenditure on dress. It is especially the rule of the conspicuous waste of goods that finds expression in dress, although the other, related principles of pecuniary repute are also exemplified in the same contrivances. Other methods of putting one's pecuniary standing in evidence serve their end effectually, and other methods are in vogue always and everywhere; but expenditure on dress has this advantage over most other methods, that our apparel is always in evidence and affords an indication of our pecuniary standing to all observers at the first glance. It is also true that admitted expenditure for display is more obviously present, and is, perhaps, more universally practiced in the matter of dress than in any other line of consumption. No one finds difficulty in assenting to the commonplace that the greater part of the expenditure incurred by all classes for apparel is incurred for the sake of a respectable appearance rather than for the protection of the person. And probably at no other point is the sense of shabbiness so keenly felt as it is if we fall short of the standard set by social usage in this matter of dress. It is true of dress in even a higher degree than of most other items of consumption, that people will undergo a very considerable degree of privation in the comforts or the necessaries of life in order to afford what is considered a decent amount of wasteful consumption; so that it is by no means an uncommon occurrence, in an inclement climate, for people to go ill clad in order to appear well dressed. And the commercial value of the goods used for clothing in any modern community is made up to a much larger extent of the fashionableness, the reputability of the goods than of the mechanical service which they render in clothing the person of the wearer. The need of dress is eminently a "higher" or spiritual need.

This spiritual need of dress is not wholly, nor even chiefly, a naïve propensity for display of expenditure. The law of conspicuous waste guides consumption in apparel, as in other things, chiefly at the second remove, by shaping the canons of taste and decency. In the common run of cases the conscious motive of the wearer or purchaser of conspicuously wasteful apparel is the need of conforming to established usage, and of living up to the accredited standard of taste and reputability. It is not only that one must be guided by the code of proprieties in dress in order to avoid the mortification that comes of unfavorable notice and comment, through that motive in itself counts for a great deal; but besides that, the requirement of expensiveness is so ingrained into our habits of thought in matters of dress that any other than expensive apparel is instinctively odious to us. Without reflection or analysis, we feel that what is inexpensive is unworthy. "A cheap coat makes a cheap man." "Cheap and nasty" is recognized to hold true in dress with even less mitigation than in other lines of consumption. On the ground both of taste and of serviceability, an inexpensive article of apparel is held to be inferior, under the maxim "cheap and nasty." We find things beautiful, as well as serviceable, somewhat in proportion as they are costly. With few and inconsequential exceptions, we all find a costly hand-wrought article of apparel much preferable, in point of beauty and of serviceability, to a less expensive imitation of it, however cleverly the spurious article may imitate the costly original; and what offends our sensibilities in the spurious article is not that it falls short in form or color, or, indeed, in visual effect in any way. The offensive object may be so close an imitation as to defy any but the closest scrutiny; and yet so soon as the counterfeit is detected, its aesthetic value, and its commercial value as well, declines precipitately. Not only that, but it may be asserted with but small risk of contradiction that the aesthetic value of a detected counterfeit in dress declines somewhat in the same proportion as the counterfeit is cheaper than its original. It loses caste aesthetically because it falls to a lower pecuniary grade.

But the function of dress as an evidence of ability to pay does not end with simply showing that the wearer consumes valuable goods in excess of what is required for physical comfort. Simple conspicuous waste of goods is effective and gratifying as far as it goes; it is good *prima facie* evidence of pecuniary success, and consequently *prima facie* evidence of social worth. But dress has subtler and more far-reaching possibilities than this crude, first-hand evidence of wasteful consumption only. If, in addition to showing that the wearer can afford to consume freely and uneconomically, it can also be shown in the same stroke that he or she is not under the necessity of earning a livelihood, the evidence of social worth is enhanced in a very considerable degree. Our dress, therefore, in order to serve its purpose effectually, should not only be expensive, but it should also make plain to all observers that the wearer is not engaged in any kind of productive labor. In the evolutionary process by which our system of dress has been elaborated into its present admirably perfect adaptation to its purpose, this subsidiary line of evidence has received due attention. A detailed examination of what passes in popular apprehension for elegant apparel will show that it is contrived at every point to convey the impression that the wearer does not habitually put forth any useful effort. It goes without saying that no apparel can be considered elegant, or even decent, if it shows the effect of manual labor on the part of the wearer, in the way of soil or wear. The pleasing effect of neat and spotless garments is chiefly, if not altogether, due to their carrying the suggestion of leisure—exemption from personal contact with industrial processes of any kind. Much of the charm that invests the patent-leather shoe, the stainless linen, the lustrous cylindrical hat, and the walking-stick, which so greatly enhance the native dignity of a gentleman, comes of their pointedly suggesting that the wearer cannot when so attired bear a hand in any employment that is directly and immediately of any human use. Elegant dress serves its purpose of elegance not only in that it is expensive, but also because it is the insignia of leisure. It not only shows that the wearer is able to consume a relatively large value, but it argues at the same time that he consumes without producing.

The dress of women goes even farther than that of men in the way of demonstrating the wearer's abstinence from productive employment. It needs no argument to enforce the generalization that the more elegant styles of feminine bonnets go even farther towards making work impossible than does the man's high hat. The woman's shoe adds the so-called French heel to the evidence of enforced leisure afforded by its polish; because this high heel obviously makes any, even the simplest and most necessary manual work extremely difficult. The like is true even in a higher degree of the skirt and the rest of the drapery which characterizes woman's dress. The substantial reason for our tenacious attachment to the skirt is just this: it is expensive and it hampers the wearer at every turn and incapacitates her for all useful exertion. The like is true of the feminine custom of wearing the hair excessively long.

But the woman's apparel not only goes beyond that of the modern man in the degree in which it argues exemption from labor; it also adds a peculiar and highly characteristic feature which differs in kind from anything habitually practiced by the men. This feature is the class of contrivances of which the corset is the typical example. The corset is, in economic theory, substantially a mutilation, undergone for the purpose of lowering the subject's vitality and rendering her permanently and obviously unfit for work. It is true, the corset impairs the personal attractions of the wearer, but the loss suffered on that score is offset by the gain in reputability which comes of her visibly increased expensiveness and infirmity. It may broadly be set down that the womanliness of woman's apparel resolves itself, in point of substantial fact, into the more effective hindrance to useful exertion offered by the garments peculiar to women. This difference between masculine and feminine apparel is here simply pointed out as a characteristic feature. The ground of its occurrence will be discussed presently.

So far, then, we have, as the great and dominant norm of dress, the broad principle of conspicuous waste. Subsidiary to this principle, and as a corollary under it, we get as a second norm the principle of conspicuous leisure. In dress construction this norm works out in the shape of diverse contrivances going to show that the wearer does not and, as far as it may conveniently be shown, cannot engage in productive labor. Beyond these two principles there is a third of scarcely less constraining force, which will occur to any one who reflects at all on the subject. Dress must not only be conspicuously expensive and inconvenient; it must at the same time be up to date. No explanation at all satisfactory has hitherto been offered of the phenomenon of changing fashions. The imperative requirement of dressing in the latest accredited manner, as well as the fact that this accredited fashion constantly changes from season to season, is sufficiently familiar to every one, but the theory of this flux and change has not been worked out. We may of course say, with perfect consistency and truthfulness, that this principle of novelty is another corollary under the law of conspicuous waste. Obviously, if each garment is permitted to serve for but a brief term, and if none of last season's apparel is carried over and made further use of during the present season, the wasteful expenditure on dress is greatly increased. This is good as far as it goes, but it is negative only. Pretty much all that this consideration warrants us in saying is that the norm of conspicuous waste exercises a controlling surveillance in all matters of dress, so that any change in the fashions must conform to the requirement of wastefulness; it leaves unanswered the question as to the motive for making and accepting a change in the prevailing styles, and it also fails to explain why conformity to a given style at a given time is so imperatively necessary as we know it to be.

For a creative principle, capable of serving as motive to invention and innovation in fashions, we shall have to go back to the primitive, non-economic motive with which apparel originated—the motive of adornment. Without going into an extended discussion of how and why this motive asserts itself under the guidance of the law of expensiveness, it may be stated broadly that each successive innovation in the fashions is an effort to reach some form of display which shall be more acceptable to our sense of form and color or of effectiveness, than that which it displaces. The changing styles are the expression of a restless search for something which shall commend itself to our aesthetic sense; but as each innovation is subject to the selective action of the norm of conspicuous waste, the range within which innovation can take place is somewhat restricted. The innovation must not only be more beautiful, or perhaps oftener less offensive, than that which it displaces, but it must also come up to the accepted standard of expensiveness.

It would seem at first sight that the result of such an unremitting struggle to attain the beautiful in dress should be a gradual approach to artistic perfection. We might naturally expect that the fashions should show a well-marked trend in the direction of some one or more types of apparel eminently becoming to the human form; and we might even feel that we have substantial ground for the hope that today, after all the ingenuity and effort which have been spent on dress these many years, the fashions should have achieved a relative perfection and a relative stability, closely approximating to a permanently tenable artistic ideal. But such is not the case. It would be very hazardous indeed to assert that the styles of today are intrinsically more becoming than those of ten years ago, or than those of twenty, or fifty, or one hundred years ago. On the other hand, the assertion freely goes uncontradicted that styles in vogue two thousand years ago are more becoming than the most elaborate and painstaking constructions of today.

The explanation of the fashions just offered, then, does not fully explain, and we shall have to look farther. It is well known that certain relatively stable styles and types of costume have been worked out in various parts of the world; as, for instance, among the Japanese, Chinese, and other Oriental nations; likewise among the Greeks, Romans, and other Eastern peoples of antiquity; so also, in later times, among the peasants of nearly every country of Europe. These national or popular costumes are in most cases adjudged by competent critics to be more becoming, more artistic, than the fluctuating styles of modern civilized apparel. At the same time they are also, at least usually less obviously wasteful; that is to say, other elements than that of a display of expense are more readily detected in their structure.

These relatively stable costumes are, commonly, pretty strictly and narrowly localized, and they vary by slight and systematic gradations from place to place. They have in every case been worked out by peoples or classes which are poorer than we, and especially they belong in countries and localities and times where the population, or at least the class to which the costume in question belongs, is relatively homogeneous, stable, and immobile. That is to say, stable costumes which will bear the test of time and perspective are worked out under circumstances where the norm of conspicuous waste asserts itself less imperatively than it does in the large modern civilized cities, whose relatively mobile, wealthy population today sets the pace in matters of fashion. The countries and classes which have in this way worked out stable and artistic costumes have been so placed that the pecuniary emulation among them has taken the direction of a competition in conspicuous leisure rather than in conspicuous consumption of goods. So that it will hold true in a general way that fashions are least stable and least becoming in those communities where the principle of a conspicuous waste of goods asserts itself most imperatively, as among ourselves. All this points to an antagonism between expensiveness and artistic apparel. In point of practical fact, the norm of conspicuous waste is incompatible with the requirement that dress should be beautiful or becoming. And this antagonism offers an explanation of that restless change in fashion which neither the canon of expensiveness nor that of beauty alone can account for.

The standard of reputability requires that dress should show wasteful expenditure; but all wastefulness is offensive to native taste. The psychological law has already been pointed out that all men—and women perhaps even in a higher degree—abhor futility, whether of effort or of expenditure—much as Nature was once said to abhor a vacuum. But the principle of conspicuous waste requires an obviously futile expenditure; and the resulting conspicuous expensiveness of dress is therefore intrinsically ugly. Hence we find that in all innovations in dress, each added or altered detail strives to avoid instant condemnation by showing some ostensible purpose, at the same time that the requirement of conspicuous waste prevents the purposefulness of these innovations from becoming anything more than a somewhat transparent pretense. Even in its freest flights, fashion rarely if ever gets away from a simulation of some ostensible use. The ostensible usefulness of the fashionable details of dress, however, is always so transparent a make-believe, and their substantial futility presently forces itself so baldly upon our attention as to become unbearable, and then we take refuge in a new style. But the new style must conform to the requirement of reputable wastefulness and futility. Its futility presently becomes as odious as that of its predecessor; and the only remedy which the law of waste allows us is to seek relief in some new construction, equally futile and equally untenable. Hence the essential ugliness and the unceasing change of fashionable attire.

Having so explained the phenomenon of shifting fashions, the next thing is to make the explanation tally with everyday facts. Among these everyday facts is the well-known liking which all men have for the styles that are in vogue at any given time. A new style comes into vogue and remains in favor for a season, and, at least so long as it is a novelty, people very generally find the new style attractive. The prevailing fashion is felt to be beautiful. This is due partly to the relief it affords in being different from what went before it, partly to its being reputable. As indicated in the last chapter, the canon of reputability to some extent shapes our tastes, so that under its guidance anything will be accepted as becoming until its novelty wears off, or until the warrant of reputability is transferred to a new and novel structure serving the same general purpose. That the alleged beauty, or "loveliness," of the styles in vogue at any given time is transient and spurious only is attested by the fact that none of the many shifting fashions will bear the test of time. When seen in the perspective of half-a-dozen years or more, the best of our fashions strike us as grotesque, if not unsightly. Our transient attachment to whatever happens to be the latest rests on other than aesthetic grounds, and lasts only until our abiding aesthetic sense has had time to assert itself and reject this latest indigestible contrivance.

The process of developing an aesthetic nausea takes more or less time; the length of time required in any given case being inversely as the degree of intrinsic odiousness of the style in question. This time relation between odiousness and instability in fashions affords ground for the inference that the more rapidly the styles succeed and displace one another, the more offensive they are to sound taste. The presumption, therefore, is that the farther the community, especially the wealthy classes of the community, develop in wealth and mobility and in the range of their human contact, the more imperatively will the law of conspicuous waste assert itself in matters of dress, the more will the sense of beauty tend to fall into abeyance or be overborne by the canon of pecuniary reputability, the more rapidly will fashions shift and change, and the more grotesque and intolerable will be the varying styles that successively come into vogue.

There remains at least one point in this theory of dress yet to be discussed. Most of what has been said applies to men's attire are well as to that of women; although in modern times it applies at nearly all points with greater force to that of women. But at one point the dress of women differs substantially from that of men. In woman's dress there is an obviously greater insistence on such features as testify to the wearer's exemption from or incapacity for all vulgarly productive employment. This characteristic of woman's apparel is of interest, not only as completing the theory of dress, but also as confirming what has already been said of the economic status of women, both in the past and in the present.

As has been seen in the discussion of woman's status under the heads of Vicarious Leisure and Vicarious Consumption, it has in the course of economic development become the office of the woman to consume vicariously for the head of the household; and her apparel is contrived with this object in view. It has come about that obviously productive labor is in a peculiar degree derogatory to respectable women, and therefore special pains should be taken in the construction of women's dress, to impress upon the beholder the fact (often indeed a fiction) that the wearer does not and can not habitually engage in useful work. Propriety requires respectable women to abstain more consistently from useful effort and to make more of a show of leisure than the men of the same social classes. It grates painfully on our nerves to contemplate the necessity of any well-bred woman's earning a livelihood by useful work. It is not "woman's sphere." Her sphere is within the household, which she should "beautify," and of which she should be the "chief ornament." The male head of the household is not currently spoken of as its ornament. This feature taken in conjunction with the other fact that propriety requires more unremitting attention to expensive display in the dress and other paraphernalia of women, goes to enforce the view already implied in what has gone before. By virtue of its descent from a patriarchal past, our social system makes it the woman's function in an especial degree to put in evidence her household's ability to pay. According to the modern civilized scheme of life, the good name of the household to which she belongs should be the special care of the woman; and the system of honorific expenditure and conspicuous leisure by which this good name is chiefly sustained is therefore the woman's sphere. In the ideal scheme, as it tends to realize itself in the life of the higher pecuniary classes, this attention to conspicuous waste of substance and effort should normally be the sole economic function of the woman.

At the stage of economic development at which the women were still in the full sense the property of the men, the performance of conspicuous leisure and consumption came to be part of the services required of them. The women being not their own masters, obvious expenditure and leisure on their part would redound to the credit of their master rather than to their own credit; and therefore the more expensive and the more obviously unproductive the women of the household are, the more creditable and more effective for the purpose of the reputability of the household or its head will their life be. So much so that the women have been required not only to afford evidence of a life of leisure, but even to disable themselves for useful activity.

It is at this point that the dress of men falls short of that of women, and for a sufficient reason. Conspicuous waste and conspicuous leisure are reputable because they are evidence of pecuniary strength; pecuniary strength is reputable or honorific because, in the last analysis, it argues success and superior force; therefore the evidence of waste and leisure put forth by an individual in his own behalf cannot consistently take such a form or be carried to such a pitch as to argue incapacity or marked discomfort on his part; as the exhibition would in that case show not superior force, but inferiority, and so defeat its own purpose. So, then, wherever wasteful expenditure and the show of abstention from effort is normally, or on an average, carried to the extent of showing obvious discomfort or voluntarily induced physical disability, there the immediate inference is that the individual in question does not perform this wasteful expenditure and undergo this disability for her own personal gain in pecuniary repute, but in behalf of some one else to whom she stands in a relation of economic dependence; a relation which in the last analysis must, in economic theory, reduce itself to a relation of servitude.

To apply this generalization to women's dress, and put the matter in concrete terms: the high heel, the skirt, the impracticable bonnet, the corset, and the general disregard of the wearer's comfort which is an obvious feature of all civilized women's apparel, are so many items of evidence to the effect that in the modern civilized scheme of life the woman is still, in theory, the economic dependent of the man—that, perhaps in a highly idealized sense, she still is the man's chattel. The homely reason for all this conspicuous leisure and attire on the part of women lies in the fact that they are servants to whom, in the differentiation of economic functions, has been delegated the office of putting in evidence their master's ability to pay.

There is a marked similarity in these respects between the apparel of women and that of domestic servants, especially liveried servants. In both there is a very elaborate show of unnecessary expensiveness, and in both cases there is also a notable disregard of the physical comfort of the wearer. But the attire of the lady goes farther in its elaborate insistence on the idleness, if not on the physical infirmity of the wearer, than does that of the domestic. And this is as it should be; for in theory, according to the ideal scheme of the pecuniary culture, the lady of the house is the chief menial of the household.

Besides servants, currently recognized as such, there is at least one other class of persons whose garb assimilates them to the class of servants and shows many of the features that go to make up the womanliness of woman's dress. This is the priestly class. Priestly vestments show, in accentuated form, all the features that have been shown to be evidence of a servile status and a vicarious life. Even more strikingly than the everyday habit of the priest, the vestments, properly so called, are ornate, grotesque, inconvenient, and, at least ostensibly, comfortless to the point of distress. The priest is at the same time expected to refrain from useful effort and, when before the public eye, to present an impassively disconsolate countenance, very much after the manner of a well-trained domestic servant. The shaven face of the priest is a further item to the same effect. This assimilation of the priestly class to the class of body servants, in demeanor and apparel, is due to the similarity of the two classes as regards economic function. In economic theory, the priest is a body servant, constructively in attendance upon the person of the divinity whose livery he wears. His livery is of a very expensive character, as it should be in order to set forth in a beseeming manner the dignity of his exalted master; but it is contrived to show that the wearing of it contributes little or nothing to the physical comfort of the wearer, for it is an item of vicarious consumption, and the repute which accrues from its consumption is to be imputed to the absent master, not to the servant.

The line of demarcation between the dress of women, priests, and servants, on the one hand, and of men, on the other hand, is not always consistently observed in practice, but it will scarcely be disputed that it is always present in a more or less definite way in the popular habits of thought. There are of course also free men, and not a few of them, who, in their blind zeal for faultlessly reputable attire, transgress the theoretical line between man's and woman's dress, to the extent of arraying themselves in apparel that is obviously designed to vex the mortal frame; but every one recognizes without hesitation that such apparel for men is a departure from the normal. We are in the habit of saying that such dress is "effeminate"; and one sometimes hears the remark that such or such an exquisitely attired gentleman is as well dressed as a footman.

Certain apparent discrepancies under this theory of dress merit a more detailed examination, especially as they mark a more or less evident trend in the later and maturer development of dress. The vogue of the corset offers an apparent exception from the rule of which it has here been cited as an illustration. A closer examination, however, will show that this apparent exception is really a verification of the rule that the vogue of any given element or feature in dress rests on its utility as an evidence of pecuniary standing. It is well known that in the industrially more advanced communities the corset is employed only within certain fairly well defined social strata. The women of the poorer classes, especially of the rural population, do not habitually use it, except as a holiday luxury. Among these classes the women have to work hard, and it avails them little in the way of a pretense of leisure to so crucify the flesh in everyday life. The holiday use of the contrivance is due to imitation of a higher-class canon of decency. Upwards from this lower level of indigence and manual labor, the corset was until within a generation or two nearly indispensable to a socially blameless standing for all women, including the wealthiest and most reputable. This rule held so long as there still was no large class of people wealthy enough to be above the imputation of any necessity for manual labor and at the same time large enough to form a self-sufficient, isolated social body whose mass would afford a foundation for special rules of conduct within the class, enforced by the current opinion of the class alone. But now there has grown up a large enough leisure class possessed of such wealth that any aspersion on the score of enforced manual employment would be idle and harmless calumny; and the corset has therefore in large measure fallen into disuse with this class.

The exceptions under this rule of exemption from the corset are more apparent than real. They are the wealthy classes of countries with a lower industrial structure—nearer the archaic, quasi-industrial type—together with the later accessions of the wealthy classes in the more advanced industrial communities. The latter have not yet had time to divest themselves of the plebeian canons of taste and of reputability carried over from their former, lower pecuniary grade. Such survival of the corset is not infrequent among the higher social classes of those American cities, for instance, which have recently and rapidly risen into opulence. If the word be used as a technical term, without any odious implication, it may be said that the corset persists in great measure through the period of snobbery—the interval of uncertainty and of transition from a lower to the upper levels of pecuniary culture. That is to say, in all countries which have inherited the corset it continues in use wherever and so long as it serves its purpose as an evidence of honorific leisure by arguing physical disability in the wearer. The same rule of course applies to other mutilations and contrivances for decreasing the visible efficiency of the individual.

Something similar should hold true with respect to diverse items of conspicuous consumption, and indeed something of the kind does seem to hold to a slight degree of sundry features of dress, especially if such features involve a marked discomfort or appearance of discomfort to the wearer. During the past one hundred years there is a tendency perceptible, in the development of men's dress especially, to discontinue methods of expenditure and the use of symbols of leisure which must have been irksome, which may have served a good purpose in their time, but the continuation of which among the upper classes today would be a work of supererogation; as, for instance, the use of powdered wigs and of gold lace, and the practice of constantly shaving the face. There has of late years been some slight recrudescence of the shaven face in polite society, but this is probably a transient and unadvised mimicry of the fashion imposed upon body servants, and it may fairly be expected to go the way of the powdered wig of our grandfathers.

These indices, and others which resemble them in point of the boldness with which they point out to all observers the habitual uselessness of those persons who employ them, have been replaced by other, more delicate methods of expressing the same fact; methods which are no less evident to the trained eyes of that smaller, select circle whose good opinion is chiefly sought. The earlier and cruder method of advertisement held its ground so long as the public to which the exhibitor had to appeal comprised large portions of the community who were not trained to detect delicate variations in the evidences of wealth and leisure. The method of advertisement undergoes a refinement when a sufficiently large wealthy class has developed, who have the leisure for acquiring skill in interpreting the subtler signs of expenditure. "Loud" dress becomes offensive to people of taste, as evincing an undue desire to reach and impress the untrained sensibilities of the vulgar. To the individual of high breeding it is only the more honorific esteem accorded by the cultivated sense of the members of his own high class that is of material consequence. Since the wealthy leisure class has grown so large, or the contact of the leisure-class individual with members of his own class has grown so wide, as to constitute a human environment sufficient for the honorific purpose, there arises a tendency to exclude the baser elements of the population from the scheme even as spectators whose applause or mortification should be sought. The result of all this is a refinement of methods, a resort to subtler contrivances, and a spiritualization of the scheme of symbolism in dress. And as this upper leisure class sets the pace in all matters of decency, the result for the rest of society also is a gradual amelioration of the scheme of dress. As the community advances in wealth and culture, the ability to pay is put in evidence by means which require a progressively nicer discrimination in the beholder. This nicer discrimination between advertising media is in fact a very large element of the higher pecuniary culture.

In Criticism of Economists

Industrial and Pecuniary Employments

For purposes of economic theory, the various activities of men and things about which economists busy themselves were classified by the early writers according to a scheme which has remained substantially unchanged, if not unquestioned, since their time. This scheme is the classical three-fold division of the factors of production under Land, Labor, and Capital. The theoretical aim of the economists in discussing these factors and the activities for which they stand has not remained the same throughout the course of economic discussion, and the three-fold division has not always lent itself with facility to new points of view and new purposes of theory, but the writers who have shaped later theory have, on the whole, not laid violent hands on the sacred formula. These facts must inspire the utmost reserve and circumspection in any one who is moved to propose even a subsidiary distinction of another kind between economic activities or agents. The terminology and the conceptual furniture of economics are complex and parti-colored enough without gratuitous innovation.

It is, accordingly, not the aim of this paper to set aside the time-honored classification of factors, or even to formulate an iconoclastic amendment, but rather to indicate how and why this classification has proved inadequate for certain purposes of theory which were not contemplated by the men who elaborated it. To this end a bit of preface may be in place as regards the aims which led to its formulation and the uses which the three-fold classification originally served.

The economists of the late eighteenth and early nineteenth centuries were believers in a Providential order, or an order of Nature. How they came by this belief need not occupy us here; neither need we raise a question as to whether their conviction of its truth was well or ill grounded. The Providential order or order of Nature is conceived to work in an effective and just way toward the end

Reprinted from *Publications of the American Economic Association,* series 3, 1901, pp. 190–205, by permission of the American Economic Association, Nashville, Tennessee.

to which it tends; and in the economic field this objective end is the material welfare of mankind. The science of that time set itself the task of interpreting the facts with which it dealt, in terms of this natural order. The material circumstances which condition men's life fall within the scope of this natural order of the universe, and as members of the universal scheme of things men fall under the constraining guidance of the laws of Nature, who does all things well. As regards their purely theoretical work, the early economists are occupied with bringing the facts of economic life under natural laws conceived somewhat after the manner indicated; and when the facts handled have been fully interpreted in the light of this fundamental postulate the theoretical work of the scientist is felt to have been successfully done.

The economic laws aimed at and formulated under the guidance of this preconception are laws of what takes place "naturally" or "normally", and it is of the essence of things so conceived that in the natural or normal course there is no wasted or misdirected effort. The standpoint is given by the material interest of mankind, or, more concretely, of the community, the ultimate theoretical postulate of which might, not unfairly, be stated as in some sort a law of the conservation of economic energy. When the course of things runs off naturally or normally, in accord with the exigencies of human welfare and the constraining laws of nature, economic income and outgo balance one another. The natural forces at play in the economic field may increase indefinitely through accretions brought in under man's dominion and through the natural increase of mankind, and, indeed, it is of the nature of things that an orderly progress of this kind should take place; but within the economic organism, as within the larger organism of the universe, there prevails an equivalence of expenditure and returns, an equilibrium of flux and reflux, which is not broken over in the normal course of things. So it is, by implication, assumed that the product which results from any given industrial process or operation is, in some sense or in some unspecified respect, the equivalent of the expenditure of forces, or of the effort, or what not, that has gone into the process out of which the product emerges.

This theorem of equivalence is the postulate which lies at the root of the classical theory of distribution, but it manifestly does not admit of proof—or of disproof either, for that matter; since neither the economic forces which go into the process nor the product which emerges are, in the economic respect, of such a tangible character as to admit of quantitative determination. They are in fact incommensurable magnitudes. To this last remark the answer may conceivably present itself that the equivalence in question is an equivalence in utility or in exchange value, and that the quantitative determination of the various items in terms of exchange value or of utility is, theoretically, not impossible; but when it is called to mind that the forces or factors which go to the production of a given product take their utility or exchange value from that of the product, it will easily be seen that the expedient will not serve. The equivalence between the aggregate factors of production in any given case and their product remains a dogmatic postulate whose validity cannot be demonstrated in any terms that will not reduce the whole proposition to an aimless fatuity, or to metaphysical grounds which have now been given up.

The point of view from which the early, and even the later, classical economists discussed economic life was that of "the society" taken as a collective whole and conceived as an organic unit. Economic theory sought out and formulated the laws of the normal life of the social organism, as it is conceived to work out in that natural course whereby the material welfare of society is attained. The details of economic life are construed, for purposes of general theory, in terms of their subservience to the aims imputed to the collective life process. Those features of detail which will bear construction as links in the process whereby the collective welfare is furthered, are magnified and brought into the foreground, while such features as will not bear this construction are treated as minor disturbances. Such a procedure is manifestly legitimate and expedient in a theoretical inquiry whose aim is to determine the laws of health of the social organism and the normal functions of this organism in a state of health. The social organism is, in this theory, handled as an individual endowed with a consistent life purpose and something of an intelligent apprehension of what means will serve the ends which it seeks. With these collective ends the interests of the individual members are conceived to be fundamentally at one; and, while men may not see that their own individual interests coincide with those of the social organism, yet, since men are members of the comprehensive organism of nature and consequently subject to beneficent natural law, the ulterior trend of underrestrained individual action is, on the whole, in the right direction.

The details of individual economic conduct and its consequences are of interest to such a general theory chiefly as they further or disturb the beneficent "natural" course. But if the aims and methods of individual conduct were of minor importance in such an economic theory, that is not the case as regards individual rights. The early political economy,was not simply a formulation of the natural course of economic phenomena, but it embodied an insistence on what is called "natural liberty". Whether this insistence on natural liberty is to be traced to utilitarianism or to a less specific faith in natural rights, the outcome for the purpose in hand is substantially the same. To avoid going too far afield, it may serve the turn to say that the law of economic equivalence, or conservation of economic energy, was, in early economics, backed by this second corollary of the order of nature, the closely related postulate of natural rights. The classical doctrine of distribution rests on both of these, and it is consequently not only a doctrine of what must normally take place as regards the course of life of society at large, but it also formulates what ought of right to take place as regards the remuneration for work and the distribution of wealth among men.

Under the resulting natural-economic law of equivalence and equity, it is held that the several participants or factors in the economic process severally get the equivalent of the productive force which they expend. They severally get as much as they produce; and conversely, in the normal case they severally produce as much as they get. In the earlier formulations, as, for example, in the authoritative formulation of Adam Smith, there is no clear or persistent pronouncement as regards the terms in which this equivalence between production and remuneration runs. With the later, classical economists, who had the benefit of a developed utilitarian philosophy, it seems to be somewhat consistently conceived in terms of an ill-defined serviceability. With some later writers it is an equivalence of exchange values; but as this latter reduces itself to tautology, it need scarcely be taken seriously. When we are told in the later political economy that the several agents or factors in production normally earn what they get, it is perhaps fairly to be construed as a claim that the economic service rendered the community by any one of the agents in production equals the service received by the agent in return. In terms of serviceability, then, if not in terms of productive force,[1] the individual agent, or at least the class or group of agents to which the individual belongs, normally gets as much as he contributes and contributes as much as he gets. This applies to all those employments or occupations which are ordinarily carried on in any community, throughout the aggregate of men's dealings with the material means of life. All activity which touches industry comes in under this law of equivalence and equity.

Now, to a theorist whose aim is to find the laws governing the economic life of a social organism, and who for this purpose conceives the economic community as a unit, the features of economic life which are of particular consequence are those which show the correlation of efforts and the solidarity of interests. For this purpose, such activities and such interests as do not fit into the scheme of solidarity contemplated are of minor importance, and are rather to be explained away, or construed into subservience to the scheme of solidarity than to be incorporated at their face value into the theoretical structure. Of this nature are what are here to be spoken of under the term "pecuniary employments," and the fortune which these pecuniary employments have met at the hands of classical economic theory is such as is outlined in the last sentence.

In a theory proceeding on the premise of economic solidarity, the important bearing of any activity that is taken up and accounted for is its bearing upon the furtherance of the collective life process. Viewed from the standpoint of the collective interest, the economic process is rated primarily as a process for the provision of the aggregate material means of life. As a late representative of the classical school expresses it: "Production, in fact, embraces every economic operation except consumption."[2] It is this aggregate productivity, and the bearing of all details upon the aggregate productivity, that constantly occupies the attention of the classical economists. What partially diverts their attention from this central and ubiquitous interest is their persistent lapse into natural-rights morality.

The result is that acquisition is treated as a sub-head under production, and effort directed to acquisition is construed in terms of production. The pecuniary activities of men, efforts directed to acquisition and operations incident to the acquisition or tenure of wealth, are treated as incidental to the distribution to each of his particular proportion in the production of goods. Pecuniary activities, in short, are handled as incidental features of the process of social production and consumption, as details incident to the method whereby the social interests are served, instead of being dealt with as the controlling factor about which the modern economic process turns.

Apart from the metaphysical tenets indicated above as influencing them, there are, of course, reasons of economic history for the procedure of the early economists in so relegating the pecuniary activities to the background of economic theory. In the days of Adam Smith, for instance, economic life still bore much of the character of what Professor Schmoller calls *Stadtwirtschaft*. This was the case to some extent in practice, but still more decidedly in tradition. To a greater extent than has since been the case, households produced goods for their own consumption, without the intervention of sale; and handicraftsmen still produced for consumption by their customers, without the intervention of a market. In a considerable measure, the conditions which the Austrian marginal-utility theory supposes, of a producing seller and a consuming buyer, actually prevailed. It may not be true that in Adam Smith's time the business operations, the bargain and sale of goods, were, in general, obviously subservient to their production and consumption, but it comes nearer being true at that time than at any time since then. And the tradition having once been put into form and authenticated by Adam Smith, that such was the place of pecuniary transactions in economic theory, this tradition has lasted on in the face of later and further changes. Under the shadow of this tradition the pecuniary employments are still dealt with as auxiliary to the process of production, and the gains from such employments are still explained as being due to a productive effect imputed to them.

According to ancient prescription, then, all normal, legitimate economic activities carried on in a well-regulated community serve a materially useful end, and so far as they are lucrative they are so by virtue of and in proportion to a productive effect imputed to them. But in the situation as it exists at any time there are activities and classes of persons which are indispensable to the community, or which are at least unavoidably present in modern economic life, and which draw some income from the aggregate product, at the same time that these activities are not patently productive of goods and cannot well be classed as industrial, in any but a highly sophisticated sense. Some of these activities, which are concerned with economic matters but are not patently of an industrial character, are integral features of modern economic life, and must therefore be classed as normal; for the existing situation, apart from a few minor discrepancies, is particularly normal in the apprehension of present-day economists. Now, the law of economic equivalence and equity says that those who normally receive an income must perforce serve some productive end; and since the existing organization of society is conceived to be eminently normal, it becomes imperative to find some ground on which to impute industrial productivity to those classes and employments which do not at the first view appear to be industrial at all. Hence there is commonly visible in the classical political economy, ancient and modern, a strong inclination to make the schedule of industrially productive employments very comprehensive; so that a good deal of ingenuity has been spent in economically justifying their presence by specifying the productive effect of such non-industrial factors as the courts, the army, the police, the clergy, the schoolmaster, the physician, the opera singer.

But these non-economic employments are not so much to the point in the present inquiry; the point being employments which are unmistakably economic, but not industrial in the naïve sense of the word industry, and which yield an income.

Adam Smith analyzed the process of industry in which he found the community of his time engaged, and found the three classes of agents or factors: Land, Labor, and Capital (stock). The productive factors engaged being thus determined, the norm of natural-economic equivalence and equity already referred to above, indicated what would be the natural sharers in the product. Later economists have shown great reserve about departing from this three-fold division of factors, with its correlated three-fold division of sharers of remuneration; apparently because they have retained an instinctive, indefeasible trust in the law of economic equivalence which underlies it. But circumstances have compelled the tentative intrusion of a fourth class of agent and income. The undertaker and his income presently came to be so large and ubiquitous figures in economic life that their presence could not be overlooked by the most normalizing economist. The undertaker's activity has been interpolated in the scheme of productive factors, as a peculiar and fundamentally distinctive kind of labor, with the function of coordinating and directing industrial processes. Similarly, his income has been interpolated in the scheme of distribution as a peculiar kind of wages, proportioned to the heightened productivity given the industrial process by his work.[3] His work is discussed in expositions of the theory of production. In discussions of his functions and his income the point of the argument is, how and in what degree does his activity increase the output of goods, or how and in what degree does it save wealth to the community. Beyond his effect in enhancing the effective volume of the aggregate wealth the undertaker receives but scant attention, apparently for the reason that so soon as that point has been disposed of the presence of the undertaker and his income has been reconciled with the tacitly accepted natural law of equivalence between productive service and remuneration. The normal balance has been established, and the undertaker's function has been justified and subsumed under the ancient law that Nature does all things well and equitably.

This holds true of the political economy of our grandfathers. But this aim and method of handling the phenomena of life for theoretical ends, of course, did not go out of vogue abruptly in the days of our grandfathers.[4] There is a large sufficiency of the like aim and animus in theoretical discussions of a later time;

but specifically to cite and analyze the evidence of its presence would be laborious, nor would it conduce to the general peace of mind.

Some motion towards a further revision of the scheme is to be seen in the attention which has latterly been given to the function and the profits of that peculiar class of undertakers whom we call speculators. But even on this head the argument is apt to turn on the question of how the services which the speculator is conceived to render the community are to be construed into an equivalent of his gains.[5] The difficulty of interpretation encountered at this point is considerable, partly because it is not quite plain whether the speculators as a class come out of their transactions with a net gain or with a net loss. A systematic net loss, or a no-profit balance, would, on the theory of equivalence, mean that the class which gets this loss or doubtful gain is of no service to the community; yet we are, out of the past, committed to the view that the speculator is useful—indeed economically indispensable—and shall therefore have his reward. In the discussions given to the speculator and his function some thought is commonly given to the question of the "legitimacy" of the speculator's traffic. The legitimate speculator is held to earn his gain by services of an economic kind rendered the community. The recourse to this epithet, "legitimate", is chiefly of interest as showing that the tacit postulate of a natural order is still in force. Legitimate are such speculative dealings as are, by the theorist, conceived to serve the ends of the community, while illegitimate speculation is that which is conceived to be disserviceable to the community.

The theoretical difficulty about the speculator and his gains (or losses) is that the speculator *ex professo* is quite without interest in or connection with any given industrial enterprise or any industrial plant. He is, industrially speaking, without visible means of support. He may stake his risks on the gain or on the loss of the community with equal chances of success, and he may shift from one side to the other without winking.

The speculator may be treated as an extreme case of undertaker, who deals exclusively with the business side of economic life rather than with the industrial side. But he differs in this respect from the common run of business men in degree rather than in kind. His traffic is a pecuniary traffic, and it touches industry only remotely and uncertainly; while the business man as commonly conceived is more or less immediately interested in the successful operation of some concrete industrial plant. But since the undertaker first broke into economic theory, some change has also taken place as regards the immediacy of the relations of the common run of undertakers to the mechanical facts of the industries in which they are interested. Half a century ago it was still possible to construe the average business manager in industry as an agent occupied with the superintendence of the mechanical processes involved in the production of goods or services. But in the later development the connection between the business manager and the mechanical processes has, on an average, grown more remote; so much so, that his superintendence of the plant or of the processes is frequently visible only to the scientific imagination. That activity by virtue of which the undertaker is classed as such makes him a business man, not a mechanic or foreman of the shop. His superintendence is a superintendence of the pecuniary affairs of the concern, rather than of the industrial plant; especially is this true in the higher development of the modern captain of Industry. As regards the nature of the employment which characterizes the undertaker, it is possible to distinguish him from the men who are mechanically engaged in the production of goods, and to say that his employment is of a business or pecuniary kind, while theirs is of an industrial or mechanical kind. It is not possible to draw a similar distinction between the undertaker who is in charge of a given industrial concern, and the business man who is in business but is not interested in the production of goods or services. As regards the character of employment, then, the line falls not between legitimate and illegitimate pecuniary transactions, but between business and industry.

The distinction between business and industry has, of course, been possible from the beginning of economic theory, and, indeed, the distinction has from time to time temporarily been made in the contract frequently pointed out between the proximate interest of the business man and the ulterior interest of society at large. What appears to have hindered the reception of the distinction into economic doctrine is the constraining presence of a belief in an order of Nature and the habit of conceiving the economic community as an organism. The point of view given by these postulates has made such a distinction between employments not only useless, but even disserviceable for the ends to which theory has been directed. But the fact has come to be gradually more and more patent that there are constantly, normally present in modern economic life an important range of activities and classes of persons who work for an income but of whom it cannot be said that they, either proximately or remotely, apply themselves to the production of goods. Their services, proximate or remote, to society are often of quite a problematical character. They are ubiquitous, and it will scarcely do to say that they are anomalous, for they are of ancient prescription, they are within the law and within the pale of popular morals.

Of these strictly economic activities that are lucrative without necessarily being serviceable to the community, the greater part are to be classed as "business." Perhaps the largest and most obvious illustration of these legitimate business employments is afforded by the speculators in securities. By way of further illustration may be mentioned the extensive and varied business of real-estate men (land-agents) engaged in the purchase and sale of property for speculative gain or for a commission; so, also, the closely related business of promoters and boomers of other than real-estate ventures; as also attorneys, brokers, bankers, and the like, although the work performed by these latter will more obviously bear interpretation in terms of social serviceability. The traffic of these business men shades off insensibly from that of the *bona fide* speculator who has no ulterior end of industrial efficiency to serve, to that of the captain of industry or entrepreneur as conventionally set forth in the economic manuals.

The characteristic in which these business employments resemble one another, and in which they differ from the mechanical occupations as well as from other non-economic employments, is that they are concerned primarily with the phenomena of value—with exchange or market values and with purchase and sale—and only indirectly and secondarily, if at all, with mechanical processes. What holds the interest and guides and shifts the attention of men within these employments is the main chance. These activities begin and end within what may broadly be called "the higgling of the market". Of the industrial employments in the stricter sense, it may be said, on the other hand, that they begin and end outside the higgling of the market. Their proximate aim and effect is the shaping and guiding of material things and processes. Broadly, they may be said to be primarily occupied with the phenomena of material serviceability, rather than with those of exchange value. They are taken up with the phenomena which make the subject matter of Physics and the other material sciences.

The business man enters the economic life process from the pecuniary side, and so far as he works an effect in industry he works it through the pecuniary dispositions which he makes. He takes thought most immediately of men's convictions regarding market values; and his efforts as a business man are directed to the apprehension, and commonly also to the influencing, of men's beliefs regarding market values. The objective point of business is the diversion of purchase and sale into some particular channel, commonly involving a diversion from other channels. The laborer and the man engaged in directing industrial processes, on the other hand, enter the economic process from the material side; in their characteristic work they take thought most immediately of mechanical effects, and their attention is directed to turning men and things to account for the compassion of some material end. The ulterior aim, and the ulterior effect, of these industrial employments may be some pecuniary result; work of this class commonly results in an enhancement, or at least an alteration, of market values. Conversely, business activity may, and in a majority of cases it probably does, effect an enhancement of the aggregate material wealth of the community, or the aggregate serviceability of the means at hand; but such an industrial outcome is by no means bound to follow from the nature of the business man's work.

From what has just been said it appears that, if we retain the classical division of economic theory into Production, Distribution, and Consumption, the pecuniary employments do not properly fall under the first of these divisions, Production, if that term is to retain the meaning commonly assigned to it. In an earlier and less specialized organization of economic life, particularly, the undertaker frequently performs the work of a foreman or a technological expert, as well as the work of business management. Hence in most discussions of his work and his theoretical relations his occupation is treated as a composite one. The technological side of his composite occupation has even given a name to his gains (wages of superintendence), as if the undertaker were primarily a master-workman. The distinction at this point has been drawn between classes of persons instead of between classes of employments; with the result that the evident necessity of discussing his technological employment under Production has given countenance to the endeavor to dispose of the undertaker's business activity under the same head. This endeavor has, of course, not wholly succeeded.

In the later development, the specialization of work in the economic field has at this point progressed so far, and the undertaker now in many cases comes so near being occupied with business affairs alone, to the exclusion of technological direction and supervision, that, with this object lesson before us, we no longer have the same difficulty in drawing a distinction between business and industrial employments. And even in the earlier days of the doctrines, when the aim was to dispose of the undertaker's work under the theoretical head of Production, the business side of his work persistently obtruded itself for discussion in the books and chapters given to Distribution and Exchange. The course taken by the later theoretical discussion of the entrepreneur leaves no question but that the characteristic fact about his work is that he is a business man, occupied with pecuniary affairs.

Such pecuniary employments, of which the purely fiscal or financiering forms of business are typical, are nearly all and nearly throughout conditioned by the institution of property or ownership—an institution which, as John Stuart Mill remarks, belongs entirely within the theoretical realm of Distribution. Ownership, no doubt, has its effect upon productive industry, and, indeed, its effect upon industry is very large, both in scope and range, even if we should not be prepared to go the length of saying that it fundamentally conditions all industry; but ownership is not itself primarily or immediately a contrivance for production. Ownership directly touches the results of industry, and only indirectly the methods and processes of industry. If the institution of property be compared with such a feature of our culture, for instance, as the domestication of plants or the smelting of iron, the meaning of what has just been said may seem clearer.

So much then of the business man's activity as is conditioned by the institution of property is not to be classed, in economic theory, as productive or industrial activity at all. Its objective point is an alteration of the distribution of wealth. His business is, essentially, to sell and buy—sell in order to buy cheaper, buy in order to sell dearer.[6] It may or may not, indirectly, and in a sense incidentally, result in enhanced production. The business man may be equally successful in his enterprise, and he may be equally well remunerated, whether his activity does or does not enrich the community. Immediately and directly, so long as it is confined to the pecuniary or business sphere, his activity is incapable of enriching or impoverishing the community as a whole except, after the fashion conceived by the mercantilists, through his dealings with men of other communities. The circulation and distribution of goods incidental to the business man's traffic is commonly, though not always or in the nature of the case, serviceable to the community; but the distribution of goods is a mechanical, not a pecuniary transaction, and it is not the objective point of business nor its invariable outcome. From the point of view of business, the distribution or circulation of goods is a means of gain, not an end sought.

It is true, industry is closely conditioned by business. In a modern community, the business man finally decides what may be done in industry, or at least in the greater number and the more conspicuous branches of industry. This is particularly true of those branches that are currently thought of as peculiarly modern. Under existing circumstances of ownership, the discretion in economic matters, industrial or otherwise, ultimately rests in the hands of the business men. It is their business to have to do with property, and property means the discretionary control of wealth. In point of character, scope and growth, industrial processes and plants adapt themselves to the exigencies of the market, wherever there is a developed market, and the exigencies of the market are pecuniary exigencies. The business man, through his pecuniary dispositions, enforces his choice of what industrial processes shall be in use. He can, of course, not create or initiate methods or aims for industry; if he does so he steps out of the business sphere into the material domain of industry. But he can decide whether and which of the known processes and industrial arts shall be practiced, and to what extent. Industry must be conducted to suit the business man in his quest for gain; which is not the same as saying that it must be conducted to suit the needs or the convenience of the community at large. Ever since the institution of property was definitely installed, and in proportion as purchase and sale has been practiced, some approach has been made to a comprehensive system of control of industry by pecuniary transactions and for pecuniary ends, and the industrial organization is nearer such a consummation now than it ever has been. For the great body of modern industry the final term of the sequence is not the production of the goods but their sale; the endeavor is not so much to fit the goods for use as for sale. It is well known that there are many lines of industry in which the cost of marketing the goods equals the cost of making and transporting them.

Any industrial venture which falls short in meeting the pecuniary exigencies of the market declines and yields ground to others that meet them with better effect. Hence shrewd business management is a requisite to success in any industry that is carried on within the scope of the market. Pecuniary failure carries with it industrial failure, whatever may be the cause to which the pecuniary failure is due—whether it be inferiority of the goods produced, lack of salesmanlike tact, popular prejudice, scanty or ill-devised advertising, excessive truthfulness, or what not. In this way industrial results are closely dependent upon the presence of business ability; but the cause of this dependence of industry upon business in a given case is to be sought in the fact that other rival ventures have the backing of shrewd business management, rather than in any help which business management in the aggregate affords to the aggregate industry of the community. Shrewd and farsighted business management is a requisite of survival in the competitive pecuniary struggle in which the several industrial concerns are engaged, because shrewd and farsighted business management abounds and is employed by all the competitors. The ground of survival in the selective process is fitness for pecuniary gain, not fitness for serviceability at large. Pecuniary management is of an emulative character and gives primarily relative success only. If the change were equitably distributed, an increase or decrease of the aggregate or average business ability in the community need not immediately affect the industrial efficiency or the material welfare of the community. The like cannot be said with respect to the aggregate or average industrial capacity of the men at work. The latter are, on the whole, occupied with production of goods; the business men, on the other hand, are occupied with the acquisition of them.

Theoreticians who are given to looking beneath the facts and to contemplating the profounder philosophical meaning of life speak of the function of the undertaker as being the guidance and coordination of industrial processes with a view to economies of production. No doubt, the remoter effect of business transactions often is such coordination and economy, and, no doubt, also, the undertaker has such economy in view and is stimulated to his maneuver of combination by the knowledge that certain economies of this kind are feasible and will inure to his gain if the proper business arrangements can be effected. But it is practicable to class even this indirect furthering of industry by the undertaker as a permissive guidance only. The men in industry must first create the mechanical possibility of such new and more economical methods and arrangements, before the undertaker sees the chance, makes the necessary business arrangements, and gives directions that the more effective working arrangements be adopted.

It is notorious, and it is a matter upon which men dilate, that the wide and comprehensive consolidations and coordinations of industry, which often add so greatly to its effectiveness, take place at the initiative of the business men who are in control. It should be added that the fact of their being in control precludes such coordination from being effected except by their advice and consent. And it should also be added, in order to a passably complete account of the undertaker's function, that he not only can and does effect economizing coordinations of a large scope, but he also can and does at times inhibit the process of consolidation and coordination. It happens so frequently that it might fairly be said to be the common run that business interests and undertaker's maneuver delay consolidation, combination, coordination, for some appreciable time after they have become patently advisable on industrial grounds. The industrial advisability or practicability is not the decisive point. Industrial advisability must wait on the eventual convergence of jarring pecuniary interests and on the strategical moves of business men playing for position.

Which of these two offices of the business man in modern industry, the furthering or the inhibitory, has the more serious or more far-reaching consequences is, on the whole, somewhat problematical. The furtherance of coordination by the modern captain of industry bulks large in our vision, in great part because the process of widening coordination is of a cumulative character. After a given step in coordination and combination has been taken, the next step takes place on the basis of the resulting situation. Industry, that is to say the working force engaged in industry, has a chance to develop new and larger possibilities to be taken further advantage of. In this way each successive move in the enhancement of the efficiency of industrial processes, or in the widening of coordination in industrial processes, pushes the captain of industry to a further concession, making possible a still farther industrial growth. But as regards the undertaker's inhibitory dealings with industrial coordination the visible outcome is not so striking. The visible outcome is simply that nothing of the kind then takes place in the premises. The potential cumulative sequence is cut off at the start, and so it does not figure in our appraisement of the disadvantage incurred. The loss does not commonly take the more obtrusive form of an absolute retreat, but only that of a failure to advance where the industrial situation admits of an advance.

It is, of course, impracticable to foot up and compare gain and loss in such a case, where the losses, being of the nature of inhibited growth, cannot be ascertained. But since the industrial serviceability of the captain of industry is, on the whole, of a problematical complexion, it should be advisable for a cautious economic theory not to rest its discussion of him on his serviceability.[7]

It appears, then, as all economists are no doubt aware, that there is in modern society a considerable range of activities, which are not normally present, but which constitute the vital core of our economic system; which are not directly concerned with production, but which are nevertheless lucrative. Indeed, the group comprises most of the highly remunerative employments in modern economic life. The gains from these employments must plainly be accounted for on other grounds than their productivity, since they need have no productivity.

But it is not only as regards the pecuniary employments that productivity and remuneration are constitutionally out of touch. It seems plain, from what has already been said, that the like is true for the remuneration gained in the industrial employments. Most wages, particularly those paid in the industrial employments proper, as contrasted with those paid for domestic or personal service, are paid on account of pecuniary serviceability to the employer, not on grounds of material serviceability to mankind at large. The product is valued, sought and paid for on account of and in some proportion to its vendibility, not for more recondite reasons of ulterior human welfare at large. It results that there is no warrant, in general theory, for claiming that the work of highly paid persons (more particularly that of highly paid business men) is of greater substantial use to the community than that of the less highly paid. At the same time, the reverse could, of course, also not be claimed. Wages, resting on a pecuniary basis, afford no consistent indication of the relative productivity of the recipients, except in comparisons between persons or classes whose products are identical except in amount—that is to say, where a resort to wages as an index of productivity would be of no use anyway.[8]

A result of the acceptance of the theoretical distinction here attempted between industrial and pecuniary employments and an effective recognition of the pecuniary basis of the modern economic organization would be to dissociate the two ideas of productivity and remuneration. In mathematical language, remuneration could no longer be conceived and handled as a "function" of productivity—unless productivity be taken to mean pecuniary serviceability to the person who pays the remuneration. In modern life remuneration is, in the last analysis, uniformly obtained by virtue of an agreement between individuals who commonly proceed on their own interest in point of pecuniary gain. The remuneration may, therefore, be said to be a "function" of the pecuniary service rendered the person who grants the remuneration; but what is pecuniarily serviceable to the individual who exercises the discretion in the matter need not be productive of material gain to the community as a whole. Nor does the algebraic sum of individual pecuniary gains measure the aggregate serviceability of the activities for which the gains are got.

In a community organized, as modern communities are, on a pecuniary basis, the discretion in economic matters rests with the individuals, in severalty; and the aggregate of discrete individual interests nowise expresses the collective interest. Expressions constantly recur in economic discussions which imply that the transactions discussed are carried out for the sake of the collective good or at the initiative of the social organism, or that "society" rewards so and so for their services. Such expressions are commonly of the nature of figures of speech and are serviceable for homiletical rather than for scientific use. They serve to express their user's faith in a beneficent order of nature, rather than to convey or to formulate information in regard to facts.

Of course, it is still possible consistently to hold that there is a natural equivalence between work and its reward, that remuneration is naturally, or normally, or in the long run, proportioned to the material service rendered the community by the recipient; but that proposition will hold true only if "natural" or "normal" be taken in such a sense as to admit of our saying that the natural does not coincide with the actual; and it must be recognized that such a doctrine of the "natural" apportionment of wealth or of income disregards the efficient facts of the case. Apart from effects of this kind in the way of equitable arrangements traceable to grounds of sentiment, the only recourse which modern science would afford the champion of a doctrine of natural distribution, in the sense indicated, would be a doctrine of natural selection; according to which all disserviceable or unproductive, wasteful, employments would, perforce, be weeded out as being incompatible with the continued life of any community that tolerated them. But such a selective elimination of unserviceable or wasteful employments would presume the following two conditions, neither of which need prevail: (1) it must be assumed that the disposable margin between the aggregate productivity of industry and the aggregate necessary consumption is so narrow as to admit of no appreciable waste of energy or of goods; (2) it must be assumed that no deterioration of the condition of society, in the economic respect, does or can "naturally" take place. As to the former of these two assumptions, it is to be said that in a very poor community, and under exceptionally hard economic circumstances, the margin of production may be as narrow as the theory would require. Something approaching this state of things may be found, for instance, among some Eskimo tribes. But in a modern industrial community—where the margin of admissible waste probably always exceeds fifty per cent of the output of goods—the facts make no approach to the hypothesis. The second assumed condition is, of course, the old-fashioned assumption of a beneficent, providential order or meliorative trend in human affairs. As such, it needs no argument at this day. Instances are not far to seek of communities in which economic deterioration has taken place while the system of distribution, both of income and of accumulated wealth, has remained on a pecuniary basis.

I am sensible of having dwelt at an unseemly length on this question of an organic or natural equivalence between social service and remuneration, on the one hand, and on the bearing of the attempted distinction between industrial and pecuniary employments upon this theory of a natural equivalence, on the other hand. My excuse for so doing is that this doctrine of a natural equivalence has had a far-reaching and enduring effect upon the received theories of distribution and production, and that, with a change of phrase rather than of substance, it still continues to afford ground for further elaboration of like theories; while at the same time it seems plain that a scrutiny of the metaphysics of the doctrine of equivalence must immediately put it out of court as being groundless as well as useless for the purposes of modern science. I am also sensible of having said very little in the course of this long argument that is not already contained, explicitly, or by broad implication, in the accepted body of doctrines. What has been attempted is to follow out the direction of latter-day economic discussion one step beyond the point at which those who have been making economic science have been content to rest their analysis of phenomena. This one step crosses the frontier between the normal and the actual, at a point where the line has not usually been crossed.

To return to the main drift of the argument. The pecuniary employments have to do with wealth in point of ownership, with market values, with transactions of exchange, purchase and sale, bargaining for the purpose of pecuniary gain. These employments make up the characteristic occupations of business men, and the gains of business are derived from successful endeavors of the pecuniary kind. These business employments are the characteristic activity (constitute the "function") of what are in theory called undertakers. The dispositions which undertakers, *qua* business men, make are pecuniary dispositions—whatever industrial sequel they may or may not have—and are carried out with a view to pecuniary gain. The wealth of which they have the discretionary disposal may or may not be in the form of "production goods"; but in whatever form the wealth in question is conceived to exist, it is handled by the undertakers in terms of values and is disposed of by them in the pecuniary respect. When, as may happen, the undertaker steps down from the pecuniary plane and directs the mechanical handling and functioning of "production goods," he becomes for the time a foreman. The undertaker, if his business venture is of the industrial kind, of course takes cognizance of the aptness of a given industrial method or process for his purpose, and he has to choose between different industrial processes in which to invest his values; but his work as undertaker, simply, is the investment and shifting of the values under his hand from the less to the more gainful point of investment. When the investment takes the form of material means of industry, or industrial plant, the sequel of a given business transaction is commonly some particular use of such means; and when such industrial use follows, it commonly takes place at the hands of other men than the undertaker, although it takes place within limits imposed by the pecuniary exigencies of which the undertaker takes cognizance. Wealth turned to account in the way of investment or business management may, or may not, in consequence, be turned to account, materially for industrial effect. Wealth, values so employed for pecuniary ends, is capital in the business sense of the word.[9] Wealth, material means of industry, physically employed for industrial ends is capital in the industrial sense. Theory, therefore, would require that care be taken to distinguish between capital as a pecuniary category, and capital as an industrial category, if the term capital is retained to cover the two concepts.[10] The distinction here made substantially coincides with a distinction which many late writers have arrived at from a different point of approach and have, with varying success, made use of under different terms.[11]

A further corollary touching capital may be pointed out. The gains derived from the handling of capital in the pecuniary respect have no immediate relation, stand in no necessary relation of proportion, to the productive effect compassed by the industrial use of the material means over which the undertaker may dispose; although the gains have a relation of dependence to the effects achieved in point of vendibility. But vendibility need not, even approximately, coincide with serviceability, except serviceability be construed in terms of marginal utility or some related conception, in which case the outcome is a tautology. Where, as in the case commonly assumed by economists as typical, the investing undertaker seeks his gain through the production and sale of some useful article, it is commonly also assumed that his effort is directed to the most economical production of as large and serviceable a product as may be, or at least it is assumed that such production is the outcome of his endeavors in the natural course of things. This account of the aim and outcome of business enterprise may be natural, but it does not describe the facts. The facts being, of course, that the undertaker in such a case seeks to produce economically as vendible a product as may be. In the common run vendibility depends in great part on the serviceability of the goods, but it depends also on several other circumstances; and to that highly variable, but nearly always considerable, extent to which vendibility depends on other circumstances than the material serviceability of the goods, the pecuniary management of capital must be held not to serve the ends of production. Neither immediately, in his purely pecuniary traffic, nor indirectly, in the business guidance of industry through his pecuniary traffic, therefore, can the undertaker's dealings with his pecuniary capital be accounted a productive occupation, nor can the gains of capital be taken to mark or to measure the productivity, due to the investment. The "cost of production" of goods in the case contemplated is to an appreciable, but indeterminable, extent a cost of production of vendibility—an outcome which is often of doubtful service to the body of consumers, and which often counts in the aggregate as waste. The material serviceability of the means employed in industry, that is to say the functioning of industrial capital in the service of the community at large, stands in no necessary or consistent relation to the gainfulness of capital in the pecuniary respect. Productivity can accordingly not be predicted of pecuniary capital. . . .

It is, further, to be remarked that pecuniary capital and industrial capital do not coincide in respect of the concrete things comprised under each. From this and from the considerations already indicated above, it follows that the magnitude of pecuniary capital may vary independently of variations in the magnitude of industrial capital—not indefinitely, perhaps, but within a range which, in its nature, is indeterminate. Pecuniary capital is a matter of market values, while industrial capital is, in the last analysis, a matter of mechanical efficiency, or rather of mechanical effects not reducible to a common measure or a collective magnitude. So far as the latter may be spoken of as a homogenous aggregate—itself a doubtful point at best—the two categories of capital are disparate magnitudes, which can be mediated only through a process of valuation conditioned by other circumstances besides the mechanical efficiency of the material means valued. Market values being a psychological outcome, it follows that pecuniary capital, an aggregate of market values, may vary in magnitude with a freedom which gives the whole an air of caprice—such as psychological phenomena, particularly the psychological phenomena of crowds, frequently present, and such as becomes strikingly noticeable in times of panic or of speculative inflation. On the other hand, industrial capital, being a matter of mechanical contrivances and adaptation, cannot similarly vary through a revision of valuations. If it is taken as an aggregate, it is a physical magnitude, and as such it does not alter its complexion or its mechanical efficiency in response to the greater or less degree of appreciation with which it is viewed. Capital pecuniarily considered rests on a basis of subjective value; capital industrially considered rests on material circumstances reducible to objective terms of mechanical, chemical and physiological effect.

The point has frequently been noted that it is impossible to get at the aggregate social (industrial) capital by adding up the several items of individual (pecuniary) capital. A reason for this, apart from variations in the market values of given material means of production, is that pecuniary capital comprises not only material things but also conventional facts, psychological phenomena not related in any rigid way to material means of production—as, e.g., good will, fashions, customs, prestige, effrontery, personal credit. Whatever ownership touches, and whatever affords ground for pecuniary discretion, may be turned to account for pecuniary gain and may therefore be comprised in the aggregate of pecuniary capital. Ownership, the basis of pecuniary capital, being itself a conventional fact, that is to say a matter of habits of thought, it is intelligible that phenomena of convention and opinion should figure in an inventory of pecuniary capital; whereas, industrial capital being of a mechanical character, conventional circumstances do not affect it—except as the future production of material means to replace the existing outfit may be guided by convention—and items having but a conventional existence are, therefore, not comprised in its aggregate. The disparity between pecuniary and industrial capital, therefore, is something more than a matter of an arbitrarily chosen point of view, as some recent discussions of the capital concept would have us believe; just as the difference between the pecuniary and the industrial employments, which are occupied with the one or the other category of capital, means something more than the same thing under different aspects.

But the distinction here attempted has a farther hearing, beyond the possible correction of a given point in the theory of distribution. Modern economic science is to an increasing extent concerning itself with the question of what men do and how and why they do it, as contrasted with the older question of how Nature, working through human nature, maintains a favorable balance in the output of goods. Neither the practical questions of our generation, nor the pressing theoretical questions of the science, run on the adequacy or equity of the share that goes to any class in the normal case. The questions are rather such realistic ones as these: Why do we, now and again, have hard times and unemployment in the midst of excellent resources, high efficiency and plenty of unmet wants? Why is one-half our consumable product contrived for consumption that yields no material benefit? Why are large coordinations of industry, which greatly reduce cost of production, a cause of perplexity and alarm? Why is the family disintegrating among the industrial classes, at the same time that the wherewithal to maintain it is easier to compass? Why are large and increasing portions of the community penniless in spite of a scale of remuneration which is very appreciably above the subsistence minimum? Why is there a widespread disaffection among the intelligent workmen who ought to know better? These and the like questions, being questions of fact, are not to be answered on the grounds of normal equivalence. Perhaps it might better be said that they have so often been answered on those grounds, without any approach to disposing of them, that the outlook for help in that direction has ceased to have a serious meaning. These are, to borrow Professor Clark's phrase, questions to be answered on dynamic, not on static grounds. They are questions of conduct and sentiment, and so far as their solution is looked for at the hands of economists it must be looked for along the line of the bearing which economic life has upon the growth of sentiment and canons of conduct. That is to say, they are questions of the bearing of economic life upon the cultural changes that are going forward.

For the present it is the vogue to hold that economic life, broadly, conditions the rest of social organization or the constitution of society. This vogue of the proposition will serve as an excuse from going into an examination of the grounds on which it may be justified, as it is scarcely necessary to persuade any economist that it has substantial merits even if he may not accept it in an unqualified form. What the Marxists have named the "Materialistic Conception of History" is assented to with less and less qualification by those who make the growth of culture their subject of inquiry. This materialistic conception says that institutions are shaped by economic conditions; but, as it left the hands of the Marxists, and as it still functions in the hands of many who knew not Marx, it has very little to say regarding the efficient force, the channels, or the methods by which the economic situation is conceived to have its effect upon institutions. What answer the early Marxists gave to this question, of how the economic situation shapes institutions, was to the effect that the causal connection lies through a selfish, calculating class interest. But, while class interest may count for much in the outcome, this answer is plainly not a competent one, since, for one thing, institutions by no means change with the alacrity which the sole efficiency of a reasoned class interest would require.

Without discrediting the claim that class interest counts for something in the shaping of institutions, and to avoid getting entangled in preliminaries, it may be said that institutions are of the nature of prevalent habits of thought, and that therefore the force which shapes institutions is the force of forces which shape the habits of thought prevalent in the community. But habits of thought are the outcome of habits of life. Whether it is intentionally directed to the education of the individual or not, the discipline of daily life acts to alter or re-enforce the received institutions under which men live. And the direction in which, on the whole, the alteration proceeds is conditioned by the trend of the discipline of daily life. The point here immediately at issue is the divergent trend of this discipline in those occupations which are prevailingly of an industrial character, as contrasted with those which are prevailingly of a pecuniary character. So far as regards the different cultural outcome to be looked for on the basis of the present economic situation as contrasted with the past, therefore, the question immediately in hand is as to the greater or less degree in which occupations are differentiated into industrial and pecuniary in the present as compared with the past.

The characteristic feature which is currently held to differentiate the existing economic situation from that out of which the present has developed, or out of which it is emerging, is the prevalence of the machine industry with the consequent larger and more highly specialized organization of the market and of the industrial force and plant. As has been pointed out above, and as is well enough known from the current discussions of the economists, industrial life is organized on a pecuniary basis and managed from the pecuniary side. This, of course, is true in a degree both of the present and of the nearer past, back at least as far as the middle ages. But the larger scope of organizations in modern industry means that the pecuniary management has been gradually passing into the hands of a relatively decreasing class, whose contract with the industrial classes proper grows continually less immediate. The distinction between employments above spoken of is in an increasing degree coming to coincide with a differentiation of occupations and of economic classes. Some degree of such specialization and differentiation there has, of course, been, one might almost say, always. But in our time, in many branches of industry, the specialization has been carried so far that large bodies of the working population have but an incidental contract with the business side of the enterprise, while a minority have little if any other concern with the enterprise than its pecuniary management. This was not true, e.g., at the time when the undertaker was still salesman, purchasing agent, business manager, foreman of the shop, and master workman. Still less was it true in the days of the self-sufficing manor or household, or in the days of the closed town industry. Neither is it true in our time of what we call the backward or old-fashioned industries. These latter have not been and are not organized on a large scale, with a consistent division of labor between the owners and business managers on the one side and the operative employees on the other. Our standing illustrations of this less highly organized class of industries are the surviving handcrafts and the common run of farming as carried on by relatively small proprietors. In that earlier phase of economic life, out of which the modern situation has gradually grown, all the men engaged had to be constantly on their guard, in a pecuniary sense, and were constantly disciplined in the driving of their means and in the driving of bargains—as is still true, e.g., of the American farmer. The like was formerly true also of the consumer, in his purchases, to a greater extent than at present. A good share of the daily attention of those who were engaged in the handicrafts was still perforce given to the pecuniary or business side of their trade. But for that great body of industry which is conventionally recognized as eminently modern, specialization of function has gone so far as, in great measure, to exempt the operative employees from taking thought of pecuniary matters.

Now, as to the bearing of all this upon cultural changes that are in progress or in the outlook. Leaving the "backward," relatively unspecialized, industries on one side, as being of an equivocal character for the point in hand and as not differing characteristically from the corresponding industries in the past so far as regards their disciplinary value; modern occupations may, for the sake of the argument, be broadly distinguished, as economic employments have been distinguished above, into business and industrial. The modern industrial and the modern business occupations are fairly comparable as regards the degree of intelligence required in both, if it be borne in mind that the former occupations comprise the highly trained technological experts and engineers as well as the highly skilled mechanics. The two classes of occupations differ in that the men in the pecuniary occupations work within the lines and under the guidance of the great institution of ownership, with its ramifications of custom, prerogative, and legal right; whereas those in the industrial occupations are, in their work, relatively free from the constraint of this conventional norm of truth and validity. It is, of course, not true that the work of the latter class lies outside the reach of the institution of ownership; but it is true that, in the beat and strain of the work, when the agent's powers and attention are fully taken up with the work which he has in hand, that of which he has perforce to take cognizance is not conventional law, but the conditions impersonally imposed by the nature of material things. This is the meaning of the current commonplace that the required close and continuous application of the operative in mechanical industry bars him out of all chance for an all-around development of the cultural graces and amenities. It is the periods of close attention and hard work that seem to count for most in the formation of habits of thought.

An *a priori* argument as to what cultural effects should naturally follow from such a difference in discipline between occupations, past and present, would probably not be convincing, as *a priori* arguments from half-authenticated premises commonly are not. And the experiments along this line which later economic developments have so far exhibited have been neither neat enough, comprehensive enough, nor long continued enough to give definitive results. Still, there is something to be said under this latter head, even if this something may turn out to be somewhat familiar.

It is, e.g., a commonplace of current vulgar discussions of existing economic questions, that the classes engaged in the modern mechanical or factory industries are improvident and apparently incompetent to take care of the pecuniary details of their own life. In this indictment may well be included not only factory hands, but the general class of highly skilled mechanics, inventors, technological experts. The rule does not hold in any hard and fast way, but there seems to be a substantial ground of truth in the indictment in this general form. This will be evident on comparison of the present factory population with the class of handicraftsmen of the older culture whom they have displaced, as also on comparison with the farming population of the present time, especially the small proprietors of this and other countries. The inferiority which is currently conceded to the modern industrial classes in this respect is not due to scantier opportunities for saving, whether they are compared with the earlier handicraftsmen or with the modern farmer or peasant. This phenomenon is commonly discussed in terms which impute to the improvident industrial classes something in the way of total depravity, and there is much preaching of thrift and steady habits. But the preaching of thrift and self-help, unremitting as it is, is not producing an appreciable effect. The trouble seems to run deeper than exhortation can reach. It seems to be of the nature of habit rather than of reasoned conviction. Other causes may be present and may be competent partially to explain the improvidence of these classes, but the inquiry is at least a pertinent one how far the absence of property and thrift among them may be traceable to the relative absence of pecuniary training in the discipline of their daily life. If, as the general lay of the subject would indicate, this peculiar pecuniary situation of the industrial classes is in any degree due to comprehensive disciplinary causes, there is material in it for an interesting economic inquiry.

The surmise that the trouble with the industrial class is something of this character is strengthened by another feature of modern vulgar life, to which attention is directed as a further, and, for the present, a concluding illustration of the character of the questions that are touched by the distinction here spoken for. The most insidious and most alarming malady, as well as the most perplexing and unprecedented, that threatens the modern social and political structure is what is vaguely called socialism. The point of danger to the social structure, and at the same time the substantial core of the socialistic disaffection, is a growing disloyalty to the institution of property, aided and abetted as it is by a similarly growing lack of deference and affection for other conventional features of social structure. The classes affected by socialistic vagaries are not consistently averse to a competent organization and control of society, particularly not in the economic respect, but they are averse to organization and control on conventional lines. The sense of solidarity does not seem to be either defective or in abeyance, but the ground of solidarity is new and unexpected. What their constructive ideals may be need not concern nor detain us; they are vague and inconsistent and for the most part negative. Their disaffection has been set down to discontent with their lot by comparison with others, and to a mistaken view of their own interests; and much and futile effort has been spent in showing them the error of their ways of thinking. But what the experience of the past suggests that we should expect under the guidance of such motives and reasoning as these would be a demand for a redistribution of property, a reconstitution of the convention of ownership on such new lines as the apprehended interests of these classes would seem to dictate. But such is not the trend of socialistic thinking, which contemplates rather the elimination of the institution of property. To the socialists property or ownership does not seem inevitable or inherent in the nature of things; to those who criticize and admonish them it commonly does.

Compare them in this respect with other classes who have been moved by hardship or discontent, whether well or ill advised, to put forth denunciations and demands for radical economic changes; as, e.g., the American farmers in their several movements, of grangerism, populism, and the like. These have been loud enough in their denunciations and complaints, and they have been accused of being socialistic in their demand for a virtual redistribution of property. They have not felt the justice of the accusation, however, and it is to be noted that their demands have consistently run on a rehabilitation of property on some new basis of distribution, and have been uniformly put forth with the avowed purpose of bettering the claimants in point of ownership. Ownership, property "honestly" acquired, has been sacred to the rural malcontents, here and elsewhere; what they have aspired to do has been to remedy what they have conceived to be certain abuses under the institution, without questioning the institution itself.

Not so with the socialists, either in this country or elsewhere. Now, the spread of socialistic sentiment shows a curious tendency to affect those classes particularly who are habitually employed in the specialized industrial occupations, and are thereby in great part exempt from the intellectual discipline of pecuniary management. Among these men, who by the circumstances of their daily life are brought to do their serious and habitual thinking in other than pecuniary terms, it looks as if the ownership preconception were becoming obsolescent through disuse. It is the industrial population, in the modern sense, and particularly the more intelligent and skilled men employed in the mechanical industries, that are most seriously and widely affected. With exceptions both ways, but with a generality that is not to be denied, the socialistic disaffection spreads through the industrial towns, chiefly and most potently among the better classes of operatives in the mechanical employments; whereas the relatively indigent and unintelligent regions and classes, which the differentiation between pecuniary and industrial occupations has not reached, are relatively free from it. In like manner the upper and middle classes, whose employments are of a pecuniary character, if any, are also not seriously affected; and when avowed socialistic sentiment is met with among these upper and middle classes it commonly turns out to be merely a humanitarian aspiration for a more "equitable" redistribution of wealth—a readjustment of ownership under some new and improved method of control—not a contemplation of the traceless disappearance of ownership.

Socialism, in the sense in which the word connotes a subversion of the economic foundations of modern culture, appears to be found only sporadically and uncertainly outside the limits, in time and space, of the discipline exercised by the modern mechanical, non-pecuniary occupations. This state of the case need of course not be due solely to the disciplinary effects of the industrial employments, nor even solely to effects traceable to those employments whether in the way of disciplinary results, selective development, or what not. Other factors, particularly factors of an ethnic character, seem to cooperate to the result indicated; but, so far as evidence bearing on the point is yet in hand and has been analyzed, it indicates that this differentiation of occupations is a necessary requisite to the growth of a consistent body of socialistic sentiment; and the indication is also that wherever this differentiation prevails in such a degree of accentuation and affects such considerable and compact bodies of people as to afford ground for a consistent growth of common sentiment, a result is some form of iconoclastic socialism. The differentiation may of course have a selective as well as a disciplinary effect upon the population affected, and an off-hand separation of these two modes of influence can of course not be made. In any case, the two modes of influence seem to converge to the outcome indicated; and, for the present purpose of illustration simply, the tracing out of the two strands of sequence in the case neither can nor need be undertaken. By force of this differentiation, in one way and another, the industrial classes are learning to think in terms of material cause and effect, to the neglect of prescription and conventional grounds of validity; just as, in a faintly incipient way, the economists are also learning to do in their discussion of the life of these classes. The resulting decay of the popular sense of conventional validity of course extends to other matters than the pecuniary conventions alone, with the outcome that the socialistically affected industrial classes are pretty uniformly affected with an effortless iconoclasm in other directions as well. For the discipline to which their work and habits of life subject them gives not so much a training away from the pecuniary conventions, specifically, as a positive and somewhat unmitigated training in methods of observation and inference proceeding on grounds alien to all conventional validity. But the practical experiment going on in the specialization of discipline, in the respect contemplated, appears still to be near its beginning, and the growth of aberrant views and habits of thought due to the peculiar disciplinary trend of the late and unprecedented specialization of occupations has not yet had time to work itself clear.

The effects of the like one-sided discipline are similarly visible in the highly irregular, conventionally indefensible attitude of the industrial classes in the current labor and wage disputes, not of an avowedly socialistic aim. So also as regards the departure from the ancient norm in such non-economic, or secondarily economic matters as the family relation and responsibility, where the disintegration of conventionalities in the industrial towns is said to threaten the foundations of domestic life and morality; and again as regards the growing inability of men trained to materialistic, industrial habits of thought to appreciate, or even to apprehend, the meaning of religious appeals and consolations that proceed on the old-fashioned conventional or metaphysical grounds of validity. But these and other like directions in which the cultural effects of the modern specialization of occupations, whether in industry or in business, may be traceable cannot be followed up here.

Notes

1. Some later writers, as, e.g., J.B. Clark, apparently must be held to conceive the equivalence in terms of productive force rather than of serviceability; or, perhaps, in terms of serviceability on one side of the equation and productive force on the other.

2. J.B. Clark, *The Distribution of Wealth*, p. 20.

3. The undertaker gets an income; therefore he must produce goods. But human activity directed to the production of goods is labor; therefore the undertaker is a particular kind of laborer. There is, of course, some dissent from this position.

4. The change which has supervened as regards the habitual resort to a natural law of equivalence is in large part a change with respect to the degree of immediacy and "reality"

imputed to this law, and to a still greater extent a change in the degree of overtness with which it is avowed.

5. See, e.g., a paper by H.C. Emery in the *Papers and Proceedings of the Twelfth Annual Meeting of the American Economic Association,* on "The Place of the Speculator in the Theory of Distribution," and more particularly the discussion following the paper.

6. Cf., e.g., Marx's *Capital,* especially bk. I, ch. IV.

7. It is not hereby intended to depreciate the services rendered the community by the captain of industry in his management of business. Such services are no doubt rendered and are also no doubt of substantial value. Still less is it the intention to decry, the pecuniary incentive as a motive to thrift and diligence. It may well be that the pecuniary traffic which we call business is the most effective method of conducting the industrial policy of the community; not only the most effective that has been contrived, but perhaps the best that can be contrived. But that is a matter of surmise and opinion. In a matter of opinion on a point that cannot be verified, a reasonable course is to say that the majority are presumably in the right. But all that is beside the point. However probable or reasonable such a view may be, it can find no lodgement in modern scientific theory, except as a corollary of secondary importance. Nor can scientific theory build upon the ground it may be conceived to afford. Policy may so build, but science cannot. Scientific theory is a formulation of the laws of phenomena in terms of the efficient forces at work in the sequence of phenomena. So long as (under the old dispensation of the order of nature) the animistically conceived natural laws, with their God-given objective end, were considered to exercise a constraining guidance over the course of events whereof they were claimed to be laws, so long it was legitimate scientific procedure for economists to formulate their theory in terms of these laws of the natural course; because so long as they were speaking in terms of what was, to them, the efficient forces and so soon as these natural laws were reduced to the plane of colorless empirical generalization as to what commonly happens, while the efficient forces at work are conceived to be of quite another cast, but so soon must theory abandon the ground of the natural course, sterile for modern scientific purposes, and shift to the ground of the causal sequence, where alone it will have to do with the forces at work as they are conceived in our time. The generalizations regarding the normal course, as "normal" has been defined in economics since J.S. Mill, are not of the nature of theory, but only rule-of-thumb. And the talk about the "function" of this and that factor of production, etc., in terms of the collective life purpose, goes to the same limbo; since the collective life purpose is no longer avowedly conceived to cut any figure in the every-day guidance of economic activities or the shaping of economic results.

The doctrine of the social-economic function of the undertaker may for the present purpose be illustrated by a suppositions parallel from Physics. It is an easy generalization, which will scarcely be questioned, that, in practice, pendulums commonly vibrate in a plane approximately parallel with the nearest wall of the clock-case in which they are placed. The normality of this parallelism is fortified by the further observation that the vibrations are also commonly in a plane parallel with the nearest wall of the room; and when it is further called to mind that the balance which serves the purpose of a pendulum in watches similarly vibrates in a plane parallel with the walls of its case, the absolute normality of the whole arrangement is placed beyond question. It is true, the parallelism is not claimed to be related to the working of the pendulum, except as a matter of fortuitous convenience; but it should be manifest from the generality of the occurrence that in the normal case, in the absence of disturbing causes, and in the long run, all pendulums will "naturally" tend to swing in a plane faultlessly parallel with the nearest wall. The use which has been made of the "organic concept", in economics and in social science at large, is fairly comparable with this suppositions argument concerning the pendulum.

8. Since the ground of payment of wages is the vendibility of the product, and since

the ground of a difference in wages is the different vendibility of the product acquired through the purchase of the labor for which the wages are paid, it follows that wherever the difference in vendibility rests on a difference in the magnitude of the product alone, there wages should be somewhat in proportion to the magnitude of the product.

9. All wealth so used is capital, but it does not follow that all pecuniary capital is social wealth.

10. In current theory the term capital is used in these two senses; while in business usage it is employed pretty consistently in the former sense alone. The current ambiguity in the term capital has often been adverted to by economists, and there may be need of a revision of the terminology at this point; but this paper is not concerned with that question.

11. Professor Fetter, in a recent paper (*Quarterly Journal of Economics*, November, 1900), is, perhaps, the writer who has gone the farthest in this direction, in the definition of the capital concept. Professor Fetter wishes to confine the term capital to pecuniary capital, or rather to such pecuniary capital as is based on the ownership of material goods. The wisdom of such a terminology expedient is, of course, not in question here.

Why Is Economics Not an Evolutionary Science?

M.G. De Lapouge recently said, "Anthropology is destined to revolutionize the political and the social sciences as radically as bacteriology has revolutionized the science of medicine."[1] In so far as he speaks of economics, the eminent anthropologist is not alone in his conviction that the science stands in need of rehabilitation. His words convey a rebuke and an admonition, and in both respects he speaks the sense of many scientists in his own and related lines of inquiry. It may be taken as the consensus of those men who are doing the serious work of modern anthropology, ethnology, and psychology, as well as of those in the biological sciences proper, that economics is helplessly behind the times, and unable to handle its subject-matter in a way to entitle it to standing as a modern science. The other political and social sciences come in for their share of this obloquy, and perhaps on equally cogent grounds. Nor are the economists themselves buoyantly indifferent to the rebuke. Probably no economist today has either the hardihood or the inclination to say that the science has now reached a definitive formulation, either in the detail of results or as regards the fundamental features of theory. The nearest recent approach to such a position on the part of an economist of accredited standing is perhaps to be found in Professor Marshall's Cambridge address of a year and a half ago.[2] But these utterances are so far from the jaunty confidence shown by the classical economists of half a century ago that what most forcibly strikes the reader of Professor Marshall's address is the exceeding modesty and the uncalled-for humility of the spokesman for the "old generation." With the economists who are most attentively looked to for guidance, uncertainty as to the definitive value of what has been and is being done, and as to what we may, with effect, take to next, is so common as to suggest that indecision is a meritorious work. Even the Historical School, who

Reprinted from the *Quarterly Journal of Economics* (July 1898): pp. 373–97. Used by permission.

made their innovation with so much home-grown applause some time back, have been unable to settle down contentedly to the pace which they set themselves.

The men of the sciences that are proud to own themselves "modern" find fault with the economists for being still content to occupy themselves with repairing a structure and doctrines and maxims resting on natural rights, utilitarianism, and administrative expediency. This aspersion is not altogether merited, but is near enough to the mark to carry a sting. These modern sciences are evolutionary sciences, and their adepts contemplate that characteristic of their work with some complacency. Economics is not an evolutionary science—by the confession of its spokesmen; and the economists turn their eyes with something of envy and some sense of baffled emulation to these rivals that make broad their phylacteries with the legend, "Up to date."

Precisely wherein the social and political sciences, including economics, fall short of being evolutionary sciences, is not so plain. At least, it has not been satisfactorily pointed out by their critics. Their successful rivals in this matter—the sciences that deal with human nature among the rest—claim as their substantial distinction that they are realistic: they deal with facts. But economics, too, is realistic in this sense: it deals with facts, often in the most painstaking way, and latterly with an increasingly strenuous insistence on the sole efficacy of data. But this "realism" does not make economics an evolutionary science. The insistence on data could scarcely be carried to a higher pitch than it was carried by the first generation of the Historical School; and yet no economics is farther from being an evolutionary science than the received economics of the Historical School. The whole broad range of erudition and research that engaged the energies of that school commonly falls short of being science, in that, when consistent, they have contented themselves with an enumeration of data and a narrative account of industrial development, and have not presumed to offer a theory of anything or to elaborate their results into a consistent body of knowledge.

Any evolutionary science, on the other hand, is a close-knit body of theory. It is a theory of a process, of an unfolding sequence. But here, again, economics seems to meet the test in a fair measure, without satisfying its critics that its credentials are good. It must be admitted, e.g., that J.S. Mill's doctrines of production, distribution, and exchange are a theory of certain economic processes, and that he deals in a consistent and effective fashion with the sequences of fact that make up his subject-matter. So, also, Cairnes's discussion of normal value, of the rate of wages, and of international trade are excellent instances of a theoretical handling of economic processes of sequence and the orderly unfolding development of fact. But an attempt to cite Mill and Cairnes as exponents of an evolutionary economics will produce no better effect than perplexity, and not a great deal of that. Very much of monetary theory might be cited to the same purpose and with the like effect. Something similar is true even of late writers who have avowed some penchant for the evolutionary point of view; as, e.g., Professor Hadley—to cite a work of unquestioned merit and unusual reach.

Measurably, he keeps the word of promise to the ear; but any one who may cite his *Economics* as having brought political economy into line as an evolutionary science will convince neither himself nor his interlocutor. Something to the like effect may fairly be said of the published work of that later English strain of economists represented by Professors Cunningham and Ashley, and Mr. Cannan, to name but a few of the more eminent figures in the group.

Of the achievements of the classical economists, recent and living, the science may justly be proud; but they fall short of the evolutionist's standard of adequacy, not in failing to offer a theory of process or of a developmental relation, but through conceiving their theory in terms alien to the evolutionist's habits of thought. The difference between the evolutionary and the pre-evolutionary sciences lies not in the insistence on facts. There was a great and fruitful activity in the natural sciences in collecting and collating facts before these sciences took on the character which marks them as evolutionary. Nor does the difference lie in the absence of efforts to formulate and explain schemes of process, sequence, growth, and development in the pre-evolutionary days. Efforts of this kind abounded, in number and diversity; and many schemes of development, of great subtlety and beauty, gained a vogue both as theories of organic and inorganic development and as schemes of the life history of nations and societies. It will not even hold true that our elders overlooked the presence of cause and effect in formulating their theories and reducing their data in a body of knowledge. But the terms which were accepted as the definitive terms of knowledge were in some degree different in the early days from what they are now. The terms of thought in which the investigators of some two or three generations back definitively formulated their knowledge of facts, in their last analyses, were different in kind from the terms in which the modern evolutionist is content to formulate his results. The analysis does not run back to the same ground, or appeal to the same standard of finality or adequacy, in the one case as in the other.

The difference is a difference of spiritual attitude or point of view in the two contrasted generations of scientists. To put the matter in other words, it is a difference in the basis of valuation of the facts for the scientific purpose, or in the interest from which the facts are appreciated. With the earlier as with the later generation the basis of valuation of the facts handled is, in matters of detail, the causal relation which is apprehended to subsist between them. This is true to the greatest extent for the natural sciences. But in their handling of the more comprehensive schemes of sequence and relation—in their definitive formulation of the results—the two generations differ. The modern scientist is unwilling to depart from the test of causal relation or quantitative sequence. When he asks the question, Why? he insists on an answer in terms of cause and effect. He wants to reduce his solution of all problems to terms of the conservation of energy or the persistence of quantity. This is his last recourse. And this last recourse has in our time been made available for the handling of schemes of development and theories of a comprehensive process by the notion of a cumulative causation. The great deserts of the evolutionist leaders—if they have great deserts as leaders—lie, on the one hand, in their refusal to go back of the colorless sequence of phenomena and seek higher ground for their ultimate syntheses, and, on the other hand, in their having shown how this colorless impersonal sequence of cause and effect can be made use of for theory proper, by virtue of its cumulative character.

For the earlier natural scientists, as for the classical economists, this ground of cause and effect is not definitive. Their sense of truth and substantiality is not satisfied with a formulation of mechanical sequence. The ultimate term in their systematization of knowledge is a "natural law." This natural law is felt to exercise some sort of a coercive surveillance over the sequence of events, and to give a spiritual stability and consistence to the causal relation at any given juncture. To meet the high classical requirement, a sequence—and a development process especially—must be apprehended in terms of a consistent propensity tending to some spiritually legitimate end. When facts and events have been reduced to these terms of fundamental truth and have been made to square with the requirements of definitive normality, the investigator rests his case. Any causal sequence which is apprehended to traverse the imputed propensity in events is a "disturbing factor." Logical congruity with the apprehended propensity is, in this view, adequate ground of procedure in building up a scheme of knowledge or of development. The objective point of the efforts of the scientists working under the guidance of this classical tradition is to formulate knowledge in terms of absolute truth; and this absolute truth is a spiritual fact. It means a coincidence of facts with the deliverance of an enlightened and deliberate common sense.

The development and the attenuation of this preconception of normality or of a propensity in events might be traced in detail from primitive animism down through the elaborate discipline of faith and metaphysics, over-ruling Providence, order of nature, natural rights, natural law, underlying principles. But all that may be necessary here is to point out that, by descent and by psychological content, this constraining normality is of a spiritual kind. It is for the scientific purpose and imputation of spiritual coherence to the facts dealt with. The question of interest is how this preconception of normality has fared at the hands of modern science, and how it has come to be superseded in the intellectual primacy by the latter-day preconception of a non-spiritual sequence. This question is of interest because its answer may throw light on the question as to what chance there is for the indefinite persistence of this archaic habit of thought in the methods of economic science.

Under primitive conditions, men stand in immediate personal contact with the material facts of the environment; and the force and discretion of the individual in shaping the facts of the environment count obviously, and to all appearance solely, in working out the conditions of life. There is little of impersonal or mechanical sequence visible to primitive men in their every-day life; and what there is of this kind in the processes of brute nature about them is in large part inexplicable and passes for inscrutable. It is accepted as malignant or beneficent, and is construed in the terms of personality that are familiar to all men at first hand—the terms known to all men by first-hand knowledge of their own acts. The inscrutable movements of the seasons and of the natural forces are apprehended as actions guided by discretion, will power, or propensity looking to an end, much as human actions are. The processes of inanimate nature are agencies whose habits of life are to be learned, and who are to be coerced, outwitted, circumvented, and turned to account, much as the beasts are. At the same time the community is small, and the human contact of the individual is not wide. Neither the industrial life nor the non-industrial social life forces upon men's attention the ruthless impersonal sweep of events that no man can withstand or deflect, such as becomes visible in the more complex and comprehensive life process of the large community of a later day. There is nothing decisive to hinder men's knowledge of facts and events being formulated in terms of personality—in terms of habit and propensity and will power.

As time goes on and as the situation departs from this archaic character—where it does depart from it—the circumstances which condition men's systematization of facts change in such a way as to throw the impersonal character of the sequence of events more and more into the foreground. The penalties for failure to apprehend facts in dispassionate terms fall surer and swifter. The sweep of events is forced home more consistently on men's minds. The guiding hand of a spiritual agency or a propensity in events becomes less readily traceable as men's knowledge of things grows ampler and more searching. In modern times, and particularly in the industrial countries, the coercive guidance of men's habits of thought in the realistic direction has been especially pronounced; and the effect shows itself in a somewhat reluctant but cumulative departure from the archaic point of view. The departure is most visible and has gone farthest in those homely branches of knowledge that have to do immediately with modern mechanical processes, such as engineering designs and technological contrivances generally. Of the sciences, those have wandered farthest on this way (of integration or disintegration, according as one may choose to view it) that have to do with mechanical sequence and process; and those have best and longest retained the archaic point of view intact which—like the moral, social, or spiritual sciences—have to do with process and sequence that is less tangible, less traceable by the use of the senses, and that therefore less immediately forces upon the attention the phenomenon of sequence as contrasted with that of propensity.

There is no abrupt transition from the pre-evolutionary to the post-evolutionary standpoint. Even in those natural sciences which deal with the processes of life and the evolutionary sequence of events the concept of dispassionate cumulative causation has often and effectively been helped out by the notion that there is in all this some sort of a meliorative trend that exercises a constraining guidance over the course of causes and effects. The faith in this meliorative trend as a concept useful to the science has gradually weakened, and it has repeatedly been disavowed; but it can scarcely be said to have yet disappeared from the field.

The process of change in the point of view, or in the terms of definitive formulation of knowledge, is a gradual one; and all the sciences have shared, though in an unequal degree, in the change that is going forward. Economics is not an exception to the rule, but it still shows too many reminiscences of the "natural" and the "normal," of "verities" and "tendencies," of "controlling principles" and "disturbing causes" to be classed as an evolutionary science. This history of the science shows a long and devious course of disintegrating animism—from the days of the scholastic writers, who discussed usury from the point of view of its relation to the divine suzerainty, to the Physiocrats, who rested their case on an "*ordre naturel*" and a "*loi naturelle*" that decides what is substantially true and, in a general way, guides the course of events by the constraint of logical congruence. There has been something of a change from Adam Smith, whose recourse in perplexity was to the guidance of "an unseen hand," to Mill and Cairnes, who formulated the laws of "natural" wages and "normal" value, and the former of whom was so well content with his work as to say, "Happily, there is nothing in the laws of Value which remains for the present or any future writer to clear up: the theory of the subject is complete."[3] But the difference between the earlier and the later point of view is a difference of degree rather than of kind.

The standpoint of the classical economists, in their higher or definitive syntheses and generalizations, may not ineptly be called the standpoint of ceremonial adequacy. The ultimate laws and principles which they formulated were laws of the normal or the natural, according to a preconception regarding the ends to which, in the nature of things, all things tend. In effect, this preconception imputes to things a tendency to work out what the instructed common sense of the time accepts as the adequate or worthy end of human effort. It is a projection of the accepted ideal of conduct. This ideal of conduct is made to serve as a canon of truth, to the extent that the investigator contents himself with an appeal to its legitimation for premises that run back of the facts with which he is immediately dealing, for the "controlling principles" that are conceived intangibly to underlie the process discussed, and for the "tendencies" that run beyond the situation as it lies before him. As instances of the use of this ceremonial canon of knowledge may be cited the "conjectural history" that plays so large a part in the classical treatment of economic institutions, such as the normalized accounts of the beginnings of barter in the transactions of the putative hunter, fisherman, and boatbuilder, or the man with the plane and the two planks, or the two men with the basket of apples and the basket of nuts.[4] Of a similar import is the characterization of money as "the great wheel of circulation"[5] or as "the medium of exchange." Money is here discussed in terms of the end which, "in the normal case," it should work out according to the given writer's ideal of economic life, rather than in terms of causal relation.

With later writers especially, this terminology is no doubt to be commonly taken as a convenient use of metaphor, in which the concept of normality and propensity to an end has reached an extreme attenuation. But it is precisely in this use of figurative terms for the formulation of theory that the classical normality still lives its attenuated life in modern economics; and it is this facile recourse to inscrutable figures of speech as the ultimate terms of theory that has saved the economists from being dragooned into the ranks of modern science. The metaphors are effective, both in their homiletical use and as a labor-saving device—more effective than their user designs them to be. By their use the theorist is enabled serenely to enjoin himself from following out an exclusive train of causal sequence. He is also enabled, without misgivings, to construct a theory of such an institution as money or wages or land-ownership without descending to a consideration of the living items concerned, except for convenient corroboration of his normalized scheme of symptoms. By this method the theory of an institution or a phase of life may be stated in conventionalized terms of the apparatus whereby life is carried on, the apparatus being invested with a tendency to an equilibrium at the normal, and the theory being a formulation of the conditions under which this putative equilibrium supervenes. In this way we have come into the usufruct of a cost-of-production theory of value which is pungently reminiscent of the time when Nature abhorred a vacuum. The ways and means and the mechanical structure of industry are formulated in a conventionalized nomenclature, and the observed motions of this mechanical apparatus are then reduced to a normalized scheme of relations. The scheme so arrived at is spiritually binding on the behavior of the phenomena contemplated. With the normalized scheme as a guide, the permutations of a given segment of the apparatus are worked out according to the values assigned the several items and features comprised in the calculation; and a ceremonially consistent formula is constructed to cover that much of the industrial field. This is the deductive method. The formula is then tested by comparison with observed permutations, by the polariscopic use of the "normal case"; and the results arrived at are thus authenticated by induction. Features of the process that do not lend themselves to interpretation in the terms of the formula are abnormal cases and are due to disturbing causes. In all this the agencies or forces causally at work in the economic life process are neatly avoided. The outcome of the method, at its best, is a body of logically consistent propositions concerning the normal relations of things—a system of economic taxonomy. At its worst, it is a body of maxims for the conduct of business and a polemical discussion of disputed points of policy.

In all this, economic science is living over again in its turn the experiences which the natural sciences passed through some time back. In the natural sciences the work of the taxonomist was and continues to be of great value, but the scientists grew restless under the regime of symmetry and system-making. They took to asking why, and so shifted their inquiries from the structure of the coral reefs to the structure and habits of life of the polyp that lives in and by them. In the science of plants, systematic botany has not ceased to be of service; but the stress of investigation and discussion among the botanists today falls on the biological value of any given feature of structure, function, or tissue rather than on its taxonomic bearing. All the talk about cytoplasm, centrosomes, and karyokinetic process means that the inquiry now looks consistently to the life process, and aims to explain it in terms of cumulative causation.

What may be done in economic science of the taxonomic kind is shown at its best in Cairnes's work, where the method is well conceived and the results effectively formulated and applied. Cairnes handles the theory of the normal case in economic life with a master hand. In his discussion the metaphysics of propensity and tendencies no longer avowedly rules the formulation of theory, nor is the inscrutable meliorative trend of a harmony of interests confidently appealed to as an engine of definitive use in giving legitimacy to the economic situation at a given time. There is less of an exercise of faith in Cairnes's economic discussions than in those of the writers that went before him. The definitive terms of the formulation are still the terms of normality and natural law, but the metaphysics underlying this appeal to normality is so far removed from the ancient ground of the beneficent "order of nature" as to have become at least nominally impersonal and to proceed without a constant regard to the humanitarian bearing of the "tendencies" which it formulates. The metaphysics has been attenuated to something approaching in colorlessness the naturalist's conception of natural law. It is a natural law which, in the guise of "controlling principles," exercises a constraining surveillance over the trend of things; but it is no longer conceived to exercise its constraint in the interest of certain ulterior human purposes. The element of beneficence has been well-nigh eliminated, and the system is formulated in terms of the system itself. Economics as it left Cairnes's hand, so far as this theoretical work is concerned, comes near being taxonomy for taxonomy's sake.

No equally capable writer has come as near making economics the ideal "dismal" science as Cairnes in his discussion of pure theory. In the days of the early classical writers economics had a vital interest for the laymen of the time, because it formulated the common-sense metaphysics of the time in its application to a department of human life. But in the hands of the later classical writers the science lost much of its charm in this regard. It was no longer a definition and authentication of the deliverance of current common sense as to what ought to come to pass; and it, therefore, in large measure lost the support of the people out of doors, who were unable to take an interest in what did not concern them; and it was also out of touch with that realistic or evolutionary habit of mind which got under way about the middle of the century in the natural sciences. It was neither vitally metaphysical nor matter-of-fact, and it found comfort with very few outside of its own ranks. Only for those who by the fortunate accident of birth or education have been able to conserve the taxonomic animus has the science during the last third of a century continued to be of absorbing interest. The result has been that from the time when the taxonomic structure stood forth as a completed whole in its symmetry and stability the economists themselves, beginning with Cairnes, have been growing restive under its discipline of stability, and have made many efforts, more or less sustained, to galvanize it into movement. At the hands of the writers of the classical line these excursions have chiefly aimed at a more complete and comprehensive taxonomic scheme of permutations; while the historical departure threw away the taxonomic ideal without getting rid of the preconceptions on which it is based; and the later Austrian group struck out on a theory of process, but presently came to a full stop because the process about which they busied themselves was not, in their apprehension of it, a cumulative or unfolding sequence.

But what does all this signify? If we are getting restless under the taxonomy of a monocotyledonous wage doctrine and a cryptogamic theory of interest, with involute, loculicidal, tomentous and moniliform variants, what is the cytoplasm, centrosome, or karyokinetic process to which we may turn, and in which we may find surcease from the metaphysics of normality and controlling principles? What are we doing about it? There is the economic life process still in great measure awaiting theoretical formulation. The active material in which the economic process goes on is the human material of the industrial community. For the purpose of economic science the process of cumulative change that is to be accounted for is the sequence of change in the methods of doing things—the methods of dealing with the material means of life.

What has been done in the way of inquiry into this economic life process? The ways and means of turning material objects and circumstances to account lie before the investigator at any given point of time in the form of mechanical contrivances and arrangements for compassing certain mechanical ends. It has therefore been easy to accept these ways and means as items of inert matter having a given mechanical structure and thereby serving the material ends of man. As such, they have been scheduled and graded by the economists under the head of capital, this capital being conceived as a mass of material objects serviceable of human use. This is well enough for the purposes of taxonomy; but it is not an effective method of conceiving the matter for the purpose of a theory of the developmental process. For the latter purpose, when taken as items in a process of cumulative change or as items in the scheme of life, these productive goods are facts of human knowledge, skill and predilection; that is to say, they are substantially prevalent habits of thought, and it is as such that they enter into the process of industrial development. The physical properties of the materials accessible to man are constants: it is the human agent that changes—his insight and his appreciation of what these things can be used for is what develops. The accumulation of goods already on hand conditions his handling and utilization of the materials offered, but even on this side—the "limitation of industry by capital"—the limitation imposed is on what men can do and on the methods of doing it. The changes that take place in the mechanical contrivances are an expression of changes in the human factor. Changes in the material facts breed further change only through the human factor. It is in the human material that the continuity of development is to be looked for; and it is here, therefore, that the motor forces of the process of economic development must be studied if they are to be studied in action at all. Economic action must be the subject-matter of the science if the science is to fall into line as an evolutionary science.

Nothing new has been said in all this. But the fact is all the more significant for being a familiar fact. It is a fact recognized by common consent throughout much of the later economic discussion, and this current recognition of the fact is a long step towards centering discussion and inquiry upon it. If economics is to follow the lead or the analogy of the other sciences that have to do with a life process, the way is plain so far as regards the general direction in which the move will be made.

The economists of the classical trend have made no serious attempt to depart from the standpoint of taxonomy and make their science a genetic account of the economic life process. As has just been said, much the same is true for the Historical School. The latter have attempted an account of developmental sequence, but they have followed the lines of pre-Darwinian speculations on development rather than lines which modern science would recognize as evolutionary. They have given a narrative survey of phenomena, not a genetic account of an unfolding process. In this work they have, no doubt, achieved results of permanent value; but the results achieved are scarcely to be classed as economic theory. On the other hand, the Austrians and their precursors and their coadjutors in the value discussion have taken up a detached portion of economic theory, and have inquired with great nicety into the process by which the phenomena within their limited field are worked out. The entire discussion of marginal utility and subjective value as the outcome of a valuation process must be taken as a genetic study of this range of facts. But here, again, nothing further has come of the inquiry, so far as regards a rehabilitation of economic theory as a whole. Accepting Menger as their spokesman on this head, it must be said that the Austrians have on the whole showed themselves unable to break with the classical tradition that economics is a taxonomic science.

The reason for the Austrian failure seems to lie in a faulty conception of human nature—faulty for the present purpose, however adequate it may be for any other. In all the received formulations of economic theory, whether at the hands of English economists or those of the Continent, the human material with which the inquiry is concerned is conceived in hedonistic terms; that is to say, in terms of a passive and substantially inert and immutably given human nature. The psychological and anthropological preconceptions of the economists have been those which were accepted by the psychological and social sciences some generations ago. The hedonistic conception of man is that of a lightning calculator of pleasures and pains, who oscillates like a homogeneous globule of desire of happiness under the impulse of stimuli that shift him about the area, but leave him intact. He has neither antecedent nor consequent. He is an isolated, definitive human datum, in stable equilibrium except for the buffets of the impinging forces that displace him in one direction or another. Self-imposed in elemental space, he spins symmetrically about his own spiritual axis until the parallelogram of forces bears down upon him, whereupon he follows the line of the resultant. When the force of the impact is spent, he comes to rest, a self-contained globule of desire as before. Spiritually, the hedonistic man is not a prime mover. He is not the seat of a process of living, except in the sense that he is subject to a series of permutations enforced upon him by circumstances external and alien to him.

The later psychology, reinforced by modern anthropological research, gives a different conception of human nature. According to this conception, it is the characteristic of man to do something, not simply to suffer pleasures and pains through the impact of suitable forces. He is not simply a bundle of desires that are to be saturated by being placed in the path of the forces of the environment, but rather a coherent structure of propensities and habits which seeks realization and expression in an unfolding activity. According to this view, human activity, and economic activity among the rest, is not apprehended as something incidental to the process of saturating given desires. The activity is itself the substantial fact of the process, and the desires under whose guidance the action takes place are circumstances of temperament which determine the specific direction in which the activity will unfold itself in the given case. These circumstances of temperament are ultimate and definitive for the individual who acts under them, so far as regards his attitude as agent in the particular action in which he is engaged. But, in the view of the science, they are elements of the existing frame of mind of the agent, and are the outcome of his antecedents and his life up to the point at which he stands. They are the products of his hereditary traits and his past experience, cumulatively wrought out under a given body of traditions, conventionalities, and material circumstances; and they afford the point of departure for the next step in the process. The economic life history of the individual is a cumulative process of adaptation of means to ends that cumulatively change as the process goes on, both the agent and his environment being at any point the outcome of the last process. His methods of life today are enforced upon him by his habits of life carried over from yesterday and by the circumstances left as the mechanical residue of the life of yesterday.

What is true of the individual in this respect is true of the group in which he lives. All economic change is a change in the economic community—a change in the community's methods of turning material things to account. The change is always in the last resort a change in habits of thought. This is true even of changes in the mechanical processes of industry. A given contrivance for effecting certain material ends becomes a circumstance which affects the further growth of habits of thought—habitual methods of procedure—and so becomes a point of departure for further development of the methods of compassing the ends sought and for the further variation of ends that are sought to be compassed. In all this flux there is no definitively adequate method of life and no definitive or absolutely worthy end of action, so far as concerns the science which sets out to formulate a theory of the process of economic life. What remains as a hard and fast residue is the fact of activity directed to an objective end. Economic action is teleological, in the sense that men always and everywhere seek to do something. What, in specific detail, they seek, is not to be answered except by a scrutiny of the details of their activity; but, so long as we have to do with their life as members of the economic community, there remains the generic fact that their life is an unfolding activity of a teleological kind.

It may or may not be a teleological process in the sense that it tends or should tend to any end that is conceived to be worthy or adequate by the inquirer or by the consensus of inquirers. Whether it is or is not, is a question with which the present inquiry is not concerned; and it is also a question of which an evolutionary economics need take no account. The question of a tendency in events can evidently not come up except on the ground of some preconception or prepossession on the part of the person looking for the tendency. In order to search for a tendency, we must be possessed of some notion of a definitive end to be sought, or some notion as to what is the legitimate trend of events. The notion of a legitimate trend in a course of events is an extra-evolutionary preconception, and lies outside the scope of an inquiry into the causal sequence in any process. The evolutionary point of view, therefore, leaves no place for a formulation of natural laws in terms of definitive normality, whether in economics or in any other branch of inquiry. Neither does it leave room for the other question of normality. What should be the end of the developmental process under discussion?

The economic life history of any community is its life history in so far as it is shaped by men's interest in the material means of life. This economic interest has counted for much in shaping the cultural growth of all communities. Primarily and most obviously, it has guided the formation, the cumulative growth, of that range of conventionalities and methods of life that are currently recognized as economic institutions; but the same interest has also pervaded the community's life and its cultural growth at points where the resulting structural features are not chiefly and most immediately of an economic bearing. The economic interest goes with men through life, and it goes with the race throughout its process of cultural development. It affects the cultural structure at all points, so that all institutions may be said to be in some measure economic institutions. This is necessarily the case, since the base of action—the point of departure—at any step in the process is the entire organic complex of habits of thought that have been shaped by the past process. The economic interest does not act in isolation, for it is but one of several vaguely isolable interests on which the complex of teleological activity carried out by the individual proceeds. The individual is but a single agent in every case; and he enters into each successive action as a whole, although the specific end sought in a given action may be sought avowedly on the basis of a particular interest; as e.g., the economic, aesthetic, sexual, humanitarian, devotional interests. Since each of these passably isolable interests is a propensity of the organic agent man, with his complex of habits of thought, the expression of each is affected by habits of life formed under the guidance of all the rest. There is, therefore, no neatly isolable range of cultural phenomena that can be rigorously set apart under the head of economic institutions, although a category of "economic institutions" may be of service as a convenient caption, comprising those institutions in which the economic interest most immediately and consistently finds expression, and which most immediately and with the least limitation are of an economic bearing.

From what has been said it appears that an evolutionary economics must be the theory of a process of cultural growth as determined by the economic interest, a theory of a cumulative sequence of economic institutions stated in terms of the process itself. Except for the want of space to do here what should be done in some detail if it is done at all, many efforts by the later economists in this direction might be cited to show the trend of economic discussion in this direction. There is not a little evidence to this effect, and much of the work done must be rated as effective work for this purpose. Much of the work of the Historical School, for instance, and that of its later exponents especially, is too noteworthy to be passed over in silence, even with all due regard to the limitations of space.

We are now ready to return to the question why economics is not an evolutionary science. It is necessarily the aim of such an economics to trace the cumulative working-out of the economic interest in the cultural sequence. It must be a theory of the economic life process of the race or the community. The economists have accepted the hedonistic preconceptions concerning human nature and human action, and the conception of the economic interest which a hedonistic psychology gives does not afford material for a theory of the development of human nature. Under hedonism the economic interest is not conceived in terms of action. It is therefore not readily apprehended or appreciated in terms of a cumulative growth of habits of thought, and does not provoke, even if it did lend itself to, treatment by the evolutionary method. At the same time the anthropological preconceptions current in that common-sense apprehension of human nature to which economists have habitually turned has not enforced the formulation of human nature in terms of a cumulative growth of habits of life. These received anthropological preconceptions are such as have made possible the normalized conjectural accounts of primitive barter with which all economic readers are familiar, and the no less normalized conventional derivation of landed property and its rent, or the sociologic-philosophical discussions of the "function" of this or that class in the life of society or of the nation.

The premises and the point of view required for an evolutionary economics have been wanting. The economists have not had the materials for such a science ready to their hand, and the provocation to strike out in such a direction has been absent. Even if it has been possible at any time to turn to the evolutionary line of speculation in economics, the possibility of a departure is not enough to bring it about. So long as the habitual view taken of a given range of facts is of the taxonomic kind and the material lends itself to treatment by the method, the taxonomic method is the easiest, gives the most gratifying immediate results, and best fits into the accepted body of knowledge of the range of facts in question. This has been the situation in economics. The other sciences of its group have likewise been a body of taxonomic discipline, and departures from the accredited method have lain under the odium of being meretricious innovations. The well-worn paths are easy to follow and lead into good company. Advance along them visibly furthers the accredited work which the science has in hand. Divergence from the paths means tentative work, which is necessarily slow and fragmentary and of uncertain value.

It is only when the methods of the science and the syntheses resulting from their use come to be out of line with habits of thought that prevail in other matters that the scientist grows restive under the guidance of the received methods and standpoints, and seeks a way out. Like other men, the economist is an individual with but one intelligence. He is a creature of habits and propensities given through the antecedents, hereditary and cultural, of which he is an outcome; and the habits of thought formed in any one line of experience affect his thinking in any other. Methods of observation and of handling facts that are familiar through habitual use in the general range of knowledge gradually assert themselves in any given special range of knowledge. They may be accepted slowly and with reluctance where their acceptance involves innovation; but, if they have the continued backing of the general body of experience, it is only a question of time when they shall come into dominance in the special field. The intellectual attitude and the method of correlation enforced upon us in the apprehension and assimilation of facts in the more elementary ranges of knowledge that have to do with brute facts assert themselves also when the attention is directed to those phenomena of the life process with which economics has to do; and the range of facts which are habitually handled by other methods than that in traditional vogue in economics has now become so large and so insistently present at every turn that we are left restless, if the new body of facts cannot be handled according to the method of mental procedure which is in this way becoming habitual.

In the general body of knowledge in modern times the facts are apprehended in terms of causal sequence. This is especially true of that knowledge of brute facts which is shaped by the exigencies of the modern mechanical industry. To men thoroughly imbued with this matter-of-fact habit of mind the laws and theorems of economics, and of the other sciences that treat of the normal course of things, have a character of "unreality" and futility that bars out any serious interest in their discussion. The laws and theorems are "unreal" to them because they are not to be apprehended in the terms which these men make use of in handling the facts with which they are perforce habitually occupied. The same matter-of-fact spiritual attitude and mode of procedure have now made their way well up into the higher levels of scientific knowledge, even in the sciences which deal in a more elementary way with the same human material that makes the subject-matter of economics, and the economists themselves are beginning to feel the unreality of their theorems about "normal" cases. Provided the practical exigencies of modern industrial life continue of the same character as they now are, and so continue to enforce the impersonal method of knowledge, it is only a question of time when that (substantially animistic) habit of mind which proceeds on the notion of a definitive normality shall be displaced in the field of economic inquiry by that (substantially materialistic) habit of mind which seeks a comprehension of facts in terms of a cumulative sequence.

The later method of apprehending and assimilating facts and handling them for the purposes of knowledge may be better or worse, more or less worthy or adequate, than the earlier; it may be of greater or less ceremonial or aesthetic effect; we may be moved to regret the incursion of underbred habits of thought into the scholar's domain. But all that is beside the present point. Under the stress of modern technological exigencies, men's everyday habits of thought are falling into the lines that in the sciences constitute the evolutionary method; and knowledge which proceeds on a higher, more archaic plane is becoming alien and meaningless to them. The social and political sciences must follow the drift, for they are already caught in it.

Notes

1. "The Fundamental Laws of Anthropo-sociology," *Journal of Political Economy*, December, 1897, p. 54. The same paper, in substance, appears in the *Rivista Italiana di Sociologia* for November, 1897.
2. "The Old Generation of Economists and the New," *Quarterly Journal of Economics*, January, 1897, p. 133.
3. *Political Economy*, Book III, ch i.
4. Marshall, *Principles of Economics* (2d ed.), Book V, ch. ii, p. 395, note.
5. Adam Smith, *Wealth of Nations* (Bohn ed.), Book II, ch. ii, p. 289.

The Preconceptions of Economic Science

Adam Smith's animistic bent asserts itself more plainly and more effectually in the general trend and aim of his discussion than in the details of theory. "Adam Smith's *Wealth of Nations* is, in fact, so far as it has one single purpose, a vindication of the unconscious law present in the separate actions of men when these actions are directed by a certain strong personal motive."[1] Both in the *Theory of the Moral Sentiments* and in the *Wealth of Nations* there are many passages that testify to his abiding conviction that there is a wholesome trend in the natural course of things, and the characteristically optimistic tone in which he speaks for natural liberty is but an expression of this conviction. An extreme resort to this animistic ground occurs in his plea for freedom of investment.[2]

In the proposition that men are "led by an invisible hand," Smith does not fall back on a meddling Providence who is to set human affairs straight when they are in danger of going askew. He conceives the Creator to be very continent in the matter of interference with the natural course of things. The Creator has established the natural order to serve the ends of human welfare; and he has very nicely adjusted the efficient causes comprised in the natural order, including human aims and motives, to this work that they are to accomplish. The guidance of the invisible hand takes place not by way of interposition, but through a comprehensive scheme of contrivances established from the beginning. For the purpose of economic theory, man is conceived to be consistently self-seeking; but this economic man is a part of the mechanism of nature, and his self-seeking traffic is but a means whereby, in the natural course of things, the general welfare is worked out. The scheme as a whole is guided by the end to be reached, but the sequence of events through which the end is reached is a causal

Part II of a three-part essay, reprinted from the *Quarterly Journal of Economics* (July 13, 1898): 396–426. Used by permission.

sequence which is not broken into episodically. The benevolent work of guidance was performed in first establishing an ingenious mechanism of forces and motives capable of accomplishing an ordained result, and nothing beyond the enduring constraint of an established trend remains to enforce the divine purpose in the resulting natural course of things.

The sequence of events, including human motives and human conduct, is a causal sequence; but it is also something more, or, rather, there is also another element of continuity besides that of brute cause and effect, present even in the step-by-step process whereby the natural course of things reaches its final term. The presence of such a quasi-spiritual or non-causal element is evident for two (alleged) facts. (1) The course of things may be deflected from the direct line of approach to the consummate human welfare which is its legitimate end. The natural trend of things may be overborne by an untoward conjuncture of causes. There is a distinction, often distressingly actual and persistent, between the legitimate and the observed course of things. If "natural," in Adam Smith's use, meant necessary, in the sense of causally determined, no divergence of events from the natural or legitimate course of things would be possible. If the mechanism of nature, including man, were a mechanically competent contrivance for achieving the great artificer's design, there could be no such episodes of blundering and perverse departure from the direct path as Adam Smith finds in nearly all existing arrangements. Institutional facts would then be "natural."[3] (2) When things have gone wrong, they will right themselves if interference with the course ceases; whereas, in the case of a causal sequence simply, the mere cessation of interference will not leave the outcome the same as if no interference had taken place. This recuperative power of nature is of an extra-mechanical character. The continuity of sequence by force of which the natural course of things prevails is, therefore, not of the nature of cause and effect, since it bridges intervals and interruptions in the causal sequence.[4] Adam Smith's use of the term "real" in statements of theory—as, for example, "real value," "real price"[5]—is evidence to this effect. "Natural" commonly has the same meaning as "real" in this connection.[6] Both "natural" and "real" are placed in contrast with the actual; and, in Adam Smith's apprehension, both have a substantiality different from and superior to facts. The view involves a distinction between reality and fact, which survives in a weakened form in the theories of "normal" prices, wages, profits, costs, in Adam Smith's successors.

This animistic prepossession seems to pervade the earlier of his two monumental works in a greater degree than the later. In the *Moral Sentiments* recourse is had to the teleological ground of the natural order more freely and with perceptibly greater insistence. There seems to be reason for holding that the animistic preconception weakened or, at any rate, fell more into the background as his later work of speculation and investigation proceeded. The change shows itself also in some details of his economic theory, as first set forth in the *Lectures*, and afterwards more fully developed in the *Wealth of Nations*. So, for instance, in the earlier presentation of the matter, "the division of labor is the immediate cause of opulence"; and this division of labor, which is the chief condition of economic well-being, "flows from a direct propensity in human nature for one man to barter with another."[7] The "propensity" in question is here appealed to as a natural endowment immediately given to man with a view to the welfare of human society, and without any attempt at further explanation of how man has come by it. No causal explanation of its presence or character is offered. But the corresponding passage of the *Wealth of Nations* handles the question more cautiously.[8] Other parallel passages might be compared, with much the same effect. The guiding hand has withdrawn farther from the range of human vision.

However, these and other like filial expressions of a devout optimism need, perhaps, not be taken as integral features of Adam Smith's economic theory, or as seriously affecting the character of his work as an economist. They are the expression of his general philosophical and theological views, and are significant for the present purpose chiefly as evidences of an animistic and optimistic bent. They go to show what is Adam Smith's accepted ground of finality—the ground to which all his speculations on human affairs converge; but they do not in any great degree show the teleological bias guiding his formulation of economic theory in detail.

The effective working of the teleological bias is best seen in Smith's more detailed handling of economic phenomena—in his discussion of what may loosely be called economic institutions—and in the criteria and principles of procedure by which he is guided in incorporating these features of economic life into the general structure of his theory. A fair instance, though perhaps not the most telling one, is the discussion of the "real and nominal price," and of the "natural and market price" of commodities, already referred to above.[9] The "real" price of commodities is their value in terms of human life. At this point Smith differs from the Physiocrats, with whom the ultimate terms of value are afforded by human sustenance taken as a product of the functioning of brute nature; the cause of the difference being that the Physiocrats conceived the natural order which works towards the material well-being of man to comprise the non-human environment only, whereas Adam Smith includes man in this concept of the natural order, and, indeed, makes him the central figure in the process of production. With the Physiocrats, production is the work of nature: with Adam Smith, it is the work of man and nature, with man in the foreground. In Adam Smith, therefore, labor is the final term in valuation. This "real" value of commodities is the value imputed to them by the economist under the stress of his teleological preconception. It has little, if any, place in the course of economic events, and no bearing on human affairs, apart from the sentimental influence which such a preconception in favor of a "real value" in things may exert upon men's notions of what is the good and equitable course to pursue in their transactions. It is impossible to gauge this real value of goods; it cannot be measured or expressed in concrete terms. Still, if labor exchanges for a varying quality of goods, "it is their value which varies, not that of the labor which purchases them."[10] The values which practically attach to goods in men's handling of them are conceived to be determined without regard to the real value which Adam Smith imputes to the goods; but, for all that, the substantial fact with respect to these market values is their presumed approximation to the real values teleologically imputed to the goods under the guidance of inviolate natural laws. The real, or natural, value of articles has no causal relation to the value at which they exchange. The discussion of how values are determined in practice runs on the motives of the buyers and sellers, and the relative advantage enjoyed by the parties to the transaction.[11] It is a discussion of a process of valuation quite unrelated to the "real," or "natural," price of things, and quite unrelated to the grounds on which things are held to come by their real, or natural, price; and yet, when the complex process of valuation has been traced out in terms of human motives and the exigencies of the market, Adam Smith feels that he has only cleared the ground. He then turns to the serious business of accounting for value and price theoretically, and making the ascertained facts articulate with his theological theory of economic life.[12]

The occurrence of the words "ordinary" and "average" in this connection need not be taken too seriously. The context makes it plain that the equality which commonly subsists between the ordinary or average rates, and the natural rates, is a matter of coincidence, not of identity. Not only are there temporary deviations, but there may be a permanent divergence between the ordinary and the natural price of a commodity; as in case of a monopoly or of produce grown under peculiar circumstances of soil or climate.[13]

The natural price coincides with the price fixed by competition, because competition means the unimpeded play of those efficient forces through which the nicely adjusted mechanism of nature works out the design to accomplish [that for] which it was contrived. The natural price is reached through the free interplay of the factors of production, and it is itself an outcome of production. Nature, including the human factor, works to turn out the goods; and the natural value of the goods is their appraisement from the standpoint of this productive process of nature. Natural value is a category of production: whereas, notoriously exchange value or market price is a category of distribution. And Adam Smith's theoretical handling of market price aims to show how the factors of human predilection and human wants at work in the higgling of the market bring about a result in passable consonance with the natural laws that are conceived to govern production.

The natural price is a composite result of the blending of the three "component parts of the price of commodities,"—the natural wages of laborer, the natural profits of stock, and the natural rent of land; and each of these three components is in its turn the measure of the productive effect of the factor to which it pertains. The further discussion of these shares in distribution aims to account for the facts of distribution on the ground of the productivity of the factors which are held to share the product between them. That is to say, Adam Smith's preconception of a productive natural process as the basis of his economic theory dominates his aims and procedure, when he comes to deal with phenomena that cannot be stated in terms of production. The causal sequence in the process of distribution is, by Adam Smith's own showing, unrelated to the causal sequence in the process of production; but, since the latter is the substantial fact, as viewed from the standpoint of a teleological natural order, the former must be stated in terms of the latter before Adam Smith's sense of substantiality, or "reality," is satisfied. Something of the same kind is, of course, visible in the Physiocrats and in Cantillon. It amounts to an extension of the natural-rights preconception to economic theory. Adam Smith's discussion of distribution as a function of productivity might be traced in detail through his handling of Wages, Profits, and Rent; but, since the aim here is a brief characterization only, and not an exposition, no farther pursuit of this point seems feasible.

It may, however, be worth while to point out another line of influence along which the dominance of the teleological preconception shows itself in Adam Smith. This is the normalization of data, in order to bring them into consonance with an orderly course of approach to the putative natural end of economic life and development. The result of this normalization of data is, on the one hand, the use of what James Steuart calls "conjectural history" in dealing with past phases of economic life, and, on the other hand, a statement of present-day phenomena in terms of what legitimately ought to be according to the God-given end of life rather than in terms of unconstrued observation. Account is taken of the facts (supposed or observed) ostensibly in terms of causal sequence, but the imputed causal sequence is construed to run on lines of teleological legitimacy.

A familiar instance of this "conjectural history," in a highly and effectively normalized form, is the account of "that early and rude state of society which precedes both the accumulation of stock and the appropriation of land."[14] It is needless at this day to point out that this "early and rude state," in which "the whole produce of labor belongs to the laborer," is altogether a figment. The whole narrative, from the putative origin down, is not only supposititious, but it is merely a schematic presentation of what should have been the course of past development, in order to lead up to that ideal economic situation which would satisfy Adam Smith's preconception.[15] As the narrative comes nearer the region of known latter-day facts, the normalization of the data becomes more difficult and receives more detailed attention; but the change in method is a change of degree rather than of kind. In the "early and rude state" the coincidence of the "natural" and the actual course of events is immediate and undisturbed, there being no refractory data at hand; but in the later stages and in the present situation, where refractory facts abound, the co-ordination is difficult, and the coincidence can be shown only by a free abstraction from phenomena that are irrelevant to the teleological trend and by a laborious interpretation of the rest. The facts of modern life are intricate, and lend themselves to statement in the terms of the theory only after they have been subjected to a "higher criticism."

The chapter "Of the Origin and Use of Money"[16] is an elegantly normalized account of the origin and nature of an economic institution, and Adam Smith's further discussion of money runs on the same lines. The origin of money is stated in terms of the purpose which money should legitimately serve in such a community as Adam Smith considered right and good, not in terms of the motives and exigencies which have resulted in the use of money and in the gradual rise of the existing method of payment and accounts. Money is "the great wheel of circulation," which effects the transfer of goods in process of production and the distribution of the finished goods to the consumers. It is an organ of the economic commonwealth rather than an expedient of accounting and a conventional repository of wealth.

It is perhaps superfluous to remark that to the "plain man," who is not concerned with the "natural course of things" in a consummate *Geldwirtschaft*, the money that passes his hand is not a "great wheel of circulation." To the Samoyed, for instance, the reindeer which serves him as unit of value is wealth in the most concrete and tangible form. Much the same is true of coin, or even of bank-notes, in the apprehension of unsophisticated people among ourselves today. And yet it is in terms of the habits and conditions of life of these "plain people" that the development of money will have to be accounted for if it is to be stated in terms of cause and effect.

The few scattered passages already cited may serve to illustrate how Adam Smith's animistic or teleological bent shapes the general structure of his theory and gives it consistency. The principle of definitive formulation in Adam Smith's economic knowledge is afforded by a putative purpose that does not at any point enter causally into the economic life process which he seeks to know. This formative or normative purpose or end is not freely conceived to enter as an efficient agent in the events discussed, or to be in any way consciously present in the process. It can scarcely be taken as an animistic agency engaged in the process. It sanctions the course of things, and gives legitimacy and substance to the sequence of events, so far as this sequence may be made to square with the requirements of the imputed end. It has therefore a ceremonial or symbolical force only, and lends the discussion a ceremonial competency; although with economists who have been in passable agreement with Adam Smith as regards the legitimate end of economic life this ceremonial consistency, or consistency *de jure*, has for many purposes been accepted as the formulation of a causal continuity in the phenomena that have been interpreted in its terms. Elucidations of what normally ought to happen, as a matter of ceremonial necessity, have in this way come to pass for an account of matters of fact.

But, as has already been pointed out, there is much more to Adam Smith's exposition of theory than a formulation of what ought to be. Much of the advance he achieved over his predecessors consists in a larger and more painstaking scrutiny of facts, and a more consistent tracing out of causal continuity in the facts handled. No doubt, his superiority over the Physiocrats, that characteristic of his work by virtue of which it superseded theirs in the farther growth of economic science, lies to some extent in his recourse to a different, more modern ground of normality—a ground more in consonance with the body of preconceptions that have had the vogue in later generations. It is a shifting of the point of view from which the facts are handled; but it comes in great part to a substitution of a new body of preconceptions for the old, or a new adaptation of the old ground of finality, rather than an elimination of all metaphysical or animistic norms of valuation. With Adam Smith, as with the Physiocrats, the fundamental question, the answer to which affords the point of departure and the norm of procedure, is a question of substantiality or economic "reality." With both, the answer to this question is given naïvely, as a deliverance of common sense. Neither is disturbed by doubts as to this deliverance of common sense or by any need of scrutinizing it. To the Physiocrats this substantial ground of economic reality is the nutritive process of Nature. To Adam Smith it is Labor. His reality has the advantage of being the deliverance of the common sense of a more modern community, and one that has maintained itself in force more widely and in better consonance with the facts of latter-day industry. The Physiocrats owe their preconception of the productiveness of nature to the habits of thought of a community in whose economic life the dominant phenomenon was the owner of agricultural land. Adam Smith owes his preconception in favor of labor to a community in which the obtrusive economic feature of the immediate past was handicraft and agriculture, with commerce as a scarcely secondary phenomenon.

So far as Adam Smith's economic theories are a tracing out of the causal sequence in economic phenomena, they are worked out in terms given by these two main directions of activity—human effort directed to the shaping of the material means of life, and human effort and discretion directed to a pecuniary gain. The former is the great, substantial productive force: the latter is not immediately, or proximately, productive.[17] Adam Smith still has too lively a sense of the nutritive purpose of the order of nature freely to extend the concept of productiveness to any activity that does not yield a material increase of the creature comforts. His instinctive appreciation of the substantial virtue of whatever effectually furthers nutrition even leads him into the concession that "in agriculture nature labors along with man," although the general tenor of his argument is that the productive force with which the economist always has to count is human labor. This recognized substantiality of labor as productive is, as has already been remarked, accountable for his effort to reduce to terms of productive labor such a category of distribution as exchange value.

With but slight qualification, it will hold that, in the causal sequence which Adam Smith traces out in his economic theories proper (contained in the first three books of the *Wealth of Nations*), the causally efficient factor is conceived to be human nature in these two relations—of productive efficiency and pecuniary gain through exchange. Pecuniary gain—gain in the material means of life through barter—furnishes the motive force to the economic activity of the individual; although productive efficiency is the legitimate, normal end of the community's economic life. To such an extent does this concept of man's seeking his ends through "truck, barter, and exchange" pervade Adam Smith's treatment of economic processes that he even states production in its terms, and says that "labour was the first price, the original purchase-money, that was paid for all things."[18] The human nature engaged in this pecuniary traffic is conceived in somewhat hedonistic terms, and the motives and movements of men are normalized to fit the requirements of a hedonistically conceived order of nature. Men are very much alike in their native aptitudes and propensities;[19] and, so far as economic theory need take account of these aptitudes and propensities, they are aptitudes for the production of the "necessaries and conveniences of life," and propensities to secure as great a share of these creature comforts as may be.

Adam Smith's conception of normal human nature—that is to say, the human factor which enters causally in the process which economic theory discusses—comes, on the whole, to this: Men exert their force and skill in a mechanical process of production, and their pecuniary sagacity in a competitive process of distribution, with a view to individual gain in the material means of life. These material means are sought in order to the satisfaction of men's natural wants through their consumption. It is true, much else enters into men's endeavors in the struggle for wealth, as Adam Smith points out; but this consumption comprises the legitimate range of incentives, and a theory which concerns itself with the natural course of things need take but incidental account of what does not come legitimately in the natural course. In point of fact, there are appreciable "actual," through scarcely "real," departures from this rule. They are spurious and insubstantial departures, and do not properly come within the purview of the stricter theory. And, since human nature is strikingly uniform, in Adam Smith's apprehension, both the efforts put forth and the consumptive effect accomplished may be put in quantitative terms and treated algebraically, with the result that the entire range of phenomena comprised under the head of consumption need be but incidentally considered; and the theory of production and distribution is complete when the goods or the values have been traced to their disappearance in the hands of their ultimate owners. The reflex effect of consumption upon production and distribution is, on the whole, quantitative only.

Adam Smith's preconception of a normal teleological order of procedure in the natural course, therefore, affects not only those features of theory where he is avowedly concerned with building up a normal scheme of the economic process. Through his normalizing the chief causal factor engaged in the process, it affects also his arguments from cause to effect.[20] What makes this latter feature worth particular attention is the fact that his successors carried this normalization farther, and employed it with less frequent reference to the mitigating exceptions which Adam Smith notices by the way.

The reason for that farther and more consistent normalization of human nature which gives us the "economic man" at the hands of Adam Smith's successors lies, in great part, in the utilitarian philosophy that entered in force and in consummate form at about the turning of the century. Some credit in the work of normalization is due also to the farther supersession of handicraft by the "capitalistic" industry that came in at the same time and in pretty close relation with the utilitarian views.

After Adam Smith's day, economics fell into profane hands. Apart from Malthus, who, of all the greater economists, stands nearest to Adam Smith on such metaphysical heads as have an immediate bearing upon the premises of economic science, the next generation do not approach their subject from the point of view of a divinely instituted order; nor do they discuss human interests with that gently optimistic spirit of submission that belongs to the economist who goes to his work with the fear of God before his eyes. Even with Malthus the recourse to the divinely sanctioned order of nature is somewhat sparing and temperate. But it is significant for the later course of economic theory that, while Malthus may well be accounted the truest continuer of Adam Smith, it was the undevout utilitarians that became the spokesmen of the science after Adam Smith's time.

There is no wide breach between Adam Smith and the utilitarians, either in details of doctrine or in the concrete conclusions arrived at as regards questions of policy. On these heads Adam Smith might well be classed as moderate utilitarian, particularly so far as regards his economic work. Malthus has still more of a utilitarian air—so much so, indeed, that he is not infrequently spoken of as a utilitarian. This view, convincingly set forth by Mr. Bonar,[21] is no doubt well borne out by a detailed scrutiny of Malthus's economic doctrines. His humanitarian bias is evident throughout, and his weakness for considerations of expediency is the great blemish of his scientific work. But, for all that, in order to an appreciation of the change that came over classical economics with the rise of Benthamism, it is necessary to note that the agreement in this matter between Adam Smith and the disciples of Bentham, and less decidedly that between Malthus and the latter, is a coincidence of conclusions rather than an identity of preconceptions.[22]

With Adam Smith the ultimate ground of economic reality is the design of God, the teleological order; and his utilitarian generalizations, as well as the hedonistic character of his economic man, are but methods of the working-out of this natural order, not the substantial and self-legitimating ground. Shifty as Malthus's metaphysics are, much the same is to be said for him.[23] Of the utilitarians proper the converse is true, although here, again, there is by no means utter consistency. The substantial economic ground is pleasure and pain: the teleological order (even the design of God, where that is admitted) is the method of its working-out.

It may be unnecessary here to go into the farther implications, psychological and ethical, which this preconception of the utilitarians involves. And even this much may seem a taking of excessive pains with a distinction that marks no tangible difference. But a reading of the classical doctrines, with something of this metaphysics of political economy in mind, will show how, and in great part why, the later economists of the classical line diverged from Adam Smith's tenets in the early years of the century, until it has been necessary to interpret Adam Smith somewhat shrewdly in order to save him from heresy.

The post-Bentham economics is substantially a theory of value. This is altogether the dominant feature of the body of doctrines; the rest follows from, or is adapted to, this central discipline. The doctrine of value is of very great importance also in Adam Smith; but Adam Smith's economics is a theory of the production and apportionment of the material means of life.[24] With Adam Smith, value is discussed from the point of view of production. With the utilitarians, production is discussed from the point of view of value. The former makes value an outcome of the process of production: the latter make production the outcome of a valuation process.

The point of departure with Adam Smith is the "productive power of labour."[25] With Ricardo it is a pecuniary problem concerned in the distribution of ownership;[26] but the classical writers are followers of Adam Smith, and improve upon and correct the results arrived at by him, and the difference of point of view, therefore, becomes evident in their divergence from him, and the different distribution of emphasis, rather than in a new and antagonistic departure.

The reason for this shifting of the center of gravity from production to valuation lies, proximately, in Bentham's revision of the "principles" of morals. Bentham's philosophical position is, of course, not a self-explanatory phenomenon, nor does the effect of Benthamism extend only to those who are avowed followers of Bentham; for Bentham is the exponent of a cultural change that affects the habits of thought of the entire community. The immediate point of Bentham's work, as affecting the habits of thought of the educated community, is the substitution of hedonism (utility) in place of achievement of purpose, as a ground of legitimacy and a guide in the normalization of knowledge. Its effect is most patent in speculations on morals, where it inculcates determinism. Its close connection with determinism in ethics points the way to what may be expected of its working in economics. In both cases the result is that human action is construed in terms of the causal forces of the environment, the human agent being, at the best, taken as a mechanism of commutation, through the workings of which the sensuous effects wrought by the impinging forces of the environment are, by an enforced process of valuation, transmuted without quantitative discrepancy into moral or economic conduct, as the case may be. In ethics and economics alike the subject-matter of the theory is this valuation process that expresses itself in conduct, resulting, in the case of economic conduct, in the pursuit of the greatest gain or least sacrifice.

Metaphysically or cosmologically considered, the human nature into the motions of which hedonistic ethics and economics inquire is an intermediate term in a causal sequence, of which the initial and the terminal members are sensuous impressions and the details of conduct. This intermediate term conveys the sensuous impulse without loss of force to its eventuation in conduct. For the purpose of the valuation process through which the impulse is so conveyed, human nature may, therefore, be accepted as uniform; and the theory of the valuation process may be formulated quantitatively, in terms of the material forces affecting the human sensory and of their equivalents in the resulting activity. In the language of economics, the theory of value may be stated in terms of the consumable goods that afford the incentive to effort and the expenditure undergone in order to procure them. Between these two there subsists a necessary equality; but the magnitudes between which the equality subsists are hedonistic magnitudes, not magnitudes of kinetic energy nor of vital force, for the terms handled are sensuous terms. It is true, since human nature is substantially uniform, passive, and unalterable in respect of men's capacity for sensuous affection, there may also be presumed to subsist a substantial equality between the psychological effect to be wrought by the consumption of goods, on the one side, and the resulting expenditure of kinetic or vital force, on the other side; but such an equality is, after all, of the nature of a coincidence, although there should be a strong presumption in favor of its prevailing on an average and in the common run of cases. Hedonism, however, does not postulate uniformity between men except in respect of sensuous cause and effect.

The theory of value which hedonism gives is, therefore, a theory of cost in terms of discomfort. By virtue of the hedonistic equilibrium reached through the valuation process, the sacrifice or expenditure of sensuous reality involved in acquisition is the equivalent of the sensuous gain secured. An alternative statement might perhaps be made, to the effect that the measure of the value of goods is not the sacrifice or discomfort undergone, but the sensuous gain that accrues from the acquisition of the goods; but this is plainly only an alternative statement, and there are special reasons in the economic life of the time why the statement in terms of cost, rather than in terms of "utility," should commend itself to the earlier classical economists.

On comparing the utilitarian doctrine of value with earlier theories, then, the case stands somewhat as follows. The Physiocrats and Adam Smith contemplate value as a measure of the productive force that realizes itself in the valuable article. With the Physiocrats this productive force is the "anabolism" of Nature (to resort to a physiological term); with Adam Smith it is chiefly human labor directed to heightening the serviceability of the materials with which it is occupied. Production causes value in either case. The post-Bentham economics contemplates value as a measure of, or as measured by, the irksomeness of the effort involved in procuring the valuable goods. As Mr. E.C.K. Gonner has admirably pointed out,[27] Ricardo—and the like holds true of classical economics generally—makes cost the foundation of value, not its cause. This resting of value on cost takes place through a valuation. Any one who will read Adam Smith's theoretical exposition to a good purpose as Mr. Gonner has read Ricardo will scarcely fail to find that the converse is true in Adam Smith's case. But the causal relation of cost to value holds only as regards "natural" or "real" value in Adam Smith's doctrine. As regards market price, Adam Smith's theory does not differ greatly from that of Ricardo on this head. He does not overlook the valuation process by which market price is adjusted and the course of investment is guided, and his discussion of this process runs in terms that should be acceptable to any hedonist.

The shifting of the point of view that comes into economics with the acceptance of utilitarian ethics and its correlate, the associationist psychology, is in great part a shifting to the ground of causal sequence as contrasted with that of serviceability to a preconceived end. This is indicated even by the main fact already cited—that the utilitarian economists make exchange value the central feature of their theories, rather than the conduciveness of industry to the community's material welfare. Hedonistic exchange value is the outcome of a valuation process enforced by the apprehended pleasure-giving capacities of the items valued. And in the utilitarian theories of production, arrived at from the standpoint so given by exchange value, the conduciveness to welfare is not the objective point of the argument. This objective point is rather the bearing of productive enterprise upon the individual fortunes of the agents engaged, or upon the fortunes of the several distinguishable classes of beneficiaries comprised in the industrial community; for the great immediate bearing of exchange values upon the life of the collectivity is their bearing upon the distribution of wealth. Value is a category of distribution. The result is that, as is well shown by Mr. Cannan's discussion,[28] the theories of production offered by the classical economists have been sensibly scant, and have been carried out with a constant view to the doctrines on distribution. An incidental but telling demonstration of the same facts is given by Professor Bücher;[29] and in illustration may be cited Torren's *Essay on the Production of Wealth*, which is to a good extent occupied with discussions of value and distribution. The classical theories of production have been theories of the production of "wealth"; and "wealth," in classical usage, consists of material things having exchange value. During the vogue of the classical economics the accepted characteristic by which "wealth" has been defined has been its amenability to ownership. Neither in Adam Smith nor in the Physiocrats is this amenability to ownership made so much of, nor is it in a similar degree accepted as a definite mark of the subject-matter of the science.

As their hedonistic preconception would require, then, it is to the pecuniary side of life that the classical economists give their most serious attention, and it is the pecuniary bearing of any given phenomenon or of any institution that commonly shapes the issue of the argument. The causal sequence about which the discussion centers is a process of pecuniary valuation. It runs on distribution, ownership, acquisition, gain, investment, exchange.[30] In this way the doctrines on production come to take a pecuniary coloring; as is seen in a less degree also in Adam Smith, and even in the Physiocrats, although these earlier economists very rarely, if ever, lose touch with the concept of generic serviceability as the characteristic feature of production. The tradition derived from Adam Smith, which made productivity and serviceability the substantial features of economic life, was not abruptly put aside by his successors, though the emphasis was differently distributed by them in following out the line of investigation to which the tradition pointed the way. In the classical economics the ideas of production and of acquisition are not commonly held apart, and very much of what passes for a theory of production is occupied with phenomena of investment and acquisition. Torrens's *Essay* is a case in point, though by no means an extreme case.

This is as it should be; for to the consistent hedonist the sole motive force concerned in the industrial process is the self-regarding motive of pecuniary gain, and industrial activity is but an intermediate term between the expenditure or discomfort undergone and the pecuniary gain sought. Whether the end and outcome is an invidious gain for the individual (in contrast with or at the cost of his neighbors), or an enhancement of the facility of human life on the whole, is altogether a by-question in any discussion of the range of incentives by which men are prompted to their work or the direction which their efforts take. The serviceability of the given line of activity, for the life purposes of the community or for one's neighbors, "is not of the essence of this contract." These features of serviceability come into the account chiefly as affecting the vendibility of what the given individual has to offer in seeking gain through a bargain.[31]

In hedonistic theory the substantial end of economic life is individual gain; and for this purpose production and acquisition may be taken as fairly coincident, if not identical. Moreover, society, in the utilitarian philosophy, is the algebraic sum of the individuals; and the interest of the society is the sum of the interests of the individuals. It follows by easy consequence, whether strictly true or not, that the sum of individual gains is the gain of the society, and that, in serving his own interest in the way of acquisition, the individual serves the collective interest of the community. Productivity or serviceability is, therefore, to be presumed of any occupation or enterprise that looks to a pecuniary gain; and so, by a roundabout path, we get back to the ancient conclusion of Adam Smith, that the remuneration of classes or persons engaged in industry coincides with their productive contribution to the output of services and consumable goods.

A felicitous illustration of the working of this hedonistic norm in classical economic doctrine is afforded by the theory of the wages of superintendence—an element in distribution which is not much more than suggested in Adam Smith, but which receives ampler and more painstaking attention as the classical body of doctrines reaches a fuller development. The "wages of superintendence" are the gains due to pecuniary management. They are the gains that come to the director of "business"—not those that go the director of the mechanical process or to the foreman of the shop. The latter are wages simply. This distinction is not altogether clear in the earlier writers, but it is clearly enough contained in the fuller development of the theory.

The undertaker's work is the management of investment. It is altogether of a pecuniary character, and its proximate aim is "the main chance." If it leads, indirectly, to an enhancement of serviceability or a heightened aggregate output of consumable goods, that is a fortuitous circumstance incident to that heightened vendibility on which the investor's gain depends. Yet the classical doctrine says frankly that the wages of superintendence are the remuneration of superior productivity,[32] and the classical theory of production is in good part a doctrine of investment in which the identity of production and pecuniary gain is taken for granted.

The substitution of investment in the place of industry as the central and substantial fact in the process of production is due not to the acceptance of hedonism simply, but rather to the conjunction of hedonism with an economic situation of which the investment of capital and its management for gain was the most obvious feature. The situation which shaped the common-sense apprehension of economic facts at the time was what has since been called a capitalistic system, in which pecuniary enterprise and the phenomena of the market were the dominant and tone-giving facts. But this economic situation was also the chief ground for the vogue of hedonism in economics; so that hedonistic economics may be taken as an interpretation of human nature in terms of the market-place. The market and the "business world," to which the business man in his pursuit of gain was required to adapt his motives, had by this time grown so large that the course of business events was beyond the control of any one person; and at the same time those far-reaching organizations of invested wealth which have latterly come to prevail and to coerce the market were not then in the foreground. The course of market events took its passionless way without traceable relation or deference to any man's convenience and without traceable guidance toward an ulterior end. Man's part in this pecuniary world was to respond with alacrity to the situation, and so adapt his vendible effects to the shifting demand as to realize something in the outcome. What he gained in his traffic was gained without loss to those with whom he dealt, for they paid no more than the goods were worth to them. One man's gain need not be another's loss; and, if it is not, then it is net gain to the community.

Among the striking remoter effects of the hedonistic preconception, and its working out in terms of pecuniary gain, is the classical failure to discriminate between capital as investment and capital as industrial appliances. This is, of course, closely related to the point already spoken of. The appliances of industry further the production of goods, therefore capital (invested wealth) is productive; and the rate of its average remuneration marks the degree of its productiveness.[33] The most obvious fact limiting the pecuniary gain secured by means of invested wealth is the sum invested. Therefore, capital limits the productiveness of industry; and the chief and indispensable condition to an advance in material well-being is the accumulation of invested wealth. In discussing the conditions of industrial improvement, it is usual to assume that "the state of the arts remains unchanged," which is, for all purposes but that of a doctrine of profits per cent, an exclusion of the main fact. Investments may, further, be transferred from one enterprise to another. Therefore, and in that degree, the means of production are "mobile."

Under the hands of the great utilitarian writers, therefore, political economy is developed into a science of wealth, taking that term in the pecuniary sense, as things amenable to ownership. The course of things in economic life is treated as a sequence of pecuniary events, and economic theory becomes a theory of what should happen in that consummate situation where the permutation of pecuniary magnitudes takes place without disturbance and without retardation. In this consummate situation the pecuniary motive has its perfect work, and guides all the acts of economic man in a guileless, colorless, unswerving quest of the greatest gain at the least sacrifice. Of course, this perfect competitive system, with its untainted "economic man," is a feat of the scientific imagination, and is not intended as a competent expression of fact. It is an expedient of abstract reasoning; and its avowed competency extends only to the abstract principles, the fundamental laws of the science, which hold only so far as the abstraction holds. But, as happens in such cases, having once been accepted and assimilated as real, though perhaps not as actual, it becomes an effective constituent in the inquirer's habits of thought, and goes to shape his knowledge of facts. It comes to serve as a norm of substantiality or legitimacy; and facts in some degree fall under its constraint, as is exemplified by many allegations regarding the "tendency" of things.

To this consummation, which Senior speaks of as "the natural state of man,"[34] human development tends by force of the hedonistic character of human nature; and in terms of its approximation to this natural state, therefore, the immature actual situation had best be stated. The pure theory, the "hypothetical science" of Cairnes, "traces the phenomena of the production and distribution of wealth up to their causes, in the principles of human nature and the laws and events—physical, political, and social—of the external world."[35] But since the principles of human nature that give the outcome in men's economic conduct, so far as it touches the production and distribution of wealth, are but the simple and constant sequence of hedonistic cause and effect, the element of human nature may fairly be eliminated from the problem, with great gain in simplicity and expedition. Human nature being eliminated, as being a constant intermediate term, and all institutional features of the situation being also eliminated (as being similar constants under that natural or consummate pecuniary régime with which the pure theory is concerned), the laws of the phenomena of wealth may be formulated in terms of the remaining factors. These factors are the vendible items that men handle in these processes of production and distribution; and economic laws come, therefore, to be expressions of the algebraic relations subsisting between the various elements of wealth and investment—capital, labor, land, supply and demand of one and the other, profits, interest, wages. Even such items as credit and population become dissociated from the personal factor, and figure in the computation as elemental factors acting and reacting through a permutation of values over the heads of the good people whose welfare they are working out.

To sum up: the classical economics, having primarily to do with the pecuniary side of life, is a theory of a process of valuation. But since the human nature at whose hands and for whose behoof the valuation takes place is simple and constant in its reaction to pecuniary stimulus, and since no other feature of human nature is legitimately present in economic phenomena than this reaction to pecuniary stimulus, the valuer concerned in the matter is to be overlooked or eliminated; and the theory of the valuation process then becomes a theory of the pecuniary interaction of the facts valued. It is a theory of valuation with the element of valuation left out—a theory of life stated in terms of the normal paraphernalia of life.

In the preconceptions with which classical economics set out were comprised the remnants of natural rights and of the order of nature, infused with the peculiarly mechanical natural theology that made its way into popular vogue on British ground during the eighteenth century and was reduced to a neutral tone by the British penchant for the commonplace—stronger at this time than at any earlier period. The reason for this growing penchant for the commonplace, for the explanation of things in casual terms, lies partly in the growing resort to mechanical processes and mechanical prime movers in industry, partly in the (consequent) continued decline of the aristocracy and the priesthood, and partly in the growing density of population and the consequent greater specialization and wider organization of trade and business. The spread of the discipline of the natural sciences, largely incident to the mechanical industry, counts in the same direction; and obscurer factors in modern culture may have had their share.

The animistic preconception was not lost, but it lost tone; and it partly fell into abeyance, particularly so far as regards its avowal. It is visible chiefly in the unavowed readiness of the classical writers to accept as imminent and definitive any possible outcome which the writer's habit or temperament inclined him to accept as right and good. Hence the visible inclination of classical economists to a doctrine of the harmony of interests, and their somewhat uncircumspect readiness to state their generalizations in terms of what ought to happen according to the ideal requirements of the consummate *Geldwirtschaft* to which men "are impelled by the provisions of nature."[36] By virtue of their hedonistic preconceptions, their habituation to the ways of a pecuniary culture, and their unavowed animistic faith that nature is in the right, the classical economists knew that the consummation to which, in the nature of things, all things tend, is the frictionless and beneficent competitive system. This competitive ideal, therefore, affords the normal, and conformity to its requirements affords the test of absolute economic truth. The standpoint so gained selectively guides the attention of the classical writers in their observation and apprehension of facts, and they come to see evidence of conformity or approach to the normal in the most unlikely places. Their observation is, in great part, interpretative, as observation commonly is. What is peculiar to the classical economists in this respect is their particular norm of procedure in the work of interpretation. And, by virtue of having achieved a standpoint of absolute economic normality, they become a "deductive" school, so called, in spite of the patent fact that they were pretty consistently employed with an inquiry into the causal sequence of economic phenomena.

The generalization of observed facts becomes a normalization of them, a statement of the phenomena in terms of their coincidence with, or divergence from, that normal tendency that makes for the actualization of the absolute economic reality. This absolute or definitive ground of economic legitimacy lies beyond the causal sequence in which the observed phenomena are conceived to be interlined. It is related to the concrete facts neither as cause nor as effect in any such way that the causal relation may be traced in a concrete instance. It has little causally to do either with the "mental" or with the "physical" data with which the classical economist is avowedly employed. Its relation to the process under discussion is that of an extraneous—that is to say, a ceremonial—legitimation. The body of knowledge gained by its help and under its guidance is, therefore, a taxonomic science.

So, by way of a concluding illustration, it may be pointed out that money, for instance, is normalized in terms of the legitimate economic tendency. It becomes a measure of value and a medium of exchange. It has become primarily an instrument of pecuniary commutation, instead of being, as under the earlier normalization of Adam Smith, primarily a great wheel of circulation for the diffusion of consumable goods. The terms in which the laws of money, as of the other phenomena of pecuniary life, are formulated, are terms which connote its normal function in the life history of objective values as they live and move and have their being in the consummate pecuniary situation of the "natural" state. To a similar work of normalization we owe those creatures of the myth-maker, the quantity theory and the wages-fund.

Notes

1. Bonar, *Philosophy and Political Economy*, pp. 177, 178.

2. "Every individual is continually exerting himself to find out the most advantageous employment for whatever capital he can command. It is his own advantage, and not that of the society, which he has in view. But the study of his own advantage naturally, or rather necessarily, leads him to prefer that employment which is most advantageous to the society. . . . By directing that industry in such a manner as its produce may be of the greatest value, he intends only his own gain; and he is in this, as in many other cases, led by an invisible hand to promote an end which was no part of his intention. Nor is it always the worse for society that it was no part of it. By pursuing his own interest he

frequently promotes that of the society more effectually than when he really intends to promote it." *Wealth of Nations*, Book IV, ch. ii.

3. The discrepancy between the actual, causally determined situation and the divinely intended consummation is the metaphysical ground of all that inculcation of morality and enlightened policy that makes up so large a part of Adam Smith's work. The like, of course, holds true for all moralists and reformers who proceed on the assumption of a providential order.

4. "In the political body, however, the wisdom of nature has fortunately made ample provision for remedying many of the bad effects of the folly and injustice of man; in the same manner as it has done in the natural body, for remedying those of his sloth and intemperance." *Wealth of Nations*, Book IV, ch. ix.

5. E.g., "the real measure of the exchangeable value of all commodities." *Wealth of Nations*, Book I, ch. v., and repeatedly in the like connection.

6. E.g., Book I, ch. vii: "When the price of any commodity is neither more nor less than what is sufficient to pay the rent of the land, the wages of the labor, and the profits of the stock employed in raising, preparing, and bringing it to market, according to their natural rates, the commodity is then sold for what may be called its natural price." "The actual price at which any commodity is commonly sold is called its market price. It may be either above or below or exactly the same with its natural price."

7. Lectures of Adam Smith (Ed. Cannan, 1896), p. 169.

8. "This division of labor, from which so many advantages are derived, is not originally the effect of any human wisdom, which foresees and intends that general opulence to which it gives occasion. It is the necessary though very slow and gradual consequence of a certain propensity in human nature which has in view no such extensive utility—the propensity to truck, barter, and exchange one thing for another. Whether this propensity be one of those original principles in human nature of which no further account can be given, or whether, as seems more probable, it be the necessary consequence of the faculties of reason and speech, it belongs not to our present subject to inquire." *Wealth of Nations*, Book I, ch. ii.

9. *Wealth of Nations*, Book I, chs. v–vii.

10. *Wealth of Nations*, Book I, ch. v.

11. As, e.g., the entire discussion of the determination of Wages, Profits and Rent, in Book I, chs. viii–xi.

12. "There is in every society or neighborhood an ordinary or average rate both of wages and profit in every different employment of labor and stock. This rate is naturally regulated, . . . partly by the general circumstances of the society. . . . There is, likewise, in every society or neighborhood an ordinary or average rate of rent, which is regulated, too. . . . These ordinary or average rates may be called the natural rates of wages, profit, and rent, at the time and place in which they commonly prevail. When the price of any commodity is neither more nor less than what is sufficient to pay the rent of the land, the wages of the labour, and the profits of the stock employed in raising, preparing, and bringing it to market, according to their natural rates, the commodity is then sold for what may be called its natural price." *Wealth of Nations*, Book I, ch. vii.

13. "Such commodities may continue for whole centuries together to be sold at this high price; and that part of it which resolves itself into the rent of land is, in this case, the part which is generally paid above its natural rate." Book I, ch. vii.

14. *Wealth of Nations*, Book I, ch. vi; also ch. viii.

15. For an instance of how these early phases of industrial development appear, when not seen in the light of Adam Smith's preconception, see, among others, Bücher, *Entstehung der Volkswirtschaft*.

16. Book I, ch. iv.

17. See *Wealth of Nations*, Book II, ch. v, "Of the Different Employment of Capitals."

18. *Wealth of Nations*, Book I, ch. v. See also the plea for free trade, Book IV, ch. ii: "But the annual revenue of every society is always precisely equal to the exchangeable value of the whole annual produce of its industry, or, rather, is precisely the same thing with that exchangeable value."

19. "The difference of natural talents in different men is in reality much less than we are aware of." *Wealth of Nations*, Book I, ch. ii.

20. "Mit diesen philosophischen Ueberzeugungen tritt nun Adam Smith an die Welt der Enfahrung heran, und es ergiebt sich ihm die Richtigkeit der Principien. Der Reiz der Smith'schen Schriften beruht zum grossen Teile darauf, dass Smith die Principien in so innige Verbindung mit dem Thatsächlichen gebracht. Hie und da werden dann auch die Principien, was durch diese Verbindung veranlasst wird, an ihren Spitzen etwas abgeschliffen, ihre allzuscharfe Ausprägung dadurch vermieden. Nichtsdestoweniger aber bleiben sie stets die leitenden Grundgedanken." Richard Zeyss, *Adam Smith und der Eigennutz* (Tübingen, 1889), p. 110.

21. See, e.g., Malthus and his Work, especially Book III, as also the chapter on Malthus in Philosophy and Political Economy, Book III, Modern Philosophy: Utilitarian Economics, ch. i, "Malthus."

22. Ricardo is here taken as a utilitarian of the Benthamite Colour, although he cannot be classed as a disciple of Bentham. His hedonism is but the uncritically accepted metaphysics comprised in the common sense of his time, and his substantial coincidence with Bentham goes to show how well diffused the hedonist preconception was at the time.

23. Cf. Bonar, *Malthus and his Work*, pp. 323–36.

24. His work is an inquiry into "The Nature and Causes of the Wealth of Nations."

25. "The annual labour of every nation is the fund which originally supplies it with all the necessaries and conveniences of life which it annually consumes, and which consist always either in the immediate produce of the labor or in what is purchased with the produce from other nations." *Wealth of Nations*, "Introduction and Plan," opening paragraph.

26. "The produce of the earth—all that is derived from its surface by the united application of labour, machinery, and capital—is divided among three classes of the community.... To determine the laws which regulate this distribution is the principal problem of political economy." *Political Economy*, Preface.

27. In the introductory essay to his edition of Ricardo's *Political Economy*. See, e.g., paragraphs 9 and 24.

28. *Theories of Production and Distribution,* 1776–1848.

29. *Entstehung der Volkswirtschaft* (second edition). Cf. especially chs. ii, iii, vi, and vii.

30. "Even if we put aside all questions which involve a consideration of the effects of industrial institutions in modifying the habits and character of the classes of the community, . . . that enough still remains to constitute a separate science, the mere enumeration of the chief terms of economics—wealth, value, exchange, credit, money, capital, and commodity—will suffice to show." Shirres, *Analysis of the Ideas of Economics* (London, 1893), pp. 8 and 9.

31. "If a commodity were in no way useful, . . . it would be destitute of exchangeable value; . . . (but), possessing utility, commodities derive their exchangeable value from two sources," etc. Ricardo, *Political Economy*, ch. i, sec. 1.

32. Cf., for instance, Senior, *Political Economy* (London, 1872), particularly pp. 88, 89 and 130–135, where the wages of superintendence are, somewhat reluctantly, classed under profits; and the work of superintendence is thereupon conceived as being, immediately or remotely, an exercise of "abstinence" and a productive work. The illustration

the bill-broker is particularly apt. The like view of the wages of superintendence is an article of theory with more than one of the later descendants of the classical line.

33. Cf. Böhm-Bawerk, *Capital and Interest*, Books II and IV, as well as the Introduction and ch. iv and v of Book I. Böhm-Bawerk's discussion bears less immediately on the present point than the similarity of the terms employed would suggest.

34. *Political Economy*, p. 8.

35. *Character and Logical Method of Political Economy* (New York, 1875), p. 71. Cairnes may not be altogether representative of the high tide of classicism, but his characterization of the science is none the less to the point.

36. Senior, *Political Economy*, p. 87.

The Socialist Economics of Karl Marx and His Followers

The system of doctrines worked out by Marx is characterized by a certain boldness of conception and a great logical consistency. Taken in detail, the constituent elements of the system are neither novel nor iconoclastic, nor does Marx at any point claim to have discovered previously hidden facts or to have invented recondite formulations of facts already known; but the system as a whole has an air of originality and initiative such as is rarely met with among the sciences that deal with any phase of human culture. How much of this distinctive character the Marxian system owes to the personal traits of its creator is not easy to say, but what marks it off from all other systems of economic theory is not a matter of personal idiosyncrasy. It differs characteristically from all systems of theory that have preceded it, both in its premises and in its aims. The (hostile) critics of Marx have not sufficiently appreciated the radical character of his departure in both of these respects, and have, therefore, commonly lost themselves in a tangled scrutiny of supposedly abstruse details; whereas those writers who have been in sympathy with his teachings have too commonly been disciples bent on exegesis and on confirming their fellow-disciples in the faith.

Except as a whole and except in the light of its postulates and aims, the Marxian system is not only not tenable, but it is not even intelligible. A discussion of a given isolated feature of the system (such as the theory of value) from the point of view of classical economics (such as that offered by Böhm-Bawerk) is as futile as a discussion of solids in terms of two dimensions.

Neither as regards his postulates and preconceptions nor as regards the aim of his inquiry is Marx's position an altogether single-minded one. In neither respect

---

The first of a two-part lecture before students at Harvard University in April 1906; later published in the *Quarterly Journal of Economics* 20 (August 1906): 578–95. Used by permission.

does his position come of a single line of antecedents. He is of no single school of philosophy, nor are his ideals those of any single group of speculators living before his time. For this reason he takes his place as an originator of a school of thought as well as the leader of a movement looking to a practical end.

As to the motives which drive him and the aspirations which guide him, in destructive criticism and in creative speculation alike, he is primarily a theoretician busied with the analysis of economic phenomena and their organization into a consistent and faithful system of scientific knowledge; but he is, at the same time, consistently and tenaciously alert to the bearing which each step in the progress of his theoretical work has upon the propaganda. His work has, therefore, an air of bias, such as belongs to an advocate's argument; but it is not, therefore, to be assumed, nor indeed to be credited, that his propagandist aims have in any substantial way deflected his inquiry or his speculations from the faithful pursuit of scientific truth. His socialistic bias may color his polemics, but his logical grasp is too neat and firm to admit of any bias, other than that of his metaphysical preconceptions, affecting his theoretical work.

There is no system of economic theory more logical than that of Marx. No member of the system, no single article of doctrine, is fairly to be understood, criticized, or defended except as an articulate member of the whole and in the light of the preconceptions and postulates which afford the point of departure and the controlling norm of the whole. As regards these preconceptions and postulates, Marx draws on two distinct lines of antecedents—the Materialistic Hegelianism and the English system of Natural Rights. By his earlier training he is an adept in the Hegelian method of speculation and inoculated with the metaphysics of development underlying the Hegelian system. By his later training he is an expert in the system of Natural Rights and Natural Liberty, ingrained in his ideals of life and held inviolate throughout. He does not take a critical attitude toward the underlying principles of Natural Rights. Even his Hegelian preconceptions of development never carry him the length of questioning the fundamental principles of that system. He is only more ruthlessly consistent in working out their content than his natural-rights antagonists in the liberal-classical school. His polemics run against the specific tenets of the liberal school, but they run wholly on the ground afforded by the premises of that school. The ideals of his propaganda are natural-rights ideals, but his theory of the working out of these ideals in the course of history rests on the Hegelian metaphysics of development, and his method of speculation and construction of theory is given by the Hegelian dialectic.

What first and most vividly centered interest on Marx and his speculations was his relation to the revolutionary socialistic movement; and it is those features of his doctrines which bear immediately on the propaganda that still continue to hold the attention of the greater number of his critics. Chief among these doctrines, in the apprehension of his critics, is the theory of value, with its corollaries: (a) the doctrines of the exploitation of labor by capital; and (b) the laborer's claim to the whole product of his labor. Avowedly, Marx traces his doctrine of labor-value to Ricardo, and through him to the classical economists.[1] The laborer's claim to the whole product of labor, which is pretty constantly implied, though not frequently avowed by Marx, he has in all probability taken from English writers of the early nineteenth century,[2] more particularly from William Thompson. These doctrines are, on their face, nothing but a development of the conceptions of natural rights which then pervaded English speculation and afforded the metaphysical ground of the liberal movement. The more formidable critics of the Marxian socialism have made much of these doctrinal elements that further the propaganda, and have, by laying the stress on these, diverted attention from other elements that are of more vital consequence to the system as a body of theory. Their exclusive interest in this side of "scientific socialism" has even led them to deny the Marxian system all substantial originality, and make it a (doubtfully legitimate) offshoot of English Liberalism and natural rights.[3] But this is one-sided criticism. It may hold as against certain tenets of the so-called "scientific socialism," but it is not altogether to the point as regards the Marxian system of theory. Even the Marxian theory of value, surplus value, and exploitation, is not simply the doctrine of William Thompson, transcribed and sophisticated in a forbidding terminology, however great the superficial resemblance and however large Marx's unacknowledged debt to Thompson may be on these heads. For many details and for much of his animus Marx may be indebted to the Utilitarians; but, after all, his system of theory, taken as a whole, lies within the frontiers of neo-Hegelianism, and even the details are worked out in accord with the preconceptions of that school of thought and have taken on the complexion that would properly belong to them on that ground. It is, therefore, not by an itemized scrutiny of the details of doctrine and by tracing their pedigree in detail that a fair conception of Marx and his contribution to economics may be reached, but rather by following him from his own point of departure out into the ramification of his theory, and so overlooking the whole in the perspective which the lapse of time now affords us, but which he could not himself attain, since he was too near to his own work to see why he went about it as he did.

The comprehensive system of Marxism is comprised within the scheme of the Materialistic Conception of History.[4] This materialistic conception is essentially Hegelian,[5] although it belongs with the Hegelian Left, and its immediate affiliation is with Feuerbach, not with the direct line of Hegelian orthodoxy. The chief point of interest here, in identifying the materialistic conception with Hegelianism, is that this identification throws it immediately and uncompromisingly into contrast with Darwinism and the post-Darwinian conceptions of evolution. Even if a plausible English pedigree should be worked out for this Materialistic Conception, or "Scientific Socialism," as has been attempted, it remains none the less true that the conception with which Marx went to his work was a transmuted framework of Hegelian dialectic.[6]

Roughly, Hegelian materialism differs from Hegelian orthodoxy by inventing the main logical sequence, not by discarding the logic or resorting to the new tests of truth or finality. One might say, though perhaps with excessive crudity, that, where Hegel pronounces his dictum, *Das Denken ist das Sein*, the materialists, particularly Marx and Engels, would say *Das Sein macht das Denken*. But in both cases some sort of a creative primacy is assigned to one or the other member of the complex, and in neither case is the relation between the two members a causal relation. In the materialistic conception man's spiritual life—what man thinks—is a reflex of what he is in the material respect, very much in the same fashion as the orthodox Hegelian would make the material world a reflex of the spirit. In both, the dominant norm of speculation and formulation of theory is the conception of movement, development, evolution, progress; and in both the movement is conceived necessarily to take place by the method of conflict or struggle. The movement is of the nature of progress—gradual advance toward a goal, toward the realization in explicit form of all that is implicit in the substantial activity involved in the movement. The movement is, further, self-conditioned and self-acting; it is an unfolding by inner necessity. The struggle which constitutes the method of movement or evolution is, in the Hegelian system proper, the struggle of the spirit for self-realization by the process of the well-known three-phase dialectic. In the materialistic conception of history this dialectical movement becomes the class struggle of the Marxian system.

The class struggle is conceived to be "material," but the term "material" is in this connection used in a metaphorical sense. It does not mean mechanical or physical, or even physiological, but economic. It is material in the sense that it is a struggle between classes for the material means of life. "The materialistic conception of history proceeds on the principle that production and, next to production, the exchange of its products is the groundwork of every social order."[7] The social order takes its form through the class struggle, and the character of the class struggle at any given phase of the unfolding development of society is determined by "the prevailing mode of economic production and exchange." The dialectic of the movement of social progress, therefore, moves on the spiritual plane of human desire and passion, not on the (literally) material plane of mechanical and physiological stress, on which the developmental process of brute creation unfolds itself. It is a sublimated materialism, sublimated by the dominating presence of the conscious human spirit; but it is conditioned by the material facts of the production of the means of life.[8] The ultimately active forces involved in the process of unfolding social life are (apparently) the material agencies engaged in the mechanics of production; but the dialectic of the process—the class struggle—runs its course only among and in terms of the secondary (epigenetic) forces of human consciousness engaged in the valuation of the material products of industry. A consistently materialistic conception, consistently adhering to a materialistic interpretation of the process of development as well as of the facts involved in the process, could scarcely avoid making its putative dialectic struggle a mere unconscious and irrelevant conflict of the brute material forces. This would have amounted to an interpretation in terms of opaque cause and effect, without recourse to the concept of a conscious class struggle, and it might have led to a concept of evolution similar to the unteleological Darwinian concept of natural selection. It could scarcely have led to the Marxian notion of a conscious class struggle as the one necessary method of social progress, though it might conceivably, by the aid of empirical generalization, have led to a scheme of social process in which a class struggle would be included as an incidental though perhaps highly efficient factor.[9] It would have led, as Darwinism has, to a concept of a process of cumulative change in social structure and function; but this process, being essentially a cumulative sequence of causation, opaque and unteleological, could not, without an infusion of pious fancy by the speculator, be asserted to involve progress as distinct from retrogression or to tend to a "realization" or "self-realization" of the human spirit or of anything else. Neither could it conceivably be asserted to lead up to a final term, a goal to which all lines of the process should converge and beyond which the process would not go, such as the assumed goal of the Marxian process of class struggle, which is conceived to cease in the classless economic structure of the socialistic final term. In Darwinism there is no such final or perfect term, and no definitive equilibrium.

The disparity between Marxism and Darwinism, as well as the disparity within the Marxian system between the range of material facts that are conceived to be the fundamental forces of the process, on the one hand, and the range of spiritual facts within which the dialectic movement proceeds—this disparity is shown in the character assigned the class struggle by Marx and Engels. The struggle is asserted to be a conscious one, and proceeds on a recognition by the competing classes of their mutually incompatible interests with regard to the material means of life. The class struggle proceeds on motives of interest, and a recognition of class interest can, of course, be reached only by reflection on the facts of the case. There is, therefore, not even a direct causal connection between the material forces in the case and the choice of a given interested line of conduct. The attitude of the interested party does not result from the material forces so immediately as to place it within the relation of direct cause and effect, nor even with such a degree of intimacy as to admit of its being classed as a tropismatic, or even instinctive, response to the impact of the material force in question. The sequence of reflection, and the consequent choice of sides to a quarrel, run entirely alongside of a range of material facts concerned.

A further characteristic of the doctrine of class struggle requires mention. While the concept is not Darwinian, it is also not legitimately Hegelian, whether of the Right or the Left. It is of a utilitarian origin and of English pedigree, and it belongs to Marx by virtue of his having borrowed its elements from the system of self-interest. It is in fact a piece of hedonism, and is related to Bentham rather than to Hegel. It proceeds on the grounds of the hedonistic calculus, which is equally foreign to the Hegelian notion of an unfolding process and to the post-Darwinian notions of cumulative causation. As regards the tenability of the doctrine, apart from the question of its derivation and its compatibility with the neo-Hegelian postulates, it is to be added that it is quite out of harmony with the later results of psychological inquiry—just as is true of the use made of the hedonistic calculus by the classical (Austrian) economics.

Within the domain covered by the materialistic conception, that is to say within the domain of unfolding human culture, which is the field of Marxian speculation at large, Marx has more particularly devoted his efforts to an analysis and theoretical formulation of the present situation—the current phase of the process, the capitalistic system. And, since the prevailing mode of the production of goods determines the institutional, intellectual, and spiritual life of the epoch, by determining the form and method of the current class struggle, the discussion necessarily begins with the theory of "capitalistic production," or production as carried on under the capitalistic system.[10] Under the capitalistic system, that is to say under the system of modern business traffic, production is a production of commodities, merchantable goods, with a view to the price to be obtained by them in the market. The great fact on which all industry under this system hinges is the price of marketable goods. Therefore it is at this point that Marx strikes into the system of capitalistic production, and therefore the theory of value becomes the dominant feature of his economics and the point of departure for the whole analysis, in all its voluminous ramifications.[11]

It is scarcely worth while to question what serves as the beginning of wisdom in the current criticisms of Marx; namely, that he offers no adequate proof of his labor-value theory.[12] It is even safe to go farther, and say that he offers no proof of it. The feint which occupies the opening paragraphs of the *Capital* and the corresponding passages of *Zur Kritik*, etc., is not to be taken seriously as an attempt to prove his position on this head by the ordinary recourse to argument. It is rather a self-satisfied superior's playful mystification of those readers (critics) whose limited powers do not enable them to see that his proposition is self-evident. Taken on the Hegelian (neo-Hegelian) ground, and seen in the light of the general materialistic conception, the proposition that value = labor-cost is self-evident, not to say tautological. Seen in any other light, it has no particular force.

In the Hegelian scheme of things the only substantial reality is the unfolding life of the spirit. In the neo-Hegelian scheme, as embodied in the materialistic conception, this reality is translated into terms of the unfolding (material) life of man in society.[13] In so far as the goods are products of industry, they are the output of this unfolding life of man, a material residue embodying a given fraction of this forceful life-process. In this life-process lies all substantial reality, and all finally valid relations of quantivalence between the products of this life-process must run in its terms. The life-process, which, when it takes the specific form of an expenditure of labor power, goes to produce goods, is a process of material forces, the spiritual or mental features of the life-process and of labor being only its insubstantial reflex. It is consequently only in the material changes wrought by this expenditure of labor power that the metaphysical substance of life—labor power—can be embodied; but in these changes of material fact it cannot but be embodied, since these are the end to which it is directed.

This balance between goods in respect of their magnitude as output of human labor holds good indefeasibly, in point of the metaphysical reality of the life-process, whatever superficial (phenomenal) variations from this norm may occur in men's dealings with the goods under the stress of the strategy of self-interest. Such is the value of the goods in reality; they are equivalents of one another in the proportion in which they partake of this substantial quality, although their true ratio of equivalence may never come to an adequate expression in the transactions involved in the distribution of the goods. This real or true value of goods is a fact of production, and holds true under all systems and methods of production, whereas the exchange value (the "phenomenal form" of the real value) is a fact of distribution and expresses the real value more or less closely to the equities given by production. If the output of industry were distributed to the productive agents strictly in proportion to their shares in production, the exchange value of the goods would be presumed to conform to their real value. But, under the current, capitalistic system, distribution is not in any sensible degree based on the equities of production, and the exchange value of goods under this system can therefore express their real value only with a very rough, and in the main fortuitous, approximation. Under a socialistic regime, where the laborer would get the full product of his labor, or where the whole system of ownership, and consequently the system of distribution, would lapse, values would reach a true expression, if any.

Under the capitalistic system the determination of exchange value is a matter of competitive profit-making, and exchange values therefore depart erratically and incontinently from the proportions that would legitimately be given them by the real values whose only expression they are. Marx's critics commonly identify the concept of "value" with that of "exchange value,"[14] and show that the theory of "value" does not square with the run of the facts of price under the existing system of distribution, piously hoping thereby to have refuted the Marxian doctrine; whereas, of course, they have for the most part not touched it. The misapprehension of the critics may be due to a (possibly international) oracular obscurity on the part of Marx. Whether by his fault or their own, their refutations have hitherto been quite inconclusive. Marx's severest stricture on the iniquities of the capitalistic system is that contained by implication in his development of the manner in which actual exchange value of goods systematically diverges from their real (labor-cost) value. Herein, indeed, lies not only the inherent iniquity of the existing system, but also its fateful infirmity, according to Marx.

The theory of value, then, is contained in the main postulates of the Marxian system rather than derived from them. Marx identifies this doctrine, in its elements, with the labor-value theory of Ricardo,[15] but the relationship between the two is that of a superficial coincidence in their main propositions rather than a substantial identity of theoretic contents. In Ricardo's theory the source and measure of value is sought in the effort and sacrifice undergone by the producer, consistently, on the whole, with the Benthamite-utilitarian position to which Ricardo somewhat loosely and uncritically adhered. The decisive fact about labor, that quality by virtue of which it is assumed to be the final term in the theory of production, is its irksomeness. Such is of course not the case in the labor-value theory of Marx, to whom the question of the irksomeness of labor is quite irrelevant, so far as regards the relation between labor and production. The substantial diversity or incompatibility of the two theories shows itself directly when each is employed by its creator in the further analysis of economic phenomena. Since with Ricardo the crucial point is the degree of irksomeness of labor, which serves as a measure both of the labor expended and the value produced, and since in Ricardo's utilitarian philosophy there is no more vital fact underlying this irksomeness, therefore no surplus-value theory follows from the main position. The productiveness of labor is not cumulative, in its own working; and the Ricardian economics goes on to seek the cumulative productiveness of industry in the functioning of the products of labor when employed in further production and in the irksomeness of the capitalist's abstinence. From which duly follows the general position of classical economics on the theory of production.

With Marx, on the other hand, the labor power expended in production being itself a product and having a substantial value corresponding to its own labor-cost, the value of the labor power expended and the value of the product created by its expenditure need not be the same. They are not the same, by supposition, as they would be in any hedonistic interpretation of the facts. Hence a discrepancy arises between the value of the labor power expended in production and the value of the product created, and this discrepancy is covered by the concept of surplus value. Under the capitalistic system, wages being the value (price) of the labor power consumed in industry, it follows that the surplus product of their labor cannot go the laborers, but becomes the profits of capital and the source of its accumulation and increase. From the fact that wages are measured by the value of labor power rather than by the (greater) value of the product of labor, it follows also that the laborers are unable to buy the whole product of their labor, and so that the capitalists are unable to sell the whole product of industry continuously at its full value, whence arise difficulties of the gravest nature in the capitalistic system, in the way of over production and the like.

But the gravest outcome of this systematic discrepancy between the value of labor power and the value of its product is the accumulation of capital out of unpaid labor, and the effect of this accumulation on the laboring population. The law of accumulation, with its corollary, the doctrine of the industrial reserve army, is the final term and the objective point of Marx's theory of capitalist production, just as the theory of labor value is his point of departure.[16] While the theory of value and surplus value are Marx's explanation of the possibility of existence of the capitalistic system, the law of the accumulation of capital is his exposition of the causes which must lead to the collapse of that system and the manner in which the collapse will come. And since Marx is, always and everywhere, a socialist agitator as well as a theoretical economist, it may be said without hesitation that the law of accumulation is the climax of his great work, from whatever point of view it is looked at, whether as an economic theorem or as a tenet of socialistic doctrine.

The law of capitalistic accumulation may be paraphrased as follows:[17] Wages being the (approximately exact) value of the labor power brought in the wage contract; the price of the product being the (similarly approximate) value of the goods produced; and since the value of the product exceeds that of the labor power by a given amount (surplus value), which by force of the wage contract passes into the possession of the capitalist and is by him in part laid by as savings and added to the capital already in hand, it follows (a) that, other things equal, the larger the surplus value, the more rapid the increase of capital; and, also (b) that the greater the increase of capital relatively to the labor force employed, the more productive the labor employed and the larger the surplus product available for accumulation. The process of accumulation, therefore, is evidently a cumulative one; and, also evidently, the increase added to capital is an unearned increment drawn from the unpaid surplus product of labor.

But with an appreciable increase of the aggregate capital a change takes place in its technological composition, whereby the "constant" capital (equipment and raw materials) increases disproportionately as compared with the "variable" capital (wages fund). "Labor-saving devices" are used to a greater extent than before, and labor is saved. A larger proportion of the expenses of production goes for the purchase of equipment and raw materials, and a smaller proportion—though perhaps an absolutely increased amount—goes for the purchase of labor power. Less labor is needed relatively to the aggregate capital employed as well as relatively to the quantity of goods produced. Hence some portion of the increasing labor supply will not be wanted, and an "industrial reserve army," a "surplus labor population," an army of unemployed, comes into existence. This reserve grows relatively larger as the accumulation of capital proceeds and as technological improvements consequently gain ground; so that there result two divergent cumulative changes in the situation—antagonistic, but due to the same set of forces and, therefore, inseparable: capital increases, and the number of unemployed laborers (relatively) increases also.

This divergence between the amount of capital and output, on the one hand, and the amount received by laborers as wages, on the other hand, has an incidental consequence of some importance. The purchasing power of the laborers, represented by their wages, being the largest part of the demand for consumable goods, and being at the same time, in the nature of the case, progressively less adequate for the purchase of the product, represented by the price of the goods produced, it follows that the market is progressively more subject to glut from over production, and hence to commercial crises and depression. It has been argued, as if it were a direct inference from Marx's position, that this maladjustment between production and markets, due to the laborer not getting the full product of his labor, leads directly to the breakdown of the capitalistic system, and so by its own force will bring on the socialistic consummation. Such is not Marx's position, however, although crises and depression play an important part in the course of development that is to lead up to socialism. In Marx's theory, socialism is to come by way of a conscious class movement on the part of the propertyless laborers, who will act advisedly on their own interest and force the revolutionary movement for their own gain. But crises and depression will have a large share in bringing the laborers to a frame of mind suitable for such a move.

Given a growing aggregate capital, as indicated above, and a concomitant reserve of unemployed laborers growing at a still higher rate, as is involved in Marx's position, this body of unemployment labor can be, and will be, used by the capitalists to depress wages, in order to increase profits. Logically, it follows that, the farther and faster capital accumulates, the larger will be the reserve of unemployed, both absolutely and relatively to the work to be done, and the more severe will be the pressure acting to reduce wages and lower the standard of living, and the deeper will be the degradation and misery of the working class and the more precipitately will their condition decline to a still lower depth. Every period of depression, with its increased body of unemployed labor seeking work, will act to hasten and accentuate the depression of wages, until there is no warrant even for holding that wages will, on an average, be kept up to the subsistence minimum.[18] Marx, indeed, is explicit to the effect that such will be the case—that wages will decline below the subsistence minimum; and he cites English conditions of child labor, misery, and degeneration to substantiate his views.[19] When this has gone far enough, when capitalist production comes near enough to occupying the whole field of industry and has depressed the condition of its laborers sufficiently to make them an effective majority of the community with nothing to lose, then, having taken advice together, they will move, by legal or extra-legal means, by absorbing the state or by subverting it, to establish the social revolution.

Socialism is to come through class antagonism due to the absence of all property interests from the laboring class, coupled with a generally prevalent misery so profound as to involve some degree of physical degeneration. This misery is to be brought about by the heightened productivity of labor due to an increased accumulation of capital and large improvements in the industrial arts; which in turn is caused by the fact that under a system of private enterprise with hired labor the laborer does not get the whole product of his labor; which, again, is only saying in other words that private ownership of capital goods enables the capitalist to appropriate and accumulate the surplus product of labor. As to what the regime is to be which the social revolution will bring in, Marx has nothing particular to say, beyond the general thesis that there will be no private ownership, at least not of the means of production.

Such are the outlines of the Marxian system of socialism. In all that has been said so far no recourse is had to the second and third volume of *Capital*. Nor is it necessary to resort to these two volumes for the general theory of socialism. They add nothing essential, although many of the details of the processes concerned in the working out of the capitalist scheme are treated with greater fullness, and the analysis is carried out with great consistency and with admirable results. For economic theory at large these further two volumes are important enough, but an inquiry into their contents in that connection is not called for here.

Nothing much need be said as to the tenability of this theory. In its essentials, or at least in its characteristic elements, it has for the most part been given up by latter-day socialist writers. The number of those who hold to it without essential deviation is growing gradually smaller. Such is necessarily the case, and for more than one reason. The facts are not bearing it out on certain critical points, such as the doctrine of increasing misery; and the Hegelian philosophical postulates, without which the Marxism of Marx is groundless, are for the most part forgotten by the dogmatists of today. Darwinism has largely supplanted Hegelianism in their habits of thought.

The particular point at which the theory is most fragile, considered simply as a theory of social growth, is its implied doctrine of population—implied in the doctrine of a growing reserve of unemployed workmen. The doctrine of the reserve of unemployed labor involves as a postulate that population will increase anyway, without reference to current or prospective means of life. The empirical facts give at least a very persuasive apparent support to the view expressed by Marx, that misery is, or has hitherto been, no hindrance to the propagation of the race; but they afford no conclusive evidence in support of a thesis to the effect that the number of laborers must increase independently of an increase of the means of life. No one since Darwin would have the hardihood to say that the increase of the human species is not conditioned by the means of living.

But all that does not really touch Marx's position. To Marx, the neo-Hegelian, history, including the economic development, is the life-history of the human species; and the main fact in this life-history, particularly in the economic aspect of it, is the growing volume of human life. This, in a manner of speaking, is the base-line of the whole analysis of the process of economic life, including the phase of capitalist production with the rest. The growth of population is the first principle, the most substantial, most material factor in this process of economic life, so long as it is a process of growth, of unfolding, of exfoliation, and not a phase of decrepitude and decay. Had Marx found that his analysis led him to a view adverse to this position, he would logically have held that the capitalist system is the mortal agony of the race and the manner of its taking off. Such a conclusion is precluded by his Hegelian point of departure, according to which the goal of the life-history of the race in a large way controls the course of that life-history in all its phases, including the phase of capitalism. This goal or end, which controls the process of human development, is the complete realization of life in all its fullness, and the realization is to be reached by a process analogous to the three-phase dialectic, of thesis, antithesis, and synthesis, into which scheme the capitalist system, with its overflowing measure of misery and degradation, fits as the last and most dreadful phase of antithesis. Marx, as a Hegelian—that is to say, a romantic philosopher—is necessarily an optimist, and the evil (antithetical element) in life is to him a logically necessary evil, as the antithesis is a necessary phase of the dialectic; and it is a means to the consummation, as the antithesis is a means to the synthesis.

Notes

1. Cf. *Critique of Political Economy*, ch. i, "Notes on the History of the Theory of Commodities," pp. 56–73 (English translation, New York, 1904).

2. See Menger, *Right to the Whole Produce of Labor*, sections iii–v and viii–ix, and Foxwell's admirable *Introduction to Menger.*

3. See Menger and Foxwell, as above, and Schaeffle, *Quintessence of Socialism* and *The Impossibility of Social Democracy.*

4. See Engels, *The Development of Socialism from Utopia to Science*, especially section ii and the opening paragraphs of section iii, also the preface of *Zur Kritik der politischen Oekonomie.*

5. See Engels, as above, and also his Feuerbach: *The Roots of Socialist Philosophy* (translation, Chicago, Kerr & Co., 1903).

6. E.g., Seligman, *The Economic Interpretation of History*, Part I.

7. Engels, *Development of Socialism*, beginning of section iii.

8. Cf., on this point, Max Adler, "Kausalität und Teleologie im streite um die Wissenschaft" (included in *Marx-Studien,* edited by Adler and Hilferding, vol. i), particularly section xi; cf. also Ludwig Stein, *Die soziale Frage im Lichte der Philosophie,* whom Adler criticizes and claims to have refuted.

9. Cf. Adler, as above.

10. It may be noted, by way of caution to readers familiar with the terms only as employed by the classical (English and Austrian) economists, that in Marxian usage "capitalistic production" means production of goods for the market by hired labor under the direction of employers who own (or control) the means of production and are engaged in industry for the sake of a profit. "Capital" is wealth (primarily funds) so employed. In these and other related points of terminological usage Marx is, of course, much more closely in touch with colloquial usage than those economists of the classical line who make capital signify "the products of past industry used as aids to further production." With Marx "Capitalism" implies certain relations of ownership, no less than the "productive use" which is alone insisted on by so many later economists in defining the term.

11. In the sense that the theory of value affords the point of departure and the fundamental concepts out of which the further theory of the workings of capitalism is constructed—in this sense, and in this sense only, is the theory of value the central doctrine and the critical tenet of Marxism. It does not follow that the Marxist doctrine of an irresistible drift toward a socialistic consummation hangs on the defensibility of the labor-value theory, nor even that the general structure of the Marxist economics would collapse if translated into other terms than those of this doctrine of labor-value. Cf. Böhm-Bawerk, *Karl Marx and the Close of His System*; and, on the other hand, Franz Oppenheimer, *Das*

Grundgesetz der Marx'schen Gesellschaftslehre; and Rudolf Goldscheid, *Verelendungs- oder Meliorationstheorie.*

12. Cf., e.g., Böhm-Bawerk, as above; Georg Adler, *Grundlagen der Karl Marx'schen Kritik.*

13. In much the same way, and with an analogous effect on their theoretical work, in the preconceptions of the classical (including the Austrian) economists, the balance of pleasure and pain is taken to be the ultimate reality in terms of which all economic theory must be stated and to terms of which all phenomena should finally be reduced in any definitive analysis of economic life. It is not the present purpose to inquire whether the one of these uncritical assumptions is in any degree more meritorious or more serviceable than the other.

14. Böhm-Bawerk, *Capital and Interest,* Book VI, ch. iii; also *Karl Marx and the Close of His System,* particularly ch. iv; Adler, *Grundlagen,* chs. ii. and iii.

15. Cf. *Capital,* vol. i, ch. xv, p. 486 (4th ed.). See also notes 9 and 16 to ch. i of the same volume, where Marx discusses the labor-value doctrines of Adam Smith and an earlier (anonymous) English writer, and compares them with his own. Similar comparisons with the early—classical—value theories recur from time to time in the later portions of *Capital.*

16. Oppenheimer (*Das Grundgesetz der Marx'schen Gesellschaftslehre*) is right in making the theory of accumulation the central element in the doctrines of Marxist socialism, but it does not follow, as Oppenheimer contends, that this doctrine is the keystone of Marx's economic theories. It follows logically from the theory of surplus value, as indicated above, and rests on that theory in such a way that it would fail (in the form in which it is held by Marx) with the failure of the doctrine of surplus value.

17. See *Capital,* vol. i, ch. xxiii.

18. The "subsistence minimum" is here taken in the sense used by Marx and the classical economists, as meaning what is necessary to keep up the supply of labor at its current rate of efficiency.

19. See *Capital,* vol. i, ch. xxiii, sections 4 and 5.

The Basis of Social Institutions

Races and Peoples

Among men who have no articulate acquaintance with matters of ethnology it is usual to speak of the several nations of Europe as distinct races. Even official documents and painstaking historians are not free from this confusion of ideas. In this colloquial use "race" is not conceived to be precisely synonymous with "nation," nor with "people"; although it would often be a difficult matter to make out from the context just what distinctive meaning is attached to one or another of these terms. They are used loosely and suggestively, and for many purposes they may doubtless be so used without compromise or confusion to the argument; so that it might seem the part of reason to take them as they come, with allowance for such margin of error as necessarily attaches to their colloquial use, and without taking thought of a closer definition or a more discriminate use than what contents those who so find these terms convenient for use in all their colloquial ambiguity.

But through all the current ambiguity in the use of these terms, and of others that serve as their virtual equivalents, there runs a certain consistent difference of connotation, such as to work confusion in much of the argument in which they are employed. Whatever else it may be taken to convey, "race" always implies a solidarity of inheritance within the group so designated; it always implies that the complement of hereditary traits is substantially the same for all the individuals comprised in the group. "Race" is a biological concept, and wherever it is applied it signifies common descent of the group from an ancestry possessed of a given specific type and transmitting the traits that mark this type, intact to all members of the group so designated. The other terms, that are currently used as interchangeable with "race," as, e.g., "nation" or "people," do not necessarily imply such a biological solidarity of the group to which they are applied; although the notion of a common descent is doubtless frequently present in a loose way in the mind of those who so use them.

Reprinted from chapter 1, "Introduction: Races and Peoples," *Imperial Germany and the Industrial Revolution,* New York: The Macmillan Company, 1915.

In this colloquial use of terms, when the distinction between these several peoples or alleged races is not allowed to rest quite uncritically on a demarcation of national frontiers, the distinguishing mark to which recourse is usually had is the community of language. So it comes about that habituation to a given type of speech has come to do duty as a conventional mark of racial derivation. A certain (virtual) uniformity of habit is taken to mean a uniformity of hereditary endowment. And many historians and publicists who discuss these matters have been led into far-reaching generalizations touching hereditary characteristics of temperament, intelligence and physique, in cases where there is in fact ground for nothing more substantial than a discriminating comparison between divergent schemes of use and wont. Such differences of use and wont as mark off one people from another may be a sufficiently consequential matter, of course; but their reach and effect are after all of quite another character, and have quite another place and bearing in the cultural growth, than differences of racial type.

The scheme of institutions in force in any given community—as exemplified, e.g., by the language—being of the nature of habit, is necessarily unstable and will necessarily vary incontinently with the passage of time, though it may be in a consistent manner; whereas the type of any given racial stock is stable, and the hereditary traits of spiritual and physical endowment that mark the type are a matter of indefeasible biological heritage, invariable throughout the life-history of the race. A meticulous discrimination between the two concepts—of habit and heredity—is the beginning of wisdom in all inquiry into human behavior; and confusion of the two is accountable for much of the polemical animus, and not a little recrimination, in recent and current writing on historical, political and economic matters. And, of course, the larger the burden of chauvinism carried by the discussion the more spectacular and sweeping has been its output of systematic blunders.

If an inquiry into the case of Germany is to profit the ends of theoretical generalization bearing on the study of human institutions, their nature and causes, it is necessary to discriminate between those factors in the case that are of a stable and enduring character and those that are variable, and at the same time it is necessary to take thought of what factors are peculiar to the case of the German people and what others are common to them and to their neighbors with whom their case will necessarily be compared. It happens that these two lines of discrimination in great part coincide. In respect of the stable characteristics of race heredity the German people do not differ in any sensible or consistent manner from the neighboring peoples; whereas in the character of their past habituation—in their cultural scheme—as well as in respect of the circumstances to which they have latterly been exposed, their case is at least in some degree peculiar. It is in the matter of received habits of thought—use and wont—and in the conditions that have further shaped their scheme of use and wont in the recent past, that the population of this country differs from the population of Europe at large.

In view of the prevalent confusion or ignorance on this head among the historians and publicists who have been dealing with these matters, it seems necessary, even at the cost of some tedium, to recite certain notorious facts bearing on the racial complexion of the German people. In so far as many bear on the question of race for the German people taken as a whole, these facts are no longer in controversy. Students of European race questions still are, and no doubt long will be, engaged on many difficult problems of local displacement, migration and infiltration of racial elements, even within the frontiers of the Fatherland; but for the purpose in hand recourse need scarcely be had to any of these matters of recondite detail. Even if more might be convenient, nothing is required for present use beyond those general features of the case on which a secure consensus has already been reached.

It is only in so far as we can make shift to conceive that the linguistic frontiers coincide in some passable way with the political frontiers of German dominion that we can make use of the name as it is currently employed in historical, polemical and patriotic writing, without phase or abatement. Taking the name, then, as loosely designating the Empire with its German-speaking population—*das deutsche Volk*—and overlooking any discrepancies in so doing, the aggregate so designated is in no defensible sense to be spoken of as a distinct race, even after all allowance has been made for intrusive elements in the population, such as the Jews or the Germanized Poles and Danes. The German people is not a distinct race either as against the non-German population of Europe or within itself. In both of these respects the case of this population is not materially different from that of any other national population in Europe. These facts are notorious.

Like the populations of the neighboring countries, the German population, too, is thoroughly and universally hybrid; and the hybrid mixture that goes to make up the German people is compounded out of the same racial elements that enter into the composition of the European population at large. Its hybrid character is perhaps more pronounced than is the case in the countries lying farther south, but the difference in degree of hybridization as between the Germans and their southern neighbors is not a serious one. On the other hand the case of the Germans is in this respect virtually identical with that of the peoples lying immediately to the east and west.

In point of race the population of south Germany is substantially identical with that of northern France or the neighboring parts of Belgium; while in the same respect the population of north Germany has substantially the same composition as that of Holland and Denmark on the west and of western Russia on the east; and, taking the Fatherland as a whole, its population is in point of race substantially identical with that of the British Isles. The variations in local detail within this broad belt of mixed populations are appreciable, no doubt, but they are after all of much the same character in one country as in another, and taken one with another they run to much the same effect both east, west and middle.

When taken in the large there is, in other words, no sensible difference of race between the English, Dutch, Germans and the Slavs of Great Russia.

In the current exposition of national merit and notability, when a pure-bred German, Germanic or Anglo-Saxon race is spoken for, the context presently brings into view that what is present in the eulogist's conception, if anything in the way of a definite biological category, is the dolicho-blond. Now it happens, unfortunately for the invidious insistence on purity of race, that this particular racial stock is less frequently to be found unmixed than either of the other two with which it is associated. It is, indeed, quite safe to affirm that there is no community extant, great or small, that is made up even approximately of pure-bred blonds to the exclusion of other racial elements.

One may even safely go further and assert that there is not by any chance an individual to be found in the population of Europe who, in point of pedigree, is of unmixed blond extraction. Nor is there any reasonable chance, nor any evidence available, that a community of pure-bred blonds ever has existed in any part of Europe. And the like assertion may be made, with but a slightly less degree of assurance, as regards pure-bred specimens of the other main European races.

The variation in race characters is very appreciable within each of these national populations; in the German case being quite pronounced between north and south. Whereas the differences which go to make the distinction between these nationalities taken as aggregates are of an institutional kind—differences in acquired traits not transmissible by inheritance, substantially differences of habituation. On this side, however, the divergences between one nationality and another may be large, and they are commonly of a systematic character; so that while no divergence of racial type may be alleged, the divergence in the cultural type may yet be serious enough.

The hybrid composition of these peoples affects their character in yet another bearing, which is of grave consequence in the growth of culture, at the same time that it affects the fortunes of all the peoples of Europe in much the same fashion, though perhaps not in the same degree. By consequence of their hybrid composition the individual members of these nationalities vary more widely in respect of their native capacities and aptitudes than would be the case in any pure-bred people.[1] So that these peoples each present a much larger diversity of personalities than would be found among them if they were not cross-bred. On the physical side, in respect of such traits as can be measured and compared by mechanical methods, this great range and complexity of variations within each nationality is obvious enough—in stature, color, mass and anatomical proportions. But it no less indubitably comprises also those (spiritual and intellectual) traits that are less amenable to anthropometrical statistic, at the same time that they are of greater consequence to the fortunes of the people among whom they are found. It is these psychological traits—spiritual and intellectual proclivities, capacities, aptitudes, sensibilities—that afford the raw material out of which any given scheme of civilization is built up and on which its life-history and the sequence of its permutations run their course. It is, of course, a trite matter-of-course that no people can work out a scheme of culture that lies beyond or outside the range of its capacities; and it is likewise a matter-of-course that a nation whose population is gifted with many and various capacities is thereby better fitted to meet the exigencies that arise in the course of its life-history, and so will be in a position more promptly to respond to any call. A larger, fuller, more varied and more broadly balanced scheme of culture will, under tolerable circumstances, be found among such a people than in a community made up of individuals that breed true with close approximation to a single specific type.

Such a hybrid population will, of course, also have the faults of its qualities. The divergence of temperament and proclivities will be as wide as that of its capacities and aptitudes; and the unrest that works out in a multiform ramification of achievement on the one side is likely to work out also in a profuse output of irritation and dissentient opinions, ideals and aspirations on the other side. For good or ill, such has been the congenital make-up of the Western peoples, and such, it may be called to mind, has also been the history of Western civilization.

All the while it may as well be kept in mind that in this respect, as regards the range and multifarious character of their native endowment, these Western peoples are today what they once were in neolithic time. The range of variations in each and all is very appreciably wider than would be had within any pure-bred stock; but it is no wider, nor is it in any sensible degree different, among the hybrid generations that inhabit these countries today than it once was among the similarly hybrid generations that carried this Western culture in that earlier time. This wide-ranging heritage is after all a neolithic heritage; and however multiform and picturesquely varied the cultural scheme of the Western peoples in later times may seem, the stream does not, after all, rise higher than its neolithic source. The population that makes up and carries forward this civilization is, after all, endowed with the faults of its qualities, and they are the neolithic qualities.

Notes

1. It is evident that under the Mendelian rules held to govern matters of heredity in hybrids it follows that the cross offspring of two (or three) distinct specific types may vary by approximately as many permutations as the number of viable combinations possible between their double (or treble) range of determinants, or "factors," comprised in the double (or treble) ancestry. That is to say, while the pure-bred representatives of a given specific type vary within the narrow limits of the type, through varying stress on the several determinants comprised in the type constitution during the growth of the filial individual (zygote); it is on the other hand contained in the premises that the cross-bred individual may vary not only by consequence of such differences of stress during its growth (what may be called variation in initially acquired characters) but also (what may be called variation in hereditary characters) by a number of new combinations of characters coming in from the two (or three) sides of his double (or treble) ancestry and amount-

ing approximately to the square (or cube)—1 of the number of determinants comprised in the type constitution—barring such combinations, more numerous the more divergent the two (or three) parent types, as may not be viable, and provided always that the filial generation in question is sufficiently numerous to provide scope for so extensive a variation. The extreme variants in such a case may easily go beyond the extreme range of either parent type in any given direction, owing to the fact that a given determinant coming in from one side may be fortified or inhibited (perhaps more easily the latter) by a determinant coming in from the other side and affecting the same group of tissues.

The Instinct of Workmanship

What is known of heredity goes to say that the various racial types of man are stable; so that during the life-history of any given racial stock, it is held, no heritable modification of its typical make-up, whether spiritual or physical, is to be looked for. The typical human endowment of instincts, as well as the typical make-up of the race in the physical respect, has according to this current view been transmitted intact from the beginning of humanity—that is to say from whatever point in the mutational development of the race it is seen fit to date humanity—except so far as subsequent mutations have given rise to new racial stocks, to and by which this human endowment of native proclivities has been transmitted in a typically modified form. On the other hand the habitual elements of human life change unremittingly and cumulatively, resulting in a continued proliferous growth of institutions. Changes in the institutional structure are continually taking place in response to the altered discipline of life under changing cultural conditions, but human nature remains specifically the same.

The ways and means, material and immaterial, by which the native proclivities work out their ends, therefore, are forever in process of change, being conditioned by the changes cumulatively going forward in the institutional fabric of habitual elements that govern the scheme of life. But there is no warrant for assuming that each or any of these successive changes in the scheme of institutions affords successively readier, surer or more facile ways and means for the instinctive proclivities to work out their ends, or that the phase of habituation in force at any given point in this sequence of change is more suitable to the untroubled functioning of these instincts than any phase that has gone before. Indeed, the presumption is the other way. On grounds of selective survival it is reasonably to be presumed that any given racial type that has endured the test of selective elimination, including the complement of instinctive dispositions by

Reprinted from chapter 1 of *The Instinct of Workmanship and the State of the Industrial Arts*, New York: The Macmillan Company, 1914.

virtue of which it has endured the test, will on its first emergency have been passably suited to the circumstances, material and cultural, under which the type emerged as a mutant and made good its survival; and in so far as the subsequent growth of institutions has altered the available scope and method of instinctive action it is therefore to be presumed that any such subsequent change in the scheme of institutions will in some degree hinder or divert the free play of its instinctive proclivities and will thereby hinder the direct and unsophisticated working-out of the instinctive dispositions native to this given racial type.

What is known of the earlier phases of culture in the life-history of the existing races and peoples goes to say that the initial phase in the life of any given racial type, the phase of culture which prevailed in its environment when it emerged, and under which the stock first proved its fitness to survive, was presumably some form of savagery. Therefore the fitness of any given type of human nature for life after the manner and under the conditions imposed by any later phase in the growth of culture is a matter of less and less secure presumption the farther the sequence of institutional change has departed from that form of savagery which marked the initial stage in the life-history of the given racial stock. Also, presumably, though by no means assuredly, the younger stocks, those which have emerged from later mutation of type, have therefore initially fallen into and made good their survival under the conditions of a relatively advanced phase of savagery—these younger races should therefore conform with greater facility and better effect to the requirements imposed by a still farther advance in that cumulative complication of institutions and intricacy of ways and means that is involved in cultural growth. The older or more primitive stocks, those which arose out of earlier mutations of type and made good their survival under a more elementary scheme of savage culture, are presumably less capable of adaptation to an advanced cultural scheme.

But at the same time it is on the same grounds to be expected that in all races and peoples there should always persist an ineradicable sentimental disposition to take back to something like that scheme of savagery for which their particular type of human nature once proved its fitness during the initial phase of its life-history. This seems to be what is commonly intended in the cry, "Back to Nature!" The older known racial stocks, the offspring of earlier mutational departures from the initially generic human type, will have been selectively adapted to more archaic forms of savagery, and these show an appreciably more refractory penchant for elementary savage modes of life, and conform to the demands and opportunities of a "higher" civilization only with a relatively slight facility, amounting in extreme cases to a practical unfitness for civilized life. Hence the "White Man's Burden" and the many perplexities of the missionaries.

Under the Mendelian theories of heredity some qualification of these broad generalizations is called for. As has already been noted above, the people of Europe, each and several, are hybrid mixtures made up of several racial stocks. The like is true in some degree of most of the peoples outside of Europe;

particularly of the more important and better known nationalities. These various peoples show more or less distinct and recognizable national types of physique—or perhaps rather of physiognomy—and temperament, and the lines of differentiation between these national types incontinently traverse the lines that divide the racial stocks. At the same time these national types have some degree of permanence; so much so that they are colloquially spoken of as types of race. While no modern anthropologist would confuse nationality with race, it is not to be overlooked that these national hybrid types are frequently so marked and characteristic as to simulate racial characters and perplex the student of race who is intent on identifying the racial stocks out of which any one of these hybrid populations has been compounded. Presumably these national and local types of physiognomy and temperament are to be rated as hybrid types that have been fixed by selective breeding, and for an explanation of this phenomenon recourse is to be taken to the latter-day theories of heredity.

To any student familiar with the simpler phenomena of hybridism it will be evident that under the Mendelian rules of hybridization the number of biologically successful—viable—hybrid forms arising from any cross between two or more forms may diverge very widely from one another and from either of the parent types. The variation must be extreme both in the number of hybrid types so constructed and in the range over which the variation extends—much greater in both respects than the range of fluctuating (non-typical) variations obtainable under any circumstances in a pure-bred race, particularly in the remoter filial generations. It is also well known, by experiment, that by selective breeding from among such hybrid forms it is possible to construct a composite type that will breed true in respect of the characters upon which the selection is directed, and that such a "pure line" may be maintained indefinitely, in spite of its hybrid origin, so long as it is not crossed back on one or other of the parent stocks, or on a hybrid stock that is not pure-bred in respect of the selected characters.

So, if the conditions of life in any community consistently favor a given type of hybrid, whether the favoring conditions are of a cultural or of a material nature, something of a selective trend will take effect in such a community and set toward a hybrid type which shall meet these conditions. The result will be the establishment of a composite pure line showing the advantageous traits of physique and temperament, combined with a varying complement of other characters that have no such selective value. Traits that have no selective value in the given case will occur with fortuitous freedom, combining in unconstrained diversity with the selectively decisive traits, and so will mark the hybrid derivation of this provisionally established composite pure line. With continued intercrossing within itself any given population of such hybrid origin as the European peoples would tend cumulatively to breed true to such a selectively favorable hybrid type, rather than to any one of the ultimate racial types represented by the parent stocks out of which the hybrid population is ultimately made up. So would emerge a national or local type, which would show the selectively decisive traits with a great degree of consistency but would vary indefinitely in respect of the selectively idle traits comprised in the composite heredity of the population. Such a composite pure line would be provisionally stable only; it should break down when crossed back on either of the parent stocks. This "provisionally stable composite pure line" should disappear when crossed on pure-bred individuals of one or other of the parent stocks from which it is drawn—pure-bred in respect of the allelomorphic characters which give the hybrid type its typical traits.

But whatever the degree of stability possessed by these hybrid national or local types, the outcome for the present purpose is much the same; the hybrid populations afford a greater scope and range of variation in their human nature than could be had within the limits of any pure-bred race. Yet, for all the multifarious diversity of racial and national types, early and late, and for all the wide divergence of hybrid variants, there is no difficulty about recognizing a generical human type of spiritual endowment, just as the zoologists have no difficulty in referring the various races of mankind to a single species on the ground of their physical characters. The distribution of emphasis among the several instinctive dispositions may vary appreciably from one race to another, but the complement of instincts native to the several races is after all of much the same kind, comprising substantially the same ends. Taken simply in their first incidence, the racial variations of human nature are commonly not considerable; but a slight bias of this kind, distinctive of any given race, may come to have decisive weight when it works out cumulatively through a system of institutions, for such a system embodies the cumulative sophistication of untold generations during which the life of the community has been dominated by the same slight bias.[1]

Racial differences in respect of these hereditary spiritual traits count for much in the outcome, because in the last resort any race is at the mercy of its instincts. In the course of cultural growth most of those civilizations or peoples that have had a long history have from time to time been brought up against an imperative call to revise their scheme of institutions in the light of their native instincts, on pain of collapse or decay; and they have chosen variously, and for the most part blindly to live or not to live, according as their instinctive bias has driven them. In the cases where it has happened that those instincts which make directly for the material welfare of the community, such as the parental bent and the sense of workmanship, have been present in such potent force, or where the institutional elements at variance with the continued life-interests of the community or the civilization in question have been in a sufficiently infirm state, there the bonds of custom, prescription, principles, precedent, have been broken—or loosened or shifted so as to let the current of life and cultural growth go on, with or without substantial retardation. But history records more frequent and more spectacular instances of the triumph of imbecile institutions over life and culture than of peoples who have by force of instinctive insight saved themselves alive out of a desperately precarious institutional situation, such, for instance, as now faces the peoples of Christendom.

Chief among those instinctive dispositions that conduce directly to the material well-being of the race, and therefore to its biological success, is perhaps the instinctive bias here spoken of as the sense of workmanship. The only other instinctive factor of human nature that could with any likelihood dispute this primacy would be the parental bent. Indeed, the two have much in common. They spend themselves on much the same concrete objective ends, and the mutual furtherance of each by the other is indeed so broad and intimate as often to leave it a matter of extreme difficulty to draw a line between them. Any discussion of either, therefore, must unavoidably draw the other into the inquiry to a greater or less extent, and a characterization of the one will involve some dealing with the other.

As the expression is here understood, the "Parental Bent" is an instinctive disposition of much larger scope than a mere proclivity to the achievement of children.[2] This latter is doubtless to be taken as a large and perhaps as a primary element in the practical working of the parental solicitude; although, even so, it is in no degree to be confused with the quasi-tropismatic impulse to the procreation of offspring. The parental solicitude in mankind has a much wider bearing than simply the welfare of one's own children. This wider bearing is particularly evident in those lower cultures where the scheme of consanguinity and inheritance is not drawn on the same close family lines as among civilized peoples, but it is also to be seen in good vigor in any civilized community. So, for instance, what the phrase-makers have called "race-suicide" meets the instinctive and unsolicited reprobation of all men, even of those who would not conceivably go the length of contributing in their own person to the incoming generation. So also, virtually all thoughtful persons—this is to say all persons who hold an opinion in these premises—will agree that it is a despicably inhuman thing for the current generation willfully to make the way of life harder for the next generation, whether though neglect of due provision for their subsistence and proper training or though wasting their heritage of resources and opportunity by improvident greed and indolence. Providence is a virtue only so far as its aim is provision for posterity.

It is difficult or impossible to say how far the current solicitude for the welfare of the race at large is to be credited to the parental bent, but it is beyond question that this instinctive disposition has a large part in the sentimental concern entertained by nearly all persons for the life and comfort of the community at large, and particularly for the community's future welfare. Doubtless this parental bent in its wider bearing greatly reinforces that sentimental approval of economy and efficiency for the common good and disapproval of wasteful and useless living that prevails so generally throughout both the highest and the lowest cultures, unless it should rather be said that this animus for economy and efficiency is a simple expression of the parental disposition itself. It might on the other hand be maintained that such an animus of economy is an essential function of the instinct of workmanship, which would then be held to be strongly sustained at this point by a parental solicitude for the common good.

In making use of the expression, "instinct of workmanship" or "sense of workmanship," it is not here intended to assume or to argue that the proclivity so designated is in the psychological respect a simple or irreducible element; still less, of course, is there any intention to allege that it is to be traced back in the physiological respect to some one isolable tropismatic sensibility or some single enzymatic or visceral stimulus. All that is matter for the attention of those whom it may concern. The expression may as well be taken to signify a concurrence of several instinctive aptitudes, each of which might or might not prove simple or irreducible when subjected to psychological or physiological analysis. For the present inquiry it is enough to note that in human behavior this disposition is effective in such consistent, ubiquitous and resilient fashion that students of human culture will have to count with it as one of the integral hereditary traits of mankind.[3]

As has already appeared, neither this nor any other instinctive disposition works out its functional content in isolation from the instinctive endowment at large. The instincts, all and several, though perhaps in varying degrees, are so intimately engaged in a play of give and take that the work of any one has its consequences for all the rest, though presumably not for all equally. It is this endless[4] complication and contamination of instinctive elements in human conduct, taken in conjunction with the pervading and cumulative effects of habit in this domain, that makes most of the difficulty and much of the interest attaching to this line of inquiry.

There are few lines of instinctive proclivity that are not crossed and colored by some ramification of the instinct of workmanship. No doubt, response to the direct call of such half-tropismatic, half-instinctive impulses as hunger, anger, or the promptings of sex, is little if at all troubled with any sentimental suffusion of workmanship; but in the more complex and deliberate activities, particularly where habit exerts an appreciable effect, the impulse and sentiment of workmanship comes in for a large share in the outcome. So much so, indeed that, for instance, in the arts, where the sense of beauty is the prime mover, habitual attention to technique will often put the original, and only ostensible, motive in the background. So, again, in the life of religious faith and observance it may happen now and again that theological niceties and ritual elaboration will successfully, and in great measure satisfactorily, substitute themselves for spiritual communion; while in the courts of law a tenacious following out of legal technicalities will not infrequently defeat the ends of justice.

As the expression is here understood, all instinctive action is intelligent in some degree; though the degree in which intelligence is engaged may vary widely from one instinctive disposition to another, and it may even fall into an extremely automatic shape in the case of some of the simpler instincts, whose functional content is of a patently physiological character. Some approach to automatism is even more evident in some of the lower animals, where, as for instance in the case of some insects, the response to the appropriate stimuli is so far uniform and mechanically determinate as to leave it doubtful whether the behavior of the animal might not best be construed as tropismatic action simply.[5] Such tropismatic directness of instinctive response is less characteristic of man even in the case of the simpler instinctive proclivities; and the indirection which so characterizes instinctive action in general, and the higher instincts of man in particular, and which makes off the instinctive dispositions from the tropisms, is the indirection of intelligence. It enters more largely in the discharge of some proclivities than of others; but all instinctive action is intelligent in some degree. This is what makes it off from the tropisms and takes it out of the category of automatism.[6]

Hence all instinctive action is theological. It involves holding to a purpose. It aims to achieve some end and involves some degree of intelligent faculty to compass the instinctively given purpose, under surveillance of the instinctive proclivity that prompts the action. And it is in this surveillance and direction of the intellectual processes to the appointed end that the instinctive dispositions control and condition human conduct; and in this work of direction the several instinctive proclivities may come to conflict and offset, or to concur and "reënforce" one another's action.

The position of the instinct of workmanship in this complex of theological activities is somewhat peculiar, in that its functional content is serviceability for the ends of life, whatever these ends may be; whereas these ends to be subserved are, at least in the main, appointed and made worth while by the various other instinctive dispositions. So that this instinct may in some sense be said to be auxiliary to all the rest, to be concerned with the ways and means of life rather than with any one given ulterior end. It has essentially to do with proximate rather than ulterior ends. Yet workmanship is none the less an object of attention and sentiment in its own right. Efficient use of the means at hand and adequate management of the resources available for the purposes of life is itself an end of endeavor, and accomplishment of this kind is a source of gratification.

All instinctive action is intelligent and teleological. The generality of instinctive dispositions prompt simply to the direct and unambiguous attainment of their specific ends, and in his dealings under their immediate guidance the agent goes as directly as may be to the end sought—he is occupied with the objective end, not with the choice of means to the end sought; whereas under the impulse of workmanship the agent's interest and endeavor are taken up with the contriving of ways and means to the end sought.

The point of contrast may be unfamiliar, and an illustration may be pertinent. So, in the instinct of pugnacity and its attendant sentiment of anger[7] the primary impulse is doubtless to a direct frontal attack, assault and battery pure and simple; and the more highly charged the agent is with the combative impulse, and the higher the pitch of animation to which he has been wrought up, the less is he inclined or able to take thought of how he may shrewdly bring mechanical devices to bear on the object of his sentiment and compass his end with the largest result per unit of force expended. It is only the well-trained fighter that will take without reflection to workmanlike ways and means at such a juncture; and in case of extreme exasperation and urgency even such a one, it is said, may forget his workmanship in the premises and throw himself into the middle of things instead of resorting to the indirections and leverages to which his workmanlike training in the art of fighting has habituated him. So, again, the immediate promptings of the parental bent urge to direct personal intervention and service in behalf of the object of solicitude. In persons highly gifted in this respect the impulse asserts itself to succor the helpless with one's own hands, to do for them in one's own person not what might on reflection approve itself as the most expedient line of conduct in the premises, but what will throw the agent most personally into action in the case. Notoriously, it is easier to move well-meaning people to unreflecting charity on an immediate and concrete appeal than it is to secure a sagacious, well sustained and well organized concert of endeavor for the amelioration of the lot of the unfortunate. Indeed, refinements of workmanlike calculation of causes and effects in such a case are instinctively felt to be out of touch with the spirit of the thing. They are distasteful; not only are they not part and parcel of the functional content of the generous impulse, but an undue injection of these elements of workmanship into the case may even induce a revulsion of feeling and defeat its own intention.

The instinct of workmanship, on the other hand, occupies the interest with practical expedients, ways and means, devices and contrivances of efficiency and economy, proficiency, creative work and technological mastery of facts. Much of the functional content of the instinct of workmanship is a proclivity for taking pains. The best or most finished outcome of this disposition is not had under stress of great excitement or under extreme urgency from any of the instinctive propensities with which its work is associated or whose ends it serves. It shows at its best, both in the individual workman's technological efficiency and in the growth of technological proficiency and insight in the community at large, under circumstances of moderate exigence, where there is work in hand and more of it in sight, since it is initially a disposition to do the next thing and do it as well as may be; whereas when interest falls off unduly through failure of provocation from the instinctive dispositions that afford an end to which to work, the stimulus to workmanship is likely to fail, and the outcome is as likely to be an endless fabrication of meaningless details and much ado about nothing. On the other hand, in seasons of great stress, when the call to any one or more of the instinctive lines of conduct is urgent beyond measure, there is likely to result a crudity of technique and presently a loss of proficiency and technological mastery.

It is, further, pertinent to note in this connection that the instinct of workmanship will commonly not run to passionate excesses; that it does not, under pressure, tenaciously hold its place as a main interest in competition with the other, more elemental instinctive proclivities; but that it rather yields ground somewhat readily, suffers repression and falls into abeyance, only to reassert itself when the pressure of other, urgent interests is relieved. What was said above as to the paramount significance of the instinct of workmanship for the life of the race will of course suffer no abatement in so recognizing its characteristically temperate urgency. The grave importance that attaches to it is a matter of its ubiquitous subservience to the ends of life, and not a matter of vehemence.

The sense of workmanship is also peculiarly subject to bias. It does not commonly, or normally, work to an independent, creative end of its own, but is rather concerned with the ways and means whereby instinctively given purposes are to be accomplished. According, therefore, as one or another of the instinctive dispositions is predominant in the community's scheme of life or in the individual's every-day interest, the habitual trend of the sense of workmanship will be bent to one or another line of proficiency and technological mastery. By cumulative habituation a bias of this character may come to have very substantial consequences for the range and scope of technological knowledge, the state of the industrial arts, and for the rate and direction of growth in workmanlike ideals.

Changes are going forward constantly and incontinently in the institutional apparatus, the habitual scheme of rules and principles that regulate the community's life, and not least in the technological ways and means by which the life of the race and its state of culture are maintained; but changes come rarely—in effect not at all—in the endowment of instincts whereby mankind is enabled to employ these means and to live under the institutions which its habits of life have cumulatively created. In the case of hybrid populations, such as the peoples of Christendom, some appreciable adaptation of this spiritual endowment to meet the changing requirements of civilization may be counted on, through the establishment of composite pure lines of a hybrid type more nearly answering to the later phases of culture than any one of the original racial types out of which the hybrid population is made up. But in so slow-breeding a species as man, and with changes in the conditions of life going forward at a visibly rapid pace, the chance of an adequate adaptation of hybrid human nature to new conditions seems doubtful at the best. It is also to be noted that the vague character of many of the human instincts, and their consequent pliability under habituation, affords an appreciable margin of adaptation with which human nature may adjust itself to new conditions of life. But after all has been said it remains true that the margin within which the instinctive nature of the race can be effectively adapted to changing circumstances is relatively narrow—narrow as contrasted with the range of variation in institutions—and the limits of such adaptation are somewhat rigid. As the matter stands, the race is required to meet changing conditions of life to which its relatively unchanging endowment of instincts is presumably not wholly adapted, and to meet these conditions by the use of technological ways and means widely different from those that were at the disposal of the race from the outset. In the initial phases of the life-history of the race, or of any given racial stock, the exigencies to which its spiritual (instinctive) nature was selectively required to conform were those of the savage culture, as has been indicated above—presumably in all cases a somewhat "low" or elementary form of savagery. This savage mode of life, which was, and is, in a sense, native to man, would be characterized by a considerable group solidarity within a relatively small group, living very near the soil, and unremittingly dependent for their daily life on the workmanlike efficiency of all the members of the group. The prime requisite for survival under these conditions would be a propensity unselfishly and impersonally to make the most of the material means at hand and a penchant for turning all resources of knowledge and material to account to sustain the life of the group.

At the outset, therefore, as it first comes into the life-history of any one or all of the racial stocks with which modern inquiry concerns itself, this instinctive disposition will have borne directly on workmanlike efficiency in the simple and obvious sense of the word. By virtue of the stability of the racial type, such is still its character, primarily and substantially, apart from its sophistication by habit and tradition. The instinct of workmanship brought the life of mankind from the brute to the human plane, and in all the later growth of culture it has never ceased to pervade the works of man. But the extensive complication of circumstances and the altered outlook of succeeding generations, brought on by the growth of institutions and the accumulation of knowledge, have led to an extension of its scope and of its canons and logic to activities and conjunctures that have little traceable bearing on the means of subsistence.

Notes

1. The all-pervading modern institution of private property appears to have been of such an origin, having cumulatively grown out of the self-regarding bias of men in their oversight of the community's material interests.

2. Cf. McDougall, *Social Psychology*, ch. x.

3. Latterly the question of instincts has been a subject of somewhat extensive discussion among students of animal behavior, and throughout this discussion the argument has commonly been conducted on neurological, or at the most on physiological ground. This line of argument is well and lucidly presented in a volume recently published (*The Science of Human Behavior*, New York, 1913) by Mr. Maurice Parmalee. The book offers an incisive critical discussion of the *Nature of Instinct* (ch. xi) with a specific reference to the instinct of workmanship (p. 252). The discussion runs, faithfully and competently, on neurological ground and reaches the outcome to be expected in an endeavor to reduce instinct to neurological (or physiological) terms. As has commonly been true of similar endeavors, the outcome is essentially negative, in that "instinct" is not so much explained as explained away. The reason of this outcome is sufficiently evident; "instinct," being not a neurological or physiological concept, is not statable in neurological or physiological terms. The instinct of workmanship no more than any other instinctive proclivity is an isolable, discrete neural function; which, however, does not touch the question of its status as a psychological element. The effect of such an analysis as is offered by Mr. Parmalee is

not to give terminological precision to the concept of "instinct" in the sense assigned it in current usage, but to dispense with it; which is an untoward move in that it deprives the student of the free use of this familiar term in its familiar sense and therefore constrains him to bring the indispensable concept of instinct in again surreptitiously under cover of some unfamiliar term or some terminological circumlocution. The current mechanistic analyses of animal behavior are of great and undoubted value to any inquiry into human conduct, but their value does not lie in an attempt to make them supersede those psychological phenomena which it is their purpose to explain. That such supersession of psychological phenomena by the mechanistic formulations need nowise follow and need not be entertained appears, e.g., in such work as that of Mr. Loeb, referred to above, *Comparative Physiology of the Brain and Comparative Psychology*.

4. Endless in the sense that the effects of such concatenation do not run to a final term in any direction.

5. Many students of animal behavior are still, as psychologists generally once were, inclined to contrast instinct with intelligence, and to confine the term typically to such automatically determinate action as takes effect without deliberation or intelligent oversight. This view would appear to be a remnant of an earlier theoretical position, according to which all the functions of intelligence were referred to a distinct immaterial entity, entelechy, associated in symbiosis with the physical organism. If all such preconceptions of a substantial dichotomy between physiological and psychological activity be abandoned it becomes a matter of course that intellectual functions themselves take effect only on the initiative of the instinctive dispositions and under their surveillance, and the antithesis between instinct and intelligence will consequently fall away. What expedients of terminology and discrimination may then be resorted to in the study of those animal instincts that involve a minimum of intellect is of course a question for the comparative psychologists. Cf., for instance, C. Lloyd Morgan, *Introduction to Comparative Psychology* (2nd edition, 1906), ch. xii, especially pp. 206–209, and *Habit and Instinct*, chs. i and vi.

6. Cf. H.S. Jennings, *Behavior of the Lower Animals*, chs. xii, xx, xxi.

7. See McDougall, *Introduction to Social Psychology*, chs. iii and x.

Ownership and the Industrial Arts

The scheme of technological insight and proficiency current in any given culture is manifestly a product of group life and is held as a common stock, and as manifestly the individual workman is helpless without access to it. It is none too broad to say that he is a workman only because and so far as he effectually shares in this common stock of technological equipment. He may be gifted in a special degree with workmanlike aptitudes, may by nature be stout or dexterous or keen-sighted or quick-witted or sagacious or industrious beyond his fellows; but with all these gifts, so long as he has assimilated none of this common stock of workmanlike knowledge he remains simply an admirable parcel of human raw material; he is of no effect in industry. With such special gifts or with special training based on this common stock an individual may stand out among his fellows as a workman of exceptional merit and value, and without the common run of workmanlike aptitudes he may come to nothing worth while as a workman even with the largest opportunities and most sedulous training. It is the two together than make the working force of the community; and in both respects, both in his inherited and in his acquired traits, the individual is a product of group life.

Using the term in a sufficiently free sense, pedigree is no less and no more requisite to the workman's effectual equipment than the common stock of technological mastery which the community offers him. But his pedigree is a group pedigree, just as his technology is a group technology. As is sometimes said to the same effect, the individual is a creature of heredity and circumstances. And heredity is always group heredity,[1] perhaps peculiarly so in the human species.

In the lower cultures, where the division of labor is slight and the diversity of occupations is mainly such as marks the changes of the seasons, the common stock of technological knowledge and proficiency is not so extensive or so

Reprinted from chapter 4 of *The Instinct of Workmanship and the State of the Industrial Arts*, New York: The MacMillan Company, 1914.

recondite but that the common man may compass it in some fashion, and in its essentials it is accessible to all members of the community by common notoriety, and the training required by the state of the industrial arts comes to everyone as a matter of course in the routine of daily life. The necessary material equipment of tools and appliances is slight and the acquisition of it is a simple matter that also arranges itself as an incident in the routine of daily life. Given the common run of aptitude for the industrial pursuits incumbent on the members of such a community, the material equipment needful to find a livelihood or to put forth the ordinary productive effort and turn out the ordinary industrial output can be compassed without strain by an individual in the course of his work as he goes along. The material equipment, the tools, implements, contrivances necessary and conducive to productive industry, is incidental to the day's work; in much the same way but in a more unqualified degree than the like is true as to the technological knowledge and skill required to make use of this equipment.[2]

As determined by the state of the industrial arts in such a culture, the members of the community cooperate in much of their work, to the common gain and to no one's detriment, since there is substantially no individual, or private, gain to be sought. There is substantially no bartering or hiring, though there is a recognized obligation in all members to lend a hand; and there is of course no price, as there is no property and no ownership, for the sufficient reason that the habits of life under these circumstances do not provoke such a habit of thought. Doubtless, it is a matter of course that articles of use and adornment pertain to their makers or users in an intimate and personal way; which will come to be construed into ownership when in the experience of the community an occasion for such a concept as ownership arises and persists in sufficient force to shape the current habits of thought to that effect. There is also more or less of reciprocal service and assistance, with a sufficient sense of mutuality to establish a customary scheme of claims and obligations in that respect. So also it is true that such a community holds certain lands and customary usufruct and that any trespass on these customary holdings is resented. But it would be a vicious misapprehension to read ideas and rights of ownership into these practices, although where civilized men have come to deal with instances of the kind they have commonly been unable to put any other construction on the customs governing the case; for the reason that civilized men's relations with these peoples of the lower culture have been of a pecuniary kind and for a pecuniary purpose, and they have brought no other than pecuniary conceptions from home.[3] There being little in hand worth owning and little purpose to be served by its ownership, the habits of thought which go to make the institution of ownership and property rights have not taken shape. The slight facts which would lend themselves to ownership are not of sufficient magnitude or urgency to call the institution into effect and are better handled under customs which do not yet take cognizance of property rights. Naturally, in such a cultural situation there is no appreciable accumulation of wealth and no inducement to it; the nearest approach being an accumulation of trinkets and personal belongings, among which should, at least in some cases, be included certain weapons and perhaps tools.[4] These things belong to their owner or bearer in much the same sense as his name, which was not held on tenure of ownership or as a pecuniary asset before the use of trademarks and merchantable goodwill.

The workman—more typically perhaps the work-woman—in such a culture, as indeed in any other, is a "productive agent" in the manner and degree determined by the state of the industrial arts. What is obvious in this respect here holds only less visibly for any other, more complicated and technologically full-charged cultural situation, such as has come on with the growth of population and wealth among the more advanced peoples. He or she, or rather they—for there is substantially no industry carried on in strict severalty in these communities—are productive factors or industrial agents, in the sense that they will on occasion turn out a surplus above their necessary current consumption, only because and so far as the state of the industrial arts enables them to do so. As workman, laborer, producer, breadwinner, the individual is a creature of the technological scheme; which in turn is a creation of the group life of the community. Apart from the common stock of knowledge and training the individual members of the community have no industrial effect. Indeed, except by grace of this common technological equipment no individual and no family group in any of the known communities of mankind could support their own life; for in the long course of mankind's life-history, since the human plane was first reached, the early mutants which were fit to survive in a ferine state without tools and without technology have selectively disappeared, as being unfit to survive under the conditions of domesticity imposed by so highly developed a state of the industrial arts as any of the savage cultures now extant.[5] The *Homo Javensis* and his like are gone, because there is technologically no place for them between the anthropoids to the one side and the extant types of man on the other. And never since the brave days when *Homo Javensis* took up the "white man's burden" for the better regulation of his anthropoid neighbors has the technological scheme admitted of any individual's carrying on his life in severalty. So that industrial efficiency, whether of an individual workman or of the community at large, is a function of the state of the industrial arts.[6]

The simple and obvious industrial system of this archaic plan leaves the individuals, or rather the domestic groups, that make up the community, economically independent of one another and of the community at large, except that they depend on the common technological stock for the immaterial equipment by means of which to get their living. This is of course not felt by them as a relation of dependence; though there seems commonly to be some sense of indebtedness on part of the young, and of responsibility on part of the older generation, for the proper transmission of the recognized elements of technological proficiency. It is impossible to say just at what point in the growth and complication of technology this simple industrial scheme will begin to give way to new exigencies and give occasion to a new scheme of institutions governing the economic relations of men; such that the men's powers and functions in the industrial community come to be decided on other grounds than workmanlike aptitude and special training. In the nature of things there can be no hard and fast limit to this phase of industrial organization. It disappearance or supersession in any culture appears always to have been brought on by the growth of property, but the institution of property need by no means come in abruptly at any determinate juncture in the sequence of technological development. So that this archaic phase of culture in which industry is organized on the ground of workmanship alone may come very extensively to overlap and blend with the succeeding phase in which property relations chiefly decide the details of the industrial organization—as is shown in varying detail by the known lower cultures.

The forces which may bring about such a transition are often complex and recondite, and they are seldom just the same in any given two instances. Neither the material situation nor the human raw material involved are precisely the same in all or several instances, and there is no coercively normal course of things that will constrain the growth of institutions to take a particular typical form or to follow a particular typical sequence in all cases. Yet, in a general way such a supersession of free workmanship by a pecuniary control of industry appears to have been necessarily involved in any considerable growth of culture. Indeed, at least in the economic respect, it appears to have been the most universal and most radical mutation which human culture has undergone in its advance from savagery to civilization; and the causes of it should be of a similarly universal and intrinsic character.

It may be taken as a generalization grounded in the instinctive endowment of mankind that the human sense of workmanship will unavoidably go on turning to account what there is in hand of technological knowledge, and so will in the course of time, by insensible gains perhaps, gradually change the technological scheme, and therefore also the scheme of customary canons of conduct answering to it; and in the absence of overmastering circumstances this sequence of change must, in a general way, set in the direction of greater technological mastery. Something in the way of an "advance" in workmanlike mastery is to be looked for, in the absence of inexorable limitations of environment. The limitations may be set by the material circumstances or by circumstance of the institutional situation, but on the lower levels of culture the insurmountable obstacles to such an advance appear to have been those imposed by the material circumstances; although institutional factors have doubtless greatly retarded the advance in most cases, and may well have defeated it in many. In some of the known lower cultures such an impassable conjuncture in the affairs of technology has apparently been reached now and again, resulting in a "stationary state" of the industrial arts and of social arrangements, economic and otherwise. Such an instance of "arrested development" is afforded by the Eskimo, who have to all appearance reached the bounds of technological mastery possible in the material circumstances in which they have been placed and with the technological antecedents which they have had to go on. At the other extreme of the American continent the Fuegians and Patagonians may similarly have reached at least a provisional limit of the same nature; though such a statement is less secure in their case, owing to the scant and fragmentary character of the available evidence. So also the Bushmen, the Ainu, various representative communities of the Negrito and perhaps of the Dravidian stocks, appear to have reached a provisional limit—barring intervention from without. In these latter instances the decisive obstacles, if they are to be accepted as such, seem to lie in the human-nature of the case rather than in the material circumstances. In these latter instances the sense of workmanship, though visibly alert and active, appears to have been inadequate to carry out the technological scheme into further new ramifications for want of the requisite intellectual aptitudes—a failure of aptitudes not in degree but in kind.

The manner in which increasing technological mastery has led over from the savage plan of free workmanship to the barbarian system of industry under pecuniary control is perhaps a hazardous topic of speculation; but the known facts of primitive culture appear to admit at least a few general propositions of a broad and provisional character. It seems reasonably safe to say that the archaic savage plan of free workmanship will commonly have persisted through the paleolithic period of technology, and indeed somewhat beyond the transition to the neolithic. This is fairly borne out by the contemporary evidence from savage cultures. In the prehistory of the north-European culture there is also reason to assume that the beginnings of a pecuniary control fall in the early half of the neolithic period.[7] There seems to be no sharply definable point in the technological advance that can be said of itself to bring on this revolutionary change in the institutions governing economic life. It appears to be loosely correlated with technological improvement, so that it sets in when a sufficient ground for it is afforded by the state of the industrial arts, but what constitutes a sufficient ground can apparently not be stated in terms of the industrial arts alone. Among the early consequences of an advance in technology beyond the state of the industrial arts schematically indicated above, and coinciding roughly with the palaeolithic stage, is on the one hand an appreciable resort to "indirect methods of production," involving a systematic cultivation of the soil, domestication of plants and animals; or an appreciable equipment of industrial appliances, such as will in either case require a deliberate expenditure of labor and will give the holders of the equipment something more than a momentary advantage in the quest of a livelihood. On the other hand it leads also to an accumulation of wealth beyond the current necessaries of subsistence and beyond that slight parcel of personal effects that have no value to anyone but their savage bearer.

Hereby the technological basis for a pecuniary control of industry is given, in that the "roundabout process of production" yields an income above the subsistence of the workmen engaged in it, and the material equipment of appliances (crops, fruit-trees, live stock, mechanical contrivances) binds this roundabout process of industry to a more or less determinate place and routine, such as to make surveillance and control possible. So far as the workman under the new phase of technology is dependent for his living on the apparatus and the orderly sequence of the "roundabout process," his work may be controlled and the surplus yielded by his industry may be turned to account; it becomes worth while to own the material means of industry, and ownership of the material means in such a situation carries with it the usufruct of the community's immaterial equipment of technological proficiency.

The substantial fact upon which the strategy of ownership converges is this usufruct of the industrial arts, and the tangible items of property to which the claims of ownership come to attach will accordingly vary from time to time, according as the state of the industrial arts will best afford an effectual exploitation of this usufruct through the tenure of one or another of the material items requisite to the pursuit of industry. The chief subject of ownership may accordingly be the cultivated trees, as in some of the South Sea islands; or the tillable land, as happens in many of the agricultural communities; or fish weirs and their location, as on some of the salmon streams of the American north-west coast; or domestic animals, as is typical of the pastoral culture; or it may be the persons of the workman, as happens under diverse circumstances both in pastoral and in agricultural communities; or, with an advance in technology of such a nature as to place the mechanical appliances of industry in a peculiarly advantageous position for engrossing the roundabout processes of production, as in the latter day machine industry, these mechanical appliances may become the typical category of industrial wealth and so come to be accounted "productive goods" in some eminent sense.

The institutional change by which a pecuniary regulation of industry comes into effect may take one form or another, but its outcome has commonly been some form of ownership of tangible goods. Particularly has that been the outcome in the course of development that has led on to those great pecuniary cultures of which Occidental civilization is the most perfect example. But just in what form the move will be made, if at all, from free workmanship to pecuniary industry and ownership, is in good part a question of what the material situation of the community will permit.

Notes

1. Except for species that habitually breed by parthenogenesis.

2. See, e.g., Skeat and Blagden, *Pagan Races of the Malay Peninsula*, vol. ii, part ii; *Report, Bureau of American Ethnology*, 1884–1885, F. Boas, "The Central Eskimo."

3. Cf. Basil Thomson, *The Diversions of a Prime Minister*, and *The Figians*.

4. The extent of this "quasi-personal fringe" of objects of intimate use varies considerably from one culture to another. It may often be inferred from the range of articles buried or destroyed with the dead among peoples on this level of culture.

5. A doubt may suggest itself in this connection touching such cultures and peoples as the pagan races of the Malay peninsula, the Mincopies of the Andaman Islands, or (possibly) the Negritos of Luzon, but these conceivable exceptions to the rule evidently do not lessen its force.

6. It may be pertinent to take note of the bearing of these considerations on certain dogmatic concepts that have played a part in the theoretical and controversial speculations of the last century. Much importance has been given by economists of one school and another to the "productivity of labor," particularly as affording a basis for a just and equitable distribution of the product; one school of controversialists having gone so far against the current of received economic doctrine as to allege that labor is the sole productive factor in industry and that the Laborer is on this ground entitled, in equity, to "the full product of his labour." It is of course not conceived that the consideration here set forth will dispose of these doctrinal contentions; but they make it at least appear that the productivity of labor, or of any other conceivable factor in industry, is an imputed productivity—imputed on grounds of convention afforded by institutions that have grown up in the course of technological development and that have consequently only such validity as attached to habits of thought induced by any given phase of collective life. These habits of thought (institutions and principles) are themselves the indirect product of the technological scheme. The controversy as to the productivity of labor should accordingly shift its ground from "the nature of things" to the exigencies of ingrained preconceptions, principles and expediencies as seen in the light of current technological requirement and the current drift of habituation.

7. See Sophus Müller, *Vor Oldtid,* "Stenalderen," and *Aarböger for nordisk Oldkyndighed,* 1906.

The Discipline of the Machine

The machine process pervades the modern life and dominates it in a mechanical sense. Its dominance is seen in the enforcement of precise mechanical measurements and adjustment and the reduction of all manner of things, purposes and acts, necessities, conveniences, and amenities of life, to standard units. . . . The point of immediate interest here is the further bearing of the machine process upon the growth of culture—the disciplinary effect which this movement for standardization and mechanical equivalence has upon the human material.

This discipline falls more immediately on the workmen engaged in the mechanical industries, and only less immediately on the rest of the community which lives in contact with this sweeping machine process. Wherever the machine process extends, it sets the pace for the workmen, great and small. The pace is set, not wholly by the particular processes in the details of which the given workman is immediately engaged, but in some degree by the more comprehensive process at large into which the given detail process fits. It is no longer simply that the individual workman makes use of one or more mechanical contrivances for effecting certain results. Such used to be his office in the earlier phases of the use of machines, and the work which he now has in hand still has much of that character. But such a characterization of the workman's part in industry misses the peculiarly modern feature of the case. He now does this work as a factor involved in a mechanical process whose movement controls his motions. It remains true, of course, as it always has been true, that he is the intelligent agent concerned in the process, while the machine, furnace, roadway, or retort are inanimate structures devised by man and subject to the workman's supervision. But the process comprises him and his intelligent motions, and it is by virtue of his necessarily taking an intelligent part in what is going forward that the mechanical process has its chief effect upon him. The process standard-

Reprinted from chapter 9 of *The Theory of Business Enterprise*, New York: Charles Scribner's Sons, 1904.

izes his supervision and guidance of the machine. Mechanically speaking, the machine is not his to do with it as his fancy may suggest. His place is to take thought of the machine and its work in terms given him by the process that is going forward. His thinking in the premises is reduced to standard units of gauge and grade. If he fails of the precise measure, by more or less, the exigencies of the process check the aberration and drive home the absolute need of conformity.

There results a standardization of the workman's intellectual life in terms of mechanical process, which is more unmitigated and precise the more comprehensive and consummate the industrial process in which he plays a part. This must not be taken to mean that such work need lower the degree of intelligence of the workman. No doubt the contrary is nearer the truth. He is a more efficient workman the more intelligent he is, and the discipline of the machine process ordinarily increases his efficiency even for work in a different line from that by which the discipline is given. But the intelligence required and inculcated in the machine industry is of a peculiar character. The machine process is a severe and insistent disciplinarian in point of intelligence. It requires close and unremitting thought, but it is thought which runs in standard terms of quantitative precision. Broadly, other intelligence on the part of the workman is useless; or it is even worse than useless, for a habit of thinking in other than quantitative terms blurs the workman's quantitative apprehension of the facts with which he has to do.[1]

In so far as he is a rightly gifted and fully disciplined workman, the final term of his habitual thinking is mechanical efficiency, understanding "mechanical" in the sense in which it is used above. But mechanical efficiency is a matter of precisely adjusted cause and effect. What the discipline of the machine industry inculcates, therefore, in the habits of life and of thought of the workman, is regularity of sequence and mechanical precision; and the intellectual outcome is an habitual resort to terms of measurable cause and effect, together with a relative neglect and disparagement of such exercise of the intellectual faculties as does not run on these lines.

Of course, in no case and with no class does the discipline of the machine process mould the habits of life and of thought fully into its own image. There is present in the human nature of all classes too large a residue of the propensities and aptitudes carried over from the past and working to a different result. The machine's regime has been of too short duration, strict as its discipline may be, and the body of inherited traits and traditions is too comprehensive and consistent to admit of anything more than a remote approach to such a consummation.

The machine process compels a more or less unremitting attention to phenomena of an impersonal character and to sequences and correlations not dependent for their force upon human predilection nor created by habit and custom. The machine throws out anthropomorphic habits of thought. It compels the adaptation of the workman to his work, rather than the adaptation of the work to the workman. The machine technology rests on a knowledge of impersonal, material cause and effect, not on the dexterity, diligence, or personal force of the workman, still less on the habits and propensities of the workman's superiors. Within the range of this machine-guided work, and within the range of modern life so far as it is guided by the machine process, the course of things is given mechanically, impersonally, and the resultant discipline is a discipline in the handling of impersonal facts for mechanical effect. It inculcates thinking in terms of opaque, impersonal cause and effect, to the neglect of those norms of validity that rest on usage and on the conventional standards handed down by usage. Usage counts for little in shaping the processes of work of this kind or in shaping the modes of thought induced by work of this kind.

The machine process gives no insight into questions of good and evil, merit and demerit, except in point of material causation, nor into the foundations or the constraining force of law and order, except such mechanically enforced law and order as may be stated in terms of pressure, temperature, velocity, tensile strength, etc.[2] The machine technology takes no cognizance of conventionally established rules of precedence; it knows neither manners nor breeding and can make no use of any of the attributes of worth. Its scheme of knowledge and of inference is based on the laws of material causation, not on those of immemorial custom, authenticity, or authoritative enactment. Its metaphysical basis is the law of cause and effect, which in the thinking of its adepts has displaced even the law of sufficient reason.[3]

The range of conventional truths, or of institutional legacies, which it traverses is very comprehensive, being, indeed, all-inclusive. It is but little more in accord with the newer, eighteenth-century conventional truths of natural rights, natural liberty, natural law, or natural religion, than with the older norms of the true, the beautiful, and the good which these displaced. Anthropomorphism, under whatever disguise, is of no use and of no force here.

The discipline exercised by the mechanical occupations, in so far as it is in question here, is a discipline of the habits of thought. It is, therefore, as processes of thought, methods of apperception, and sequences of reasoning, that these occupations are of interest for the present purpose; it is as such that they have whatever cultural value belongs to them. They have such a value, therefore, somewhat in proportion as they tax the mental faculties of those employed; and the largest effects are to be looked for among those industrial classes who are required to comprehend and guide the processes, rather than among those who serve merely as mechanical auxiliaries of the machine process. Not that the latter are exempt from the machine's discipline, but it falls upon them blindly and enforces an uncritical acceptance of opaque results, rather than a theoretical insight into the causal sequences which make up the machine process. The higher degree of training in such matter-of-fact habits of thought is accordingly to be looked for among the higher ranks of skilled mechanics, and perhaps still more decisively among those who stand in an engineering or supervisory relation to the processes. It counts more forcibly and farthest among those who are required to exercise what may be called a mechanical discretion in the guidance of the industrial processes, who, as one might say, are required to administer the laws of causal sequence that run through material phenomena, who therefore must learn to think in the terms in which the machine processes work.[4] The metaphysical ground, the assumptions, on which such thinking proceeds must be such as will hold good for the sequence of material phenomena; that is to say, it is the metaphysical assumption of modern material science—the law of cause and effect, cumulative causation, conservation of energy, persistence of quantity, or whatever phrase be chosen to cover the concept. The men occupied with the modern material sciences are, accordingly, for the purpose in hand, in somewhat the same case as the higher ranks of those employed in mechanical industry.[5]

Leaving aside the archaic vocations of war, politics, fashion, and religion, the employments in which men are engaged may be distinguished as pecuniary or business employments on the one hand, and industrial or mechanical employments on the other hand.[6] In earlier times, and indeed until an uncertain point in the nineteenth century, such a distinction between employments would not to any great extent have coincided with a difference between occupations. But gradually, as time has passed and production for a market has come to be the rule in industry, there has supervened a differentiation of occupations, or a division of labor, whereby one class of men has taken over the work of purchase and sale and of husbanding a store of accumulated values. Concomitantly, of course, the rest, who may, for lack of means or of pecuniary aptitude, have been less well fitted for pecuniary pursuits, have been relieved of the cares of business and have with increasing specialization given their attention to the mechanical processes involved in this production for a market. In this way the distinction between pecuniary and industrial activities or employments has come to coincide more and more nearly with a difference between occupations. Not that the specialization has even yet gone so far as to exempt any class from all pecuniary care;[7] for even those whose daily occupation is mechanical work still habitually bargain with their employers for their wages and with others for their supplies. So that none of the active classes in modern life is fully exempt from pecuniary work.

But the need of attention to pecuniary matters is less and less exacting, even in the matter of wages and supplies. The scale of wages, for instance, is, for the body of workmen, and also for what may be called the engineering force, becoming more and more a matter of routine, thereby lessening at least the constancy with which occasions for detail bargaining in this respect recur. So also as regards the purchase of consumable goods. In the cities and industrial towns, particularly, the supplying of the means of subsistence has, in great part, become a matter of routine. Retail prices are in an increasing degree fixed by the seller, and in great measure fixed in an impersonal way. This occurs in a particularly evident and instructive way in the practice of the department stores, where the seller fixes the price, and comes in contact with the buyer only through the intervention of a salesman who has no discretion as to the terms of sale. The change that has taken place and that is still going on in this respect is sufficiently striking on comparison with the past in any industrial community, or with the present in any of those communities which we are in the habit of calling "industrially backward."

Conversely, as regards the men in the pecuniary occupations, the business men. Their exemption from taking thought of mechanical facts and processes is likewise only relative. Even those business men whose business is in a peculiar degree remote from the handling of tools or goods, and from the oversight of mechanical process, as, for example, bankers, lawyers, brokers, and the like, have still, at the best, to take some cognizance of the mechanical apparatus of everyday life; they are at least compelled to take some thought of what may be called the mechanics of consumption. Whereas those business men whose business is more immediately concerned with industry commonly have some knowledge and take some thought of the processes of industry; to some appreciable extent they habitually think in mechanical terms. Their cogitations may habitually run to pecuniary conclusions, and the test to which the force and validity of their reasoning is brought may habitually be the pecuniary outcome; the beginning and end of their more serious thinking is of a pecuniary kind, but it always takes in some general features of the mechanical process along the way. Their exemption from mechanical thinking, from thinking in terms of cause and effect, is, therefore, materially qualified.

But after all qualifications have been made, the fact still is apparent that the everyday life of those classes which are engaged in business differs materially in the respect cited from the life of the classes engaged in industry proper. There is an appreciable and widening difference between the habits of life of the two classes; and this carries with it a widening difference in the discipline to which the two classes are subjected. It induces a difference in the habits of thought and the habitual grounds and methods of reasoning resorted to by each class. There results a difference in the point of view, in the facts dwelt upon, in the methods of argument, in the grounds of validity appealed to; and this difference gains in magnitude and consistency as the differentiation of occupations goes on. So that the two classes come to have an increasing difficulty in understanding one another and appreciating one another's convictions, ideals, capacities, and shortcomings.

The ultimate ground of validity for the thinking of the business classes is the natural-rights ground of property—a conventional, anthropomorphic fact having an institutional validity, rather than a matter-of-fact validity such as can be formulated in terms of material cause and effect; while the classes engaged in the machine industry are habitually occupied with matters of causal sequence, which do not lend themselves to statement in anthropomorphic terms of natural rights and which afford no guidance in questions of institutional right and wrong, or of conventional reason and consequence. Arguments which proceed on material cause and effect cannot be met with arguments from conventional precedent or dialectically sufficient reason, and conversely.

The thinking required by the pecuniary occupations proceeds on grounds of conventionality, whereas that involved in the industrial occupations runs, in the main, on grounds of mechanical sequence or causation, to the neglect of conventionality. The institution (habit of thought) of ownership or property is a conventional fact; and the logic of pecuniary thinking—that is to say, of thinking on matters of ownership—is a working out of the implications of this postulate, this concept of ownership or property. The characteristic habits of thought given by such work are habits of recourse to conventional grounds of finality or validity, to anthropomorphism, to explanations of phenomena in terms of human relation, discretion, authenticity, and choice. The final ground of certainty in inquiries on this natural-rights plane is always a ground of authenticity, of precedent, or accepted decision. The argument is an argument *de jure*, not *de facto*, and the training given lends facility and certainty in the pursuit of *de jure* distinctions and generalizations, rather than in the pursuit or the assimilation of a *de facto* knowledge of impersonal phenomena. The end of such reasoning is the interpretation of new facts in terms of accredited precedents, rather than a revision of the knowledge drawn from past experience in the matter-of-fact light of new phenomena. The endeavor is to make facts conform to law, not to make the law or general rule conform to facts. The bent so given favors the acceptance of the general, abstract, custom-made rule as something real with a reality superior to the reality of impersonal, non-conventional facts. Such training gives reach and subtlety in metaphysical argument and in what is known as the "practical" management of affairs; it gives executive or administrative efficiency, so-called, as distinguished from mechanical work. "Practical" efficiency means the ability to turn facts to account for the purposes of the accepted conventions, to give a large effect to the situation in terms of the pecuniary conventions in force.[8]

The spiritual attitude given by this training in reasoning *de jure*, from pecuniary premises to pecuniary conclusions, is necessarily conservative. This species of reasoning assumes the validity of the conventionally established postulates, and is consequently unable to take a skeptical attitude toward these postulates or toward the institutions in which these postulates are embodied. It may lead to skepticism touching other, older, institutions that are at variance with its own (natural-rights) postulates, but its skepticism cannot touch the natural-rights ground on which it rests its own case. In the same manner, of course, the thinking which runs in material causal sequence cannot take a skeptical attitude toward its fundamental postulate, the law of cause and effect; but since reasoning on this materialistic basis does not visibly go to uphold the received institutions, the attitude given by the discipline of the machine technology cannot, for the present, be called a conservative attitude.

The business classes are conservative, on the whole, but such a conservative bent is, of course, not peculiar to them. These occupations are not the only ones whose reasoning prevailingly moves on a conventional plane. Indeed, the intellectual activity of other classes, such as soldiers, politicians, the clergy, and men of fashion, moves on a plane of still older conventions; so that if the training given by business employments is to be characterized as conservative, that given by these other, more archaic employments should be called reactionary.[9] Extreme conventionalization means extreme conservatism. Conservatism means the maintenance of conventions already in force. On this head, therefore, the discipline of modern business life may be said simply to retain something of the complexion which marks the life of the higher barbarian culture, at the same time that it has not retained the disciplinary force of the barbarian culture in so high a state of preservation as some of the other occupations just named.

The discipline of the modern industrial employments is relatively free from the bias of conventionality, but the difference between the mechanical and the business occupations in this respect is a difference of degree. It is not simply that conventional standards of certainty fall into abeyance for lack of exercise, among the industrial classes. The positive discipline exercised by their work in good part runs counter to the habit of thinking in conventional, anthropomorphic terms, whether the conventionality is that of natural rights or any other. And in respect of this positive training away from conventional norms, there is a large divergence between the several lines of industrial employment. In proportion as a given line of employment has more of the character of a machine process and less of the character of handicraft, the matter-of-fact training which it gives is more pronounced. In a sense more intimate than the inventors of the phrase seem to have appreciated, the machine has become the master of the man who works with it and an arbiter in the cultural fortunes of the community into whose life it has entered.

The intellectual and spiritual training of the machine in modern life, therefore, is very far-reaching. It leaves but a small proportion of the community untouched; but while its constraint is ramified throughout the body of the population, and constrains virtually all classes at some points in their daily life, it falls with the most direct, intimate, and unmitigated impact upon the skilled mechanical classes, for these have no respite from its mastery, whether they are at work or at play.

The ubiquitous presence of the machine, with its spiritual concomitant—workday ideals and skepticism of what is only conventionally valid—is the unequivocal mark of the western culture of today as contrasted with the culture of other times and places. It pervades all classes and strata in a varying degree, but on an average in a greater degree than at any time in the past, and most potently in the advanced industrial communities and in the classes immediately in contact with the mechanical occupations. As the comprehensive mechanical organization of the material side of life has gone on, a heightening of this cultural effect throughout the community has also supervened, and with a farther and faster movement in the same direction a farther accentuation of this "modern" complexion of culture is fairly to be looked for, unless some remedy be found. And as the concomitant differentiation and specialization of occupation goes on, a still more unmitigated discipline falls upon ever-widening classes of the population, resulting in an ever-weakening sense of conviction, allegiance, or piety toward the received institutions.

Notes

1. If, e.g., he takes to myth-making and personifies the machine or the process and imputes purpose and benevolence to the mechanical appliances, after the manner of current nursery tales and pulpit oratory, he is sure to go wrong.

2. Such expressions as "good and ill," "merit and demerit," "law and order," when applied to technological facts or to the outcome of material science, are evidently only metaphorical expressions, borrowed from older usage and serviceable only as figures of speech.

3. Tarde, *Psychologie Economique*, vol. I, pp. 122–31, offers a characterization of the psychology of modern work, contrasting, among other things, the work of the machine workman with that of the handicraftsman in respect of its psychological requirements and effects. It may be taken as a temperate formulation of the current commonplaces on this topic, and seems to be fairly wide of the mark.

4. For something more than a hundred years past this change in the habits of thought of the workman has been commonly spoken of as a deterioration or numbing of his intelligence. But that seems too sweeping a characterization of the change brought on by habituation to machine work. It is safe to say that such habituation brings a change in the workman's habits of thought—in the direction, method, and content of his thinking—heightening his intelligence for some purposes and lowering it for certain others. No doubt, on the whole, the machine's discipline lowers the intelligence of the workman for such purposes as were rated high as marks of intelligence before the coming of the machine, but it appears likewise to heighten his intelligence for such purposes as have been brought to the front by the machine. If he is by nature scantily endowed with the aptitudes that would make him think effectively in terms of the machine process, if he has intellectual capacity for other things and not for this, then the training of the machine may fairly be said to lower his intelligence, since it hinders the full development of the only capacities of which he is possessed. The resulting difference in intellectual training is a difference in kind and direction, not necessarily in degree. Cf. Schmoller, *Grundriss der Volkswirtschaftslehre,* vol. I, secs. 85–6, 132; Hobson, *Evolution of Modern Capitalism*, ch. 9, secs. 4 and 5; Cooke Taylor, *Modern Factory System*, pp. 434–5; Sidney and Beatrice Webb, *Industrial Democracy*, e.g., pp. 327 et seq.; K. Th. Reinhold, *Arbeit und Werkzeug,* ch. 10 (particularly pp. 190–8) and ch. 11 (particularly pp. 221–40).

5. Cf. J.C. Sutherland, "The Engineering Mind," *Popular Science Monthly*, Jan. 1903, pp. 254–6.

6. Cf. "Industrial and Pecuniary Employments" [especially pp. 287–306 as republished in *The Place of Science in Modern Civilization*, 1919, from the Papers and Proceedings of the Thirteenth Annual Meeting of the American Economic Association, 1901].

7. As G.F. Steffen has described it: "Those who hire out their labour power or their capital or their land to the entrepreneurs are as a rule not absolutely passive as seen from the point of view of business enterprise. They are not simply inanimate implements in the hands of the entrepreneurs. They are 'enterprising implements' (företagande verktyg) who surrender their undertaking functions only to the extent designated in the contract with the entrepreneur."—*Ekonomisk Tidskrift*, vol. V, p. 256.

8. Cf., on the other hand, Reinhold, *Arbeit und Werkzeug,* chs. 12 and 14, where double-dealing is confused with workmanship, very much after the manner familiar to readers or expositions of the "wages of superintendence," but more broadly and ingeniously than usual.

9. Individual exceptions are, of course, to be found in all classes, but there is, after all, a more or less consistent, prevalent class attitude. As is well known, clergymen, lawyers, soldiers, civil servants, and the like are popularly held to be of conservative, if not reactionary temper. This vulgar apprehension may be faulty in detail, and especially it may be too sweeping in its generalizations; but there are, after all, few persons not belonging to these classes who will not immediately recognize that this vulgar appraisement of them rests on substantial grounds, even though the appraisement may need qualification. So, also, a conservative animus is seen to pervade all classes more generally in earlier times or on more archaic levels of culture than our own. At the same time, in those early days and in the more archaic cultural regions, the structure of conventionally accepted truths and the body of accredited spiritual or extra-material facts are more comprehensive and rigid, and the thinking on all topics is more consistently held to tests of authenticity as contrasted with tests of sense perception. On the whole, the number and variety of things that are fundamentally and eternally true and good increase as one goes outward from the modern west-European cultural centers into the earlier barbarian past or into the remoter barbarian present.

On the Merits of Borrowing

The efficiency of borrowing that so comes to light in the life-history of the Baltic culture, as also in a less notorious manner in other instances of cultural intercourse, puts up to the student of institutions a perplexing question, or rather a group of perplexing questions. Something has just been said on the question of why one people borrows elements of culture or of technology with greater facility and effect than another. But the larger question stands untouched: Why do the borrowed elements lend themselves with greater facility and effect to their intrinsic use in the hands of the borrower people than in the hands of the people to whose initiative they are due? Why are borrowed elements of culture more efficiently employed than home-grown innovations? or more so than the same elements at the hands of their originators? It would of course be quite bootless to claim that such is always or necessarily the case, but it is likewise not to be denied that, as a matter of history, technological innovations and creations of an institutional nature have in many cases reached their fullest serviceability only at the hands of other communities and other peoples than those to whom these cultural elements owed their origin and initial success. That such should ever be the case is a sufficiently striking phenomenon—one might even say a sufficiently striking discrepancy.

An explanation, good as far as it goes, though it may not go all the way, is to be looked for in the peculiar circumstances attending the growth, as well as the eventual transmission by borrowing, of any article of the institutional equipment. Technological elements affecting the state of the industrial arts, as being the more concrete and more tangible, will best serve to demonstrate the proposition. Any far-reaching innovation or invention, such as may eventually find a substantial place in the inventory of borrowed elements, will necessarily begin in a small way, finding its way into use and wont among the people where it takes its rise

Reprinted from chapter 2 of *Imperial Germany and the Industrial Revolution,* New York: The Macmillan Company, 1915.

rather tentatively and by tolerance than with a sweeping acceptance and an adequate realization of its uses and ulterior consequences. Such will have been the case, e.g., with the domestication of the crop plants and the beginnings of tillage, or the domestication of the useful animals, or the use of the metals, or, again, with the rise of the handicraft system, or the industrial revolution that brought in the machine industry. The innovation finds its way into the system of use and wont at the cost of some derangement to the system, provokes to new usages, conventions, beliefs, and principles of conduct, in part directed advisedly to its utilization or to the mitigation of its immediate consequences, or to the diversion of its usufruct to the benefit of given individuals or classes; but in part there also grow up new habits of thought due to the innovation which it brings into the routine of life, directly in the way of new requirements of manipulation, surveillance, attendance or seasonal time-schedule, and indirectly by affecting the economic relations between classes and localities, as well as the distribution and perhaps the aggregate supply of consumable wealth.

In the early times, such as would come immediately in question here, it is a virtual matter-of-course that any material innovation, or indeed any appreciable unit of technological ways and means, will be attended with a fringe of magical or superstitious conceits and observances. The evidences of this are to be found in good plenty in all cultures, ancient or contemporary, on the savage and barbarian levels; and indeed they are not altogether wanting in civilized life. Many students of ethnology, folk-psychology and religion have busied themselves to good effect with collecting and analyzing such material afforded by magical and superstitious practice, and in most instances they are able to trace these practices to some ground of putative utility, connecting them with the serviceable working of the arts of life at one point or another, or with the maintenance of conditions conducive to life and welfare in some essential respect. Where the ethnologist is unable to find such a line of logical connection between superstitious practice and the exigencies of life and welfare, he commonly considers that he has not been able to find what is in the premises, not that the premises do not contain anything of the kind he is bound to expect. But if magical and superstitious practices, or such of them as are at all of material consequence, are with virtual universality to be traced back through the channels of habituation to some putative ground of serviceability for human use, it follows that the rule should work, passably at least, the other way; that the state of the industrial arts which serve human use in such a culture will be shot through with magical and superstitious conceits and observances having an indispensable but wholly putative efficacy.

In many of the lower cultures, or perhaps rather in such of the lower cultures as are at all well known, the workday routine of getting a living is encumbered with a ubiquitous and pervasive scheme of such magical or superstitious conceits and observances, which are felt to constitute an indispensable part of the industrial processes in which they mingle. They embody the putatively efficacious immaterial constituent of all technological procedure; or, seen in detail, they are the spiritual half that completes and animates any process of device throughout its participation in the industrial routine. Like the technological elements with which they are associated, and concomitantly with them, these magically efficacious devices have grown into the prevalent habits of thought of the population and have become an integral part of the common-sense notion of how these technological elements are and are to be turned to account.[1] And at a slightly farther shift in the current of sophistication, out of the same penchant for anthropomorphic interpretation and analogy, a wide range of religious observances, properly so called, will also presently come to bear on the industrial process and the routine of economic life; with a proliferous growth of ceremonial, of propitiation and avoidance, designed to further the propitious course of things to be done. . . .

But aside from these simple-minded institutional inhibitions on industrial efficiency that seem so much a matter of course in the lower cultures, there are others that run to much the same effect and hold their place among the more enlightened peoples in much the same matter-of-course way. These are in part rather obscure, not having been much attended to in popular speculation, and in part quite notorious, having long been subjects of homiletical iteration. And since this growth of what may be called secular, as contrasted with magical or religious, institutional inhibitions on efficiency, has much to do with latter-day economic affairs, as well as with the material fortunes of our prehistoric forebears, a more detailed exposition of their place in economic life will be in place.

On the adoption of new industrial ways and means, whether in the way of specific devices and expedients or of comprehensive changes in methods and processes, there follows a growth of conventional usages governing the utilization of the new ways and means. This applies equally whether the new expedients are home-bred innovations or technological improvements borrowed from outside; and in any case such a growth of conventions takes time, being of the nature of adaptive habituation. A new expedient, in the way of material appliances or of improved processes, comes into the industrial system and is adapted to the requirements of the state of things into which it is introduced. Certain habitual ways of utilizing the new device come to be accepted; as would happen, e.g., on the introduction of domestic animals among a people previously living by tillage alone and having no acquaintance with the use of such animals under other conditions than those prevailing among purely pastoral peoples. So, again, the gradual improvement of boat-building and navigation, such as took place among the prehistoric Baltic peoples, would induce a progressive change in the conventional scheme of life and bring on a specialization of occupations, with some division of economic and social classes. Or, again, in such a large systematic shift as is involved in the coming of the handicraft industry and its spread and maturing; class distinctions, occupational divisions, standardization of methods and products, together with trade relations and settled markets and trade routes, came gradually into effect. In part these conventional features resulting from and answering to the new industrial factors continued to have the force of common-sense conventional arrangement only; in part they also acquired the added stability given by set agreement, authoritative control and statutory enactment.

So, in the case of the handicraft system such matters as trade routes, methods of package, transportation and consignment, credit relations, and the like, continued very largely, though not wholly nor throughout the vogue of the system, to be regulated by conventional vogue rather than by authoritative formulation; while on the other hand the demarcation between crafts and classes of craftsman, as well as the standardization of methods and output, were presently, in the common run, brought under rigorous surveillance by authorities vested with specific powers and acting under carefully formulated rules.

But whether this standardization and conventionalization takes the set form of authoritative agreement and enactment or is allowed to rest on the looser ground of settled use and wont, it is always of the nature of a precipitate of past habituation, and is designed to meet exigencies that have come into effect in past experience; it always embodies something of the principle of the dead hand; and along with all the salutary effects of stability and harmonious working that may be credited to such systematization, it follows also that these standing conventions out of the past unavoidably act to retard, deflect or defeat adaptation to new exigencies that arise in the further course. Conventions that are in some degree effete continue to cumber the ground.

All this apparatus of conventions and standard usage, whether it takes the simpler form of use and wont or the settled character of legally competent enactment and common-law rule, necessarily has something of this effect of retardation in any given state of the industrial arts, and so necessarily acts in some degree to lower the net efficiency of the industrial system which it pervades. But this work of retardation is also backed by the like character attaching to the material equipment by use of which the technological proficiency of the community takes effect. The equipment is also out of the past, and it too lies under the dead hand. In a general way, any minor innovation in processes or in the extension of available resources, or in the scale of organization, is taken care of as far as may be by a patchwork improvement and amplification of the items of equipment already in hand; the fashion of plant and appliances already in use is adhered to, with concessions in new installations, but it is adhered to more decisively so in any endeavor to bring the equipment in hand up to scale and grade. Changes so made are in part of a concessive nature, in sufficiently large part, indeed, to tell materially on the aggregate; and the fact of such changes being habitually made in a concessive spirit so lessens the thrust in the direction of innovation that even the concessions do not carry as far as might be.[2]

It is in the relatively advanced stages of the industrial arts that this retardation due to use and wont, as distinguished from magical and religious waste and inhibitions on innovation, become of grave consequence. There appears, indeed, to be in some sort a systematic symmetry or balance to be observed in the way in which the one of these lines of technological inhibition comes into effectual bearing as fast as the other declines. At the same time, as fast as commercial considerations, considerations of investment, come to rule industry, the investor's interest comes also to exercise an inhibitory surveillance over technological efficiency, both by the well-known channel of limiting the output and holding up the price to what the traffic will bear—that is to say what it will bear in the pecuniary sense of yielding the largest net gain to the business men in interest—and also by the less notorious reluctance of investors and business concerns to replace obsolete methods and plants with new and more efficient equipment.

Beyond these simple and immediate inhibitory convolutions within the industrial system itself, there lies a fertile domain of conventions and institutional arrangements induced as secondary consequences of the growth of industrial efficiency and contrived to keep its net serviceability in bounds, by diverting its energies to industrially unproductive uses and its output to unproductive consumption.

With any considerable advance in the industrial arts business enterprise presently takes over the control of the industrial process; with the consequence that the net pecuniary gain to the business man in control becomes the test of industrial efficiency. This may result in a speeding up of the processes of industry, as is commonly noted by economists. But it also results in "unemployment" whenever a sustained working of the forces engaged does not, or is not believed to, conduce to the employer's largest net gain, as may notoriously happen in production for a market. Also, it follows that industry is controlled and directed with a view to sales, and a wise expenditure of industrial efficiency, in the business sense, comes to mean such expenditure as contributes to sales; which may often mean that the larger share of costs, as the goods reach their users, is the industrially wasteful cost of advertising and other expedients of salesmanship.

The normal result of business control in industry—normal in the sense of being uniformly aimed at and also in that it commonly follows—is the accumulation of wealth and income in the hands of a class. Under the well-accepted principle of "conspicuous waste" wealth so accumulated is to be put in evidence in visible consumption and visible exemption from work. So that with due, but ordinarily not a large, lapse of time, an elaborate scheme of proprieties establishes itself, bearing on this matter of conspicuous consumption, so contrived as to "take up the slack." This system of conspicuous waste is a scheme of proprieties, decencies, and standards of living, the economic motive of which is competitive spending. It works out in a compromise between the immediate spending of income on conspicuous consumption—together with the conspicuous avoidance of industrial work—on the one side, and deferred spending—commonly called "saving"—on the other side. The deferred spending may be deferred to a later day in the lifetime of the saver, or to a later generation; its effects are substantially the same in either case. There is the further reservation to be noted, that in so far as property rights, tenures and the conjunctures of business gain are in any degree insecure, measures will be taken to insure against the risks of loss and eventual inability to keep up appearances according to the accepted standard of living. This insurance takes the shape of accumulation, in one form or another—provision for future revenue.

Like other conventions and institutional regulations, the scheme of spending rests on current, i.e., immediately past, experience, and as was noted above it is so contrived as to take up the calculable slack—the margin between production and productive consumption. It is perhaps needless to enter the caution that such a scheme of conspicuous waste does not always, perhaps not in the common run of cases, go to the full limit of what the traffic will bear; but it is also to be noted that it will sometimes, and indeed not infrequently, exceed that limit. Perhaps in all cases, but particularly where the industrial efficiency of the community is notably high, so as to yield a very appreciable margin between productive output and necessary current consumption, some appreciable thought has to be spent on the question of ways and means of spending; and a technique of consumption grows up.

It will be appreciated how serious a question this may become, of the ways and means of reputable consumption, when it is called to mind that in the communities where the modern state of the industrial arts has adequately taken effect this margin of product disposable for wasteful consumption will always exceed fifty per cent of the current product, and will in the more fortunate cases probably exceed seventy-five per cent of the whole. So considerable a margin is not to be disposed of to good effect by haphazard impulse. The due absorption of it in competitive spending takes thought, skill and time for the organization of ways and means. It is also not a simple problem of conspicuously consuming time and substance, without more ado; men's sense of fitness and beauty requires that the spending should take place in an appropriate manner, such as will not offend good taste and not involve an odiously aimless ostentation. And it takes time and habituation, as well as a discriminate balancing of details, before a scheme of reputable standardized waste is perfected; of course, it also costs time and specialized effort to take due care of the running adjustment of such a scheme to current conditions of taste, ennui and consumptive distinction—as seen, e.g., in the technique of fashions. It has, indeed, proved to be a matter of some difficulty, not to say of serious strain, in the industrially advanced communities, to keep the scheme of conspicuous waste abreast of the times; so that, besides the conspicuous consumers in their own right, there have grown up an appreciable number of special occupations devoted to the technical needs of reputable spending. The technology of wasteful consumption is large and elaborate and its achievements are among the monuments of human initiative and endeavor; it has its victories and its heroes as well as the technology of production.

But any technological scheme is more or less of a balanced system, in which the interplay of parts has such a character of mutual support and dependence that any substantial addition or subtraction at any one point will involve more or less of derangement all along the line. Neither can an extremely large contingent of reputable waste be suddenly superinduced in the accepted standard of living of any given community—though this difficulty is not commonly a sinister one—nor can a large retrenchment in this domain of what is technically called "the moral standard of living" be suddenly effected without substantial hardship or without seriously disturbing the spiritual balance of the community. To realize the import of such disturbance in the scheme of wasteful consumption one need only try to picture the consternation that would, e.g., fall on the British community consequent on the abrupt discontinuance of the Court and its social and civil manifestations, or of horse-racing, or of the established church, or of evening dress.

But since the growth and acceptance of any scheme of wasteful expenditure is after all subsequent to and consequent upon the surplus productivity of the industrial system on which it rests, the introduction, in whole or in part, of a new and more efficient state of the industrial arts does not carry with it from the outset a fully developed system of standardized consumption; particularly, it need not follow that the standard scheme of consumption will be carried over intact in case a new industrial technology is borrowed. There is no intimate or intrinsic mutuality of mechanical detail between the technology of industry and the technique of conspicuous waste; the high-heeled slipper and the high-wrought "picture hat," e.g., are equally well accepted in prehistoric Crete and in twentieth-century France; and the Chinese lady bandages her foot into deformity where the Manchu lady, in evidence of the same degree of opulence in the same town, is careful to let her foot run loose. It is only that, human nature being what it is, a disposable margin of production will, under conditions of private ownership, provoke a competent scheme of wasteful consumption.

Owing to this mechanical discontinuity between any given state of the industrial arts and the scheme of magical, religious, conventional, or pecuniary use and wont with which it lives in some sort of symbiosis, the carrying-over of such a state of the industrial arts from one community to another need not involve the carrying-over of this its spiritual complement. Such is particularly the case where the borrowing takes place across a marked cultural frontier, in which case it follows necessarily that the alien scheme of conventions will not be taken over intact in taking over an alien technological system, whether in whole or in part. The borrowing community or cultural group is already furnished with its own system of conceits and observances—in magic, religion, propriety, and any other line of conventional necessity—and the introduction of a new scheme, or the intrusion of new and alien elements into the accredited scheme already in force, is a work of habituation that takes time and special provocation. All of which applies with added force to the introduction of isolated technological elements from an alien culture, still more particularly, of course, where the technological expedients borrowed are turned to other uses and utilized by other methods than those employed in the culture from which they were borrowed—as, e.g., would be the case in the acquisition of domestic cattle by a sedentary farming community from a community of nomadic or half-nomadic pastoral people, as appears to have happened in the prehistoric culture of the Baltic peoples. The interposition of a linguistic frontier between the borrower and creditor communities would still farther lessen the chance of immaterial elements of culture being carried over in the transmission of technological knowledge. The borrowed elements of industrial efficiency would be stripped of their fringe of conventional inhibitions and waste, and the borrowing community would be in a position to use them with a freer hand and with a better chance of utilizing them to their full capacity, and also with a better chance of improving on their use, turning them to new uses, and carrying the principles (habits of thought) involved in the borrowed items out, with unhampered insight, into farther ramifications of technological proficiency. The borrowers are in a position of advantage, intellectually, in that the new expedient comes into their hands more nearly in the shape of a theoretical principle applicable under given physical conditions; rather than in the shape of a concrete expedient applicable within the limits of traditional use, personal, magical, conventional. It is, in other words, taken over in a measure without the defects of its qualities.

Here, again, is a secondary effect of borrowing, that may not seem of first-rate consequence but is none the less necessarily to be taken into account. The borrowed elements are drawn into a cultural scheme in which they are aliens and into the texture of which they can be wrought only at the cost of some, more or less serious, derangement of the accustomed scheme of life and the accepted system of knowledge and belief. Habituation to their use and insight into their working acts in its degree to incapacitate the borrowers for holding all their home-bred conceits and beliefs intact and in full conviction. They are vehicles of cultural discrepancy, conduce to a bias of skepticism, and act, in their degree, to loosen the bonds of authenticity. Incidentally, the shift involved in such a move will have its distasteful side and carry its burden of disturbance and discomfort; but the new elements, it is presumed, will make their way, and the borrowing community will make its peace with them on such terms as may be had; that assumption being included in the premises.

In some instances of such communication of alien technological and other cultural elements the terms on which a settlement has been effected have been harsh enough, as, e.g., on the introduction of iron tools and fire-arms among the American Indians, or the similar introduction of distilled spirits, of the horse, and of trade—especially in furs—among the same general group of peoples. Polynesia, Australia, and other countries new to the European technology, and to the European conceits and conceptions in law, religion and morals, will be called to mind to the same effect. In these cases the intrusion of alien, but technologically indefeasible, elements of culture has been too large to allow the old order to change; so it has gone to pieces. This result may, of course, have been due in part to a temperamental incapacity of these peoples for the acquisition of new and alien habits of thought; they may not have been good borrowers, at least they appear not to have been sufficiently good borrowers. The same view, in substance, is often formulated to the effect that these are inferior or "backward" races, being apparently not endowed with the traits that conduce to a facile apprehension of the modern European technological system.

Notes

1. For illustration from contemporary lower cultures, cf. W.W. Skeat, *Malay Magic,* perhaps especially ch. v; for classic antiquity cf. Jane E. Harrison, *Prolegomena to the Study of Greek Religion,* ch. iv.

2. An illustrative instance of this obsolescence of equipment on a large scale and in modern circumstances is afforded by several of the underlying companies of the United States Steel Corporation. The plants in question had been installed at a period when the later methods of steel production had not been perfected and before the later and richer sources of raw materials had become available by the latest methods of transportation; they were also located with a view to smaller markets, distributed on an earlier and now obsolete plan, which has become obsolete through changes in the railway system and the growth of new centers of population. It was technologically impossible to bring them up to date as independent industrial plants, and as a business proposition it was impracticable abruptly to discard them and replace them by new equipment placed to better advantage and organized on a scale to take full advantage of available resources and methods. The remedy sought in the formation of the Steel Corporation was a compromise, whereby the obsolete items of equipment—in part obsolete only in the geographical sense that the industrial situation had shifted out of their way—were gradually discarded and replaced with new plants designed for specialized lines of production, at the same time that the monopolistic position of the new Corporation enabled the shift to be made at a sufficiently slow rate to mask the substitution and make the community at large pay for this temporary lower efficiency due to a gradual disuse of obsolete equipment and methods, in place of such an abrupt and sweeping shift to a new basis as the altered technological situation called for.

At a later juncture the Steel Corporation found itself also face to face with a serious difficulty due to "obsolescence through improvement" of the same general kind; when it appeared that by the later improved processes steel of the first quality could be made from ore peculiar to the southern field as cheaply as from the Minnesota supply on which the Corporation's mills were in the habit of depending, and with special advantages of access to certain markets. How far the resulting acquisition of the southern coal, ore and lime by the Corporation may have resulted in a retardation of efficiency in steel production would be hazardous to guess.

On the Penalty of Taking the Lead

The modern state of the industrial arts that so has led to the rehabilitation of a dynastic State in Germany on a scale exceeding what had been practicable in earlier times—this technological advance was not made in Germany but was borrowed, directly or at the second remove, from the English-speaking peoples; primarily, and in the last resort almost wholly, from England. What has been insisted on above is that British use and wont in other than the technological respect was not taken over by the German community at the same time. The result being that Germany offers what is by contrast with England an anomaly, in that it shows the working of the modern state of the industrial arts as worked out by the English, but without the characteristic range of institutions and convictions that have grown up among English-speaking peoples concomitantly with the growth of this modern state of the industrial arts. Germany combines the results of English experience in the development of modern technology with a state of the other arts of life more nearly equivalent to what prevailed in England before the modern industrial regime came on; so that the German people have been enabled to take up the technological heritage of the English without having paid for it in the habits of thought, the use and wont, induced in the English community by the experience involved in achieving it. Modern technology has come to the Germans ready-made, without the cultural consequences which its gradual development and continued use has entailed among the people whose experience initiated it and determined the course of its development.

The position of the Germans is not precisely unique in this respect; in a degree the same general proposition will apply to the other Western nations,[1] but it applies to none with anything like the same breadth. The case of Germany is unexampled among Western nations both as regards the abruptness, thorough-

Reprinted from chapters 3 and 4 of *Imperial Germany and the Industrial Revolution,* New York: The Macmillan Company, 1915.

ness and amplitude of its appropriation of this technology, and as regards the archaism of its cultural furniture at the date of this appropriation.

It will be in place to call to mind, in this connection, what has been said in an earlier chapter on the advantage of borrowing the technological arts rather than developing them by home growth. In the transit from one community to another the technological elements so borrowed do not carry over the fringe of other cultural elements that have grown up about them in the course of their development and use. The new expedients come to hand stripped of whatever has only a putative or conventional bearing on their use. On the lower levels of culture this fringe of conventional or putative exactions bound up with the usufruct of given technological devices would be mainly of the nature of magical or religious observances; but on the higher levels, in cases of the class here in question, they are more likely to be conventionalities embedded in custom and to some extent in law, of a secular kind, but frequently approaching the mandatory character of religious observances, as, e.g., the requirement of a decently expensive standard of living.

Propounded in this explicit fashion, the view that a given technological system will have an economic value and a cultural incidence on a community which takes it over ready-made, different from the effects it has already wrought in the community from which it is taken over and in which it has cumulatively grown to maturity in correlation with other concomitant changes in the arts of life—when so stated as an articulate generalization this proposition may seem unfamiliar, and perhaps dubious. But apart from its formal recognition as a premise to go on, the position has long had the assured standing of commonplace. Where such an instance of borrowing comes up for attention among historians and students of human culture, the people that so has taken over an unfamiliar system of industrial ways and means will commonly be characterized as "raw," "immature," "unbalanced," "crude," "underbred"; the spokesmen of such a community on the other hand are likely to speak of its being "youthful," "sturdy," "unspoiled," "in the prime of full-blooded manhood." The meaning in either case, invidious emotions apart, being that such a people has on the one hand not acquired those immaterial elements of culture, those habits of thought on other than industrial matters, that should, and in due course will, come into effect as the necessary correlate of such an advance in technological efficiency, and on the other hand that the people with the new-found material efficiency has not come in for the wasteful and inhibitory habits and fashions with which in the course of time the same technological assets have come to be encumbered among those peoples who have long had the use of them. There is no need of quarreling with either view. Seen as a phenomenon of habituation, and so of the growth of use and wont, the two supplement one another. They are two perspectives of the same view. And the difference between the case of Germany and that of the British, and indeed of the other industrially advanced peoples of Europe, is of this nature. The German people have come in for the modern technology without taking over the graces of the modern industrial culture in which this technology belongs by right of birth; but it is at least equally to the point to note that they have taken over this technological system without the faults of its qualities. . . .

At the transition from medieval to modern time the English people were in arrears, culturally, as compared with the rest of west and central Europe, including west and south Germany; whether that epoch is to be dated from the close of the fifteenth century or from any earlier period, and whether the comparison is to be made in industry and material civilization or in immaterial terms of intellectual achievement and the arts of life. But during the succeeding century the English community had made such gains that by its close they stood (perhaps doubtfully) abreast of their Continental neighbors. This British gain was both absolute and relative, and was due both to an accelerated advance in the Island and a retardation of the rate of gain in much of the Continental territory, although the retardation is more visible on the Continent during the seventeenth than even toward the close of the sixteenth century. Relatively, by comparison again with the state of things among the rival states on the Continent, the English community at this time experienced a respite from political, military and religious disturbances; though this respite is a matter of mitigation, not of surcease. It doubtless has much to do with the advance of the new trade, industry and learning of that classic age, particularly in the increased security of life which it brought; and it is at the same time noteworthy as the initial period of that British peace that has held since then, at times precariously, no doubt, but after all with sufficient consistency to have marked a difference in this respect between the conditions of life offered in the Island and those that have prevailed on the Continent. So that, with reservations, the arts of peace have claimed the greater attention throughout modern times. It may be doubtful whether one can with equal confidence say that the arts of war and of dynastic politics and religion have claimed the chief attention of the Continental peoples during the same period; but in any case the contrast in this respect is too broad to be overlooked, and of too profound a character not to have had its effect in a divergent growth of the institutions and preconceptions that govern human relations and human ends.

For the purpose in hand this modern period of British life may best be divided into two phases or stages, contrasted in some respects; the earlier phase running from an indefinite date in the early sixteenth to somewhere in the early seventeenth century, while the later begins loosely in the later seventeenth and runs to the historical present. The former phase, of course, comes to its most pronounced manifestation in the Elizabethan era; although its cultural consequences are more fully realized at a later date. The high tide of the latter is marked by the Industrial Revolution, conventionally so called, and leaves its mark on British culture chiefly in the nineteenth century.

The criteria as well as the reasons for so subdividing British modern time are chiefly of a technological or industrial nature and bearing. The earlier of these two periods is the high tide of English borrowing and assimilation in the industrial arts, and so corresponds in some sense with the Imperial era of Germany;

the latter period is to be remarked as in a special sense a creative era in English life, which has engendered the current technological system, characterized and dominated by the machine industry; and which has no counterpart in the life-history of the German people hitherto. There would accordingly appear to be an interval of, loosely, some three or four hundred years' experience included in the life-history of the English community, but omitted from the experience that has gone to make the national genius of the German people. . . .

Modern writers who have handled this segment of English history from a large and genial outlook are apt to look on Elizabethan England as a self-contained cultural epoch, which made its own growth out of vital forces comprised within its own historical limits; and such is doubtless a competent view of that exuberant season of British achievement in so far as touches the exploits of the new learning, the warlike and commercial enterprise of the period, and the swift and sure advance of its literature, provided one confines one's attention to these works of fruition and their immediate ground in the wealth of unfolding energy that created them. But Elizabethan England is not an episode that happened by the way; no more than Imperial Germany. Like the Imperial era in Germany the Elizabethan era grew out of and carried out a new situation, a new posture of the material forces that conditioned the life and endeavors of the community. And like the corresponding German case this new posture of economic forces is in great part an outcome of new acquisitions in the industrial arts, largely drawn from abroad.

Earlier Tudor times that led up to the Elizabethan period proper began the movement of bringing English industry abreast of the neighboring countries on the Continent; which was continued through the greater part of Elizabeth's reign. This movement is chiefly occupied with borrowing processes, devices, workmen and methods, and with adapting all these things shrewdly to the needs and uses of the island community. In so borrowing, the English had the advantage that comes to any borrower in like case. They took over what approved itself, and took it over without the conventional limitations that attached to the borrowed elements in the countries of their origin. These conventional elements were those characteristic of the handicraft system, with its gild and charter regulations and the settled usages, routes and methods of the petty trade that went with that system. Among the new gains a not inconsiderable item is what the English learned from the Dutch, of ship-building and navigation.

An immediate though secondary effect of the new departure in the industrial system—a departure which is better expressed in terms of improvement and innovation that in those of a new start—is the (virtual) discovery of resources made available in the new posture which industrial forces are taking, and the consequent freedom with which these new resources were turned to account. New and wide opportunities offered, by contrast with what had been the run of things before, and these opportunities for enterprise, then as ever, played into the posture of affairs as provocations to enterprise; which then as ever brought on its cumulative run of prosperity. The wealth in hand increased in utility under the stimulus of new opportunities for its gainful utilization, and the men in whose hands lay the discretion in industrial matters saw opportunities ahead which their own faith in these opportunities enabled them to realize through adventurous enterprise inspired by the new outlook itself.

It is the tale familiar to all students of periodic prosperity in trade and industry—periods of cumulatively increasing confidence, speculative advance, enhanced buoyancy, expansion, inflation, or whatever term is chosen as the antithesis of depression—the chief distinguishing trait of this particular period of prosperity being that it grew out of the acquirement of a new efficiency, due to what was in effect a discovery of new technological resources backed by a concomitant discovery that the natural resources at hand were acquiring an increased industrial regime; together with the further characteristic feature that this virtual discovery of powers went forward progressively over a considerable space of time, so that no stagnation due to an exhaustion of the stimulus overtook this era of prosperity and enterprise within the lifetime of the generation which first caught the swing of its impulsion.

In this respect the case of Imperial Germany shows a parallel, although the greater scale and rate of their acquiring the new industrial system, as well as the swifter pace of modern trade and industrial enterprise, has so foreshortened the corresponding experience of the Germans as to compress within a lifetime the rounded movement from initiative to climax that would correspond with what occupied the English for more than a century. This very different tempo grows out of the different character of the machine technology, as contrasted with the handicraft system and its petty trade. . . .

The time so allowed the English for the acquirement of the technological wisdom of Continental Christendom, and for the unimpeded usufruct of it, exceeds the corresponding time allowance of Imperial Germany by some six-fold, and the enforced rate of utilization and transition to a new scheme would be correspondingly temperate. The new scheme of habituation in the material arts of life would accordingly have a more adequate chance to work out its consequences in the way of a revision of the community's habits of thought on other heads; the technological institutions so taken into the scheme of life would enforce their discipline upon the population that so became addicted to this new economic situation, and would bend their thinking on other matters in consonance with the frame of mind inbred in the industrial system.

The system which the English borrowed and worked out into its farther consequences was the system of handicraft and petty trade, and the frame of mind native or normal to this industrial system is that which stands for self-help and an equal chance.[2] All this pervasive discipline of the industrial occupations and of the scheme of interests and regulations embodied in this system worked slowly, with a temperate but massive and steady drift, to induce in the English people an animus of democratic equity and non-interference, self-help and local autonomy; which came to a head on the political side in the revolution of 1688, and which continued to direct the course of sentiment through the subsequent development of a scheme of common law based on the metaphysics of Natural Rights.

An effect of the English forward move into the early modern regime of handicraft and self-help, therefore, was, among other things, the collapse of autocracy and the decay of coercive surveillance on the part of self-constituted authorities. With the redistribution of discretion and initiative in economic matters, consequent on and enforced by the new industrial system, the ancient animus of insubordination again took effect in the affairs of the community, threw the material interests and initiative of the individual into the foreground of policy, changed the "subject" into a "citizen," and went near to reducing the State to a condition of "innocuous desuetude" by making it a bureau for the administration of the public peace and the regulation of equity between private interests. All this drift of things away from the landmarks of the ancient dynastic regime has never reached a consummate outcome—the proliferation of English Natural Rights has never matured into a system of regulated anarchy, after the prehistoric pattern, although a speculative excursion in that direction has made its appearance now and again. Neither the large scale and intricate organization of modern industry and trade, nor the ever-present shadow of international discord, has permitted such an eventuality. . . .

An industrial system which, like the English, has been long engaged in a course of improvement, extension, innovation and specialization, will in the past have committed itself, more than once and in more than one connection, to what was at the time an adequate scale of appliance and schedule of processes and time adjustments. Partly by its own growth, and by force of technological innovations designed to enlarge the scale or increase the tempo of production or service, the accepted correlations in industry and in business, as well as the established equipment, are thrown out of date. And yet it is by no means an easy matter to find a remedy; more particularly is it difficult to find a remedy that will approve itself as a sound business proposition to a community of conservative businessmen who have a pecuniary interest in the continued working of the received system, and who will (commonly) not be endowed with much insight into technological matters anyway. So long as the obsolescence in question gives rise to no marked differential advantage of one or a group of these business men as against competing concerns, it follows logically that no remedy will be sought. An adequate remedy by detail innovation is not always practicable; indeed, in the more serious conjunctures of the kind it is virtually impossible, in that new items of equipment are necessarily required to conform to the specifications already governing the old.

So, e.g., it is well known that the railways of Great Britain, like those of other countries, are built with too narrow a gauge, but while this item of "depreciation through obsolescence" has been known for some time, it has not even in the most genial speculative sense come up for consideration as a remediable defect. In the same connection, American, and latterly German observers have been much impressed with the silly little bobtailed carriages used in the British goods traffic; which were well enough in their time, before American or German railway traffic was good for anything much, but which have at the best a playful air when brought up against the requirements of today. Yet the remedy is not a simple question of good sense. The terminal facilities, tracks, shunting facilities, and all the ways and means of handling freight on this oldest and most complete of railway systems, are all adapted to the bobtailed car. So, again, the roadbed and metal, as well as the engines, are well and substantially constructed to take care of such traffic as required to be taken care of when they first went into operation, and it is not easy to make a piecemeal adjustment to later requirements. It is perhaps true that as seen from the standpoint of the community at large and its material interest, the out-of-date equipment and organization should profitably be discarded—"junked," as the colloquial phrase has it—and the later contrivances substituted throughout; but it is the discretion of the business men that necessarily decides these questions, and the whole proposition has a different value as seen in the light of the competitive pecuniary interests of the business men in control.

This instance of the British railway system and its shortcomings in detail is typical of the British industrial equipment and organization throughout, although the obsolescence will for the most part, perhaps, be neither so obvious nor so serious a matter in many other directions. Towns, roadways, factories, harbors, habitations, were placed and constructed to meet the exigencies of what is now in a degree an obsolete state of the industrial arts, and they are, all and several, "irrelevant, incompetent and impertinent" in the same degree in which the technological scheme has shifted from what it was when these appliances were installed.[3] They have all been improved, "perfected," adapted, to meet changing requirements in some passable fashion; but the chief significance of this work of improvement, adaptation and repair in this connection is that it argues a fatal reluctance or inability to overcome this all-pervading depreciation by obsolescence.

All this does not mean that the British have sinned against the canons of technology. It is only that they are paying the penalty for having been thrown into the lead and so having shown the way.

Notes

1. It applies with at least equal cogency to the case of Japan, and indeed the Japanese case is strikingly analogous to that of Germany in this connection. Cf. "The Opportunity of Japan," in the *Journal of Race Development*, July 1915.

2. Cf. Werner Sombart, *Der moderne Kapitalismus,* bk. i,. chs. v, vi, vii, De Bourgeois, "Einleitung," ch. ii; W. J. Ashley, *English Economic History and Theory*, bk. ii. ch. vi.; and authors referred to by these writers.

3. Even in such an all-underlying and specifically British line of work as the iron industry, observers from other countries—e.g., German, Swedish or American—have latterly had occasion to find serious and sarcastic fault with the incompetently diminutive blast-furnaces, the antiquated appliances for moving materials, and the out-of-date contrivances for wasting labor and fuel.

The Case of the United States

The Captain of Industry

The Captain of Industry is one of the major institutions of the nineteenth century. He has been an institution of civilized life—a self-sufficient element in the scheme of law and custom—in much the same sense as the Crown, or the Country Gentlemen, or the Priesthood, have been institutions, or as they still are in those places where the habits of thought which they embody still have an institutional force.[1] For a hundred years or so he was, cumulatively, the dominant figure in civilized life, about whose deeds and interest law and custom have turned, the central and paramount personal agency in Occidental civilization. Indeed, his great vogue and compelling eminence are not past yet, so far as regards his place in popular superstition and in the make-believe of political strategy, but it is essentially a glory standing over out of the past, essentially a superstition.[2] As regards the material actualities of life, the captain of industry is no longer the central and directive force in that business traffic that governs the material fortunes of mankind; not much more so than the Crown, the Country Gentleman, or the Priesthood.

Considered as an institution, then, the captain of industry is the personal upshot of that mobilization of business enterprise that arose out of the industrial use of the machine process. And the period of his ascendancy is, accordingly, that era of (temperately) free competition that lies between the Industrial Revolution of the eighteenth century and the rise of corporation finance in the nineteenth, and so tapering off into the competitive twilight-zone of the later time when competition was shifting from industry to finance. But in the time of his ascendancy the old-fashioned competitive system came up, flourished, and eventually fell into decay, all under the ministering hand of the Captain.

As is likely to be true of any institution that eventually counts for much in

The editor wishes to thank Becky Veblen Meyers for permission to reprint from chapter 6 of *Absentee Ownership and Business Enterprise in Recent Times*, New York: B.W. Huebsch, 1923.

human life and culture, so also the captain of industry arose out of small beginnings which held no clear promise of a larger destiny. The prototype rather than the origin of the captain of industry is to be seen in the Merchant Adventurer of an earlier age, or as he would be called after he had grown to larger dimensions and become altogether sessile, the Merchant Prince. In the beginning the captain was an adventurer in industrial enterprise—hence the name given him; very much as the itinerant merchant of the days of the petty trade had once been an adventurer in commerce. He was a person of insight—perhaps chiefly industrial insight—and of initiative and energy, who was able to see something of the industrial reach and drive of that new mechanical technology that was finding its way into the industries, and who went about to contrive ways and means of turning these technological resources to new uses and a larger efficiency; always with a view to his own gain from turning out a more serviceable product with greater expedition. He was a captain of workmanship at the same time that he was a business man; but he was a good deal of a pioneer in both respects, inasmuch as he was on new ground in both respects. In many of the industrial ventures into which initiative led him, both the mechanical working and the financial sanity of the new ways and means were yet to be tried out, so that in both respects he was working out an adventurous experiment rather than watchfully waiting for the turn of events. In the typical case, he was business manager of the venture as well as foreman of the works, and not infrequently he was the designer and master builder of the equipment, of which he was also the responsible owner.[3] Typical of the work and spirit of these Captains of the early time are the careers of the great tool-builders of the late eighteenth and early nineteenth century.[4]

Such, it is believed, were many of those to whom the mechanical industries owed their rapid growth and sweeping success in the early time, both in production and in earning-capacity; and something of this sort is the typical Captain of Industry as he has lived, and still lives, in the affections of his countrymen. Such also is the type-form in terms of which those substantial citizens like to think of themselves, who aspire to the title. If this characterization may appear large and fanciful to an unbelieving generation, at least the continued vogue of it both as a popular superstition and as a business man's day-dream will go to show that the instinct of workmanship is not dead yet even in those civilized countries where it has become eternally right and good that workmanship should wait on business. The disposition to think kindly of workmanlike service is still extant in these civilized nations, at least in their day-dreams; although business principles have put it in abeyance so far as regards any practical effect.

In fact, it seems to be true that many, perhaps most, of those persons who amassed fortunes out of the proceeds of industry during this early period (say, 1760–1860), and who thereby acquired merit, were not of this workmanlike or pioneering type, but rather came in for large gains by shrewd investment and conservative undertakings, such as would now be called safe and sane business.

Yet there will at the same time also have been so much of this spirit of initiative and adventure abroad in the conduct of industry, and it will have been so visible an element of industrial business-as-usual at that time, as to have enabled this type-form of the captain of industry to find lodgement in the popular belief; a man of workmanlike force and creative insight into the community's needs, who stood out on a footing of self-help, took large chances for large ideals, and came in for his gains as a due reward for work well done in the service of the common good, in designing and working out a more effective organization of industrial forces and in creating and testing out new and better processes of production. It is by no means easy at this distance to make out how much of popular myth-making went to set up this genial conception of the Captain in the popular mind, or how much more of the same engaging conceit was contributed toward the same preconception by the many-sided self-esteem of many substantial business men who had grown great by "buying in" and "sitting tight," and who would like to believe that they had done something to merit their gains. But however the balance may lie, between workmanship and salesmanship, in the make-up of the common run of those early leaders of industrial enterprise, it seems that there will have been enough of the master-workman in a sufficient number of them, and enough of adventure and initiative in a sufficient number of undertakings, to enable the popular fancy to set up and hold fast this genial belief in the typical captain of industry as a creative factor in the advance of the industrial arts; at the same time that the economists were able presently to set him up, under the name of "Entrepreneur," as a fourth factor of production, along with Land, Labor, and Capital. Indeed, it is on some such ground that men have come to be called "Captains of Industry" rather than captains of business. Experience and observation at any later period could scarcely have engendered such a conception of those absentee owners who control the country's industrial plant and trade on a restricted output.

By insensible degrees, as the volume of industry grew larger, employing a larger equipment and larger numbers of workmen, the business concerns necessarily also increased in size and in the volume of transactions, personal supervision of the work by the owners was no longer practicable, and personal contact and personal arrangements between the employer-owner and his workmen tapered off into impersonal wage contracts governed by custom and adjusted to the minimum which the traffic would bear. The employer-owner, an ever increasingly impersonal business concern, shifted more and more to a footing of accountancy in its relations with the industrial plant and its personnel, and the oversight of the works passed by insensible degrees into the hands of technical experts who stood in a business relation to the concern, as its employees responsible to the concern for working the plant to such a fraction of its productive capacity as of the condition the market warranted for the time being.

So the function of the entrepreneur, the captain of industry, gradually fell apart in a two-fold division of labor, between the business manager and industrial work on the one side and the technician and the office work on the other side. Gradually more and more, by this shift and division, the captain of industry developed into a captain of business, and that part of his occupation which had given him title to his name and rank as captain of "industry" passed into alien hands. Expert practical men, practical in the way of tangible performance, men who had, or need have, no share in the prospective net gain and no responsibility for the concern's financial transactions, unbusinesslike technicians, began to be drawn into the management of the industry on the tangible side. It was a division of labor and responsibility, between the employer-owners who still were presumed to carry on the business of the concern and who were responsible to themselves for its financial fortunes, and on the other hand the expert industrial men who took over the tangible performance of production and were responsible to their own sense of workmanship.

Industry and business gradually split apart, in so far as concerned the personnel and the day's work. The employer-owners shifted farther over on their own ground as absentee owners, but continued to govern the volume of production and the conditions of life for the working personnel on the businesslike principle of the net gain in terms of price. While the tangible performance of so much work as the absentee owners considered to be wise fell increasingly under the management of that line of technicians out of which there grew in time the engineering profession, with its many duties, grades, and divisions and its ever numerous and increasingly specialized personnel. It was a gradual shift and division, of course. So gradual, indeed, that while it had set in in a small way before the close of the eighteenth century, it had not yet been carried through to so rigorous a finish as to have warranted its recognition in the standard economic theories. In the manuals the captain of industry still figures as the enterprising investor-technician of the days of the beginning, and as such he still is a certified article of economic doctrine under the caption of the "Entrepreneur."

The industrial arts are a matter of tangible performance directed to work that is designed to be of material use to man, and all the while they are calling for an increasingly exhaustive knowledge of material fact and an increasingly close application to the work in hand. The realities of the technician's world are mechanistic realities, matters of material fact. And the responsibilities of the technician, as such, are responsibilities of workmanship only; in the last resort responsibilities to his own sense of workmanlike performance, which might well be called the engineer's conscience. On the other hand the arts of business are arts of bargaining, effrontery, salesmanship, make-believe, and are directed to the gain of the business man at the cost of the community, at large and in detail. Neither tangible performance nor the common good is a business proposition. Any material use which his traffic may service is quite beside the business man's purpose, except indirectly, in so far as it may serve to influence his clientele to his advantage.

But the arts of business, too, call all the while for closer application to the work in hand. Throughout recent times salesmanship has come in for a steadily increasing volume and intensity of attention, and great things have been achieved along that line. But the work in hand in business traffic is not tangible performance. The realities of the business world are money-values; that is to say matters of make-believe which have the sanction of law and custom and are upheld by the policies in case of need. The business man's care is to create needs to be satisfied at a price paid to himself. The engineer's care is to provide for these needs, so far as the business men in the background find their advantage in allowing it. But law and custom have little to say to the engineer, except to keep his hands off the work when the interests of business call for a temperate scarcity.

So, by force of circumstances the captain of industry came in the course of time and growth to be occupied wholly with the financial end of those industrial ventures of which he still continued to be the captain. The spirit of enterprise in him took a turn of sobriety. He became patient and attentive to details, with an eye single to his own greater net gain in terms of price. His conduct came to be framed more and more on lines of an alert patience, moderation, assurance, and conservatism; that is to say, his conduct would have to fall into these lines if he was to continue as a Captain under the changing circumstances of the time. Changing circumstances called for a new line of strategy in those who would survive as Captains and come into the commanding positions in the business community, and so into control of the industrial system. It should perhaps rather be said that the force of changing circumstances worked a change in the character of the Captains by eliminating the Captains of the earlier type from the more responsible position and favoring the substitution of persons endowed with other gifts and trained to other ideals and other standards of conduct; in short, men more nearly on the order of safe and sane business, such as have continued to be well at home in responsible affairs since then.

Under the changing circumstances the captains of industry of the earlier type fell to second rank, became lieutenants, who presently more and more lost standing, as being irresponsible, fanciful project-makers, footless adventures, fit only to work out innovations that were of doubtful expediency in a business way, creators of technological disturbances that led to obsolescence of equipment and therefore to shrinkage of assets. Such men are persons whom it is not for the safe and sane Captains of the newer type to countenance; but who should be handled with circumspection and made the most of, as project-makers whose restless initiative and immature versatility is counted on to bring about all sorts of unsettling and irritating changes in the conditions of industry; but who may also, now and again, bring in something that will give some patiently alert business man a new advantage over his rivals in business, if he has the luck or the shrewdness to grasp it firmly and betimes. Under the changed circumstances the spirit of venturesome enterprise is more than likely to foot up as a hunting of trouble, and wisdom in business enterprise has more and more settled down to the wisdom of "Watchful Waiting."[5]

The changing circumstances by force of which the conduct of industrial business so gradually came under the hands of a saner generations of Captains, actuated more singly by a conservative estimate of the net gain for themselves—these circumstances have already been recited in an earlier passage, in sketching the rise and derivation of the business corporation and the conditions which brought corporation finance into action as the ordinary means of controlling the output of industry and turning it to the advantage of absentee owners. So far as these determining circumstances admit of being enumerated in an itemized way they were such as follows: (a) the industrial arts, in the mechanical industries, grew gradually into a complex and extensive technology which called for a continually more exhaustive and more exact knowledge of material facts, such as to give rise to engineers, technicians, industrial experts; (b) the scale on which industrial processes were carried out grew greater in the leading industries, so as to require the men in charge to give their undivided attention to the technical conduct, the tangible performance of the work in hand; (c) the business concerns in which was vested the ownership and control of the industrial equipment and its working also grew larger, carried a larger volume of transactions, took on more of an impersonally financial character, and eventually passed over into the wholly impersonal form of the corporation or joint-stock company, with limited liability; (d) the continued advance of the industrial arts, in range, scope, and efficiency, increased the ordinary productive capacity of the leading industries to such a degree that there was continually less and less question of their being able to supply the market and continually more and more danger that the output would exceed what the market could carry off at prices that would yield a reasonable profit—that is to say the largest obtainable profit; (e) loosely speaking, production had overtaken the market; (f) eventually corporation finance came into action and shifted the point of businesslike initiative and discretion from the works and their management, and even from the running volume of transactions carried by the business office of the concern, to the negotiation and maintenance of a running volume of credit; (g) the capitalization of credit with fixed charges, as involved in the corporate organization, precluded shrinkage, recession, or retrenchment of assets or earnings, and so ordinarily precluded a lowering of prices or an undue increase of output—undue for purposes of the net gain. Business enterprise, therefore, ceased progressively to be compatible with free-swung industrial enterprise, and a new order of businesslike management went progressively into action, and shuffled a new type of persons into the positions of responsibility; men with an eye more single to the main chance at the cost of any whom it may concern.

Among these circumstances that so made for a new order in industrial business the one which is, presumably, the decisive one beyond the rest is the growing productive capacity of industry wherever and so far as the later advances in industrial process are allowed to go into effect. By about the middle of the nineteenth century it can be said without affectation that the leading industries were beginning to be inordinately productive, as rated in terms of what the traffic would bear; that is to say as counted in terms of net gain. Free-swung production, approaching the full productive capacity of the equipment and the available manpower, was no longer to be tolerated in ordinary times. It became ever more imperative to observe a duly graduated moderation and to govern the volume of output, not by the productive capacity of the plant or the working capacity of the workmen, nor by the consumptive needs of the consumers, but by what the traffic would bear; which was then habitually and increasingly coming to mean a modicum of employment both of the plant and the available manpower. It was coming to be true, increasingly, that the ordinary equipment of industry and the available complement of workmen were not wanted for daily use, but only for special occasions and during seasons of exceptionally brisk trade. Unemployment, in other words sabotage, to use a word of later date, was becoming an everyday care of the business management in the mechanical industries, and was already on the way to become, what it is today, the most engrossing care that habitually engages the vigilance of the business executives. And sabotage can best be taken care of in the large; so that the corporations, and particularly the larger corporations, would be in a particularly fortunate position to administer the routine of salutary sabotage. And when the Captain of Industry then made the passage from industrial adventurer to corporation financier it become the ordinary care of his office as Captain to keep a restraining hand on employment and output, and so administer a salutary running margin of a sabotage on production, at the cost of the underlying populations.[6]

But the account is not complete with a description of what the Captain of Industry has done toward the standardization of business methods and the stabilization of industrial enterprise, and of what the new order of business-as-usual has done toward the standardization of the Captain and eventually towards his neutralization and abeyance. As has already been remarked, he was one of the major institutions of the nineteenth century, and as such he has left his mark on the culture of that time and after, in other bearings as well as in the standards of business enterprise. As has also been remarked above, the Captain of Industry and his work and interests presently became the focus of attention and deference. The Landed Interest, the political buccaneers, and the priesthood, yielded him the first place in affairs and in the councils of the nation, civil and political. With the forward movement from that state of things in which business was conceived to be the servant of industry to that more mature order of things under which industry became the servant of business which lives and moves on the higher level of finance at large—as this progression took effect and reshaped the Captain to its uses, the growth of popular sentiment kept pace with the march of facts, so that the popular ideal came to be the prehensile business man rather than the creative driver of industry; the sedentary man of means, the Captain of Solvency. And all the while the illusions of nationalism allowed the underlying population to believe that the common good was bound up with the business advantage of these captains of solvency, into whose service the national establishment was gradually driven, more and more unreservedly, until it has become an axiomatic rule that all the powers of government and diplomacy must work together for the benefit of the business interests of the larger sort. Not that the constituted authorities have no other cares, but these other cares are, after all, in all the civilized nations, in the nature of secondary considerations, matters to be taken care of when and so far as the paramount exigencies of business will allow.

In all this there is, of course, nothing radically new, in principle. In principle it all comes to much the same thing as the older plan which this era of business, big and little, has displaced. So long as nationalism has held sway, the care and affectionate price of the underlying population has, in effect, ever centered on the due keep of the nation's kept classes. It is only that by force of circumstances the captain of industry, or in more accurate words the captain of solvency, has in recent times come to be the effectual spokesman and type-form of the kept classes as well as the keeper and dispenser of their keep; very much as the War Lord of the barbarian raids, or the baron of the Middle Ages, or the Prince of the era of statemaking, or the Priesthood early and late in Christendom, have all and several, each in their time, place and degree, stood out as the spokesman and exemplar of the kept classes, and served as the legitimate channel by which the community's surplus product has been drained off and consumed, to the greater spiritual comfort of all parties concerned.

It is only that the superstitions of absentee ownership and business principles have come into the first place among those "Superstitions of the Herd" which go to make up the spirit of national integrity. The moral excellence and public utility of the kept classes that now march under the banners of absentee ownership and business enterprise are no more to be doubted by the loyal citizens of the Christian nations today than the similar excellence and utility of the princely establishment and the priestly ministrations which have drained the resources of the underlying population in an earlier and ruder age. And the princes of solvency and free income no more doubt their own excellence and utility than the princes of the divine grace or the prelates of the divine visitations have done in their time. It is only a shifting of the primacy among the civilized institutions, with the effect that the princes and the priests of the Grace and the Mercy now habitually creep in under the now impervious cloak of the prince and priest of business; very much as the business adventurer of an earlier day crept in under the sheltering cloak of the prince and the priest of the Grace and the Mercy, on whom the superstitions that were dominant in that time then bestowed the usufruct of the underlying population. For in the nineteenth century the captain of business became, in the popular apprehension, a prince after the order of Melchizedech, holding the primacy in secular and spiritual concerns.

Men are moved by many impulses and driven by many instinctive dispositions. Among these abiding dispositions are a strong bent to admire and defer to persons of achievement and distinction, as well as a workmanlike disposition to find merit in any work that serves the common good. The distinction which is admired and deferred to may often be nothing more to the point than a conventional investiture of rank attained by the routine of descent, as, e.g., a king, or by the routine of seniority, as, e.g., a prelate.

There is commonly no personal quality which a bystander can distinguish in these personages. The case of the Mikado in the times of the Shogunate is perhaps extreme, but it can by no means be said to be untrue or unfair as an illustrative instance of how the predilection for deference will find merit even in a personage who, for all that is known of him, has no personal attributes, good, bad, or indifferent. The kings and prelates of Christendom are only less perfect instances of the same. It is in these cases a matter of distinction, of course, with no hint of achievement, except such achievement as a loyal deference is bound to impute.[7] It is usual, indeed it seems inevitable, in all such instances of the conventional exaltation of nothing-in-particular, that there is also imputed to the person who so becomes a personage something in the way of service to the common good. Men like to believe that the personages whom they so admire by force of conventional routine are also of some use, as well as of great distinction—that they even somehow contribute, or at least conduce, to the material well-being at large. Which is presumably to be set down as one of the wonders wrought by the instinct of workmanship, which will not let men be content without some colorable serviceability in the personages which they so create out of nothing-in-particular.

But where there is also achievement, great deeds according to that fashion of exploits that has the vogue for the time being, this will of itself create distinction and erect a personage. Such is the derivation of the captain of industry in the nineteenth century. Men had learned, at some cost, that their exalted personages created *ad hoc* by incantation were of something less than no use to the common good, that at the best and cheapest they were something in the nature of a blameless bill of expense. The civilized nations had turned democratic, so much of them as had a fairly colorable claim to be called civilized; and so they had been left without their indispensable complement of personages to whom to defer and to whom to impute merit. In so far as the ground had been cleared of institutional holdovers from predemocratic times, there remained but one workable ground of distinction on which a practicable line of personages at large could be erected, such as would meet the ever-insistent need of some intoxicating make-believe of the kind. Democratically speaking, distinction at large could be achieved only in the matter of ownership, but when ownership was carried well out along the way of absentee ownership it was found to do very nicely as a base on which to erect a colorable personage, sufficient to carry decently full charge of imputed merit.[8] It results that under the aegis of democracy one's betters must be better in point of property qualification, from which the civic virtues flow by ready force of imputation.

So the captain of industry came into the place of first consequence and took up the responsibilities of exemplar, philosopher and friend at large to civilized mankind; and no man shall say that he has not done as well as might be expected. Neither has he fallen short in respect of a becoming gravity through it all. The larger the proportion of the community's wealth and income which he has taken over, the larger the deference and imputation of merit imputed to him, and the larger and graver that affable condescension and stately benevolence that habitually adorn the character of the large captains of solvency. There is no branch or department of the humanities in which the substantial absentee owner is not competent to act as guide, philosopher and friend, whether in his own conceit or in the estimation of his underlying population—in art and literature, in church and state, in science and education, in law and morals—and the underlying population is well content. And nowhere does the pecuniary personage stand higher or more secure as the standard container of the civic virtues than in democratic America; as should be the case, of course, since America is the most democratic of them all. And nowhere else does the captain of big business rule the affairs of the nation, civil and political, and control the conditions of life so unreservedly as in democratic America; as should also be the case, inasmuch as the acquisition of absentee ownership is, after all, in the popular apprehension, the most meritorious and the most necessary work to be done in this country.

Notes

1. An institution is of the nature of a usage which has become axiomatic and indispensable by habituation and general acceptance. Its physiological counterpart would presumably be any one of those habitual addictions that are now attracting the experts in sobriety.

2. He is also still a dominant figure in the folklore of Political Economy.

3. Cf. *The Engineers and the Price System*, ch. ii, "The Industrial System and the Captains of Industry."

4. Cf. Roes, *British and American Tool-Builders.*

5. Doubtless this form of words, "watchful waiting," will have been employed in the first instance to describe the frame of mind of a toad who has reached years of discretion and has found his appointed place along some frequented run where many flies and spiders pass and repass on their way to complete that destiny to which it has pleased an all-seeing and merciful Providence to call them; but by an easy turn of speech it has also been found suitable to describe the safe and sane strategy of that mature order of captains of industry who are governed by sound business principles. There is a certain bland sufficiency spread across the face of such a toad so circumstanced, while his comely personal bulk gives assurance of a pyramidal stability of principles.

And the sons of Mary smile and are blessed—
they know the angels are on their side,
They know in them is the Grace confessed,
and for them are the Mercies multiplied.

They sit at the Feet, and they hear the Word—
they know how truly the Promise runs.
They have cast their burden upon the Lord,
and—the Lord, He lays it on Martha's sons.
—Rudyard Kipling

6. As someone with a taste for slang and aphorism has said it, "In the beginning the Captain of industry set out to do something, and in the end he sat down to do somebody."

7. As a blameless instance of this human avidity for deference and exaltation of personages, a certain Square on Manhattan Island has lately been renamed in honor of a certain military personage who was once, in an emergency, appointed to high rank and responsibility because there was nothing better available under the routine of seniority, and of whose deeds and attainments the most laudatory encomium has found nothing substantially better to say than that it might have been worse. And it is by no means an isolated case.

8. Exception may be taken to all this, to the effect that the requisite personages can always be found in the shape of gentlemen at large—"country gentlemen" or "Southern Gentlemen," or what not—and "Best Families" who sit secure on a prescriptive gentility of birth and breeding. But in this bearing and seen in impersonal perspective, Gentlemen and Best Families are best to be defined as "absentee ownership in the consumptive phase," just as the captain of industry may likewise be spoken of impersonally as absentee ownership in the acquisitive phase; which brings the case back to the point of departure.

The Independent Farmer

The case of the American farmer is conspicuous; though it can scarcely be called singular, since in great part it is rather typical of the fortune which has overtaken the underlying populations throughout Christendom under the dominion of absentee ownership in its later developed phase. Much the same general run of conditions recurs elsewhere in those respects which engage the fearsome attention of these farmers. By and large, the farmer is so placed in the economic system that both as producer and as consumer he deals with business concerns which are in a position to make the terms of the traffic, which it is for him to take or leave. Therefore the margin of benefit that comes to him from his work is commonly at a minimum. He is commonly driven by circumstances over which he has no control, the circumstances being made by the system of absentee ownership and its business enterprise. Yet he is, on the whole, an obstinately loyal supporter of the system of law and custom which so make the conditions of life for him.

His unwavering loyalty to the system is in part a holdover from that obsolete past when he was the Independent Farmer of the poets; but in part it is also due to the still surviving persuasion that he is on his way, by hard work and shrewd management, to acquire a "competence"; such as will enable him some day to take his due place among the absentee owners of the land and so come in for an easy livelihood at the cost of the rest of the community; and in part it is also due to the persistent though fantastic opinion that his own present interest is bound up with the system of absentee ownership, in that he is himself an absentee owner by so much as he owns land and equipment which he works with hired help—always presuming that he is such an owner, in effect or in prospect.

It is true, the farmer-owners commonly are absentee owners to this extent.

The editor wishes to thank Becky Veblen Meyers for permission to reprint from chapter 7 of *Absentee Ownership and Business Enterprise in Recent Times,* New York: B. W. Huebsch, 1923.

Farming is team-work. As it is necessarily carried on by current methods in the great farming sections, farm work runs on such a scale that no individual owner can carry on by use of his own personal work alone, or by use of the man-power of his own household alone—which makes him an absentee owner by so much. But it does not, in the common run, make him an absentee owner of such dimensions as are required in order to create an effectual collusive control of the market, or such as will enable him, singly or collectively, to determine what charges the traffic shall bear. It leaves him still effectually in a position to take or leave what is offered at the discretion of those massive absentee interests that move in the background of the market.[1]

Always, of course, the farmer has with him the abiding comfort of his illusions, to the effect that he is in some occult sense the "Independent Farmer," and that he is somehow by way of achieving a competence of absentee ownership by hard work and sharp practice, some day; but in practical effect, as things habitually work out, he is rather to be called a quasi-absentee owner, or perhaps a pseudo-absentee owner, being too small a parcel of absentee ownership to count as such in the outcome. But it is presumably all for the best, or at least it is expedient for business-as-usual, that the farmer should continue to nurse his illusions and go about his work; that he should go on his way to complete that destiny to which it has pleased an all-seeing and merciful Providence to call him.

From colonial times and through the greater part of its history as a republic America has been in the main an agricultural country. Farming has been the staple occupation and has employed the greater part of the population. And the soil has always been the chief of those natural resources which the American people have taken over and made into property. Through the greater part of its history the visible growth of the country has consisted in the extension of the cultivated area and the increasing farm output, farm equipment, and farm population. This progressive taking-over and settlement of the farming lands is the most impressive material achievement of the American people, as it is also the most serviceable work which they have accomplished hitherto. It still is, as it ever has been, the people's livelihood; and the rest of the industrial system has in the main, grown up, hitherto, as a subsidiary or auxiliary, adopted to and limited by the needs and the achievements of the country's husbandry. The incentives and methods engaged in this taking-over of the soil, as well as the industrial and institutional consequences that have followed, are accordingly matters of prime consideration in any endeavor to understand or explain the national character and the temperamental bent which underlies it.

The farm population—that farm population which has counted substantially toward this national achievement—have been a ready, capable and resourceful body of workmen. And they have been driven by the incentives already spoken of in an earlier passage as being characteristic of the English-speaking colonial enterprise—individual self-help and cupidity. Except transiently and provisionally, and with doubtful effect, this farm population has nowhere and at no time been actuated by a spirit of community interest in dealing with any of their material concerns. Their community spirit, in material concerns, has been quite notably scant and precarious, in spite of the fact that they have long been exposed to material circumstances of a wide-sweeping uniformity such as should have engendered a spirit of community interest and made for collective enterprise, and such as could have made any effectual collective enterprise greatly remunerative to all concerned. But they still stand sturdily by the timeworn make-believe that they still are individually self-sufficient masterless men, and through good report and evil report they have remained Independent Farmers, as between themselves, which is all that is left of their independence—Each for himself, etc.

Of its kind, this is an admirable spirit, of course; and it has achieved many admirable results, even though the results have not all been to the gain of the farmers. Their self-help and cupidity have left them at the mercy of any organization that is capable of mass action and a steady purpose. So they have, in the economic respect—incidently in the civil and political respect—fallen under the dominion of those massive business interests that move obscurely in the background of the market and buy and sell and dispose of the farm products and the farmers' votes and opinions very much on their own terms and at their ease.

But all the while it remains true that they have brought an unexampled large and fertile body of soil to a very passable state of service, and their work continues to yield a comfortably large food supply to an increasing population, at the same time that it yields a comfortable run of free income to the country's kept classes. It is true, in the end the farm population find themselves at work for the benefit of business-as-usual, on a very modest livelihood. For farming is, perhaps necessarily, carried on in severalty and on a relatively small scale, even though the required scale exceeds what is possible on a footing of strict self-ownership of land and equipment by the cultivators; and there is always the pervading spirit of self-help and cupidity, which unavoidably defeats even that degree of collusive mass action that might otherwise be possible. Whereas the system of business interests in whose web the farmers are caught is drawn on a large scale, its units are massive, impersonal, imperturbable and, in effect, irresponsible, under the established order of law and custom, and they are interlocked in an unbreakable framework of common interests.

By and large, the case of America is as the case of the American farm population, and for the like reasons. For the incentives and ideals, the law and custom and the knowledge and belief, on which the farm population has gone about its work and has come to this pass, are the same as have ruled the growth and shaped the outcome for the community at large. Nor does the situation in America differ materially from the state of things elsewhere in the civilized countries, in so far as these others share in the same material civilization of Christendom.

In the American tradition, and in point of historical fact out of which the tradition has arisen, the farmer has been something of a pioneer. Loosely it can be said that the pioneering era is now closing, at least provisionally and regards farming. But while the pioneer-farmer is dropping out of the work of husbandry, his pioneer soul goes marching on. And it has been an essential trait of this American pioneering spirit to seize upon so much of the country's natural resources as the enterprising pioneer could lay hands on—in the case of the pioneer-farmer, so much of the land as he could get and hold possession of. The land had, as it still has, a prospective use and therefore a prospective value, a "speculative" value as it is called; and the farmer-pioneer was concerned with seizing upon this prospective value and turning it into net gain by way of absentee ownership, as much as the pioneer-farmer was concerned with turning the fertile soil to present use in the creation of a livelihood for himself and his household from day to day.

Habitually and with singular uniformity the American farmers have aimed to acquire real estate at the same time that they have worked at their trade as husbandmen. And real estate is a matter of absentee ownership, an asset whose value is based on the community's need of this given parcel of land for use as a means of livelihood, and the value of which is measured by the capitalized free income which the owner may expect to come in for by holding it for as high a rental as the traffic in this need will bear. So that the pioneering aim, in American farming, has been for the pioneer-farmers, each and several, to come in for as much of a free income at the cost of the rest of the community as the law would allow; which has habitually worked out in their occupying, each and several, something more than they could well take care of. They have habitually "carried" valuable real estate at the same time that they have worked the soil of so much of their land as they could take care of, in as effectual a manner as they could under these circumstances. They have been cultivators of the main chance as well as of the fertile soil; with the result that, by consequence of this intense and unbroken habituation, the farm population is today imbued with that penny-wise spirit of self-help and cupidity that now leaves them and their work and holdings at the disposal of those massive vested interests that know the uses of collusive mass action, as already spoken of above.

But aside from this spiritual effect which this protracted habituation to a somewhat picayune calculation of the main chance has had on the farmers' frame of mind, and aside from their consequent unfitness to meet the business-like maneuvers of the greater vested interests, this manner of pioneering enterprise which the farmers have habitually mixed into their farming has also had a more immediate bearing on the country's husbandry, and, indeed, on the industrial system as a whole. The common practice has been to "take up" more land than the farmer could cultivate, with his available means, and to hold it at some cost. Which has increased the equipment required for cultivation of the acres cultivated, and has also increased the urgency of the farmer's need of credit by help of which to find the needed equipment and meet the expenses incident to his holding his idle and semi-idle acres intact. And farm credit has been notoriously usurious. All this has had the effect of raising the cost of production of farm products; partly by making the individual farm that much more unwieldy as an instrument of production, partly by further enforcing the insufficiency and the make-shift character for which American farm equipment is justly famed, and partly also by increasing the distances over which the farm supplies and the farm products have had to be moved.

This last point marks one of the more serious handicaps of American farming, at the same time that it has contributed materially to enforce that "extensive," "superficial," and exhausting character of American farming which has arrested the attention of all foreign observers. In American practice the "farm area" has always greatly exceeded the "acreage under cultivation," even after all due allowance is made for any unavoidable inclusion of waste and half-waste acreage within the farm boundaries. Even yet, at the provisional close of the career of the American pioneer-farmer, the actual proportion of unused and half-used land included within and among the farms will materially exceed what the records show, and it greatly exceeds what any inexperienced observer will be able to credit. The period is not long past—if it is past—when, taking one locality with another within the great farming sections of the country, the idle and half-idle lands included in and among the farms equalled the acreage that was fully employed, even in that "extensive" fashion in which American farming has habitually been carried on.

But there is no need of insisting on this proportion of idle acreage, which none will credit who has not a wide and intimate knowledge of the facts in the case. For more or less—for as much as all intelligent observers will be ready to credit—this American practice has counted toward an excessively wide distribution of the cultivated areas, excessively long distances of transport, over roads which have by consequence been excessively bad—necessarily and notoriously so—and which have hindered communication to such a degree as in many instances to confine the cultivation to such crops as can be handled with a minimum of farm buildings and will bear the crudest kind of carriage over long distances and with incalculable delays. This applies not only to the farm-country's highways, but to its railway facilities as well. The American practice has doubled the difficulty of transportation and retarded the introduction of the more practicable and more remunerative methods of farming; until make-shift and haphazard have in many places become so ingrained in the habits of the farm population that nothing but abounding distress and the slow passing of generations can correct it all.[2] At the same time, as an incident by the way, this same excessive dispersion of the farming communities over long distances, helped out by bad roads, has been perhaps the chief factor in giving the retail business communities of the country towns their strangle-hold on the underlying farm population.

And it should surprise no one if a population which has been exposed to unremitting habituation of this kind has presently come to feel at home in it all;

so that the bootless chicanery of their self-help is rated as a masterly fabric of axiomatic realities, and sharp practice has become a matter of conscience. In such a community it should hold true that "An honest man will bear watching," that the common good is a by-word, that "Everybody's business is nobody's business," that public office is a private job, where the peak of aphoristic wisdom is reached in that red-letter formula of democratic politics, "Subtraction, division, and silence." So it has become a democratic principle that public office should go by rotation, under the rule of equal opportunity—equal opportunity to get something for nothing—but should go only to those who value the opportunity highly enough to make a desperate run for it. Here men "run" for office, not "stand" for it. Subtraction is the aim of this pioneer cupidity, not production; and salesmanship is its line of approach, not workmanship; and so, being in no way related quantitatively to a person's workmanlike powers or to his tangible performance, it has no "saturation point."[3]

The spirit of the American farmers, typically, has been that of the pioneer rather than the workman. They have been efficient workmen, but that is not the trait which marks them for its own and sets them off in contrast with the common run. Their passion for acquisition has driven them to work, hard and painfully, but they have never been slavishly attached to their work; their slavery has been not to an imperative bent of workmanship and human service, but to an indefinitely extensible cupidity which strives to work when other expedients fail; at least so they say. So they have been somewhat footloose in their attachment to the soil as well as somewhat hasty and shiftless in its cultivation. They have always, in the typical case, wanted something more than their proportionate share of the soil; not because they were driven by a felt need of doing more than their fair share of work or because they aimed to give the community more service than would be a fair equivalent of their own livelihood, but with a view to cornering something more than their proportion of the community's indispensable means of life and so getting a little something for nothing in allowing their holdings to be turned to account, for a good and valuable consideration.

The American farmers have been footloose, on the whole, more particularly that peculiarly American element among them who derive their traditions from a colonial pedigree. There has always been an easy shifting from country to town, and this steady drift into the towns of the great farming sections has in the main been a drift from work into business. And it has been the business of these country towns—what may be called their business-as-usual—to make the most of the necessities and the ignorance of their underlying farm population. The farmers have on the whole been ready to make such a shift whenever there has been an "opening"; that is to say, they have habitually been ready to turn their talents to more remunerative use in some other pursuit whenever the chance has offered, and indeed they have habitually been ready to make the shift out of husbandry into the traffic of the towns even at some risk whenever the prospect of a wider margin of net gain has opened before their eager eyes.

In all this pursuit of the net gain the farm population and their country-town cousins have carried on with the utmost good nature. The business communities of the country towns have uniformly got the upper hand. But the farmers have shown themselves good losers; they have in the main gracefully accepted the turn of things and have continued to count on meeting with better luck or making a shrewder play next time. But the upshot of it so far has habitually been that the farm population find themselves working for a very modest livelihood and the country towns come in for an inordinately wide margin of net gains; that is to say, net gain over necessary outlay and over the value of the services which they render their underlying farm populations.

To many persons who have some superficial acquaintance with the run of the facts it may seem, on scant reflection, that what is said above of the inordinate gains that go the country towns is a rash overstatement, perhaps even a malicious overstatement. It is not intended to say that the gains *per capita* of the persons currently engaged in business in the country towns, or the gains per cent, on the funds invested, are extraordinarily high; but only that as counted on the necessary rather than the actual cost of the useful work done, and as counted on the necessary rather than the actual number of persons engaged, the gains which go to the business traffic of the country towns are inordinately large.[4]

Notes

1. Cf. Wallace, *Farm Prices*.

2. As a side issue to this arrangement of magnificent distances in the fertile farm country, it may be called to mind that the education of the farm children has on this account continually suffered from enforced neglect, with untoward results. And there are those who believe that the noticeably high rate of insanity among farmers' wives in certain sections of the prairie country is traceable in good part to the dreary isolation enforced upon them by this American plan of "country life."

3. This civilized man's cupidity is one of those "higher wants of man" which the economists have found to be "indefinitely extensible," and like other spiritual needs it is self-authenticating, its own voucher.

The Latin phrase is *auri sacra fames,* which goes to show the point along the road to civilization reached by that people. They had reached a realization of the essentially sacramental virtue of this indefinitely extensible need of more; but the aurum in terms of which they visualized the object of their passion is after all a tangible object, with physical limitations of weight and space, such as to impose a mechanical "saturation point" on the appetite for its accumulation. But the civilized peoples of Christendom at large, and more particularly America, the most civilized and most Christian of them all, have in recent times removed this limitation. The object of this "higher want of man" is no longer specie, but some form of credit instrument which conveys title to a run of free income; and it can accordingly have no "saturation point," even in fancy, inasmuch as credit is also indefinitely extensible and stands in no quantitative relation to tangible fact.

4. It may be added, though it should scarcely be necessary, that a good part of the gains which are taken by the country-town business community passes through their hands into the hands of those massive vested interests that move obscurely in the background of the market, and to whom the country towns stand in a relation of feeders,

analogous to that in which the farm population stands to the towns. In good part the business traffic of the country towns serves as ways and means of net gain to the business interests in the background. But when all due allowance is made on this and other accounts, and even if this element which may be called net gains in transit be deducted, the statement as made above remains standing without material abatement; the business gains which come to the country towns in their traffic with their underlying farm populations are inordinately large, as counted on the necessary cost and use-value of the service rendered, or on the necessary work done. But whether these net gains, in so far as they are "inordinate"—that is in so far as they go in under the caption of Something for Nothing—are retained by the business men of the town or are by them passed on to the larger business interests which dominate them, that is an idle difference for all that concerns the fortunes of the underlying farm population or the community at large. In either case it is idle waste, so far as concerns the material well-being of any part of the farm population.

The Country Town

The country town of the great American farming region is the perfect flower of self-help and cupidity standardized on the American plan. Its name may be Spoon River or Gopher Prairie, or it may be Emporia or Centralia or Columbia. The pattern is substantially the same, and is repeated several thousand times with a faithful perfection which argues that there is no help for it, that it is worked out by uniform circumstances over which there is no control, and that it wholly falls in with the spirit of things and answers to the enduring aspirations of the community. The country town is one of the great American institutions; perhaps the greatest, in the sense that it has had and continues to have a greater part than any other in shaping public sentiment and giving character to American culture.

The location of any given town has commonly been determined by collusion between "interested parties" with a view to speculation in real estate, and it continues through its life-history (hitherto) to be managed as a real estate "proposition." Its municipal affairs, its civic pride, its community interest, converge upon its real estate values, which are invariably of a speculative character, and which all its loyal citizens are intent on "booming" and "boosting"—that is to say, lifting still farther off the level of actual ground-values as measured by the uses to which the ground is turned. Seldom do the current (speculative) values of the town's real estate exceed the use-value of it by less than 100 per cent.; and never do they exceed the actual values by less than 200 per cent., as shown by the estimates of the tax assessor; nor do the loyal citizens ever cease their endeavors to lift the speculative values to something still farther out of touch with the material facts. A country town which does not answer to these specifications is "a dead one," one that has failed to "make good," and need not be counted with, except as a warning to the unwary "boomer."[1] Real estate is the

The editor wishes to thank Becky Veblen Meyers for permission to reprint from chapter 7 of *Absentee Ownership and Business Enterprise in Recent Times,* New York: B. W. Huebsch, 1923.

one community interest that binds the townsmen with a common bond; and it is highly significant—perhaps it is pathetic, perhaps admirable—that those inhabitants of the town who have no holdings of real estate and who never hope to have any will commonly also do their little best to inflate the speculative values by adding the clamor of their unpaid chorus to the paid clamor of the profession publicity-agents, at the cost of so adding a little something to their own cost of living in the enhanced rentals and prices out of which the expense of publicity are to be met.

Real estate is an enterprise in "futures," designed to get something for nothing from the unwary, of whom it is believed by experienced persons that "there is one born every minute." So, farmers and townsmen together throughout the great farming region are pilgrims of hope looking forward to the time when the community's advancing needs will enable them to realize on the inflated values of their real estate, or looking more immediately to the chance that one or another of those who are "born every minute" may be so ill-advised as to take them at their word and become their debtors in the amount which they say their real estate is worth. The purpose of country-town real estate, as of farm real estate in a less extreme degree, is to realize on it. This is the common bond of community interest which binds and animates the business community of the country town. In this enterprise there is concerted action and a spirit of solidarity, as well as a running business of mutual maneuvering to get the better of one another. For eternal vigilance is the price of country-town real estate, being an enterprise in salesmanship.

Aside from this common interest in the town's inflated real estate, the townsmen are engaged in a vigilant rivalry, being competitors in the traffic carried on with the farm population. The town is a retail trading-station, where farm produce is bought and farm supplies are sold, and there are always more traders than are necessary to take care of this retail trade. So that they are each and several looking to increase their own share in this trade at the expense of their neighbors in the same line. There is always more or less active competition, often underhand. But this does not hinder collusion between the competitors with a view to maintain and augment their collective hold on the trade with their farm population.

From an early point in the life-history of such a town collusion habitually becomes the rule, and there is commonly a well-recognized ethical code of collusion governing the style and limits of competitive maneuvers which any reputable trader may allow himself. In effect, the competition among business concerns engaged in any given line of traffic is kept well in hand by a common understanding, and the traders as a body direct their collective efforts to getting what can be got out of the underlying farm population. It is on this farm trade also, and on the volume and increase of it, past and prospective, that the real estate values of the town rest. As one consequence, the volume and profit of the farm trade is commonly over-stated, with a view to enhancing the town's real estate values.

Quite as a matter of course the business of the town arranges itself under such regulations and usages that it foots up to a competition, not between the business concerns, but between town and country, between traders and customers. And quite as a matter of course, too, the number of concerns doing business in any one town greatly exceeds what is necessary to carry on the traffic; with the result that while the total profits of the business in any given town are inordinately large for the work done, the profits of any given concern are likely to be modest enough. The more successful ones among them commonly do very well and come in for large returns on their outlay, but the average returns per concern or per man are quite modest, and the less successful ones are habitually doing business within speaking-distance of bankruptcy. The number of failures is large, but they are habitually replaced by others who still have something to lose. The conscientiously habitual overstatements of the real estate interests continually draw new traders into the town, for the retail trade of the town also gets its quota of such persons as are born every minute, who then transiently become supernumerary retail traders. Many fortunes are made in the country towns, often fortunes of very respectable proportions, but many smaller fortunes are also lost.

Neither the causes nor the effects of this state of things have been expounded by the economists, nor has it found a place in the many formulations of theory that have to do with the retail trade; presumably because it is all, under the circumstances, so altogether "natural" and unavoidable. Exposition of the obvious is a tedious employment, and a recital of commonplaces does not hold the interest of readers or audience. Yet, for completeness of argument, it seems necessary here to go a little farther into the details and add something on the reasons for this arrangement. However obvious and natural it may be it is after all serious enough to merit the attention of anyone who is interested in the economic situation as it stands, or in finding a way out of this situation; which is just now (1923) quite perplexing, as the futile endeavors of the statesmen will abundantly demonstrate.

However natural and legitimate it all undoubtedly may be, the arrangement as it runs today imposes on the country's farm industry an annual overhead charge which runs into ten or twelve figures, and all to the benefit of no one. This overhead charge of billions, due to duplication of work, personnel, equipment, and traffic, in the country towns is, after all, simple and obvious waste. Which is perhaps to be deprecated, although one may well hesitate to find fault with it all, inasmuch as it is all a simple and obvious outcome of those democratic principles of self-help and cupidity on which the commonwealth is founded. These principles are fundamentally and eternally right and good—so long as popular sentiment runs to that effect—and they are to be accepted gratefully, with the defects of their qualities. The whole arrangement is doubtless all right and worth its cost; indeed it is avowed to be the chief care and most righteous solicitude of the constituted authorities to maintain and cherish it all.

To an understanding of the country town and its place in the economy of

American farming it should be noted that in the great farming regions any given town has a virtual monopoly of the trade within the territory tributary to it. This monopoly is neither complete nor indisputable; it does not cover all lines of traffic equally nor is outside competition completely excluded in any line. But the broad statement is quite sound, that within its domain any given country town in the farming country has a virtual monopoly of trade in those main lines of business in which the townsmen are chiefly engaged. And the townsmen are vigilant in taking due precautions that this virtual monopoly shall not be broken in upon. It may be remarked by the way that this characterization applies to the country towns of the great farming country, and only in a less degree to the towns of the industrial and outlying sections.

Under such a (virtual) monopoly the charge collected on the traffic adjusts itself, quite as a matter of course, to what the traffic will bear. It has no other relation to the costs or the use-value of the service rendered. But what the traffic will bear is something to be determined by experience and is subject to continued readjustment and revision, with the effect of unremittingly keeping the charge close up to the practicable maximum. Indeed, there is reason to believe that the townsmen are habitually driven by a conscientious cupidity and a sense of equity to push the level of charges somewhat over the maximum; that is to say, over the rate which would yield them the largest net return. Since there are too many of them they are so placed as habitually to feel that they come in for something short of their just desserts, and their endeavor to remedy this state of things is likely to lead to overcharging rather than the reverse.

What the traffic will bear in this retail trade is what the farm population will put up with, without breaking away and finding their necessary supplies and disposing of their marketable products elsewhere, in some other town, through itinerant dealers, by recourse to brokers at a distance, through the mail-order concerns, and the like. The two dangerous outside channels of trade appear to be the rival country towns and the mail-order houses, and of these the mail-order houses are apparently the more real menace as well as the more dreaded. Indeed they are quite cordially detested by right-minded country-town dealers. The rival country towns are no really grave menace to the usurious charges of any community of country-town business men, since they are all and several in the same position, and none of them fails to charge all comers all that the traffic will bear.

There is also another limiting condition to be considered in determining what the traffic will bear in this retail trade, though it is less, or at least less visibly, operative; namely, the point beyond which the charges can not enduringly be advanced without discouraging the farm population unduly; that is to say, the point beyond which the livelihood of the farm population will be cut into so severely by the overcharging of the retail trade that they begin to decide that they have nothing more to lose, and so give up and move out. This critical point appears not commonly to be reached in the ordinary retail trade—as, e.g., groceries, clothing, hardware—possibly because there still remains, practicable in an extremity, the recourse to outside dealers of one sort or another. In the business of country-town banking, however, and similar money-lending by other persons than the banks, the critical point is not infrequently reached and passed. Here the local monopoly is fairly complete and rigorous, which brings on an insistent provocation to over-reach.

And then, too, the banker deals in money-values, and money-values are forever liable to fluctuate; at the same time that the fortunes of the banker's farm clients are subject to the vicissitudes of the seasons and of the markets; and competition drives both banker and client to base their habitual rates, not on a conservative anticipation of what is likely to happen but on the lucky chance of what may come to pass barring accidents and the acts of God. And the baker is under necessity—"inner necessity," as the Hegelians would say—of getting all he can and securing himself against all risk, at the cost of any whom it may concern, by such charges and stipulations as will insure his net gain in any event.

It is the business of the country-town business community, one with another, to charge what the traffic will bear; and the traffic will bear charges that are inordinately high as counted on the necessary cost or the use-value of the work to be done. It follows, under the common-sense logic of self-help, cupidity, and business-as-usual, that men eager to do business on a good margin will continue to drift in and cut into the traffic until the number of concerns among whom the gains are to be divided is so large that each one's share is no more than will cover costs and leave a "reasonable" margin of net gain. So that while the underlying farm population continues to yield inordinately high rates on the traffic, the business concerns engaged, one with another, come in for no more than what will induce them to go on; the reasons being that in the retail trade as conducted on this plan of self-help and equal opportunity the stocks, equipment and man-power employed will unavoidably exceed what is required for the work, by some 200 to 1000 percent—those lines of the trade being the more densely over-populated which enjoy the nearest approach to a local monopoly, as, e.g., groceries, or banking.[2]

It is perhaps not impertinent to call to mind that the retail trade throughout, always and everywhere, runs on very much the same plan of inordinately high charges and consequently extravagant multiplication of stock, equipment, work, personnel, publicity, credits, and costs. It runs to the same effect in city, town and country. And in city, town or country town it is in all of these several respects the country's largest business enterprise in the aggregate; and always something like three-fourths to nine-tenths of it is idle waste, to be canceled out of the community's working efficiency as lag, leak and friction. When the statesmen and the newspapers—and other publicity-agencies—speak for the security and the meritorious work of the country's business men, it is something of this sort they are talking about. The bulk of the country's business is the retail trade, and in an eminent sense the retail trade is business-as-usual.

The retail trade, and therefore in its degree the country town, have been the home ground of American culture and the actuating center of public affairs and public sentiment throughout the nineteenth century, ever more securely and unequivocally as the century advanced and drew toward its close. In American parlance "The Public," so far as it can be defined, has meant those persons who are engaged in and about the business of the retail trade, together with such of the kept classes as draw their keep from this traffic. The road to success has run into and through the country town, or its retail-trade equivalent in the cities, and the habits of thought engendered by the preoccupations of the retail trade have shaped popular sentiment and popular morals and have dominated public policy in what was to be done and what was to be left undone, locally and at large, in political, civil, social, ecclesiastical, and educational concern. The country's public men and official spokesmen have come up through and out of the country-town community, on passing the test of fitness according to retail-trade standards, and have carried with them into official responsibility the habits of thought induced by these interests and these habits of life.

This is also what is meant by democracy in American parlance, and it was for this country-town pattern of democracy that the Defender of the American Faith once aspired to make the work safe. Meantime democracy, at least in America, has moved forward and upward to a higher business level, where larger vested interest dominates and bulkier margins of net gain are in the hazard. It has come to be recognized that the country-town situation of the nineteenth century is now by way of being left behind; and so it is now recognized, or at least acted on, that the salvation of twentieth-century democracy is best to be worked out by making the world safe for Big Business and then let Big Business take care of the interests of the retail trade and the country town, together with much else. But it should not be overlooked that in and through all this it is the soul of the country town that goes marching on.

Toward the close of the century, and increasingly since the turn of the century, the trading community of the country towns has been losing its initiative as a maker of charges and has by degrees become tributary to the great vested interests that move in the background of the market. In a way the country towns have in an appreciable degree fallen into the position of toll-gate keepers for the distribution of goods and collection of customs for the large absentee owners of the business. Grocers, hardware dealers, meat-markets, druggists, shoe-shops, are more and more extensively falling into the position of local distributors for jobbing houses and manufacturers. They increasingly handle "package goods" bearing the brand of some (ostensible) maker, whose chief connection with the goods is that of advertiser of the copyright brand which appears on the label. Prices, and margins, are made for the retailer, which they can take or leave. But leaving, in this connection, will commonly mean leaving the business—which is not included in the premises. The bankers work by affiliation with and under surveillance of their correspondents in the sub-centers of credit, who are similarly tied in under the credit routine of the associated banking houses in the great centers. And the clothiers duly sell garments under the brand of "Cost-Plus," or some such apocryphal token of merit.

All this reduction of the retailer to simpler terms has by no means lowered the overhead charges of the retail trade as they bear upon the underlying farm population; rather the reverse. Nor has it hitherto lessened the duplication of stocks, equipment, personnel and work, that goes into the retail trade; rather the reverse, indeed, whatever may yet happen in that connection. Nor has it abated the ancient spirit of self-help and cupidity that has always animated the retail trade and the country town; rather the reverse; inasmuch as their principles back in the jungle of Big Business cut into the initiative and the margins of the retailers with "package goods," brands, advertising, and agency contracts; which irritates the retailers and provokes them to retaliate and recoup where they see an opening, that is at the cost of the underlying farm population. It is true, the added overcharge which so can effectually be brought to rest on the farm population may be a negligible quantity; there never was much slack to be taken up on that side.

The best days of the retail trade and the country town are past. The retail trader is passing under the hand of Big Business and so is ceasing to be a masterless man ready to follow the line of his own initiative and help to rule his corner of the land in collusion with his fellow townsmen. Circumstances are prescribing for him. The decisive circumstances that hedge him about have been changing in such a way as to leave him no longer fit to do business on his own, even in collusion with his fellow townsmen. The retail trade and the country town are an enterprise in salesmanship, of course, and salesmanship is a matter of buying cheap and selling dear; all of which is simple and obvious to any retailer, and holds true all around the circle from grocer to banker and back again. During the period while the country town has flourished and grown into the texture of the economic situation, the salesmanship which made the outcome was a matter of personal qualities, knack and skill that gave the dealer an advantage in meeting his customers man to man, largely a matter of fact, patience and effrontery; those qualities, in short, which have qualified the rustic horse-trader and have cast a glamour of adventurous enterprise over American country life. In this connection it is worth recalling that the personnel engaged in the retail trade of the country towns has in the main been drawn by self-selection from the farm population, prevailingly from the older-settled sections where this traditional animus of the horse-trader is of older growth and more untroubled.

All this was well enough, at least, during the period of what may be called the masterless country town, before Big Business began to come into its own in these premises. But this situation has been changing, becoming obsolete, slowly by insensible degrees. The factors of change have been such as: increased facilities of transport and communication; increasing use of advertising, largely made possible by facilities of transport and communication; increased size and combination of the business concerns engaged in the wholesale trade, as packers, jobbers, warehouse-concerns handling farm products; increased resort to package-goods, brands, and trademarks, advertised on a liberal plan which runs over the heads of the retailers; increased employment of chain-store methods and agencies; increased dependence of local bankers on the greater credit establishments of the financial centers. It will be seen, of course, that this new growth finally runs back to and rests upon changes of a material sort, in the industrial arts, and more immediately on changes in the means of transport and communication.

In effect, salesmanship, too, has been shifting to the wholesale scale and plane, and the country-town retailer is not in a position to make use of the resulting wholesale methods of publicity and control. The conditioning circumstances have outgrown him. Should he make the shift to the wholesale plan of salesmanship he will cease to be a country-town retailer and take on the character of a chain-store concern, a line-yard lumber syndicate, a mail-order house, a Chicago packer instead of a meat market, a Reserve Bank instead of a county-seat banker, and the like; all of which is not contained in the premises of the country-town retail trade.

The country town, of course, still has its uses, and its use so far as bears on the daily life of the underlying farm population is much the same as ever; but for the retail trade and for those accessory persons and classes who draw their keep from its net gains the country town is no longer what it once was. It has been falling into the position of a way-station in the distributive system, instead of a local habituation where a man of initiative and principle might reasonably hope to come in for a "competence"—that is a capitalized free livelihood—and bear his share in the control of affairs without being accountable to any master-concern "higher-up" in the hierarchy of business. The country town and the townsmen are by way of becoming ways and means in the hands of Big Business. Barring accidents, Bolshevism, and the acts of God or of the United States Congress, such would appear to be the drift of things in the calculable future; that is to say, in the absence of disturbing causes.

This does not mean that the country town is on the decline in point of population or the volume of its traffic; but only that the once masterless retailer is coming in for a master, that the retail trade is being standardized and reparcelled by and in behalf of those massive vested interests that move obscurely in the background, and that these vested interests in the background now have the first call on the "income stream" that flows from the farms through the country town. Nor does it imply that that spirit of self-help and collusive cupidity that made and animated the country town at its best has faded out of the mentality of this people. It has only moved upward and onward to higher duties and wider horizons. Even if it should appear that the self-acting collusive store-keeper and banker of the nineteenth century country town "lies a-moldering in his grave," yet "his soul goes marching on." It is only that the same stock of men with the same traditions and ideals are doing Big Business on the same general plan on which the country town was built. And these men who know the country town "from the ground up" now find it ready to their hand, ready to be turned to account according to the methods and principles bred in their own bone. And the habit of mind induced by and conducive to business-as-usual is much the same whether the balance sheet runs in four figures or in eight.

It is an unhappy circumstance that all this plain speaking about the country town, its traffic, its animating spirit, and its standards of merit, unavoidably has an air of finding fault. But even slight reflection will show that this appearance is unavoidable even where there is no inclination to disparage. It lies in the nature of the case, unfortunately. No unprejudiced inquiry into the facts can content itself with anything short of plain speech, and in this connection plain speech has an air of disparagement because it has been the unbroken usage to avoid plain speech touching these things, these motives, aims, principles, ways and means and achievements, of these substantial citizens and their business and fortunes. But for all that, all these substantial citizens and their folks, fortunes, works, and opinions are no less substantial and meritorious, in fact. Indeed one can scarcely appreciate the full measure of their stature, substance and achievements, and more particularly the moral costs of their great work in developing the country and taking over its resources, without putting it all in plain terms, instead of the salesmanlike parables that have to be employed in the make-believe of trade and politics.

The country town and the business of its substantial citizens are and have ever been an enterprise in salesmanship; and the beginning of wisdom in salesmanship is equivocation. There is a decent measure of equivocation which runs its course on the hither side of prevarication or duplicity, and an honest salesman—such "an honest man as will bear watching"—will endeavor to confine his best efforts to this highly moral zone where stands the upright man who is not under oath to tell the whole truth. But "self-preservation knows no moral law"; and it is not to be overlooked that there habitually enter into the retail trade of the country towns many competitors who do not falter at prevarication and who even do not hesitate at outright duplicity; and it will not do for an honest man to let the rogues get away with the best—or any—of the trade, at the risk of too narrow a margin of profit on his own business—that is to say a narrower margin than might be had in the absence of scruple. And then there is always the base-line of what the law allows; and what the law allows can not be far wrong. Indeed, the sane presumption will be that whoever lives within the law has no need to quarrel with his conscience. And a sound principle will be to improve the hour today and, if worse comes to worst, let the courts determine tomorrow, under protest, just what the law allows, and therefore what the moral code exacts. And then, too it is believed and credible that the courts will be wise enough to see that the law is not allowed to apply with such effect as to impede the volume or narrow the margins of business-as-usual.

"He either fears his fate too much, Or his deserts are small, Who dare not put it to the touch" and take a chance with the legalities and the moralities for once in a way, when there is easy money in sight and no one is looking, particularly in case his own solvency—that is his life as a business concern—should be in the balance. Solvency is always a meritorious work, however it may be achieved or maintained; and so long as one is quite sound on this main count one is sound on the whole, and can afford to forget peccadillos, within reason. The country-town code of morality at large as well as its code of business ethics, is quite sharp, meticulous; but solvency always has a sedative value in these premises, at large and in personal detail. And then, too, solvency not only puts a man in the way of acquiring merit, but it makes him over into a substantial citizen whose opinions and preferences have weight and who is therefore enabled to do much good for his fellow citizens—that is to say, shape them somewhat to his own pattern. To create mankind in one's own image is a work that partakes of the divine, and it is a high privilege which the substantial citizen commonly makes the most of. Evidently this salesmanlike pursuit of the net gain has a high cultural value at the same time that it is invaluable as a means to a competence.

The country-town pattern of moral agent and the code of morals and proprieties, manners and customs, which come up out of this life of salesmanship is such as this unremitting habituation is fit to produce. The scheme of conduct for the business man and for "his sisters and his cousins and his aunts" is a scheme of salesmanship, seven days in the week. And the rule of life of country-town salesmanship is summed up in what the older logicians have called *suppressio veri* and *suggestio falsi*. The dominant note of this life is circumspection.[3] One must avoid offense, cultivate good-will, at any reasonable cost, and continue unfailing in taking advantage of it; and, as a corollary to this axiom, one should be ready to recognize and recount the possible short-comings of one's neighbors, for neighbors are (or may be) rivals in the trade, and in trade one man's loss is another's gain, and a rival's disabilities count in among one's assets and should not be allowed to go to waste.

One must be circumspect, acquire merit, and avoid offense. So one must eschew opinions, or information, which are not acceptable to the common run of those whose good-will has or may conceivably come to have any commercial value. The country-town system of knowledge and belief can admit nothing that would annoy the prejudices of any appreciable number of the respectable towns-folk. So it becomes a system of intellectual, institutional, and religious hold-overs. The country town is conservative; aggressively and truculently so, since any assertion or denial that runs counter to any appreciable set of respectable prejudices would come in for some degree of disfavor, and any degree of disfavor is intolerable to men whose business would presumably suffer from it. Whereas there is no (business) harm done in assenting to, and so in time coming to believe in, any or all of the commonplaces of the day before yesterday. In this sense the country town is conservative, in that it is by force of business expediency intolerant of anything but holdovers. Intellectually, institutionally, and religiously, the country towns of the great farming country are "standing pat" on the ground taken somewhere about the period of the Civil War; or according to the wider chronology, somewhere about Mid-Victorian times. And the men of affairs and responsibility in public life, who have passed the test of country-town fitness, as they must, are men who have come through and made good according to the canons of faith and conduct imposed by this system of holdovers.

Again it seems necessary to enter the caution that in so speaking of this system of country-town holdovers and circumspection there need be no hint of disparagement. The colloquial speech of our time, outside of the country-town hives of expedient respectability, carries a note of disallowance and disclaimer in all that it has to say of holdovers; which is an unfortunate but inherent defect of the language, and which it is necessary to discount and make one's peace with. It is only that outside of the country towns, where human intelligence has not yet gone into abeyance and where human speech accordingly is in continued process of remaking, sentiment and opinion run to the unhappy effect which this implicit disparagement of these holdovers discloses.

Indeed, there is much, or at least something, to be said to the credit of this country-town system of holdovers, with its canons of salesmanship and circumspection. It has to its credit many deeds of Christian charity and Christian faith. It may be—as how should it not?—that many of these deeds of faith and charity are done in the businesslike hope that they will have some salutary effect on the doer's balance sheet; but the opaque fact remains that these businessmen do these things, and it is to be presumed that they would rather not discuss the ulterior motives.

It is a notorious commonplace among those who get their living by promoting enterprises of charity and good deeds in general that no large enterprise of this description can be carried through to a successful and lucrative issue without due appeal to the country towns and due support by the businesslike townsmen and their associates and accessory folks. And it is likewise notorious that the country-town community of businessmen and substantial households will endorse and contribute to virtually any enterprise of the sort, and ask few questions. The effectual interest which prompts to endorsement of and visible contribution to these enterprises is a salesmanlike interest in the "prestige value" that comes to those persons who endorse and visibly contribute; and perhaps even more insistently there is the loss of "prestige value" that would come to anyone who should dare to omit due endorsement and contribution to any ostensibly public-spirited enterprise of this kind that has caught the vogue and does not violate the system of prescriptive holdovers.

Other interest there may well be, as , e.g., human charity or Christian charity—that is to say solicitude for the salvation of one's soul—but without due appeal to salesmanlike respectability the clamor of any certified solicitor of these good deeds will be but as sounding brass and tinkling cymbal. One need only try to picture what would be the fate, e.g., of the campaigns and campaigners for Red

Cross, famine relief, Liberty Bonds, foreign missions, Inter-Church fund, and the like, in the absence of such appeal and of the due response. It may well be, of course, that the salesmanlike townsman endorses with the majority and pays his contribution as a mulct, under compunction of expediency, a choice between evils, for fear of losing good-will. But the main fact remains. It may perhaps all foot up to this with the common run, that no man who values his salesmanlike well-being will dare follow his own untoward propensity in dealing with these certified enterprises in good deeds, and speak his profane mind to the certified campaigners. But it all comes to the same in the upshot. The substantial townsman is shrewd perhaps, or at least he aims to be, and it may well be that with a shrewd man's logic he argues that two birds in the bush are worth more than one in the hand; and so pays his due peace-offering to the certified solicitor of good deeds somewhat in the spirit of those addicts of the faith who once upon a time brought Papal indulgences. But when all is said, it works; and that it does so, and that these many adventures and adventurers in certified mercy and humanity are so enabled to subsist in any degree of prosperity and comfort is to be credited, for the major part, to the salesmanlike tact of the substantial citizens of the country towns.

One hesitates to imagine what would be the fate of the foreign missions, e.g., in the absence of this salesmanlike solicitude for the main chance in the country towns. And there is perhaps less comfort in reflecting on what would be the terms of liquidation for those many churches and churchmen that now adorn the land, if they were driven to rest their fortunes on unconstrained gifts from *de facto* worshippers moved by the first-hand fear of God, in the absence of that more bounteous subvention that so comes in from the quasi-consecrated respectable townsmen who are so constrained by their salesmanlike fear of a possible decline in their prestige.

Any person who is seriously addicted to devout observances and who takes his ecclesiastical verities at their face might be moved to deprecate this dependence of the good cause on these mixed motives. But there is no need of entertaining doubts here as to the ulterior goodness of these businesslike incentives. Seen in perspective from the outside—as any economist must view these matters—it should seem to be the part of wisdom, for the faithful and for their businesslike benefactors alike, to look steadfastly to the good end and leave ulterior questions of motive on one side. There is also some reason to believe that such a view of the whole matter is not infrequently acted upon. And when all is said and allowed for, the main fact remains, that in the absence of this spirit of what may without offense be called salesmanlike pusillanimity in the country towns, both the glory of God and the good of man would be less bountifully served, on all these issues that engage the certified solicitors of good deeds.

This system of innocuous holdover, then, makes up what may be called the country-town profession of faith, spiritual and secular. And so it comes to pass that the same general system of holdovers imposes its bias on the reputable organs of expression throughout the community—pulpit, public press, courts, schools—and dominates the conduct of public affairs; inasmuch as the constituency of the country town, in the main and in the everyday run, shapes the course of reputable sentiment and conviction for the American community at large. Not because of any widely prevalent aggressive preference for that sort of thing, perhaps, but rather because it would scarcely be a "sound business proposition" to run counter to the known interests of the ruling class; that is to say, the substantial citizens and their folks. But the effect is much the same and will scarcely be denied.

It will be seen that in substantial effect this country-town system of holdovers is of what would be called a "salutary" character; that is to say, it is somewhat intolerantly conservative. It is a system of professions and avowals, which may perhaps run to no deeper ground than a salesmanlike pusillanimity, but the effect is much the same. In the country-town community and its outlying ramifications, as in any community of men, the professions made and insisted on will unavoidably shape the effectual scheme of knowledge and belief. Such is the known force of inveterate habit. To the young generation the prescriptive holdovers are handed down as self-evident and immutable principles of reality, and the (reputable) schools can allow themselves no latitude and no question. And what is more to the point, men and women come to believe in the truths which they continue stubbornly to profess, on whatever ground, provided only that they continue stubbornly to profess them. Their professions may have come out of expedient make-believe, but, all the same, they serve as premises in all the projects, reflections, and reveries of these folks who profess them. And it will be only on provocation of harsh and protracted exposure to material facts running unbroken to the contrary that the current of their sentiments and convictions can be brought to range outside of the lines drawn for them by these professed articles of truth.

The case is illustrated, e.g., by the various and widely-varying systems of religious verities current among the outlying peoples, the peoples of the lower cultures, each and several of which are indubitable and immutably truthful to their respective believers, throughout all the bizarre web of their incredible conceits and grotesqueries, none of which will bear the light of alien scrutiny.[4] Having come in for these professions of archaic make-believe, and continuing stubbornly to profess implicit faith in these things as a hopeful sedative of the wrath to come, these things come to hedge about the scheme of what is to be done or left undone. In much the same way the country-town system of prescriptive holdovers has gone into action as the safe and sane body of American common sense; until it is now self-evident to American public sentiment that any derangement of these holdovers would bring the affairs of the human race to a disastrous collapse. And all the while the material conditions are progressively drawing together into such shape that this country-town common sense will no longer work.

Notes

1. "The great American game," they say, is Poker. Just why Real Estate should not come in for honorable mention in that way is not to be explained off hand. And an extended exposition of the reasons why would be tedious and perhaps distasteful, besides calling for such expert discrimination as quite exceeds the powers of a layman in these premises. But even persons who are laymen on both heads will recognize the same family traits in both.

2. The round numbers named above are safe and conservative, particularly so long as the question concerns the staple country towns of the great farming regions. As has already been remarked, they are only less securely applicable in the case of similar towns in the industrial and outlying parts of the country. To some they may seem large and loose. They are based on a fairly exhaustive study of statistical materials gathered by special inquiry in the spring of 1918 for the Statistical Division of the Food Administration, but not published hitherto.

There has been little detailed or concrete discussion of the topic. See, however, a very brief paper by Isador Lubin on "The Economic Costs of Retail Distribution," published in the Twenty-second Report of the Michigan Academy of Science, which runs in great part on the same material.

It is, or should be, unnecessary to add that the retail trade of the country towns is neither a unique nor an extravagant development of business-as-usual. It is in fact very much the sort of thing that is to be met with in the retail trade everywhere, in America and elsewhere.

3. It might also be called salesmanlike pusillanimity.

4. There is, of course, no call in this Christian land to throw doubt or question touching any of the highly remarkable verities of the Christian confession at large. While it will be freely admitted on all hands that many of the observances and beliefs current among the "non-Christian tribes" are grotesque and palpable errors of mortal mind; it must at the same time, and indeed by the same token, be equally plain to any person of cultivated tastes in religious superstition, and with a sound bias, that the corresponding convolutions of unreason in the Christian faith are in the nature of a divine coagulum of the true, the beautiful, and the good, as it was in the beginning, is now, and ever shall be: World without end. But all the while it is evident that all these "beastly devices of the heathen," just referred to, are true, beautiful and good to their benighted apprehension only because their apprehension has been benighted by the stubborn profession of these articles of misguided make-believe, through the generations; which is the point of the argument.

Culture, Religion, and Education

The Place of Science in Modern Civilization

It is commonly held that modern Christendom is superior to any and all other system of civilized life. Other ages and other cultural regions are by contrast spoken of as lower, or more archaic, or less mature. The claim is that the modern culture is superior on the whole, not that it is the best or highest in all respects and at every point. It has, in fact, not an all-around superiority, but a superiority within a closely limited range of intellectual activities, while outside this range many other civilizations surpass that of the modern occidental peoples. But the peculiar excellence of the modern culture is of such a nature as to give it a decisive practical advantage over all other cultural schemes that have gone before or that have come into competition with it. It has proved itself fit to survive in a struggle for existence as against those civilizations which differ from it in respect of its distinctive traits.

Modern civilization is peculiarly matter-of-fact. It contains many elements that are not of this character, but these other elements do not belong exclusively or characteristically to it. The modern civilized people are in a peculiar degree capable of an impersonal, dispassionate insight into the material facts with which mankind has to deal. The apex of cultural growth is at this point. Compared with this trait the rest of what is comprised in the cultural scheme is adventitious, or at the best it is a by-product of this hard-headed apprehension of facts. This quality may be a matter of habit or of racial endowment, or it may be an outcome of both; but whatever be the explanation of its prevalence, the immediate consequence is much the same for the growth of civilization. A civilization which is dominated by this matter-of-fact insight must prevail against any cultural scheme that lacks this element. This characteristic of western civilization comes to a

Reprinted from *American Journal of Sociology* 11 (March 1906): 585–609. Used by permission.

head in modern science, and it finds its highest material expression in the technology of the machine industry. In these things modern culture is creative and self-sufficient; and these being given, the rest of what may seem characteristic in western civilization follows by easy consequence. The cultural structure clusters about this body of matter-of-fact knowledge as its substantial core. Whatever is not consonant with these opaque creations of science is an intrusive feature in the modern scheme, borrowed or standing over from the barbarian past.

Other ages and other peoples excel in other things and are known by other virtues. In creative art, as well as in critical taste, the faltering talent of Christendom can at the best follow the lead of the ancient Greeks and the Japanese. In deft workmanship the handicraftsmen of the middle Orient, as well as of the Far East, stand on a level securely above the highest European achievement, old or new. In myth-making, folklore, and occult symbolism many of the lower barbarians have achieved things beyond what the latter-day priests and poets know how to propose. In metaphysical insight and dialectical versatility many orientals, as well as the Schoolmen of the Middle Ages, easily surpass the highest reaches of the New Thought and the Higher Criticism. In a shrewd sense of the religious verities, as well as in an unsparing faith in devout observances, the people of India or Tibet, or even the medieval Christians, are past-masters in comparison even with the select of the faith of modern times. In political finesse, as well as in unreasoning, brute loyalty, more than one of the ancient peoples give evidence of a capacity to which no modern civilized nation may aspire. In warlike malevolence and abandon, the hosts of Islam, the Sioux Indian, and the "heathen of the northern sea" have set the mark above the reach of the most strenuous civilized warlord.

To modern civilized men, especially in their intervals of sober reflection, all these things that distinguish the barbarian civilizations seem of dubious value and are required to show cause why they should not be slighted. It is not so with the knowledge of facts. The making of states and dynasties, the founding of families, the prosecution of feuds, the propagation of creeds and the creation of sects, the accumulation of fortunes, the consumption of superfluities—these have all in their time been felt to justify themselves as an end of endeavor; but in the eyes of modern civilized men all these things seem futile in comparison with the achievements of science. They dwindle in men's esteem as time passes, while the achievements of science are held higher as time passes. This is the one secure holding-ground of latter-day conviction, that "the increase and diffusion of knowledge among men" is indefeasibly right and good. When seen in such perspective as will clear it of the trivial perplexities of workday life, this proposition is not questioned within the horizon of the western culture, and no other cultural ideal holds a similar unquestioned place in the convictions of civilized mankind.

On any large question which is to be disposed of for good and all the final appeal is by common consent taken to the scientist. The solution offered in the name of science is decisive so long as it is not set aside by a still more searching scientific inquiry. The state of things may not be altogether fortunate, but such is the fact. There are other, older grounds of finality that may conceivably be better, nobler, worthier, more profound, more beautiful. It might conceivably be preferable, as a matter of cultural ideals, to leave the last word with the lawyer, the duelist, the priest, the moralist, or the college of heraldry. In past times people have been content to leave their weightiest question to the decision of some one or other of these tribunals, and, it cannot be denied, with very happy results in those respects that were then looked to with the greatest solicitude. But whatever the commonsense of earlier generations may have held in this respect, modern commonsense holds that the scientists's answer is the only ultimately true one. In the last resort enlightened commonsense sticks by the opaque truth and refuses to go behind the returns given by the tangible facts.

Quasi lignum vitae in paradiso Dei, et quasi lucerna fulgoris in domo Domini, such is the place of science in modern civilization. This latter-day faith in matter-of-fact knowledge may be well grounded or it may not. It has come about that men assign it this high place, perhaps idolatrously, perhaps to the detriment of the best and most intimate interests of the race. There is room for much more than a vague doubt that this cult of science is not altogether a wholesome growth—that the unmitigated quest of knowledge, of this matter-of-fact kind, makes for race-deterioration and discomfort on the whole, both in its immediate effects upon the spiritual life of mankind, and in the material consequences that follow from a great advance in matter-of-fact knowledge.

But we are not here concerned with the merits of the case. The question here is: How has this cult of science arisen? What are its cultural antecedents? How far is it in consonance with hereditary human nature? and, What is the nature of its hold on the convictions of civilized men?

In dealing with pedagogical problems and the theory of education, current psychology is nearly at one in saying that all learning is of a "pragmatic character; that knowledge is inchoate action inchoately directed to an end; that all knowledge—is "functional;" that it is of the nature of use. This, of course, is only a corollary under the main postulate of the latter-day psychologists, whose catchword is that The Idea is essentially active. There is no need of quarreling with this "pragmatic" school of psychologists. Their aphorism may not contain the whole truth, perhaps, but at least it goes nearer to the heart of the epistemological problem than any earlier formulation. It may confidently be said to do so because, for one thing, its argument meets the requirements of modern science. It is such a concept as matter-of-fact science can make effective use of; it is drawn in terms which are, in the last analysis, of an impersonal, not to say tropismatic, character; such as is demanded by science, with its insistence on opaque cause and effect. While knowledge is construed in teleological terms, in terms of personal interest and attention, this teleological aptitude is itself reducible to a product of unteleological natural selection. The teleological bent of intelligence is a hereditary trait settled upon the race by the selective action of forces that look to no end. The foundations of pragmatic intelligence are not pragmatic, nor even personal or sensible.

This impersonal character of intelligence is, of course, most evident on the lower levels of life. If we follow Mr. Loeb, e.g., in his inquiries into the psychology of that life that lies below the threshold of intelligence, what we meet with is an aimless but unwavering motor response to stimulus.[1] The response is of the nature of motor impulse, and in so far it is "pragmatic," if that term may fairly be applied to so rudimentary a phase of sensibility. The responding organism may be called an "agent" in so far. It is only by a figure of speech that these terms are made to apply to tropismatic reactions. Higher in the scale of sensibility and nervous complication instincts work to a somewhat similar outcome. On the human plane, intelligence (the selective effect of inhibitive complication) may throw the response into the form of a reasoned line of conduct looking to an outcome that shall be expedient for the agent. This is naive pragmatism of the developed kind. There is no longer a question but that the responding organism is an "agent," and that his intelligent response to stimulus is of a teleological character. But that is not all. The inhibitive nervous complication may also detach another chain of response to the given stimulus, which does not send itself in a line of motor conduct and does not fall into a system of uses. Pragmatically speaking, this outlying chain of response is unintended and irrelevant. Except in urgent cases, such an idle response seems commonly to be present as a subsidiary phenomenon. If credence is given to the view that intelligence is, in its elements, of the nature of an inhibitive selection, it seems necessary to assume some such chain of idle and irrelevant response to account for the further course of the elements eliminated in giving the motor response the character of a reasoned line of conduct. So that associated with the pragmatic attention there is found more or less of an irrelevant attention, or idle curiosity. This is more particularly the case where a higher range of intelligence is present. This idle curiosity is, perhaps, closely related to the aptitude for play, observed both in man and in the lower animals.[2] The aptitude for play, as well as the functioning of idle curiosity, seems peculiarly lively in the young, whose aptitude for sustained pragmatism is at the same time relatively vague and unreliable.

This idle curiosity formulates its response to stimulus, not in terms of an expedient line of conduct, nor even necessarily in a chain of motor activity, but in terms of the sequence of activities going on in the observed phenomena. The "interpretation" of the facts under the guidance of this idle curiosity may take the form of anthropomorphic or animistic explanations of the "conduct" of the objects observed. The interpretation of the facts takes a dramatic form. The facts are conceived in an animistic way, and a pragmatic animus is imputed to them. Their behavior is construed as a reasoned procedure on their part looking to the advantage of these animistically conceived objects, or looking to the achievements of some end which these objects are conceived to have at heart for reasons of their own.

Among the savage and lower barbarian peoples there is commonly current a large body of knowledge organized in this way into myths and legends, which need have no pragmatic value for the learner of them and no intended bearing on his conduct of practical affairs. They may come to have a practical value imputed to them as a ground of superstitious observances, but they may also not.[3] All students of the lower cultures are aware of the dramatic character of the myths current among these peoples, and they are also aware that, particularly among the peaceable communities, the great body of mythical lore is of an idle kind, as having very little intended bearing on the practical conduct of those who believe in these myth-dramas. The myths on the one hand, and the workday knowledge of uses, materials, appliances, and expedients on the other hand, may be neatly independent of one another. Such is the case in an especial degree among those peoples who are prevailingly of a peaceable habit of life, among whom the myths have not in any great measure been canonized into precedents of divine malevolence.

The lower barbarian's knowledge of the phenomena of nature, in so far as they are made the subject of deliberate speculation and are organized into a consistent body, is of the nature of life-histories. This body of knowledge is in the main organized under the guidance of an idle curiosity. In so far as it is systematized under the canons of curiosity rather than of expediency, the test of truth applied throughout this body of barbarian knowledge is the test of dramatic consistency. In addition to their dramatic cosmology and folk legends, it is needless to say, these peoples have also a considerable body of worldly wisdom in a more or less systematic form. In this the test of validity is usefulness.[4]

The pragmatic knowledge of the early days differs scarcely at all in character from that of the maturest phases of culture. Its highest achievements in the direction of systematic formulation consist of didactic exhortations to thrift, prudence, equanimity, and shrewd management—a body of maxims of expedient conduct. In this field there is scarcely a degree of advance from Confucius to Samuel Smiles. Under the guidance of the idle curiosity, on the other hand, there has been a continued advance toward a more and more comprehensive system of knowledge. With the advance in intelligence and experience there come closer observation and more detailed analysis of facts.[5] The dramatization of the sequence of phenomena may then fall into somewhat less personal, less anthropomorphic formulations of the processes observed; but at no stage of its growth—at least at no stage hitherto reached—does the output of this work of the idle curiosity lose its dramatic character. Comprehensive generalizations are made and cosmologies are built up, but always in dramatic form. General principles of explanation are settled on, which in the earlier days of theoretical speculation seem invariably to run back to the broad vital principle of generation. Procreation, birth, growth, and decay constitute the cycle of postulates within which the dramatized processes of natural phenomena run their course. Creation is procreation in these archaic theoretical systems, and causation is gestation and birth. The archaic cosmological schemes of Greece, India, Japan, China, Polynesia, and America, all run to the same general effect on this head.[6]

Throughout this biological speculation there is present, obscurely in the background, the tacit recognition of a material causation, such as conditions the vulgar operations of workday life from hour to hour. But this causal relation between vulgar work and product is vaguely taken for granted and not made a principle for comprehensive generalizations. It is overlooked as a trivial matter of course. The higher generalizations take their color from the broader features of the current scheme of life. The habits of thought that rule in the working-out of a system of knowledge are such as are fostered by the more impressive affairs of life, by the institutional structure under which the community lives. So long as the ruling institutions are those of blood-relationship, descent, and clannish discrimination, so long the canons of knowledge are of the same complexion.

When presently a transformation is made in the scheme of culture from peaceable life with sporadic predation to a settled scheme of predaceous life, involving mastery and servitude, gradations of privilege and honor, coercion and personal dependence, then the scheme of knowledge undergoes an analogous change. The predaceous, or higher barbarian, culture is, for the present purpose, peculiar in that it is ruled by an accentuated pragmatism. The institutions of this cultural phase are conventionalized relations of force and fraud. The questions of life are questions of expedient conduct as carried on under the current relations of mastery and subservience. The habitual distinctions are distinctions of personal force, advantage, precedence, and authority. A shrewd adaptation to this system of graded dignity and servitude becomes a matter of life and death, and men learn to think in these terms as ultimate and definitive. The system of knowledge, even in so far as its motives are of a dispassionate or idle kind, falls into the like terms, because such are the habits of thought and the standards of discrimination enforced by daily life.[7]

The theoretical work of such a cultural era, as, for instance, the Middle Ages, still takes the general shape of dramatization, but the postulates of the dramaturgic theories and the tests of theoretic validity are no longer the same as before the scheme of graded servitude came to occupy the field. The canons which guide the work of the idle curiosity are no longer those of generation, blood-relationship, and homely life, but rather those of graded dignity, authenticity, and dependence. The higher generalizations take on a new complexion, it may be without formally discarding the older articles of belief. The cosmologies of these higher barbarians are cast in terms of a feudalistic hierarchy of agents and elements, and the causal nexus between phenomena is conceived animistically after the manner of sympathetic magic. The laws that are sought to be discovered in the natural universe are sought in terms of authoritative enactment. The relation in which the deity, or deities, are conceived to stand to facts is no longer the relation of progenitor, so much as that of suzerainty. Natural laws are corollaries under the arbitrary rules of status imposed on the natural universe by an all-powerful Providence with a view to the maintenance of his own prestige. The science that grows in such a spiritual environment is of the class represented by alchemy and astrology, in which the imputed degree of nobility and prepotency of the objects and the symbolic force of their names are looked to for an explanation of what takes place.

The theoretical output of the Schoolmen has necessarily an accentuated pragmatic complexion, since the whole cultural scheme under which they lived and worked was of a strenuously pragmatic character. The current concepts of things were then drawn in terms of expediency, personal force, exploit, prescriptive authority, and the like, and this range of concepts was by force of habit employed in the correlation of facts for purposes of knowledge even where no immediate practical use of the knowledge so gained was had in view. At the same time a very large proportion of the scholastic researches and speculations aimed directly at rules of expedient conduct, whether it took the form of a philosophy of life under temporal law and custom, or of a scheme of salvation under the decrees of an autocratic Providence. A naive apprehension of the dictum that all knowledge is pragmatic would find more satisfactory corroboration in the intellectual output of scholasticism than in any system of knowledge of an older or later date.

With the advent of modern times a change comes over the nature of the inquiries and formulations worked out under the guidance of the idle curiosity—which from this epoch is often spoken of as the scientific spirit. The change in question is closely correlated with an analogous change in institutions and habits of life, particularly with the changes which the modern era brings in industry and in the economic organization of society. It is doubtful whether the characteristic intellectual interests and teachings of the new era can properly be spoken of as less "pragmatic," as that term is sometimes understood, than those of the scholastic times; but they are of another kind, being conditioned by a different cultural and industrial situation.[8] In the life of the new era conceptions of authentic rank and differential dignity have grown weaker in practical affairs, and notions of preferential reality and authentic tradition similarly count for less in the new science. The forces at work in the external world are conceived in a less animistic manner, although anthropomorphism still prevails, at least to the degree required in order to give a dramatic interpretation of the sequence of phenomena.

The changes in the cultural situation which seem to have had the most serious consequences for the methods and animus of scientific inquiry are those changes that took place in the field of industry. Industry in early modern times is a fact of relatively greater preponderance, more of a tone-giving factor, than it was under the régime of feudal status. It is the characteristic trait of the modern culture, very much as exploit and fealty were the characteristic cultural traits of the earlier times. This early-modern industry is, in an obvious and convincing degree, a matter of workmanship. The same has not been true in the same degree either before or since. The workman, more or less skilled and with more or less specialized efficiency, was the central figure in the cultural situation of the time; and so the concepts of the scientists came to be drawn in the image of the workman. The dramatizations of the sequence of external phenomena worked out under the impulse of the idle curiosity were then conceived in terms of workmanship. Workmanship gradually supplanted differential dignity as the authoritative canon of scientific truth, even on the higher levels of speculation and research. This, of course, amounts to saying in other words, that the law of cause and effect was given the first place, as contrasted with dialectical consistency and authentic tradition. But this early-modern law of cause and effect—the law of efficient causes—is of an anthropomorphic kind. "Like causes produce like effects," in much the same sense as the skilled workman's product is like the workman; "nothing is found in the effect that was not contained in the cause," in much the same manner.

These dicta are, of course, older than modern science, but it is only in the early days of modern science that they come to rule the field with an unquestioned sway and to push the higher grounds of dialectical validity to one side. They invade even the highest and most recondite fields of speculation, so that at the approach to the transition from the early-modern to the late-modern period, in the eighteenth century, they determine the outcome even in the counsels of the theologians. The deity, from having been in medieval times primarily a suzerain concerned with the maintenance of his own prestige, becomes primarily a creator engaged in the workmanlike occupation of making things useful for man. His relation to man and the natural universe is no longer primarily that of a progenitor, as it is in the lower barbarian culture, but rather that of a talented mechanic. The "natural laws" which the scientists of that era make so much of are no longer decrees of a preternatural legislative authority, but rather details of the workshop specifications handed down by the master-craftsman for the guidance of handicraftsmen working out his designs. In the eighteenth-century science these natural laws are laws specifying the sequence of cause and effect, and will bear characterization as a dramatic interpretation of the activity of the causes at work, and these causes are conceived in a quasi-personal manner. In later modern times the formulations of causal sequence grow impersonal and more objective, more matter-of-fact; but the imputation of activity to the observed objects never ceases, and even in the latest and maturest formulations of scientific research the dramatic tone is not wholly lost. The causes at work are conceived in a highly impersonal way, but hitherto no science (except ostensibly mathematics) has been content to do its theoretical work in terms of inert magnitude alone. Activity continues to be input to the phenomena with which science deals; and activity is, of course, not a fact of observation, but is imputed to the phenomena by the observer.[9] This is, also of course, denied by those who insist on a purely mathematical formulation of scientific theories, but the denial is maintained only at the cost of consistency. Those eminent authorities who speak for a colorless mathematical formulation invariably and necessarily fall back on the (essentially metaphysical) preconception of causation as soon as they go into the actual work of scientific inquiry.[10]

Since the machine technology has made great advances during the nineteenth century and has become a cultural force of wide-reaching consequence, the formulations of science have made another move in the direction of impersonal matter-of-fact. The machine process has displaced the workman as the archetype in whose image causation is conceived by the scientific investigators. The dramatic interpretation of natural phenomena has thereby become less anthropomorphic; it no longer constructs the life-history of a cause working to produce a given effect—after the manner of a skilled workman producing a piece of wrought goods—but it constructs the life-history of a process in which the distinction between cause and effect need scarcely be observed in an itemized and specific way, but in which the run of causation unfolds itself in an unbroken sequence of cumulative change. By contrast with the pragmatic formulations of worldly wisdom these latter-day theories of the scientists appear highly opaque, impersonal, and matter-of-fact; but taken by themselves they must be admitted still to show the constraint of the dramatic prepossessions that once guided the savage myth-makers.

In so far as touches the aims and the animus of scientific inquiry, as seen from the point of view of the scientist, it is a wholly fortuitous and insubstantial coincidence that much of the knowledge gained under machine-made canons of research can be turned to practical account. Much of this knowledge is useful, or may be made so, by applying it to the control of the processes in which natural forces are engaged. This employment of scientific knowledge for useful ends is technology, in the broad sense in which the term includes, besides the machine industry proper, such branches of practice as engineering, agriculture, medicine, sanitation, and economic reforms. The reason why scientific theories can be turned to account for these practical ends is not that these ends are included in the scope of scientific inquiry. These useful purposes lie outside the scientist's interest. It is not that he aims, or can aim, at technological improvements. His inquiry is as "idle" as that of the Pueblo myth-maker. But the canons of validity under whose guidance he works are those imposed by the modem technology, through habituation to its requirements; and therefore his results are available for the technological purpose. His canons of validity are made for him by the cultural situation; they are habits of thought imposed on him by the scheme of life current in the community in which he lives; and under modern conditions this scheme of life is largely machine-made. In the modern culture, industry, industrial processes, and industrial products have progressively gained upon humanity, until these creations of man's ingenuity have latterly come to take the dominant place in the cultural scheme; and it is not too much to say that they have become the chief force in shaping men's daily life, and therefore the chief factor in shaping men's habits of thought. Hence men have learned to think in the terms in which the technological processes act. This is particularly true of those men who by virtue of a peculiarly strong susceptibility in this direction become addicted to that habit of matter-of-fact inquiry that constitutes scientific research

Modern technology makes use of the same range of concepts, thinks in the same terms, and applies the same tests of validity, as modern science. In both, the terms of standardization, validity, and finality are always terms of impersonal sequence, not terms of human nature or of preternatural agencies. Hence the easy copartnership between the two. Science and technology play into one another's hands. The processes of nature with which science deals and which technology turns to account, the sequence of changes in the external world, animate and inanimate, run in terms of brute causation, as do the theories of science. These processes take no thought of human expediency or inexpediency. To make use of them they must be taken as they are, opaque and unsympathetic. Technology, therefore, has come to proceed on an interpretation of these phenomena in mechanical terms, not in terms of imputed personality nor even of workmanship. Modern science, deriving its concepts from the same source, carries on its inquiries and states its conclusions in terms of the same objective character as those employed by the mechanical engineer.

So it has come about, through the progressive change of the ruling habits of thought in the community, that the theories of science have progressively diverged from the formulations of pragmatism ever since that modern era set in. From an organization of knowledge on the basis of imputed personal or animistic propensity the theory has changed its base to an imputation of brute activity only, and this latter is conceived in an increasingly matter-of-fact manner; until, latterly, the pragmatic range of knowledge and the scientific are more widely out of touch than ever, differing not only in aim, but in matter as well. In both domains knowledge runs in terms of activity, but it is on the one hand knowledge of what had best be done, and on the other hand knowledge of what takes place; on the one hand knowledge of ways and means, on the other hand knowledge without any ulterior purpose. The latter range of knowledge may serve the ends of the former, but the converse does not hold true.

These two divergent ranges of inquiry are to be found together in all phases of human culture. What distinguishes the present phase is that the discrepancy between the two is now wider than ever before. The present is nowise distinguished above other cultural eras by any exceptional urgency or acumen in the search for pragmatic expedients. Neither is it safe to assert that the present excels all other civilizations in the volume or the workmanship of that body of knowledge that is to be credited to the idle curiosity. What distinguishes the present in these premises is (1) that the primacy in the cultural scheme has passed from pragmatism to a disinterested inquiry whose motive is idle curiosity, and (2) that in the domain of the latter the making of myths and legends in terms of imputed personality, as well as the construction of a dialectical system in terms of differential reality, has yielded the first place to the making of theories in terms of matter-of-fact sequence.[11]

Pragmatism creates nothing but maxims of expedient conduct. Science creates nothing but theories.[12] It knows nothing of policy or utility, of better or worse. None of all that is comprised in what is today accounted scientific knowledge. Wisdom and proficiency of the pragmatic sort does not contribute to the advance of a knowledge of fact. It has only an incidental bearing on scientific research, and its bearing is chiefly that of inhibition and misdirection. Wherever canons of expediency are intruded into or are attempted to be incorporated in the inquiry, the consequence is an unhappy one for science, however happy it may be for some other purpose extraneous to science. The mental attitude of worldly wisdom is at cross-purposes with the disinterested scientific spirit, and the pursuit of it induces an intellectual bias that is incompatible with scientific insight. Its intellectual output is a body of shrewd rules of conduct, in great part designed to take advantage of human infirmity. Its habitual terms of standardization and validity are terms of human nature, of human preference, prejudice, aspiration, endeavor, and disability, and the habit of mind that goes with it is such as is consonant with these terms. No doubt, the all-pervading pragmatic animus of the older and non-European civilizations has had more than anything else to do with their relatively slight and slow advance in scientific knowledge. In the modern scheme of knowledge it holds true, in a similar manner and with analogous effect, that training in divinity, in law, and in the related branches of diplomacy, business tactics, military affairs, and political theory, is alien to the skeptical scientific spirit and subversive of it.

The modern scheme of culture comprises a large body of worldly wisdom, as well as of science. This pragmatic lore stands over against science with something of a jealous reserve. The pragmatists value themselves somewhat on being useful as well as being efficient for good and evil. They feel the inherent antagonism between themselves and the scientists, and look with some doubt on the latter as being merely decorative triflers, although they sometimes borrow the prestige of the name of science—as is only good and well, since it is of the essence of worldly wisdom to borrow anything that can be turned to account. The reasoning in these fields turns about questions of personal advantage of one kind or another, and the merits of the claims canvassed in these discussions are decided on grounds of authenticity. Personal claims make up the subject of the inquiry, and these claims are construed and decided in terms of precedent and choice, use and wont, prescriptive authority, and the like. The higher reaches of generalization in these pragmatic inquiries are of the nature of deductions from authentic tradition, and the training in this class of reasoning gives discrimination in respect of authenticity and expediency. The resulting habit of mind is a bias for substituting dialectical distinctions and decisions *de jure* in the place of explanations *de facto*. The so-called "sciences" associated with these pragmatic disciplines, such as jurisprudence, political science, and the like, are a taxonomy of credenda. Of this character was the greater part of the "science" cultivated by the Schoolmen, and large remnants of the same kind of authentic conviction are, of course, still found among the tenets of the scientists, particularly in the social sciences, and no small solicitude is still given to their cultivation. Substantially the same value as that of the temporal pragmatic inquiries belongs also, of course, to the "science" of divinity. Here the questions to which an answer is sought, as well as the aim and method of inquiry, are of the same pragmatic character, although the argument runs on a higher plane of personality, and seeks a solution in terms of a remoter and more metaphysical expediency.

In the light of what has been said above, the questions recur: How far is the scientific quest of matter-of-fact knowledge consonant with the inherited intellectual aptitudes and propensities of the normal man? and, what foothold has science in the modern culture? The former is a question of the temperamental heritage of civilized mankind, and therefore it is in large part a question of the circumstances which have in the past selectively shaped the human nature of civilized mankind. Under the barbarian culture, as well as on the lower levels of what is currently called civilized life, the dominant note has been that of competitive expediency for the individual or the group, great or small, in an avowed struggle for the means of life. Such is still the ideal of the politician and business man, as well as of other classes whose habits of life lead them to cling to the inherited barbarian traditions. The upper-barbarian and lower-civilized culture, as has already been indicated, is pragmatic, with a thoroughness that nearly bars out any non-pragmatic ideal of life or of knowledge. Where this tradition is strong there is but a precarious chance for any consistent effort to formulate knowledge in other terms than those drawn from the prevalent relations of personal mastery and subservience and the ideals of personal gain.

During the Dark and Middle Ages, for instance, it is true in the main that any movement of thought not controlled by considerations of expediency and conventions of status are to be found only in the obscure depths of vulgar life, among those neglected elements of the population that lived below the reach of the active class struggle. What there is surviving of this vulgar, non-pragmatic intellectual output takes the form of legends and folktales, often embroidered on the authentic documents of the Faith. These are less alien to the latest and highest culture of Christendom than are the dogmatic, dialectical, and chivalric productions that occupied the attention of the upper classes in medieval times. It may seem a curious paradox that the latest and most perfect flower of the western civilization is more nearly akin to the spiritual life of the serfs and villeins than it is to that of the grange or the abbey. The courtly life and the chivalric habits of thought of that past phase of culture have left as nearly no trace in the culture scheme of later modern times as could well be. Even the romancers who ostensibly rehearse the phenomena of chivalry unavoidably make their knights and ladies speak the language and the sentiments of the slums of that time, tempered with certain schematized modern reflections and speculations. The gallantries, the genteel inanities and devout imbecilities of medieval high-life would be insufferable even to the meanest and most romantic modern intelligence. So that in a later, less barbarian age the precarious remnants of folklore that have come down through the vulgar channel—half savage and more than half pagan—are treasured as containing the largest spiritual gains which the barbarian ages of Europe have to offer.

The sway of barbarian pragmatism has, everywhere in the western world, been relatively brief and relatively light; the only exceptions would be found in certain parts of the Mediterranean seaboard. But wherever the barbarian culture has been sufficiently long-lived and unmitigated to work out a thoroughly selective effect in the human material subjected to it, there the pragmatic animus may be expected to have become supreme and to inhibit all movement in the direction of scientific inquiry and eliminate all effective aptitude for other than worldly wisdom. What the selective consequences of such a protracted regime of pragmatism would be for the temper of the race may be seen in the human flotsam left by the great civilizations of antiquity, such as Egypt, India, Persia. Science is not at home among these leavings of barbarism. In these instances of its long and unmitigated dominion the barbarian culture has selectively worked out a temperamental bias and a scheme of life from which objective, matter-of-fact knowledge is virtually excluded in favor of pragmatism, secular and religious. But for the greater part of the race, at least for the greater part of civilized mankind, the régime of the mature barbarian culture has been of relatively short duration, and has had a correspondingly superficial and transient selective effect. It has not had force and time to eliminate certain elements of human nature handed down from an earlier phase of life, which are not in full consonance with the barbarian animus or with the demands of the pragmatic scheme of thought. The barbarian-pragmatic habit of mind, therefore, is not properly speaking a temperamental trait of the civilized peoples, except possibly within certain class limits (as, e.g., the German nobility). It is rather a tradition, and it does not constitute so tenacious a bias as to make head against the strongly materialistic drift of modern conditions and set aside that increasingly urgent resort to matter-of-fact conceptions that makes for the primacy of science. Civilized mankind does not in any great measure take back atavistically to the upper-barbarian habit of mind. Barbarism covers too small a segment of the life-history of the race to have given an enduring temperamental result. The unmitigated discipline of the higher barbarism in Europe fell on a relatively small proportion of the population, and in the course of time this select element of the population was crossed and blended with the blood of the lower elements whose life always continued to run in the ruts of savagery rather than in those of the high-strung, finished barbarian culture that gave rise to the chivalric scheme of life.

Of the several phases of human culture the most protracted, and the one which has counted for most in shaping the abiding traits of the race, is unquestionably that of savagery. With savagery, for the purpose in hand, is to be classed the lower, relatively peaceable barbarism that is not characterized by wide and sharp class discrepancies or by an unremitting endeavor of one individual or group to get the better of another. Even under the full-grown barbarian culture—as, for instance, during the Middle Ages—the habits of life and the spiritual interests of the great body of the population continue in large measure to bear the character of savagery. The savage phase of culture accounts for by far the greater portion of the life-history of mankind, particularly if the lower barbarism and the vulgar life of later barbarism be counted in with savagery, as in a measure they properly should. This is particularly true of those racial elements that have entered into the composition of the leading peoples of Christendom.

The savage culture is characterized by the relative absence of pragmatism from the higher generalizations of its knowledge and beliefs. As has been noted above, its theoretical creations are chiefly of the nature of mythology shading off into folklore. This genial spinning of apocryphal yarns is, at its best, an amiably inefficient formulation of experiences and observations in terms of something like a life-history of the phenomena observed. It has, on the one hand, little value, and little purpose, in the way of pragmatic expediency, and so it is not closely akin to the pragmatic-barbarian scheme of life; while, on the other hand, it is also ineffectual as a systematic knowledge of matter-of-fact. It is a quest of knowledge, perhaps of systematic knowledge, and it is carried on under the incentive of the idle curiosity. In this respect it falls in the same class with the civilized man's science; but it seeks knowledge not in terms of opaque matter-of-fact, but in terms of some sort of a spiritual life imputed to the facts. It is romantic and Hegelian rather than realistic and Darwinian. The logical necessities of its scheme of thought are necessities of spiritual consistency rather than of quantitative equivalence. It is like science in that it has no ulterior motive beyond the idle craving for a systematic correlation of data; but it is unlike science in that its standardization and correlation of data run in terms of the free play of imputed personal initiative rather than in terms of the constraint of objective cause and effect.

By force of the protracted selective discipline of this past phase of culture, the human nature of civilized mankind is still substantially the human nature of savage man. The ancient equipment of congenital aptitudes and propensities stands over substantially unchanged, though overlaid with barbarian traditions and conventionalities and readjusted by habituation to the exigencies of civilized life. In a measure, therefore, but by no means altogether, scientific inquiry is native to civilized man with his savage heritage, since scientific inquiry proceeds on the same general motive of idle curiosity as guided the savage myth-makers, though it makes use of concepts and standards in great measure alien to the myth-makers' habit of mind. The ancient human predilection for discovering a dramatic play of passion and intrigue in the phenomena of nature still asserts itself. In the most advanced communities, and even among the adepts of modern science, there comes up persistently the revulsion of the native savage against the inhumanly dispassionate sweep of the scientific quest, as well as against the inhumanly ruthless fabric of technological processes that have come out of this search for matter-of-fact knowledge. Very often the savage need of a spiritual interpretation (dramatization) of phenomena breaks through the crust of acquired materialistic habits of thought, to find such refuge as may be had in articles of faith seized on and held by sheer force of instinctive conviction. Science and its creations are more or less uncanny, more or less alien, to that fashion of craving for knowledge that by ancient inheritance animates mankind. Furtively or by an overt breach of consistency, men still seek comfort in marvelous articles of savage-born lore, which contradict the truths of that modern science whose dominion they dare not question, but whose findings at the same times go beyond the breaking point of their jungle-fed spiritual sensibilities.

The ancient ruts of savage thought and conviction are smooth and easy; but however sweet and indispensable the archaic ways of thinking may be to the civilized man's peace of mind, yet such is the binding force of matter-of-fact analysis and inference under modern conditions that the findings of science are not questioned on the whole. The name of science is after all a word to conjure with. So much so that the name and the mannerisms, at least, if nothing more of science, have invaded all fields of learning and have even overrun territory that belongs to the enemy. So there are "sciences" of theology, law, and medicine, as has already been noted above. And there are such things as Christian Science, and "scientific" astrology, palmistry, and the like. But within the field of learning proper there is a similar predilection for an air of scientific acumen and precision where science does not belong. So that even that large range of knowledge that has to do with general information rather than with theory—what is loosely termed scholarship—tends strongly to take on the name and forms of theoretical statement. However decided the contrast between these branches of knowledge on the one hand, and science properly so called on the other hand, yet even the classical learning, and the humanities generally, fall in with this predilection more and more with each succeeding generation of students. The students of literature, for instance, are more and more prone to substitute critical analysis and linguistic speculation, as the end of their endeavors, in the place of that discipline of taste and that cultivated sense of literary form and literary feeling that must always remain the chief end of literary training, as distinct from philology and the social sciences. There is, of course, no intention to question the legitimacy of a science of philology or of the analytical study of literature as a fact in cultural history, but these things do not constitute training in literary taste, nor can they take the place of it. The effect of this straining after scientific formulations in a field alien to the scientific spirit is as curious as it is wasteful. Scientifically speaking, those quasi-scientific inquiries necessarily begin nowhere and end in the same place; while in point of cultural gain they commonly come to nothing better than spiritual abnegation. But these blindfold endeavors to conform to the canons of science serve to show how wide and unmitigated the sway of science is in the modern community.

Scholarship—that is to say, an intimate and systematic familiarity with past cultural achievements—still holds its place in the scheme of learning, in spite of the unadvised efforts of the short-sighted to blend it with the work of science, for it affords play for the ancient genial propensities that ruled men's quest of knowledge before the coming of science or of the out-spoken pragmatic barbarism. Its place may not be so large in proportion to the entire field of learning as it was before the scientific era got fully under way. But there is no intrinsic antagonism between science and scholarship, as there is between pragmatic training and scientific inquiry. Modern scholarship shares with modern science the quality of not being pragmatic in its aim. Like science it has no ulterior end. It may be difficult here and there to draw the line between science and scholarship, and it may even more be unnecessary to draw such a line; yet while the two ranges of discipline belong together in many ways, and while there are many points of contact and sympathy between the two; while the two together make up the modern scheme of learning; yet there is no need of confounding the one with the other, nor can the one do the work of the other. The scheme of learning has changed in such manner as to give science the more commanding place, but the scholar's domain has not thereby been invaded, nor has it suffered contraction at the hands of science, whatever may be said of the weak-kneed abnegation of some whose place, if they have one, is in the field of scholarship rather than of science.

All that has been said above has of course nothing to say as to the intrinsic merits of this quest of matter-of-fact knowledge. In point of fact, science gives its tone to modern culture. One may approve or one may deprecate the fact that this opaque, materialistic interpretation of things pervades modern thinking. That is a question of taste, about which there is no disputing. The prevalence of this matter-of-fact inquiry is a feature of modern culture, and the attitude which critics take toward this phenomenon is chiefly significant as indicating how far their own habit of mind coincides with the enlightened common-sense of civilized mankind. It shows in what degree they are abreast of the advance of culture. Those in whom the savage predilection or the barbarian tradition is stronger than their habituation to civilized life will find that this dominant factor of modern life is perverse, if not calamitous; those whose habits of thought have been fully shaped by the machine process and scientific inquiry are likely to find it good. The modern western culture, with its core of matter-of-fact knowledge, may be better or worse than some other cultural scheme, such as the classic Greek, the medieval Christian, the Hindu, or the Pueblo Indian. Seen in certain lights, tested by certain standards, it is doubtless better; by other standards, worse. But the fact remains that the current cultural scheme, in its maturest growth, is of that complexion; its characteristic force lies in this matter-of-fact insight; its highest discipline and its maturest aspirations are these.

In point of fact, the sober common-sense of civilized mankind accepts no other end of endeavor as self-sufficient and ultimate. That such is the case seems to be due chiefly to the ubiquitous presence of the machine technology and its creations in the life of modern communities. And so long as the machine process continues to hold its dominant place as a disciplinary factor in modern culture, so long must the spiritual and intellectual life of this cultural era maintain the character which the machine process gives it.

But while the scientist's spirit and his achievements stir an unqualified admiration in modern men, and while his discoveries carry conviction as nothing else does, it does not follow that the manner of man which this quest of knowledge produces or requires comes near answering to the current ideal of manhood, or that his conclusions are felt to be as good and beautiful as they are true. The ideal man, and the ideal of human life, even in the apprehension of those who most rejoice in the advances of science, is neither the finikin skeptic in the laboratory nor the animated slide-rule. The quest of science is relatively new. It is a cultural factor not comprised, in anything like its modern force, among those circumstances whose selective action in the far past has given to the race the human nature which it now has. The race reached the human plane with little of this searching knowledge of facts; and throughout the greater part of its life-history on the human plane it has been accustomed to make its higher generalizations and to formulate its larger principles of life in other terms than those of passionless matter-of-fact. This manner of knowledge has occupied an increasing share of men's attention in the past, since it bears in a decisive way upon the minor affairs of workday life; but it has never until now been put in the first place, as the dominant note of human culture. The normal man, such as his inheritance has made him, has therefore good cause to be restive under its dominion.

Notes

1. Jacques Loeb, *Heliotropismus der Thiere* and *Comparative Psychology and Physiology of the Brain.*
2. Cf. Gross, *Spiele der Thiere*, ch. 2 (esp. pp. 65–76), and ch. 5; *The Play of Man, Part III,* sec. 3; Spencer, *Principles of Psychology*, secs. 533–35.
3. The myths and legendary lore of the Eskimo, the Pueblo Indians, and some tribes of the northwest coast afford good instances of such idle creations. Cf. various *Reports of the Bureau of American Ethnology;* also, e.g., Tylor, *Primitive Culture,* esp. the chapters on "Mythology" and "Animism."
4. "Pragmatic" is here used in a more restricted sense than the distinctively pragmatic school of modern psychologists would commonly assign the term. "Pragmatic," "teleological," and the like terms have been extended to cover imputation of purpose as well as conversion to use. It is not intended to criticize this ambiguous use of terms, nor to correct it; but the terms are here used only in the latter sense, which alone belong to them by force of early usage and etymology. "Pragmatic" knowledge, therefore, is such as is designed to serve an expedient end for the knower, and is here contrasted with the imputation of expedient conduct to the facts observed. The reason for preserving this distinction is simply the present need of a simple term by which to mark the distinction between worldly wisdom and idle learning.
5. Cf. Ward, *Pure Sociology,* esp. pp. 437–48.
6. Cf., e.g., Tylor, *Primitive Culture*, chap. 8.
7. Cf. James, *Psychology,* chap. 9, esp. sec. 5.

8. As currently employed, the term "pragmatic" is made to cover both conduct looking to the agent's preferential advantage, expedient conduct and workmanship directed to the production of things that may or may not be of advantage to the agent. If the term be taken in the latter meaning, the culture of modern times is no less "pragmatic" than that of the Middle Ages. It is here intended to be used in the former sense.

9. Epistemologically speaking, activity is imputed to phenomena for the purpose of organizing them into a dramatically consistent system.

10. Cf., e.g., Karl Pearson, *Grammar of Science,* and compare his ideal of inert magnitudes as set forth in his exposition with his actual work as shown in chaps. 9, 10, and 12, and more particularly in his discussion of "Mother Right" and related topics in *The Chances of Death.*

11. Cf. James, *Psychology*, Vol. II, chap. 28, pp. 633–71, esp, p. 640 note.

12. Cf. Ward, *Principles of Psychology,* pp. 439–43.

The Intellectual Pre-Eminence of Jews in Modern Europe

Among all the clamorous projects of national self-determination which surround the return of peace, the proposal of the Zionists is notable for sobriety, good will, and a pose of self-assurance. More confidently and perspicuously than all the others, the Zionists propose a rehabilitation of their national integrity under a régime of live and let live, "with charity for all, with malice toward none." Yet it is always a project for withdrawal upon themselves, a scheme of national demarcation between Jew and gentile; indeed, it is a scheme of territorial demarcation and national frontiers of the conventional sort, within which Jews and Jewish traits, traditions, and aspirations are to find scope and breathing space for a home-bred culture and a free unfolding of all that is best and most characteristic in the endowment of the race. There runs through it all a dominant bias of isolation and inbreeding, and a confident persuasion that this isolation and inbreeding will bring great and good results for all concerned. The Zionists aspire to bring to full fruition all that massive endowment of spiritual and intellectual capacities of which their people have given evidence throughout their troubled history, and not least during these concluding centuries of their exile.

The whole project has an idyllic and engaging air. And any disinterested bystander will be greatly moved to wish them godspeed. Yet there comes in a regret that this experiment in isolation and inbreeding could not have been put to the test at an earlier date, before the new order of large-scale industry and universal intercourse had made any conclusive degree of such national isolation impracticable, before this same new order had so shaped the run of things that any nation or community drawn on this small scale would necessarily be dependent on and subsidiary to the run of things at large. It is now, unhappily, true that

Reprinted from *Political Science Quarterly* 34 (March 1919): 33–42. Used by permission of Political Science Quarterly.

any "nation" of the size and geographical emplacement of the projected Zion will, for the present and the calculable future, necessarily be something of a national make-believe. The current state of the industrial arts will necessarily deny it a round and self-balanced national integrity in any substantial sense. The days of Solomon and the caravan trade which underlay the glory of Solomon are long past.

Yet much can doubtless be done by taking thought and making the most of that spirit of stubborn clannishness which has never been the least among the traits of this people. But again, to any disinterested bystander there will come the question: What is the use of it all? It is not so much a question of what is aimed at, as of the chances of its working-out. The logic of the Zionist project plainly runs to the effect that, whereas this people have achieved great things while living under conditions of great adversity, scattered piecemeal among the gentiles of Europe, they are due to achieve much greater things and to reach an unexampled prosperity so soon as they shall have a chance to follow their own devices untroubled within the shelter of their own frontiers. But the doubt presents itself that the conditioning circumstances are not the same or of the same kind in the occidental twentieth century A.D. as in the oriental twelfth century B.C.; nor need it follow that those things which scattered Jews have achieved during their dispersion among the gentiles of Europe are a safe index of what things may be expected of a nation of Jews turned in upon themselves within the insulating frontiers of the Holy Land. It is on this latter point that a question is raised here as to the nature and causes of Jewish achievement in gentile Europe; and the contrast of the conditions offered by the projected Zion will present itself without argument.

It is a fact which must strike any dispassionate observer that the Jewish people have contributed much more than the Jewish people have contributed much more than an even share to the intellectual life of modern Europe. So also it is plain that the civilization of Christendom continues today to draw heavily on the Jews for men devoted to science and scholarly pursuits. It is not only that men of Jewish extraction continue to supply more than a proportionate quota to the rank and file engaged in scientific and scholarly work, but a disproportionate number of the men to whom modern science and scholarship look for guidance and leadership are of the same derivation. Particularly is this true of the modern sciences, and it applies perhaps especially in the field of scientific theory, even beyond the extent of its application in the domain of workday detail. So much is notorious.

This notable and indeed highly creditable showing has, of course, not escaped the attention of those men of Jewish race who interest themselves in the fortunes of their own people. Not unusually it is set down as a national trait, as evidence of a peculiarly fortunate intellectual endowment, native and hereditary, in the Jewish people. There is much to be said for such a view, but it should not follow that any inquiry into the place and value of the Jewish people in western civilization should come to rest with this broad assertion of pre-eminence in point of native endowment.

It is true that the history of the Chosen People, late and early, throws them into a position of distinction among the nations with which they have been associated; and it will commonly be accepted without much argument that they have, both late and early, shown distinctive traits of temperament and aptitude, such as to mark them off more or less sharply from all the gentiles among whom it has been their lot to be thrown. So general is the recognition of special Jewish traits, of character and of capacity, that any refusal to recognize something which may be called a Jewish type of hereditary endowment would come to nothing much better than a borrowing of trouble.

That there should be such a tenacious spiritual and intellectual heritage transmissible within the Jewish community and marking that people off in any perceptible degree from their gentile neighbors is all the more notable in view of the known life-history of the children of Israel. No unbiased ethologist will question the fact that the Jewish people are a nation of hybrids; that gentile blood of many kinds has been infused into the people in large proportions in the course of time. Indeed, none of the peoples of Christendom has been more unremittingly exposed to hybridization, in spite of all the stiff conventional precautions that have been taken to keep the breed pure. It is not a question of a surreptitious hybrid strain, such as would show itself in sporadic reversions to an alien type; but rather it is a question whether the Jewish strain itself, racially speaking, can at all reasonably be held to account for one half of the pedigree of the Jewish nation as it stands.

The hybrid antecedents of the Children of Israel are not a mere matter of bookish record. Evidence of their hybrid descent is written all over them wherever they are to be met with, so that in this respect the Jews of Europe are in the same case as the other Europeans, who are also universally cross-bred. It would perplex any anthropologist to identify a single individual among them all who could safely be set down as embodying the Jewish racial type without abatement. The variations in all the measurable traits that go to identify any individual in the schedules of the anthropologists are wide and ubiquitous as regards both their physical and their spiritual traits, in respect of anthropometric measurements as well as in temperament and capacities. And yet, when all is said in abatement of it, the Jewish type, it must be admitted, asserts itself with amazing persistence through all the disguises with which it has been overlaid in the course of agelong hybridization. Whatever may be found true elsewhere, in their contact with other racial types than those of Europe, it still appears that within this European racial environment the outcome given by any infusion of Jewish blood in these cross-bred individuals is something which can be identified as Jewish. Crossbreeding commonly results in a gain to the Jewish community rather than conversely; and the hybrid offspring is a child of Israel rather than of the gentiles.

In effect, therefore, it is the contribution of this Jewish-hybrid people to the culture of modern Europe that is in question. The men of this Jewish extraction count for more than their proportionate share in the intellectual life of western civilization; and they count particularly among the vanguard, the pioneers, the uneasy guild of pathfinders and iconoclasts, in science, scholarship, and institutional change and growth. On its face it appears as if an infusion of Jewish blood, even in some degree of hybrid attenuation, were the one decisive factor in the case; and something of that sort may well be allowed, to avoid argument if for no more substantial reason. But even a casual survey of the available evidence will leave so broad a claim in doubt.

Of course, there is the fact to be allowed for at the outset, so far as need be, that these intellectuals of Jewish extraction are, after all, of hybrid extraction as well; but this feature of the case need be given no undue weight. It is of consequence in its bearing on the case of the Jews only in the same manner and degree as it is of consequence for any other hybrid people. Cross-breeding gives a wider range of variation and a greater diversity of individual endowment than can be had in any passably pure-bred population; from which results a greater effectual flexibility of aptitudes and capacities in such a people when exposed to conditions that make for change. In this respect the Jews are neither more nor less fortunate than their gentile compatriots.

It may be more to the purpose to note that this intellectual pre-eminence of the Jews has come into bearing within the gentile community of peoples, not from the outside; that the men who have been its bearers have been men immersed in this gentile culture in which they have played their part of guidance and incitement, not bearers of a compelling message from afar or proselytes of enlightenment conjuring with a ready formula worked out in the ghetto and carried over into the gentile community for its mental regeneration. In point of fact, neither these nor other Jews have done effectual missionary work, in any ordinary sense of that term, in this or any other connection; nor have they entertained a design to do so. Indeed, the Chosen People have quite characteristically never been addicted to missionary enterprise; nor does the Jewish scheme of light and honest living comprise anything of the kind. This, too, is notorious fact; so much so that this allusion to it may well strike any Jew as foolish insistence on a commonplace matter of course. In their character of a Chosen People, it is not for them to take thought of their unblest neighbors and seek to dispel the darkness that overlies the soul of the gentiles.

The cultural heritage of the Jewish people is large and rich, and it is of ancient and honorable lineage. And from time immemorial this people has shown aptitude for such work as will tax the powers of thought and imagination. Their home-bred achievements of the ancient time, before the Diaspora, are among the secure cultural monuments of mankind; but these achievements of the Jewish ancients neither touch the frontiers of modern science nor do they fall in the lines of modern scholarship. So also the later achievements of the Jewish scholars and savants, in so far as their intellectual enterprise has gone forward on what may be called distinctively Jewish lines, within the confines of their own community and by the leading of their own home-bred interest, untouched by that peculiar drift of inquiry that characterizes the speculations of the modern gentile world—this learning of the later generations of home-bred Jewish scholars is also reputed to have run into lucubrations that have no significance for contemporary science or scholarship at large.

It appears to be only when the gifted Jew escapes from the cultural environment created and fed by the particular genius of his own people, only when he falls into the alien lines of gentile inquiry and becomes a naturalized, through hyphenate, citizen in the gentile republic of learning, that he comes into his own as a creative leader in the world's intellectual enterprise. It is by loss of allegiance, or at the best by force of a divided allegiance to the people of his origin, that he finds himself in the vanguard of modern inquiry.

It will not do to say that none but renegade Jews count effectually in the modern sciences. Such a statement would be too broad; but, for all its excessive breadth, it exceeds the fact only by a margin. The margin may seem wide, so wide as to vitiate the general statement, perhaps, or at least wide enough materially to reduce its cogency. But it would be wider of the mark to claim that the renegades are to be counted only as sporadic exceptions among a body of unmitigated Jews who make up the virtual total of that muster of creative men of science which the Jewish people have thrown into the intellectual advance of Christendom.

The first requisite for constructive work in modern science, and indeed for any work of inquiry that shall bring enduring results, is a skeptical frame of mind. The enterprising skeptic alone can be counted on to further the increase of knowledge in any substantial fashion. This will be found true both in the modern sciences and in the field of scholarship at large. Much good and serviceable workmanship of a workday character goes into the grand total of modern scientific achievement; but that pioneering and engineering work of guidance, design, and theoretical correlation, without which the most painstaking collection and canvass of information is irrelevant, incompetent, and impertinent—this intellectual enterprise that goes forward presupposes a degree of exemption from hard-and-fast preconceptions, a skeptical animus, *Unbefangenheit*, release from the dead hand of conventional finality.

The intellectually gifted Jew is in a peculiarly fortunate position in respect of this requisite immunity from the inhibitions of intellectual quietism. But he can come in for such immunity only at the cost of losing his secure place in the scheme of conventions into which he has been born, and at the cost, also, of finding no similarly secure place in that scheme of gentile conventions into which he is thrown. For him as for other men in the like case, the skepticism that goes to make him an effectual factor in the increase and diffusion of knowledge among men involves a loss of that peace of mind that is the birthright of the safe and sane quietest. He becomes a disturber of the intellectual peace, but only at the cost of becoming an intellectual wayfaring man, a wanderer in the intellectual no-man's-land, seeking another place to rest, farther along the road, somewhere over the horizon. They are neither a complaisant nor a contented lot, these aliens of the uneasy feet; but that is, after all, not the point in question.

The young Jew who is at all gifted with a taste for knowledge will unavoidably go afield into that domain of learning where the gentile interests dominate and the gentile orientation gives the outcome. There is nowhere else to go on the quest. He comes forthwith to realize that the scheme of traditions and conventional verities handed down within the pale of his own people are matters of habit handed down by tradition, that they have only such force as belongs to matters of habit and convention, and that they lose their binding force so soon as the habitually accepted outlook is given up or seriously deranged. These nationally binding convictions of what is true, good, and beautiful in the world of the human spirit are forthwith seen to be only contingently good and true; to be binding only so far as the habitual will to believe in them and to seek the truth along their lines remains intact. That is to say, only so long as no scheme of habituation alien to the man's traditional outlook has broken in on him, and has forced him to see that those convictions and verities which hold their place as fundamentally and eternally good and right within the balanced scheme of received traditions prove to be, after all, only an ephemeral web of habits of thought; so soon as his current habits of life no longer continue to fall in those traditional lines that keep these habits of thought in countenance.

Now it happens that the home-bred Jewish scheme of things, human and divine, and the ways and means of knowledge that go with such a scheme, are of an archaic fashion, good and true, perhaps, beyond all praise, for the time and conditions that gave rise to it all, that wove that web of habituation and bound its close-knit tissue of traditional verities and conventions. But it all bears the date-mark, "B.C." It is of a divine complexion, monotheistic even, and perhaps intrinsically the thearchic; it is ritualistic, with an exceedingly and beautifully magical efficacy of ritual necessity. It is imperiously self-balanced and self-sufficient, to the point of sanctity; and as is always true of such schemes of sanctity and magical sufficiency, it runs on a logic of personal and spiritual traits, qualities and relations, a class of imponderables which are no longer of the substance of those things that are inquired into by men to whom the ever increasingly mechanistic orientation of the modern time becomes habitual.

When the gifted young Jew, still flexible in respect of his mental habits, is set loose among the iron pots of this mechanistic orientation, the clay vessel of Jewish archaism suffers that fortune which is due and coming to clay vessels among the iron pots. His beautifully rounded heirloom, trade-marked "B.C.," goes to pieces between his hands, and they are left empty. He is divested of those archaic conventional preconceptions which will not comport with the intellectual environment in which he finds himself. But he is not thereby invested with the gentile's peculiar heritage of conventional preconceptions which have stood over, by inertia of habit, out of the gentile past, which go, on the one hand, to make the safe and sane gentile, conservative and complacent, and which conduce also, on the other hand, to blur the safe and sane gentile's intellectual vision, and to leave him intellectually sessile.

The young Jew finds his own heritage of usage and outlook untenable; but this does not mean that he therefore will take over and inwardly assimilate the traditions of usage and outlook which the gentile world has to offer; or at the most he does not uncritically take over all the intellectual prepossessions that are always standing over among the substantial citizens of the republic of learning. The idols of his own tribe have crumbled in decay and no longer cumber the ground, but that release does not induce him to set up a new line of idols borrowed from an alien tribe to do the same disservice. By consequence he is in a peculiar degree exposed to the unmediated facts of the current situation; and in a peculiar degree, therefore, he takes his orientation from the run of the facts as he finds them, rather than from the traditional interpretation of analogous facts in the past. In short, he is a skeptic by force of circumstances over which he has no control. Which comes to saying that he is in line to become a guide and leader of men in that intellectual enterprise out of which comes the increase and diffusion of knowledge among men, provided always that he is by native gift endowed with that net modicum of intelligence which takes effect in the play of the idle curiosity.

Intellectually he is likely to become an alien; spiritually he is more than likely to remain a Jew; for the heart-strings of affection and consuetude are tied early, and they are not readily retied in after life. Nor does the animus with which the community of safe and sane gentiles is wont to meet him conduce at all to his personal incorporation in that community, whatever may befall the intellectual assets which he brings. Their people need not become his people nor their gods his gods, and indeed the provocation is forever and irritably present all over the place to turn back from following after them. The most amiable share in the gentile community's life that is likely to fall to his lot is that of being interned. One who goes away from home will come to see many unfamiliar things, and to take note of them; but it does not follow that he will swear by all the strange gods whom he meets along the road.

As bearing on the Zionist's enterprise in isolation and nationality, this fable appears to teach a two-fold moral: If the adventure is carried to that consummate outcome which seems to be aimed at, it should apparently be due to be crowned with a large national complacency and, possibly, a profound and self-sufficient content on the part of the Chosen People domiciled once more in the Chosen Land; and when and in so far as the Jewish people in this way turn inward on themselves, their prospective contribution to the world's intellectual output should, in the light of the historical evidence, fairly be expected to take on the complexion of Talmudic lore, rather than that character of free-swung skeptical initiative which their renegades have habitually infused into the pursuit of the modern sciences abroad among the nations. Doubtless, even so the supply of Jewish renegades would not altogether cease, though it should presumably fall off to a relatively inconsiderable residue. And not all renegades are fit guides and leaders of men on the quest of knowledge, nor is their dominant incentive always or ordinarily the quest of the idle curiosity.

There should be some loss to Christendom at large, and there might be some gain to the repatriated Children of Israel. It is a sufficiently difficult choice between a life of complacent futility at home and a thankless quest of unprofitable knowledge abroad. It is, after all, a matter of the drift of circumstances; and behind that lies a question of taste, about which there is no disputing.

Christian Morals and the Competitive System

In the light of the current materialistic outlook and the current skepticism touching supernatural matters, some question may fairly be entertained as to the religious cult of Christianity. Its fortunes in the proximate future, as well as its intrinsic value for the current scheme of civilization, may be subject to doubt. But a similar doubt is not readily entertained as regards the morals of Christianity. In some of its elements this morality is so intimately and organically connected with the scheme of western civilization that its elimination would signify a cultural revolution whereby occidental culture would lose its occidental characteristics and fall into the ranks of ethnic civilization at large. Much the same may be said of that pecuniary competition which today rules the economic life of Christendom and in large measure guides western civilization in much else than the economic respect.

Both are institutional factors of first-rate importance in this culture, and as such it might be difficult or impracticable to assign the primacy to the one or the other, since each appears to be in a dominant position. Western civilization is both Christian and competitive (pecuniary); and it seems bootless to ask whether its course is more substantially under the guidance of the one than of the other of these two institutional norms. Hence, if it should appear, as is sometimes contended, that there is an irreconcilable discrepancy between the two, the student of this culture might have to face the question: Will western civilization dwindle and decay if one or the other, the morals of competition or the morals of Christianity, definitively fall into abeyance?

In a question between the two codes, or systems of conduct, each must be taken at its best and simplest. That is to say, it is a question of agreement or

Reprinted by permission of University of Chicago Press. Originally appeared in *International Journal of Ethics* 20 (January 1910):168–85.

discrepancy in the larger elementary principles of each, not a question of the variegated details, nor of the practice of the common run of Christians, on the one hand, and of competitive business men, on the other. The variety of detailed elaboration and sophistication is fairly endless in both codes; at the same time many Christians are engaged in competitive business, and conversely. Under the diversified exigencies of daily life neither the accepted principles of morality nor those of business competition work out in an untroubled or untempered course of conduct. Circumstances constrain men unremittingly to shrewd adaptions, if not to some degree of compromise, in their endeavors to live up to their accustomed principles of conduct. Yet both of these principles, or codes of conduct, are actively present throughout life in any modern community. For all the shrewd adaptation to which they may be subject in the casuistry of individual practice, they will not have fallen into abeyance so long as the current scheme of life is not radically altered. Both the Christian morality and the morality of pecuniary competition are intimately involved in this occidental scheme of life; for it is out of these and the like habits of thought that the scheme of life is made up. Taken at their best, do the two further and fortify one another? Do they work together without mutual help or hindrance? Or do they mutually inhibit and defeat each other?

In the light of modern science the principles of Christian morality or of pecuniary competition must, like any other principles of conduct, be taken simply as prevalent habits of thought. And in this light no question can be entertained as to the intrinsic merit, the eternal validity, of either. They are, humanly speaking, institutions which have arisen in the growth of the western civilization. Their genesis and growth are incidents, or possible episodes, in the life-history of this culture—habits of thought induced by the discipline of life in the course of this culture's growth, and more or less intrinsic and essential to its character as a phase of civilization. Therefore, the question of their consistency with one another, or with the cultural scheme in which they are involved, turns into a question as to the conditions to which they owe their rise and continued force as institutions—as to the discipline of experience in the past, out of which each of them has come and to which, therefore, each is (presumably) suited. The exigencies of life and the discipline of experience in a complex cultural situation are many and diverse, and it is always possible that any given phase of culture may give rise to divergent lines of institutional growth, to habits of conduct which are mutually incompatible, and which may at the same time be incompatible with the continued life of that cultural situation which has brought them to pass. The dead civilizations of history, particularly the greater ones, seem commonly to have died of some such malady. If Christian morality and pecuniary competition are the outgrowth of the same or similar lines of habituation, there should presumably be no incompatibility or discrepancy between them; otherwise it is an open question.

Leaving on one side, then, all question of its divine or supernatural origin, force, and warrant, as well as of its truth and its intrinsic merit or demerit, it may be feasible to trace the human line of derivation of this spirit of Christianity, considered as a spiritual attitude habitual to civilized mankind. The details and mutations of the many variants of the cult and creed might likewise be traced back, by shrewd analysis, to their origins in the habits enforced by past civilized life, and might on this ground be appraised in respect of their fitness to survive under the changing conditions of later culture; but such a work of detailed inquiry is neither practicable nor necessary here. The variants are many and diverse, but for all the diversity and discord among them they have certain large features in common, by which they are identified as Christian and are contrasted with the ethnic cults and creeds. There is a certain Christian animus which pervades most of them, and marks them off against the non-Christian spiritual world. This is, perhaps, more particularly true of the moral principles of Christianity than of the general fabric of its many creeds and cults. Certain elemental features of this Christian animus stand forth obtrusively in its beginnings, and have, with varying fortunes of dominance and decay, persisted or survived unbroken, on the whole, to the present day. These are non-resistance (humility) and brotherly love. Something further might be added, perhaps, but this much is common, in some degree, to the several variants of Christianity, late or early; and the inclusion of other common principles besides these would be debatable and precarious, except in case of such moral principles as are also common to certain of the ethnic cults as well as to Christianity. Even with respect to the two principles named, there might be some debate as to their belonging peculiarly and characteristically to the Christian spirit, exclusive of all other spiritual habits of mind. But it is at least a tenable position that these principles are intrinsic to the Christian spirit, and that they habitually serve as competent marks of identification. With the exclusion or final obsolescence of either of these, the cult would no longer be Christian, in the current acceptation of the term; though much else, chiefly not of an ethical character, would have to be added to make up a passably complete characterization of the Christian system, as, e.g., monotheism, sin and atonement, eschatological retribution, and the like. But the two principles named bear immediately on the morals of Christianity; they are, indeed, the spiritual capital with which the Christian movement started out, and they are still the characteristics by force of which it survives.

It is commonly held that these principles are not inherent traits of human nature as such, congenital and hereditary traits of the species which assert themselves instinctively, impulsively, by force of the mere absence of repression. Such, at least, in effect, is the teaching of the Christian creeds, in that they hold these spiritual qualities to be a gift of divine grace, not a heritage of sinful human nature. Such an account of their origin and their acquirement by the successive generations of men does not fit these two main supports of Christian morality in the same degree. It may fairly be questioned as regards the principle of brotherly love, or the impulse to mutual service. While this seems to be a characteristic trait of Christian morals and may serve as a specific mark by which to distinguish this morality from the greater non-Christian cults, it is apparently a trait which Christendom shares with many of the obscurer cultures, and which does not in any higher degree characterize Christendom than it does these other, lower cultures. In the lower, non-Christian cultures, particularly among the more peaceable communities of savages, something of the kind appears to prevail by mere force of hereditary propensity; at least it appears, in some degree, to belong in these lower civilizations without being traceable to special teaching or to a visible interposition of divine grace. And in an obscure and dubious fashion, perhaps sporadically, it recurs throughout the life of human society with such an air of ubiquity as would argue that it is an elemental trait of the species, rather than a cultural product of Christendom. It may not be an overstatement to say that this principle is, in its elements, in some sort an atavistic trait, and that Christendom comes by it through a cultural reversion to the animus of the lower (peaceable) savage culture. But even if such an account be admitted as substantially sound, it does not account for that cultural reversion to which Christendom owes its peculiar partiality for this principle; nor is its association with its fellow principle, non-resistance, thereby accounted for. The two come into play together in the beginnings of Christianity, and are henceforward associated together, more or less inseparable, throughout the later vicissitudes of the cult and its moral code.

The second-named principle, of non-resistance and renunciation, is placed first in order of importance in the earlier formulations of Christian conduct. This is not similarly to be traced back as a culturally atavistic trait, as the outgrowth of such an archaic cultural situation as if offered by the lower savagery. Non-resistance has no such air of ubiquity and spontaneous recrudescence, and does not show itself, even sporadically, as a matter of course in cultures that are otherwise apparently unrelated; particularly not in the lower cultures, where the hereditary traits of the species should presumably assert themselves, on occasion in a less sophisticated expression than on the more highly conventionalized levels of civilization. On the contrary, it belongs almost wholly to the more highly developed, more coercively organized civilizations, that are possessed of a consistent monotheistic religion and a somewhat arbitrary secular authority; and it is not always, indeed not commonly, present in these.

Christianity at its inception did not take over this moral principle, ready-made, from any of the older cults or cultures from which the Christian movement was in a position to draw. It is not found, at least not in appreciable force, in the received Judaism; nor can it be derived from the classical (Graeco-Roman) cultures, which had none of it; nor is it to be found among the pagan antiquities of these barbarians whose descendants make up the great body of Christendom today. Yet Christianity sets out with the principle of non-resistance full-blown, in the days of its early diffusion, and finds assent and acceptance for it with such readiness as seems to argue that mankind was prepared beforehand for just such a principle of conduct. Mankind, particularly the populace, within the confines of that Roman dominion within which the early diffusion of Christianity took place, was apparently in a frame of mind to accept such a principle of morality, or such a maxim of conduct; and the same is progressively true for the outlying populations to which Christianity spread in the next four centuries.

To any modern student of human culture, this ready acceptance of such principle (habit of thought) gives evidence that the section of mankind which had thus shifted its moral footing to a new and revolutionary moral principle must have been trained, by recently past experience, by the discipline of daily life in the immediate past, into such a frame of mind as predisposed them for its acceptance; that is to say, they must have been disciplined into a spiritual attitude to which such a new principle of conduct would commend itself as reasonable, if not as a matter of course. And in due process, as this suitable attitude was enforced upon the other, outlying populations by suitable disciplinary means, Christianity with its gospel of renunciation tended to spread and supplant the outworn cults that no longer fitted the altered cultural situation. But in its later diffusion, among peoples not securely under Roman rule and not reduced to such a frame of mind by a protracted experience of Roman discipline, Christianity makes less capital of the morality of non-resistance.

It was among the peoples subject to the Roman rule that Christianity first arose and spread; among the lower orders of the populace especially, who had been beaten to a pulp by the hard-handed, systematic, inexorable power of the imperial city; who had no rights which the Roman master was bound to respect; who were aliens and practically outlaws under the sway of the Caesars; and who had acquired, under high pressure, the conviction that non-resistance was the chief of virtues if not the whole duty of man. They had learned to render unto Caesar that which is Caesar's, and were in a frame of mind to render unto God that which is God's.

It is a notable fact also that, as a general rule, in its subsequent diffusion to regions and peoples not benefited by the Roman discipline, Christianity spread in proportion to the more or less protracted experience of defeat and helpless submission undergone by these peoples; and that it was the subject populace rather than the master classes that took kindly to the doctrine of non-resistance. In the outlying corners of the western world, such as the Scandinavian and British countries, where subjection to arbitrary rule in temporal matters had been less consistently and less enduringly enforced, the principle of non-resistance took less firm root. And in the days when the peoples of Christendom were sharply differentiated into ruling and subject classes, non-resistance was accepted by the lower rather than by the upper classes.

Much the same, indeed, is true of the companion principle of mutual succor. On the whole, it is not too bold a generalization to say that these elements of the moral code which distinguish Christianity from the ethnic cults are elements of the morals of low life, of the subject populace. There is, in point of practical morality, not much to choose, e.g., between the upper-class medieval Christianity and the contemporary Mohammedan morality. It is only in later times, after the western culture had lost its aristocratic-feudalistic character and had become, in its typical form, though not in all its ramifications, a kind of universalized low-life culture—it is only at this later period that these principles of low-life morality also became in some degree universalized principles of Christian duty; and it still remains true that these principles are most at home in the more vulgar divisions of the Christian cult. The higher-class variants of Christianity still differ little in the substance of their morality from Judaism or Islam. The morality of the upper class is in a less degree the morality of non-resistance and brotherly love, and is in a greater degree the morality of coercive control and kindly tutelage, which are in no degree distinctive traits of Christianity, as contrasted with the other great religious systems.

In their experience of Roman devastation and punishment-at-large, which predisposed the populace for this principle of non-resistance, the subject peoples commonly also lost such class distinctions and differential rights and privileges as they had previously enjoyed. They were leveled down to a passably homogeneous state of subjection, in which one class or individual had little to gain at the cost of another, and in which, also, each and all palpably needed the succor of all the rest. The institutional fabric had crumbled, very much as it does in an earthquake. The conventional differentiations, handed down out of the past, had proved vain and meaningless in the face of the current situation. The pride of caste and all the principles of differential dignity and honor fell away, and left mankind naked and unashamed and free to follow the prompting of hereditary savage human nature which make for fellowship and Christian charity.

Barring repressive conventionalities, reversion to the spiritual state of savagery is always easy; for human nature is still substantially savage. The discipline of savage life, selective and adaptive, has been by far the most protracted and probably the most exacting of any phase of culture in all the life-history of the race; so that by heredity human nature still is, and must indefinitely continue to be, savage human nature. This savage spiritual heritage that "springs eternal" when the pressure of conventionality is removed or relieved seems highly conducive to the two main traits of Christian morality, though more so to the principle of brotherly love than to that of renunciation. And this may well be the chief circumstance that has contributed to the persistence of these principles of conduct even in later times, when the external conditions have not visibly favored or called for their continued exercise.

The principles of conduct underlying pecuniary competition are the principles of Natural Rights, and as such date from the eighteenth century. In respect of their acceptance into the body of commonplace morality and practice and the constraining force which they exercise, they are apparently an outgrowth of modern civilization—whatever older antiquity may be assigned them in respect of their documentary pedigree. Comparatively speaking, they are absent from the scheme of life and from the common-sense apprehension of rights and duties in medieval times. They derive their warrant as moral principles from the discipline of life under the cultural situation of early modern times. They are accordingly of relatively recent date as prevalent habits of thought, at least in their fuller and freer development; even though the underlying traits of human nature which have lent themselves to the formation of these habits of thought may be as ancient as any other. The period of their growth coincides somewhat closely with that of the philosophy of egoism, self-interest, or "individualism," as it is less aptly called. This egoistic outlook gradually assumes a dominant place in the occidental scheme of thought during and after the transition from medieval to modern times; it appears to be a result of the habituation to those new conditions of life which characterize the modern, as contrasted with the medieval, situation. Assuming, as is now commonly done, that the fundamental and controlling changes which shape and guide the transition from the institutional situation of the medieval to that of the modern world are economic changes, one may with fair confidence trace a connection between these economic changes and the concomitant growth of modern business principles. The vulgar element, held cheap, kept under but massive, in the medieval order of society, comes gradually into the foreground and into the controlling position in economic life; so that the aristocratic or chivalric standards and ideals are gradually supplanted or displaced by the vulgar apprehension of what is right and best in the conduct of life. The chivalric canons of destructive exploit and of status give place to the more sordid canons of workmanlike efficiency and pecuniary strength. The economic changes which thus gave a new and hitherto impotent element of society the primacy in the social order and in the common-sense apprehensions of what is worth while, are, in the main characteristically, the growth of handicraft and petty trade; giving rise to the industrial towns, to the growth of markets, to a pecuniary field of individual enterprise and initiative, and to a valuation of men, things and events in pecuniary terms.

It is impossible here to go narrowly into the traits of culture and of human nature which were evolved in the rise and progress of handicraft and the petty trade, and brought about the decay of medievalism and the rise of the modern cultural scheme. But so much seems plain on the face of things: there is at work in all this growth of the new, pecuniary culture, a large element of emulation, both in the acquisition of goods and in their conspicuous consumption. Pecuniary exploit in a degree supplies the place of chivalric exploit. But emulation is not the whole of the motive force of the new order, nor does it supply all the canons of conduct and standards of merit under the new order. In its earlier stages, while dominated by the exigencies of handicraft and the petty trade, the modern culture is fully as much shaped and guided by considerations of livelihood, as by the ideals of differential gain.

The material conditions of the new economic situation would not tolerate the institutional conditions of the old situation. There was being enforced upon the community, primarily upon that workday element into whose hands the new industrial exigencies were shifting the directive force, a new range of habitual notions as to what was needful and what was right. In both of the characteristically modern lines of occupation—handicraft and the petty trade—the individual, the workman or trader, is the central and efficient factor, on whose initiative, force, diligence, and discretion his own economic fortunes and those of the community visibly turn. It is an economic situation in which, necessarily, individual deals with individual on a footing of pecuniary efficiency; where the ties of group solidarity, which control the individual's economic (and social) relations, are themselves of a pecuniary character, and are made or broken more or less at the individual's discretion and in pecuniary terms; and it is, moreover, a cultural situation in which the social and civil relations binding the individual are prevailing and increasingly formed for pecuniary ends, and enforced by pecuniary sanctions. The individualism of the modern era sets out with industrial aims and makes its way by force of industrial efficiency. And since the individual relations under this system take the pecuniary form, the individualism thus worked out and incorporated in the modern institutional fabric is a pecuniary individualism, and is therefore also typically egoistic.

The principles governing right conduct according to the habits of thought native to this individualistic era are the egoistic principles of natural rights and natural liberty. These rights and this liberty are egoistic rights and liberty of the individual. They are to be summed up as freedom and security of person and of pecuniary transactions. It is a curious fact, significant of the extreme preponderance of the vulgar element in this cultural revolution, that among these natural rights there are included no remnants of those prerogatives and disabilities of birth, office, or station, which seemed matters of course and of common-sense to the earlier generations of men who had grown up under the influence of the medieval social order. Nor, curiously, are there remnants of the more ancient rights and duties of the bond of kinship, the blood feud, or clan allegiance, such as were once also matters of course and of commonsense in the cultural eras and areas in which the social order of the kinship group or the clan organization had prevailed. On the other hand, while these institutional elements have (in theory) lost all standing, the analogous institution of property has become an element of the natural order of things. The system of natural rights is natural in the sense of being consonant with the nature of handicraft and petty trade.

Meanwhile, times have changed since the eighteenth century, when this system of pecuniary egoism reached its mature development. That is to say, the material circumstances, the economic exigencies, have changed, and the discipline of habit resulting from the changed situation has, as a consequence, tended to a somewhat different effect—as is evidenced by the fact that the sanctity and sole efficacy of the principles of natural rights are beginning to be called in question. The excellence and sufficiency of an enlightened pecuniary egoism are no longer a matter of course and of commonsense to the mind of this generation, which has experienced the current era of machine industry, credit delegated corporation management, and distant markets. What fortune may overtake these business principles, these habits of thought native to the handicraft era, in the further sequence of economic changes can, of course, not be foretold; but it is at least certain that they cannot remain standing and effective, in the long run, unless the modern community should return to an economic regime equivalent to the era of handicraft and petty trade. For the business principles in question are of the nature of habits of thought, and habits of thought are made by habits of life; and the habits of life necessary to maintain these principles and to give them their effective sanction in the commonsense convictions of the community are the habits of life enforced by the system of handicraft and petty trade.

It appears, then, that these two codes of conduct, Christian morals and business principles, are the institutional by-products of two different cultural situations. The former, in so far as they are typically Christian, arose out of the abjectly and precariously servile relations in which the populace stood to their masters in late Roman times, as also, in a great, though perhaps less, degree, during the "Dark" and the Middle Ages. The latter, the morals of pecuniary competition, on the other hand, are habits of thought induced by the exigencies of vulgar life under the rule of handicraft and petty trade, out of which has come the peculiar system of rights and duties characteristic of modern Christendom. Yet there is something in common between the two. The Christian principles inculcate brotherly love, mutual succor: Love thy neighbor as thyself; *Mutuum date, nihil inde sperantes.* This principle seems, in its elements at least, to be a culturally atavistic trait, belonging to the ancient, not to say primordial, peaceable culture of the lower savagery. The natural-rights analogue of this principle of solidarity and mutual succor is the principle of fair play, which appears to be the nearest approach to the golden rule that the pecuniary civilization will admit. There is no reach of ingenuity or of ingenuousness by which the one of these may be converted into the other; nor does the regime of fair play—essentially a regime of emulation—conduce to the reinforcement of the golden rule. Yet throughout all the vicissitudes of cultural change, the golden rule of the peaceable savage has never lost the respect of occidental mankind, and its hold on men's convictions is, perhaps, stronger now than at any earlier period of the modern time. It seems incompatible with business principles, but appreciably less so than with the principles of conduct that ruled the western world in the days before the Grace of God was supplanted by the Rights of Man. The distaste for the spectacle of contemporary life seldom rises to the pitch of "renunciation of the world" under the new dispensation. While one half of the Christian moral code, that pious principle which inculcates humility, submission to irresponsible authority, found easier lodgement in the medieval culture, the more humane moral element of mutual succor seems less alien to the modern culture of pecuniary self-help.

The presumptive degree of compatibility between the two codes of morality may be shown by a comparison of the cultural setting, out of which each has arisen and in which each should be at home. In the most general outline, and neglecting details as far as may be, we may describe the upshot of this growth of occidental principles as follows: The ancient Christian principle of humility, renunciation, abnegation, or non-resistance has been virtually eliminated from the moral scheme of Christendom; nothing better than a sophisticated affectation of it has any extensive currency in modern life. The conditions to which it owes its rise—bare-handed despotism and servile helplessness—are, for the immediate present and the recent past, no longer effectual elements in the cultural situation; and it is, of course, in the recent past that the conditions must be sought which have shaped the habits of thought of the immediate present. Its companion principle, brotherly love or mutual service, appears, in its elements at least, to be a very deeprooted and ancient cultural trait, due to an extremely protracted experience of the race in the early stages of human culture, reinforced and defined by the social conditions prevalent in the early days of Christianity. In the naïve and particular formulation given it by the early Christians, this habit of thought has also lost much of its force, or has fallen somewhat into abeyance; being currently represented by a thrifty charity, and, perhaps, by the negative principle of fair play, neither of which can fairly be rated as a competent expression of the Christian spirit. Yet this principle is forever reasserting itself in economic matters, in the impulsive approval of whatever conduct is serviceable to the common good and in the disapproval of disservicable conduct even within the limits of legality and natural right. It seems, indeed, to be nothing else than a somewhat specialized manifestation of the instinct of workmanship, and as such it has the indefeasible vitality that belongs to the hereditary traits of human nature.

The pecuniary scheme of right conduct is of recent growth, but it is an outcome of a recently past phase of modern culture rather than of the immediate present. This system of natural rights, including the right of ownership and the principles of pecuniary good and evil that go with it, no longer has the consistent support of current events. Under the conditions prevalent in the era of handicraft, the rights of ownership made for equality rather than the reverse, so that their exercise was in effect not notably inconsistent with the ancient bias in favor of mutual aid and human brotherhood. This is more particularly apparent if the particular form of organization and the spirit of the regulations then ruling in vulgar life be kept in mind. The technology of handicraft, as well as the market relations of the system of petty trade, pushed the individual workman into the foreground and led men to think of economic interests in terms of this workman and his work; the situation emphasized his creative relation to his product, as well as his responsibility for this product and for its serviceability to the common welfare. It was a situation in which the acquisition of property depended, in the main, on the workmanlike serviceability of the man who acquired it, and in which, on the whole, honesty was the best policy. Under such conditions the principles of fair play and the inviolability of ownership would be somewhat closely in touch with the ancient human instinct of workmanship, which approves mutual aid and serviceability to the common good. On the other hand, the current experience of men in the communities of Christendom, now no longer acts to reinforce these habits of thought embodied in the system of natural rights; and it is scarcely conceivable that a conviction of the goodness, sufficiency, and inviolability of the rights of ownership could arise out of such a condition of things, technological and pecuniary, as now prevails.

Hence, there are indications in current events that these principles—habits of thought—are in process of disintegration rather than otherwise. With the revolutionary changes that have supervened in technology and in pecuniary relations, there is no longer such a close and visible touch between the workman and his product as would persuade men that the product belongs to him by force of an extension of his personality; nor is there a visible relation between serviceability and acquisition; nor between the discretionary use of wealth and the common welfare. The principles of fair play and pecuniary discretion have, in great measure, lost the sanction once afforded them by the human propensity for serviceability to the common good, neutral as that sanction has been at its best. Particularly is this true since business has taken on the character of an impersonal, dispassionate, not to say graceless, investment for profit. There is little in the current situation to keep the natural right of pecuniary discretion in touch with the impulsive bias of brotherly love, and there is in the spiritual discipline of this situation much that makes for an effectual discrepancy between the two. Except for a possible reversion to a cultural situation strongly characterized by ideals of emulation and status, the ancient racial bias embodied in the Christian principle of brotherhood should logically continue to gain ground at the expense of the pecuniary morals of competitive business.

Salesmanship and the Churches

Writers who discuss these matters have not directed attention to the Propaganda of the Faith as an object-lesson in sales-publicity, its theory and practice, its ways and means, its benefits and its possibilities of gain. Yet it is altogether the most notable enterprise of the kind. The Propaganda of the Faith is quite the largest, oldest, most magnificent, most unabashed, and most lucrative enterprise in sales-publicity in all Christendom. Much is to be learned from it as regards media and suitable methods of approach, as well as due perseverance, tact, and effrontery. By contrast, the many secular adventures in salesmanship are no better than up-starts, raw recruits, late and slender capitalizations out of the ample fund of human credulity. It is only quite recently, and even yet only with a dawning realization of what may be achieved by consummate effrontery in the long run, that these others are beginning to take on anything like the same air of stately benevolence and menacing solemnity. No pronouncement on rubber-heels, soap-powders, lip-sticks, or yeast-cakes, not even Sapphira Buncombe's Vegetative Compound, are yet able to ignore material facts with the same magisterial detachment, and none has yet commanded the same unreasoning assent or acclamation. None other has achieved that pitch of unabated assurance which has enabled the publicity-agents of the Faith to debar human reason from scrutinizing their pronouncements. These others are doing well enough, no doubt; perhaps as well as might reasonably be expected under the circumstances, but they are a feeble thing in comparison. Saul has slain his thousands, perhaps, but David has slain his tens of thousands.

There is, of course, no occasion for levity in so calling to mind these highly significant works of human infatuation, past and current. Nor should it cast any shadow of profanation on any of the sacred verities when it is so called to mind

The editor wishes to thank Becky Veblen Meyers for permission to reprint from a note to chapter 11, "Manufactures ans Salesmanship," of *Absentee Ownership and Business Enterprise in Recent Times*, New York: B. W. Huebsch, 1923.

that, when all is said, they, too, rest after all on the same ubiquitously human ground of unreasoning fear, aspiration, and credulity, as do the familiar soap-powders, yeast-cakes, lip-sticks, rubber tires, chewing-gum, and restoratives of lost manhood, whose profitable efficacy is likewise created and kept in repair by a well-advised sales-publicity. Indeed, it should rather seem the other way about. That the same principles of self-publicity are found good and profitable for the traffic in spiritual amenities and in these material comforts should serve to show how deep and pervasively the scheme of deliverance and rehabilitation is rooted in the merciful gift of credulous infatuation. It should redound to the credit of the secular arm of sales-publicity rather than cast an aspersion on those who traffic in man's spiritual needs; and should go to show how truly business-as-usual articulates with the business of the Kingdom of Heaven. As it is with the traffic in these divinely beneficial intangibles, so it is with the like salesmanship on the material plane; the marvels of commercial make-believe, too, seek and find a lodgement in the popular knowledge and belief by way of a tireless publicity, such as blessed experience has long and profitably proved and found good in the Propaganda of the Faith. Ways and means which so have proved gainful to His publicity-agents and conducive to the Glory of God—indeed indispensable to the continued upkeep of that Glory—are being drawn into the service of the secular Good of Man; so attesting the excellence of that devoutly familiar form of words which describes the *summum bonum* as a balanced ration of divine glory and human use. It is worth noting in this connection that those Godfearing business men who administer the nation's affairs appear to realize this congruity between sacred and secular salesmanship; so much so that they have on due consideration found that investment in commercial advertising is rightfully exempt from the income tax, very much as the assets and revenues of the churches are tax-exempt. The one line of publicity, it appears is intrinsic to the good of man, as the other is essential to the continued Glory of God.

There is more than one reason for speaking of these matters here, and for speaking of them in a detached and objective way as mere workday factors of human conduct—leaving all due sanctimony on one side for the time being, without thereby questioning the need and merit of such sanctimony as ordinary means of grace, or the expediency of it as a standard vehicle of sales-publicity in putting over the transcendent verities of the Faith. It all implies no call and no inclination to lay profane hands on these verities. Taken objectively as a human achievement, the high example of the Propaganda of the Faith should serve as a moral stimulus and a pacemaker. The whole duty of sales-publicity is to "put it over," as the colloquial phrasing has it; and in the matter of putting it over, it is plain that the laurel, the palms, and the paean are due to go to the publicity-agents of the Faith, without protest. The large and enduring success of the Propaganda through the ages is an object-lesson to show how great is the efficacy of *ipse dixit* when it is put over with due perseverance and audacity. It also carries a broad suggestion as to what may be the practical limits eventually to be attained by commercial advertising in the way of capitalizable earning-capacity.

Commercial sales-publicity of the secular sort evidently falls short, hitherto, in respect of the pitch and volume of make-believe which can be put over effectually and profitably. But it also falls short conspicuously at another critical point. It is of the nature of sales-publicity, to promise much and deliver a minimum. *Suppressio veri, suggestio falsi.* Worked out to its ideal finish, as in the promises and performance of the publicity-agents of the Faith, it should be the high good fortune of the perfect salesman in the secular field also to promise everything and deliver nothing.

Hitherto this climax of salesmanlike felicity has not been attained in the secular merchandising enterprise, except in a sporadic and dubious fashion. On the other hand, hitherto the publicity-agents of the Faith have habitually promised much and have delivered substantially none of the material advertised, and have "come through" with none of the tangible performances promised by their advertising matter. All that has been delivered hitherto has—perhaps all for the better—been in the nature of further publicity, often with a use of more pointedly menacing language; but it has always been more language, with a moratorium on the liquidation of the promises to pay, and a penalty on any expressed doubt of the solvency of the concern. There have of course, from time to time, been staged certain sketchy prodigies, in the nature of what the secular outdoor advertisers would call "spectacular displays," apparently designed to demonstrate the nature and merits of the goods kept in stock. These have not infrequently been highly ingenious, and also quite convincing to such persons as are fit to be convinced by them. They have carried conviction to those persons whose habitual beliefs are of a suitable kind. But as viewed objectively and as seen in any other than their own dim religious light, these admirable feats of manifestation have been after all essentially ephemeral and nugatory hitherto; very much of a class with those lunch-counter sample-packages that are designed to demonstrate the expansive powers of some noted baking-powder, in miniature and with precautions. They are after all in the nature of publicity-gestures, eloquent, no doubt, and graceful, but they are not the goods listed in the doctrinal pronouncements; no more than the wriggly gestures with which certain spear-headed manikins stab the nightly firmament over Times Square are an effectual delivery of chewing-gum. *Bona-fide* delivery of the listed goods would have to be a tangible performance of quite another complexion, inasmuch as the specifications call for Hell-fire and the Kingdom of Heaven; to which the most heavily capitalized of these publicity concerns of the supernatural adds a broad margin of Purgatory.

There is, of course, no call and no inclination to take the publicity-agents of the Faith to task for failure to deliver the goods listed in their advertising matter. Quite otherwise, indeed. Since the sales-publicity from which these publicity-concerns derive their revenue plays on unreasoning fear and unreasoning aspiration, the output of goods listed in their advertising matter falls under the two general heads of Hell-fire and the Kingdom of Heaven; so that, on the whole, their failure to deliver the goods is perhaps fortunate rather than otherwise. Hell-fire is after all a commodity the punctual delivery of which is not desired by the ultimate consumers; and according to such descriptive matter as is available the Kingdom of Heaven, on the other hand, should not greatly appeal to persons of sensitive taste, being presumably something of a dubiously gaudy affair, something in the nature of three rings and a steam-calliope, perhaps. It might have been worse.

This failure to deliver the goods is brought up here only as an object-lesson which goes to show what and how great are the powers of sales-publicity at its best; as exemplified in a publicity enterprise which has over a long period of time very profitably employed a very large personnel and a very extensive and costly material equipment, coupled with no visible ability or intention to deliver any material part of the commodities advertised, or indeed to deliver anything else than a further continued volume of the same magisterial publicity that has procured a livelihood for its numerous personnel and floated its magnificent overhead charges in the past. In the lucrative enterprise the Propaganda of the Faith employs a larger and more expensive personnel and a larger equipment of material appliances, with larger running expenses and larger revenues—not only larger than any given one line among the secular enterprises in sales-publicity, but larger than the total of all that goes into secular sales-publicity in all the nations of Christendom.

Of such sacred sales-publicity concerns operating as certified agents for this marketing of supernatural intangibles, the Census of 1916 enumerates 202 chain-store organizations, comprising a total of 203,432 retail establishments occupied exclusively with the sale of such publicity to the ultimate consumers; of whom there is one born every minute, and who are said to be carried on the books of these retailers to the number of 41,926,854. It has been confidently estimated, on the ground of these data, that the effectual number of paying customers will be approximately 90,000,000; regard being had to the very appreciable floating clientele and the great number of effectual consumers attached to and associated with the customers of record. The stated value of "church property" is $1,676,600,582. These tangible assets are exempt from taxation.

The figures of this enumeration are suggestive, but it takes account of only such establishments as are formally chartered to do business exclusively in the retail distribution of sacred sales-publicity. It covers no more than the certified apparatus for retail merchandising of the output. If regard be had to the equipment and personnel engaged in the fabrication, sorting, storage, ripening and mobilization of the output, these figures will be found impossibly scant. If regard be had to the very considerable number of schools for the training of certified publicity-agents in Divinity and for generating a suitable bias of credulity in the incoming generation, as well as to the mighty multitude of convents, clubs, camps, infirmaries, retreats, missions, charities, cemeteries, and periodicals, in whole or in part given over to this work and its personnel, at home and abroad, it will be evident that any of the figures commonly assigned, whether for the material equipment, the receipts and disbursements, or for the operative personnel engaged on the propaganda, should freely be doubled, at least.[1]

The man-power employed in this work of the Propaganda is also more considerable than that engaged in any other calling, except Arms, and possibly Husbandry. Prelates and parsons abound all over the place, in the high, the middle, and the low degree; too many and too diversified, in person, station, nomenclature, and vestments, to be rightly enumerated or described—bishops, deans, canons, abbots and abbesses, rectors, vicars, curates, monks and nuns, elders, deacons and deaconesses, secretaries, clerks and employees of Y.M.C.A., Epworth Leagues, Christian Endeavors, etc., beadles, janitors, sextons, Sunday-school teachers, missionaries, writers, editors, printers and vendors of sacred literature, in books, periodicals and ephemera. All told—if it were possible—it will be evident that the aggregate of human talent currently consumed in this fabrication of vendible imponderables in the *n*th dimension, will foot up to a truly massive total, even after making a reasonable allowance, of, say, some thirty-three and one-third percent, for average mental deficiency in the personnel which devotes itself to this manner of livelihood.[2]

Notes

1. Cf. Part I of *Report on Religious Bodies*, 1916, by the Bureau of the Census.
2. Extra Services at St. Patrick's.

Special Holy Week services are scheduled for each day at St. Patrick's Cathedral.

Tomorrow night there will be a sermon by the Rev. W. B. Martin and benediction of the Blessed Sacrament, while the tenebrae will be sung at 4 P.M. in commemoration of the sufferings and death of Christ.

On Holy Thursday communion will be given every half hour between 6 and 9 A.M. and at 10 A.M. There will be pontifical mass, blessing of the holy oils, and procession to the repository. The tenebrae will be sung at 4 P.M. and the holy hour will begin at 8 P.M.

On Good Friday adoration at the repository will take place from 8 to 10 A.M., followed by singing of the sacred psalms, sermon, unveiling of the holy cross, procession to the repository, mass of the presanctified, and reverencing of the holy cross.

The Passion sermon on Friday will be preached by Mgr. Lavelle, rector, The tenebrae will be sung at 4 P.M.

The blessing of the new fire will take place at 8 o'clock on Saturday. The paschal candle and the baptismal font also will be blessed.

Mass on Easter Sunday will be pontificated by the archbishop, who also will give the papal blessing. Pontifical vespers will take place at 4 P.M.—*The Globe and Commercial Advertiser*, New York, Tuesday, March 27, 1923.

The Higher Learning

The older American universities have grown out of underlying colleges—undergraduate schools. Within the memory of men still living it was a nearly unbroken rule that the governing boards of these higher American schools were drawn largely from the clergy and were also guided mainly by ecclesiastical, or at least by devotional, notions of what was right and needful in matters of learning. This state of things reflected the ingrained devoutness of that portion of the American community to which the higher schools then were of much significance. At the same time it reflected the historical fact that the colleges of the early days had been established primarily as training schools for ministers of the church. In their later growth, in the recent past, while the chief purpose of these seminaries has no longer been religious, yet ecclesiastical prepossessions long continued to mark the permissible limits of the learning which they cultivated, and continued also to guard the curriculum and discipline of the schools.

That phase of academic policy is past. Due regard at least is, of course, still had to the religious proprieties—the American community, by and large, is still the most devout of civilized countries—but such regard on the part of the academic authorities now proceeds on grounds of businesslike expediency rather than on religious conviction or on an ecclesiastical or priestly bias in the ruling bodies. It is a concessive precaution on the part of a worldly-wise directorate, in view of the devout prejudices of those who know no better.

The rule of the clergy belongs virtually to the pre-history of the American universities. While that rule held there were few if any schools that should properly be rated as of university grade. Even now, it is true, much of the secondary school system, including the greater part, though a diminishing number, of the smaller colleges, is under the tutelage of the clergy; and the academic heads of these schools

Reprinted from chapters 2, 5, and 8 of *The Higher Learning in America*, New York: B. W. Huebsch, 1918.

are almost universally men of ecclesiastical standing and bias rather than of scholarly attainments. But that fact does not call for particular notice here, since these schools lie outside the university field, and so outside the scope of this inquiry.

For a generation past, while the American universities have been coming into line as seminaries of the higher learning, there has gone on a wide-reaching substitution of laymen in the place of clergymen on the governing boards. This progressive secularization is sufficiently notorious, even though there are some among the older establishments the terms of whose charters require a large proportion of clergymen on their boards. This secularization is entirely consonant with the prevailing drift of sentiment in the community at large, as is shown by the uniform and uncritical approval with which it is regarded. The substitution is a substitution of businessmen and politicians; which amounts to saying that it is a substitution of businessmen. So that the discretionary control in matters of university policy now rests finally in the hands of businessmen.

The reason which men prefer to allege for this state of things is the sensible need of experienced men of affairs to take care of the fiscal concerns of these university corporations; for the typical modern university is a corporation possessed of large property and disposing of large aggregate expenditures, so that it will necessarily have many and often delicate pecuniary interests to be looked after. It is at the same time held to be expedient in case of emergency to have several wealthy men identified with the governing board, and such men of wealth are also commonly businessmen. It is apparently believed, though on just what ground this sanguine belief rests does not appear, that in case of emergency the wealthy members of the boards may be counted on to spend their substance in behalf of the university. In point of fact, at any rate, poor men and men without large experience in business affairs are felt to have no place in these bodies. If by any chance such men, without the due pecuniary qualifications, should come to make up a majority, or even an appreciable minority of such a governing board, the situation would be viewed with some apprehension by all persons interested in the case and cognizant of the facts. The only exception might be cases where, by tradition, the board habitually includes a considerable proportion of clergymen:

> "Such great regard is always lent
> By men to ancient precedent."

The reasons alleged are no doubt convincing to those who are ready to be so convinced, but they are after all more plausible at first sight than on reflection. In point of fact these businesslike governing boards commonly exercise little if any current surveillance of the corporate affairs of the university, beyond a directive oversight of the distribution of expenditures among the several academic purposes for which the corporate income is to be used; that is to say, they control the budget of expenditures; which comes to saying that they exercise a pecuniary discretion in the case mainly in the way of deciding what the body of academic men that constitutes the university may or may not do with the means in hand; that is to say, their pecuniary surveillance comes in the main to an interference with the academic work, the merits of which these men of affairs on the governing board are in no special degree qualified to judge. Beyond this, as touches the actual running administration of the corporation's investments, income and expenditures—all that is taken care of by permanent officials who have, as they necessarily must, sole and responsible charge of those matters. Even the auditing of the corporation's accounts is commonly vested in such officers of the corporation, who have none but a formal, if any, direct connection with the governing board. The governing board, or more commonly a committee of the board, on the other hand, will then formally review the balance sheets and bundles of vouchers duly submitted by the corporation's fiscal officers and their clerical force—with such effect of complaisant oversight as will best be appreciated by any person who has had the fortune to look into the accounts of a large corporation.

So far as regards its pecuniary affairs and their due administration, the typical modern university is in a position, without loss or detriment, to dispense with the services of any board of trustees, regents, curators, or what not. Except for the insuperable difficulty of getting a hearing for such an extraordinary proposal, it should be no difficult matter to show that these governing boards of business men commonly are quite useless to the university for any businesslike purpose. Indeed, except for a stubborn prejudice to the contrary, the fact should readily be seen that the boards are of no material use in any connection; their sole effectual function being to interfere with the academic management in matters that are not of the nature of business, and that lie outside their competence and outside the range of their habitual interest.

The governing boards—trustees, regents, curators, fellows, whatever their style and title—are an aimless survival from the days of clerical rule, when they were presumably of some effect in enforcing conformity to orthodox opinions and observances, among the academic staff. At that time, when means for maintenance of the denominational colleges commonly had to be procured by an appeal to impecunious congregations, it fell to these bodies of churchmen to do service as sturdy beggars for funds with which to meet current expenses. So that as long as the boards were made up chiefly of clergymen they served a pecuniary purpose; whereas, since their complexion has been changed by the substitution of business men in the place of ecclesiastics, they have ceased to exercise any function other than a bootless meddling with academic matters which they do not understand. The sole ground of their retention appears to be an unreflecting deferential concession to the usages of corporate organization and control, such as have been found advantageous for the pursuit of private gain by business men banded together in the exploitation of joint-stock companies with limited liability.[1]

The fact remains, the modern civilized community is reluctant to trust its serious interests to others than men of pecuniary substance, who have proved their fitness for the direction of academic affairs by acquiring, or by otherwise being possessed of considerable wealth.[2] It is not simply that experienced business men are, on mature reflection, judged to be the safest and most competent trustees of the university's fiscal interests. The preference appears to be almost wholly impulsive, and a matter of habitual bias. It is due for the greater part to the high esteem currently accorded to men of wealth at large, and especially to wealthy men who have succeeded in business, quite apart from any special capacity shown by such success for the guardianship of any institution of learning. Business success is by common consent, and quite uncritically, taken to be conclusive evidence of wisdom even in matters that have no relation to business affairs. So that it stands as a matter of course that business men must be preferred to the guardianship and control of that intellectual enterprise for the pursuit of which the university is established, as well as to take care of the pecuniary welfare of the university corporation. And, full of the same naïve faith that business success "answereth all things," these businessmen into whose hands this trust falls are content to accept the responsibility and confident to exercise full discretion in these matters with which they have no special familiarity. Such is the outcome, to the present date, of the recent and current secularization of the governing boards. The final discretion in the affairs of the seats of learning is entrusted to men who have proved their capacity for work that has nothing in common with the higher learning.[3]

As bearing on the case of the American universities, it should be called to mind that the businessmen of this country, as a class, are of a notably conservative habit of mind. In a degree scarcely equalled in any community that can lay claim to a modicum of intelligence and enterprise, the spirit of American business is a spirit of quietism, caution, compromise, collusion, and chicane. It is not that the spirit of enterprise or of unrest is wanting in this community, but only that, by selective effect of the conditioning circumstances, persons affected with that spirit are excluded from the management of business, and so do not come into the class of successful businessmen from which the governing boards are drawn. American inventors are bold and resourceful, perhaps beyond the common run of their class elsewhere, but it has become a commonplace that American inventors habitually die poor; and one does not find them represented on the boards in question. American engineers and technologists are as good and efficient as their kind in other countries; but they do not as a class accumulate wealth enough to entitle them to sit on the directive board of any self-respecting university, nor can they claim even a moderate rank as "safe and sane" men of business. American explorers, prospectors and pioneers can not be said to fall short of the common measure in hardihood, insight, temerity or tenacity; but wealth does not accumulate in their hands, and it is a common saying, of them as of the inventors, that they are not fit to conduct their own (pecuniary) affairs; and the reminder is scarcely needed that neither they nor their qualities are drawn into the counsels of these governing boards. The wealth and the serviceable results that come of the endeavors of these enterprising and temerarious Americans habitually inure to the benefit of such of their compatriots as are endowed with a "safe and sane" spirit of "watchful waiting"—of caution, collusion and chicane. There is a homely but well-accepted American colloquialism which says that "The silent hog eats the swill". . . .

Apart from outside resources the livelihood that comes to a university man is, commonly, somewhat meager. The tenure is uncertain and the salaries, at an average, are not large. Indeed, they are notably low in comparison with the high conventional standard of living which is by custom incumbent on university men. University men are conventionally required to live on a scale of expenditure comparable with that in vogue among the well-to-do business men, while their university incomes compare more nearly with the lower grades of clerks and salesmen. The rate of pay varies quite materially, as is well known. For the higher grades of the staff, whose scale of pay is likely to be publicly divulged, it is, perhaps, adequate to the average demands made on university incomes by polite usage; but the large majority of university men belong on the lower levels of grade and pay; and on these lower levels the pay is, perhaps, lower than any outsider appreciates.[4]

With men circumstanced as the common run of university men are, the temptation to parsimony is ever present, while on the other hand, as has already been noted, the prestige of the university—and of the academic head—demands of all its members a conspicuously expensive manner of living. Both of these needs may, of course, be met in some poor measure by saving in the obscurer items of domestic expense, such as food, clothing, heating, lighting, floor-space, books, and the like; and making all available funds count toward the collective end of reputable publicity, by throwing the stress on such expenditures as come under the public eye, as dress and equipage, bric-a-brac, amusements, public entertainments, etc. It may seem that it should also be possible to cut down the proportion of obscure expenditures for creative comforts by limiting the number of births in the family, or by foregoing marriage. But, by and large, there is reason to believe that this expedient has been exhausted. As men have latterly been at pains to show, the current average of children in academic households is not high; whereas the percentage of celibates is. There appears, indeed, to be little room for additional economy on this head, or in the matter of household thrift, beyond what is embodied in the family budgets already in force in academic circles.

So also, the tenure of office is somewhat precarious; more so than the documents would seem to indicate. This applies with greater force to the lower grades than to the higher. Latterly, under the rule of business principles, since the prestige value of a conspicuous consumption has come to a greater currency in academic policy, a member of the staff may render his tenure more secure, and may perhaps assure his due preferment, by a sedulous attention to the academic social amenities, and to the more conspicuous items of his expense account; and he will then do well in the same connection also to turn his best attention in the day's work to administrative duties and schoolmasterly discipline, rather than to the increase of knowledge. Whereas he may make his chance of preferment less assured, and may even jeopardize his tenure, by a conspicuously parsimonious manner of life, or by too pronounced an addiction to scientific or scholarly pursuits, to the neglect of those polite exhibitions of decorum that conduce to the maintenance of the university's prestige in the eyes of the (pecuniarily) cultured laity.

A variety of other untoward circumstances, of a similarly extra-scholastic bearing, may affect the fortunes of academic men to a like effect; as, e.g., unearned newspaper notoriety that may be turned to account in ridicule; unconventional religious, or irreligious convictions—so far as they become known; an undesirable political affiliation; an impecunious marriage, or such domestic infelicities as might become subject of remark. None of these untoward circumstances need touch the serviceability of the incumbent for any of the avowed, or avowable, purposes of the seminary of learning; and where action has to be taken by the directorate on provocation of such circumstances it is commonly done with the (unofficial) admission that such action is taken not on the substantial merits of the case but on compulsion of appearances and the exigencies of advertising. That some such effect should be had follows from the nature of things, so far as business principles rule.

In the degree, then, in which these and the like motives of expediency are decisive, there results a husbanding of time, energy and means in the less conspicuous expenditures and duties, in order to a freer application to more conspicuous uses, and a meticulous cultivation of the bourgeois virtues. The workday duties of instruction, and more particularly of inquiry, are, in the nature of the case, less conspicuously in evidence than the duties of the drawing-room, the ceremonial procession, the formal dinner, or the grandstand on some red-letter day of intercollegiate athletics.[5] For the purposes of a reputable notoriety the everyday work of the classroom and laboratory is also not so effective as lectures to popular audiences outside; especially, perhaps, addresses before an audience of devout and well-to-do women. Indeed, all this is well approved by experience. In many and devious ways, therefore, a university man may be able to serve the collective enterprise of his university to better effect than by an exclusive attention to the scholastic work on which alone he is ostensibly engaged.

Among the consequences that follow is a constant temptation for the members of the staff to take on work outside of that for which the salary is nominally paid. Such work takes the public eye; but a further incentive to go into this outside and non-academic work, as well as to take on supernumerary work within the academic schedule, lies in the fact that such outside or supernumerary work is specially paid, and so may help to eke out a sensibly scant livelihood. So far as touches the more scantily paid grades of university men, and so far as no alien considerations come in to trouble the working-out of business principles, the outcome may be schematized somewhat as follows. These men have, at the outset, gone into the university presumably from an inclination to scholarly or scientific pursuits; it is not probable that they have been led into this calling by the pecuniary inducements, which are slight as compared with the ruling rates of pay in the open market for other work that demands an equally arduous preparation and an equally close application. They have then been apportioned rather more work as instructors than they can take care of in the most efficient manner, at a rate of pay which is sensibly scant for the standard of (conspicuous) living conventionally imposed on them. They are, by authority, expected to expend time and means in such polite observances, spectacles, and quasi-learned exhibitions as are presumed to enhance the prestige of the university. They are so induced to divert their time and energy to spreading abroad the university's good repute by creditable exhibitions of a quasi-scholarly character, which have no substantial bearing on a university man's legitimate interests; as well as in seeking supplementary work outside of their mandatory schedule, from which to derive an adequate livelihood and to fill up the complement of politely wasteful expenditures expected of them. The academic instruction necessarily suffers by this diversion of forces to extra-scholastic objects; and the work of inquiry, which may have primarily engaged their interest and which is indispensable to their continued efficiency as teachers, is, in the common run of cases, crowded to one side and presently drops out of mind. Like other workmen, under pressure of competition the members of the academic staff will endeavor to keep up their necessary income by cheapening their product and increasing their marketable output. And by consequence of this pressure of bread-winning and genteel expenditure, these university men are so barred out from the serious pursuit of those scientific and scholarly inquiries which alone can, academically speaking, justify their retention of the university faculty, and for the sake of which, in great part at least, they have chosen this vocation. No infirmity more commonly besets university men than this going to seed in routine work and extra-scholastic duties. They have entered on the academic career to find time, place, facilities and congenial environment for the pursuit of knowledge, and under pressure they presently settle down to a round of perfunctory labor by means of which to simulate the life of gentlemen.[6]

Before leaving the topic it should further be remarked that the dissipation incident to these polite amenities, that so are incumbent on the academic personnel, apparently also has something of a deteriorative effect on their working capacity, whether for scholarly or for worldly uses. *Prima facie* evidence to this effect might be adduced, but it is not easy to say how far the evidence would bear closer scrutiny. There is an appreciable amount of dissipation, in its several sorts, carried forward in university circles in an inconspicuous manner, and not designed for publicity. How far this is induced by a loss of interest in scholarly work, due to the habitual diversion of the scholars' energies to other and more exacting duties, would be hard to say; as also how far it may be due to the lead given by men-of-the-world retained on the faculties for other than scholarly reasons. At the same time there is the difficulty that many of those men who bear a large part in the ceremonial dissipation incident to the enterprise in publicity are retained, apparently, for their proficiency in this line as much as for their scholarly attainments, or at least so one might infer; and these men must be accepted with the defects of their qualities.

As bearing on this whole matter of pomp and circumstance, social amenities and ritual dissipation, quasi-learned demonstrations and meretricious publicity, in academic life, it is difficult beyond hope of a final answer to determine how much of it is due directly to the masterful initiative of the strong man who directs the enterprise, and how much is to be set down to an innate proclivity for all that sort of thing on the part of the academic personnel. A near view of these phenomena leaves the impression that there is, on the whole, less objection felt than expressed among the academic men with regard to this routine of demonstration; that the reluctance with which they pass under the ceremonial yoke is not altogether ingenuous; all of which would perhaps hold true even more decidedly as applied to the faculty households.[7] But for all that, it also remains true that without the initiative and countenance of the executive head these boyish movements of sentimental spectacularity on the part of the personnel would come to little, by comparison with what actually takes place. It is after all a matter for executive discretion, and, from whatever motives, this diversion of effort to extra-scholastic ends has the executive sanction;[8] with the result that an intimate familiarity with current academic life is calculated to raise the question whether make-believe does not, after all, occupy a larger and more urgent place in the life of these thoughtful adult male citizens than in the life of their children. . . .

Throughout the foregoing inquiry, the argument continually returns to or turns about two main interests—notoriety and the academic executive. These two might be called the two foci about which swings the orbit of the university world. These conjugate foci lie on a reasonably short axis; indeed, they tend to coincide, so that the orbit comes near the perfection of a circle; having virtually but a single center, which may perhaps indifferently be spoken of as the university's president or as its renown, according as one may incline to conceive these matters in terms of tangible fact or of intangible.

The system of standardization and accountancy has this renown or prestige as its chief ulterior purpose—the prestige of the university or of its president, which largely comes to the same net result. Particularly will this be true in so far as this organization is designed to serve competitive ends; which are, in academic affairs, chiefly the ends of notoriety, prestige, advertising in all its branches and bearings. It is through increased creditable notoriety that the universities seek their competitive ends, and it is on such increase of notoriety, accordingly, that the competitive endeavors of a businesslike management are chiefly spent. It is in and through such accession of renown, therefore, that the chief and most tangible gains due to the injection of competitive business principles in the academic policy should appear.

Of course, this renown, as such, has no substantial value to the corporation of learning; nor indeed, to any one but the university executive by whose management it is achieved. Taken simply in its first incidence, as prestige or notoriety, it conduces in no degree to the pursuit of knowledge; but in its ulterior consequences, it appears currently to be believed, at least ostensibly, that such notoriety must greatly enhance the powers of the corporation of learning. These ulterior consequences are (believed to be) a growth in the material resources and the volume of traffic.

Such good effects as may follow from a sedulous attention to creditable publicity, therefore, are the chief gains to be set off against the mischief incident to "scientific management" in academic affairs. Hence any line of inquiry into the business management of the universities continually leads back to the cares of publicity, with what might to an outsider seem undue insistence. The reason is that the businesslike management and arrangements in question are habitually—and primarily—required either to serve the ends of this competitive campaign of publicity or to conform to its schedule of expediency. The felt need of notoriety and prestige has a main share in shaping the work and bearing of the university at every point. Whatever will not serve this end of prestige has no secure footing in current university policy. The margin of tolerance on this head is quite narrow; and it is apparently growing incontinently narrower.

So far as any university administration can, with the requisite dignity, permit itself to avow a pursuit of notoriety, the gain that is avowedly sought by its means is an increase of funds—more or less ingenuously spoken of as an increase of equipment. An increased enrollment of students will be no less eagerly sought after, but the received canons of academic decency require this object to be kept even more discreetly masked than the quest of funds.

The duties of publicity are large and arduous, and the expenditures incurred in this behalf are similarly considerable. So that it is not unusual to find a Publicity Bureau—often apologetically masquerading under a less tell-tale name—incorporated in the university organization to further this enterprise in reputable notoriety. Not only must a creditable publicity be provided for, as one of the running cares of the administration, but every feature of academic life, and of the life of all members of the academic staff, must unremittingly (though of course unavowedly) be held under surveillance at every turn, with a view to furthering whatever may yield a reputable notoriety, and to correcting or eliminating whatever may be conceived to have a doubtful or untoward bearing in this respect.

This surveillance of appearances, and of the means of propagating appearances, is perhaps the most exacting detail of duty incumbent on the enterprising executive. Without such a painstaking cultivation of a reputable notoriety, it is believed, a due share of funds could not be procured by any university for the prosecution of its work as a seminary of the higher learning. Its more alert and unabashed rivals, it is presumed, would in that case be able to divert the flow of loose funds to their own use, and would so outstrip their dilatory competitor in the race of size and popular acclaim, and therefore, it is sought to be believed, in scientific and scholarly application.

In the absence of all reflection—not an uncommon frame of mind in this connection—one might be tempted to think that all the academic enterprise of notoriety and conciliation should add something appreciable to the aggregate of funds placed at the disposal of the university; and that each of these competitive advertising concerns should so gain something appreciable, without thereby cutting into the supply of funds available for the rest. But such is probably not the outcome, to any appreciable extent; assuredly not apart from the case of the state universities that are dependent on the favor of local politicians, and perhaps apart from gifts for conspicuous buildings.

With whatever (slight) reservation may be due, publicity in university management is of substantially the same nature and effect as advertising in other competitive business; and with such reservation as may be called for in the case of other advertising, it is an engine of competition, and has no aggregate effect. As is true of competitive gains in business at large, so also these differential gains of the several university corporations can not be added together to make an aggregate. They are differential gains in the main, of the same nature as the gains achieved in any other game of skill and effrontery. The gross aggregate funds contributed to university uses from all sources would in all probability be nearly as large in the absence of such competitive notoriety and conformity. Indeed, it should seem likely that such donors as are gifted with sufficient sense of the value of science and scholarship to find it worth while to sink any part of their capital in that behalf would be somewhat deterred by the spectacle of competitive waste and futile clamor presented by this academic enterprise; so that the outcome might as well be a diminution of the gross aggregate of donations and allowances. But such an argument doubtless runs on very precarious grounds; it is by no means evident that these munificent patrons of learning habitually distinguish between scholarship and publicity. But in any case it is quite safe to presume that to the cause of learning at large, and therefore to the community in respect of its interest in the advancement of learning, no appreciable net gain accrues from this competitive publicity of the seats of learning.

In some slight, or doubtful, degree this competitive publicity, including academic pageants, genteel solemnities, and the like, may conceivably augment the gross aggregate means placed at the disposal of the universities, by persuasively keeping the well-meaning men of wealth constantly in mind of the university's need of additional funds, as well as of the fact that such gifts will not be allowed to escape due public notice. But the aggregate increase of funds due to these endeavors is doubtless not large enough to offset the aggregate expenditure on notoriety. Taken as a whole, and counting in all the wide-ranging expenditure entailed by this enterprise in notoriety and the maintenance of academic prestige, university publicity doubtless costs appreciably more than it brings. So far as it succeeds in its purpose, its chief effect is to divert the flow of funds from one to another of the rival establishments. In the aggregate this expedient for procuring means for the advancement of learning doubtless results in an appreciable net loss.

The net loss, indeed, is always much more considerable than would be indicated by any statistical showing; for this academic enterprise involves an extensive and almost wholly wasteful duplication of equipment, personnel and output of instruction, as between the rival seats of learning, at the same time that it also involves an excessively parsimonious provision for actual scholastic work, as contrasted with publicity; so also it involves the overloading of each rival corps of instructors with a heterogeneous schedule of courses, beyond what would conduce to their best efficiency as teachers. This competitive parcelment, duplication and surreptitious thrift, due to a businesslike rivalry between the several schools, is perhaps the gravest drawback to the American university situation.

It should be added that no aggregate gain for scholarship comes of diverting any given student from one school to another duplicate establishment by specious offers of a differential advantage; particularly when, as frequently happens, the differential inducement takes the form of the extra-scholastic amenities spoken of in an earlier chapter, or the greater alleged prestige of one school as against another, or, as also happens, a surreptitiously greater facility for achieving a given academic degree.

In all its multifarious ways and means, university advertising carried beyond the modicum that would serve a due "publicity of accounts" as regards the work to be done, accomplishes no useful aggregate result. And, as is true of advertising in other competitive business, current university publicity is not an effective means of spreading reliable information; nor is it designed for that end. Here as elsewhere, to meet the requirements of competitive enterprise, advertising must somewhat exceed the point of maximum veracity.

In no field of human endeavor is competitive notoriety and a painstaking conformity to extraneous standards of living and of conduct so gratuitous a burden, since learning is in no degree a competitive enterprise; and all mandatory observance of the conventions—pecuniary or other—is necessarily a drag on the pursuit of knowledge. In ordinary competitive business, as, e.g., merchandising, advertisement is a means of competitive selling, and is justified by the increased profits that come to the successful advertiser from the increased traffic; and on the like grounds a painstaking conformity to conventional usage, in appearances and expenditure, is there wisely cultivated with the same end in view. In the affairs of science and scholarship, simply as such and apart from the personal ambitions of the university's executive, there is nothing that corresponds to this increased traffic or these competitive profits[9]—nor will the discretionary officials avow that such increased traffic is the purpose of academic publicity. Indeed, an increased enrollment of students yields no increased net income, nor is the corporation of learning engaged (avowedly, at least) in an enterprise that looks to a net income. At the same time, such increased enrollment as comes of this competitive salesmanship among the universities is made up almost wholly of wasters, accessions from the genteel and sporting classes, who seek the university as a means of respectability and dissipation, and who serve the advancement of the higher learning only as fire, flood and pestilence serve the needs of the husband-man. . . .

The executive heads of these competitive universities are a picked body of men, endowed with a particular bent, such as will dispose them to be guided by the run of motives indicated. This will imply that they are, either by training or by native gift, men of a somewhat peculiar frame of mind—peculiarly open to the appeal of parade and ephemeral celebrity, and peculiarly facile in the choice of means by which to achieve these gaudy distinctions; peculiarly solicitous of appearances, and peculiarly heedless of the substance of their performance. It is not that this characterization would imply exceptionally great gifts, or otherwise notable traits of character; they are little else than an accentuation of the more commonplace frailties of commonplace men. As a side light on this spiritual complexion of the typical academic executive, it may be worth noting that much the same characterization will apply without abatement to the class of professional politicians, particularly to that large and long-lived class of minor politicians who make a living by keeping well in the public eye and avoiding blame.[10]

There is, indeed more than a superficial or accidental resemblance between the typical academic executive and the professional politician of the familiar and more vacant sort, both as regards the qualifications requisite for entering on this career and as regards the conditions of tenure. Among the genial make-believe that goes to dignify the executive office is a dutiful protest, indeed, a somewhat clamorous protest, of conspicuous self-effacement on the part of the incumbent, to the effect that the responsibilities of office have come upon him unsought, if not unawares; which is related to the facts in much the same manner and degree as the like holds true for the manoeuvres of those wise politicians that "heed the call of duty" and so find themselves "in the hands of their friends." In point of fact, here as in political office-seeking, the most active factor that goes to decide the selection of the eventual incumbents of office is a tenacious and aggressive self-selection. With due, but by no means large, allowance for exceptions, the incumbents are chosen from among a self-selected body of candidates, each of whom has, in the common run of cases, been resolutely in pursuit of such an office for some appreciable time, and has spent much time and endeavor on fitting himself for its duties. Commonly it is only after the aspirant has achieved a settled reputation for eligibility and a predilection for the office that he will finally secure an appointment. The number of aspirants, and of eligibles, considerably exceeds the number of such executive offices, very much as is true for the parallel case of aspirants for political office.

As to the qualifications, in point of character and attainments, that so go to make eligibility for the executive office, it is necessary to recall what has been said in an earlier chapter, on the characteristics of those boards of control with whom rests the choice in these matters of appointment. These boards are made up of well-to-do businessmen, with a penchant for popular notability; and the qualifications necessary to be put in evidence by aspirants for executive office are such as will convince such a board of their serviceability. Among the indispensable general qualifications, therefore, will be a "businesslike" facility in the management of affairs, an engaging address and fluent command of language before a popular audience, and what is called "optimism"—a serene and voluble loyalty to the current convetionalities and a conspicuously profound conviction that all things are working out for good, except for such untoward details as do not visibly conduce to the vested advantage of the well-to-do businessmen under the established law and order. To secure an appointment to executive office it is not only necessary to be possessed of these qualifications, and contrive to put them in evidence; the aspirant must ordinarily also, to use a colloquialism, be willing and able to "work his passage" by adroit negotiation and detail engagements on points of policy, appointments and administration.

The greater proportion of such aspirants for executive office work their apprenticeship and manage their campaign of office-seeking while engaged in some university employment. To this end the most likely line of university employment is such as will comprise a large share of administrative duties, as, e.g., the deanships that are latterly receiving much attention in this behalf; while of the work of instruction the preference should be given to such undergraduate class-work as will bring the aspirant in wide contact with the less scholalrly element of the student body, and with those "student activities" that come favorably under public observation; and more particularly should one go in for the quasi-scholarly pursuits of "university extension"; which will bring the candidate into favorable notice among the quasi-literate leisure class; at the same time this employment conduces greatly to assurance and a flow of popular speech.

It is by no means here intended to convey the assumption that appointments to executive office are currently made exclusively from among aspiring candidates answering the description outlined above, or that the administrative deanships that currently abound in the universities are uniformly looked on by their incumbents as in some sort a hopeful novitiate to the presidential dignity. The exceptions under both of these general propositions would be too numerous to be set aside as negligible, although scarcely numerous enough or consequential enough entirely to vitiate these propositions as a competent formulation of the typical line of approach to the coveted office. The larger and more substantial exception would, of course, be taken to the generalization as touching the use of the deanships in preparation for the presidency.

The course of training and publicity afforded by the deanships and extension lectures appears to be the most promising, although it is not the only line of approach. So, e.g., as has been remarked in an earlier passage, the exigencies of academic administration will ordinarily lead to the formation of an unofficially organized corps of counselors and agents or lieutenants, who serve as aids to the executive head. While these aids, factors, and gentlemen-in-waiting are vested with no official status proclaiming their relation to the executive office or their share in its administration, it goes without saying that their vicarious discretion and their special prerogatives of access and advisement with the executive head do not commonly remain hidden from their colleagues on the academic staff, or from interested persons outside the university corporation; nor, indeed does it appear that they commonly desire to remain unknown.

In the same connection, as has also been remarked above, and as is sufficiently notorious, among the large and imperative duties of executive office is public discourse. This is required, both as a measure of publicity at large and as a means of divulging the ostensible aims, advantages and peculiar merits of the given university and its chief. The volume of such public discourse, as well as the incident attendance at many public and ceremonial functions, is very considerable; so much so that in the case of any university of reasonable size and spirit the traffic in these premises is likely to exceed the powers of any one man, even where, as is not infrequently the case, the "executive" head is presently led to make this business of stately parade and promulgation his chief employment. In effect, much of this traffic will necessarily be delegated to such representatives of the chief as may be trusted duly to observe its spirit and intention; and the indicated bearers of these vicarious dignities and responsibilities will necessarily be the personal aids and counselors of the chief; which throws them, again, into public notice in a most propitious fashion.

So also, by force of the same exigencies of parade and discourse, the chief executive is frequently called away from home on a more or less extended itinerary; and the burden of dignity attached to the chief office is such as to require that its ostensible duties be delegated to some competent lieutenant during these extensive absences of the chief; and here, again, this temporary discretion and dignity will most wisely and fittingly be delegated to some member of the corps of personal aids who stands in peculiarly close relations of sympathy and usefulness to the chief. It has happened more than once that such an habitual "acting head" has come in for the succession to the executive office.

It comes, therefore, to something like a general rule, that the discipline which makes the typical captain of erudition, as he is seen in the administration of executive office, will have set in before his induction into office, not infrequently at an appreciable interval before that event, and involving a consequent, more or less protracted, term of novitiate, probation and preliminary seasoning; and the aspirants so subjected to this discipline of initiation are at the same time picked men, drawn into the running chiefly by force of a facile conformity and a self-selective predisposition for this official dignity.

The resulting captain of erudition then falls under a certain exacting discipline exercised by the situation in which the exigencies of office place him. These exigencies are of diverse origin, and are systematically at variance among themselves. So that the dominant note of his official life necessarily becomes that ambiguity. By tradition—indeed, by that tradition to which the presidential office owes its existence, and except by force of which there would apparently be no call to institute such an office at all—by tradition the president of the university is the senior member of the faculty, its confidential spokesman in official and corporate concerns, and the "moderator" of its town meeting-like deliberative assemblies. As chairman of its meetings he is, by tradition, presumed to exercise no peculiar control, beyond such guidance as the superior experience of the senior member may be presumed to afford his colleagues. As spokesman for the faculty he is, by tradition, presumed to be a scholar of such erudition, breadth and maturity as may fairly command something of filial respect and affection from his associates in the corporation of learning; and it is by virtue of these qualities of scholarly wisdom, which gives him his place as senior member of a corporation of scholars, that he is, by tradition, competent to serve as their spokesman and to occupy the chair in their deliberative assembly.

Such is the tradition of the American College President—and, in so far, of the university president—as it comes down from that earlier phase of academic history from which the office derive its ostensible character, and to which it owes its hold on life under the circumstances of the later growth of the schools. And it will be noted that this office is distinctly American; it has no counterpart elsewhere, and there appears to be no felt need of such an office in other countries, where no similar tradition of a college president has created a presumptive need of a similar official in the universities—the reason being evidently that these universities in other lands have not, in the typical case, grown out of an underlying college.

In the sentimental apprehension of the laity out of doors, and in a degree even in the unreflecting esteem of men within the academic precincts, the presidential office still carries something of this traditionally preconceived scholarly character; and it is this still surviving traditional preconception, which confuses induction into the office with scholarly fitness for its dignities, that still makes the office of the academic executive available for those purposes of expensive publicity and businesslike management that it has been made to serve. Except for this uncritical esteem of the office and its incumbency, so surviving out of an inglorious past, no great prestige could attach to that traffic in spectacular solemnities, edifying discourse and misdirected business control, that makes up the substantial duties of the office as now conducted. It is therefore of the utmost moment to keep up, or rather to magnify, that appearance of scholarly competence and of intimate solidarity with the corporation of learning that gives the presidential office this prestige value. But since it is only for purposes external, not to say extraneous, to the corporation of learning that this prestige value is seriously worth while, it is also only toward the outside that the make-believe of presidential erudition and scholarly ideals need seriously be kept up. For the common run of the incumbents today to pose before their faculties as in an eminent degree conversant with the run of contemporary science or scholarship, or as rising to the average even of their own faculties in this respect, would be as bootless as it is uncalled for. But the faculties, as is well enough understood, need of course entertain no respect for their executive head as a citizen of the republic of learning, so long as they at all adequately appreciate his discretionary power of use and abuse, as touches them and their fortunes and all the ways, means and opportunities of academic work. By tradition, and in the genial legendary lore that colors the proceedings of the faculty-meeting, he is still the senior member of an assemblage of scholarly gentlemen; but in point of executive fact he is their employer, who does business with and by them on a commercial footing. To the faculty, the presidential office is a business proposition, and its incumbent is chiefly an object of circumspection, to whom they owe "hired-man's loyalty.". . .

All of which points unambiguously to the only line of remedial measures that can be worth serious consideration; and at the same time it carries the broad implication that in the present state of popular sentiment, touching these matters of control and administration, any effort that looks to reinstate the universities as effectual seminaries of learning will necessarily by nugatory; inasmuch as the popular sentiment runs plainly to the effect that magnitude, arbitrary control, and businesslike administration is the only sane rule to be followed in any human enterprise. So that, while the measures called for are simple, obvious, and effectual, they are also sure to be impracticable, and for none but extraneous reasons.

While it still remains true that the long-term common-sense judgment of civilized mankind places knowledge above business traffic, as an end to be sought, yet workday habituation under the stress of competitive business has induced a frame of mind that will tolerate no other method of procedure, and no rule of life that does not approve itself as a faithful travesty of competitive enterprise. And since the quest of learning cannot be carried on by the methods or with the apparatus and incidents of competitive business, it follows that the only remedial measures that hold any promise of rehabilitation for the higher learning in the universities cannot be attempted in the present state of public sentiment.

All that is required is the abolition of the academic executive and of the governing board. Anything short of this heroic remedy is bound to fail, because the evils sought to be remedied are inherent in these organs, and intrinsic to their functioning.

Notes

1. An instance showing something of the measure of incidence of fiscal service rendered by such a businesslike board may be suggestive, even though it is scarcely to be taken as faithfully illustrating current practice, in that the particular board in question has exercised an uncommon measure of surveillance over its university's pecuniary concerns.

A university corporation endowed with a large estate (appraised at something over $30,000,000) has been governed by a board of the usual form, with plenary discretion, established on a basis of co-optation. In point of practical effect, the board, or rather that fraction of the board which takes an active interest in the university's affairs, has been made up of a group of local business men engaged in diverse enterprises of the kind familiar to men of relatively large means, with somewhat extensive interests of the nature of banking and underwriting, where large extensions of credit and the temporary use of large funds are of substantial consequence. By terms of the corporate charter the board was required to render to the governor of the state a yearly report of all the pecuniary affairs of the university; but no penalty was attached to their eventual failure to render such report, though some legal remedy could doubtless have been had on due application by the parties in interest, as, e.g., by the academic head of the university. No such report has been rendered, however, and no steps appear to have been taken to procure such a report, or any equivalent accounting. But on persistent urging from the side of his faculty, and after some courteous delay, the academic head pushed an inquiry into the corporation's finances so far as to bring out facts somewhat to the following effect: The board, or the group of local business men who constituted the habitual working majority of the board, appear to have kept a fairly close and active oversight of the corporate funds entrusted to them, and to have seen to their investment and disposal somewhat in detail—and, it has been suggested, somewhat to their own pecuniary advantage. With the result that the investments were found to yield a current income of some three percent. (rather under than over)—in a state where investment on good security in the open market commonly yielded from six percent, to eight percent. Of this income approximately one-half (apparently some forty-five percent) practically accrued to the possible current use of the university establishment. Just what disposal was made of the remainder is not altogether clear; though it is loosely presumed to have been kept in hand with an eventual view to the erection and repair of buildings. Something like one-half of what so made up the currently disposable income was further set aside in the character of a sinking fund, to accumulate for future use and to meet contingencies; so that what effectually accrued to the university establishment for current use to meet academic expenditures would amount to something like one percent. (or less) on the total investment. But of this finally disposable fraction of the income, again, an appreciable sum was set aside as a special sinking fund to accumulate for the eventual use of the university library—which, it may be remarked, was in the meantime seriously handicapped for want of funds with which to provide for current needs. So also the academic establishment at large was perforce managed on a basis of penurious economy, to the present inefficiency and the lasting damage of the university.

The figures and percentages given above are not claimed to be exact; it is known that a more accurate specification of details would result in a less favorable showing.

At the time when these matters were disclosed (to a small number of the uneasy persons interested) there was an ugly suggestion afloat touching the pecuniary integrity of the board's management, but this is doubtless to be dismissed as being merely a loose expression of ill-will; and the like is also doubtless to be said as regards the suggestion that there may have been an interested collusion between the academic head and the active members of the board. These were "all honorable men," of great repute in the community and well known as sagacious and successful men in their private business ventures.

2. Cf. *The Instinct of Workmanship*, ch. vii, pp. 343–52.

3. A subsidiary reason of some weight should not be overlooked in seeking the cause of this secularism of the boards, and of the peculiar color which the secularization has given them. In any community where wealth and business enterprise are held in such high esteem, men of wealth and of affairs are not only deferred to, but their countenance is sought from one motive and another. At the same time election to one of these boards has come to have a high value as an honorable distinction. Such election or appointment therefore is often sought from motives of vanity, and it is at the same time a convenient means of conciliating the good will of the wealthy incumbent.

It may be added that now and again the discretionary control of large funds which so falls to the members of the board may come to be pecuniarily profitable to them, so that the office may come to be attractive as a business proposition as well as in point of prestige. Instances of the kind are not wholly unknown, though presumable exceptional.

4. In a certain large and enterprising university, e.g., the pay of the lowest, the numerous, rank regularly employed to do full work as teachers, is proportioned to that of the highest—much less numerous—rank about as one to twelve at the most, perhaps even as low as one to twenty. And it may not be out of place to enter the caution that the nominal rank of a given member of the staff is no secure index of his income, even where the salary "normally" attached to the given academic rank is known. Not unusually a "normal" scale of salaries is formally adopted by the governing board and spread upon their records, and such a scale will then be surreptitiously made public. But departures from the scale habitually occur, whereby the salaries actually paid come to fall short of the "normal" perhaps as frequently as they conform to it.

There is no trades-union among university teachers, and no collective bargaining. There appears to be a feeling prevalent among them that their salaries are not of the nature of wages, and that there would be species of moral obliquity implied in overtly so dealing with the matter. And in the individual bargaining by which the rate of pay is determined the directorate may easily be tempted to seek an economical way out, by offering a low rate of pay coupled with a higher academic rank. The plea is always ready to hand that the university is in want of the necessary funds and is constrained to economize where it can. So an advance in nominal rank is made to serve in place of an advance in salary, the former being the less costly commodity for the time being. Indeed, so frequent are such departures from the normal scale as to have given rise to the (no doubt ill-advised) suggestion that this may be one of the chief uses of the adopted schedule of normal salaries. So an employee of the university may not infrequently find himself constrained to accept, as part payment, an expensive increment of dignity attaching to a higher rank than his salary account would indicate. Such an outcome of individual bargaining is all the more likely in the academic community, since there is no settled code of professional ethics governing the conduct of business enterprise in academic management, as contrasted with the traffic of ordinary competitive business.

5. So, e.g., the well-known president of a well and favorably known university was at pains a few years ago to distinguish one of his faculty as being his "ideal of a university man"; the grounds of this invidious distinction being a lifelike imitation of a country gentleman and a fair degree of attention to committee work in connection with the academic administration; the incumbent had no distinguishing marks either as a teacher or as a scholar, and neither science nor letters will be found in his debt. It is perhaps needless to add that for reasons of invidious distinction, no names can be mentioned in this connection. It should be added in illumination of the instance cited, that in the same university, by consistent selection and discipline of the personnel, it had come about that, in the apprehension of the staff as well as of the executive, the accepted test of efficiency was the work done on the administrative committees rather than that of the class rooms or laboratories.

6. Within the past few years an academic executive of great note has been heard repeatedly to express himself in facetious doubt of this penchant for scholarly inquiry on the part of university men, whether as "reseárch" or as "résearch"; and there is doubtless ground for skepticism as to its permeating the academic body with that sting of ubiquity that is implied in many expressions on this head. And it should also be said, perhaps in extenuation of the expression cited above, that the president was addressing delegations of his own faculty, and presumably directing his remarks to their special benefit; and that while he professed (no doubt ingenuously) a profound zeal for the cause of science at

large, it had come about, selectively, through a long course of sedulous attention on his own part to all other qualifications than the main fact, that his faculty at the time of speaking was in the main an aggregation of slack-twisted schoolmasters and men about town. Such a characterization, however, does not carry any gravely invidious discrimination, nor will it presumably serve in any degree to identify the seat of learning to which it refers.

7. The share and value of the "faculty wives" in all this routine of resolute conviviality is a large topic, an intelligent and veracious account of which could only be a work of naive brutality.

> *"But the grim, grim Ladies, Oh, my brothers!*
> *They are ladling bitterly.*
> *They are ladling in the work-time of the others.*
> *In the country of the free."*
> —Mrs. Elizabeth Harte Browning, in *The Cry of the Heathen Chinee.*

8. What takes place without executive sanction need trouble no one.

9. "Education is the one kind of human enterprise that can not be brought under the action of the economic law of supply and demand. It can not be conducted on 'business principles.' There is no 'demand' for education in the economic sense. . . . Society is the only interest that can be said to demand it, and society must supply its own demand. Those who found educational institutions or promote educational enterprise put themselves in the place of society and assume to speak and act for society, not for any economic interest."—Lester F. Ward, *Pure Sociology*, p. 575.

10. Indeed, the resemblance is visible. As among professional politicians, so also as regards incumbents and aspirants for academic office, it is not at all unusual, nor does it cause surprise, to find such persons visibly affected with those characteristic pathological marks that come of what is conventionally called "high living"—late hours, unseasonable vigils, surfeit of victuals and drink, the fatigue of sedentary ennui. A flabby habit of body, hypertrophy of the abdomen, varicose veins, particularly of the facial tissues, a blear eye and a coloration suggestive of bile and apoplexy—when this unwholesome bulk is duly wrapped in a conventionally decorous costume it is accepted rather as a mark of weight and responsibility, and so serves to distinguish the pillars of urban society. Nor should it be imagined that these grave men of affairs and discretion are in any peculiar degree prone to excesses of the table or to nerve-shattering bouts of dissipation. The exigencies of publicity, however, are, by current use and wont, such as to enjoin not indulgence in such excursions of sensual perversity, so much as a gentlemanly conformity to a large routine of conspicuous convivialities. "Indulgence" in ostensibly gluttonous bouts of this kind—banquets, dinners, etc.—is not so much a matter of taste as of astute publicity, designed to keep the celebrants in repute among a laity whose simplest and most assured award of esteem proceeds on evidence of wasteful ability to pay. But the pathological consequences, physical and otherwise, are of much the same nature in either case.

The "Great Man" and His "Just" Rewards

On a cursory acquaintance with this volume one is tempted to dismiss it with the comment that Mr. Mallock has written another of his foolish books. The objective point of the new book is still the enforcement of the author's pet fallacy, which he has expounded so felicitously on many a former occasion. It is restated here with somewhat greater circumstance than before, and is backed by much telling illustration and some substantial information that might well have served a more useful purpose. A fuller acquaintance with its contents, however, will convince the reader that the book has substantial merits, although these merits do not belong with the economic side of the argument.

While the present volume covers a wider range of phenomena and traces the working of a great man's dominating efficiency through a greater variety of human relations than Mr. Mallock's earlier books have done, the chief point of the argument is still the productive efficiency of the great man in industry and the bearing of this productive efficiency upon the equitable claim of the wealthy classes to a superior share of the product. What is to be proven is the equity and the expediency of a system of distribution in which a relatively large share of the product of industry goes to the owners of capital and the directors of business. For this purpose "the great man" in industry is tacitly identified with the captain of industry or the owner of capital. It is right that the great man, so understood, should receive a large share, because he produces a large proportion of the product of industry (book III; pp. 197–267). And it is expedient that exceptional gains should come to this exceptional wealth-producer, because on no other terms can he be induced to take care of the economic welfare of the community—and, in

Review of W. H. Mallock's "Aristocracy and Evolution," reprinted from *Journal of Political Economy* 7 (June 1898): 430–35. Used by permission from University of Chicago Press.

the nature of things, the welfare of the community, of the many, lies unreservedly in the hands of the minority of great men (book iv; pp. 271–380).

The few are the chief producers.

All the democratic formulas which for the past hundred years have represented the employed as the producers of wealth, and the capitalistic employers as the appropriators of it, are, instead of being, as they claim to be, the expressions of a profound truth, related to truth only as being direct inversions of it. Whatever appearances may seem to show to the contrary, it is the few and not the many who, in the domain of economic production, are essentially and permanently the chief repositories of power" (pp. 174–175).

"The case of labour directed by different great men is the same as the case of labour applied to different qualities of land. The great men produce the increment. Labour, however, must be held to produce that minimum necessary to the support of the labourers, both in agriculture and in all kinds of production. The great man produces the increment that would not be produced by labour if his influence ceased. Labour, it is true, is essential to the production of the increment, also; but we cannot draw any conclusions from the hypothesis of labour ceasing; for the labourers would have to labour whether the great men were there or not (pp. 202–206, margin). The efficiency of labour itself is practically constant; and for the student of wealth-production the principal force to be studied is the ability of the few, by which the labour of the many is multiplied, and which only exerts itself under special social circumstances (p. 209, note).

We are thus enabled to discriminate arithmetically between the share of the product due to the great men and that due to the many."

"Let us take the case of the United Kingdom, and consider the amount per head that was annually produced by the population a hundred years ago. This amount was about £14. At the present time it is something like £35. . . . Now, if we attribute the entire production of this country, at the close of the last century, to common or average labor (which is plainly an absurd concession), we shall gain some idea of what the utmost limits of the independent productivity of the ordinary man are; for the ordinary man's talents as a producer, when directed by nobody but himself, have, as has been said already, not appreciably increased in the course of two thousand years, and have certainly not increased within the past three generations. The only thing that has increased has been the concentration on the ordinary man's productive talents not the productive talents of the exceptional man. The talents of the exceptional man, in fact, have been the only variant in the problem; and, accordingly, the minimum which these talents produce is the total difference between £14 and £35."

This argument may be restated in more concise arithmetical form after adding a further premise, which is implied, though not fully taken account of, in Mr. Mallock's exposition. The talents of the ordinary man have not changed within the past three generations, or if they have changed it is but by a variation so small that it can only be indicated, not quantitatively registered; the like is true of the talents of the exceptional man. This latter feature of the premises has not been brought out by Mr. Mallock, although his claim that human talents have remained constant plainly involves it. The traits of human nature have not appreciably changed within the period in question. The race of British subjects is much the same as it has been. But in order to allow for a possible, though inappreciable, change in the talents of the two classes, the conceivable infinitesimal change may be indicated by the use of accents. The arithmetical problem in hand will then present the following result:

(1) o(ordinary) x g(great man) = 14.
(2) o' x g' = 35.

But since 35 may be broken up and written 14 plus 21, it follows that, in the second equation, 21 of the entire product (35) is the product of g' alone. Q.E.D.

This traverses the ancient traditions of arithmetic, but it is to be said in legitimation of this procedure that it would be extremely difficult to get the same result by a different method. Any man encumbered with a hide-bound arithmetic would find himself constrained to look for some other variable in the problem than a special segment of that human nature which is by supposition declared invariable; nor would such a one have the courage to portion out the *meum* and *tuum* as between two factors of a joint product. But Mr. Mallock is without fear.

Some account, though scant, is taken by Mr. Mallock of the phenomena of transmitted knowledge, usages, and methods of work; but these facts are not allowed to count as against the primacy of the great man. And as regards this great man, where he is first characterized and expounded, in the chapter especially devoted to him ("Great Men, as the True Cause of Progress," pp. 55–88), the chief variants of him that concern economic theory are the inventor, the overseer of industrial processes, and the business man. The impression is conveyed in this early chapter that for the industrial purpose the greatest of these is the inventor, and next to him ranks the director of mechanical processes, while the business man comes into view as a wealth-producer chiefly in an indirect way by influencing the motions of the two former, and, through them, the motions of "ordinary men" engaged in manual labor. At a later point, when the question comes to concern the appraisement of productivity and the equitable apportionment of the product, the inventor, the engineer and the foreman disappear behind the business man's ledger, as the peppercorn disappears behind the nutshell, and "the great man" becomes synonymous with "the captain of industry." By a curious inversion of his own main position, Mr. Mallock reaches the broad verdict that consumable goods are mainly produced by the captain of industry. His main position, so far as regards industrial efficiency, is that the greatness and efficiency of the great man lie in his superior knowledge, which he is able to impose upon others and so direct their efforts to the result aimed at. "The master of knowledge, as applied to production, is the inventor" (p. 138).

"The inventor . . . is an agent of 'social progression' only because the particularized knowledge of which his invention consists is embodied either in models, or drawings, or written or spoken orders, and thus affects the technical action of whole classes of other men" (p. 139). Under the capitalistic wage system "productive power has increased because capital . . . has enabled a few men to apply, with the most constant and intense effort, their intellectual faculties to industry in its minutest details" (p. 161). Productive efficiency, therefore, is a matter of a detailed knowledge of the technical processes of industry and the application of this knowledge through directing the technical movements of others. Yet the type of productive efficiency in the advanced portion of Mr. Mallock's argument is taken to be the counting-house activity of the business man, who frequently does not, and pretty uniformly need not, have any technical knowledge of the industry that goes on under his hand. His relation to the mechanical processes is always remote, and usually of a permissive kind only. This is especially true of the director of a large business, who is by that fact, if he is successful, a highly efficient great man. He delegates certain men, perhaps at the second or third remove, to assume discretion and set certain workmen and machines in motion under the guidance of technical knowledge possessed by them, not by him. The captain's efficiency is not to be called in question, but it is bold irony to call it productive efficiency under the definition of productivity set up by Mr. Mallock.

Most modern men would have been content to justify the business man's claim to a share in the product on the ground of his serviceability to the community, without specifically imputing to him the major part in the production of goods; but Mr. Mallock's abounding faith in the canons of natural rights compels him naïvely to account for the business man's income in terms of productive efficiency simply. The argument of the book, as is evident especially in the concluding portion (book iv; pp. 271–380), is chiefly directed to the confutation of the socialists. And in this confutation it is the ancient, now for the most part abandoned, socialist position that is made the point of attack. This early socialist position was summed up in the claim that to the laborer should belong the entire product of his labor. The claim is a crude application of a natural-rights dogma, and for the living generation of socialists it may fairly be said to be a discarded standpoint. It is this dead dog that Mr. Mallock chiefly belabors. Together with this, the similarly obsolete natural-rights formula that all men are born free and equal comes in for a portion of his polemical attention. In all this, the polemic proceeds on the lost ground of natural rights. Objection is taken not to the obvious groundlessness of the whole natural-rights structure, but to the scope of the application given the dogmas and to the excessive narrowness of the definitions employed.

Through it all, however, Mr. Mallock very effectively presents the current arguments going to show that the pecuniary incentive is indispensable to modern industry, and he shows, with great detail and with good effect, the weakness of the socialist contentions on this head. He goes with the socialists to the length of showing that the pecuniary incentive—the desire of wealth—is in large part a desire for distinction only, not in the last analysis a desire for the material, consumable goods. But he denies flatly—what they affirm—that an emulative incentive of another kind might serve the turn if the pecuniary incentive were to fall away. No other method of gauging success and distinction will take the place of this one as an incentive to wealth-production, whatever seems to be true as regard other directions of effort (book vi, chap. ii; pp. 284–323). It is to be regretted that nothing beyond asseveration is put forward in support of this denial, which is the central feature of the refutation of socialism. No decisive argument for the denial is adduced, but through the assertion made there runs an implication that, in order to serve their purpose at all effectively, the inducements offered the wealth-producer must mechanically resemble the results to be worked out. As on the homeopathic principle like is to be cured by like, so in industry the repugnance to effort spent on material goods must be overcome by a remedial application of material goods. While it seems to be present in the reasoning, it is by no means clear, it should be remarked, that this axiom of similarity has been present in the reasoner's mind.

Mr. Mallock is a master of pleasing diction, and his arguments are presented in a lucid and forcible way that makes the book very attractive reading. And the grotesquely devious ways of its economic argument do not prevent it from being a suggestive contribution to the discussion of cultural development. At many points it brings out in a strong light the importance of a gifted minority as an element in the process of institutional growth, although even here it is curious, and in a sense instructive, to note that as representative spokesmen of the modern social sciences, Mr. Mallock has been constrained to cite George, Laveleye, and Mr. Kidd. The discussion of the great man's place in the cultural process is at its best where it deals with other fields than the economic. Unfortunately, it is the economic bearing of the argument alone that can be taken up here.

The volume suffers from a meretricious increase of bulk, due to an excessive use of large type, wide margins and heavy paper. It should be added that the printer's work is altogether above reproach.

On War, Peace, and Capitalism

The Dynastic State: The Case of Germany

It is as difficult for the commonplace Englishman to understand what the German means by the "State" as it is for the German to comprehend the English conception of a "commonwealth," or very nearly so. The English still have the word "state" in their current vocabulary, because they once had the concept which it is designed to cover, but when they do not in current use confuse it with the notion of a commonwealth, as they commonly do in making it serve as a synonym for "nation," it is taken to designate an extensive tract of land; on the other hand, the Germans, having never had occasion for such a concept as that covered by the term "commonwealth," have no corresponding word in their vocabulary. The State is a matter not easily to be expounded in English. It is neither the territorial area, nor the population, nor the body of citizens or subjects, nor the aggregate wealth or traffic, nor the public administration, nor the government, nor the crown, nor the sovereign; yet in some sense it is all these matters, or rather all these are organs of the State. In some potent sense, the State is a personal entity, with rights and duties superior and anterior to those of the subjects, whether these latter be taken severally or collectively, in detail or in the aggregate or average. The citizen is a subject of the State. Under a commonwealth, as in the United Kingdom, the citizen is, in the ritual sense of heraldic rank, a subject of the king—whatever that may mean—but this relation of subjection is a personal relation, a relation of mutual rank between two persons. The terms to the relation are necessarily personal entities, and they enter into this relation only by virtue of their character as persons.

"The State is the people legally united as an independent power." So says one who speaks with authority in these premises. But then, also, "The State is in the

Reprinted from chapters 5 and 8 of *Imperial Germany and the Industrial Revolution*, New York: The MacMillan Company, 1915.

first instance power, that it may maintain itself; it is not the totality of the people itself—the people is not altogether amalgamated with it; but the State protects and embraces the life of the people, regulating it externally in all directions. On principle it does not ask how the people is disposed; it demands obedience." "The State is power," says the same authority, and "it is only the State that is really powerful that corresponds to our idea." It might perhaps exceed the scope of the premises to follow him farther and find that "power" here means "military power." Plainly, government by consent of the governed is not a State. The sovereignty is not in the people, but it is in the State. Failure to understand this conundrum is perhaps the most detestable trait of unreason that taints the English-speaking peoples, in the apprehension of intelligent Germans.

The German ideal of statesmanship is, accordingly, to make all the resources of the nation converge on military strength; just as the English ideal is, *per contra*, to keep the military power down to the indispensable minimum required to keep the peace. This personal—in English one is tempted to say quasi-personal—entity, impersonate perhaps in the sovereign as its avatar, is a conception and an ideal which the English-speaking peoples appear to have missed, through its not lying within the horizon of their materialistic and pecuniary cultural outlook; they appear to have lost it in losing the spiritual perspective peculiar to the medieval mind. Rated in terms of the English cultural sequence, the conception would seem to be an archaism, an insight atrophied through disuse. It should seem also that it might be recovered in case the British nation should have the fortune to fall under the personal dominion of an autocratic prince, and so set up a dynastic State after the pattern preserved in the working constitution of Prussia.

The part played by this conception of the State in the rehabilitation of Germany is so considerable, and the difference it has made between the German scheme of right and honest living and that which prevails elsewhere, among the other contemporary branches of the north-European culture, is so characteristic and consequential that it should merit more detailed scrutiny, both as to its logical and sentimental contents and as regards its derivation and its bearing on the material fortunes of the race.

In point of its sentimental content, as regards the native propensities which find expression in this concept of the State, its chief ingredient is doubtless the ancient sense of group solidarity, expanded to take in a nation seen only in fancy, instead of the original neighborhood group known by personal contact and common gossip. This group solidarity is seen somewhat baldly at work in the small communities of the lower cultures and in the local pride and loyalty of neighborhoods and hamlets, clubs and congregations, among the more naïve and commonplace elements of the civilized populations. It has been construed by the utilitarian philosophers, in their time, as a calculated outcome of material self-interest resorting to co-operation—doubtless an inadequate if not groundless account of a propensity that is frequently seen to traverse the lines of self-interest. It would rather appear to be a native and indefeasible bias in the race. That such should be the case is all the more reasonable in view of the fact that men have always lived in groups, that the existence of the race has been continued only in and by group life. That enterprising individuals now and again successfully trade on this sentiment of solidarity for their own advantage gives no degree of support to the nation that it is a derivative of self-interest; rather the contrary.

But however jealous and self-complacent this sense of solidarity may show itself to be, under circumstances which provoke its expression along lines of invidious comparison and emulation, the recognition of this temperamental bent does not of itself carry us beyond the conception of a community or commonwealth. There are still lacking the elements of personality and unfolding power, which are essential to the concept of the State as distinct from that of a community. This is the more evident if it be kept in mind that the State may—perhaps rather typically does—unfold its power and assert its initiative apart from, beyond, or even in contravention of, any consensus on the part of the community. The bias of solidarity is an essential element, no doubt, but it is a solidarity subservient to an extraneous initiative; an initiative not necessarily alien to the spontaneous consensus of the group, but also not necessarily coincident with or germane to the ends of life comprised in the consensus of the community. In the ideal case—and the Prussian case visibly approaches this ideal—the consensus of the community will, at least passably, coincide with the drift of the State's initiative; and that it does so is a fortunate circumstance and an element of power in the State, but it is a matter of coincidence rather than an organic necessity. Where the popular consensus so comes to coincide with the line of the State's initiative and unfolding power, as in the Prussian case, it will commonly happen that this happy consummation is reached through the community's accepting the State's ends as its own, and also commonly without such knowledge of the State's ends in the case as would enable the community to take stock of them and appreciate what has been accepted or assented to. In other words, the coalescence of the community's consensus of interest with the State's ambitions is a coalescence by submission or abnegation, whereby the community lends itself, willingly and even enthusiastically, as a means to the State's realization of its own higher ends.

With great uniformity, wherever such a conception of a State as an over-ruling personal—or quasi-personal—entity prevails and takes effect as a working ideal, the State is conceived as a monarchical establishment—it is what has here been spoken of as a "dynastic State." It is, as in the Prussian case, an autocratic monarchy that it had in mind as the only practical realization or incorporation of this ideal of a State; an absolute dynastic monarchy, "constitutional" by concession perhaps, but paramount and peremptory at need. The State is personalized in the person of the sovereign. And this sovereign or dynasty is not on a tenure of sufferance or good will. He does not hold his authority by gift of the community. If he did he would be only the spokesman and administrative servant of the community, and the State would so disappear in a commonwealth woven together out of expedient compromises between the several interests living together in the community. It seems doubtful if this working conception of the State can be formulated in concrete terms as anything else than or short of a dynastic monarch, absolute at least in theory.

To cast back again into European prehistory for such dim light as may so be had on the elements of human nature that come in evidence in this current conception of the State: In the petty communities, perhaps kingdoms, managed on a basis of neighborhood solidarity and administered somewhat anarchistically by force of a neighborly consensus—in these quasi-anarchistic groups of remote Baltic antiquity the common understanding that made group life practicable appears to have been in effect the rule of Live and let live. Apart from their anarchistic scheme of administration there is only one institutional fact that is confidently, or rather unavoidably, to be imputed to these communities of the Old Order on the evidence that has come down, viz., the ownership of property. But the evidence of ownership under that archaic regime goes back so near to the beginning of things in the north-European culture—as it commonly does elsewhere also—that there is not much to be surmised of an earlier antiquity. There may also have been kings in that early time—the evidence is of course not conclusive—but there can scarcely have been a State; an anarchistic State will easily be conceded to be a misnomer.

As has appeared in other passages of this inquiry, this state of culture, dimly shown in the archaeological evidence, has the sanction of natural law, in that it was seen and approved as viable by a longer series of generations than have lived since it disappeared. Such slight institutional furniture as it gives evidence of should be near-hand expressions of a native bent in the peoples concerned, and may be taken as a naïve indication of what is indefeasibly right and good in the sight of these men. Among these time-tried institutions is the right of ownership, the secure usufruct of what the owner may have achieved or acquired, under the rules of the game as approved by common consent. From some far-off point in the cultural sequence, again apparently in remote antiquity, inheritance has been a legitimate method of coming into such usufruct. All this still approves itself to the common sense of the common man today.

In later time, when this people came to deal with aliens in the way of raiding and conquest, what a man might achieve or acquire and transmit by inheritance came to include such booty and such dominion over a subject people as his fortune and initiative put him in the way of—always subject to the rules of the game as seen and approved by the community on whose consensus he leaned. Out of these predatory beginnings, legitimized by convention and settled by use and wont, presently came the feudal regime; and out of this in turn, by further working of the anarchistic principle of usufruct applicable to whatever one might achieve or acquire within the rules of the game, came the dynastic State. The principle of usufruct by right of ownership, which once applied to a subject community (originally of aliens), is in the dynastic State extended to cover the usufruct of a community which has by use and wont grown to feel itself at one with its masters and has come into authentic acceptance of a comprehensive servile status.

The ancient principle of ownership has by historical permutation taken such a turn as to vest the usufruct of the community at large in its dynastic head. And so long as the situation at large continues to be transfused with dynastic ambitions and chicane, so that the alternative effectively offered any community would be subservience to its homebred dynastic head or to an alien dynasty, so long the dynastic State continues in force, backed as it is by the sense of group solidarity and not violating the principle of Live and let live in any greater degree than the only visible alternative to its rule—subjection to another and alien power of the same complexion.

In the Prussian environment the conditions of national life have favored the conservation of this dynastic rule; whereas in England, placed as that nation has been in modern time, the dynastic conception has disintegrated under the wasting impact of the common man's native animus to Live and let live. The truth and beauty of a regime of dynastic usufruct is not realized in the absence of a suitable background of war and rapine. And one finds that the encomiasts of this regime habitually protest against any proposal to remove or soften this background.

Now it happens, perhaps as an accident involved in the historical sequence, perhaps due to a recrudescence of the ancient anarchistic bent, that in modern times the drift of sentiment sets in the direction of Live and let live, and discountenances all institutional establishments of a visibly servile order. Such is peculiarly the case in those communities—like the French, English-speaking, Dutch and Scandinavian countries—that have been most intimately engaged in the latter-day technological and scientific achievements. Now, whether by force of arrogation or by drift of sober common sense, this same group of industrial nations have at the same time come to be accounted the leaders among civilized peoples, in so far as bears on the scheme of civil and political institutions. There is in fact an apparently well-advised, or at all events well-accepted, preconception lodged in the body of current common sense to the effect that slavery, servitude and the like subjection to the dictates of an irresponsible personal master is a moral and aesthetic impossibility among civilized mankind; that such personal subservience is a relic of feudalistic barbarism and disappears irretrievably from among the usages and the ideals of any peoples so soon as they emerge upon the levels of latter-day civilized life.

While this modernism apparently owes its rise and its vogue to the growth of opinion among the advanced industrial peoples and to its congruity with the scheme of peaceable industry to which these peoples are addicted, it has also imposed itself by force of example on the later comers among the peoples of Christendom, at least to the extent of a shamefaced formal acceptance. So massive and so ubiquitous is this persuasion of the shamefulness of servitude, that even in those instances where the dynastic State still stands intact as a practical effect, and has not yet come to be felt as an irksome or insufferable grievance, it will no longer do to display its character openly as an organization of servitude based on subjection to the person of the dynastic head. When conceived in these bald terms of usufruct and submission, the uses of a dynastic establishment are seen to be of the same nature as the uses of a tapeworm; and the tapeworm's relation to his host is something not easy to beautify in words, or even to authenticate in such convincing fashion as will insure his affectionate retention on grounds of decorous use and wont.

However, by taking thought one may conserve the facts and save appearances. The dynastic establishment may be sublimated into a personalized collectivity of "the people legally united as an independent power." There is no obnoxious trait of servile subjection to an irresponsible personal master in the community's so taking collective action. This is what would be understood by a "commonwealth." But a community so constituted is not a State; it is more like a joint-stock company. Its personality must become something more than a figure of speech. If such a community is to be a power—to exercise that "will to power" that one hears of—the usufruct of the collective strength must be vested in a personal agent with plenary discretion; and the requisite efficiency and stability of initiative and discretion can be had only if this personal head is possessed of paramount authority, and in so far as his jurisdiction rests on a tenure independent of the ebb and flow of vulgar sentiment. The State must find "a local habitation and a name" in the person of a dynastic prince, in whom must vest the unqualified usufruct of the community's powers. So will the dynastic State be reinstated, in effect, unimpaired and unmitigated.

It is some such theoretical construction of a personalized collectivity that is held up to view in the expositions offered by the spokesmen of the Prussian State and its high destiny. But it is at the same time difficult to make out that the patriotic sentiments of the Prussian subject effectually center on anything more shadowy than the personal dynasty of the Hohenzollern and the personal ambitions of its head. With this feudalistic loyalty goes an enthusiastic sense of national solidarity and a self-complacent conviction of the superior merits of the views and usages current in the Fatherland—the "Culture" of Germany; but all that is not integral to the conception of the State. The dynastic State, of course, is a large element in the "Culture" of this people; very much as its repudiation is an integral feature of the cultural scheme accepted among English-speaking peoples. Indeed, there is little, if substantially anything, else in the way of incurable difference between the German and the English scheme of things than the discrepancy between this ideal of the dynastic State on the one hand and the preconception of popular autonomy on the other hand. The visible differences of principle in other bearings will commonly be found to be derivatives or ramifications of these incompatible sentiments on the head of the personal government.

The resulting difference between British and German in respect of personal freedom and subordination is less a matter of practical conduct than of "principle"; although it will not be seriously questioned, because it has been proven by experiment, that British, or English-speaking, popular sentiment will eventually submit to much less provocation before taking recourse to concerted insubordination. The margin of tolerance in this respect is visibly narrower in the British case. Yet the point of equilibrium reached by each of the two peoples in their everyday conduct of affairs and in their practical attitude toward the constituted authorities is by no means widely different; although the one may be held to reach this equilibrium of working arrangements by concessive abatement of the demands of insubordination, while much the same practical outcome is reached from the other side by expedient mitigation of the claims of absolute tutelage and fealty. The English-speaking peoples are democratic, indeed anarchistically democratic, in principle, but by reason of common-sense expediency fortified by a pervading respect of person—what is sometimes disrespectfully called flunkeyism—the effective degree of freedom enjoyed by the individual, as restrained by law and custom, is only moderately greater than that which falls to the lot of the German subject whose point of departure in the regulation of conduct would appear to be this same flunkeyism, dignified with a metaphysical nimbus and mitigated by common-sense expediency.

"Flunkeyism" has an odious sound in modern ears, but unfortunately there is no equally precise term available to cover the same range of sentiment without invidious implications; it is a fault of the current vocabulary. Both German and English-speaking peoples make much of personal liberty, as is the fashion in modern Christendom, but it would seem that in the German conception this liberty is freedom to give orders and freely to follow orders, while in the English conception it is rather an exemption from orders—a somewhat anarchistic habit of thought.

It was this dynastic power of the Prussian state, resting on an authentic tradition of personal fealty, unlimited in the last resort, that was the largest single factor of a cultural kind entering into the Imperial era from the German side. It is at least conceivable that in the course of time the protracted disintegrating impact of the discipline exercised by modern industrial habits would have brought this dynastic State and its coercive organization to much the same state of decay as that which once overtook its smaller and feebler counterpart in Elizabethan England. But the course of time has not had a chance to run in this Prussian case. Elizabethan England, and its soaring imperialistic aspirations, was exposed to the slow corrosion of peace and isolation, with the common interest converging more and more on the industrial arts and the fortunes of trade; and it took a hundred years and more to displace dynastic statecraft and eliminate imperialist politics—in so far as these elements of the ancient regime can be said to have been lost—and it took another two hundred years to reach the farthest point along the line of liberal policy and peaceable ideals eventually attained by the English community. . . .

It will be seen, then, that both in its cultural antecedents and in the current circumstances there are several factors of considerable scope peculiar to this German case and converging to an outcome different from what has resulted, so far, among the English-speaking peoples as a consequence of their taking over the modern industrial arts—different, indeed, in a very appreciable degree from what can by any dispassionate line of reasoning be looked for among the English-speaking peoples within the calculable future.

Germany carried over from a recent and retarded past a State, of the dynastic order, with a scheme of detail institutions and a popular habit of mind suitable to a coercive, centralized, and irresponsible control and to the pursuit of dynastic dominion. Quite unavoidably, the united Fatherland came under the hegemony of the most aggressive and most irresponsible—substantially the most archaic—of the several states that coalesced in its formation; and quite as a matter of course the dynastic spirit of the Prussian State has permeated the rest of the federated people, until the whole is now very appreciably nearer the spiritual bent of the militant Prussian State of a hundred years ago than it has been at any time since the movement for German union began in the nineteenth century.

This united German community, at the same time, took over from their (industrially) more advanced neighbors the latest and highly efficient state of the industrial arts—wholly out of consonance with their institutional scheme, but highly productive, and so affording a large margin disposable for the uses of the dynastic State. Being taken over ready-made and in the shortest practicable time, this new technology brought with it virtually none of its inherent drawbacks, in the way of conventional waste, obsolescent usage and equipment, or class animosities; and as it has been brought into full bearing within an unexampled short time, none of these drawbacks or handicaps have yet had time to grow to formidable dimensions.

Owing in part to the same unprecedentedly short period of its acquirement and installation, and in part to the nearly unbroken medievalism of the institutional scheme into which the new technology has been intruded, it has hitherto had but a slight effect in the way of inducing new habits of thought on institutional matters among the German population, such as have formed the institutional counterpart of its gradual development among the English-speaking peoples. Such institutional consequences of a workday habituation to any given state of the industrial arts will necessarily come on by slow degrees and be worked out only in the course of generations.

In the English case, as has been indicated in earlier passages, such growth of popular institutions and ideals of autonomy and initiative as may be observed in modern times has not placed popular autonomy in anything like a position of unqualified domination in any of the collective concerns of life. There is much standing over from the earlier, feudalistic and dynastic, regime, as e.g., the crown, the nobility with its house of lords, and the established church; although these remains so left over are in a visibly infirm state and have something of an air of incongruity and anachronism in their modern setting. "Dead letter" and "legal fiction" have a large place in English conceptions, and these archaic strands in the institutional fabric are in great part to be viewed in that light. At the same time, while the modern institutional notions of popular autonomy have been encroaching on the domain once held by feudalism and the State, there has, along with this growth, also grown into the scheme a new range of customary conceptions and usages that greatly circumscribe the *de facto* supremacy of popular institutions in the British commonwealth.

Any English-speaking community is a commonwealth rather than a State: but none of these communities, for all that, is a commonwealth of free, equal, and ungraded men; their citizens are not "masterless men," except in the cognizance of the law. Discrepancies of wealth have grown great and found secure lodgement in the institutional scheme at the same time that these modern communities have been falling back on those ancient ideals of personal insubordination that makes the substance of their free institutions. And serious discrepancies of wealth are a matter not provided for in that ancient hereditary bent that once made the petty anarchistic groups of the Baltic culture a practicable engine of social control, and that is now reasserting itself in democratic discontent. While property rights work no *de jure* disturbance of the democratic scheme, their *de facto* consequences are sufficiently grave, so that it is doubtful if a free but indigent workman in a modern industrial community is at all better off in point of material circumstances than the workman on a servile tenure under feudalism. Indeed, so grave and perplexing has the situation in the English-speaking countries become, in respect of the *de facto* control of the community's material fortunes by the owners of large property, that none but a graceless "pessimist" is conceived to be capable of calling attention to so sore a difficulty for which no remedy can be discovered. Yet, while the current administrative affairs may be carried on by bailiffs of the wealthy and well-to-do, and primarily in their interest, it remains true that in point of popular sentiment the sovereignty vests collectively in the common man; and it will scarcely be questioned that if brought to a sufficiently sharp test, this popular sentiment would stubbornly assert its paramount dominion.

Partial and incomplete as this shift to popular autonomy proves to have been in the English-speaking nations, it has taken some centuries of experience to carry the community from a position comparable to that occupied by the Germans at the formation of the Empire to the compromise in force among these peoples today. This growth of free institutions and insubordination, such as it is, has apparently come partly of the positive discipline in mechanistic habits of thought given by the modern industrial arts, but partly also as a reassertion of the hereditary anarchistic bent of this population in the absence of duly rigorous circumstances going to enforce a scheme of coercion and loyalty. The net outcome may be rated as a gain or a loss, according as one is inclined to see it. But it is an outcome of the working of the modern industrial system, and if it is to be rated as an infirmity it is also to be accepted as one of the concomitants of that system, inseparable from it in the long run because it is made of the same substance as this technological system.

It is this "long run" that is still wanting in the German case, and it must necessarily be all the longer a run for the care taken by the Imperial State to prevent such an outcome. Meantime the Imperial state has come into the usufruct of this state of the industrial arts without being hampered with its long-term institutional consequences. Carrying over a traditional bias of Romantic loyalty, infused anew with a militant patriotism by several successful wars, and irritably conscious of national power in their new-found economic efficiency, the feudalistic spirit of the population has yet suffered little if any abatement from their brief experience as a modern industrial community. And borne up by its ancient tradition of prowess and dynastic aggression, the Prussian-Imperial State has faithfully fostered this militant spirit and cultivated in the people the animus of a solidarity of prowess. Hence a pronounced retardation in the movement toward popular autonomy, due to follow from habituation to the mechanistic logic of the modern technology and industrial organization.

In this work of retarding the new and conserving the old the Imperial State has been greatly furthered by finding ready to hand a large and serviceable body of men, useless for industrial purposes by force of conventional and temperamental disabilities, who have eagerly entered the career of prowess opened to them by the warlike enterprise of the empire and have zealously fallen in with the spirit of that policy—such being the run of traditions out of which they have come in the recent past. Indeed, so large, so strongly biased, and so well entrenched in the use and wont of the Fatherland, have this contingent of specialists in prowess been, that even with a very moderate degree of moral support from the constituted authorities, perhaps even on a footing of tolerance—if such a footing were conceivable under the Imperial auspices—their organization into a specialized corps of war-leaders should have followed as a matter of course; and the presence of such a body of professional military men, pervaded with a headlong enthusiasm for warlike enterprise, would of itself have had the effect of heightening the war spirit abroad in the community at large and inducing a steady drift of sentiment leading to a warlike climax.

It has been the usual fortune of military establishments and warlike class organizations presently to fall into a certain state of moral decay, whereby rank, routine, perquisites and intemperate dissipation come to engage the best attention of the specialists in war. Like other works of use and wont this maturing of the warlike establishment takes time, and the corps of war specialists under the Imperial auspices has not yet had time to work out the manifest destiny of warlike establishments in this respect; although it may be admitted that "irregularities" of the kind alluded to have by no means been altogether wanting. The corrosion of military use and wont, in the way of routine, subordination, arrogance, indolence and dissipation, has perhaps gone so far as would unfit this picked body of men for the duties of citizenship under any but an autocratic government, but they have probably suffered no appreciable impairment in respect of their serviceability for war and its advocacy.

In the same connection, it is also credibly reported, though not officially confirmed, that the highly efficient school system of the empire, perhaps especially of Prussia, is, under Imperial auspices, made a vehicle for propaganda of the same patriotism of prowess that pervades the body of officers. Something of the kind is known to be true of the Prussian universities. Much can of course be done toward giving a bent of this kind to the incoming generation by well-directed inculcation during the impressionable period of schoolboy life.

One further item should be included in any recital of the special circumstances that go to make Imperial Germany and shape its destiny. Among the gains that have come to the Imperial State, and by no means least among these gains if one is to judge by the solicitous attention given it, is the use of the modern technology for warlike equipment and strategy. It has already been noted that the railway system, as also the merchant marine and its harbor equipment, has been developed under surveillance, with a view to its serviceability in war; in part this transportation system has been projected and built avowedly for strategic use, in part under specifications and with subventions designed to make it an auxiliary arm. The importance of such a competently organized transportation system in modern strategy needs no argument; its bearing on the animus of the statesmen at whose disposal so efficient a factor of warlike equipment is held, as well as on that of the people at large, should also not be overlooked.[1]

But beyond this, and doubtless of graver import, is the direct service rendered by the modern technology and applied science to the art of war. Since the modern technology fell into the hands of the Germans they have taken the lead in the application of this technological knowledge to what may be called the industrial arts of war, with at least no less zeal and no less effect than in its utilization in the arts of peace. In the "armed peace" of Europe, Imperial Germany has consistently aimed to be the most heavily armed and the readiest for any eventual breach of the peace. These preparations, it has been usual to declare, have been made with a view to keeping the peace. Some weight may perhaps attach to these declarations. They have been made by statesmen of the school of Frederick the Great. The run of the facts in the case is that throughout the forty-four years of its life-history hitherto, and more particularly through the later quarter of a century, preparation for war on a large scale has been going forward unremittingly, and at a constantly accelerating rate, whether as measured in terms of absolute magnitude or as measured in terms of expenditure per capita of the population, or of percentages of current income or of accumulated wealth, or as compared with the corresponding efforts of neighboring states.

This drift toward a warlike fatality has been facilitated by subsidiary consequences that should, in their immediate incidence, seem to have no bearing of the kind. So, e.g., their great success in business and industry has inspired the commonplace German subject with a degree of confidence and self-complacency that impresses their neighbors as conceit and braggadocio. Human nature being what it is, it is unavoidable that German subjects should take the German successes to heart in this way and that they should fall into something of an overbearing attitude toward other nationalities; and on similarly sufficient grounds it follows that those who are brought in contact with this very natural magisterial swagger find it insufferable. All of which engenders a resentful animosity, such as will place all international relations on a precarious footing. So, by force of circumstances over which no control could be had, and which it must be admitted have not been sought to be controlled, it has come about that their economic success has brought the German people an abundance of ill-will for all that.

It may be worth noting that something of the same sense of estrangement is visible in the attitude of the Continental peoples toward the English of the swaggering Elizabethan times, and after. But the resulting animosity in that case appears not to have reached so high a pitch, and the insular position of the English served in any case to prevent any such animosity from becoming a menace to the public peace. The consciousness of this pervading ill-will has doubtless contributed appreciably to that patriotic solidarity of prowess in the German people on which the warlike policy of the Imperial government leans, and so has served to accelerate the shifting of the Empire's forces, material and spiritual, into a strategical position incompatible with any but a warlike outcome. . . .

Again it is bootless, of course, to speculate on what might have been. It may be more to the point to inquire into the effectual value and consequence of this Prussian-Imperial diversion, in its bearing on the civilization of Christendom. The pursuit of the Imperial policy has led Christendom into an unexampled war—an outcome which all men deprecate, whether sincerely or otherwise. At the best rating that can be had, the current war will necessarily be accounted an untoward episode. In the perspective of history it may also some day be so rated. Meantime the fact should not be lost sight of that it was entered on in a sense deliberately and advisedly, and with the best intentions on both sides. This is particularly true for the Prussian-Imperial statesmen and their strategy of defensive offense, though the *bona fides* of the party of the second part are perhaps more perspicuously evident on the face of the returns. Interest, therefore, can not center on the question of praise and blame. Neither can the purpose of the contest, as seen from either side, claim sustained attention, since on the one hand the aim on either side appears to have been sufficiently creditable in the eyes of those in whom discretion vested, while on the other hand the contest will run its course to much the same outcome, and carry substantially the same consequences, whatever the aim may have been.

It is a plain and easy generalization that the more consequential and enduring effects of the conflict will be of an immaterial nature, in the way of bias and sentiment, affecting the spiritual and intellectual outlook of the peoples, and so coming to an ulterior effect in more or less of a revision of the current institutional scheme. Hitherto the distinctive gains made by this civilization have been made by way of peace and industry—by "gains" being understood whatever has conduced to an advance in the direction of the latter day cultural situation among the distinctively Occidental peoples, as contrasted with the cultural scheme of their own barbarian past, in the Dark and Middle Ages. By the generality of civilized men this advance will be rated as, on the whole, an improvement over what it has displaced. Such an appraisal, however, is a matter of taste and opinion, in which the habituation embodied in this modern cultural scheme is itself taken as a base-line of appraisal; and it could, therefore, not be accepted as definitive in any argument on the intrinsic merits of this culture, in contrast with any other. But it is useful as showing that the current consensus, such as there is, runs to the effect that the change from medievalism to the modern regime is, on the whole, to be rated as an advance, and that consequently this meaning of the term is the only one that is at home in current usage in these premises.

This modern regime, like any other cultural scheme, late or early, is possessed of a certain systematic solidarity, due to the fact that it is pervaded by a certain characteristic logic and perspective, a certain line of habitual conceptions having a degree of congruity among themselves, a "philosophy," as it would once have been called. The exceptions, digressions, excursions and discordant encumbrances carried over by tradition from earlier usage or drawn in for side lines of interest or of constraint—all this is scarcely to be rated as adventitious or negligible, and it will bulk large in any given cultural scheme, particularly in such a one where the range is wide and the changes are rapid and diverse. Yet, owing to the fact that the community which carries this scheme and is exposed to its discipline is made up of individuals each and several of which is a single agent and is therefore bent as a whole by any habituation to which he is exposed, it follows that just in so far as it is possible to conceive any given cultural complex as a distinctive scheme, it will be characterized by one generally pervading habit of mind—by no means universally prevalent, but prevalent so extensively and pronouncedly as to be effectual as a common run. Where and in so far as this solidarity of habit does not prevail, the cultural situation is currently recognized as lacking homogeneity, as being a hybrid civilization, an unstable or transitional phase, etc.

As regards the civilization of modern Christendom in this bearing, what marks it off pervasively and dynamically from its own earlier phases, as well as from other cultures with which it is contrasted, is a certain character of matter-of-fact; showing itself on the institutional side, e.g., in a nearly universal avowed repudiation—often futile enough in practice—of all personal discrimination and prerogative; and showing itself more unequivocally on the side of knowledge, in an impersonal mechanical conception of objective things and events. So, the most characteristic habit of thought that pervades this modern civilization, in high or low degree, is what has, in the simplest terms hitherto given it, been called the mechanistic conception.[2] Its practical working-out is the machine technology, of which the intellectual precipitate and counterpart is the exact sciences. Associated with these in such a way as to argue a correlation, of the nature of cause and effect, is the modern drift toward free or popular institutions.[3]

Coercion, personal dominion, self-abasement, subjection, loyalty, suspicion, duplicity, ill-will—these things do not articulate with the mechanistic conception. Whatever human experience conduces to this range of habits of thought will, by so much, act to retard and defeat the cultural drift toward matter-of-fact; and any scheme or order of control that runs on these grounds will not enduringly contain that range of conceits and convictions that make up the modern body of theoretical knowledge and the principles of the common law. Personal dominion is essentially incongruous with the logic and perspective of this modern culture, and is therefore systematically incompatible with its ascendancy. Warlike experience is experience in personal rule, spoliation, loyalty, hate, subordination and duplicity. Therefore, whatever may be the nominal balance of profit and loss in the way of what is called the "fortunes of war," the net consequences will be much the same; and these consequences can not but be of the nature of retardation to Western civilization in those respects that mark it as Western and modern.

This warlike-dynastic diversion in which the Imperial State has been the protagonist is presumably of a transient nature, even though it can by no means be expected to be ephemeral. The Prussian-Imperial system may be taken as the type-form and embodiment of this reaction against the current of modern civilization; although the State is not thereby to be accounted the sole advocate of medievalism among the nations, nor is it a whole-hearted advocate. In the long run, in point of the long-term habituation enforced by its discipline, the system is necessarily inimical to modern science and technology, as well as to the modern scheme of free or popular institutions, inasmuch as it is incompatible with the mechanistic animus that underlies these habits of thought; not necessarily hostile in respect of the sentiments that animate its statesmen and spokesmen in their attitude towards these landmarks of the Western civilization, but inimical in respect of the set and fashion of the habit of mind which it inculcates.

Yet the Imperial system of dominion, statecraft and warlike enterprise necessarily rests on the modern mechanistic science and technology, for its economic foundations and its material equipment as well as for its administrative machinery and the strategy necessary to its carrying on. In this, of course, it is in the same case with other modern states. Nothing short of the fullest usufruct of this technology will serve the material needs of the modern warlike State; yet the discipline incident to a sufficiently unreserved addiction to this mechanistic technology will unavoidably disintegrate the institutional foundations of such a system of personal dominion as goes to make up and carry on a dynastic State.

The Imperial State, therefore, may be said to be unable to get along without the machine industry, and also, in the long run, unable to get along with it; since this industrial system in the long run undermines the foundations of the State. So that what the Prussian-Imperial State is, in effect, contending for in its offensive defense of German dominion, is something in the nature of a reprieve for personal government; but the situation has this singular feature that whether the Imperial State wins or loses in the contest for the hegemony, the movement of cultural reversion for which in substance it is contending stands to gain at least to the extent of a substantial, though presumably temporary, impairment and arrest of Western civilization at large.

Notes

1. "There is something in the possession of superior strength most dangerous, in a moral view, to its possessor. Brought in contact with semi-civilized man, the European, with his endowments and effective force so immeasurably superior, holds him as little higher than the brute, and as born equally for his service. He feels that he has a natural right, as it were, to his obedience, and that this obedience is to be measured, not by the powers of the barbarian, but by the will of his conqueror. Resistance becomes a crime to be washed out only in the blood of the victim. The tale of such atrocities is not confined to the Spaniard."—Prescott, Conquest of Peru, Book IV.

Such loss of moral perspective through an overweening sense of power appears to follow equally whether the stronger is or is not superior in any other respect—perhaps even more pronouncedly in the latter case. The Huns and Turks show it in their dealings with the Romanized Europeans, just as the Children of Israel show it on contact with Canaanites and Philistines, and as it appears again in the animus of Gauls, Goths, Visigoths and Vandals, in their time. So also the swaggering Elizabethan "gentleman adventurer" in his degree, as well as the Spanish conquistador or the Prussian-Imperial statesman. It is the moral attitude of the pot-hunter towards the fur-bearing animals. One does not keep faith with the fur-bearing animals.

2. Cf. Jacques Loeb, The Mechanistic Conception of Life.

3. This pervasion of modern communities by such a mechanistic conception and by a bias inimical to prerogative and personal government is, of course, to be taken as a matter of habituation and acquired bent, not a derangement or deflection of the underlying instinctive proclivities of human nature. Yet, the habituation leading to this mechanistic, matter of fact drift in Western civilization may presumably be better conceived as a disciplined obsolescence of habitual elements derived from the recent past and no longer enforced by current circumstances, instead of newly acquired habits of thought coercively enforced upon a human nature to which they are essentially alien. It would appear to be a work of divestment or riddance, quite as much as of investiture or inculcation of a new proficiency. In the absence of, or under reduced pressure from, discipline conducive to personal subjection and abasement, or to the interpretation of objective things and relations in the personalized terms of magical or occult forces, it may be conceived that human faculty will, in a sense atavistically, assert its native bent of matter-of-fact in both of these cognate directions. With the obsolescence of putative occult powers and qualities in the conception of objective reality, such as is required by the machine technology, the like obsolescence of a similar habitual imputation of occult grounds of privilege, authority, and subservience will take effect in the institutional scheme.

Peace and the Price System

Evidently the conception of peace on which its various spokesmen are proceeding is by no means the same for all of them. In the current German conception, e.g., as seen in the utterances of its many and urgent spokesmen, peace appears to be of the general nature of a truce between nations, whose God-given destiny it is, in time, to adjust a claim to precedence by wager of battle. They will sometimes speak of it, euphemistically, with a view to conciliation, as "assurance of the national future," in which the national future is taken to mean an opportunity for the extension of the national dominion at the expense of some other national establishment. In the same connection one may recall the many eloquent passages on the State and its paramount place and value in the human economy. The State is useful for disturbing the peace. This German notion may confidently be set down as the lowest of the current conceptions of peace or perhaps rather as the notion of peace reduced to the lowest terms at which it continues to be recognizable as such. Next beyond in that direction lies the notion of armistice; which differs from this conception of peace chiefly in connoting specifically a definite and relatively short interval between warlike operations.

The conception of peace as being a period of preparation for war has many adherents outside the Fatherland, of course. Indeed, it has probably a wider vogue and a readier acceptance among men who interest themselves in questions of peace and war than any other. It goes hand in hand with that militant nationalism that is taken for granted, conventionally, as the common ground of those international relations that play a part in diplomatic intercourse. It is the diplomatist's *métier* to talk war in parables of peace. This conception of peace as a precarious interval of preparation has come down to the present out of the feudal age and is, of course, best at home where the feudal range of preconcep-

---

Reprinted from chapters 1–3, 5, and 7 of *An Inquiry into the Nature of Peace and the Terms of Its Perpetuation,* New York: The MacMillan Company, 1917.

tions has suffered least dilapidation; and it carries the feudalistic presumption that all national establishments are competitors for dominion, after the scheme of Macchiavelli. The peace which is had on this footing, within the realm, is a peace of subjection, more or less on the militant order; a war-like organization being necessarily of a servile character, in the same measure in which it is warlike.

In much the same measure and with much the same limitations as the modern democratic nations have departed from the feudal system of civil relations and from the peculiar range of conceptions which characterize that system, they have also come in for a new or revised conception of peace. Instead of its being valued chiefly as a space of time in which to prepare for war, offensive or defensive, among these democratic and provisionally pacific nations it has come to stand in the common estimation as the normal and stable manner of life, good and commendable in its own right. These modern, pacific, commonwealths stand on the defensive, habitually. They are still pugnaciously national, but they have unlearned so much of the feudal preconceptions as to leave them in a defensive attitude, under the watch-word: Peace with honor. Their quasi-feudalistic national prestige is not to be trifled with, though it has lost so much of its fascination as ordinarily not to serve the purposes of an aggressive enterprise, at least not without some shrewd sophistication at the hands of militant politicians and their diplomatic agents. Of course, an exuberant patriotism may now and again take on the ancient barbarian vehemence and lead such a provisionally pacific nation into an aggressive raid against a helpless neighbor; but it remains characteristically true, after all, that these peoples look on the country's peace as the normal and ordinary course of things, which each nation is to take care of for itself and by its own force.

The ideal of the nineteenth-century statesmen was to keep the peace by a balance of power; an unstable equilibrium of rivalries, in which it was recognized that eternal vigilance was the price of peace by equilibration. Since then, by force of the object-lesson of the twentieth-century wars, it has become evident that eternal vigilance will no longer keep the peace by equilibration, and the balance of power has become obsolete. At the same time things have so turned that an effective majority of the civilized nations now see their advantage in peace, without further opportunity to seek further dominion. These nations have also been falling into the shape of commonwealths, and so have lost something of their national spirit.

With much reluctant hesitation and many misgivings, the statesmen of these pacific nations are accordingly busying themselves with schemes for keeping the peace on the unfamiliar footing of a stable equilibrium; the method preferred on the whole being an equilibration of make-believe, in imitation of the obsolete balance of power. There is a meticulous regard for national jealousies and discriminations, which it is thought necessary to keep intact. Of course, on any one of these slightly diversified plans of keeping the peace on a stable footing of copartnery among the pacific nations, national jealousies and national integrity no longer have any substantial meaning. But statesmen think and plan in terms of precedent; which comes to thinking and planning in terms of make-believe, when altered circumstances have made the precedents obsolete. So one comes to the singular proposal of the statesmen, that the peace is to be kept in concert among these pacific nations by a provision of force with which to break it at will. The peace that is to be kept on this footing of national discriminations and national armaments will necessarily be of a precarious kind; being, in effect, a statesmanlike imitation of the peace as it was once kept even more precariously by the pacific nations in severalty.

Hitherto the movement toward peace has not gone beyond this conception of it, as a collusive safeguarding of national discrepancies by force of arms. Such a peace is necessarily precarious, partly because armed force is useful for breaking the peace, partly because the national discrepancies, by which these current peace-makers set such store, are a constant source of embroilment. What the peace-makers might logically be expected to concern themselves about would be the elimination of these discrepancies that make for embroilment. But what they actually seem concerned about is their preservation. A peace by collusive neglect of those remnants of feudalistic make-believe that still serve to divide the pacific nations has hitherto not seriously come under advisement.

Evidently, hitherto, and for the calculable future, peace is a relative matter, a matter of more or less, whichever of the several working conceptions spoken of above may rule the case. Evidently, too, a peace designed to strengthen the national establishment against eventual war will count to a different effect from a collusive peace of a defensive kind among the pacific peoples, designed by its projectors to conserve those national discrepancies on which patriotic statesmen like to dwell. Different from both would be the value of a peace by neglect of such useless national discriminations as now make for embroilment. A protracted season of peace should logically have a somewhat different cultural value according to the character of the public policy to be pursued under its cover. So that a safe and sane conservation of the received law and order should presumably best be effected under cover of a collusive peace of the defensive kind, which is designed to retain those national discrepancies intact that count for so much in the national life of today, both as a focus of patriotic sentiment and as an outlet for national expenditures. This plan would involve the least derangement of the received order among the democratic peoples, although the plan might itself undergo some change in the course of time.

Among the singularities of the latterday situation, in this connection, and brought out by the experiences of the great war, is a close resemblance between latterday war-like operations and the ordinary processes of industry. Modern warfare and modern industry alike are carried on by technological processes subject to surveillance and direction by mechanical engineers, or perhaps rather experts in engineering science of the mechanistic kind. War is not now a matter of the stout heart and strong arm. Not that these attributes do not have their place and value in modern warfare; but they are no longer the chief or decisive factors in the case. The exploits that count in this warfare are technological exploits; exploits of technological science, industrial appliances, and technological training. As has been remarked before, it is no longer a gentlemen's war, and the gentleman, as such, is no better than a marplot in the game as it is played.

Certain consequences follow from this state of the case. Technology and industrial experience, in large volume and at a high proficiency, are indispensable to the conduct of war on the modern plan, as well as a large, efficient and up-to-date industrial community and industrial plant to supply the necessary material of this warfare. At the same time the discipline of the campaign, as it impinges on the rank and file as well as on the very numerous body of officers and technicians, is not at cross purposes with the ordinary industrial employments of peace, or not in the same degree as has been the case in the past, even in the recent past. The experience of the campaign does not greatly unfit the men who survive for industrial uses; nor does it come in as a sheer interruption of their industrial training, or break the continuity of that range of habits of thought which modern industry of the technological order induces; not in the same degree as was the case under the conditions of war as carried on in the nineteenth century. The cultural, and particularly the technological, incidence of this modern warfare should evidently be appreciably different from what has been experienced in the past, and from what this past experience has induced students of these matters to look for among the psychological effects of warlike experience.

It remains true that the discipline of the campaign, however imperial it may tend to become, still inculcates personal subordination and unquestioning obedience; and yet the modern tactics and methods of fighting bear somewhat more on the individual's initiative, discretion, sagacity and self-possession than once would have been true. Doubtless the men who come out of this great war, the common men, will bring home an accentuated and acrimonious patriotism, a venomous hatred of the enemies whom they have missed killing; but it may reasonably be doubted if they come away with a correspondingly heightened admiration and affection for their betters who have failed to make good as foremen in charge of this teamwork in killing. The years of the war have been trying to the reputation of officials and officers, who have had to meet uncharted exigencies with not much better chance of guessing the way through than their subalterns have had.

By and large, it is perhaps not to be doubted that the populace now under arms will return from the experience of the war with some net gain in loyalty to the nation's honor and in allegiance to their masters; particularly the German subjects,—the like is scarcely true for the British; but a doubt will present itself as to the magnitude of this net gain in subordination, or this net loss in self-possession. A doubt may be permitted as to whether the common man in the countries of the Imperial coalition, e.g., will, as the net outcome of this war experience, be in a perceptibly more pliable frame of mind as touches his obligations toward his betters and subservience to the irresponsible authority exercised by the various governmental agencies, than he was at the outbreak of the war. At that time, there is reason to believe, there was an ominous, though scarcely threatening, murmur of discontent beginning to be heard among the working classes of the industrial towns. It is fair to presume, however, that the servile discipline of the service and the vindictive patriotism bred of the fight should combine to render the populace of the Fatherland more amenable to the irresponsible rule of the Imperial dynasty and its subaltern royal establishments, in spite of any slight effect of a contrary character exercised by the training in technological methods and in self-reliance, with which this discipline of the service has been accompanied. As to the case of the British population, under arms or under compulsion of necessity at home, something has already been said in an earlier passage; and much will apparently depend, in their case, on the further duration of the war. The case of the other nationalities involved, both neutrals and belligerents, is even more obscure in this bearing, but it is also of less immediate consequence for the present argument.

The essentially feudal virtues of loyalty and bellicose patriotism would appear to have gained their great ascendancy over all men's spirit within the Western civilization by force of the peculiarly consistent character of the discipline of life under feudal conditions, whether in war or peace; and to the same uniformity of these forces that shaped the workday habits of thought among the feudal nations is apparently due that profound institutionalization of the preconceptions of patriotism and loyalty, by force of which these preconceptions still hold the modern peoples in an unbreakable web of prejudice, after the conditions favoring their acquirement have in great part ceased to operate. These preconceptions of national solidarity and international enmity have come down from the past as an integral part of the unwritten constitution underlying all these modern nations, even those which have departed most widely from the manner of life to which the peoples owe these ancient preconceptions. Hitherto, or rather until recent times, the workday experience of these peoples has not seriously worked at cross purposes with the patriotic spirit and its bias of national animosity; and what discrepancy there has effectively been between the discipline of workday life and the received institutional preconceptions on this head, has hitherto been overborne by the unremitting inculcation of these virtues by interested politicians, priests and publicists, who speak habitually for the received order of things.

That order of things which is known on its political and civil side as the feudal system, together with that era of the dynastic State which succeeds the feudal age technically so called, was, on its industrial or technological side, a system of trained man-power organized on a plan of subordination of man to man. On the whole, the scheme and logic of that life, whether in its political (warlike) or its industrial doings, whether in war or peace, runs on terms of personal capacity, proficiency and relations. The organization of the forces engaged and the constraining rules according to which this organization worked, were of the nature of personal relations, and the impersonal factors in the case were taken for granted. Politics and war were a field for personal valor, force and cunning, in practical effect a field for personal force and fraud. Industry was a field in which the routine of life, and its outcome, turned on "the skill, dexterity and judgment of the individual workman," in the words of Adam Smith.

The feudal age passed, being done to death by handicraft industry, commercial traffic, gunpowder, and the state-making politicians. But the political States of the statemakers, the dynastic States as they may well be called, continued the conduct of political life on the personal plane of rivalry and jealousy between dynasties and between their States; and in spite of gunpowder and the new military engineering, warfare continued also to be, in the main and characteristically, a field in which manpower and personal qualities decided the outcome, by virtue of personal "skill, dexterity and judgment." Meantime industry and its technology by insensible degrees under went a change in the direction of impersonalization, particularly in those countries in which statemaking and its warlike enterprise had ceased, or were ceasing, to be the chief interests and the controlling preconception of the people.

The logic of the new, mechanical industry which has supplanted handicraft in these countries, is a mechanistic logic, which proceeds in terms of matter-of-fact strains, masses, velocities, and the like, instead of the "skill, dexterity and judgement" of personal agents. The new industry does not dispense with the personal agencies, nor can it even be said to minimize the need of skill, dexterity and judgment in their personal agents employed, but it does take them and their attributes for granted as in some sort a foregone premise to its main argument. The logic of the handicraft system took the impersonal agencies for granted; the machine industry takes the skill, dexterity and judgment of the workmen for granted. The processes of thought, and therefore the consistent habitual discipline, of the former ran in terms of the personal agents engaged, and of the personal relations of discretion, control and subordination necessary to the work; whereas the mechanistic logic of the modern technology, more and more consistently, runs in terms of the impersonal forces engaged, and inculcates an habitual predilection for matter-of-fact statement, and an habitual preconception that the findings of material science alone are conclusive.

In those nations that have made up the advance guard of Western civilization in its movement out of feudalism, the disintegrating effect of this matter-of-fact animus inculcated by the later state of the industrial arts has apparently acted effectively, in some degree, to discredit those preconceptions of personal discrimination on which dynastic rule is founded. But in no case has the discipline of this mechanistic technology yet wrought its perfect work or come to a definitive conclusion. Meantime war and politics have on the whole continued on the ancient plane; it may perhaps be fair to say that politics has so continued because warlike enterprise has continued still to be a matter of such personal forces as skill, dexterity and judgment, valor and cunning, personal force and fraud. Latterly, gradually, but increasingly, the technology of war, too, has been shifting to the mechanistic plane; until in the latest phases of it, somewhere about the turn of the century, it is evident that the logic of warfare too has come to be the same mechanistic logic that makes the modern state of the industrial arts.

What, if anything, is due by consequence to overtake the political strategy and the political preconceptions of the new century, is a question that will obtrude itself, though with scant hope of finding a ready answer. It may even seem a rash, as well as an ungraceful, undertaking to inquire into the possible manner and degree of prospective decay to which the received political ideals and virtues would appear to be exposed by consequence of this derangement of the ancient discipline to which men have been subjected. So much, however, would seem evident, that the received virtues and ideals of patriotic animosity and national jealousy can best be guarded against untimely decay by resolutely holding to the formal observance of all outworn punctilios of national integrity and discrimination, in spite of their increasing disserviceability,—as would be done, e.g., or at least sought to be done, in the installation of a league of neutral nations to keep the peace and at the same time to safeguard those "national interests" whose only use is to divide these nations and keep them in a state of mutual envy and distrust.

Those peoples who are subject to the constraining governance of this modern state of this industrial arts, as all modern peoples are in much the same measure in which they are "modern," are, therefore, exposed to a workday discipline running at cross purposes with the received law and order as it takes effect in national affairs; and to this is to be added that, with warlike enterprise also shifted to this same mechanistic-technological ground, war can no longer be counted on so confidently as before to correct all the consequent drift away from the ancient landmarks of dynastic, pseudo-dynastic, and national enterprise in dominion.

As has been noted above, modern warfare not only makes use of, and indeed depends on, the modern industrial technology at every turn of the operations in the field, but it draws on the ordinary industrial resources of the countries at war in a degree and with an urgency never equalled. No nation can hope to make a stand in modern warfare, much less to make headway in warlike enterprise, without the most thoroughgoing exploitation of the modern industrial arts. Which signifies for the purpose in hand that any Power that harbors an imperial ambition must take measures to let its underlying population acquire the ways and means of the modern machine industry, without reservation; which in turn signifies that popular education must be taken care of to such an extent as may be serviceable in this manner of industry and in the manner of life which this industrial system necessarily imposes; which signifies, of course, that only the thoroughly trained and thoroughly educated nations have a chance of holding their place as formidable Powers in this latterday phase of civilization. What is needed is the training and education that go to make proficiency in the modern fashion of technology and in those material sciences that conduce to technological proficiency of this modern order. It is a matter of course that in these premises any appreciable illiteracy is an intolerable handicap. So is also any training which discourages habitual self-reliance and initiative, or which acts as a check on skepticism; for the skeptical frame of mind is a necessary part of the intellectual equipment that makes for advance, invention and understanding in the field of technological proficiency.

But these requirements, imperatively necessary as a condition of warlike success, are at cross purposes with that unquestioning respect of persons and that spirit of abnegation that alone can hold a people to the political institutions of the old order and make them a willing instrument in the hands of the dynastic statesmen. The dynastic State is apparently caught in a dilemma. The necessary preparation for warlike enterprise on the modern plan can apparently be counted on, in the long run, to disintegrate the foundations of the dynastic State. But it is only in the long run that this effect can be counted on; and it is perhaps not securely to be counted on even in a moderately long run of things as they have run hitherto, if due precautions are taken by the interested statesmen,—as would seem to be indicated by the successful conservation of archaic traits in the German peoples during the past half century under the archaising rule of the Hohenzollern. It is matter of habituation, which takes time, and which can at the same time be neutralized in some degree by indoctrination.

Still, when all is told, it will probably have to be conceded that, e.g., such a nation as Russia will fall under this rule of inherent disability imposed by the necessary use of the modern industrial arts. Without a fairly full and free command of these modern industrial methods on the part of the Russian people, together with the virtual disappearance of illiteracy, and with the facile and far-reaching system of communication which it all involves, the Russian Imperial establishment would not be a formidable power or a serious menace to the pacific nations; and it is not easy to imagine how the Imperial establishment could retain its hold and its character under the conditions indicated.

The case of Japan, taken by itself, rests on somewhat similar lines as these others. In time, and in this case the time-allowance should presumably not be anything very large, the Japanese people are likely to get an adequate command of the modern technology; which would, here as elsewhere, involve the virtual disappearance of the present high illiteracy, and the loss, in some passable measure, of the current superstitiously crass nationalism of that people. There are indications that something of that kind, and of quite disquieting dimensions, is already under way; though with no indication that any consequent disintegrating habits of thought have yet invaded the sacred close of Japanese patriotic devotion.

Again, it is a question of time and habituation. With time and habituation the emperor may insensibly cease to be of divine pedigree, and the syndicate of statesmen who are doing business under his signature may consequently find their measure of Imperial expansion questioned by the people who pay the bills. But so long as the Imperial syndicate enjoy their present immunity from outside obstruction, and can accordingly carry on an uninterrupted campaign of cumulative predation in Korea, China and Manchuria, the patriotic infatuation is less likely to fall off, and by so much the decay of Japanese loyalty will be retarded. Yet, even if allowed anything that may seem at all probable in the way of a free hand for aggression against their hapless neighbors, the skepticism and insubordination to personal rule that seems inseparable in the long run from addiction to the modern industrial arts should be expected presently to overtake the Japanese spirit of loyal servitude. And the opportunity of Imperial Japan lies in the interval. So also does the menace of Imperial Japan as a presumptive disturber of the peace at large.

At the cost of some unavoidable tedium, the argument as regards these and similar instances may be summarized. It appears, in the (possibly doubtful) light of the history of democratic institutions and of modern technology hitherto, as also from the logical character of this technology and its underlying material sciences, that consistent addiction to the peculiar habits of thought involved in its carrying on will presently induce a decay of those preconceptions in which dynastic government and national ambitions have their ground. Continued addiction to this modern scheme of industrial life should in time eventuate in a decay of militant nationalism, with a consequent lapse of warlike enterprise. At the same time, popular proficiency in the modern industrial arts, with all that that implies in the way of intelligence and information, is indispensable as a means to any successful warlike enterprise on the modern plan. The menace of warlike aggression from such dynastic States, e.g., as Imperial Germany and Imperial Japan is due to their having acquired a competent use of this modern technology, while they have not yet had time to lose that spirit of dynastic loyalty which they have carried over from an archaic order of things, out of which they have emerged at a very appreciably later period (last half of the nineteenth century) than those democratic peoples whose peace they now menace. As has been said, they have taken over this modern state of the industrial arts without having yet come in for the defects of its qualities. This modern technology, with its underlying material sciences, is a novel factor in the history of human culture, in that addiction to its use conduces to the decay of militant patriotism, at the same time that its employment so greatly enhances the warlike efficiency of even a pacific people, at need, that they can not be seriously molested by any other peoples, however valorous and numerous, who have not a competent use of this technology. A peace at large among the civilized nations, by loss of the militant temper through addiction to this manner of arts of peace, therefore, carries no risk of interruption by an inroad of warlike barbarians,—always provided that those existing archaic people who might pass muster as barbarians are brought into line with the pacific nations on a footing of peace and equality. The disparity in point of outlook as between the resulting peace at large by neglect of bootless animosities, on the one hand, and those historic instances of a peaceable civilization that have been overwhelmed by warlike barbarian invasions, on the other hand, should be evident.

It is always possible, indeed it would scarcely be surprising to find, that the projected league of neutrals or of nations bent on peace can not be brought to realization at this juncture; perhaps not for a long time yet. But it should at the same time seem reasonable to expect that the drift toward a peaceable settlement of a national discrepancies such as has been visible in history for some appreciable time past will, in the absence of unforeseen hindrances, work out to some such effect in the course of further experience under modern conditions. And whether the projected peace compact at its inception takes one form or another, provided it succeeds in its main purpose, the long-term drift of things under its rule should logically set toward some ulterior settlement of the general character of what has here been spoken of as a peace by neglect or by neutralization of discrepancies.

It should do so, in the absence of unforeseen contingencies; more particularly if there were no effectual factor of dissension included in the fabric of institutions within the nation. But there should also, e.g., be no difficulty in assenting to the forecast that when and if national peace and security are achieved and settled beyond recall, the discrepancy in fact between those who own the country's wealth and those who do not is presently due to come to an issue. Any attempt to forecast the form which this issue is to take, or the manner, incidents, adjuncts and sequelae of this determination, would be a bolder and more ambiguous, undertaking. Hitherto attempts to bring this question to an issue have run aground on the real or fancied jeopardy to paramount national interests. How, if at all, this issue might affect national interests and international relations, would obviously depend in the first instance on the state of the given national establishment and the character of the international engagements entered into in the formation of this projected pacific league. It is always conceivable that the transactions involving so ubiquitous an issue might come to take on an international character and that they might touch the actual or fanciful interests of these diverse nations with such divergent effect as to bring on a rupture of the common understanding between them and of the peace-compact in which the common understanding is embodied.

In the beginning, that is to say in the beginnings, out of which this modern era of the Western civilization has arisen, with its scheme of law and custom, there grew into the scheme of law and custom, by settled usage, a right of ownership and of contract in disposal of ownership,—which may or may not have been a salutary institutional arrangement on the whole, under the circumstances of the early days. With the later growth of handicraft and the petty trade in Western Europe this right of ownership and contract came to be insisted on, standardized under legal specification, and secured against molestation by the governmental interest; more particularly and scrupulously among those peoples that have taken the lead in working out that system of free or popular institutions that marks the modern civilized nations. So it has come to be embodied in the common law of the modern world as an inviolable natural right. It has all the prescriptive force of legally authenticated immemorial custom.

Under the system of handicraft and petty trade this right of petty and free contract served the interest of the common man, at least in much of its incidence, and acted in its degree to shelter industrious and economical persons from hardship and indignity at the hands of their betters. There seems reason to believe, as is commonly believed, that so long as that relatively direct and simple scheme of industry and trade lasted, the right of ownership and contract was a salutary custom, in its bearing on the fortunes of the common man. It appears also, on the whole, to have been favorable to the fuller development of the handicraft technology, as well as to its eventual outgrowth into the new line of technological expedients and contrivances that presently gave rise to the machine industry and the large-scale business enterprise.

The standard theories of economic science have assumed the rights of property and contract as axiomatic premises and ultimate terms of analysis; and their theories are commonly drawn in such a form as would fit the circumstances of the handicraft industry and the petty trade, and such as can be extended to any other economic situation by shrewd interpretation. These theories, as they run from Adam Smith down through the nineteenth century and later, appear tenable, on the whole, when taken to apply to the economic situation of that earlier time, in virtually all that they have to say on questions of wages, capital, savings, and the economy and efficiency of management and production by the methods of private enterprise resting on these rights of ownership and contract and governed by the pursuit of private gain. It is when these standard theories are sought to be applied to the later situation, which has outgrown the conditions of handicraft, that they appear nugatory or meretricious. The "competitive system" which these standard theories assume as a necessary condition of their own validity, and about which they are designed to form a defensive hedge, would, under those earlier conditions of small-scale enterprise and personal contact, appear to have been both a passably valid assumption as a premise and passably expedient scheme of economic relations and traffic. At that period of its life-history it can not be said consistently to have worked hardship to the common man; rather the reverse. And the common man in that time appears to have had no misgivings about the excellence of the scheme or of that article of Natural Rights that underlies it.

This complexion of things, as touches the effectual bearing of the institution of property and the ancient customary rights of ownership, has changed substantially since the time of Adam Smith. The "competitive system," which he looked to as the economic working-out of the "simple and obvious system of natural liberty," that always engaged his best affections, has in great measure ceased to operate as a routine of natural liberty, in fact; particularly in so far as touches the fortunes of the common man, the impecunious mass of the people. *De jure*, of course, the competitive system and its inviolable rights of ownership are a citadel of Natural Liberty; but *de facto* the common man is now, and has for some time been, feeling the pinch of it. It is law, and doubtless it is good law, grounded in immemorial usage and authenticated with statute and precedent. But circumstances have so changed that this good old plan has in a degree become archaic, perhaps unprofitable, or even mischievous, on the whole, and especially as touches the conditions of life for the common man. At least, so the common man in these modern democratic and commercial countries is beginning to apprehend the matter.

Some slight and summary characterization of these changing circumstances that have affected the incidence of the rights of property during modern times may, therefore, not be out of place; with a view to seeing how far and why these rights may be due to come under advisement and possible revision, in case a state of settled peace should leave men's attention free to turn to these internal, as contrasted with national interests.

Under that order of handicraft and petty trade that led to the standardization of these rights of ownership in the accentuated form which belongs to them in modern law and custom, the common man had a practicable chance of free initiative and self-direction in his choice and pursuit of an occupation and a livelihood, in so far as rights of ownership bore on his case. At that period the workman was the main factor in industry and, in the main and characteristically, the question of his employment was a question of what he would do. The material equipment of industry—the "plant," as it has come to be called—was subject of ownership, then as now; but it was then a secondary factor and, notoriously, subsidiary to the immaterial equipment of skill, dexterity and judgment embodied in the person of the craftsman. The body of information, or general knowledge, requisite to a workmanlike proficiency as handicraftsman was sufficiently slight and simple to fall within the ordinary reach of the working class, without special schooling; and the material equipment necessary to the work, in the way of tools and appliances, was also slight enough, ordinarily, to bring it within the reach of the common man. The stress fell on the acquirement of that special personal skill, dexterity and judgment that would constitute the workman a master of his craft. Given a reasonable measure of pertinacity, the common man would be able to compass the material equipment needful to the pursuit of his craft, and so could make his way to a livelihood; and the inviolable right of ownership would then serve to secure him the product of his own industry, in provision for his own old-age and for a fair start in behalf of his children. At least in the popular conception, and presumably in some degree also in fact, the right of property served as a guarantee of personal liberty and a basis of equality. And so its apologists still look on the institution.

In a very appreciable degree this complexion of things and of popular conceptions has changed since then; although, as would be expected, the change in popular conceptions has not kept pace with the changing circumstances. In all the characteristic and controlling lines of industry the modern machine technology calls for a very considerable material equipment; so large an equipment, indeed, that this plant, as it is called, always represents a formidable amount of invested wealth; and also so large that it will, typically, employ a considerable number of workmen per unit of plant. On the transition to the machine technology the plant became the unit of operation, instead of the workman, as had previously been the case; and with the further development of this modern technology, during the past hundred and fifty years or so, the unit of operation and control has increasingly come to be not the individual or isolated plant but rather an articulated group of such plants working together as a balanced system and keeping pace in common, under a collective business management; and coincidently the individual workman has been falling into the position of an auxiliary factor, nearly into that of an article of supply, to be charged up as an item of operating expenses. Under this later and current system, discretion and initiative vest not in the workman but in the owners of the plant, if anywhere. So that at this point the right of ownership has ceased to be, in fact, a guarantee of personal liberty to the common man, and has come to be, or is coming to be, a guarantee of dependence. All of which engenders a feeling of unrest and insecurity, such as to instill a doubt in the mind of the common man as to the continued expediency of this arrangement and of the prescriptive rights of property on which the arrangement rests.

There is also an insidious suggestion, carrying a sinister note of discredit, that comes in from ethnological science at this point; which is adapted still further to derange the common man's faith in this received institution of ownership and its control of the material equipment of industry. To students interested in human culture it is a matter of course that this material equipment is a means of utilizing the state of the industrial arts; that it is useful in industry and profitable to its owners only because and in so far as it is a creation of the current technological knowledge and enables its owner to appropriate the usufruct of the current industrial arts. It is likewise a matter of course that this technological knowledge, that so enables the material equipment to serve the purposes of production and of private gain, is a free gift of the community at large to the owners of industrial plant; and under latterday condition, to them exclusively. The state of the industrial arts is a joint heritage of the community at large, but where, as in the modern countries, the work to be done by this technology requires a large material equipment, the usufruct of this joint heritage passes, in effect, into the hands of the owners of this large material equipment.

These owners have, ordinarily, contributed nothing to the technology, the state of the industrial arts, from which their control of the material equipment of industry enables them to derive a gain. Indeed, no class or condition of men in the modern community—with the possible exception of politicians and the clergy—can conceivably contribute less to the community's store of technological knowledge than the large owners of invested wealth. By one of those singular inversions due to productions being managed for private gain, it happens that these investors are not only not given to the increase and diffusion of technological knowledge, but they have a well-advised interest in retarding or defeating improvements in the industrial arts in detail. Improvements, innovations that heighten productive efficiency in the general line of production in which a given investment is placed, are commonly to be counted on to bring "obsolescence by supersession" to the plant already engaged in that line; and therefore to bring a decline in its income-yielding capacity, and so in its capital or investment value.

Invested capital yields income because it enjoys the usufruct of the community's technological knowledge; it has an effectual monopoly of this usufruct because this machine technology requires large material appliances with which to do its work; the interest of the owners of established industrial plant will not tolerate innovations designed to supersede these appliances. The bearing of ownership on industry and on the fortunes of the common man is accordingly, in the main, the bearing which it has by virtue of its monopoly control of the industrial arts, and its consequent control of the condition of employment and of the supply of vendable products. It takes effect chiefly by inhibition and privation; stoppage of production in case it brings no suitable profit to the investor, refusal of employment and of a livelihood to the workmen in case their product does not command a profitable price in the market.

The expediency of so having the nation's industry managed on a footing of private ownership in the pursuit of private gain, by persons who can show no equitable personal claim to even the most modest livelihood, and whose habitual method of controlling industry is sabotage—refusal to let production go on except it affords them an unearned income—the expediency of all this is coming to be doubted by those who have to pay the cost of it. And it does not go far to lessen their doubts to find that the cost which they pay is commonly turned to no more urgent or useful purpose than a conspicuously wasteful consumption of superfluities by the captains of sabotage and their domestic establishments.

This may not seem a veracious and adequate account of these matters; it may, in effect, fall short of the formulation: The truth, the whole truth, and nothing but the truth; nor does the question here turn on its adequacy as statement of fact. Without prejudice to the question of its veracity and adequacy, it is believed to be such an account of these matters as will increasingly come easy and seem convincing to the common man who, in an ever increasing degree, finds himself pinched with privation and insecurity by a run of acts which will consistently bear this construction, and who perforce sees these facts from the prejudiced standpoint of a loser. To such a one, there is reason to believe, the view so outlined will seem all the more convincing the more attentively the pertinent facts and their bearing on his fortunes are considered. How far the contrary prejudice of those whose interest or training inclines them the other way may lead them to a different construction of these pertinent facts does not concern the present argument, which has to do with this run of facts only as they bear on the prospective frame of mind of that unblest mass of the population who will have opportunity to present their proposals when peace at large shall have put national interest out of their preferential place in men's regard.

At the risk of what may seem an excessively wide digression, there is something further to be said of the capitalistic sabotage spoken of above. The word has by usage come to have an altogether ungraceful air of disapproval. Yet it signifies nothing more vicious than a deliberate obstruction or retardation of industry, usually by legitimate means, for the sake of some personal or partisan advantage. This morally colorless meaning is all that is intended in its use here. It is extremely common in all industry that is designed to supply merchantable goods for the market. It is, in fact, the most ordinary and ubiquitous of all expedients in business enterprise that has to do with supplying the market, being always present in the business man's necessary calculations; being not only a usual and convenient recourse but quite indispensable as an habitual measure of business sagacity. So that no personal blame can attach to its employment by any given businessman or business concern. It is only when measures of this nature are resorted to by employees, to gain some end of their own, that such conduct becomes (technically) reprehensible.

Any businesslike management of industry is carried on for gain, which is to be got only on condition of meeting the terms of the market. The price system under which industrial business is carried on will not tolerate production in excess of the market demand, or without due regard to the expense of production as determined by the market on the side of the supplies required. Hence any business concern must adjust its operation, by due acceleration, retardation or stoppage, to the market condition, with a view to what the traffic will bear; that is to say, with a view to what will yield the largest obtainable net gain. So long as the price system rules, that is to say so long as industry is managed on investment for a profit, there is no escaping this necessity of adjusting the processes of industry to the requirements of a remunerative price; and this adjustment can be taken care of only by well-advised acceleration or curtailment of the processes of industry; which answers to the definition of sabotage. Wise business management, and more particularly what is spoken of as safe and sane business management, therefore, reduces itself in the main to a sagacious use of sabotage; that is to say sagacious imitation of productive processes to something less than the productive capacity of the means in hand.

To anyone who is inclined to see these matters of usage in the light of their history and to appraise them as phenomena of habituation, adaption and supersession in the sequence of cultural proliferation, there should be no difficulty in appreciating that this institution of ownership that makes the core of the modern institutional structure is a precipitate of custom, like any other item of use and wont; and that, like any other article of institutional furniture, it is subject to the contingencies of supersession and obsolescence. If prevalent habits of thought, enforced by the prevalent exigencies of life and livelihood, come to change in such a way as to make life under the rule imposed by this institution seem irksome, or intolerable, to the mass of the population; and if at the same time things turn in such a way as to leave no other and more urgent interest or exigency to take precedence of this one and hinder its being pushed to an issue; then it should reasonably follow that contention is due to arise between the unblest mass on whose life it is a burden and the classes who live by it. But it is, of course, impossible to state beforehand what will be the precise line of cleavage or what form the division between the two parties in interest will take. Yet it is contained in the premises that, barring unforeseen contingencies of a formidable magnitude, such a cleavage is due to follow as a logical sequel of an enduring peace at large. And it is also well within the possibilities of the case that this issue may work into an interruption or disruption of the peace between the nations.

In this connection it may be called to mind that the existing governmental establishments in these pacific nations are, in all cases, in the hands of the beneficiary, or kept classes,—beneficiaries in the sense in which a distinction to that effect comes into the premises of the case at this point. The responsible officials and their chief administrative officers,—so much as may at all reasonably be called the "Government" or the "Administration,"—are quite invariably and characteristically drawn from these beneficiary classes; nobles, gentlemen, or business men, which all comes to the same thing for the purpose in hand; the point of it all being that the common man does not come within these precincts and does not share in these counsels that assume to guide the destiny of the nations.

Of course, sporadically and ephemerally, a man out of the impecunious and undistinguished mass may now and again find his way within the gates; and more frequently will a professed "Man of the People" sit in council. But that the rule holds unbroken and inviolable is sufficiently evident in the fact that no community will let the emoluments of office for any of its responsible officials, even for those of a very scant responsibility, fall to the level of the habitual livelihood of the undistinguished populace, or indeed to fall below what is esteemed to be a seemly income for a gentleman. Should such an impecunious one be thrown up into place of discretion in the government, he will forthwith cease to be a common man and will be inducted into the rank of gentleman,—so far as that feat can be achieved by taking thought or by assigning him an income adequate to a reputably expensive manner of life. So obvious is the antagonism between a vulgar station in life and a position of official trust, that many a "selfmade man" has advisedly taken recourse to governmental position, often at some appreciable cost, from no apparent motive other than its known efficacy as a Levitical corrective for a humble origin. And in point of fact, neither here nor there have the underbred majority hitherto learned to trust one of their own kind with governmental discretion; which has never yet, in the popular conviction, ceased to be a perquisite of the gently-bred and the well-to-do.

Let it be presumed that this state of things will continue without substantial alteration, so far as regards the complexion of the governmental establishments of these pacific nations, and with such allowance for overstatement in the above characterization as may seem called for. These governmental establishments are, by official position and by the character of their personnel, committed more or less consistently to the maintenance of the existing law and order. And should no substantial change overtake them as an effect of the war experience, the pacific league under discussion would be entered into by and between governments of this complexion. Should difficulties then arise between those who won and those who do not, in any one of these countries, it would become a nice question whether the compact to maintain the peace and national integrity of the several nations comprised in the league should be held to cover the case of internal dissensions and possible disorder partaking of the character of revolt against the established authorities or against the established provisions of law. A strike of the scope and character of the one recently threatened, and narrowly averted, on the American railroads, e.g., might easily give rise to disturbances sufficiently formidable to raise a question of the peace league's jurisdiction; particularly if such a disturbance should arise in a less orderly and less isolated country than the American republic; so as unavoidably to carry the effects of the disturbance across the national frontiers along the lines of industrial and commercial intercourse and correlation. It is always conceivable that a national government standing on a somewhat conservative maintenance of the received law and order might feel itself bound by its conception of the peace to make common cause with the keepers of established rights in neighboring states, particularly if the similar interest of their own nation were thought to be placed in jeopardy by the course of events.

Antecedently it seems highly probable that the received rights of ownership and disposal of property, particularly of investment, will come up for advisement and revision so soon as a settled state of peace is achieved. And there should seem to be little doubt but this revision would go toward, or at least aim at, the curtailment or abrogation of these rights; very much after the fashion in which the analogous vested rights of feudalism and the dynastic monarchy have been revised and in great part curtailed or abrogated in the advanced democratic countries. Not much can confidently be said as to the details of such a prospective revision of legal rights, but the analogy of that procedure by which these other vested rights have been reduced to a manageable disability, suggests that the method in the present case also would be by way of curtailment, abrogation and elimination. Here again, as in analogous movements of disuse and disestablishment, there would doubtless be much conservative apprehension as to the procuring of a competent substitute for the supplanted methods of doing what is no longer desirable to be done; but here as elsewhere, in a like conjuncture, the practicable way out would presumably be found to lie along the line of simple disuse and disallowance of class prerogative. Taken at its face value, without unavoidable prejudice out of the past, this question of a substitute to replace the current exploitation of the industrial arts for private gain by capitalistic sabotage is not altogether above a suspicion of drollery.

Yet it is not to be overlooked that private enterprise on the basis of private ownership is the familiar and accepted method of conducting industrial affairs, and that it has the sanction of immemorial usage, in the eyes of the common man, and that it is reinforced with the urgency of life and death in the apprehension of the kept classes. It should accordingly be a possible outcome of such a peace as would put away international dissension, that the division of classes would come on in a new form, between those who stand on their ancient rights of exploitation and mastery, and those who are unwilling longer to submit. And it is quite within the possibilities of the case that the division of opinion on these matters might presently shift back to the old familiar ground of international hostilities; undertaken partly to put down civil disturbances in given countries, partly by the more archaic, or conservative, peoples to safeguard the institutions of the received law and order against inroads from the side of the iconoclastic ones.

In the apprehension of those who are speaking for peace between the nations and planning for its realization, the outlook is that of a return to, or a continuance of, the state of things before the great war came on, with peace and national security added, or with the danger of war eliminated. Nothing appreciable in the way of consequent innovation, certainly nothing of a serious character, is contemplated as being among the necessary consequences of such a move into peace and security. National integrity and autonomy are to be preserved on the received lines, and international division and discrimination is to be managed as before, and with the accustomed incidents of punctilio and pecuniary equilibration. Internationally speaking, there is to dawn an era of diplomacy without after-thought, whatever that might conceivably mean.

There is much in the present situation that speaks for such an arrangement, particularly as an initial phase of the perpetual peace that is aimed at, whatever excursive variations might befall presently, in the course of years. The war experience in the belligerent countries and the alarm that has disturbed the neutral nations have visibly raised the pitch of patriotic solidarity in all these countries; and patriotism greatly favors the conservation of established use and wont; more particularly is it favorable to the established powers and policies of the national government. The patriotic spirit is not a spirit of innovation. The chances of survival, and indeed of stabilization, for the accepted use and wont and for the traditional distinctions of class and prescriptive rights, should therefore seem favorable, at any rate in the first instance.

Presuming, therefore, as the spokesmen of such a peace-compact are singularly ready to presume, that the era of peace and good-will which they have in view is to be of a piece with the most tranquil decades of the recent past, only more of the same kind, it becomes a question of immediate interest to the common man, as well as to all students of human culture, how the common man is to fare under this regime of law and order,—the mass of the population whose place it is to do what is to be done, and thereby to carry forward the civilization of these pacific nations. It may not be out of place to recall, by way of parenthesis, that it is here taken for granted as a matter of course that all governmental establishments are necessarily conservative in all their dealings with this heritage of culture, except so far as they may be reactionary. Their office is the stabilization of archaic institutions, the measure of archaism varying from one to another.

With due stabilization and with a sagacious administration of the established scheme of law and order, the common man should find himself working under conditions and to results of the familiar kind; but with the difference that, while legal usage and legal precedent remain unchanged, the state of the industrial arts can confidently be expected to continue its advance in the same general direction as before, while the population increases after the familiar fashion, and the investing business community pursues its accustomed quest of competitive gain and competitive spending in the familiar spirit and with cumulatively augmented means. Stabilization of the received law and order will not touch this matter; and for the present it is assumed that these matters will not derange the received law and order. The assumption may seem a violent one to the student of human culture, but it is a simple matter of course to the statesmen.

To this piping time of peace the nearest analogues in history would seem to be the Roman peace, say, of the days of Antonines, and passably the British peace of the Victorian era. Changes in the scheme of law and order supervened in both of these instances, but the changes were, after all, neither unconscionably large nor were they of a subversive nature. The scheme of law and order, indeed, appears in neither instance to have changed so far as the altered circumstances would seem to have called for. To the common man the Roman peace appears to have been a peace by submission, not widely different from what the case of China has latterly brought to the appreciation of students. The Victorian peace, which can be appreciated more in detail, was of a more genial character, as regards the fortunes of the common man. It started from a reasonably low level of hardship and *de facto* iniquity, and was occupied with many prudent endeavors to improve the lot of the unblest majority; but it is to be admitted that these prudent endeavors never caught up with the march of circumstances. Not that these prudent measures of amelioration were nugatory, but it is clear that they were not an altogether effectual corrective of the changes going on; they were, in effect, systematically so far in arrears as always to leave an uncovered margin of discontent with current conditions. It is a fact of history that very appreciable sections of the populace were approaching an attitude of revolt against what they considered to be intolerable conditions when that era closed. Much of what kept them within bounds, that is to say within legal bounds, was their continued loyalty to the nation; which was greatly, and for the purpose needfully, reinforced by a lively fear of warlike aggression from without. Now, under the projected *pax orbis terrarum* all fear of invasion, it is hopefully believed, will be removed; and with disappearance of this fear should also disappear the drag of national loyalty on the counsels of the underbred.

If this British peace of the nineteenth century is to be taken as significant indication of what may be looked for under a regime of peace at large, with due allowance for what is obviously necessary to be allowed for, then what is held in promise would appear to be an era of unexampled commercial prosperity, of investment and business enterprise on a scale hitherto not experienced. These developments will bring their necessary consequences affecting the life of the community, and some of the consequences it should be possible to foresee. The circumstances conditioning this prospective era of peace and prosperity will necessarily differ from the corresponding circumstances that conditioned the Victorian peace, and many of these points of difference it is also possible to forecast in outline with a fair degree of confidence. It is in the main these economic factors going to condition the civilization of the promised future that will have to be depended on to give the cue to any student interested in the prospective unfolding of events.

The scheme of law and order governing all modern nations, both in the conduct of their domestic affairs and in their national policies, is in its controlling elements the scheme worked out through British (and French) experience in the eighteenth century and earlier, as revised and further accommodated in the nineteenth century. Other people, particularly the Dutch, have of course had their part in the derivation and development of this modern scheme of institutional principles, but it has after all been a minor part; so that the scheme at large would not differ very materially, if indeed it should differ sensibly, from what it is, even if the contribution of these others had not been had. The backward nations, as e.g., Germany, Russia, Spain, etc., have of course contributed substantially nothing but retardation and maladjustment to this modern scheme of civil life; whatever may be due to students resident in those countries, in the way of scholarly formulation. This nineteenth century scheme it is proposed to carry over into the new era; and the responsible spokesmen of the projected new order appear to contemplate no provision touching this scheme of law and order, beyond the keeping of it intact in all substantial respects.

When and in so far as the projected peace at large takes effect, international interests will necessarily fall somewhat into the background, as being no longer a matter of precarious equilibration, with heavy penalties in the balance; and diplomacy will consequently become even more of a make-believe than today—something after the fashion of a game of bluff played with irredeemable "chips." Commercial, that is to say business, enterprise will consequently come in for a more undivided attention and be carried on under conditions of greater security and of more comprehensive trade relations. The population of the pacified world may be expected to go on increasing somewhat as in the recent past; in which connection it is to be remarked that not more than one-half, presumably something less than one-half, of the available agricultural resources have been turned to account for the civilized world hitherto. The state of the industrial arts, including means of transport and communication, may be expected to develop farther in the same general direction as before, assuming always that peace conditions continue to hold. Popular intelligence, as it is called,—more properly popular education,—may be expected to suffer a further advance; necessarily so, since it is a necessary condition of any effectual advance in the industrial arts,—every appreciable technological advance presumes, as a requisite to its working-out in industry, an augmented state of information and of logical facility in the workmen under whose hands it is to take effect.

Of the prescriptive rights carried over into the new era, under the received law and order, the rights of ownership alone may be expected to have any material significance for the routine of workday life; the other personal rights that once seemed urgent will for everyday purposes have passed into a state of half-forgotten matter-of-course. As now, but in an accentuated degree, the rights of ownership will, in effect, coincide and coalesce with the rights of investment and business management. The market—that is to say the rule of the price-system in all matters of production and livelihood—may be expected to gain in volume and inclusiveness; so that virtually all matters of industry and livelihood will turn on questions of market price, even beyond the degree in which that proposition holds today. The progressive extension and consolidation of investments, corporate solidity, and business management may be expected to go forward on the accustomed lines, as illustrated by the course of things during the past few decades. Market conditions should accordingly, in a progressively increased degree, fall under the legitimate discretionary control of businessmen, or syndicates of businessmen, who have the disposal of large blocks of invested wealth,—"big business," as it is called, should reasonably be expected to grow bigger and to exercise an increasingly more unhampered control of market conditions, including the money market and the labor market.

With such improvements in the industrial arts as may fairly be expected to come forward, and with the possible enhancement of industrial efficiency which should follow from a larger scale of organization, a wider reach of transport and communication, and an increased population,—with these increasing advantages on the side of productive industry, the per-capita product as well as the total product should be increased in a notable degree, and the conditions of life should possibly become notably easier and more attractive, or at least more conducive to efficiency and personal comfort, for all concerned. Such would be the first and unguarded inference to be drawn from the premises of the case as they offer themselves in the large; and something of that kind is apparently what floats before the prophetic vision of the advocates of a league of nations for the maintenance of peace at large. These premises, and the inferences so drawn from them, may be further fortified and amplified in the same sense on considering that certain very material economies also become practicable, and should take effect "in the absence of disturbing causes," on the establishment of such a peace at large. It will of course occur to all thoughtful persons that armaments must be reduced, perhaps to a minimum, and that the cost of these things, in point of expenditures as well as of man-power spent in the service, would consequently fall off in a corresponding measure. So also, as slight further reflection will show, would the cost of the civil service presumably fall off very appreciably; more particularly the cost of this service per unit of service rendered. Some such climax of felicities might be looked for by hopeful persons, in the absence of disturbing causes.

Under the new dispensation the standard of living, that is to say the standard of expenditure, would reasonably be expected to advance in a very appreciable degree, at least among the wealthy and well-to-do; and by pressure of imitative necessity a like effect would doubtless also be had among the undistinguished mass. It is not a question of the standard of living considered as a matter of the subsistence minimum, or even a standard of habitually prevalent creature comfort, particularly not among the wealthy and well-to-do. These latter classes have long since left all question of material comfort behind in their accepted standards of living and in the continued advance of these standards. For these classes who are often spoken of euphemistically as being "in easy circumstances," it is altogether a question of a standard of reputable expenditure, to be observed on pain of lost self-respect and of lost reputation at large. As has been remarked in an earlier passage, wants of this kind are indefinitely extensible. So that some doubt may well be entertained as to whether the higher productive efficiency spoken of will necessarily make the way of life easier, in view of this need of a higher standard of expenditure, even when due account is taken of the many economies which the new dispensation is expected to make practicable.

One of the effects to be looked for would apparently be an increased pressure on the part of aspiring men to get into some line of business enterprise; since it is only in business, as contrasted with the industrial occupations, that anyone can hope to find the relatively large income required for such an expensive manner of life as will bring any degree of content to aspirants for pecuniary good repute. So it should follow that the number of businessmen and business concerns would increase up to the limit of what the traffic could support, and that the competition between these rival, and in a sense overnumerous, concerns would push the costs of competition to the like limit. In this respect the situation would be of much the same character as what it now is, with the difference that the limit of competitive expenditures would be rather higher than at present, to answer to the greater available margin of product that could be devoted to this use; and that the competing concerns would be somewhat more numerous, or at least that the aggregate expenditure on competitive enterprise would be somewhat larger; as, e.g., cost of advertising, salesmanship, strategic litigation, procuration of legislative and municipal grants and connivance, and the like.

It is always conceivable, though it may scarcely seem probable, that these incidents of increased pressure of competition in business traffic might eventually take up all the slack, and leave no net margin of product over what is available under the less favorable conditions of industry that prevail today; more particularly when this increased competition for business gains is backed by an increased pressure of competitive spending for purposes of a reputable appearance. All this applies in retail trade and in such lines of industry and public service as partakes of the nature of retail trade, in the respect that salesmanship and the costs of salesmanship enter into their case in an appreciable measure; this is an extensive field, it is true, and incontinently growing more extensive with the later changes in the customary methods of marketing products; but it is by no means anything like the whole domain of industrial business, and by no means a field in which business is carried on without interference of a higher control from outside its own immediate limits.

All this generously large and highly expensive and profitable field of trade and of trade-like industry, in which the businessmen in charge deal somewhat directly with a large body of customers, is always subject to limitations imposed by the condition of the market; and the condition of the market is in part not under the control of these businessmen, but is also in part controlled by large concerns in the background; which in their turn are after all also not precisely free agents; in fact not much more so than their cousins in the retail trade, being confined in all their motions by the constraint of the price-system that dominates the whole and gathers them all in its impersonal and inexorable net.

There is a colloquial saying among businessmen, that they are not doing business for their health; which being interpreted means that they are doing business for a price. It is out of a discrepancy in price, between purchase and sale, or between transactions which come to the same result as purchase and sale, that the gains of business are drawn; and is in terms of price that these gains are rated, amassed and funded. It is necessary, for a business concern to achieve a favorable balance in terms of price; and the larger the balance in terms of price the more successful the enterprise. Such a balance can not achieved except by due regard to the conditions of the market, to the effect that dealings must not go on beyond what will yield a favorable balance in terms of price between income and outgo. As has already been remarked above, the prescriptive and indispensable recourse in all this conduct of business is sabotage, limitation of supply to bring a remunerative price result.

The new dispensation offers two new factors bearing on this businesslike need of a sagacious sabotage, or rather it brings a change of coefficients in two factors already familiar in business management: a greater need, for gainful business, of resorting to such limitation of traffic; and a greater facility of ways and means for enforcing the needed restriction. So, it is confidently to be expected that in the prospective piping time of peace the advance in the industrial arts will continue at an accelerated rate; which may confidently be expected to affect the practicable increased production of merchantable goods; from which it follows that it will act to depress the prices of these goods; from which it follows that if a profitable business is to be done in the conduct of productive industry a greater degree of continence than before will have to exercised in order not to let prices fall to an unprofitable figure; that is to say, the permissible output must be held short of the productive capacity of such industry by a wider margin than before. On the other hand, it is well known out of the experience of the past few decades that a larger coalition of invested capital, controlling a larger proportion of the output, can more effectually limit the supply to a salutary maximum, such as will afford reasonable profits. And with the new dispensation affording a freer scope for business enterprise on conditions of greater security, larger coalitions than before are due to come into bearing. So that the means will be at hand competently to meet this more urgent need of a stricter limitation of the output, in spite of any increased productive capacity conferred on the industrial community by any conceivable advance in the industrial arts. The outcome to be looked for should apparently be such an effectual recourse to capitalistic sabotage as will neutralize any added advantage that might otherwise accrue to the community from its continued improvements in technology.

In spite of this singularly untoward conjuncture of circumstances to be looked for there need be no serious apprehension that capitalistic sabotage, with a view to maintaining prices and the rate of profits, will go all the way to the result indicated, at least not on grounds so indicated alone. There is in the modern development of technology, and confidently to be counted on, a continued flow of new contrivances and expedients designed to supersede the old; and these are in fact successful, in greater or less measure, in finding their way into profitable use, on such terms as to displace older appliances, underbid them in the market, and render them obsolete or subject to recapitalization on a lowered earning-capacity. So far as this unremitting flow of innovations has its effect, that is to say so far as it can not be hindered from having an effect, it acts to lower the effectual cost of products to the consumer. This effect is but a partial and somewhat uncertain one, but is always to be counted in as a persistent factor, of uncertain magnitude, that will affect the results in the long run.

As has just been spoken of above, large coalitions of invested wealth are more competent to maintain, or if need be to advance, prices than smaller coalitions acting in severalty, or even when acting in collusion. This state of the case has been well illustrated by the very successful conduct of such large business organizations during the past few decades; successful, that is, in earning large returns on the investments engaged. Under the new dispensation, as has already been remarked, coalitions should reasonably be expected to grow to a larger size and achieve a greater efficiency for the same purpose.

The large gains of the large corporate coalitions are commonly ascribed by their promoters, and by sympathetic theoreticians of the ancient line, to economies of production made practicable by a larger scale of production; an explanation which is disingenuous only so far as it needs be. What is more visibly true on looking into the working of these coalitions in detail is that they are enabled to maintain prices at a profitable, indeed at a strikingly profitable, level by such a control of the output as would be called sabotage if it were put in practice by interested workmen with a view to maintain wages. The effects of this sagacious sabotage become visible in the large earnings of these investments and the large gains which, now and again, accrue to their managers. Large fortunes commonly are of this derivation.

In cases where no recapitalization has been effected for a considerable series of years the yearly earnings of such businesslike coalitions have been known to approach fifty percent on the capitalized value. Commonly, however, when earnings rise to a striking figure, the business will be recapitalized on the basis of its earning-capacity, by issue of a stock divided, by reincorporation in a new combination with an increased capitalization, and the like. Such augmentation of capital not unusually has been spoken of by theoretical writers and publicists as an increase of the community's wealth, due to savings; an analysis of any given case is likely to show that its increased capital value represents an increasingly profitable procedure for securing a high price above cost, by stopping the available output short of the productive capacity of the industries involved. Loosely speaking, and within the limits of what the traffic will bear, the gains in such a case are proportioned to the deficiency by which the production or supply under control falls short of productive capacity. So that the capitalization in the case comes to bear a rough proportion to the material loss which this organization of sabotage is enabled to inflict on the community at large; and instead of its being a capitalization of serviceable means of production it may, now and again, come to little else than a capitalization of chartered sabotage.

Under the new dispensation of peace and security at large this manner of capitalization and business enterprise might reasonably be expected to gain something in scope and security of operation. Indeed, there are few things within the range of human interest on which an opinion may more confidently be formed beforehand. If the rights of property, in their extent and amplitude, are maintained intact as they are before the law today, the hold which business enterprise on the large scale now has on the affairs and fortunes of the community at large is bound to grow firmer and to be used more unreservedly for private advantage under the new conditions contemplated.

The logical result should be an accelerated rate of accumulation of the country's wealth in the hands of a relatively very small class of wealthy owners, with a relatively inconsiderable semi-dependent middle class of the well-to-do, and with the mass of the population even more nearly destitute than they are today. At the same time it is scarcely to be avoided that this wholly dependent and impecunious mass of the population must be given an appreciably better education than they have today. The argument will return to the difficulties that are liable to arise out of this conjuncture of facts, in the way of discontent and possible disturbance.

Meantime, looking to the promise of the pacific future in the light of the pacific past, certain further consequences, particularly consequences of the economic order, that may reasonably be expected to follow will also merit attention. The experience of the Victorian peace is almost as pointed in its suggestion on this head as if it had been an experiment made *ad hoc*; but with the reservation that the scale of economic life, after all, was small in the Victorian era, and its pace was slack, compared with what the twentieth century should have to offer under suitable conditions of peace and pecuniary security. In the light of this most instructive modern instance, there should appear to be in prospect a growth of well-bred families resting on invested wealth and so living on unearned incomes; larger incomes and consequently a more imposingly well-bred body of gentlefolk, sustained and vouched for by a more munificent expenditure on superfluities, than the modern world has witnessed hitherto. Doubtless the resulting growth of gentlemen and gentlewomen would be as perfect after their kind as these unexampled opportunities of gentle breeding might be expected to engender; so that even their British precursors on the trail of respectability would fall somewhat into insignificance by comparison, whether in respect of gentlemanly qualities or in point of cost per unit.

The moral, and even more particularly the aesthetic, value of such a line of gentlefolk, and of the culture which they may be expected to place on view,—this cultural side of the case, of course, is what one would prefer to dwell on, and on the spiritual gains that might be expected to accrue to humanity at large from the steady contemplation of this meritorious respectability so displayed at such a cost.

But the prosaic necessity of the argument turns back to the economic and civil bearing of this prospective development, this virtual bifurcation of the pacified nation into a small number of gentlemen who own the community's wealth and consume its net product in the pursuit of gentility, on the one hand, and an unblest mass of the populace who do the community's work on a meager livelihood tapering down toward the subsistence minimum, on the other hand. Evidently, this prospective posture of affairs may seem "fraught with danger to the common weal," as a public spirited citizen might phrase it. Or, as it would be expressed in less eloquent words, it appears to comprise elements that should make for a change. At the same time it should be recalled, and the statement will command assent on slight reflection, that there is no avoiding substantially such a posture of affairs under the promised regime of peace and security, provided only that the price-system stands over intact, and the current rights of property continue to be held inviolate. If the known principles of competitive gain and competitive spending should need enforcement to that effect by an illustrative instance, the familiar history of the Victorian peace is sufficient to quiet all doubts.

Of course, the resulting articulation of classes in the community will not be expected to fall into such simple lines of sheer contrast as this scheme would indicate. The class of gentlefolk, the legally constituted wasters, as they would be rated from the economic point of view, can not be expected personally to take care of so large a consumption of superfluities as this posture of affairs requires at their hands. They would, as the Victorian peace teaches, necessarily have the assistance of a trained corps of experts in unproductive consumption, the first and most immediate of whom would be those whom the genial phrasing of Adam Smith designates "menial servants." Beyond these would come the purveyors of superfluities, properly speaking, and the large, indeed redundant, class of tradespeople of high and low degree,—dependent in fact but with an illusion of semi-dependence; and father out again the legal and other professional classes of the order of stewards, whose duty it will be administer the sources of income and receive, apportion and disburse the revenues so devoted to a traceless extinguishment.

There would, in other words, be something of a "substantial middle class," dependent on the wealthy and on their expenditure of wealth, but presumably imbued with the Victorian middle-class illusion that they are of some account in their own right. Under the due legal forms and sanctions this, somewhat voluminous, middle-class population would engage in the traffic which is their perquisite, and would continue to believe, in some passable fashion, that they touch the substance of things at something nearer than the second remove. They would in great part appear to be people of "independent means," and more particularly would they continue in the hope of so appearing and of some time making good the appearance. Hence their fancied, and therefore their sentimental, interest would fall out on the side of the established law and order; and they would accordingly be an element of stability in the commonwealth, and would throw in their weight, and their voice, to safeguard that private property and that fabric of prices and credit through which the "income stream" flows to the owners of preponderant invested wealth.

Judged on the state of the situation as it runs in our time, and allowing for the heightened efficiency of large-scale investment and consolidated management under the prospective conditions of added pecuniary security, it is to be expected that the middle-class population with "independent means" should come in for a somewhat meager livelihood, provided that they work faithfully at their business of managing pecuniary traffic to the advantage of their pecuniary betters,—meager, that is to say, when allowance is made for the conventionally large expenditure on reputable appearances which is necessarily to be included in their standards of living. It lies in the nature of this system of large-scale investment and enterprise that the (pecuniarily) minor agencies engaged on a footing of ostensible independence will come in for only such a share in the aggregate gains of the community as it is expedient for the greater business interests to allow them as an incentive to go on with their work as purveyors of traffic to these greater business interests.

The current, and still more this prospective, case of the quasi-self-directing middle class may fairly be illustrated by the case of the American farmers, of the past and present. The American farmer rejoices to be called "The Independent Farmer." He once was independent, in a meager and toil-worn fashion, in the days before the price-system had brought him and all his works into the compass of the market; but that was some time ago. He now works for the market, ordinarily at something like what is called a "living wage," provided he has "independent means" enough to enable him by steady application to earn a living wage; and of course, the market being controlled by the paramount investment interests in the background, his work, in effect, inures to their benefit; except so much as it may seem necessary to allow him as incentive to go on. Also of course, these paramount investment interests are in turn controlled in all their maneuver by the impersonal exigencies of the price-system, which permits no vagaries in violation of the rule that all traffic must show a balance of profit in terms of price.

The Independent Farmer still continues to believe that in some occult sense he still is independent in what he will do and what not; or perhaps rather that he can by shrewd management retain or regain a tolerable measure of such independence, after the fashion of what is held to have been the posture of affairs in the days before the coming of corporation finance; or at least he believes that he ought to have, or to regain or reclaim, some appreciable measure of such independence; which ought then, by help of the "independent means" which he still treasures, to procure him an honest and assured livelihood in return for an honest year's work. Latterly he, that is the common run of the farmers, has been taking note of the fact that he is, as he apprehends it, at a disadvantage in the market; and he is now taking recourse to concerted action for the purpose of what might be called "rigging the market" to his own advantage. In this he overlooks the impregnable position which the party of the second part, the great investment interests, occupy; in fact, he is counting without his host. Hitherto he has not been convinced of his own helplessness. And with a fine fancy he still imagines that his own interest is on the side of the propertied and privileged classes; so that the farmer constituency is the chief pillar of conservative law and order, particularly in all that touches the inviolable rights of property and at every juncture where a division comes on between those who live by investment and those who live by work. In pecuniary effect, the ordinary American farmer, who legally owns a moderate farm of the common sort, belongs among those who work for a livelihood; such a livelihood as the investment interests find it worth while to allow him under the rule of what the traffic will bear; but in point of sentiment and class consciousness he clings to a belated stand on the side of those who draw a profit from his work.

So it is also with the menial servants and middle-class people of "independent means," who are, however, in a position to see more clearly their dependence on the owners of predominant wealth. And such, with a further accentuation of the anomaly, may reasonably be expected to be the further run of these relations under the promised regime of peace and security. The class of well-kept gentlefolk will scarcely be called on to stand alone, in case of a division between those who live by investment and those who live by work; inasmuch as, for the calculable future, it should seem a reasonable expectation that this very considerable fringe of dependents and pseudo-independents will abide by their time-tried principles of right and honest living, through good days and evil, and cast in their lot unreservedly with that reputable body to whom the control of trade and industry by investment assigns the usufruct of the community's productive powers.

Something has already been said of the prospective breeding of pedigreed gentlefolk under the projected regime of peace. Pedigree, for the purpose in hand, is a pecuniary attribute and is, of course, a product of funded wealth, more or less ancient. Virtually ancient pedigree can be procured by well-advised expenditure on the conspicuous amenities; that is to say pedigree effectually competent as a background of current gentility. Gentlefolk of such syncopated pedigree may have to walk circumspectly, of course; but their being in this manner put on their good behavior should tend to heighten their effectual serviceability as gentlefolk, by inducing a single-mindedness of gentility beyond what can fairly be expected of those who are already secure in their tenure.

Except conventionally, there is no hereditary difference between the standard gentlefolk and, say, their "menial servants," or the general populations of the farms and the industrial towns. This is a well-established commonplace among ethnological students; which has, of course, nothing to say with respect to the conventionally distinct lines of descent of the "Best Families." These Best Families are nowise distinguishable from the common run in point of hereditary traits; the difference that makes the gentleman and the gentlewoman being wholly a matter of habituation during the individual's lifetime. It is something of a distasteful necessity to attention to this total absence of native difference between the well-born and the common, but it is a necessity of the argument in hand, and recalling of it may, therefore, be overlooked for once in a way. There is no harm and no annoyance intended. The point of it all is that, on the premises which this state of the case affords, the body of gentlefolk created by such an accumulation of invested wealth will have no less of an effectual cultural value than they would have had if their virtually ancient pedigree had been actual.

At this point, again, the experience of the Victorian peace and the functioning of its gentlefolk come in to indicate what may fairly be hoped for in this way under this prospective regime of peace at large. But with the difference that the scale of things is to be larger, the pace swifter, and the volume and dispersion of this prospective leisure class somewhat wider. The work of this leisure class—and there is neither paradox nor inconsistency in the phase—should be patterned on the lines worked out by their prototypes of the Victorian time, but with some appreciable accentuation in the direction of what chiefly characterized the leisure class of that era of tranquillity. The characteristic feature to which attention naturally turns at this suggestion is the tranquillity that has marked that body of gentlefolk and their code of clean and honest living. Another word than "tranquillity" might be hit upon to designate this characteristic animus, but any other word that should at all adequately serve the turn would carry a less felicitous suggestion of those upper-class virtues that have constituted the substantial worth of the Victorian gentleman. The conscious worth of these gentlefolk has been a beautifully complete achievement. It has been an achievement of "faith without works," of course; but, needless to say, that is as it should be, also of course. The place of gentlefolk in the economy of Nature is tracelessly to consume the community's net product, and in doing so to set a standard of decent expenditure for the others emulatively to work up to as near as may be. It is scarcely conceivable that this could have been done in a more unobtrusively efficient manner, or with a more austerely virtuous conviction of well-doing, than by the gentlefolk bred of the Victorian peace. So also, in turn, it is not to be believed that the prospective breed of gentlefolk derivable from the net product of the pacific nations under the promised regime of peace at large will prove in any degree less effective for the like ends. More will be required of them in the way of a traceless consumption of superfluities and an unexampled expensive standard of living. But this situation that so faces them may be construed as a larger opportunity, quite as well as a more difficult task.

A theoretical exposition of the place and cultural value of a leisure class in modern life would scarcely be in place here; and it has also been set out in some detail elsewhere.[1] For the purpose in hand it may be sufficient to recall that the canons of taste and the standards of valuation worked out and inculcated by leisure-class life have in all ages run, with unbroken consistency, to pecuniary waste and personal futility. In its economic bearing, and particularly in its immediate bearing on the material well-being of the community at large, the leadership of the leisure class can scarcely be called by a less derogatory epithet than "untoward." But that is not the whole of the case, and the other side should be heard. The leisure-class life of tranquillity, running detached as it does above the turmoil out of which the material of their sustenance is derived, enables a growth of all those virtues that mark, or make, the gentleman; and that affect the life of the underlying community throughout, pervasively, by imitation; leading to a standardization of the everyday proprieties on a, presumably, higher level of urbanity and integrity than might be expected to result in the absence of this prescriptive model.

Integer vitae scelerisque purus, the gentleman of assured station turns a placid countenance to all those petty vexations of breadwinning that touch him not. Serenely and with an impassive fortitude he faces those common vicissitudes of life that are impotent to make or mar his material fortunes and that can neither impair his creature comforts nor put a slur on his good repute. So that without afterthought he deals fairly in all everyday conjunctures of give and take; for they are at the most inconsequential episodes to him, although the like might spell irremediable disaster to his impecunious counterfoil among the common men who have the community's work to do. In short, he is a gentleman, in the best acceptation of the word,—unavoidably, by force of circumstance. As such his example is of invaluable consequence to the underlying community of common folk, in that it keeps before their eyes an object-lesson in habitual fortitude and visible integrity such as could scarcely have been created except under such shelter from those disturbances that would go to mar habitual fortitude and integrity. There can be little doubt but the high example of the Victorian gentlefolk has had much to do with stabilizing the animus of the British common man on lines of integrity and fair play. What else and more in the way of habitual preconceptions he may, by competitive imitation, owe to the same high sources is not immediately in question here.

Recalling once more that the canon of life whereby folk are gentlefolk sums itself up in the requirements of pecuniary waste and personal futility, and that these requirements are indefinitely extensible, at the same time that the management of the community's industry by investment for a profit enables the owners of invested wealth to divert to their own use the community's net product, wherewith to meet these requirements, it follows that the community at large which provides this output of product will be allowed so much as is required by their necessary standard of living,—with an unstable margin of error in the adjustment. This margin of error should tend continually to grow narrower as the businesslike management of industry grows more efficient with experience; but it will also continually be disturbed in the contrary sense by innovations of a technological nature that require continual readjustment. This margin is probably not to be got rid of, though it may be expected to become less considerable under more settled conditions.

It should also not be overlooked that the standard of living here spoken of as necessarily to be allowed the working population by no means coincides with the "physical subsistence minimum," from which in fact it always departs by something appreciable. The necessary standard of living of the working community is in fact made up of two distinguishable factors: the subsistence minimum, and the requirements of decorously wasteful consumption—the "decencies of life." These decencies are no less requisite than the physical necessaries, in point of workday urgency, and their amount is a matter of use and wont. This composite standard of living is a practical minimum, below which consumption will not fall, except by a fluctuating margin of error; the effect being the same, in point of necessary consumption, as if it were all of the nature of a physical subsistence minimum.

Loosely speaking the arrangement should leave nothing appreciable over, after the requirements of genteel waste and of the workday standard of consumption have been met. From which in turn it should follow that the rest of what is comprised under the general caption of "culture" will find a place only in the interstices of leisure-class expenditure and only at the hands of aberrant members of the class of the gently-bred. The working population should have no effectual margin of time, energy or means for other pursuits than the day's work in the service of the price-system; so that aberrant individuals in this class, who might by native propensity incline, e.g., to pursue the sciences or the fine arts, should have (virtually) no chance to make good. It would be a virtual suppression of such native gifts among the common folk, not a definitive and all-inclusive suppression. The state of the case under the Victorian peace may, again, be taken in illustration of the point; although under the presumably more effectual control to be looked for in the pacific future the margin might reasonably be expected to run somewhat narrower, so that this virtual suppression of cultural talent among the common men should come nearer a complete suppression.

The working of that free initiative that makes the advance of civilization, and also the greater part of its conservation, would in effect be allowed only in the erratic members of the kept classes; where at the same time it would have to work against the side-draught of conventional usage, which discountenances any pursuit that is not visibly futile according to some accepted manner of futility. Now under the prospective perfect working of the price-system, bearers of the banners of civilization could effectually be drawn only from the kept classes, the gentlefolk who alone would have the disposal of such free income as is required for work that has no pecuniary value. And numerically the gentlefolk are an inconsiderable fraction of the population. The supply of competently gifted bearers of the community's culture would accordingly be limited to such as could be drawn by self-selection from among this inconsiderable proportion of the community at large.

It may be recalled that in point of heredity, and therefore in point of native fitness for the maintenance and advance of civilization, there is no difference between the gentlefolk and the populace at large; or at least there is no difference of such a nature as to count in abatement of the proposition set down above. Some slight, but after all inconsequential, difference there may be, but such difference as there is, if any, rather counts against the gentlefolk as keepers of the cultural advance. The gentlefolk are derived from business; the gentlemen represents a filial generation of the businessman; and if the class typically is gifted with any peculiar hereditary traits, therefore, they should presumably be such as typically mark the successful businessman—astute, prehensile, unscrupulous. For a generation or two, perhaps to the scriptural third and fourth generation, it is possible that a diluted rapacity and cunning may continue to mark the businessman's well-born descendants; but these are not serviceable traits for the conservation and advancement of the community's cultural heritage. So that no consideration of special hereditary fitness in the well-born need be entertained in this connection.

As to the limitation imposed by the price-system on the supply of candidates suited by native gift for the human work of civilization; it would, no doubt, be putting the figure extravagantly high to say that the gentlefolk, properly speaking, comprise as much as ten percent of the total population; perhaps something less than one-half of that percentage would still seem a gross overstatement. But, to cover loose ends and vagrant cases, the gentlefolk may for the purpose be credited with so high a percentage of the total population. If ten percent be allowed, as an outside figure, it follows that the community's scientists, artists, scholars, and like individuals given over to the workday pursuits of the human spirit, are by conventional restriction to drawn from one-tenth of the current supply of persons suited by native gift for these pursuits. Or as it may also be expressed, in so far as the projected scheme takes effect it should result in the suppression of nine (or more) out of every ten persons available for the constructive work of civilization. The cultural consequence to be looked for, therefore, should be quite markedly of the conservative order.

Of course, in actual effect, the retardation or repression of civilization by this means, as calculated on these premises, should reasonably be expected to count up to something appreciably more than nine-tenths of the gains that might presumably be achieved in the conceivable absence of the price-system and the regime of investment. All work of this kind has much of the character of teamwork; so that the efforts of isolated individuals count for little, and a few working in more or less of concert and understanding will count for proportionally much less than many working in concert. The endeavors of the individuals engaged count cumulatively, to such effect that doubling their forces will more than double the aggregate efficiency; and conversely, reducing the number will reduce the effectiveness of their work by something more than the simple numerical proportion. Indeed, an undue reduction of numbers in such a case may lead to the total defeat of the few that are left, and the best endeavors of a dwindling remnant may be wholly nugatory. There is needed a sense of community and solidarity, without which the assurance necessary to the work is bound to falter and dwindle out; and there is also needed a degree of popular countenance, not to be had by isolated individuals engaged in an unconventional pursuit of things that are neither to be classed as spendthrift decorum nor as merchantable goods. In this connection an isolated one does not count for one, and more than the critical minimum will count for several per capita. It is a case where the "minimal dose" is wholly inoperative.

There is not a little reason to believe that consequent upon the installation of the projected regime of peace at large and secure investment the critical point in the repression of talent will very shortly be reached and passed, so that the principle of the "minimal dose" will come to apply. The point may readily be illustrated by the case of many British and American towns and neighborhoods during the past few decades; where the dominant price-system and its commercial standards of truth and beauty have over-ruled all inclination to cultural sanity and put it definitively in abeyance. The cultural, or perhaps the conventional, residue left over in these cases where civilization has gone stale through inefficiency of the minimal dose is not properly to be found fault with; it is of a blameless character, conventionally; nor is there any intention here to cast aspersion on the desolate. The like effects of the like causes are to be seen in the

American colleges and universities, where business principles have supplanted the pursuit of learning, and where the commercialization of aims, ideals, tastes, occupations and personnel is following much the same lines that have led so many of the country towns effectually outside the cultural pale. The American university or college is coming to be an outlier of the price-system, in point of aims, standards and personnel; hitherto the tradition of learning as a trait of civilization, as distinct from business, has not been fully displaced, although it is now coming to face the passage of the minimal dose. The like, in a degree, is apparently true latterly for many English, and still more evidently for many German schools.

In these various instances of what may be called dry-rot or local blight on the civilized world's culture the decline appears to be due not to a positive infection of a malignant sort, so much as to a failure of the active cultural ferment, which has fallen below the critical point of efficacy; perhaps through an unintended refusal of a livelihood to persons given over to cultivating the elements of civilization; perhaps through the conventional disallowance of the pursuit of any other ends than competitive gain and competitive spending. Evidently it is something much more comprehensive in this nature that is reasonably to be looked for under the prospective regime of peace, in case the price-system gains that farther impetus and warrant which it should come in for if the rights of ownership and investment stand over intact, and so come to enjoy the benefit of a further improved state of the industrial arts and a further enlarged scale of operation and enhanced rate of turnover.

To turn back to the point from which this excursion branched off. It has been presumed all the while that the technological equipment, or the state of the industrial arts, must continue to advance under the conditions offered by this regime of peace at large. But the last few paragraphs will doubtless suggest that such a single-minded addiction to competitive gain and competitive spending as the stabilized and amplified price-system would enjoin, must lead to an effectual retardation, perhaps to a decline, of those material sciences on which modern technology draws; and that the state of the industrial arts should therefore cease to advance, if only the scheme of investment and businesslike sabotage can be made sufficiently secure. That such may be the outcome is a contingency which the argument will have to meet and to allow for; but it is after all a contingency that need not be expected to derange the sequence of events, except in the way of retardation. Even without further advance in technological expedients or in the relevant material sciences, there will still necessarily ensue an effectual advance in the industrial arts, in the sense that further organization and enlargement of the material equipment and industrial processes on lines already securely known and not to be forgotten must bring an effectually enhanced efficiency of the industrial process as a whole.

In illustration, it is scarcely to be assumed even as a tentative hypothesis that the system of transport and communication will not undergo extension and improvement on the lines already familiar, even in the absence of new technological contrivances. At the same time a continued increase of population is to be counted on; which has, for the purpose in hand, much the same effect as an advance in the industrial arts. Human contact and mutual understanding will necessarily grow wider and closer, and will have its effect on the habits of thought prevalent in the communities that are to live under the promised regime of peace. The system of transport and communications having to handle a more voluminous and exacting traffic, in the service of a larger and more compact population, will have to be organized and administered on mechanically drawn schedules of time, place, volume, velocity, and price, of a still more exacting accuracy than hitherto. The like will necessarily apply throughout the industrial occupations that employ extensive plant or processes, or that articulate with industrial processes of that nature; which will necessarily comprise a larger proportion of the industrial process at large than hitherto.

As has already been remarked more than once in the course of the argument, a population that lives and does its work, and such play as is allowed it, in and by an exactingly articulate mechanical system of this kind will necessarily be an "intelligent" people, in the colloquial sense of the word; that is to say it will necessarily be a people that uses printed matter freely and that has some familiarity with the elements of those material science that underlie this mechanically organized system of appliances and processes. Such a population lives by and within the framework of the mechanistic logic, and is in a fair way to lose faith in any proposition that can not be stated convincingly in terms of this mechanistic logic. Superstitions are liable to lapse by neglect or disuse in such a community; that is to say propositions of a nonmechanistic complexion are liable to insensible disestablishment in such a case; "superstition" in these premises coming to signify whatever is not of this mechanistic, or "materialistic" character. An exception to this broad characterization of non-mechanistic propositions as "superstition" would be matters that are of the nature of an immediate deliverance of the senses or of the aesthetic sensibilities.

By a simile it might be said that what so falls under the caption of "superstition" in such a case is subject to decay by inanition. It should not be difficult to conceive the general course of such a decay of superstitions under this unremitting discipline of mechanistic habits of life. The recent past offers an illustration, in the unemotional progress of decay that has overtaken religious beliefs in the more civilized countries, and more particularly among the intellectually trained workmen of the mechanical industries. The elimination of such non-mechanistic propositions of the faith has been visibly going on, but it has not worked out on any uniform plan, nor has it overtaken any large or compact body of people consistently or abruptly, being of the nature of obsolescence rather than of set repudiation. But in a slack and unreflecting fashion the divestment has gone on until the aggregate effect is unmistakable.

A similar divestment of superstitions is reasonably to be looked for also in that domain of preconceptions that lies between the supernatural and the mechanistic. Chief among these time-warped preconceptions—or superstitions—that so stand over out of the alien past among these democratic peoples is the institution of property. As is true of preconceptions touching the supernatural verities, so here too the article of use and wont in question will not bear formulation in mechanistic terms and is not congruous with that mechanistic logic that is incontinently bending the habits of thought of the common man more and more consistently to its own bent. There is, of course, the difference that while no class—apart from the servants of the church—have a material interest in the continued integrity of the articles of the supernatural faith, there is a strong and stubborn material interest bound up with the maintenance of this article of the pecuniary faith; and the class in whom this material interest vests are also, in effect, invested with the coercive powers of the law.

The law, and the poplar preconceptions that give the law its binding force, go to uphold the established usage and the established prerogatives on this head; and the disestablishment of the rights of property and investment therefore is not a simple matter of obsolescence through neglect. It may confidently be counted on that all the apparatus of the law and all the coercive agencies of law and order, will be brought in requisition to uphold the ancient rights of ownership, whenever any move is made toward their disallowance or restriction. But then, on the other hand, the movement to disallow or diminish the prerogatives of ownership is also not to take the innocuous shape of unstudied neglect. So soon, or rather so far, as the common man comes to realize that these rights of ownership and investment uniformly work to his material detriment, at the same time that he has lost the "will to believe" in any argument that does not run in terms of the mechanistic logic, it is reasonable to expect that he will take a stand on this matter; and it is more than likely that the stand taken will be of an uncompromising kind,—presumably something in the nature of the stand once taken by recalcitrant Englishmen in protest against the irresponsible rule of the Stuart sovereign. It is also not likely that the beneficiaries under these proprietary rights will yield their ground at all amicably; all the more since they are patently within their authentic rights in insisting on full discretion in the disposal of their own possessions; very much as Charles I or James II once were within their prescriptive right,—which had little to say in the outcome.

Even apart from "time immemorial" and the patent authenticity of the institution, there were and are many cogent arguments to be alleged in favor of the position for which the Stuart sovereigns and the spokesmen contended. So there are and will be many, perhaps more, cogent reasons to be alleged for the maintenance of the established law and order in respect of the rights of ownership and investment. Not least urgent, nor least real, among these arguments is the puzzling question of what to put in the place of these rights and of the methods of control based on them, very much as the analogous question puzzled the public spirited men of the Stuart times. All of which goes to argue that there may be expected to arise a conjuncture of perplexities and complications, as well as a division of interests and claims. To which should be added that the division is likely to come to a head soon as the balance of forces between the two parties in interest becomes doubtful, so that either party comes to surmise that the success of its own aims may depend on its own efforts. And as happens where two antagonistic parties are each convinced of the justice of its cause, and in the absence of an umpire, the logical recourse is the wager of battle.

Granting the premises, there should be no reasonable doubt as to this eventual cleavage between those who own and those who do not; and of the premises the only item that is not already an accomplished fact is the installation of peace at large. The rest of what goes into the argument is the well-known modern state of the industrial arts, and the equally well-known price-system; which, in combination, give its character to the modern state of business enterprise. It is only an unusually broad instance of an institutional arrangement which has in the course of time and changing conditions come to work at cross purposes with that underlying ground of institutional arrangements that takes form in the commonplace aphorism, Live and let live. With change setting in the direction familiar to all men today, it is only a question of limited time when the discrepancy will reach a critical pass, and the installation of peace may be counted on to hasten this course of things.

That a decision will be sought by recourse to forcible measures, is also scarcely open to question; since the established law and order provides for a resort to coercion in the enforcement of these prescriptive rights, and since both parties in interest, in this as in other cases, are persuaded of the justice of their claims. A decision either way is an intolerable iniquity in the eyes of the losing side. History teaches that in such a quarrel the recourse has always been to force.

History teaches also, but with an inflection of doubt, that the outworn institution in such a conjuncture faces disestablishment. At least, so men like to believe. What the experience of history does not leave in doubt is the grave damage, discomfort and shame incident to the displacement of such an institutional discrepancy by such recourse to force. What further appears to be clear in the premises, at least to the point of a strong presumption, is that in the present case the decision, or the choice, lies between two alternatives; either the price-system and its attendant business enterprise will yield and pass out; or the pacific nations will conserve their pecuniary scheme of law and order at the cost of returning to a war footing and letting their owners preserve the rights of ownership by force of arms.

The reflection obviously suggests itself that this prospect of consequences to follow from the installation of peace at large might well be taken into account beforehand by those who are aiming to work out an enduring peace. It has appeared in the course of the argument that the preservation of the present pecuniary law and order, with all its incidents of ownership and investment, is incompatible with an unwarlike state of peace and security. This current scheme of investment, business, and sabotage, should have an appreciably better chance of survival in the long run if the present conditions of warlike preparation and national insecurity were maintained, or if the projected peace were left in a somewhat problematical state, sufficiently precarious to keep national animosities alert, and thereby to the neglect of domestic interest, particularly of such interest as touch the popular well-being. On the other hand, it has also appeared that the cause of peace and its perpetuation might be materially advanced if precautions were taken beforehand to put out of the way as much as may be of those discrepancies of interest and sentiment between nations and between classes which make for dissension and eventual hostilities.

So, if the projectors of this peace at large are in any degree inclined to seek concessive terms on which the peace might hopefully be made enduring, it should evidently be part of their endeavors from the outset to put events in train for the present abatement and eventual abrogation of the rights of ownership and of the price-system in which these rights take effect. A hopeful beginning along this line would manifestly be the neutralization of all pecuniary rights of citizenship, as has been indicated in an earlier passage. On the other hand, if peace is not desired at the cost of relinquishing the scheme of competitive gain and competitive spending, the promoters of peace should logically observe due precaution and move only so far in the direction of a peaceable settlement as should result in a sufficiently unstable equilibrium of mutual jealousies; such as might expeditiously be upset whenever discontent with pecuniary affairs should come to threaten this established scheme of pecuniary prerogatives.

Note

1. Cf. *The Theory of the Leisure Class,* especially chs. v–ix and xiv.

Review of J.M. Keynes, *The Economic Consequences of the Peace*

It is now something like a year since this book was written. And much of its argument is in the nature of forecast which has in great part been overtaken by the precipitate run of events during these past months. Therefore it would scarcely be fair to read the author's argument as a presentation of current fact. It is rather to be taken as a presentation of the diplomatic potentialities of the Treaty and the League, as seen beforehand, and of the further consequences which may be expected to follow in the course of a statesmanlike management of things under the powers conferred by the Treaty and by the Covenant of the League. It is an altogether sober and admirably candid and facile argument, by a man familiar with diplomatic usage and trained in the details of large financial policy; and the wide vogue and earnest consideration which have been given to this volume reflect its very substantial merit. At the same time the same facts go to show how faithfully its point of view and its line of argument fall in with the prevailing attitude of thoughtful men toward the same range of questions. It is the attitude of men accustomed to take political documents at their face value.

Writing at about the date of its formulation and before its effectual working had been demonstrated, Mr. Keynes accepts the Treaty as a definitive formulation of the terms of peace, as a conclusive settlement rather than a strategic point of departure for further negotiations and a continuation of warlike enterprise—and this in spite of the fact that Mr. Keynes was continuously and intimately in touch with the Peace Conference during all those devious negotiations by which the Elder Statesmen of the Great Powers arrived at the bargains embodied in this instrument. These negotiations were quite secret, of course, as is fitting that negotiations among Elder Statesmen should be. But for all their vulpine secrecy,

Review of John Maynard Keynes, *The Economic Consequences of the Peace, Political Science Quarterly*, 35 (September 1920): 467–72. Reprinted by permission of Political Science Quarterly.

the temper and purposes of that hidden Conclave of political hucksters were already becoming evident to outsiders a year ago, and it is all the more surprising to find that an observer so shrewd and so advantageously placed as Mr. Keynes has been led to credit them with any degree of *bona fides* or to ascribe any degree of finality to the diplomatic instruments which came out of their bargaining.

The Treaty was designed, in substance, to re-establish the *status quo ante*, with a particular view to the conservation of international jealousies. Instead of its having brought a settlement of the world's peace, the Treaty (together with the League) has already shown itself to be nothing better than a screen of diplomatic verbiage behind which the Elder Statesmen of the Great Powers continue their pursuit of political chicane and imperialistic aggrandisement. All this is patent now, and it needs no peculiar degree of courage to admit it. It is also scarcely too much to say that all this should have been sufficiently evident to Mr. Keynes a year ago. But in failing to take note of this patent state of the case Mr. Keynes only reflects the commonplace attitude of thoughtful citizens. His discussion, accordingly, is a faithful and exceptionally intelligent commentary on the language of the Treaty, rather than the consequences which were designed to follow from it or the uses to which it is lending itself. It would perhaps be an ungraceful overstatement to say that Mr. Keynes has successfully avoided the main facts in the case; but an equally broad statement to the contrary would be farther from the truth.

The events of the past months go to show that the central and most binding provision of the Treaty (and of the League) is an unrecorded clause by which the governments of the Great Powers are banded together for the suppression of Soviet Russia—unrecorded unless record of it is to be found somewhere among the secret archives of the League or of the Great Powers. Apart from this unacknowledged compact there appears to be nothing in the Treaty that has any character of stability or binding force. (Of course, this compact for the reduction of Soviet Russia was not written into the text of the Treaty; it may rather be said to have been the parchment upon which the text was written.) A formal avowal of such a compact for continued warlike operations would not comport with the usages of secret diplomacy, and then it might also be counted on unduly to irritate the underlying populations of the Great Powers, who are unable to see the urgency of the case in the same perspective as the Elder Statesmen. So this difficult but imperative task of suppressing Bolshevism, which faced the Conclave from the outset, has no part in Mr. Keynes's analysis of the consequences to be expected from the conclave's Treaty. Yet it is sufficiently evident now that the exigencies of the Conclave's campaign against Russian Bolshevism have shaped the working-out of the Treaty hitherto, beyond any other consideration. This appears to be the only interest which the Elder Statesmen of the Great Powers hold in common; in all else they appear to be engrossed with mutual jealousies and cross purposes, quite in the spirit of that imperialistic *status quo* out of which the Great War arose. And the like promises to hold true for the future, until after Soviet Russia or the Powers banded together in this surreptitious war on Russia shall reach the breaking-point. In the nature of things it is a war without quarter; but in the nature of things it is also an enterprise which cannot be avowed.

It is quite needless to find fault with this urgent campaign of the governments of the Great Powers against Soviet Russia or to say anything in approval of it all. But it is necessary to take note of its urgency and the nature of it, as well as of the fact that this major factor in the practical working-out of the Peace has apparently escaped attention in the most competent analysis of the Peace and its consequences that has yet been offered. It has been overlooked, perhaps, because it is a foregone matter of course. Yet this oversight is unfortunate. Among other things, it has led Mr. Keynes into an ungracious characterization of the President and his share in the negotiations. Mr. Keynes has much that is uncomplimentary to say of the many concessions and comprehensive defeat in which the President and his avowed purposes became involved in the course of those negotiations with the Elder Statesmen of the Great Powers. Due appreciation of the gravity of this anti-Bolshevist issue, and of its ubiquitous and paramount force in the deliberations of the Conclave, should have saved Mr. Keynes from those expressions of scant courtesy which mar his characterization of the President and of the President's work as peacemaker.

The intrinsic merits of the quarrel between the Bolsheviki and the Elder Statesmen are not a matter for off-hand decision; nor need they come in consideration here. But the difficulties of the President's work as peacemaker are not to be appreciated without some regard to the nature of this issue that faced him. So, without prejudice, it seems necessary to call to mind the main facts of the case, as these facts confronted him in the negotiations with the Conclave. It is to be remarked, then, that Bolshevism is a menace to absentee ownership. At the same time the present economic and political order rests on absentee ownership. The imperialist policies of the Great Powers, including America, also look to the maintenance and extension of absentee ownership as the major and abiding purpose of all their political traffic. Absentee ownership, accordingly, is the foundation of law and order, according to that scheme of law and order which has been handed down out of the past in all the civilized nations, and to the perpetuation of which the Elder Statesmen are committed by native bent and by the duties of office. This applies to both the economic and the political order, in all these civilized nations, where the security of property rights has become virtually the sole concern of the constituted authorities.

The Fourteen Points were drawn up without due appreciation of this paramount place which absentee ownership has come to occupy in the modern civilized countries and without due appreciation of the intrinsically precarious equilibrium in which this paramount institution of civilized mankind has been placed by the growth of industry and education. The Bolshevist demonstration had not yet shown the menace, at the time when the Fourteen Points were drawn up. The Fourteen Points were drawn in the humane spirit of Mid-Victorian Liberalism, without due realization of the fact that democracy has in the meantime outgrown the Mid-Victorian scheme of personal liberty and has grown into a democracy of property rights. Not until the Bolshevist overturn and the rise of Soviet Russia did this new complexion of things become evident to men trained in the good old way of thinking on questions of policy. But at the date of the Peace Conference Soviet Russia had come to be the largest and most perplexing fact within the political and economic horizon. Therefore, so soon as a consideration of details was entered upon it became evident, point by point, that the demands of absentee ownership coincide with the requirements of the existing order, and that these paramount demands of absentee ownership are at the same time incompatible with the humane principles of Mid-Victorian Liberalism. Therefore, regretfully and reluctantly, but imperatively, it became the part of wise statesmanship to save the existing order by saving absentee ownership and letting the Fourteen Points go in the discard. Bolshevism is a menace to absentee ownership; and in the light of events in Soviet Russia it became evident, point by point, that only with the definitive suppression of Bolshevism and all its works, at any cost, could the world be made safe for that Democracy of Property Rights on which the existing political and civil order is founded. So it became the first concern of all the guardians of the existing order to root out Bolshevism at any cost, without regard to international law.

If one is so inclined, one may find fault with the premises of this argument as being out of date and reactionary; and one might find fault with the President for being too straightly guided by considerations of this nature. But the President was committed to the preservation of the existing order of commercialized imperialism, by conviction and by his high office. His apparent defeat in the face of this unforeseen situation, therefore, was not so much a defeat, but rather a strategic realignment designed to compass what was indispensable, even at some cost to his own prestige—the main consideration being the defeat of Bolshevism at any cost—so that a well-considered view of the President's share in the deliberations of the Conclave will credit him with insight, courage, facility, and tenacity of purpose rather than with that pusillanimity, vacillation, and ineptitude which is ascribed to him in Mr. Keynes's too superficial review of the case.

So also his oversight of this paramount need of making the world safe for a democracy of absentee owners has led Mr. Keynes to take an unduly pessimistic view of the provisions covering the German indemnity. A notable leniency, amounting to something like collusive remissness, has characterized the dealings of the Powers with Germany hitherto. As should have seemed altogether probable beforehand, the stipulations touching the German indemnity have proved to be provisional and tentative only—if they should not rather be characterized as a diplomatic bluff, designed to gain time, divert attention, and keep the various claimants in a reasonably patient frame of mind during the period of rehabilitation needed to reinstate the reactionary régime in Germany and erect it into a bulwark against Bolshevism. These stipulations have already suffered substantial modifications at every point that has come to a test hitherto, and there is no present indication and no present reason to believe that any of them will be lived up to in any integral fashion. They are apparently in the nature of a base for negotiations and are due to come up for indefinite further adjustment as expediency may dictate. And the expediencies of the case appear to run on two main considerations: (a) the defeat of Bolshevism, in Russia and elsewhere; and (b) the continued secure tenure of absentee ownership in Germany. It follows that Germany must not be crippled in such a degree as would leave the imperial establishment materially weakened in its campaign against Bolshevism abroad or radicalism at home. From which it also follows that no indemnity should effectually be levied on Germany such as will at all seriously cut into the free income of the propertied and privileged classes, who alone can be trusted to safeguard the democratic interests of absentee ownership. Such burden as the indemnity may impose must accordingly not exceed an amount which may conveniently be made to fall somewhat immediately on the propertyless working class, who are to be kept in hand. As required by these considerations of safety for the established order, it will be observed that the provisions of the Treaty shrewdly avoid any measures that would involve confiscation of property; whereas, if these provisions had not been drawn with a shrewd eye to the continued security of absentee ownership, there should have been no serious difficulty in collecting an adequate indemnity from the wealth of Germany without materially deranging the country's industry and without hardship to others than the absentee owners. There is no reason, other than the reason of absentee ownership, why the Treaty should not have provided for a comprehensive repudiation of the German war debt, imperial, state, and municipal, with a view to diverting that much of German income to the benefit of those who suffered from German aggression. So also no other reason stood in the way of a comprehensive confiscation of German wealth, so far as that wealth is covered by securities and is therefore held by absentee owners, and there is no question as to the war guilt of these absentee owners.

But such a measure would subvert the order of society, which is an order of absentee ownership in so far as concerns the Elder Statesmen and the interests whose guardians they are. Therefore it would not do, nor has the notion been entertained, to divert any part of this free income from the German absentee owners to the relief of those who suffered from the war which these absentee owners carried into the countries of the Allies. In effect, in their efforts to safeguard the existing political and economic order—to make the world safe for a democracy of investors—the statesmen of the victorious Powers have taken sides with the war-guilty absentee owners of Germany and against their underlying population. All of which, of course, is quite regular and beyond reproach; nor does it all ruffle the course of Mr. Keynes's exposition of economic consequences, in any degree.

Even such conservative provisions as the Treaty makes for indemnifying the war victims have hitherto been enforced only with a shrewdly managed leniency, marked with an unmistakable partisan bias in favor of the German-Imperial *status quo ante*; as is also true for the provisions touching disarmament and the discontinuance of warlike industries and organization—which provisions have been administered in a well-conceived spirit of *opéra bouffe*. Indeed, the measures hitherto taken in the execution of this Peace Treaty's provisional terms throw something of an air of fantasy over Mr. Keynes's apprehensions on this head.

Books and Articles by Thorstein Veblen

The Theory of the Leisure Class: An Economic Study of Institutions. New York: The Macmillan Company, 1899.

The Theory of Business Enterprise. New York: Charles Scribner's Sons, 1904.

The Instinct of Workmanship and the State of the Industrial Arts. New York: The Macmillan Company, 1914.

Imperial Germany and the Industrial Revolution. New York: The MacMillan Company, 1915.

An Inquiry into the Nature of Peace and the Terms of Its Perpetuation. New York: The Macmillan Company, 1917.

The Higher Learning in America: A Memorandum on the Conduct of Universities by Businessmen. New York: B. W. Huebsch, 1918.

*The Place of Science in Modern Civilization and Other Essays**. New York: B. W. Huebsch, 1919.

The Vested Interests and the State of the Industrial Arts. New York: B. W. Huebsch, 1919. (Title changed in 1920 to *The Vested Interests and the Common Man.*)

The Engineers and the Price System. New York: B. W. Huebsch, 1921.

Absentee Ownership and Business Enterprise in Recent Times. New York: B.W. Huebsch, 1923.

Introduction and Translation of *The Laxdaela Saga.* New York: B. W. Huebsch, 1925.

*Essays in Our Changing Order.** Edited by Leon Ardzrooni. New York: Viking Press, 1934.

*Thorstein Veblen: Essays, Reviews, and Reports, Previously Uncollected Writings.** Edited and with an introduction by Joseph Dorfman. New York: Augustus M. Kelley, 1973.

*These books are compilations of articles, reviews, or reports written by Veblen. For a complete bibliography of Veblen's writings, the reader is also advised to consult Joseph Dorfman, *Thorstein Veblen and His America* (New York: Viking Press, 1966).

Suggestions for Further Reading

Dente, Leonard A. *Veblen's Theory of Social Change*. New York: Arno Press, 1977.

Diggins, John P. *The Bard of Savagery: Thorstein Veblen and Modern Social Theory*. New York: Seabury Press, 1978.

Dorfman, Joseph. *Thorstein Veblen and His America*. New York: Viking Press, 1934.

Edgell, Stephen, and Tilman, Rick. "The Intellectual Antecedents of Thorstein Veblen: A Reappraisal." *Journal of Economic Issues* 23 (December 1989): 1003–26.

Leibenstein, Harvey. "Bandwagon, Snob, and Veblen Effects in the Theory of Consumer's Demand." *Quarterly Journal of Economics* 64 (May 1950): 183–207.

Lerner, Max. "What is Usable in Veblen." *New Republic* 83 (May 1935): 7–10.

Mason, Roger S. *Conspicuous Consumption*. New York: St. Martin's Press, 1981.

Mead, George H. Review of *The Nature of Peace* in *Journal of Political Economy* 26 (June 1918): 752–62.

Mills, C. Wright. Introduction to *The Theory of the Leisure Class*. New York: Mentor Books, 1953.

Steiner, Robert L. and Weiss, Joseph, "Veblen Revised in the Light of Counter-Snobbery." *Journal of Aesthetics and Art Criticism* 9 (March 1951): 263–68.

Tilman, Rick. "Veblen's Ideal Political Economy and Its Critics." *American Journal of Economics and Sociology* 31 (July 1972): 307–17.

———. "Thorstein Veblen: Incrementalist and Utopian." *American Journal of Economics and Sociology* 32 (April 1973): 155–69.

———. *Thorstein Veblen and His Critics, 1891–1963: Conservative, Liberal and Radical Perspectives*. Princeton: Princeton University Press, 1992.

———. ed. "Thorstein Veblen as Social Theorist and Critic." Special issue of *International Review of Sociology* (No. 3, 1992).

Index

About the Editor

Rick Tilman is a Professor of Public Administration at the University of Nevada, Las Vegas whose research interests are political economy, and American and European intellectual history. He is author of *C. Wright Mills: A Native Radical and His American Intellectual Roots* and *Thorstein Veblen and His Critics, 1891–1963: Conservative, Liberal and Radical Perspectives.*